AP®
Human Geography
Prep Plus
2020 & 2021

AP® is a registered trademark of the College Board, which was not involved in the production of, and does not endorse, this product.

Lead Editor
Katy Haynicz-Smith, MA

Special thanks to our writers and reviewers on this edition: Steve Bartley, Leslie Buchanan, Sterling Davenport, M. Dominic Eggert, Mark Feery, Paula Fleming, Peter Haynicz-Smith, Melissa McLaughlin, Kelly Swanson, Amanda Swearingen, and Caroline Sykes.

Additional special thanks to the following for their contributions to this text: Laura Aitcheson, Joanna Graham, Adam Grey, Maria Hauser, Jesika Islam, Rebecca Knauer, Mandy Luk, Jenn Moore, Camellia Mukherjee, Kristin Murnuer, Samantha Nealer, Monica Ostolaza, Rebecca Truong, Oscar Velazquez, Robert Verini, Shayna Webb-Dray, and Amy Zarkos.

AP® is a registered trademark of the College Board, which was not involved in the production of, and does not endorse, this product.

Published by Kaplan Publishing, a division of Kaplan, Inc.
750 Third Avenue
New York, NY 10017

Printed in the United States of America

10 9 8 7 6 5 4 3 2 1

Retail ISBN: 978-1-5062-5981-9
Course ISBN: 978-1-5062-5983-3

Kaplan Publishing print books are available at special quantity discounts to use for sales promotions, employee premiums, or educational purposes. For more information or to purchase books, please call the Simon & Schuster special sales department at 866-506-1949.

TABLE OF CONTENTS

Table of Contents

PART 3: COMPREHENSIVE REVIEW

PART 4: PRACTICE EXAMS

PART 1

Getting Started

CHAPTER 1

What You Need to Know about the AP Human Geography Exam

Congratulations—you have chosen Kaplan to help you get a top score on your AP Human Geography exam. Kaplan understands your goals and what you're up against: conquering a tough exam while participating in everything else that high school has to offer.

You expect realistic practice, authoritative advice, and accurate, up-to-the-minute information on the exam, and that's exactly what you'll find in this book. To help you reach your goals, we have conducted extensive research and incorporated insights from an AP expert who has 20 years of experience with AP Human Geography.

ABOUT THE AP EXPERT

Dr. Kelly Swanson has been involved with AP Human Geography since 1997, when 50 teachers from across the United States were brought together to structure the curriculum for the course. Dr. Swanson's course syllabus was published in the first edition of the AP Human Geography Teachers Guide, and he has been active in the Minnesota Alliance for Geographic Education (MAGE) since 1996. Dr. Swanson served as a geographic consultant for the Onion's *Our Dumb World* atlas published in 2007 and the *Korean National Atlas* published in 2016. His travels and speaking engagements have taken him around the world, and he brings this passion for travel and curriculum writing to the AP Human Geography course.

Dr. Swanson has been a reader for the AP Human Geography exam since 2003 and was a table leader for the 2006, 2007, 2008, 2015, and 2017 exams. For the 2009 through 2013 exams, he was selected as a Lead Table Leader. Dr. Swanson has taught different geography methods to teachers in the United States and around the world, promoting geography as a core academic discipline in any well-rounded education. In addition to teaching the AP Human Geography course at the high school level, Dr. Swanson is also currently a community faculty member at Metropolitan State University in St. Paul, Minnesota, teaching introductory geography courses at the collegiate level. He has a PhD in Learning Technologies specializing in Geography Assessment and Instruction.

ABOUT THIS BOOK

In preparing for the AP exam, you certainly will have built a solid foundation of geography knowledge. While this knowledge is critical to your learning, keep in mind that rote memorization of facts alone does not ensure success on the exam! Memorizing state capitals and world cities builds general knowledge but does little for understanding what the world is like in various locations.

Human geography is about the interconnections between people and places. This book follows the College Board's thematic approach to the multifaceted field of geography. For example, one cannot discuss a place or region without considering agricultural issues, such as how people produce or obtain their food and how this connects to their population; additionally, agriculture directly affects a country's economic development and how the people use the land, as well as the ways natural resources are allocated. This is just one example of how various geography topics intersect. On the official exam, you'll need to understand these connections at a deeper level and apply the knowledge you've learned in order to show evidence of college-level abilities.

That's where this book comes in. This guide offers much more than a review of human geography. We'll show you how to put your knowledge to brilliant use on the AP exam. We'll explain the ins and outs of the exam structure and question formats, so you won't experience any surprises. We'll even give you test-taking strategies that successful students use to earn high scores.

Are you ready for your adventure in the study and mastery of everything AP Human Geography? Good luck!

EXAM STRUCTURE

The Human Geography exam is divided into two sections, with a brief break in between. Section I gives you 60 minutes to answer 60 multiple-choice questions covering a variety of topics. The topics covered, along with the frequency of questions on each topic, are as follows:

Thinking Geographically (8%–10%)

Population and Migration Patterns and Processes (12%–17%)

Cultural Patterns and Processes (12%–17%)

Political Patterns and Processes (12%–17%)

Agriculture and Rural Land-Use Patterns and Processes (12%–17%)

Cities and Urban Land-Use Patterns and Processes (12%–17%)

Industrial and Economic Development Patterns and Processes (12%–17%)

Section II gives you 75 minutes to answer three free-response questions. These multi-part prompts can involve any of the content tested in the multiple-choice section, but they will require you to make connections across a variety of ideas that relate to each question's theme.

EXAM SCORING

The score from the multiple-choice section of the exam counts for 50% of your total exam score. Student answer sheets for the multiple-choice section are scored by machine. Scores are based on the number of questions answered correctly. No points are deducted for wrong answers.

The other 50% of your exam score comes from the three free-response questions. The free-response section is evaluated and scored manually by trained AP readers. Rubrics based on each specific free-response prompt are released on the AP central website after the exams are administered. The rubrics contain information about what needs to be present in each student response in order to earn points.

After your total scores from Sections I and II are calculated, your results are converted to a scaled score from 1 to 5. The range of points for each scaled score varies depending on the difficulty of the exam in a particular year, but the significance of each value is constant from year to year. According to the College Board, AP scores should be interpreted as follows:

5 = Extremely well qualified

4 = Well qualified

3 = Qualified

2 = Possibly qualified

1 = No recommendation

Colleges will generally award credit for a score of 3, with more selective schools requiring a 4 or 5. Note that some schools will not award college credit regardless of score. Be sure to research schools that you plan to apply to so you can determine the score you need to aim for on the AP Human Geography exam.

REGISTRATION AND FEES

To register for the exam, contact your school guidance counselor or AP coordinator. If your school does not administer the AP exam, contact the College Board for a listing of schools that do.

There is a fee for taking AP exams, the current value of which can be found at the official exam website listed below. For students with acute financial need, the College Board offers a fee reduction. In addition, most states offer exam subsidies to cover all or part of the remaining cost for eligible students. To learn about other sources of financial aid, contact your AP coordinator.

For more information on all things AP, contact the Advanced Placement Program:

Phone: (888) 225-5427 or (212) 632-1780

Email: apstudents@info.collegeboard.org

Website: https://apstudent.collegeboard.org/home

CHAPTER 2

How to Get the Score You Need

Kaplan's *AP Human Geography Prep Plus* contains precisely what you'll need to get the score you want in the time you have to study. The unique format of this book allows you to customize your prep experience to make the most of your time.

Start by going to **kaptest.com/moreonline** to register your book and get a glimpse of the additional online resources available to you.

HOW TO GET THE MOST OUT OF THIS BOOK

Specific AP Human Geography Strategies

This chapter features both general test-taking strategies and strategies tailored specifically to the AP Human Geography exam. You'll learn about the types of questions you'll see on the official exam and how to best approach them to get a top score.

Customizable Study Plans

We recognize that every student is a unique individual, and there is no single recipe for success that works for everyone. To give you the best chance to succeed, we have developed three customizable study plans. Each offers guidance on how to make the most of your available study time. In addition, we have split this book into "Rapid Review" and "Comprehensive Review" sections for each topic. There is guidance in both the study plans and the Rapid Review sections to help you determine how to best move through this book and optimize your study time.

Rapid Review and Practice

Chapters 3–9 aim to cover the most high-yield content in the shortest amount of time. Each Rapid Review and Practice chapter begins with a "Test What You Already Know" section containing a multiple-choice quiz and a checklist of key terms; this combination allows you to see where you stand with this topic before you even begin studying the content. The "Next Steps" chart (example shown below) will guide you in customizing your further study. In the middle of the Rapid Review chapter, the section entitled "Essential Content" contains a summary of key takeaways and a complete list of definitions for all of the key terms. Finally, the "Test What You Learned" section contains another multiple-choice quiz and the same key terms checklist so you can see how you're doing after some studying.

If You Got...	Do This
80% or more of the Test What You Already Know assessment correct	• Read the definitions in this chapter for all the key terms you didn't check off. • Complete the Test What You Learned assessment in this chapter.
50% or less of the Test What You Already Know assessment correct	• Read the comprehensive review for this topic. ○ If you are short on time, read only the High-Yield sections. • Read through all of the key term definitions in this chapter. • Complete the Test What You Learned assessment in this chapter.
Any other result	• Read the High-Yield sections in the comprehensive review of this topic. • Read the definitions in this chapter for all the key terms you didn't check off. • Complete the Test What You Learned assessment in this chapter.

Comprehensive Review

Chapters 10–16 feature the same topics as the Rapid Review chapters, but they offer a more detailed look at all of the specifics tested on the AP exam. You'll be directed to these Comprehensive Review chapters, for studying the High-Yield topics or for reading the whole chapter, based on your results in the corresponding Rapid Review chapter.

The Comprehensive Review chapters are like an abbreviated version of a textbook you would use in class. The key terms in bold are the same (and appear in the same order as) the terms in the Rapid Review and Practice chapters. Chapter 17 is an in-depth review of the free-response section of the exam, including sample essays and grading information. High-Yield icons appear throughout the Comprehensive Review chapters to help you recognize when information is absolutely essential to know. You will also see AP Expert Notes that highlight important connections between topics and provide tips about how to better apply your knowledge on the official exam.

Full-Length Practice Exams

In addition to the exam-like practice questions featured in the chapter quizzes, this book contains three full-length practice exams. These full-length exams mimic the multiple-choice and free-response questions on the real AP exam. Taking a practice full-length exam gives you an idea of what it's like to answer exam-like questions for about three hours. Granted, that's not exactly a fun experience, but it is a helpful one. The best part is that it doesn't count; mistakes you make on our practice exams are mistakes you won't make on your real exam.

After taking each practice exam, you'll score your multiple-choice and free-response sections using the answers and explanations. Then, you'll navigate to the scoring section in your online resources and input your raw scores to see what your overall score would be with a similar performance on the official exam.

Online Quizzes

While this book contains dozens of exam-like multiple-choice questions, you may still find yourself wanting additional practice on particular topics. That's what the online quizzes are for! Your online resources contain additional quizzes for each topic. Go to **kaptest.com/moreonline** to find them all.

HOW TO CHOOSE THE BEST STUDY PLAN FOR YOU

There's a lot of material to review before the AP exam, so it's essential to have a solid game plan that optimizes your available study time. The sheet in the front of the book consists of three separable bookmarks, each of which covers a specific, customizable study plan. You can use one of these bookmarks to not only hold your place in the book, but also to keep track of your progress in completing one of these study plans. But how do you choose the study plan that's right for you?

Fortunately, all you need to know to make this decision is how much time you have to prep. If you have two months or more, with plenty of time to study, then we recommend using the Two-Month Study Plan. If you only have about a month, or if you have more than a month but your time will be split among competing priorities, you should probably choose the One-Month Study Plan. Finally, if you have less than a month to prep, your best bet is the Two-Week Study Plan.

Regardless of your chosen plan, you have flexibility in how you follow the instructions. You can stick to the order and timing that the plan recommends or tailor those recommendations to fit your particular study schedule. For example, if you have six weeks before your exam, you could use the One-Month Study Plan but spread out the recommended activities for Week 1 across the first two weeks of your studying.

You can further customize any of the study plans by skipping over chapters or sections that you've already mastered or by adjusting the recommended time to better suit your schedule. Don't forget to also use the guidelines in the Rapid Review chapters to further customize how you study.

STRATEGIES FOR EACH QUESTION TYPE

The AP Human Geography exam can be challenging, but with the right strategic mindset, you can get yourself on track for earning the 3, 4, or 5 that you need to qualify for college credit or advanced placement. The following are strategies to aid you on each section of the exam. These strategies and the information reviewed in the following chapters will set you up for success on the official exam.

Multiple-Choice Questions

Multiple-choice questions will ask about a variety of topics, ranging from more straightforward to more complex. One question might ask you to identify a type of diffusion, while the next question might ask you to apply a geography model to a hypothetical scenario, and the question after that might ask you to analyze relevant trends based on a map.

Terminology

There are many important key terms in human geography, and multiple-choice questions will fold these terms into both the question and the answer choices. Therefore, in order to answer the questions, you'll need to have a solid foundation of geography terminology. Free-response questions (as you'll see below) also rely on knowledge of terminology, so learning these terms and practicing with them in the multiple-choice section will help prepare you for the AP exam as a whole.

When studying terminology, it's crucial to learn both the definitions of terms and the connections they have to other terms and topics. For example, to answer a question about the findings of Thomas Malthus, you need to know about birth rate, death rate, and exponential population growth; furthermore, you need to know how Malthusian theory relates to modern-day population and food production trends.

The Rapid Review and Practice chapters (3–9) in this book focus heavily on lists of key terms and practice questions. We do this precisely so you can master all of the proper terminology more efficiently in preparation for your exam!

Stimulus Analysis

Recently, the College Board has begun adding more stimulus-based questions. These are questions with some type of chart, map, graph, or other visual element attached to the question. Before you spend too much time studying the stimulus, make sure you read the question stem and understand what is being asked. It may be that the question is only focused on a certain part of a map or section of a chart, or that the question is about the general topic that the image depicts.

For any stimulus, focusing on just a few main aspects will often yield what you need to answer the question at hand.

- **Titles or captions:** Students are often tempted to skip these seemingly simple features, but a lot of information can be gleaned from them. Read any titles or captions carefully, noting the subject as well as any years, sources, or other pertinent details.

- **Keys or labels:** There might be shading in a map, or bars in a graph, that you need to understand in order to answer the question. The AP exam will always provide a key or label to help you decode this information.

- **Trends:** Think about what trends or patterns this stimulus is depicting, where they are occurring, and where they are *not* occurring. It may help to think about why people would have created the image. What were they trying to convey? Why did they choose to include certain information? After all, maps, charts, and other visuals are ways we organize information to better understand it.

Keep in mind that you'll need to both analyze the stimulus *and* use your prior knowledge in order to answer these questions. Plan your time accordingly with stimulus-based questions, as they will take more time than typical multiple-choice questions.

Pacing and Strategy

With 60 minutes to answer 60 multiple-choice questions, you have an average of one minute per question. Keep in mind, however, that some questions, such as stimulus-based questions, may naturally take longer to answer, while other questions may take less time. As you move through the exam, answer questions as efficiently as you can in order to save extra time for the questions that need it.

The questions on the exam are numbered, but that doesn't mean you have to answer them in the order presented. Every question, regardless of how hard or easy it seems, is worth the same amount. That means you should feel free to answer the questions in an order that plays to your strengths and minimizes your weaknesses. A solid strategy is to do multiple passes:

1. On your first pass, answer all of the questions that you know and are sure about.

2. Next, go back through the remaining questions. If you can eliminate at least two answer choices and the topic is familiar, take your best educated guess as to the answer. If you look at the question and do not remember the topic, mark the question with an X in your exam booklet and move on. (If you skip a question, make sure that you skip that line on the answer grid!)

3. Go back through the exam for a third time to answer the questions you marked with an X. Again, try to eliminate at least two choices, and take an educated guess. If you're still not sure, at this point, just bubble in an answer for the question; remember that there is no penalty for guessing on the AP exam multiple-choice questions.

4. With the time remaining, remove any extraneous marks in your answer grid (such as any X's you may have written in), and make sure that the answers you have bubbled in correspond to the correct numbers in the test booklet.

Educated Guessing

The AP exam does not deduct points for wrong answers, so never leave a multiple-choice question unanswered! A blind guess on the AP Human Geography exam gives you a 1-in-5 (20%) chance of getting the correct answer. Even better, every incorrect answer you can confidently eliminate increases those odds, and if you eliminate all four incorrect answer choices, you just got the question right. So, whenever the correct answer isn't immediately clear, start eliminating and see where it gets you.

When guessing, keep in mind that you should *not* change an answer you have made unless you are absolutely sure that your initial answer is incorrect. Research shows that your first attempt is usually the correct one.

Scoring

The multiple-choice section is scored electronically. Each correct question is awarded one point, and no points are deducted for incorrect or unanswered questions. The multiple-choice section is worth half of your total score, with the other half coming from the free-response section.

Free-Response Questions

The 75-minute free-response section consists of three questions. You must answer all three. You do not have the option, as in some other AP exams, to choose the questions that you would like to answer.

Each question will include a geographic scenario and address multiple topics in AP Human Geography; for instance, a question might describe demographic conditions in a particular country and then ask you to relate the topic of the country's economic development to the topic of its urbanization.

Each question consists of seven tasks, labeled (A)–(G). Although this may sound like a lot of parts to answer, the questions are structured to ask progressively more challenging tasks that will help you think through the prompt and build your answer. For example, Part A may ask you to identify a concept; Part B, to describe an example of that concept; and Part C, to explain how that concept relates to another topic.

Some free-response questions will include a source stimulus, such as a map, image, or graph. Question 1 will always have no source stimulus, Question 2 will always contain one source stimulus, and Question 3 will always have two source stimuli to consider. See Chapter 17 for more information about how to approach free-response questions with and without stimuli.

Unlike some other AP tests, the AP Human Geography exam does not require you to write a long essay with a thesis statement. Instead, you should write a sentence or paragraph for each part of the prompt and label each part (A, B, etc.). Do everything you can to make it straightforward for the readers to follow your responses and easily locate your quality content. Make them want to give you those points!

Pacing

Because each of the three questions counts equally in your overall score, you should practice pacing yourself to make sure you have adequate time to answer each prompt fully. When practicing, use a watch, and devote about 25 minutes to each question, divided into 5 minutes for planning and 20 minutes for writing each response. See Chapter 17 for a simple 4-step method to help you successfully approach every free-response question.

You must respond to all three prompts to earn a high score, but the order in which you answer the prompts doesn't matter. Therefore, begin with the prompt(s) that you feel you can write about most confidently, with the strongest supporting information. Just be sure to write each response on the corresponding page of your answer booklet so the readers know which question you are answering.

Practice, Practice, Practice

Now you've learned about the structure of the exam sections and the types of questions you'll encounter. This knowledge will help you confidently approach the official AP exam; but to maximize your scoring potential, you'll need to practice. The Rapid Review quizzes (Chapters 3–9), the free-response chapter (Chapter 17), the full-length exams, and the additional quizzes in your online resources provide the perfect opportunity to practice your skills with hundreds of exam-like questions!

✔ AP Expert Note

Practice your Test Day mindset

Having the right mindset plays a large part in how well people do on a test. Students who practice consciously reframing feelings of nervousness as excitement when taking tests can approach their AP exams with a more confident attitude; this helps sharpen their focus and often leads to higher scores. Practice developing a confident mindset—no matter what happens, you've prepared for this exam and you *can* do well. As you work your way through the exam, devote your attention to just one question at a time, and don't be afraid to pause and take a few refocusing, deep breaths as needed. You've got this!

COUNTDOWN TO THE EXAM

This book contains detailed review, guidance, and practice for you to utilize in the weeks leading up to your AP exam. In the final few days before the official exam, we recommend the following steps.

Three Days Before the Exam

Take a full-length practice exam under timed conditions. Use the techniques and strategies you've learned in this book. Approach the exam strategically, actively, and confidently. Note that you should *not* take a full-length practice exam with fewer than 48 hours left before your real exam. Doing so will probably exhaust you and hurt your score.

Two Days Before the Exam

Go over the results of your latest practice exam. Don't worry too much about your score or whether you got a specific question right or wrong. Instead, examine your overall performance on the different topics, choose a few of the topics where you struggled the most, and brush up on them one final time.

The Night Before the Exam

DO NOT STUDY. Get together an "AP Exam Kit" containing the following items:

- A few No. 2 pencils (Pencils with slightly dull points fill the ovals better; mechanical pencils are NOT permitted.)

- A few pens with black or dark blue ink (for the free-response questions)

- Erasers

- A watch (as long as it doesn't have Internet access, have an alarm, or make noise)

- Your 6-digit school code (Home-schooled students will be provided with their state's or country's home-school code at the time of the exam.)

- Photo ID card

- Your AP Student Pack

- If applicable, your Student Accommodation Letter, which verifies that you have been approved for a testing accommodation such as braille or large-type exams

Make sure that you don't bring anything that is *not* allowed in the exam room. You can find a complete list on the College Board's website (https://apstudent.collegeboard.org/home). Your school may have additional restrictions, so make sure you get this information from your school's AP coordinator prior to the exam.

Know exactly where you're going, how you're getting there, and how long it takes to get there. It's probably a good idea to visit your testing center sometime before the day of your exam so that you know what to expect: what the rooms are like, how the desks are set up, and so on.

Relax the night before the exam: read a good book, take a hot shower, watch something you'll enjoy. Get a good night's sleep. Go to bed early and leave yourself extra time in the morning.

The Morning of the Exam

First, make sure you wake up on time. Then:

- Eat breakfast. Make it something substantial, but nothing too heavy or greasy.

- Don't drink a lot of caffeine, especially if you're not used to it. Bathroom breaks cut into your time, and too much caffeine is a bad idea.

- Dress in layers so that you can adjust to the temperature of the testing room.

- Read something. Warm up your brain with a newspaper or a magazine. You shouldn't let the exam be the first thing you read that day.

- Be sure to get there early. Allow yourself extra time for traffic, mass transit delays, and/or detours.

During the Exam

Don't be shaken. If you find your confidence slipping, remind yourself how well you've prepared. You know the structure of the exam and you've had practice with every question type.

If something goes really wrong, don't panic. If you accidentally misgrid your answer page or put the answers in the wrong section, raise your hand and tell the proctor. He or she may be able to arrange for you to regrid your exam after it's over, when it won't cost you any time.

After the Exam

You might walk out of the AP exam thinking that you blew it. This is a normal reaction. Lots of people—even the highest scorers—feel that way. You tend to remember the questions that stumped you, not the ones that you knew. Keep in mind that almost nobody gets everything correct. You can still score a 4 or 5 even if you get some multiple-choice questions incorrect or miss several points on a free-response question.

We're positive that you will have performed well and scored your best on the exam because you followed the Kaplan strategies outlined in this chapter and reviewed all the content provided in the other chapters. Be confident in your preparation, and celebrate the fact that, after many hours of hard work, you have just completed the AP Human Geography exam!

PART 2

Rapid Review and Practice

CHAPTER 3

Thinking Geographically

LEARNING OBJECTIVES

- Define major geographical concepts and geography's importance.

- Interpret map data.

- Analyze data across different scales.

- Interpret quantitative, qualitative, and geospatial geographic data.

- Explain the nature of regions and the regionalization process, and give examples of regions.

- Describe the human organization of space using landscape analysis and spatial thinking.

- Describe how people interact and exchange resources differently over time.

- Interpret geographic concepts using mathematical formulas and graphs.

- Apply major geographic models to specific topics and questions.

TEST WHAT YOU ALREADY KNOW

Part A: Quiz

> **Questions 1–2 refer to the following table.**

Metropolitan Area	African American Population, 1940	African American Population, 1970
New York City	661,100	2,347,100
Chicago	346,800	1,328,600
Los Angeles	76,200	765,800
Detroit	168,600	753,800
Washington, D.C.	251,600	695,100

1. The table above best exemplifies which of the following concepts?

    (A) Contagious diffusion

    (B) Stimulus diffusion

    (C) Relocation diffusion

    (D) Hierarchical diffusion

    (E) Expansion diffusion

2. In analyzing population movements in a country, which of the following would be most helpful?

    (A) Historical data about population movements in that country

    (B) Contemporaneous accounts of population movements

    (C) Historical data about population movements across the world

    (D) Population density maps of the country's largest cities

    (E) Maps showing all the physical features of that country

3. A geographer who supports the theory of environmental determinism would most likely agree with which of the following statements?

    (A) Humans are not entirely a product of their environment, and they possess the skills to adapt their environment to fit their needs.

    (B) A society's physical and intellectual attributes are shaped by the location and climate in which they develop.

    (C) Human activity has resulted in global climate change and increasingly severe weather patterns.

    (D) Most societies can control their environment to their benefit, resulting in higher levels of economic development.

    (E) Societies are not influenced by their environments, instead developing independently of environmental factors.

4. Which of the following statements is most clearly an instance of the ecological fallacy?

    (A) Climate and ecosystems remain constant over time.

    (B) Extrapolations between scales are permissible as long as the data is accurate.

    (C) The environment dictates the development and customs of any society.

    (D) Slash-and-burn agriculture has a low impact on pollution.

    (E) Regions rich in natural resources always have advanced economies.

5. Which of the following best explains the primary difference between "site" and "situation"?

(A) Site refers to a location's physical characteristics, while situation refers to the relationship between that location and the surrounding area.

(B) Site refers to the relationship between a location and the surrounding area, while situation refers to that location's intrinsic characteristics.

(C) Site refers to a permanent location, while situation refers to the temporary location of a society.

(D) Site refers to the natural resources available in a region, while situation refers to the manufactured products created from them.

(E) Site refers to an intentionally built community, while situation refers to a community that originates organically.

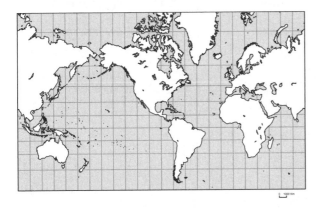

6. The above image of the Mercator map projection best illustrates which problem in mapping?

(A) Distortion

(B) Projection

(C) Extrapolation

(D) Regionalism

(E) Situation

7. Which of the following maps would likely have the largest scale?

(A) A map of a country

(B) A map of a region

(C) A map of the world

(D) A map of a city

(E) A map of weather patterns

8. Which of the following statements best demonstrates the effect that natural features like mountain ranges and oceans have on human geography?

(A) Natural features shape the diffusion of cultural ideas and populations.

(B) Natural features determine the material utility of natural resources.

(C) Natural features control the population of surrounding countries.

(D) Natural features determine the creation of new societal organizations.

(E) Natural features shape the societal structure of surrounding countries.

9. To an average American, who has never traveled outside of the United States, what does "Western Europe" best represent?

(A) An economic region

(B) A technological region

(C) A geographic region

(D) A perceptual region

(E) A functional region

10. Which of the following latitudes would go through the state of Alaska?

(A) 90 degrees north

(B) 60 degrees north

(C) 0 degrees

(D) 60 degrees south

(E) 90 degrees south

3

Part B: Key Terms

The following is a list of the major concepts for the AP Human Geography topic of Thinking Geographically. You will likely see many of these on the official AP exam.

For each key term, ask yourself the following questions:

①. Can I define this key term and use it in a sentence?

②. Can I provide an example related to this key term? *(past and/present)*

• Could I correctly answer a multiple-choice question about this key term?

• Could I correctly answer a free-response question about this key term?

Check off the key terms if you can answer "yes" to at least three of these questions.

Directions: For any you can't ☆, create a google slide completing #1 and #2

Historical Foundations of Geography

☐ Geography   ☐ Possibilism   ☐ Geographic information systems (GIS)

☐ Environmental determinism   ☐ Global positioning systems (GPS)

Maps: An Introduction

☐ Scale   ☐ Planar maps   ☐ Isoline maps

☐ Equal-area projection   ☐ Conic maps   ☐ Flow-line maps

☐ Oval maps   ☐ Choropleth maps

☐ Conformal maps   ☐ Thematic maps   ☐ Cartograms

☐ Cylindrical maps

Themes of Geography

- ☐ Human geography
- ☐ Built landscape
- ☐ Sequent occupance
- ☐ Physical geography
- ☐ Place
- ☐ Region
- ☐ Formal regions
- ☐ Functional regions

- ☐ Perceptual/ vernacular region
- ☐ Relative location
- ☐ Absolute location
- ☐ Site
- ☐ Situation
- ☐ Latitudes (parallels)
- ☐ Equator

- ☐ Longitudes (meridians)
- ☐ Prime meridian
- ☐ Time zone
- ☐ International Date Line
- ☐ Human-environment interaction
- ☐ Spatial interaction/ movement

Diffusion

- ☐ Hearth
- ☐ Relocation diffusion

- ☐ Expansion diffusion
- ☐ Hierarchical diffusion

- ☐ Contagious diffusion
- ☐ Stimulus diffusion

Distribution

- ☐ Density
- ☐ Physiological density

- ☐ Arithmetic density
- ☐ Agricultural density

- ☐ Concentration
- ☐ Pattern

Mathematical Principles and Geographic Models

- ☐ Ecological fallacy
- ☐ Rank-size rule

Next Steps

Step 1: Tally your correct answers from Part A and review the quiz explanations at the end of this chapter.

1.	C	6.	A
2.	A	7.	D
3.	B	8.	A
4.	B	9.	D
5.	A	10.	B

_____ out of 10 questions

Step 2: Count the number of key terms you checked off in Part B.

_____ out of 52 key terms

Step 3: Read the Key Takeaways in this chapter.

Step 4: Consult the table below, and follow the instructions based on your performance.

If You Got...	Do This
80% or more of the Test What You Already Know assessment correct (8 or more questions from Part A and 42 or more key terms from Part B)	• Read the definitions in this chapter for all the key terms you didn't check off. • Complete the Test What You Learned assessment in this chapter.
50% or less of the Test What You Already Know assessment correct (5 or fewer questions from Part A and 26 or fewer key terms from Part B)	• Read the comprehensive review for this topic in Chapter 10. ◦ If you are short on time, read only the High-Yield sections. • Read through all of the key term definitions in this chapter. • Complete the Test What You Learned assessment in this chapter.
Any other result	• Read the High-Yield sections in the comprehensive review of this topic in Chapter 10. • Read the definitions in this chapter for all the key terms you didn't check off. • Complete the Test What You Learned assessment in this chapter.

ESSENTIAL CONTENT

Key Takeaways: Thinking Geographically

1. The five themes of geography allow geographers to make each place unique and to tie them together. Humans alter the environment to meet their needs.

2. Diffusion is the spread or movement of a principle or phenomenon. Relocation and expansion diffusion are means by which an idea or phenomenon spreads. Expansion diffusion is further broken down into contagious, stimulus, and hierarchical diffusion.

3. There are three types of regions: formal, functional, and perceptual/vernacular.

4. There are three main aspects of distribution: density, concentration, and patterns. All are used to assist in determining spatial characteristics of the landscape.

5. Geography is a multidisciplinary approach to studying the world around us. Logic, data analysis, and models are thus important tools.

3

Key Terms: Thinking Geographically

Historical Foundations of Geography

Geography: The description of the Earth's surface and the people and processes that shape those landscapes.

Environmental determinism: A philosophy of geography that stated that human behaviors are a direct result of the surrounding environment. While discredited for decades due to its use as a justification for European imperialism, it has undergone a recent revival in the form of neo-environmental determinism. This variation emphasizes how natural resources and ecology affect the development, expansion, and potential collapse of societies.

Possibilism: An approach to geography favored by most contemporary geographers. Possibilism suggests that humans are not a product of their environment; instead, they possess the skills necessary to change their environment to satisfy human needs. People can determine their own outcomes without regard to location.

Global positioning systems (GPS): A way for geographers to obtain new information, GPS technology is found in cars and cellphones; it uses the Earth's latitude and longitude coordinates to determine an exact location. It is owned by the U.S. government. GLONASS is the Russian competitor and counterpart to GPS.

Geographic information systems (GIS): A way for geographers to obtain new information, GIS layers geographic information into a map, showing specific types of geographic data. Watersheds, population density, highways, and agricultural data are geographic features that can be used as layers of data. Satellite imagery is important for GIS.

Maps: An Introduction

Scale: The relationship of the size of the map to the amount of area it represents on the planet. In other words, scale is the abstract dimension into which one renders the real world.

Equal-area projection: Maps that try to distribute distortion equally throughout the map; these maps distort shapes.

Conformal maps: Maps that distort area but keep shapes intact.

Cylindrical maps: Maps that distort shapes but show true direction (e.g., a Mercator map).

Planar maps: Maps that show true direction and examine the Earth from one point, usually from a pole or a polar direction (e.g., any azimuthal map).

Conic maps: Maps that put a cone over the Earth and keep distance intact but lose directional qualities.

Oval maps: Maps that combine the cylindrical and conic projections (e.g., the Molleweide projection).

Maps: An Introduction (cont.)

Thematic maps: Used to determine some type of geographic phenomenon, thematic maps can be represented in various ways: area class maps, area symbol maps, cartograms, choropleth maps, digital images, dot maps, flow-line maps, isoline maps, point symbol maps, and proportional symbol maps.

Isoline maps: An abstract map which outlines and connects points of identical value. An example is the weather map, which shows temperature or rainfall as overlapping colored blobs.

Flow-line maps: Maps that are good for determining movement, such as migration trends.

Choropleth maps: Maps that put data into a spatial format and are useful for determining demographic data by assigning colors or patterns to areas.

Cartograms: Maps that assign space by the size of some datum. For example, world population by country is often illustrated in a cartogram, with countries with larger populations appearing larger on the map.

Themes of Geography

Human geography: The study of human characteristics on the landscape, including population, agriculture, urbanization, and culture.

Built landscape: The sum of tangible human creations on the landscape.

Sequent occupance: The idea that each civilization leaves an influence on the cultural landscape of place, affecting the civilizations that come after them.

Physical geography: The study of the physical features of the Earth and the attempt to define how they work.

Place: The description of what we see and of how we experience a certain aspect of the Earth's surface.

Region: A concept used to link different places together based on any parameter the geographer chooses.

Formal regions: Regions where anything and everything inside has the same characteristics or phenomena.

Functional regions: Regions that can be defined around a certain point or node; functional regions are most intense around the center but lose their characteristics as the distance from the focal point increases.

Perceptual/vernacular region: A region that exists primarily in the individual's perception or feelings (e.g., the concept of "the South" differs depending on where someone lives in the United States).

Relative location: A location that is based on, or refers to, another feature on the Earth's surface.

Absolute location: Location based on latitude and longitude coordinates.

Site: The internal characteristics of a place based on its physical features.

Situation: The relationship that a particular location has with the locations around it.

Latitudes (parallels): Parallel lines that run east/west on the surface of the Earth; the highest degree of latitude is 90 degrees.

3

Themes of Geography (cont.)

Equator: The latitude line that runs through the middle of the Earth. It is at 0 degrees latitude. Anything to the north of the equator is in the northern hemisphere, and anything to the south of the equator is in the southern hemisphere.

Longitudes (meridians): Parallel lines that run north/south on the surface of the Earth.

Prime meridian: The 0 degree longitude line, which runs through Greenwich, in southeast London, England. It divides the eastern hemisphere and the western hemisphere.

Time zone: Based largely on the 15-degree longitude principle, although the exact location of the line may vary to take into account other factors, such as political boundaries and domestic political policy.

International Date Line: An imaginary boundary between one day and the next. It was created alongside the international system of time zones. The farthest that one can go on the longitude scale is 180 degrees, and that longitude roughly represents the International Date Line. It zigzags its way through the Pacific Ocean, owing to the location of countries there.

Human-environment interaction: How people modify or alter the environment to fit individual or societal needs.

Spatial interaction/movement: Concerned with how linked a place is to the outside world, because how well an area is connected to the world determines its importance.

Diffusion

Hearth: The place where a given characteristic began.

Relocation diffusion: The spreading of a custom when people move; language tends to be spread through relocation diffusion.

Expansion diffusion: The term used to describe the spread of a characteristic from a central node through various means. There are three different types of expansion diffusion: hierarchical, contagious, and stimulus diffusion.

Hierarchical diffusion: The notion that a phenomenon spreads as a result of the social elite, such as political leaders, entertainment leaders, or famous athletes, spreading societal ideas or trends.

Contagious diffusion: The process of spreading a culture from one place to another through direct contact, similar to the way disease spreads.

Stimulus diffusion: The spread of a particular concept that is then used in another product.

Distribution

Density: A term used to describe how often an object occurs within a given area or space; most often used in terms of population density, or the average number of inhabitants per unit area.

Physiological density: Refers to the total number of people divided by the arable (farmable) land; a more accurate measure of population density than arithmetic density.

Arithmetic density: Determined by dividing the population of a country by the total land area.

Distribution (cont.)

Agricultural density: The number of farmers per unit area of arable (farmable) land.

Concentration: The density of particular phenomena over an area; in terms of concentration, objects can either be clustered (close together) or dispersed (scattered).

Pattern: Patterns are related to how objects are organized in their space. May be anything from triangular to linear or even three-dimensional, as with high-rise buildings. Geometric shapes are used to describe how the phenomena are laid out. If the items are laid out on a singular line, the pattern is linear. If they're clustered together, the pattern is centralized. The lack of a pattern on the landscape is called a random distribution.

Mathematical Principles and Geographic Models

Ecological fallacy: The assumption that the relationships at one scale also exist at other scales.

Rank-size rule: The principle that relates cities' relative population sizes to their rank within a country.

TEST WHAT YOU LEARNED

Part A: Quiz

3

1. What is the most significant difference between GPS and GIS?

    (A) GPS uses computer software, whereas GIS uses satellite triangulation.

    (B) GPS is used for creating maps, whereas GIS is used for navigation.

    (C) GPS is solely used for military purposes, whereas GIS is available to civilians.

    (D) GPS finds one specific location, whereas GIS finds multiple different locations.

    (E) GPS provides one type of data, whereas GIS combines multiple types of data.

2. Which of the following terms does NOT refer to a class of map used by cartographers?

    (A) Cylindrical

    (B) Planar

    (C) Regional

    (D) Oval

    (E) Conic

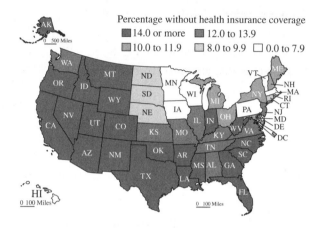

Uninsured Rate by State: 2012

3. The map demonstrates which of the following data representation concepts?

    (A) Concentration

    (B) Density

    (C) Pattern

    (D) Diffusion

    (E) Time–space compression

4. The theory that holds that human societies can shape their environments to suit their needs rather than being constrained by their environments is called

    (A) possibilism

    (B) neo-possibilism

    (C) environmental determinism

    (D) neo-environmental determinism

    (E) geocentrism

Country	Population	Area in square miles
United States	327,000,000	3,979,000
Bangladesh	163,000,000	56,980

5. Based on the information in the table, which of the following measurements is higher in Bangladesh than in the United States?

   (A) Physiological density

   (B) Arithmetic density

   (C) Agricultural density

   (D) Cultural density

   (E) National density

6. Which of the following would NOT be described as a culture hearth?

   (A) The Fertile Crescent

   (B) The Indus River Valley

   (C) The Swiss Alps

   (D) Hollywood

   (E) Tokyo

7. The prime meridian establishes

   (A) the location of longitude zero degrees

   (B) the center of population of the United Kingdom

   (C) the equator

   (D) the reference point for Daylight Savings Time

   (E) the division of northern and southern hemispheres

8. Which of the following scenarios best exemplifies the concept of distance decay?

   (A) A person who lives in Nebraska but reads *The New York Times*

   (B) A person who lives far away from a shopping mall and therefore visits it infrequently

   (C) A person who lives in a neighborhood with few supermarkets but many fast-food chains

   (D) A person who sees a celebrity wearing a particular style and purchases similar garments

   (E) A viral video spreading all around the world via the Internet

9. The European Union (EU) is comprised of 28 member states, many of which share a common currency, and allows freedom of movement between countries within its boundaries. The EU can best be characterized as an example of which of the following?

   (A) Perceptual region

   (B) Functional region

   (C) Agricultural region

   (D) Formal region

   (E) Cultural region

10. In what pattern would rural settlements around a large water source be arranged for best access to the water source?

   (A) Random distribution

   (B) Centralized

   (C) Dispersed

   (D) Scattered

   (E) Linear

3

Part B: Key Terms

This key terms list is the same as the list in the Test What You Already Know section earlier in this chapter. Based on what you have now learned, again ask yourself the following questions:

- Can I define this key term and use it in a sentence?
- Can I provide an example related to this key term?
- Could I correctly answer a multiple-choice question about this key term?
- Could I correctly answer a free-response question about this key term?

Check off the key terms if you can answer "yes" to at least three of these questions.

Historical Foundations of Geography

- ☐ Geography
- ☐ Environmental determinism
- ☐ Possibilism
- ☐ Global positioning systems (GPS)
- ☐ Geographic information systems (GIS)

Maps: An Introduction

- ☐ Scale
- ☐ Equal-area projection
- ☐ Conformal maps
- ☐ Cylindrical maps
- ☐ Planar maps
- ☐ Conic maps
- ☐ Oval maps
- ☐ Thematic maps
- ☐ Isoline maps
- ☐ Flow-line maps
- ☐ Choropleth maps
- ☐ Cartograms

Themes of Geography

- ☐ Human geography
- ☐ Built landscape
- ☐ Sequent occupance
- ☐ Physical geography
- ☐ Place
- ☐ Region
- ☐ Formal regions
- ☐ Functional regions

- ☐ Perceptual/ vernacular region
- ☐ Relative location
- ☐ Absolute location
- ☐ Site
- ☐ Situation
- ☐ Latitudes (parallels)
- ☐ Equator
- ☐ Longitudes (meridians)

- ☐ Prime meridian
- ☐ Time zone
- ☐ International Date Line
- ☐ Human-environment interaction
- ☐ Spatial interaction/ movement

Diffusion

- ☐ Hearth
- ☐ Relocation diffusion

- ☐ Expansion diffusion
- ☐ Hierarchical diffusion

- ☐ Contagious diffusion
- ☐ Stimulus diffusion

Distribution

- ☐ Density
- ☐ Physiological density

- ☐ Arithmetic density
- ☐ Agricultural density

- ☐ Concentration
- ☐ Pattern

Mathematical Principles and Geographic Models

- ☐ Ecological fallacy
- ☐ Rank-size rule

Next Steps

Step 1: Tally your correct answers from Part A, and review the quiz explanations at the end of this chapter.

1. E   6. C

2. C   7. A

3. A   8. B

4. A   9. D

5. B   10. B

_____ out of 10 questions

Step 2: Count the number of key terms you checked off in Part B.

_____ out of 52 key terms

Step 3: Compare your Test What You Already Know results to these Test What You Learned results to see how exam-ready you are for this topic.

For More Practice:

- Read (or reread) the comprehensive review for this topic in Chapter 10.
- Go to kaptest.com to complete the online quiz questions for Thinking Geographically.
  - Haven't registered your book yet? Go to **kaptest.com/moreonline** to begin.

CHAPTER 3 ANSWERS AND EXPLANATIONS

Test What You Already Know

1. C

The table shows how African American populations greatly increased in major U.S. cities from 1940 to 1970 (during the second wave of the Great Migration). Relocation diffusion includes the physical spread of people and ideas from one place to another; thus, **(C)** is correct. The rest of the answer choices cannot be derived from the data at hand. Contagious diffusion is a rapid spread of culture, analogous to the way disease can spread through a population; (A) is incorrect. Stimulus diffusion occurs when an idea spreads to create an innovative product; (B) is incorrect. Hierarchical diffusion results when an idea spreads due to the influence of a particular group, so (D) is incorrect. Expansion diffusion is the spread of a characteristic from a central node or a hearth through various means, and it encompasses hierarchical, contagious, and stimulus diffusion; (E) is also incorrect.

2. A

To make an analysis, you must have some frame of reference for evaluating your data. In this case, the best comparison would be with historical population movements in the given country, which would allow you to see if recent data were a continuation of an older pattern or something new. **(A)** is thus correct. Accounts from the time of the population movements would be interesting but not necessary for a geographic analysis; (B) is incorrect. Worldwide population movements would be too diffuse, and to apply them to a specific case in a specific country would be an example of the ecological fallacy; (C) is incorrect. Similarly, (D) and (E) would not make for a direct comparison, though they could be used as supporting evidence.

3. B

At its simplest, the theory of environmental determinism states that human societies are formed by the environments in which they originate. Thus, **(B)** is correct. (A) and (E) are incorrect because they reference the opposing theory of environmental possibilism. Though (C) is a true statement, it refers to anthropogenic changes in the environment, not the theory of environmental determinism, so it is incorrect. Although many human societies modify their environment through farming and landscaping, this does not always correlate with economic development, nor does it reflect the theory of environmental determinism; (D) is incorrect.

4. B

The ecological fallacy is a failure in reasoning that occurs when an observation at one scale is applied to another scale. Ecological in this case refers to systems, not the environment. An example would be assuming that an individual student's favorite food is chocolate simply because chocolate was voted the favorite food at the student's school. The fact that data is correct is not enough to justify extrapolating between different scales, so **(B)** is correct. The remaining choices, (A), (C), (D), and (E), represent other fallacious or incorrect statements, but they are not examples of the ecological fallacy.

5. A

Site refers to the intrinsic characteristics of a location, which are often physical. Situation refers to the attributes of a location that are relative to the resources around it. The city of New Orleans is an example of a city with a poor site (prone to flooding) but a good situation (located in the Mississippi River delta). Thus, **(A)** is correct. (B) is incorrect because it reverses the definitions of the two terms. (C)–(E) are incorrect because neither site nor situation has to do with temporary locations, natural resources, or intentionality.

6. A

Distortion, or the misrepresentation of proportion and distance, is an unavoidable consequence of mapping three-dimensional objects. While the Mercator map projection, shown in the image, is useful for navigation and determining distance on the surface of the earth, it greatly exaggerates the land forms around the polar regions. This is why Greenland looks as though it is the size of Africa on a Mercator map projection, when in reality Greenland is only a fraction of the size of Africa. Thus, **(A)** is correct. Projection refers to the method by which a map is drawn; this is not a problem with maps, so (B) incorrect. Extrapolation is the process of applying observations from a small data set to a larger data set; (C) is incorrect. (D) is incorrect because, although regionalism could be an issue with a given map, it is not depicted in the Mercator map of the entire world shown here. Finally, situation refers to the relationship between a location and its surrounding area; (E) is incorrect.

7. D

Scale is the proportion of the size of the map to the amount of area it represents. Counterintuitively, a large-scale map shows a small area in greater detail; therefore, **(D)** is correct. (A), (B), and (C) are all likely to represent larger areas than a city map and would thus be at a small scale. Weather maps could be of any scale; (E) is incorrect.

8. A

Natural features like oceans, mountains, and deserts affect the movement of populations, languages, and religions, and shape their spread; **(A)** is correct. (B) is incorrect because it concerns a natural effect of these features, rather than an effect on human geography. Population is determined by many factors and is not necessarily controlled by natural features, particularly given the ability of humans to reshape our environment; (C) is incorrect. Similarly, natural features are not necessarily major factors in the organization of governments or societies, particularly with the compression of time and space through communication technology and the quick spread of ideas; (D) and (E) are incorrect.

9. D

A perceptual region, also called a vernacular region, represents the perception of an individual regarding a certain area. This perception could be highly accurate or highly inaccurate, and varies from person to person. **(D)** is correct. (A), (B), and (C) do not represent types of regions in geography, but might be used that way in common parlance. A functional region is defined by its organization around a focal point, or node, which does not describe Western Europe; (E) is incorrect.

10. B

Latitudes are imaginary parallel lines, measured in degrees, that run east/west on the Earth's surface. The most northern latitude measure possible is 90 degrees north: the North Pole. The most southern latitude is 90 degrees south: the South Pole. Alaska is far to the north and borders Canada, but it is not located at the North Pole; thus, **(B)** is correct. (A) represents the North Pole, (C) represents the equator, (D) is in the opposite hemisphere to Alaska, and (E) represents the South Pole.

Test What You Learned

1. E

The global positioning system (GPS) determines location using satellite triangulation. A geographic information system (GIS) is a computer system that takes multiple types of data and combines and uses it in many complex ways. For example, GIS could layer streets, bodies of water, buildings, vegetation, and population density onto the same map in order to better analyze patterns and relationships. Therefore, **(E)** is correct and (A) is incorrect. (B) is incorrect because it reverses the roles of both systems. Both systems are available to and are used by civilians, making (C) incorrect. GIS does not itself discover locations, but is instead used to gather data; (D) is incorrect.

2. C

Cartographers use four different classes of maps: cylindrical, planar, oval, and conic. These classes are defined by the different types of projection and what kind of distortion results from each. Though cartographers make regional maps, regional is not a class of map. Therefore, **(C)** is correct, and (A), (B), (D), and (E) are incorrect.

3. A

Concentration is a comparative measure of data points between areas. This is depicted in the map through the various colors that represent the percentage of people; **(A)** is correct. Density is the analysis of data points in a single area, which does not fit the above map, so (B) is incorrect. Pattern refers to the spatial orientation of objects; (C) is incorrect. Diffusion refers to the movement of things through time, and this data is a single snapshot, so (D) cannot be correct. Time–space compression refers to the changes brought about by electronic communications; (E) is incorrect.

4. A

In the 1920s, Carl Sauer promoted possibilism as an alternative to the then-dominant school of environmental determinism. There is no neo-possibilism school. Thus, **(A)** is correct, while (B) and (C) are incorrect. Neo-environmental determinism arose in the 1990s, but it is still a minority school of thought; (D) is incorrect. Geo-centrism is the belief that the sun revolves around the Earth, which was disproved in the seventeenth century; (E) is incorrect.

5. B

Arithmetic density is a simple measure of the number of people per unit of land. Bangladesh has half the population of the United States, but approximately 1/80th the land area, meaning it has a much higher arithmetic density; **(B)** is correct. Physiological density measures the number of people per unit of arable land, which is not reflected in the table, so (A) is incorrect. Agricultural density is the ratio of farmers to units of arable land, which is not reflected in the table; (C) is incorrect. (D) and (E) are incorrect because they are not measures of population density, so the table provides no information on them.

6. C

A culture hearth is a place from which ideas originate and spread. The Swiss Alps are not known for being the source of major ideas that have then spread to other areas; **(C)** is correct. The Fertile Crescent and the Indus River Valley are examples of ancient culture hearths of agriculture, making (A) and (B) incorrect. Hollywood, in the United States, and Tokyo, in Japan, are examples of modern culture hearths; thus, (D) and (E) are incorrect.

7. A

The prime meridian is the line of longitude selected to define the location of zero degrees longitude. Thus, **(A)** is correct. The prime meridian runs through Greenwich, England, but this does not represent the center of population of the United Kingdom; (B) is incorrect. The equator divides the northern and southern hemispheres; (C) and (E) are incorrect. Though the prime meridian is associated with coordinated universal time (UTC), UTC does not observe Daylight Savings Time; (D) is also incorrect.

8. B

Distance decay is defined as the decreasing influence of a node due to increasing distance from it. For example, if a person lives far away from a shopping mall (a node), then the person is less likely to be influenced by it. **(B)** is correct. (A) is incorrect because it provides an example of a functional region. *The New York Times* has a very large functional region because it has the funding to distribute newspapers across a large geographic area. (C) is incorrect because it gives an example of a food desert, where it is difficult to buy fresh produce or healthy food. (D) is an example of hierarchical diffusion, and (E) is an example of contagious diffusion; (D) and (E) are incorrect.

9. D

Formal regions are defined by common characteristics and established borders. Within the EU, citizens and visitors enjoy protections and privileges above and beyond those offered by individual member states; **(D)** is correct. Perceptual regions exist for individuals and are not always universally shared, so (A) is incorrect. Functional regions do not have defined boundaries, so (B) is incorrect. Agricultural and cultural regions may be categories in common parlance, but they are not types of regions in geography; (C) and (E) are incorrect.

10. B

Rural settlements would be clustered around a large water source in a centralized pattern to maximize access to water, so **(B)** is correct. Randomly distributed settlements would not be close to water; (A) is incorrect. Similarly, dispersed or scattered patterns would result in uneven access to water, making (C) and (D) incorrect. A linear pattern would mean the settlements are arranged in a single line, also resulting in uneven access to water; (E) is also incorrect.

CHAPTER 4

Population and Migration Patterns and Processes

LEARNING OBJECTIVES

- Identify factors influencing population distribution.

- Describe human interaction with the environment in regard to population distribution and density.

- List factors affecting population composition.

- Explain causes and effects of changes in population policies, fertility rates, and aging.

- Analyze historical and modern-day examples of migrations.

- Explain population trends using growth and decline theories.

- Evaluate the effect of push and pull factors on migration.

- Explain the ways migration affects culture, politics, economics, and the environment.

TEST WHAT YOU ALREADY KNOW

Part A: Quiz

4

1. The birth rate in the United Kingdom is 13, while the death rate is 9, and employees are more involved in services than in the production of goods. Which of the following stages of the demographic transition model would best describe the United Kingdom?

    (A) stage 1

    (B) stage 2

    (C) stage 3

    (D) stage 4

    (E) stage 5

2. Which of the following statements best describes the main difference between population clusters in Asia and Europe?

    (A) In Asia, most people live in urban areas.

    (B) In Europe, most people live in urban areas.

    (C) In Asia, most people make their living in the secondary sector of the economy.

    (D) In Europe, most people make their living in the primary sector of the economy.

    (E) In Asia, the tertiary sector of the economy is stagnant.

Region	Land area	Population
Croatia	21,851 sq mi	4,154,000
Hong Kong	427 sq mi	7,392,000
Monaco	0.8 sq mi	38,695
Singapore	278.6 sq mi	5,612,000
United States	3,797,000 sq mi	327,200,000

3. Based on the information in the table, which of the following has the highest population density?

    (A) Croatia

    (B) Hong Kong

    (C) Monaco

    (D) Singapore

    (E) United States

4. Which of the following best describes the seasonal migration of livestock to pasture lands where food is more plentiful?

    (A) Intercontinental migration

    (B) Step migration

    (C) Interregional migration

    (D) Intraregional migration

    (E) Transhumance

5. Which of the following factors best characterizes stage 2 of the demographic transition model?

    (A) High growth

    (B) Low growth

    (C) Moderate growth

    (D) Zero growth

    (E) Negative growth

6. A person is trying to move from Miami to San Diego but decides to stop and stay in Dallas because he finds a better job. This is an example of which of the following?

   (A) Intervening obstacle

   (B) Intervening opportunity

   (C) Environmental push factor

   (D) Environmental pull factor

   (E) Distance decay

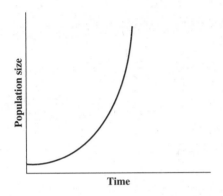

7. The J-curve, depicted in the above image, is used to illustrate which of the following geographic principles?

   (A) The tendency for cities to be associated with each other based on their population sizes

   (B) The logistic growth of a country's population

   (C) The exponential growth of a country's population

   (D) The openness and stability of countries over time

   (E) Growth that occurs evenly across each unit of time

8. The movement of people from the Rust Belt to the Sun Belt is an example of which of the following types of migration?

   (A) Intercontinental

   (B) International

   (C) Interregional

   (D) Intraregional

   (E) Intervening

9. Which of the following correctly pairs the event with its characterization as a push or pull factor?

   (A) A government persecutes a religious group: political pull factor

   (B) A new factory opens: economic push factor

   (C) A factory closes: economic pull factor

   (D) Tornadoes cause a city to evacuate: environmental push factor

   (E) An area experiences flooding: environmental pull factor

10. Enslaved Africans were brought to the Americas and the Caribbean in exchange for goods as part of the triangular trade in the sixteenth century. Which of the following best describes this type of migration?

    (A) Forced migration

    (B) Transnational migration

    (C) Internal migration

    (D) Chain migration

    (E) Step migration

4

Part B: Key Terms

The following is a list of the major concepts for the AP Human Geography topic of Population and Migration Patterns and Processes. You will likely see many of these on the official AP exam.

For each key term, ask yourself the following questions:

- Can I define this key term and use it in a sentence?
- Can I provide an example related to this key term?
- Could I correctly answer a multiple-choice question about this key term?
- Could I correctly answer a free-response question about this key term?

Check off the key terms if you can answer "yes" to at least three of these questions.

Factors Affecting Population

☐ Demography ☐ Underpopulation ☐ Environmental degradation
☐ Birth rate ☐ Overpopulation
☐ Death rate ☐ Carrying capacity

Population Distribution and Density

☐ Population density

Population and Growth

☐ Thomas Malthus ☐ Exponential growth
☐ Linear growth ☐ Neo-Malthusian

Demographic Transition Model

☐ Demographic transition model ☐ Zero population growth

Population Structure

☐ Population pyramid ☐ Demographic momentum ☐ Demographic equation
☐ Population projection ☐ Negative growth ☐ Infant mortality rate
☐ Dependency ratio

Population Equations and Scientific Methods

☐ Doubling time   ☐ Sustainability

Theories of Migration

☐ Migration
☐ Immigrants
☐ Emigrants
☐ Net migration
☐ Push factor
☐ Pull factor
☐ Refugees
☐ Place utility
☐ Internal migration
☐ Ravenstein's laws of migration

☐ Human capital model
☐ Life course theory
☐ Intercontinental migration
☐ Distance decay
☐ Acculturation
☐ Chain migration
☐ Interregional migration
☐ International migration

☐ Intraregional migration
☐ Cyclic migration
☐ Transhumance
☐ Intervening obstacle
☐ Intervening opportunity
☐ Forced migration

Next Steps

Step 1: Tally your correct answers from Part A and review the quiz explanations at the end of this chapter.

1.	D	6.	B
2.	B	7.	C
3.	C	8.	C
4.	E	9.	D
5.	A	10.	A

_____ out of 10 questions

Step 2: Count the number of key terms you checked off in Part B.

_____ out of 47 key terms

Step 3: Read the Key Takeaways in this chapter.

Step 4: Consult the table below, and follow the instructions based on your performance.

If You Got...	Do This
80% or more of the Test What You Already Know assessment correct (8 or more questions from Part A and 38 or more key terms from Part B)	• Read the definitions in this chapter for all the key terms you didn't check off. • Complete the Test What You Learned assessment in this chapter.
50% or less of the Test What You Already Know assessment correct (5 or fewer questions from Part A and 23 or fewer key terms from Part B)	• Read the comprehensive review for this topic in Chapter 11. ○ If you are short on time, read only the High-Yield sections. • Read through all of the key term definitions in this chapter. • Complete the Test What You Learned assessment in this chapter.
Any other result	• Read the High-Yield sections in the comprehensive review of this topic in Chapter 11. • Read the definitions in this chapter for all the key terms you didn't check off. • Complete the Test What You Learned assessment in this chapter.

ESSENTIAL CONTENT

Key Takeaways: Population and Migration Patterns and Processes

1. Demography is the scientific analysis of population trends, and it predicts future occurrences based on present statistics. Many factors affect a country's population growth and the allocation of resources.

2. The demographic transition model is a tool demographers use to categorize countries' population growth rates and economic structures. The model analyzes birth rates, death rates, and total population trends in a society at a given point in time.

3. The world's population is growing exponentially. Most of the growth is occurring in less developed countries (LDCs). Many of the more developed countries (MDCs) are either at or near zero population growth.

4. Population pyramids show the age and sex demographics of a particular country, city, or neighborhood. Inverted pyramids indicate a large percentage of elderly persons in the community. A large base indicates a lot of children in the society and could indicate a less developed country.

5. There are four primary push and pull factors: economic, political, environmental, and social. Each of these factors has encouraged the movement of millions of people.

Key Terms: Population and Migration Patterns and Processes

Factors Affecting Population

Demography: The study of population characteristics.

Birth rate: The number of births per 1,000 people in the population.

Death rate: The number of deaths per 1,000 people in the population.

Underpopulation: A situation where resources cannot be optimally utilized because of an insufficient number of residents in an area.

Overpopulation: A situation where resources are insufficient to meet the needs of the residents of an area.

Carrying capacity: The ability of the land to sustain a certain number of people.

Environmental degradation: The harming of the environment, which occurs when more and more humans inhabit a specific area and place a strain on the environmental resources.

Population Distribution and Density

Population density: Calculates how concentrated people are within a given area. When calculating arithmetic population density, the number of people is divided by the amount of land to arrive at a number of people per square unit of land. Besides arithmetic density, population density can be expressed in other ways, such as physiological density.

Population and Growth

Thomas Malthus: British reverend who concluded that the population was growing at a faster rate than productivity in the late 1700s; he coined the term overpopulation.

Linear growth: Growth that occurs at a constant rate over time.

Exponential growth: Growth that occurs at an increasing rate over time, typically expressed as a percentage of the total population.

Neo-Malthusian: Critics of the demographic transition model who typically advocate for population control measures.

Demographic Transition Model

Demographic transition model: A model of what will happen to a society's or country's population based on three primary factors: the birth rate, the death rate, and the total population. This model usually has four stages: hunting and gathering societies, agricultural societies, industrial societies, and tertiary societies. Sometimes a fifth stage is included, which involves quaternary activities.

Zero population growth: A phenomenon of tertiary societies (stage 4 of the demographic transition model) in which the birth rate equals the death rate.

Population Structure

Population pyramid: A tool that demographers and geographers use to chart populations on a graph that breaks down the population based on both gender and age; this can then be analyzed in terms of the demographic transition model to determine in which stage a society is grouped. Population pyramids are sometimes called age/sex structures.

Population projection: An estimate that uses demographic data to determine future population sizes and is typically analyzed with population pyramids.

Dependency ratio: The ratio of individuals aged 0–14 and over 65 (representing the population of dependents) to individuals aged 15–64 (representing the productive workforce) in a society.

Demographic momentum: A continued population increase after a decline in fertility as a result of a large segment of the population being young, which typically occurs in stage 2 countries.

Negative growth: A process that occurs when the natural increase rate falls below zero and a country (typically at stage 4) begins to lose population.

Demographic equation: An equation that determines the population growth rate for the world by subtracting the global deaths from the global births.

Infant mortality rate: The number of babies, out of every 1,000 live births, that die within their first year of life.

Population Equations and Scientific Methods

Doubling time: The number of years it takes a country to double its population.

Sustainability: The efficient utilization of resources to allow future generations to live at the same or a higher standard of living than the population today.

Theories of Migration

Migration: The movement of people.

Immigrants: People who move into a region or country.

Emigrants: People who leave a region or country.

Theories of Migration (cont.)

Net migration: The number of immigrants minus the number of emigrants.

Push factor: A negative perception about a location that encourages a person to move away from that location.

Pull factor: A positive perception about a location that encourages a person to move there.

Refugees: People who are forced to flee their homeland for reasons such as fear of persecution or death and who seek some type of asylum in another country.

Place utility: When communities offer incentives for people to move to their areas.

Internal migration: The movement of people within the same country or area.

Ravenstein's laws of migration: The ten statements related to migration trends that E. G. Ravenstein developed in 1885. Some of the migration laws are still valid in the present day, while others have become outdated.

Human capital model: Developed by Larry Sjaastad in 1962, this model states that people seek to improve their incomes over the course of their lives; therefore, people weigh the costs against the benefits of migrating. William A. V. Clark contributed to the explanation in 1986, adding psychological and social costs and benefits.

Life course theory: Developed in the 1960s; states that people make major decisions early in life (e.g., college, employment, marriage, having children) that may then dictate migration preferences and opportunities in the future.

Intercontinental migration: The movement of people across an ocean or continent.

Distance decay: The lessening of a phenomenon as the distance from the hearth or node increases.

Acculturation: The transfer of cultures in which the influence of a person's native culture in a new country is not as strong as it was in his or her original country.

Chain migration: A movement of people that is voluntary in nature and functions to reunite families and cultures; it begins with a small number of immigrants in a new location, who work to save and send resources that eventually allow other family and community members to join them.

Interregional migration: The movement of people within a country's borders, from region to region.

International migration: The movement of people between countries.

Intraregional migration: The movement of people within the same region.

Cyclic migration: The seasonal migration of people, often associated with agricultural work.

Transhumance: The seasonal movement of livestock.

Intervening obstacle: An event that forces individuals to halt their migration plans due to some negative factor, which can range from cultural to physical.

Intervening opportunity: An event that causes a migrant to stop and decide to stay at a location along his or her journey after encountering favorable economic opportunities or environmental amenities.

Forced migration: The movement of people against their will, often because of political or environmental factors.

TEST WHAT YOU LEARNED

Part A: Quiz

1. Which of the following is an example of the gravity model?

    (A) New York and Los Angeles are closely linked based on their distance.

    (B) New York and Los Angeles are not linked at all because of their distance.

    (C) New York and Los Angeles are linked due to their populations.

    (D) New York and Los Angeles are not linked due to their populations.

    (E) New York and Los Angeles are linked due to their proximity to ports.

2. Which of the following best describes the process of acculturation?

    (A) As the distance between two locations increases, their interactions decline.

    (B) The seasonal migration of livestock moves animals to areas where food is more available.

    (C) A community offers incentives for people to move to its area.

    (D) Upon migrating to an area of a different culture, a person's original customs and traditions eventually become less strong.

    (E) Upon migrating to an area of a different culture, a person completely gives up his or her original customs and traditions.

3. Which of the following countries would have the greatest demographic momentum based on its birth rate and death rate?

    (A) Mozambique: 44 birth rate and 15 death rate

    (B) Tanzania: 40 birth rate and 9 death rate

    (C) Ethiopia: 34 birth rate and 8 death rate

    (D) Zimbabwe: 33 birth rate and 11 death rate

    (E) Réunion: 17 birth rate and 5 death rate

4. With which of the following would a neo-Malthusian geographer most likely disagree?

    (A) The demographic transition model is flawed.

    (B) The United States is ripe for a return to exponential population growth.

    (C) Population is growing at a faster rate than agriculture productivity.

    (D) If there are multiple minority groups and no majority group, the growth rate will resemble the rate of growth of the fastest-growing group.

    (E) The increased fertility and birth rates within immigrant communities will eventually cause an increased growth rate in more developed countries.

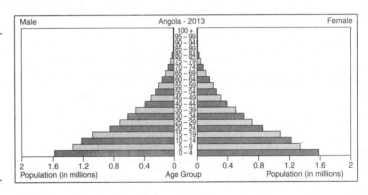

5. Based on the population pyramid above, in which stage of the demographic transition model is Angola?

    (A) Stage 1

    (B) Stage 2

    (C) Stage 3

    (D) Stage 4

    (E) Stage 5

6. Which of the following is a characteristic of a country moving from stage 3 to stage 4 of the demographic transition model?

    (A) Decrease in the percentage of children

    (B) Decrease in total population growth

    (C) A low total population

    (D) Increase in reliance on farming

    (E) Increase in reliance on mass production

7. Which of the following best explains how the Green Revolution has impacted the carrying capacity of land?

    (A) The Green Revolution produced technology that has gradually decreased the carrying capacity of land.

    (B) The Green Revolution shifted efforts from hunting and gathering to planting, leading to greater carrying capacity.

    (C) The Green Revolution led to populations exceeding a land's carrying capacity.

    (D) The Green Revolution led to environmental degradation, resulting in a lower carrying capacity.

    (E) The Green Revolution produced technology that has increased food productivity, leading to greater carrying capacity.

8. Which of the following groups would be least likely to be considered refugees?

    (A) The Jews who emigrated during World War II

    (B) Those who emigrated from Rwanda and Uganda in the 1990s

    (C) Those who moved from the former Yugoslavia to neighboring countries in the 1990s

    (D) Those who voluntarily moved from the Middle East to Dearborn, Michigan, in the 1920s

    (E) The Hmong who migrated to the United States after the Vietnam War

9. Which of the following statements describes the human capital model of migration?

    (A) People seek to improve their incomes over the course of their lives, so they weigh the costs against the benefits of migrating.

    (B) People make major decisions early on in life that dictate migration preferences and opportunities in the future.

    (C) Excessive population growth encourages people to move to another country where there is more economic opportunity.

    (D) Long-distance migrants usually move to centers of economic opportunity.

    (E) People move to certain locations due to positive perceptions of the area.

10. Which of the following would be considered a stage 4 country?

    (A) A country that has birth rates and death rates similar to world averages

    (B) A country that moves away from its reliance on industry to a more service-based economy

    (C) A country that is characterized by an industrial society

    (D) A country that has a high birth rate and declining death rate

    (E) A country with a low total population and fluctuations in both the birth and death rates

Part B: Key Terms

This key terms list is the same as the list in the Test What You Already Know section earlier in this chapter. Based on what you have now learned, again ask yourself the following questions:

- Can I define this key term and use it in a sentence?
- Can I provide an example related to this key term?
- Could I correctly answer a multiple-choice question about this key term?
- Could I correctly answer a free-response question about this key term?

Check off the key terms if you can answer "yes" to at least three of these questions.

Factors Affecting Population

- ☐ Demography
- ☐ Birth rate
- ☐ Death rate
- ☐ Underpopulation
- ☐ Overpopulation
- ☐ Carrying capacity
- ☐ Environmental degradation

Population Distribution and Density

- ☐ Population density

Population and Growth

- ☐ Thomas Malthus
- ☐ Linear growth
- ☐ Exponential growth
- ☐ Neo-Malthusian

Demographic Transition Model

- ☐ Demographic transition model
- ☐ Zero population growth

Population Structure

- ☐ Population pyramid
- ☐ Population projection
- ☐ Dependency ratio
- ☐ Demographic momentum
- ☐ Negative growth
- ☐ Demographic equation
- ☐ Infant mortality rate

Population Equations and Scientific Methods

- ☐ Doubling time
- ☐ Sustainability

4

Theories of Migration

- [ ] Migration
- [ ] Immigrants
- [ ] Emigrants
- [ ] Net migration
- [ ] Push factor
- [ ] Pull factor
- [ ] Refugees
- [ ] Place utility
- [ ] Internal migration
- [ ] Ravenstein's laws of migration

- [ ] Human capital model
- [ ] Life course theory
- [ ] Intercontinental migration
- [ ] Distance decay
- [ ] Acculturation
- [ ] Chain migration
- [ ] Interregional migration

- [ ] International migration
- [ ] Intraregional migration
- [ ] Cyclic migration
- [ ] Transhumance
- [ ] Intervening obstacle
- [ ] Intervening opportunity
- [ ] Forced migration

Next Steps

Step 1: Tally your correct answers from Part A, and review the quiz explanations at the end of this chapter.

1. C	6. A
2. D	7. E
3. B	8. D
4. C	9. A
5. B	10. B

____ out of 10 questions

Step 2: Count the number of key terms you checked off in Part B.

____ out of 47 key terms

Step 3: Compare your Test What You Already Know results to these Test What You Learned results to see how exam-ready you are for this topic.

For More Practice:

- Read (or reread) the comprehensive review for this topic in Chapter 11.
- Go to kaptest.com to complete the online quiz questions for Population and Migration Patterns and Processes.
  - Haven't registered your book yet? Go to **kaptest.com/moreonline** to begin.

CHAPTER 4 ANSWERS AND EXPLANATIONS

Test What You Already Know

1. D

Stage 4 is characterized by a more service-based economy in which the birth rates and death rates (measured as a number out of 1,000 people) are almost equal; thus, **(D)** is correct. There are no countries in stage 1, eliminating (A). (B) is incorrect because a stage 2 country would be more agricultural and have a higher birth rate. Stage 3 is characterized by higher birth rates than that of the United Kingdom and more industrial jobs, making (C) incorrect. With a birth rate of 13 and a death rate of 9, the United Kingdom has not gone past zero population growth to enter what some demographers believe is the transition into stage 5, making (E) incorrect.

2. B

The majority of people in Europe live in urban areas. Conversely, with the exception of megacities, like Tokyo in East Asia, the majority of people in East, South, and Southeast Asia live in rural, clustered settlements. Thus, **(B)** is correct and (A) is incorrect. This is primarily a function of the fact that Europe is an industrial/post-industrial society, whereas most people in Asia still engage in agriculture, which is the primary sector; (C) is incorrect. (D) is incorrect because most people work in the tertiary sector of the economy, which is service based, in Europe. In Asia, the tertiary sector is growing, making (E) incorrect.

3. C

Population density is calculated by dividing the total population by the land area. Monaco has the highest population density of 48,368.8 people per square mile, making **(C)** correct. The population densities for the other areas are less than that of Monaco; these densities, reported in people per square mile, are as follows. Croatia has a density of 190.1; Hong Kong has a density of 17,311.5; Singapore has a density of 20,143.6; and the United States has the lowest population density of 86.2. Thus, (A), (B), (D), and (E) are incorrect.

4. E

Transhumance is the seasonal migration of livestock, so **(E)** is correct. (A)–(D) are incorrect because these types of movement focus on people, not livestock.

Intercontinental migration is the movement of people across an ocean or continent. Step migration is the movement of people with different stops along the way. Interregional migration is the movement of people from one region to another within a country's borders. Lastly, intraregional migration is the movement of people within the same region.

5. A

In stage 2 of demographic transition, death rates dramatically drop while birth rates remain at the same high level or drop slightly. As a result, the population experiences high growth. Thus, **(A)** is correct, and (B) and (C) are incorrect. Stage 4 countries experience zero growth or negative growth, eliminating (D) and (E).

6. B

An intervening opportunity occurs when a migrant stops and decides to stay at a location along the journey because of favorable economic opportunities or environmental amenities; **(B)** is correct. An intervening obstacle forces a stop in migration due to a negative factor, which is not true of this example; (A) is incorrect. The reason the person stopped migrating was for a better job, which is economic, not environmental; (C) and (D) are incorrect. Distance decay occurs when a migrant's native culture is not as strong as it was in his or her original country; (E) is incorrect.

7. C

The J-curve reflects the exponential population growth that can occur in ideal environments, where food, water, and living space are plentiful. **(C)** is correct. (A) is incorrect because this statement describes the gravity model. (B) is incorrect because it describes the S-curve, the type of growth that happens when countries have a strict carrying capacity. (D) defines a different J-curve, by Ian Bremmer, pertaining to why certain countries rise and fall; this is not the same as the geographic J-curve, making (D) incorrect. Growth that occurs evenly over time is linear growth, which is not depicted by the J-curve; (E) is incorrect.

8. C

The movement from the Rust Belt to the Sun Belt is an example of interregional migration, which is defined as migrating between regions within the same country; **(C)** is correct. Intercontinental migration usually involves crossing oceans, but always means moving from one continent to another and traveling a long distance, which eliminates (A). International migration is moving from one country to another, and the Sun Belt and the Rust Belt are both in the United States; (B) is incorrect. Intra-regional migration is the movement of people within the same region, but the Sun Belt and the Rust Belt are two different regions, making (D) incorrect. (E) is incorrect because, while "intervening obstacles" and "intervening opportunities" are accepted terminology in human geography pertaining to migration, "intervening migration" is not a recognized term.

9. D

A push factor is a negative characteristic about a location that leads someone to move away from that place, while a pull factor is a positive characteristic about a location that leads someone to move to that place. A tornado that causes a city to evacuate would be a negative characteristic that may cause people to move away, making this an environmental push factor. Thus, **(D)** is correct. The persecution of a religious group by a government is negative and would be a political push factor; (A) is incorrect. (B) is incorrect because the opening of a new factory would create more job opportunities, which is positive, making this an economic pull factor. On the other hand, the closing of a factory would eliminate many job positions, which is negative, making this an economic push factor; (C) is incorrect. (E) is incorrect because an area that experiences routine flooding would be an environmental push factor.

10. A

Because of the forced migration of the slave trade, which was associated with the triangular trade in the sixteenth century, millions of people of African descent are currently in the United States, the Caribbean, and South America; **(A)** is correct. (B)–(E) are incorrect because transnational, internal, chain, and step migrations are all considered voluntary.

Test What You Learned

1. C

The gravity model suggests that areas are linked based on their populations and their importance based on those population levels; thus, **(C)** is correct and (D) is incorrect. World cities, such as New York and Los Angeles, are closely linked because of their populations, which affect trade routes and airline routes. The gravity model multiplies the populations of the two cities and divides the product by the distance between the two cities squared. Therefore, the considerable distance makes the cities less closely linked, but does not eliminate their linkage entirely; (A) and (B) are incorrect. (E) is incorrect because proximity to ports is irrelevant in the gravity model.

2. D

The process of acculturation involves a person's original culture becoming less influential after his or her migration to a new area; **(D)** is correct. (A) describes distance decay, making this choice incorrect. (B) is incorrect because transhumance, not acculturation, is the seasonal migration of livestock to areas where food is more available. The idea of a community offering incentives for others to move to its area is called place utility; (C) is incorrect. Assimilation means completely giving up one's original customs and traditions in favor of a new culture, which is distinct from and more extreme than acculturation; (E) is also incorrect.

3. B

Demographic momentum is the difference between a country's birth rate and death rate. The greater the difference between birth and death rates, the greater the rate of natural increase; the greater its rate of natural increase, the more demographic momentum a country has. **(B)** is correct because this number is highest at 31 points. (A), (C), (D), and (E) are incorrect because their totals are less than Tanzania's at 29, 26, 22, and 12, respectively.

4. C

Thomas Malthus believed that the population is growing at a faster rate than agricultural productivity and that this would lead to a population crisis; the neo-Malthusians, however, disputed this statement. **(C)** is thus correct.

Neo-Malthusians are critical of the demographic transition model, (A); they believe that the United States is ripe for a return to exponential population growth, (B), and that the increased fertility and birth rates within immigrant communities will eventually cause an increased growth rate in more developed countries, (E). Neo-Malthusians also believe that if there are many minority groups and no majority group, the growth rate will look like the rate of growth of the fastest-growing group, (D).

5. B

The population pyramid of Angola has a very wide base and becomes very narrow at the top. This is typical of a stage 2 country; **(B)** is correct. The pyramid shows that a large part of Angola's population is under the age of 15. While stage 1 countries would look similar, they would not have as many elderly people, eliminating (A). Stage 3 countries have more adults and elderly people in the population and fewer children, making the pyramid look less bottom heavy; (C) is incorrect. (D) is incorrect because the percentage of children decreases dramatically and the workforce segment bulges in stage 4 countries. Stage 5 is a hypothetical stage in which the birth rate and population decline, which is the opposite of a stage 2 country; (E) is incorrect.

6. A

When a country moves from stage 3 to stage 4 of the demographic transition model, it experiences a decrease in the percentage of children, and the workforce segment of the population actually bulges, with 20- to 50-year-old adults becoming the majority of the population. Thus, **(A)** is correct. (B) is incorrect because this is characteristic of a country moving from stage 4 to stage 5. A stage 1 country typically has a low total population, making (C) incorrect. (D) is incorrect because a country moving from stage 1 to stage 2 increasingly relies on farming. A country moving from stage 2 to stage 3 increasingly relies on mass production and factories, making (E) incorrect.

7. E

Carrying capacity is the ability of the land to sustain a certain number of people. The more people inhabit an area, the more likely they will reach the carrying capacity of the environment. Once the carrying capacity is reached, the problems of overpopulation become apparent. Technological innovations that can increase food productivity, such as those of the Green Revolution, increase the carrying capacity of land; thus, **(E)** is correct, while (A) and (D) are incorrect. The First Agricultural Revolution, not the Green Revolution, involved the transition from hunting and gathering to planting, making (B) incorrect. (C) is incorrect because high birth rates and low death rates lead to overpopulation.

8. D

Dearborn, Michigan, is home to one of the largest Muslim populations in the United States because many immigrants from the Middle East came to the area in the 1920s to work in the automobile industry. The people who participated in this voluntary migration would not be considered refugees. Thus, **(D)** is correct. Refugees are those who seek asylum or safety in another country after escaping their home country for fear of their lives. (A), (B), (C), and (E) are examples of people who would be considered refugees.

9. A

The human capital model of migration was developed by Larry Sjaastad in 1962; it states that people weigh the costs against the benefits of migrating because they seek to improve their incomes over the course of their lives, so **(A)** is correct. (B) is incorrect because this statement describes the life course theory, while (C) is incorrect because it defines migration transition. In his laws of migration, E. G. Ravenstein proposed that long-distance migrants typically move to urban areas, which are the centers of economic opportunity; (D) is incorrect. A pull factor, not the human capital model of migration, is a positive perception about a location that induces a person to move there, eliminating (E).

10. B

In stage 4, a country becomes more service based and less industrial. Thus, **(B)** is correct. (A) and (C) are incorrect because stage 3, not stage 4, is characterized by having birth and death rates near world averages and by having an industrialized society. High birth rates and declining death rates indicate a stage 2 country, making (D) incorrect. (E) is incorrect because a low total population, with fluctuations in birth and death rates, indicates a stage 1 country.

CHAPTER 5

Cultural Patterns and Processes

LEARNING OBJECTIVES

- Define culture and cultural traits.

- Explain the geographic patterns associated with different expressions of cultural identity.

- Explain how the five themes of geography (region, place, location, human-environment interaction, and movement) influence cultural patterns.

- Describe globalization's impact on cultural interaction.

- Discuss the causes and effects of cultural diffusion over time.

- Explain how geographers use maps and spatial thinking to analyze cultural groups.

TEST WHAT YOU ALREADY KNOW

Part A: Quiz

1. Which of the following statements accurately describes why Judaism is considered an ethnic religion?

   (A) Judaism is one of the most widespread faiths due to its proselytizing activity.

   (B) Some Jewish people who are not devoutly religious celebrate their Jewish cultural identity.

   (C) Jewish people are usually born into their faith rather than converting to it.

   (D) Judaism is largely a mission-based faith in which conversion is a primary pillar.

   (E) Jewish people exercise strict compliance to their faith and a literal interpretation of the Torah.

2. Which of the following languages would be considered the lingua franca of East Africa?

   (A) Hindi

   (B) English

   (C) French

   (D) Swahili

   (E) Zulu

3. Why is Missouri one of the hearths of bluegrass music?

   (A) Missouri was inhabited by a large percentage of people living in poverty, who migrated to the state from Appalachia.

   (B) Missouri was composed of a mix of Irish, Scottish, and African American people.

   (C) Missouri was inhabited by a large percentage of African American people whose ancestors were from West Africa.

   (D) Missouri was the destination of the Acadians (French Canadians), who migrated from southeastern Canada.

   (E) Missouri was where people from Scandinavia, Poland, and Germany chose to live when they immigrated to the United States.

4. Which of the following is an example of hierarchical diffusion?

   (A) McDonald's in India serving Chicken Maharaja Mac

   (B) Americans putting pineapple on pizza

   (C) Japanese baseball allowing tied games

   (D) South Korean Catholics practicing ancestor rites

   (E) A British celebrity popularizing her hairstyle in Brazil

5. At which of the following sporting events do hooligans incite violence?

   (A) Boxing matches

   (B) Hockey games

   (C) Basketball games

   (D) Baseball games

   (E) Soccer matches

6. The structure above would most likely be found in which of the following countries?

   (A) Ecuador

   (B) Germany

   (C) India

   (D) Thailand

   (E) Israel

7. A good example of a monolingual country would be

   (A) Canada

   (B) Japan

   (C) Turkey

   (D) The United Kingdom

   (E) South Africa

8. Which of the following best explains why the process of acculturation typically takes three generations?

   (A) Religion and language are often lost parts of culture by the third generation.

   (B) Food, music, and other parts of heritage are mostly lost within three generations.

   (C) Use of the home language usually fades away within three generations.

   (D) Most third-generation immigrants have become bilingual.

   (E) Language has spread via relocation diffusion by the third generation.

9. Which of the following describes a primary desire of secularists?

   (A) Follow strict behavioral guidelines aligned with holy texts

   (B) Reach a global scale and appeal to all people

   (C) Create a state that is ruled by a pastor or priest

   (D) Remove all religious practices from the world

   (E) Separate marriage from religious constraints

10. Which of the following is an example of a monument that is NOT considered a sacred space?

    (A) The Taj Mahal

    (B) The Ganges River

    (C) The Wailing Wall

    (D) The Hiroshima Peace Memorial

    (E) The Bodhi tree

Part B: Key Terms

The following is a list of the major concepts for the AP Human Geography topic of Cultural Patterns and Processes. You will likely see many of these on the official AP exam.

For each key term, ask yourself the following questions:

- Can I define this key term and use it in a sentence?
- Can I provide an example related to this key term?
- Could I correctly answer a multiple-choice question about this key term?
- Could I correctly answer a free-response question about this key term?

Check off the key terms if you can answer "yes" to at least three of these questions.

The Meaning of Culture

- [ ] Material culture
- [ ] Built environment
- [ ] Nonmaterial culture
- [ ] Folk culture
- [ ] Popular culture
- [ ] Multicultural
- [ ] Cultural relativism
- [ ] Ethnocentrism

The Cultural Landscape

- [ ] Cultural landscape
- [ ] Natural landscape
- [ ] Adaptive strategy

Language and Culture

- [ ] Language
- [ ] Monolingual country
- [ ] Multilingual country
- [ ] Lingua franca
- [ ] Dialect
- [ ] Isogloss
- [ ] Pidgin language
- [ ] Trade language
- [ ] Creole language
- [ ] Official language
- [ ] Linguistic diversity
- [ ] Language families
- [ ] Language groups

5

Religion and Culture

- ☐ Religion
- ☐ Faith
- ☐ Fundamentalism
- ☐ Monotheistic
- ☐ Polytheistic
- ☐ Ethnic religion
- ☐ Universalizing (proselytic) religion
- ☐ Atheist
- ☐ Secularist

- ☐ Jainism
- ☐ Christianity
- ☐ Denominations
- ☐ Islam
- ☐ Theocracy
- ☐ Judaism
- ☐ Zoroastrianism
- ☐ Hinduism
- ☐ Buddhism
- ☐ Syncretic religion

- ☐ Sikhism
- ☐ Bahá'í
- ☐ Animism
- ☐ Confucianism
- ☐ Taoism (Daoism)
- ☐ Shinto
- ☐ Sacred spaces
- ☐ Enclave
- ☐ Exclave

Next Steps

Step 1: Tally your correct answers from Part A and review the quiz explanations at the end of this chapter.

1.	C	6.	D
2.	D	7.	B
3.	B	8.	C
4.	E	9.	E
5.	E	10.	D

_____ out of 10 Questions

Step 2: Count the number of key terms you checked off in Part B.

_____ out of 52 key terms

Step 3: Read the Key Takeaways in this chapter.

Step 4: Consult the table below, and follow the instructions based on your performance.

If You Got...	Do This
80% or more of the Test What You Already Know assessment correct (8 or more questions from Part A and 42 or more key terms from Part B)	• Read the definitions in this chapter for all the key terms you didn't check off. • Complete the Test What You Learned assessment in this chapter.
50% or less of the Test What You Already Know assessment correct (5 or fewer questions from Part A and 26 or fewer key terms from Part B)	• Read the comprehensive review for this topic in Chapter 12. ○ If you are short on time, read only the High-Yield sections. • Read through all of the key term definitions in this chapter. • Complete the Test What You Learned assessment in this chapter.
Any other result	• Read the High-Yield sections of the comprehensive review of this topic in Chapter 12. • Read the definitions in this chapter for all the key terms you didn't check off. • Complete the Test What You Learned assessment in this chapter.

ESSENTIAL CONTENT

Key Takeaways: Cultural Patterns and Processes

1. Cultural landscapes can be read and interpreted based on cultural features such as public spaces, language of signs, architecture, and even food preferences.

2. Language is the means of mutually comprehensible communication among people. Dialects are forms of a language that differ based on vocabulary, syntax, and speed. There are thousands of languages around the world, but many are dying out.

3. The largest language family is the Indo-European family, of which there are many branches, including the Romance and the Germanic languages. The second-largest language family is the Sino-Tibetan family, which includes the most commonly spoken language in the world, Mandarin Chinese.

4. Religions are defined as monotheistic or polytheistic (whether people worship one god or multiple gods) and ethnic or universalizing (whether the religion is contained to a particular ethnicity or people can convert to the religion).

5. There are five primary religions in the world today: Christianity, Islam, and Judaism (the Western religions) and Hinduism and Buddhism (the Eastern religions). Christianity is the largest religion in the world, and Islam is the fastest-growing religion in the world.

Key Terms: Cultural Patterns and Processes

The Meaning of Culture

Material culture: Anything that can physically be seen on the landscape.

Built environment: Produced by the physical material culture, the built environment is the tangible human creation on the landscape.

Nonmaterial culture: Anything on the landscape that comprises culture that cannot be physically touched (e.g., language and religion).

Folk culture: The practice of particular customs of a relatively small group of people that increases that group's uniqueness.

Popular culture: Culture that is not tied to a specific location but rather a general location based on widespread diffusion.

Multicultural: Containing several ethnic or cultural groups within the same society.

Cultural relativism: The concept that social practices, morality, and ethics are not universal; instead, different cultures have different concepts of rightness and wrongness.

Ethnocentrism: The concept that one's own culture is paramount and is used as the lens through which to study the rest of the world.

The Cultural Landscape

Cultural landscape: Cultural attributes of an area often used to describe a place (e.g., buildings, theaters, places of worship).

Natural landscape: The physical landscape that exists before it is acted upon by human culture.

Adaptive strategy: The way humans adapt to the physical and cultural landscape they are living in.

Language and Culture

Language: The ability to communicate with others in mutual comprehension in oral and/or written form.

Monolingual country: Has one official language in which all government business is conducted.

Multilingual country: Has more than one official language.

Lingua franca: A language that is adopted as a common language between speakers whose native languages are different.

Dialect: A form of a language that is different in sound, speed, syntax, and vocabulary from the language itself.

Isogloss: The definitional boundaries of a dialect.

Pidgin language: A means of communication that develops between two or more groups that do not have a language in common; typically, a mixture of simplified languages or a simplified primary language with other languages' elements included.

Language and Culture (cont.)

Trade language: A language or dialect systematically used to make communication possible between people who do not share a native language or dialect; particularly used as a means to conduct business.

Creole language: A stable language developed from a mixture of different languages. Unlike a pidgin (a simplified form of communication), a creole language is a complete language, used in a community.

Official language: A language that is given a special legal status in a particular country, state, or other jurisdiction; used to conduct all government business.

Religion and Culture

Religion: Value system based on belief in a spiritual or divine aspect of the world, including the ways in which people worship.

Faith: Belief in something based on spirituality rather than physical proof.

Fundamentalism: Strict adherence to a set of beliefs, based on a literal interpretation of the basic principles of a religion.

Monotheistic: Believing in one god.

Polytheistic: Believing in multiple gods.

Ethnic religion: A religion associated with a particular ethnic group and passed down through birth.

Universalizing (proselytic) religion: A religion that attempts to reach a global scale and to appeal to all people in multiple parts of the world.

Atheist: Not believing that deities exist.

Secularist: Wanting to separate religion from all other aspects of society, including government and other social institutions.

Linguistic diversity: The learning of more languages; can be understood on an individual scale or a societal/global scale.

Language families: Groups of languages organized by their common ancestry. Subfamilies are smaller groups within a language family.

Language groups: Languages descended from a common ancestral language.

Jainism: A religion that is based on nonmaterialism and transcending the cycles of life and death; considered an atheist philosophy because followers do not believe in a god or gods.

Christianity: The world's largest religion; monotheistic, with a focus on the life of Jesus Christ.

Denominations: Branches of a religion that differ on specific practices or principles of the religion.

Islam: Second largest world religion; monotheistic and shares a common heritage with the Jewish and Christian religions.

Religion and Culture (cont.)

Theocracy: A state that is ruled by religious leaders, in which the church plays an integral part in the administration of the country (e.g., Iran and Saudi Arabia).

Judaism: One of the oldest religions in the world; an ethnic and monotheistic religion.

Zoroastrianism: One of the oldest religions still practiced; the belief that Zarathustra is the father of religion.

Hinduism: A polytheistic religion, thought to be the oldest religion on Earth, with three primary deities—Brahma, Shiva, and Vishnu—and many lesser deities.

Buddhism: A religion practiced mostly in East Asia; it is considered a universalizing religion, but many Buddhists would consider their practices as part of a social code rather than a strict religion.

Syncretic religion: A religion that blends two or more religious belief systems into a new system; also, a religion that incorporates beliefs from unrelated traditions into its own belief system.

Sikhism: Religion that holds a belief in one god, rejects the caste system of India, and believes that all people are created equal.

Bahá'í: A universalizing religion that is practiced in parts of Africa and Asia; similar to Sikhism in the sense that it advocates for the elimination of religious differences.

Animism: The belief that all things, including places and objects as well as plants and animals, possess a spirit or soul.

Confucianism: Based on the teachings of Confucius, who lived in China at about the same time as Siddhartha Gautama lived in India, this belief system focuses on the relationships within the world and is associated with the philosophy of feng shui.

Taoism (Daoism): Philosophy based on the release of personal desires; also emphasizes mysticism.

Shinto: Practiced mainly in Japan, with characteristics of both polytheism and monotheism; Shintoists believe that nature is divine and emphasize reverence of one's ancestors.

Sacred spaces: Certain locations that hold spiritual significance for religions.

Enclave: An area within or surrounded by a larger area whose inhabitants are culturally or ethnically distinct; a group of people or place that is different in character from those surrounding it.

Exclave: A group of people physically separated from their hearth.

5

TEST WHAT YOU LEARNED

Part A: Quiz

1. When European settlers established relations with American Indians, new languages were created to ease communication and economic exchange between both groups. What is this language type called?

   (A) Official language

   (B) Creole language

   (C) Pidgin language

   (D) Trade language

   (E) Indigenous language

2. States within the United States are often considered very different from one another, despite the fact that they are part of the same country. Which of the following best describes this situation?

   (A) An adaptive strategy

   (B) A built environment

   (C) The natural landscape

   (D) Folk culture

   (E) Regionalization

3. The modern game of soccer (football) spread to many parts of the world because of British colonization. This is best described as an example of which type of diffusion?

   (A) Expansion

   (B) Hierarchical

   (C) Relocation

   (D) Stimulus

   (E) Contagious

4. Which of the following statements is NOT true regarding language?

   (A) Languages are relatively static.

   (B) Language can divide a country.

   (C) Language can contribute to political unity.

   (D) Language can be an adaptive strategy.

   (E) Languages can diffuse through colonization.

5. "Jack tales" are best described as an example of

   (A) material culture

   (B) nonmaterial culture

   (C) popular culture

   (D) folk culture

   (E) folklore

6. Which of the following is a language from the Afro-Asiatic family?

   (A) Mandarin

   (B) Hebrew

   (C) Turkish

   (D) Persian

   (E) Nubian

5

7. Which of the following correctly connects the Christian denomination to one of its core beliefs?

   (A) Roman Catholicism recognizes the position of the Pope but not his supremacy over the Church.

   (B) Protestants believe in the idea that the edible ritual elements used during communion literally become the body and blood of Christ.

   (C) Mormonism rejects the mainstream Christian doctrine of the Trinity.

   (D) Eastern Orthodoxy includes the belief of a personal relationship with Jesus Christ, instead of communicating with God through priests.

   (E) Zoroastrianism includes the belief in a messiah who will resurrect the dead and bring everlasting life.

8. The four heads of Brahma are thought to represent

   (A) India's four seasons

   (B) the three primary deities in Hinduism, along with Parvati

   (C) the four cardinal directions

   (D) the Four Noble Truths of Hinduism

   (E) the Vedas

9. Islam's spread to parts of East Africa and Southeast Asia via trade networks is an example of what two types of cultural diffusion?

   (A) Relocation and hierarchical diffusion

   (B) Relocation and contagious diffusion

   (C) Hierarchical and contagious diffusion

   (D) Relocation and stimulus diffusion

   (E) Contagious and stimulus diffusion

10. The building depicted above is best considered an example of what kind of religious architecture?

    (A) A Roman Catholic church

    (B) An Eastern Orthodox church

    (C) A mosque

    (D) A pagoda

    (E) A sacred site

Part B: Key Terms

This key terms list is the same as the list in the Test What You Already Know section earlier in this chapter. Based on what you have now learned, again ask yourself the following questions:

- Can I define this key term and use it in a sentence?
- Can I provide an example related to this key term?
- Could I correctly answer a multiple-choice question about this key term?
- Could I correctly answer a free-response question about this key term?

Check off the key terms if you can answer "yes" to at least three of these questions.

The Meaning of Culture

☐ Material culture   ☐ Folk culture   ☐ Cultural relativism

☐ Built environment   ☐ Popular culture   ☐ Ethnocentrism

☐ Nonmaterial culture   ☐ Multicultural

The Cultural Landscape

☐ Cultural landscape   ☐ Natural landscape   ☐ Adaptive strategy

Language and Culture

☐ Language   ☐ Dialect   ☐ Official language

☐ Monolingual country   ☐ Isogloss   ☐ Linguistic diversity

☐ Multilingual country   ☐ Pidgin language   ☐ Language families

☐ Lingua franca   ☐ Trade language   ☐ Language groups

☐ Creole language

Religion and Culture

- ☐ Religion
- ☐ Faith
- ☐ Fundamentalism
- ☐ Monotheistic
- ☐ Polytheistic
- ☐ Ethnic religion
- ☐ Universalizing (proselytic) religion
- ☐ Atheist
- ☐ Secularist

- ☐ Jainism
- ☐ Christianity
- ☐ Denominations
- ☐ Islam
- ☐ Theocracy
- ☐ Judaism
- ☐ Zoroastrianism
- ☐ Hinduism
- ☐ Buddhism
- ☐ Syncretic religion

- ☐ Sikhism
- ☐ Bahá'í
- ☐ Animism
- ☐ Confucianism
- ☐ Taoism (Daoism)
- ☐ Shinto
- ☐ Sacred spaces
- ☐ Enclave
- ☐ Exclave

5

Next Steps

Step 1: Tally your correct answers from Part A, and review the quiz explanations at the end of this chapter.

1.	D	6.	B
2.	E	7.	C
3.	C	8.	E
4.	A	9.	B
5.	E	10.	C

____ out of 10 Questions

Step 2: Count the number of key terms you checked off in Part B.

____ out of 52 key terms

Step 3: Compare your Test What You Already Know results to these Test What You Learned results to see how exam-ready you are for this topic.

For More Practice:

- Read (or reread) the comprehensive review for this topic in Chapter 12.
- Go to kaptest.com to complete the online quiz questions for Cultural Patterns and Processes.
  - Haven't registered your book yet? Go to **kaptest.com/moreonline** to begin.

CHAPTER 5 ANSWERS AND EXPLANATIONS

Test What You Already Know

1. C

An ethnic religion involves being born into a faith, with little to no emphasis put on converting others to the religion. As this describes Judaism, **(C)** is correct. (A) and (D) are incorrect because they describe universalizing religions. Although some people who practice Judaism celebrate their cultural identity without being devoutly religious, this is not a defining characteristic of an ethnic religion. Therefore, (B) is incorrect. While some Jewish people, such as orthodox Jews, do take the Torah literally, this is not true of the majority of Jewish people; additionally, this would not be a reason Judaism is considered an ethnic religion. Thus, (E) is incorrect.

2. D

Even though English is the world's primary lingua franca, East Africa's lingua franca is Swahili. Over 40 million people speak Swahili as their primary language, but more than 100 million people speak Swahili as a lingua franca in a region extending from Somalia to Tanzania. Thus, **(D)** is correct and (B) is incorrect. Hindi is largely limited to India, making (A) incorrect. French is still a lingua franca in much of West Africa, but not East Africa; (C) is incorrect. Zulu is an important language spoken in southern Africa; (E) is incorrect.

3. B

Bluegrass music originated from the mix of Irish, Scottish, and African American people in the American south and some midwestern states like Missouri. **(B)** is correct. (A) is incorrect because it describes the development of country music. Nashville, Tennessee, is a hearth for country music. (C) is incorrect because it describes the cultural influence that birthed the blues; the Mississippi Delta region is where blues music is said to have originated. (D) is incorrect because it describes the demographic influence that brought about Cajun music, which was born in Louisiana, not Missouri. Finally, (E) is incorrect because it describes the group connected to polka music, which is associated with the upper Midwest.

4. E

A celebrity popularizing a hairstyle would be an example of hierarchical diffusion, which is the transmission of an idea from a powerful person (or group) to a wider group. Thus, **(E)** is correct. (A)–(D) are all examples of stimulus diffusion, in which a cultural product is modified by foreign adopters. Because cows are sacred in Hinduism, McDonald's avoids the use of beef products in India. Americans have adapted the Italian recipe for pizza into a recipe suited to U.S. tastes. Japanese baseball has modified U.S. rules. South Korean Catholics have incorporated ancestor rites from Confucianism and Buddhism.

5. E

Hooligans are fans who incite violence at soccer matches, often through hurling racial or religious epithets against opposing players and fans. While the sport is called *football* in most areas of the world, in the United States it is termed *soccer* to avoid confusion with another U.S. sport. Thus, **(E)** is correct while (A)–(D) are incorrect.

6. D

The picture shows a pagoda, which is common in Buddhist countries. Buddhism is the primary religion in East and Southeast Asia. So, **(D)** is correct. Ecuador and Germany are both Christian-majority countries, located in South America and Europe, respectively; (A) and (B) are incorrect. India is a Hindu-majority country with a sizable Muslim minority, making (C) incorrect. Israel is a Jewish state, so (E) is also incorrect.

7. B

A monolingual country is a country that speaks only one language. In Japan, almost everyone speaks Japanese. Minority languages have either died out or verge on extinction. **(B)** is correct. Canada is a bilingual country, with both French and English as official languages. In Turkey, the Kurds speak Kurdish while the Turks speak Turkish. In the United Kingdom, Welsh is an official language in the region of Wales. South Africa includes speakers of Afrikaans, English, and Zulu. Thus, (A) and (C)–(E) are incorrect.

8. C

Acculturation is the fading out of an immigrant family's culture as the family members are gradually assimilated into the dominant culture of their new home. For example, while new immigrants to the United States will often use their native tongue at home and English outside the home, this usually stops by the third generation as English use becomes universal in the family's everyday life. Thus, **(C)** is correct. Although language can often fade away by the third generation through acculturation, other parts of heritage and culture, like religion, do not and are thus not a consistent component of acculturation. So, (A) is incorrect. (B) is incorrect because many aspects of cultural heritage stay strong through generations. For example, many Italian Americans, several generations out, hold on to much of their heritage, often retaining Italian recipes passed down from generation to generation. Bilingualism is more common for first and second generation, and does not describe the assimilation of the dominant language by the third generation; thus, (D) is incorrect. (E) is incorrect because it describes the opposite idea: diffusion of culture instead of assimilation of immigrants to the dominant culture with loss of their home culture.

9. E

A secularist is a person who wants to separate religion from all other aspects of society, including government and social institutions; **(E)** is correct. (A) is incorrect because it describes the desires of fundamentalists. Fundamentalists want a literal interpretation of the basic principles of their religion, which sometimes requires the involvement of religion in government. (B) is incorrect because it describes a universalizing (proselytic) religion. (C) is incorrect because it describes the desire of theocrats. Although secularists sometimes overlap with atheists, who do not believe in any god or god-like figure, they do not want the complete removal of religion, but a separation between religion and state; (D) is also incorrect.

10. D

Sacred spaces are certain locations that hold spiritual significance for followers of a given religion. The Hiroshima Peace Memorial is a memorial to those killed in the 1945 atomic bombing of that city. It is not a site of holy significance to any religion and is thus a secular monument. **(D)** is correct. The Taj Mahal and the Ganges River are important sites to Muslims and Hindus in India, respectively, making (A) and (B) incorrect. (C) is incorrect because the Wailing Wall in Jerusalem is sacred to the Jewish religion; Muslims revere the same site, calling it the Al-Buraq Wall. Buddhists hold that the Bodhi tree is a sacred space because it is where Siddhartha Gautama gained enlightenment, so (E) is also incorrect.

Test What You Learned

1. D

A trade language uses vocabulary from two or more languages. Some trade languages were developed by American Indian and European traders to facilitate commercial activity; **(D)** is correct. When a government requires that all its business be done in a specific language, that is called an official language; (A) is incorrect. A creole language is similar to a trade language in that it is a blend of two or more languages, but it is stable, meaning that it has become so common that the majority of people in an area speak it. Thus, (B) is incorrect. While a pidgin language can develop into a full-fledged trade language, its simplicity and lack of widespread use limits it to only basic bartering, which would have been too elementary for the purposes of the European and American Indian interactions; (C) is also incorrect. An example of an indigenous language would be one that American Indians spoke before contact with the Europeans, making (E) incorrect.

2. E

When regions within the same country develop different cultural characteristics, from food to folklore, that process is known as regionalization. Thus, **(E)** is correct. (A)–(C) are incorrect because those terms do not directly involve regionalization. Adaptive strategies are simply ways in which people learn a new culture. The built environment includes the structures that humans have constructed upon the landscape. The natural landscape deals with the physical Earth, not human geography. Finally, (D) is incorrect because folk culture involves regional characteristics, such as styles of music, but it is only one aspect of regionalization.

3. C

Many British people who relocated during colonization in the 1800s brought their games with them, which is a form of relocation diffusion; **(C)** is correct. Relocation diffusion is a specific form of expansion diffusion; (A) is too broad to be correct. Soccer had mass popularity from early on, so hierarchical diffusion would not apply; (B) is incorrect. Soccer was not modified by the people exposed to British soccer, so (D) is incorrect. Contagious diffusion relies on rapid person-to-person transmission of culture; while soccer grew in popularity thanks to its increased exposure to new audiences, that exposure only took place thanks to migration. (E) is also incorrect.

4. A

While some cultures seek to keep their language relatively static, as a whole, language is constantly evolving through various means: relocation diffusion, evolving dialects, the creation of words, etc. Thus, **(A)** is correct because it is the only untrue statement. The rest of the answer choices are accurate descriptions of language and its properties.

5. E

Stories that are passed from generation to generation are known as folklore. In the Appalachian Mountain region, "Jack tales" are often passed from older to younger generations. Thus, **(E)** is correct. Material culture encompasses anything physically produced by a culture, and stories are not physical goods, making (A) incorrect. Nonmaterial culture and folk culture both include folklore; however, as labels, they are both too broad to be an accurate description of "Jack tales," so (B) and (D) are incorrect. Popular culture is the opposite of folk culture, which is a category that includes folklore. Thus, (C) is also incorrect.

6. B

Hebrew is a member of the Afro-Asiatic language family, specifically its Semitic subgroup. Therefore, **(B)** is correct. Mandarin Chinese is a member of the Sino-Tibetan language family, which is largely spoken in East Asia, making (A) incorrect. Turkish is a language in the Turkic language family. Turkic languages stretch from Turkey to Siberia, as they were spread by steppe nomad invasions; (C) is incorrect. The Indo-European family includes Middle Eastern languages like Persian, but not Hebrew, making (D) incorrect. Nubian is the language of Nubia, which extends from southern Egypt to northern Sudan, and is a member of the Nilo-Saharan language family. As its name implies, Nilo-Saharan languages are found in the Sahara and along the Nile River, so (E) is incorrect.

7. C

Mormonism is an example of a Christian denomination that does not fall under the umbrella of the three major groupings: Roman Catholicism, Protestantism, and Eastern Orthodoxy. Because it differs from those three denominations on the doctrine of the Holy Spirit, it is classified as nontrinitarian, just as Jehovah's Witnesses are. Thus, **(C)** is correct. (A) is incorrect because this belief is central to Eastern Orthodoxy and is the primary divide between Eastern Orthodoxy and Roman Catholicism. (B) is incorrect because this is a belief held by Roman Catholics and is a primary point of difference between Catholics and Protestants. (D) describes a Protestant belief, specifically a belief developed by Martin Luther in his *95 Theses*. So, (D) is incorrect. Although Christian denominations are believed to stem from Zoroastrianism (as well as Islam and Judaism), it is a separate, non-Christian religion, making (E) incorrect.

8. E

The four heads of Brahma are thought to represent the Vedas, which are holy texts in Hinduism; **(E)** is correct. There is no evidence that the four heads represent the four seasons or any deity save Brahma himself; (A) and (B) are incorrect. While his heads do face in the four cardinal directions, this does not itself represent anything, eliminating (C). The Four Noble Truths are aspects of Buddhism, not Hinduism, making (D) incorrect.

9. B

Islam's spread via trade networks is an example of relocation and contagious diffusion, as Muslim traders traveled to new locations and spread their religion person to person; **(B)** is correct. Their religion mainly spread by word of mouth, not by the popular appeal of merchants or by any other form of hierarchical diffusion; thus, (A) and (C) are incorrect. Islam as a religion was not significantly changed by those who adopted it in East Africa and Southeast Asia, so it would be inaccurate to label its spread as stimulus diffusion; thus, (D) and (E) are incorrect.

10. C

The building depicted is a mosque. Note the minarets towering over the central building, an architectural feature unique to mosques. **(C)** is correct. Both a Roman Catholic church and an Eastern Orthodox church would have Christian architectural features such as a cross. (A) and (B) are incorrect. The building does not resemble the tall central tower typical of a pagoda, so (D) is incorrect. This building is not an example of a sacred site or a place that is especially holy or important to a religion, such as the Ganges River to Hindus; (E) is incorrect.

CHAPTER 6

Political Patterns and Processes

LEARNING OBJECTIVES

- Describe the contemporary political map and its changes over time.

- Explain the power of politics and territoriality, particularly with regard to boundaries.

- Analyze globalization's impact on a state's economy, politics, culture, and technology.

- Compare and contrast forms and patterns of governance.

- Explain how geopolitical changes impact the contemporary political map.

- Explain national centripetal and centrifugal forces.

- Evaluate the intersection of politics, culture, and economy.

TEST WHAT YOU ALREADY KNOW

Part A: Quiz

1. Which of the following would best describe the type of political entity that an American Indian reservation would be classified as?

   (A) Nation-state

   (B) Multinational state

   (C) Independent state

   (D) City-state

   (E) Semiautonomous region

2. In the late 1940s, tensions between India and Pakistan escalated into armed conflict. The tensions were fueled, in part, by religious differences. Such differences are best described by which of the following?

   (A) National iconography

   (B) Devolution

   (C) Colonialism

   (D) Centrifugal forces

   (E) Centripetal forces

3. Which of the following international organizations would have the most geopolitical importance according to Spykman's rimland theory?

   (A) UN (United Nations)

   (B) EU (European Union)

   (C) NATO (North Atlantic Treaty Organization)

   (D) NAFTA (North American Free Trade Agreement)

   (E) ASEAN (Association of Southeast Asian Nations)

4. Suppose that a newly created country forms a government that is based on centralized authority and rejects the notion of locally based power centers. Which of the following terms best describes the government in this new state?

   (A) Democracy

   (B) Core country

   (C) Unitary

   (D) Federal

   (E) Confederation

5. Supranational organizations, such as the European Union (EU), North Atlantic Treaty Organization (NATO), and the United Nations (UN), often attempt to limit the political or economic actions of their member countries. As such, these organizations

   (A) violate international law

   (B) contradict the principles of democracy

   (C) threaten to end state-controlled government

   (D) challenge state sovereignty

   (E) prohibit all trade agreements with non-member states

6

6. The majority of African states entered the United Nations after 1960 because

   (A) the United Nations excluded all African states before 1960

   (B) the United States vetoed several African states' requests to join

   (C) a majority of African states were under the control of the Soviet Union

   (D) most African states sought to form the Organisation of African Unity (OAU)

   (E) the majority of the states hadn't become independent until the 1960s

7. San Marino and Vatican City are countries that are located within Italy. Lesotho is a country that is located within South Africa. Which of the following best describes the political geography of these three states?

   (A) They are enclaves.

   (B) They are perforated states.

   (C) They are theocracies.

   (D) They are autonomous regions.

   (E) They are buffer states.

8. The Berlin Wall is a good example of which of the following?

   (A) Demarcation line

   (B) Natural physical boundary

   (C) Boundary mandated by the United Nations

   (D) Geometric boundary using latitude and longitude

   (E) Antecedent boundary located within an urban area

9. Which of the following is the best example of voluntary segregation?

   (A) Ethnic neighborhoods in New York City

   (B) Ghettos during World War II in Poland

   (C) Palestinian refugee camps in Jordan

   (D) Relocation of South Africans during apartheid

   (E) 19th-century American Indian reservations in the United States

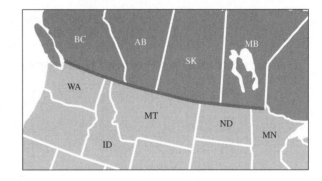

10. The border between the United States and Canada, as shown in the map above, is an example of what type of boundary?

    (A) Mountain boundary

    (B) River boundary

    (C) Religious boundary

    (D) Language boundary

    (E) Geometric boundary

6

Part B: Key Terms

The following is a list of the major concepts for the AP Human Geography topic of Political Patterns and Processes. You will likely see many of these on the official AP exam.

For each key term, ask yourself the following questions:

- Can I define this key term and use it in a sentence?
- Can I provide an example related to this key term?
- Could I correctly answer a multiple-choice question about this key term?
- Could I correctly answer a free-response question about this key term?

Check off the key terms if you can answer "yes" to at least three of these questions.

Understanding Political Geography

☐ Political geography	☐ Sovereignty	☐ Nation-state
☐ State	☐ City-state	☐ Semiautonomous
☐ Nation	☐ Stateless nation	

Boundaries

☐ Political boundary	☐ Antecedent boundary	☐ Definitional boundary dispute
☐ Frontier		
☐ Geometric boundary	☐ Subsequent boundary	☐ Locational boundary dispute
☐ Physical boundary	☐ Superimposed boundary	☐ Operational boundary dispute
☐ Ethnographic/ cultural boundary	☐ Irredentism	☐ Allocational boundary dispute
☐ Delimitation	☐ Relic boundary	
☐ Demarcation	☐ Reunification	☐ Exclusive economic zone (EEZ)
☐ Border landscape	☐ Balkanization	☐ Global commons
	☐ Annexation	

Colonialism and Imperialism

☐ Colonialism	☐ Self-determination
☐ Imperialism	☐ Democratization

6

Shapes of Countries

- ☐ Compact shape
- ☐ Elongated shape
- ☐ Fragmented shape
- ☐ Perforated shape
- ☐ Exclave
- ☐ Enclave
- ☐ Landlocked state
- ☐ Prorupted shape

The Political Organization of Space

- ☐ Nationalism
- ☐ Federal government
- ☐ Unitary government
- ☐ Embassy
- ☐ Ambassador
- ☐ Consulate
- ☐ Supranational organization
- ☐ Satellite state
- ☐ Buffer zone (buffer state)
- ☐ Shatterbelt region
- ☐ Heartland theory
- ☐ Rimland theory

Centripetal and Centrifugal Forces

- ☐ Centripetal force
- ☐ Centrifugal force
- ☐ Regionalism
- ☐ Autonomous region
- ☐ Theocracy
- ☐ Devolution

Historical Geography of the United States

- ☐ Historical geography
- ☐ Reapportionment
- ☐ Gerrymandering

Issues of Geopolitics

- ☐ Ethnicity
- ☐ Race
- ☐ Globalization
- ☐ Cultural shatterbelt
- ☐ Ethnic landscape
- ☐ Ethnic enclave

6

Next Steps

Step 1: Tally your correct answers from Part A and review the quiz explanations at the end of this chapter.

1.	E	6.	E
2.	D	7.	A
3.	C	8.	A
4.	C	9.	A
5.	D	10.	E

_____ out of 10 questions

Step 2: Count the number of key terms you checked off in Part B.

_____ out of 69 key terms

Step 3: Read the Key Takeaways in this chapter.

Step 4: Consult the table below, and follow the instructions based on your performance.

If You Got...	Do This
80% or more of the Test What You Already Know assessment correct (8 or more questions from Part A and 56 or more key terms from Part B)	• Read the definitions in this chapter for all the key terms you didn't check off. • Complete the Test What You Learned assessment in this chapter.
50% or less of the Test What You Already Know assessment correct (5 or fewer questions from Part A and 34 or fewer key terms from Part B)	• Read the comprehensive review for this topic in Chapter 13. ○ If you are short on time, read only the High-Yield sections. • Read through all of the key term definitions in this chapter. • Complete the Test What You Learned assessment in this chapter.
Any other result	• Read the High-Yield sections in the comprehensive review of this topic in Chapter 13. • Read the definitions in this chapter for all the key terms you didn't check off. • Complete the Test What You Learned assessment in this chapter.

ESSENTIAL CONTENT

Key Takeaways: Political Patterns and Processes

1. A nation is a group of people with common cultural characteristics, whereas a state is an area with defined boundaries that has sovereignty within its borders. A nation-state is a country whose political boundaries correspond with its cultural boundaries.

2. Boundary disputes arise for various reasons. Some arise from the demarcation of the boundary, while others arise from the allocation of resources along the border.

3. Colonialism has had a profound impact on the world today. The major colonial powers in the western hemisphere were Great Britain, Portugal, Spain, and France.

4. There are five shapes to countries: compact, elongated, fragmented, perforated, and prorupted. Each of these has advantages and disadvantages.

5. Supranational organizations, such as the European Union and the United Nations, have a strong influence on the world's political climate.

6

Key Terms: Political Patterns and Processes

Understanding Political Geography

Political geography: A branch of geography that studies geographical influences on political systems and power relationships. Sometimes used interchangeably with the term *geopolitics*, which is specifically the study of international political relations.

State: A politically bound area controlled by an established government that has authority over its internal affairs and foreign policy. Synonymous with the term "country."

Nation: A group of people bound together by some sense of a common culture, ethnicity, language, shared history, and attachment to a homeland.

Sovereignty: The political authority of a state to govern itself.

City-state: A small sovereign state that is made up of a town or city and the surrounding area.

Stateless nation: A nation of people without a state that it considers home.

Nation-state: A state in which the cultural borders of a nation correspond with the state borders of a country (e.g. Japan, Iceland, Denmark).

Semiautonomous: The state of affairs when a state, nation, or community has a degree of self-government but is not completely independent.

Boundaries

Political boundary: An invisible line that marks the outer limits of a state's territory.

Frontier: A zone of territory where no state has governing authority.

Geometric boundary: A boundary created by using lines of latitude and longitude and their associated arcs.

Physical boundary: A boundary based on the geographical features of the Earth's surface.

Ethnographic/cultural boundary: A boundary based on ethnographic and cultural considerations, such as language and religion.

Delimitation: The process of mapmakers representing a boundary on the map.

Demarcation: The process of physically representing a boundary on the landscape.

Border landscape: The zonal area on both sides of the boundary.

Antecedent boundary: A boundary that existed either before humans settled an area or very early during the settlement history.

Subsequent boundary: A boundary that develops along with the development of the cultural landscape.

Superimposed boundary: A political boundary that ignores the existing cultural organization on the landscape.

Irredentism: A political movement by an ethnic group or other closely aligned group that aims to reoccupy an area that the group lost. The group's territorial claims are often based on national, historic, or ethnic affiliations.

Relic boundary: A boundary that is no longer used but can still be seen on the landscape.

6

Boundaries (cont.)

Reunification: The rejoining of two regions that were previously a single state.

Balkanization: A contentious process of a state fragmenting into smaller states, which are often hostile or uncooperative with one another.

Annexation: The process of adding territory to an already existing state.

Definitional boundary dispute: A dispute that arises due to the legal language of the treaty's definition of the boundary.

Locational boundary dispute: A dispute that arises when the definition of the border is not questioned, but the interpretation of the border is in question.

Operational boundary dispute: A dispute that occurs when two countries next to each other disagree on a major issue involving the border.

Allocational boundary dispute: A dispute over the actual use of a boundary, such as the use of a resource that crosses the boundary.

Exclusive economic zone (EEZ): A sea zone over which a state has special rights over the exploration and use of marine resources stretching 200 nautical miles from the coast.

Global commons: Areas in which no country has access or exclusive right to exploit natural resources.

Colonialism and Imperialism

Colonialism: The practice of establishing political dominance over a people for economic, political, and territorial gain (e.g., European colonization of Africa).

Imperialism: The practice of taking control of an area that is already politically organized.

Self-determination: The power of a people to establish their own government the way that they see fit.

Democratization: The process of establishing representative and accountable forms of government led by popularly elected political representatives.

Shapes of Countries

Compact shape: The shape of a country in which the distance from the center of a state to any of its outer boundaries is roughly the same length (e.g., Poland).

Elongated shape: Describes a country that has long and narrow land extensions (e.g., Chile).

Fragmented shape: Describes a country that has two or more discontinuous, or separate, pieces of territory (e.g., Indonesia).

Perforated shape: Describes a state that has a smaller state located entirely within it (e.g., Italy and South Africa).

Exclave: A portion of a state that is geographically separated from the mainland by another country or countries (e.g., Alaska being separate from the U.S. mainland).

Enclave: A country that is completely surrounded by another state (e.g., Vatican City).

Landlocked state: A country that does not have direct access to the sea due to being surrounded by neighboring states (e.g., Bolivia).

Prorupted shape: A country that is characterized by having a compact shape plus a large projecting landmass (e.g., Namibia).

The Political Organization of Space

Nationalism: Doctrine based on the idea that an ethno-cultural group, or nation, has the power to control its own affairs.

Federal government: A system of governing in which the central government shares authority with regional subdivisions.

Unitary government: A system of governing in which a central government maintains control over the entire country.

Embassy: A state's main diplomatic office in a foreign state.

Ambassador: A state's chief diplomat, whose function is to represent the state in a foreign country.

Consulate: An office similar to an embassy that serves a secondary role in a foreign country.

Supranational organization: International bodies formed by three or more states to promote shared objectives. Major examples are the United Nations (UN), the North Atlantic Treaty Organization (NATO), and the European Union (EU).

Satellite state: A country that is technically independent but under heavy political, economic, and military influence from another country (e.g., Eastern European states under Soviet influence during the Cold War).

Buffer zone (buffer state): A region or state that provides territorial separation, or a "cushion," between rivals.

Shatterbelt region: A region such as a country or multiple countries caught up in a conflict between two superpowers.

Heartland theory: Suggests that whoever controls Eastern Europe and Western Asia has the political power and capital to rule the world; developed by Halford Mackinder.

Rimland theory: Claims that forming alliances and controlling the coasts and seas are necessary to maintain the political power to control the world; developed by Nicholas Spykman.

Centripetal and Centrifugal Forces

Centripetal force: An attitude or force that unifies people and increases support for a state; these forces keep the country together (e.g., national identity and patriotism).

Centrifugal force: An attitude or force that pulls people apart; these forces can limit interaction, produce regionalism, and create dissimilarity among the citizens of a country (e.g., differences in religion and language).

Regionalism: The expression of a common sense of identity and purpose combined with the creation of institutions that shape collective action within a geographical region.

Autonomous region: A segment of a country that has some degree of self-governing authority granted to it by the state.

Theocracy: A state whose government is under the control of a group of religious leaders.

Devolution: The process of a state giving up its power over another state or region.

Historical Geography of the United States

Historical geography: A subset of geography that analyzes geographical patterns through history.

Reapportionment: The political process of reallocating electoral seats to the regions of a state.

Gerrymandering: A process by which a political party manipulates political boundaries for political gain.

Issues of Geopolitics

Ethnicity: The identity within a group of people who share distinct physical and other traits as a product of common heredity and cultural traditions.

Race: The perceived physical characteristics of a group of people.

Globalization: The expansion of economic, political, and cultural processes to the point that they become global in scale and impact.

Cultural shatterbelt: An area where people are caught between the globalization or modernization of their culture and their traditional cultural identity.

Ethnic landscape: The evidence of an ethnicity on the features of the landscape.

Ethnic enclave: An ethnic neighborhood that is surrounded by people of a different ethnicity; often, the surrounding ethnicity is hostile to the group in the enclave.

6

TEST WHAT YOU LEARNED

Part A: Quiz

1. Namibia, a state in the southwestern part of Africa, has a prorupted shape: while mostly compact, it includes a nearly 300-mile protrusion called the Caprivi Strip that extends eastward to the Zambezi River.

   Which of the following is most likely a primary advantage of Namibia's proruption?

   (A) Shorter trade routes throughout a more compacted state

   (B) Control over different nationalities within the borders

   (C) Access to more raw materials and trade routes

   (D) Greater economic autonomy from colonizers

   (E) Improved transportation throughout the country

2. Which of the following best describes a primary purpose for why state and local political boundaries were defined, delimited, and demarcated in the United States?

   (A) To establish the authority of the federal government

   (B) To set the limits of political sovereignty

   (C) To prevent gerrymandering from taking place

   (D) To encourage the development of regional identity

   (E) To establish political voting districts

3. After decades of Soviet rule and control of Eastern Europe, in 1989, the Berlin Wall and the Iron Curtain fell, precipitating the end of the Soviet Union. This is best described as an example of which of the following?

   (A) Devolution

   (B) Heartland theory

   (C) Imperialism

   (D) Balkanization

   (E) Annexation

4. A family of immigrants learns the language of their new country, with each generation becoming more fluent. This process is an example of which of the following?

   (A) Irredentism

   (B) Acculturation

   (C) Centrifugal force

   (D) Cultural shatterbelt

   (E) Chain migration

5. Due to population changes, political boundaries must be redrawn so that districts are more representative of the new population numbers. Suppose a state legislature that is controlled by a dominant political party manipulates this process to help elect candidates of its party. This process would best be described as

   (A) reapportionment

   (B) district formation

   (C) gerrymandering

   (D) census taking

   (E) geopolitics

6. In the 1990s, in Rwanda, conflict between the Hutus and the Tutsis caused the deaths of hundreds of thousands of people. This is best described as an example of

   (A) a religious conflict

   (B) an ethnic conflict

   (C) a conflict between a colony and colonizer

   (D) a conflict over slavery

   (E) a conflict over communism

7. Which of the following international agreements most likely gives the details concerning the United States' legal rights to extract oil off the U.S. coast?

   (A) The Kyoto Protocol

   (B) The Paris Climate Agreement

   (C) The North American Free Trade Agreement (NAFTA)

   (D) The membership agreement with the Organization of the Petroleum Exporting Countries (OPEC)

   (E) The UN's International Law of the Sea

8. From the 1950s through the 1970s, Southeast Asia was in the middle of the conflict between two Cold War superpowers. The West, led by the United States, and the East, led by the Soviet Union and China, fought for control of the region. Which of the following would describe Southeast Asia in this situation?

   (A) A shatterbelt region where outside forces exerted influence

   (B) A high-growth area of increasing economic development

   (C) An area where theocratic governments were dominant

   (D) A contentious area where regional conflicts were common

   (E) A relatively peaceful region recovering from colonization

9. Which of the following represents an example of political fragmentation?

   (A) The creation of the United Nations

   (B) European states joining the European Union

   (C) The formation of the African Union

   (D) The signing of the North American Free Trade Agreement (NAFTA)

   (E) The end of Yugoslavia as an independent state

10. The countries of Japan, Iceland, and Denmark are examples of countries wherein one major ethnic group makes up most of the population. In these countries, the national borders correspond very closely with the state borders. Such countries are most appropriately referred to as which of the following?

    (A) Nation-states

    (B) Microstates

    (C) Core countries

    (D) Periphery countries

    (E) Ethnic enclaves

6

Part B: Key Terms

This key terms list is the same as the list in the Test What You Already Know section earlier in this chapter. Based on what you have now learned, again ask yourself the following questions:

- Can I define this key term and use it in a sentence?
- Can I provide an example related to this key term?
- Could I correctly answer a multiple-choice question about this key term?
- Could I correctly answer a free-response question about this key term?

Check off the key terms if you can answer "yes" to at least three of these questions.

Understanding Political Geography

- ☐ Political geography
- ☐ State
- ☐ Nation
- ☐ Sovereignty
- ☐ City-state
- ☐ Stateless nation
- ☐ Nation-state
- ☐ Semiautonomous

Boundaries

- ☐ Political boundary
- ☐ Frontier
- ☐ Geometric boundary
- ☐ Physical boundary
- ☐ Ethnographic/cultural boundary
- ☐ Delimitation
- ☐ Demarcation
- ☐ Border landscape
- ☐ Antecedent boundary
- ☐ Subsequent boundary
- ☐ Superimposed boundary
- ☐ Irredentism
- ☐ Relic boundary
- ☐ Reunification
- ☐ Balkanization
- ☐ Annexation
- ☐ Definitional boundary dispute
- ☐ Locational boundary dispute
- ☐ Operational boundary dispute
- ☐ Allocational boundary dispute
- ☐ Exclusive economic zone (EEZ)
- ☐ Global commons

Colonialism and Imperialism

- ☐ Colonialism
- ☐ Imperialism
- ☐ Self-determination
- ☐ Democratization

Shapes of Countries

- ☐ Compact shape
- ☐ Elongated shape
- ☐ Fragmented shape
- ☐ Perforated shape
- ☐ Exclave
- ☐ Enclave
- ☐ Landlocked state
- ☐ Prorupted shape

The Political Organization of Space

- ☐ Nationalism
- ☐ Federal government
- ☐ Unitary government
- ☐ Embassy
- ☐ Ambassador
- ☐ Consulate
- ☐ Supranational organization
- ☐ Satellite state
- ☐ Buffer zone (buffer state)
- ☐ Shatterbelt region
- ☐ Heartland theory
- ☐ Rimland theory

Centripetal and Centrifugal Forces

- ☐ Centripetal force
- ☐ Centrifugal force
- ☐ Regionalism
- ☐ Autonomous region
- ☐ Theocracy
- ☐ Devolution

Historical Geography of the United States

- ☐ Historical geography
- ☐ Reapportionment
- ☐ Gerrymandering

Issues of Geopolitics

- ☐ Ethnicity
- ☐ Race
- ☐ Globalization
- ☐ Cultural shatterbelt
- ☐ Ethnic landscape
- ☐ Ethnic enclave

6

Next Steps

Step 1: Tally your correct answers from Part A, and review the quiz explanations at the end of this chapter.

1.	C	6.	B
2.	B	7.	E
3.	A	8.	A
4.	B	9.	E
5.	C	10.	A

_____ out of 10 questions

Step 2: Count the number of key terms you checked off in Part B.

_____ out of 69 key terms

Step 3: Compare your Test What You Already Know results to these Test What You Learned results to see how exam-ready you are for this topic.

For More Practice:

- Read (or reread) the comprehensive review for this topic in Chapter 13.
- Go to kaptest.com to complete the online quiz questions for Political Patterns and Processes.
  - Haven't registered your book yet? Go to **kaptest.com/moreonline** to begin.

CHAPTER 6 ANSWERS AND EXPLANATIONS

Test What You Already Know

1. E

A certain area in a country may seek partial independence from the state. If the state grants the area some degree of self-governing authority, then the area is considered semiautonomous. This is the political status of the American Indian reservations in the United States. They possess some authority to manage their own affairs, making **(E)** correct. In a nation-state, the cultural borders of a nation correspond with the state borders of the country (e.g., Japan, Iceland, Denmark). The borders of an American Indian reservation do not correspond with the borders of the entire continental United States, so (A) is incorrect. While the United States government recognizes tribal governments as sovereign, it does not grant the status of sovereign *state* to American Indian peoples or their reservations; thus, (B), (C), and (D) are incorrect.

2. D

Unlike centripetal forces, which bring people together and unify a state, centrifugal forces are factors that tend to break up a state. One of the main factors in the breakup of India and Pakistan was religious differences. The majority of people in India are Hindu, while the majority of people in Pakistan are Muslim. Therefore, **(D)** is correct and (E) is incorrect. National iconography, such as a country's flag or the national anthem, is typically a unifying force; (A) is incorrect. Devolution is the process of a state giving up power over another state or region (e.g., the breakup of the Soviet bloc countries at the end of the Cold War). This does not accurately describe the situation between India and Pakistan, making (B) incorrect. Colonialism is the practice of establishing political dominance over a people for economic, political, and territorial gain. While both India and Pakistan were colonies of Great Britain, the term *colonialism* does not relate to the religious tensions in the region, so (C) is incorrect.

3. C

In the early 1940s, Nicholas Spykman developed the rimland theory, which claimed the key to controlling Eurasia was to control the coastal areas of Europe and Asia. To control the coastal areas, superior sea power and military alliances would be needed. NATO (the North Atlantic Treaty Organization) is a military alliance that was set up among the Western European countries, Canada, and the United States in 1949. The goal of NATO was to prevent the Soviet Union from gaining more control in Europe and Asia by protecting the rimland areas. **(C)** is correct. The United Nations was created in 1945 to promote world peace and to prevent another world war; (A) is incorrect. The European Union and ASEAN (Association of Southeast Asian Nations) were designed to promote unity, stability, and prosperity among member states, making (B) and (E) incorrect. NAFTA (the North American Free Trade Agreement) was a trade agreement signed by the United States, Mexico, and Canada in the early 1990s, so (D) is also incorrect.

4. C

A unitary government is a system of governing in which a central government maintains control over the entire country (e.g., France). A state with such a government is very different from a state with a federal system, such as the United States, in which power is shared with local governments. Therefore, **(C)** is correct and (D) is incorrect. A state with a unitary style of government may or may not be a democracy, so (A) is incorrect. A core country is any country that is well developed with a strong economic base. Such a country may or may not have a unitary government, making (B) incorrect. A confederation is an association of sovereign states by a treaty or agreement. This would not describe a strong central government; in fact, a government that is structured as a confederation is often a weak form of government, so (E) is incorrect.

5. D

Supranational organizations such as the EU, NATO, and UN place limits on what their member states can do. For example, members of NATO are supposed to reach an agreement before a member state undertakes a military engagement. As such, supranational organizations limit or challenge state sovereignty, which is the political authority of a state to govern itself. **(D)** is correct. Supranational organizations do not violate international law—in fact, they often create international law. (A) is incorrect. Most supranational organizations are founded on and operate based on the principles of democratic rule, so (B) is incorrect. Such organizations do not threaten to end state-controlled government, making (C) incorrect. While some supranational organizations (e.g., the EU) have rules on how members are to negotiate trade agreements, such organizations, in general, do not prohibit trade agreements. (E) is incorrect.

6. E

Colonialism was still prevalent in Africa up until the 1960s. From then through the 1980s, many African countries claimed their independence from colonial powers and gained statehood. Upon becoming sovereign states, most became members of the United Nations; **(E)** is correct. The United Nations, including the United States, welcomed the addition of the African states, making (A) and (B) incorrect. While the Soviet Union was able to exert some influence in Africa, it was not able to prevent African states from joining the United Nations, making (C) incorrect. A group of African states formed the Organisation of African Unity (OAU) in 1963 to promote African unity, sovereignty, and prosperity. The OAU's creation, however, did not hinder African states from joining the United Nations, so (D) is incorrect.

7. A

A country that is completely surrounded by another country is called an enclave. The surrounding country is called a perforated country. South Africa and Italy are examples of perforated countries; Italy contains both San Marino and Vatican City, and South Africa contains Lesotho. **(A)** is correct and (B) is incorrect. A theocracy is a state whose government is under the control of a group of religious leaders. While Vatican City is technically a theocracy, the other two countries are not, so (C) is incorrect. Because San Marino, Vatican City, and Lesotho are actual countries, they are not classified as autonomous regions, which are

self-governing areas but not independent states. (D) is therefore incorrect. A buffer state is a state that provides territorial separation, or a "cushion," between rivals. This does not accurately describe any of these three countries, so (E) is incorrect.

8. A

The process of physically placing a boundary on the landscape is known as demarcation. The demarcation zone can sometimes be a tense area, where the hostilities of two countries come to a head. During the Cold War, the Berlin Wall was built as a demarcation line to separate capitalist West Germany from communist East Germany; **(A)** is correct. This constructed wall is not a natural physical boundary, making (B) incorrect. The Berlin Wall was built due to geopolitical issues between the West and the former Soviet Union rather than due to a United Nations mandate or because of lines of latitude and longitude, making (C) and (D) incorrect. An antecedent boundary is a boundary that exists before many people settle in an area, so (E) is also incorrect.

9. A

New York City is a key immigrant entry point to the United States, and as such, it has many ethnic neighborhoods. This is because many immigrants, at least at first, exercise voluntary segregation owing to the language barrier, and tend to live in areas where they can communicate and feel comfortable culturally. Therefore, **(A)** is correct. All of the other answer choices describe involuntary segregation. Starting in the late 1930s, Nazi Germany forced Jewish communities to relocate to ghettos in Poland and Eastern Europe as part of its genocidal actions. Due to the Israeli-Palestinian conflict over the past several decades, many Palestinians have been forced to relocate to other countries, including Jordan. During the apartheid era in South Africa, the black population was mandated to live apart from the white population. Lastly, in the nineteenth century, the U.S. government pushed many American Indians out of their homelands and onto reservations.

10. E

A geometric boundary is based on lines of latitude and longitude. The boundary between the United States and Canada is defined along the 49th parallel, so **(E)** is correct. The boundary is not based on physical elements such as mountains or rivers, making (A) and (B) incorrect. Likewise, it is not based on cultural considerations such as religion or language, so (C) and (D) are incorrect.

Test What You Learned

1. C

Proruptions are extended landmasses that project outward from a country's mainland. Namibia's prorupted strip in the Northeast provides it with access to the Zambezi River, facilitating the country's access to natural resources and trade routes. Proruptions in other countries typically serve similar purposes. **(C)** is correct. Because proruptions are extensions of land, countries with such shapes are less compact, which tends to make transportation within the country more challenging. Thus, (A) and (E) are incorrect. The prorupted shape in Namibia's case is not about controlling its citizens; (B) is incorrect. Namibia is an independent state, not a colony, so (D) is also incorrect.

2. B

Internal political boundaries determine the jurisdiction or area governed by localities, cities, and states. For example, the state government of Ohio has no governing authority over the neighboring state of Indiana. As such, internal political boundaries are established in the United States to set the limits of political sovereignty. **(B)** is correct. The authority of the U.S. federal government is established by the U.S. Constitution, rather than through the creation of political boundaries, so (A) is incorrect. Gerrymandering describes the process in which a political party manipulates the boundaries of voting districts in order to favor the candidates of its party. Preventing this, however, is not why political boundaries are created, so (C) is incorrect. Similarly, political boundaries were not created in the United States primarily for the purpose of promoting regional identity, making (D) incorrect. While political boundaries establish political voting districts, this is not a main reason for setting boundaries; (E) is incorrect.

3. A

Devolution is the process of a state giving up its power over another state or region. The collapse of the Iron Curtain and the breakup of the Soviet bloc countries at the end of the Cold War is an example of devolution. Thus, **(A)** is correct. Heartland theory is the suggestion that whoever controls Eastern Europe and Western Asia has the political power and capital to rule the world. While that may describe why the Soviet Union sought power in Eastern Europe, it would not accurately describe the events in this question, so (B) is incorrect. Imperialism is the practice of taking control of an area that is already politically organized. This is the opposite of what this question describes, so (C) is incorrect. Balkanization describes the contentious process of a state fragmenting into smaller states, which are often hostile or uncooperative with one another (e.g., the breakup of the former state of Yugoslavia). While related to the end of the Soviet Union, this term does not accurately describe the fall of the Iron Curtain. (D) is incorrect. Annexation is the process of adding territory to an already existing state (e.g., the United States purchasing Alaska from Russia). That process does not relate to the events in this question, so (E) is incorrect.

4. B

The process of acculturation involves immigrants adapting to and adopting cultural elements of their new country, including learning the host country's language, a process that often takes several generations. Thus, **(B)** is correct. (A) is incorrect because irredentism refers to political movements, often of ethnic groups, to reclaim former territories. A centrifugal force is an influence that pushes people in a region apart, so (C) is incorrect. A cultural shatterbelt describes an area where the clash between cultures, often between modernizing and traditional identities, leads to instability; the scenario in the question stem does not describe such conflict, so (D) is incorrect. Chain migration occurs when the current immigrants in a country send resources to their families so that they too can migrate to the new country; this scenario is not mentioned in the question stem, so (E) is also incorrect.

5. C

The process of redrawing political districts for political gain is called gerrymandering; **(C)** is correct. In the case of the United States, the political party that controls the state legislature often tries to have districts redrawn in its party's favor. (A) is incorrect because it is too general; reapportionment is the process of reallocating political representatives to political districts, which may or may not include gerrymandering. (B) is incorrect because simply creating a district would not necessarily be done for political gain. (D) is incorrect because census taking is done prior to the redrawing of political districts in the United States. Geopolitics is a broad term referring to how geography and politics interact, so (E) is incorrect.

6. B

The civil war in Rwanda was fought between the Hutu and the Tutsi tribes. Both groups sought governmental power, and the power struggle stemmed from ethnic differences. In 1994, the Hutu undertook to eliminate the Tutsi population, resulting in the mass slaughter of hundreds of thousands of the Tutsi people. **(B)** is correct. The conflict was not the result of religion, slavery, or communism, making (A), (D), and (E) incorrect. Rwanda was a colony of Belgium until 1962, but Belgium was not a participant in the Rwandan Civil War; (C) is incorrect.

7. E

The United Nations held a conference in 1958 to establish the United Nations Convention on the Law of the Sea. When finally adopted as international law in 1983, part of the law created exclusive economic zones (EEZs). EEZs are areas up to 200 miles off a country's coast in which the country has the right to explore for resources. For example, the United States can drill for oil and natural gas in the Gulf of Mexico out to 200 miles. Thus, **(E)** is correct. The Kyoto Protocol and the Paris Climate Agreement are international treaties that deal with global climate change, making (A) and (B) incorrect. NAFTA is a free trade pact with the United States, Mexico, and Canada, so (C) is incorrect. OPEC is an international organization that deals with oil resources; (D) is also incorrect.

8. A

A shatterbelt is defined as a region that is in the middle of two superpowers fighting for control. Therefore, **(A)** is correct and (E) is incorrect. Given the conflict in Southeast Asia, economic development stagnated, so (B) is incorrect. Theocratic governments are governments run by a religious organization, which was not the case in Southeast Asia, making (C) incorrect. Because of the international influence in Southeast Asia, the conflict could not be characterized as regional; (D) is incorrect.

9. E

During the 1980s, ethnic tensions grew to a volatile level in the former country Yugoslavia. As the Cold War came to a close, the state of Yugoslavia experienced a civil war that resulted in a breaking apart of the country into multiple states, including Bosnia and Herzegovina, Macedonia, Serbia, Montenegro, Croatia, and Slovenia. **(E)** is correct. (A)–(D) are all incorrect because they are examples of supranationalism: states coming together into larger wholes, which is effectively the opposite of political fragmentation.

10. A

The nation-state is a state in which the cultural borders of a nation correspond with the state borders of a country. In a textbook nation-state, there would only be one ethnicity. As such, nearly every person would speak the same language, practice the same religion, and generally share the same cultural characteristics. While there is no such nation-state in existence, examples of countries that are considered nation-states include Japan, Iceland, and Denmark. **(A)** is correct. A microstate is a country that is small in both population and area; Vatican City is an example of a microstate. This term would not accurately describe the countries in this question, so (B) is incorrect. A core country is a country that is well developed with a strong economic base, and a periphery country is a less developed, economically poor country. These are terms often used by geographers to describe economic development patterns throughout the world. While Japan, Denmark, and Iceland are considered core countries, the term "core country" does not describe a country wherein the national and state borders coincide. (C) and (D) are incorrect. An ethnic enclave is an ethnic neighborhood that is surrounded by people of a different ethnicity; often, the surrounding ethnicity is hostile to the group in the enclave. This term would not accurately describe a country, however. (E) is incorrect.

CHAPTER 7

Agriculture and Rural Land-Use Patterns and Processes

LEARNING OBJECTIVES

- Describe the impacts of the First and Second Agricultural Revolutions.

- Evaluate the Green Revolution's positive and negative effects.

- Explain how agricultural practices shape the surrounding environment.

- Define real-world applications of von Thünen's land use model.

- Describe the interrelationship of agribusiness and economic factors.

- Analyze the intersection of gender and food production and consumption.

- List pertinent issues of modern-day agriculture and food production.

- Explain the global nature of food supply chains, particularly in terms of production and consumption.

- Define the major bioclimatic zones' impact on agricultural production regions.

TEST WHAT YOU ALREADY KNOW

Part A: Quiz

1. Which of the following correctly pairs the agricultural hearth with its type?

    (A) Southeast Asia and seed agriculture

    (B) West Africa and seed agriculture

    (C) Southern Mexico and seed agriculture

    (D) Northeastern Africa and vegetative planting

    (E) Northern China and vegetative planting

2. Which of the following agricultural practices would most likely be used in tropical forested areas of southeast Asia and central Africa?

    (A) Crop rotation

    (B) Shifting cultivation

    (C) Pastoral nomadism

    (D) Mediterranean agriculture

    (E) Transhumance

3. Which of the following was most likely the first form of agriculture in human history?

    (A) Slash-and-burn farming

    (B) Seed agriculture

    (C) Hunting and gathering

    (D) Pastoral nomadism

    (E) Shifting cultivation

4. The Tuareg people of the Sahara and their animals seasonally migrate to the higher lands in the summer and the valleys in the winter. This is best considered an example of

    (A) pastoral nomadism

    (B) livestock ranching

    (C) livestock fattening

    (D) dairy farming

    (E) transhumance

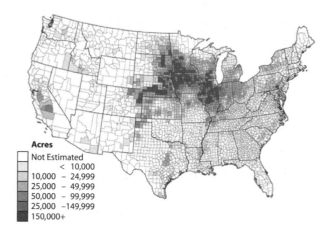

Acres
Not Estimated
< 10,000
10,000 – 24,999
25,000 – 49,999
50,000 – 99,999
25,000 –149,999
150,000+

5. The map above shows corn production for selected U.S. states. Which of the following conclusions can be made based on the map?

    (A) Corn is linked with the livestock-fattening region of the United States.

    (B) Corn is a high-bulk food and therefore must be grown closer to urban centers.

    (C) Corn is a staple food in the American diet.

    (D) Corn is not grown much in the West due to dietary preferences.

    (E) Corn is not as profitable as other major crops due to the influence of ethanol and other biofuels.

6. Which of the following best explains recent trends in agriculture in the United States?

    (A) The average size of farms is decreasing as American farmers' efficiency increases.

    (B) The number of family-owned farms is continuing to increase.

    (C) The total revenue of agricultural sales is becoming more concentrated in a small number of large corporate farms.

    (D) The cost of converting a conventional farm into a farm that grows certified organic crops is relatively quick and easy.

    (E) Sustainable farms make up only a small percentage of total agricultural sales, and their numbers are declining.

7. A group of farmers decide to grow crops in tropical areas for sale in more developed countries. Which of the following best describes this type of farming?

    (A) Slash-and-burn farming

    (B) Plantation agriculture

    (C) Intensive subsistence agriculture

    (D) Shifting cultivation

    (E) Commercial agriculture

8. In the 1930s in the United States, a Dust Bowl was created in the Great Plains area due to a combination of drought, overgrazing by cattle, and farming practices that overtaxed the soil. Which of the following terms describes this type of process?

    (A) Soil erosion

    (B) Climate change

    (C) Desertification

    (D) Food desert

    (E) Farm crisis

9. Which of the following is NOT a form of commercial farming?

    (A) Grain farming

    (B) Fruit farming

    (C) Mediterranean agriculture

    (D) Livestock ranching

    (E) Slash-and-burn farming

10. Which of the following best explains the role of women in the First Agricultural Revolution?

    (A) Labor-saving devices freed women from toil in the fields, offering them financial independence through factory work.

    (B) Women cultivated crops based on their observations of seasonal patterns in plant growth.

    (C) Women helped secure food for their tribe by gathering roots and other wild plants.

    (D) Women performed specialized jobs such as caring for the children, weaving cloth, and making cheese from milk.

    (E) Labor-saving devices made plantation agriculture a more profitable system, leading to an increase in female slaves.

7

Part B: Key Terms

The following is a list of the major concepts for the AP Human Geography topic of Agriculture and Rural Land-Use Patterns and Processes. You will likely see many of these on the official AP exam.

For each key term, ask yourself the following questions:

- Can I define this key term and use it in a sentence?
- Can I provide an example related to this key term?
- Could I correctly answer a multiple-choice question about this key term?
- Could I correctly answer a free-response question about this key term?

Check off the key terms if you can answer "yes" to at least three of these questions.

A Historical Perspective

- ☐ Farming
- ☐ Hunting and gathering
- ☐ Agriculture
- ☐ First (Neolithic) Agricultural Revolution
- ☐ Plant domestication
- ☐ Animal domestication
- ☐ Second Agricultural Revolution
- ☐ Third Agricultural (Green) Revolution
- ☐ Environmental modification
- ☐ Globalized agriculture
- ☐ Agribusiness
- ☐ Monoculture
- ☐ Biotechnology
- ☐ Genetically modified organisms (GMOs)
- ☐ Organic farming
- ☐ Fourth Agricultural Revolution

Agricultural Hearths

- ☐ Agricultural origins
- ☐ Vegetative planting
- ☐ Seed agriculture

Agricultural Regions and Patterns of Change

- ☐ Cultivation regions
- ☐ Rural settlement
- ☐ Village form
- ☐ Agricultural landscape
- ☐ Subsistence farmers
- ☐ Shifting cultivation
- ☐ Slash-and-burn agriculture
- ☐ Crop rotation
- ☐ Pastoral nomadism
- ☐ Transhumance

- ☐ Extensive subsistence agriculture
- ☐ Intensive subsistence agriculture
- ☐ Intertillage
- ☐ Commercial farming
- ☐ Mediterranean agriculture
- ☐ Dairy farming (dairying)
- ☐ Mixed livestock with crop production

- ☐ Livestock ranching
- ☐ Specialized fruit production
- ☐ Irrigation
- ☐ Plantation agriculture
- ☐ Large-scale commercial agriculture
- ☐ Agricultural industrialization
- ☐ Grain farming

Von Thünen's Model of Agricultural Land Use

- ☐ Model of agricultural land use
- ☐ Food chain
- ☐ Commodity chain

Economic Systems and Activities

- ☐ Adaptive strategies
- ☐ Farm crisis
- ☐ Fair trade

Agriculture and Gender

- ☐ Specialization

Agriculture in the United States

- ☐ Metes and bounds
- ☐ Township and range
- ☐ Survey pattern

- ☐ Long lots
- ☐ Desertification
- ☐ Soil erosion

- ☐ Aquaculture
- ☐ Fishing
- ☐ Forestry

Agriculture and the Environment

- ☐ Sustainable yield

World Crop Regions

- ☐ Planned economy
- ☐ Collective farm

7

Next Steps

Step 1: Tally your correct answers from Part A and review the quiz explanations at the end of this chapter.

1.	C	6.	C
2.	B	7.	B
3.	C	8.	C
4.	E	9.	E
5.	A	10.	B

_____ out of 10 questions

Step 2: Count the number of key terms you checked off in Part B.

_____ out of 62 key terms

Step 3: Read the Key Takeaways in this chapter.

Step 4: Consult the table below, and follow the instructions based on your performance.

If You Got...	Do This
80% or more of the Test What You Already Know assessment correct (8 or more questions from Part A and 50 or more key terms from Part B)	• Read the definitions in this chapter for all the key terms you didn't check off. • Complete the Test What You Learned assessment in this chapter.
50% or less of the Test What You Already Know assessment correct (5 or fewer questions from Part A and 31 or fewer key terms from Part B)	• Read the comprehensive review for this topic in Chapter 14. 　◦ If you are short on time, read only the High-Yield sections. • Read through all of the key term definitions in this chapter. • Complete the Test What You Learned assessment in this chapter.
Any other result	• Read the High-Yield sections in the comprehensive review of this topic in Chapter 14. • Read the definitions in this chapter for all the key terms you didn't check off. • Complete the Test What You Learned assessment in this chapter.

ESSENTIAL CONTENT

Key Takeaways: Agriculture and Rural Land-Use Patterns and Processes

1. There were three agricultural revolutions that changed history. The First Agricultural Revolution was the transition from hunting and gathering to planting and sustaining. The Second Agricultural Revolution increased the productivity of farming through mechanization and access to market areas due to better transportation. The Third Agricultural Revolution involved hybridization and genetic engineering of products and the increased use of pesticides and fertilizers.

2. There are two primary methods of farming in the world. Subsistence farming involves producing agricultural products for use by the farmer's family. Commercial farming involves agriculture for the purpose of sale.

3. The von Thünen model of agricultural land use focuses on transportation. The distance and the weight of crops, as well as their distance to the market, affect which crops are grown in a specific location.

4. Modern agriculture is becoming more industrialized and more specialized. To compete with agribusiness in the United States, many family farms are turning to sustainable methods of production, organic agriculture, and catering to the local food movement.

5. Many of the settlement patterns in the United States have been based on the agricultural possibilities of specific areas.

6. Many of the world's crop products are dictated by the climate of the regions where they are grown.

Key Terms: Agriculture and Rural Land-Use Patterns and Processes

A Historical Perspective

Farming: The methodical cultivation of plants and/or animals.

Hunting and gathering: The first way humans obtained food. Nomadic groups around the world depended on migratory animals, wild fruit, berries, and roots for sustenance.

Agriculture: The raising of animals or the growing of crops on tended land to obtain food for primary consumption by a farmer's family or for sale off the farm.

First (Neolithic) Agricultural Revolution: The slow change from hunter and gather societies to more agriculturally based ones through the gradual understanding of seeds, watering, and plant care.

Plant domestication: The process by which wild plants are cultivated into productive crops, often with more desirable traits.

Animal domestication: The process by which wild animals are cultivated into a resource supply for humans, often resulting in physical and behavioral changes.

Second Agricultural Revolution: Coinciding with the Industrial Revolution, the Second Agricultural Revolution used the increased technology from the Industrial Revolution as a means to increase farm productivity through mechanization. This contributed to exponential population increase.

Third Agricultural (Green) Revolution: This transformation began in the latter half of the twentieth century and corresponded with exponential population growth around the world. Hybridization, pesticides, and chemical fertilizers were key aspects.

Environmental modification: The introduction of manufactured chemicals and practices that, at times, have drastic effects on native soil and vegetation.

Globalized agriculture: A system of agriculture built on economic and regulatory practices that are global in scope and organization.

Agribusiness: The mass production of agricultural products; a form of large-scale commercial agriculture.

Monoculture: The farming of a single crop in a given area of land.

Biotechnology: A precise science that involves altering the DNA of agricultural products to increase productivity.

Genetically modified organisms (GMOs): Plants and animals that have been genetically engineered in some way.

Organic farming: Farming that uses natural processes and seeds that are not genetically altered. To be certified as organic in the United States, farmers must demonstrate organic methods on a number of different measures.

Fourth Agricultural Revolution: A movement in which food is both grown and sold locally, and fertilizers and pesticides are minimized or eliminated in favor of pure organic farming.

7

Agricultural Hearths

Agricultural origins: The origin points of vegetative planting and seed agriculture; determined by Carl Sauer, a professor of geography who started the field of cultural ecology.

Vegetative planting: Removing part of a plant and putting it in the ground to grow a new plant. Contrast with seed agriculture.

Seed agriculture: The taking of seeds from existing plants and planting them to produce new plants.

Agricultural Regions and Patterns of Change

Cultivation regions: Areas that are specifically used for agriculture production.

Rural settlement: Points of human habitation in non-urban and non-suburban areas. Often associated with agricultural labor.

Village form: Refers to the layout of the rural settlement, of which there are several variations (cluster, grid, linear, round, or walled).

Agricultural landscape: The land people choose to farm, as well as the products they choose to farm.

Subsistence farming: Farmers grow crops and raise animals based on what they and their families need for daily sustenance, with very little surplus.

Shifting cultivation: The moving of farm fields, after several years, in search of more productive soil because of depleted nutrients in the original field.

Slash-and-burn agriculture: The process of burning the physical landscape to create space and add nutrients to the soil.

Crop rotation: The planting of different crops each year to replenish the soil's nutrients that were lost to the previous crops.

Pastoral nomadism: A form of subsistence agriculture that revolves around herding domesticated animals; usually practiced in arid climates.

Transhumance: The seasonal moving of herds by nomadic groups in order to access resources needed for the animals; nomadic groups often go to higher elevations in the summer and return to the valley floor in the winter.

Extensive subsistence agriculture: A form of subsistence farming that uses more land but requires less labor and is more productive than other forms. Both pastoral nomadism and shifting cultivation are this farming type, which has been criticized for causing environmental problems.

Intensive subsistence agriculture: A high-labor form of subsistence agriculture that involves farmers devoting a large amount of effort into making an area of land maximally productive.

Intertillage: The clearing of rows in the field with the use of hoes, rakes, and other manual equipment.

Commercial farming: The farming of products for sale off the farm; commercial farming is usually popular in developed countries and requires the use of heavy machinery.

Mediterranean agriculture: A type of farming which must be practiced in a climate that has a dry summer and a cool, moist winter. The crops associated with the Mediterranean Sea region include grapes, dates, and olives.

Agricultural Regions and Patterns of Change (cont.)

Dairy farming (dairying): A form of commercial farming which has become highly mechanized in recent years. Dairy farming is not limited to milk production and also includes anything that can be made with milk, like butter and cheese.

Mixed livestock with crop production: A type of farming where livestock raised on a farm are fed with crops that are grown on the same farm.

Livestock ranching: A form of commercial farming where animals are raised for their meat and other products. This type of farming always occurs in more developed countries and is done on the fringes of productive land.

Specialized fruit production: A form of commercial farming devoted to producing fruit.

Irrigation: The supplying of water to farmland in order to support agriculture.

Plantation agriculture: A type of agriculture that occurs in less developed countries; it involves the cultivation of one crop to be sold in more developed countries (e.g., coffee plantations in Costa Rica). The plantation and most of its profits often belong to owners residing in a more developed country.

Large-scale commercial agriculture: Agriculture on an industrial level, using standardized techniques and seed stock.

Agricultural industrialization: The increased mechanization of the farming process to boost profits and productivity.

Grain farming: The planting and harvesting of grain crops, such as wheat, barley, and millet; these crops are known as staple grains because a large percentage of the world population depends on them for survival.

Von Thünen's Model of Agricultural Land Use

Model of agricultural land use: A model developed by Johann Heinrich von Thünen that suggested that certain crops were grown in direct relation to their distance to the market. This model is also called the agricultural location model.

Food chain: The process of food reaching customers after harvesting. For example, after harvesting, commercial grain is sent to the market area, usually in semitrailers, where it is sold to a manufacturer who makes a product with the grain, such as bread. The product is then sold to a wholesaler, who sells it to a grocery store, where individual customers can purchase it.

Commodity chain: The process that food goes through to get from the primary (resource based) sector of the economy to the tertiary (service based) sector. The in-between players include the transportation systems and two, three, or more different sellers before the consumer has the opportunity to purchase the item.

Economic Systems and Activities

Adaptive strategies: Culture and behaviors that humans adopt to thrive in a given region based on its cultural and physical landscape.

Farm crisis: Occurs when farmers are too productive, causing a surplus of crops. This leads to lower prices and less revenue for the farmers.

Agriculture and Gender

Specialization: The process by which jobs in human society became focused on certain tasks, starting when ancient farmers first developed a surplus of food following the invention of agriculture.

Agriculture in the United States

Metes and bounds: A traditional English system of measuring property that uses the land's physical features to describe ownership claims. The bounds system uses more generalized features, while the metes system uses traditional distance measurements.

Township and range: A form of land division in the Midwest and Great Plains in which land is divided into regular squares, known as sections.

Survey pattern: A system used to survey the Earth's surface.

Long lots: A system of surveying, established by the French, in which lots up to a half mile or more extend back from a river, which farmers use as their primary means of hauling their agricultural products to the market.

Desertification: The expansion of deserts in arid regions.

Soil erosion: The loss of topsoil to flowing water or wind.

Fair trade: Designation for goods produced in such a way that protects the rights of workers and the environment.

Aquaculture: The farming of aquatic organisms for sale off the farm. An example of an organism that can be grown using aquaculture is fish; fish may be raised in pools and then sold for food or to stock lakes for the tourism industry.

Fishing: The hunting of fish for food and sport.

Forestry: The act of managing, using, conserving, replenishing, and even creating a forest. Forestry can also be utilized to extract useful resources, like medicinal herbs, from forests. Some people do not consider forestry a type of farming, but rather the harvesting of a natural resource.

7

Agriculture and the Environment

Sustainable yield: The amount of a resource that can be harvested regularly without endangering the supply to future generations.

World Crop Regions

Planned economy: An economy in which the government dictates the quantity and type of agricultural products that farmers can produce.

Collective farm: A farm type where workers are not paid with money, but instead receive a share of the crop. This arrangement can begin due to the farmers having a common religious or political ideal, or because they are forced to accept it by those in power.

7

TEST WHAT YOU LEARNED

Part A: Quiz

1. The image above shows which of the following types of survey pattern used in the United States?

    (A) Dispersed village

    (B) Township and range

    (C) Long lots

    (D) Metes and bounds

    (E) Nucleated format

2. Which of the following is a circumstance that often leads to desertification?

    (A) Land becoming exposed to too much precipitation in a short period of time

    (B) Herds of animals grazing on land that does not receive enough rainfall

    (C) Farms overproducing crops and leading to price reductions

    (D) Populations moving away from the land in great numbers

    (E) Farmers moving their animals elsewhere and abandoning the land

3. Which of the following best explains the primary difference between livestock ranching and livestock fattening?

    (A) Livestock fattening requires more space than livestock ranching.

    (B) Livestock ranching has more profit per head of cattle than livestock fattening.

    (C) Livestock fattening requires less feed per head of cattle than livestock ranching.

    (D) Livestock ranching requires more land than livestock fattening.

    (E) Livestock ranching requires more capital investment for feed products.

4. The majority of the world's farming population is involved in which type of agriculture?

    (A) Pastoral nomadism

    (B) Mediterranean agriculture

    (C) Shifting cultivation

    (D) Subsistence farming

    (E) Plantation agriculture

5. Which of the following best describes the Second Agricultural Revolution?

    (A) The Second Agricultural Revolution saw the beginning of seed agriculture.

    (B) The Second Agricultural Revolution involved the mechanization of farming.

    (C) The Second Agricultural Revolution prompted farmers to develop new crops.

    (D) The Second Agricultural Revolution saw the genetic engineering of crops.

    (E) The Second Agricultural Revolution saw the rise of large-scale farms.

7

6. Which of the following trends best describes farming in the United States in the late twentieth century?

   (A) Movement to industrial agriculture

   (B) Debt-for-nature swap

   (C) "Tragedy of the commons"

   (D) More sustainable organic yields

   (E) More work with intertillage practices

7. Which of the following statements describes an impact of the double-cropping practice that started during the Green Revolution?

   (A) It allows subsistence farmers to receive more income from selling their products.

   (B) It provides consumers with more choices of foods to eat.

   (C) It relies exclusively on natural processes in order to boost crop yields.

   (D) It allows farmers to alter natural processes to increase crop yields.

   (E) It gives producers the profit margins to meet the demands of investors.

Questions 8–10 refer to the following image.

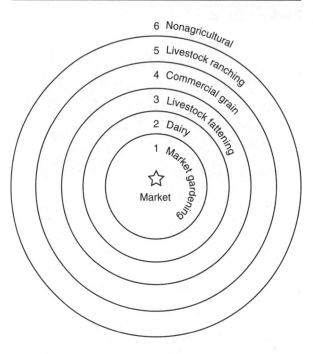

8. Von Thünen's model of agricultural land use revolves around which of the following fundamental principles?

   (A) The climate and agricultural conditions worsen farther away from the market area.

   (B) The fertility of the soil decreases farther away from the urban area or market.

   (C) Access to transportation improves as one moves closer to the urban area.

   (D) In the village system, farmers are involved in subsistence agriculture, and an urban area serves as a cultural hub.

   (E) The farmers in the area are all involved in commercial agriculture, selling their products to a centrally located market.

7

9. Which of the following zones of von Thünen's model is the best fit for the fruit production method of farming?

    (A) Market gardening

    (B) Dairy

    (C) Livestock fattening

    (D) Commercial grain

    (E) Livestock ranching

10. Three of the largest U.S. dairy regions are in the Northeast (New York and Pennsylvania), the Upper Midwest (Wisconsin and Minnesota), and California. Which of the following best explains this phenomenon?

    (A) The transportation systems are much better in these areas.

    (B) The climates are more conducive to raising dairy cattle.

    (C) Large urban centers are located near each region.

    (D) Industrial output is much greater due to the crops produced in these regions.

    (E) There are more milk drinkers in these parts of the country than in other parts.

7

Part B: Key Terms

This key terms list is the same as the list in the Test What You Already Know section earlier in this chapter. Based on what you have now learned, again ask yourself the following questions:

- Can I define this key term and use it in a sentence?
- Can I provide an example related to this key term?
- Could I correctly answer a multiple-choice question about this key term?
- Could I correctly answer a free-response question about this key term?

Check off the key terms if you can answer "yes" to at least three of these questions.

A Historical Perspective

- [ ] Farming
- [ ] Hunting and gathering
- [ ] Agriculture
- [ ] First (Neolithic) Agricultural Revolution
- [ ] Plant domestication
- [ ] Animal domestication
- [ ] Second Agricultural Revolution
- [ ] Third Agricultural (Green) Revolution
- [ ] Environmental modification
- [ ] Globalized agriculture
- [ ] Agribusiness
- [ ] Monoculture
- [ ] Biotechnology
- [ ] Genetically modified organisms (GMOs)
- [ ] Organic farming
- [ ] Fourth Agricultural Revolution

Agricultural Hearths

- [ ] Agricultural origins
- [ ] Vegetative planting
- [ ] Seed agriculture

Agricultural Regions and Patterns of Change

- [ ] Cultivation regions
- [ ] Rural settlement
- [ ] Village form
- [ ] Agricultural landscape
- [ ] Subsistence farmers
- [ ] Shifting cultivation
- [ ] Slash-and-burn agriculture
- [ ] Crop rotation
- [ ] Pastoral nomadism
- [ ] Transhumance
- [ ] Extensive subsistence agriculture
- [ ] Intensive subsistence agriculture
- [ ] Intertillage
- [ ] Commercial farming
- [ ] Mediterranean agriculture
- [ ] Dairy farming (dairying)

Agricultural Regions and Patterns of Change (cont.)

- ☐ Mixed livestock with crop production
- ☐ Livestock ranching
- ☐ Specialized fruit production

- ☐ Irrigation
- ☐ Plantation agriculture
- ☐ Large-scale commercial agriculture

- ☐ Agricultural industrialization
- ☐ Grain farming

Von Thünen's Model of Agricultural Land Use

- ☐ Model of agricultural land use

- ☐ Food chain
- ☐ Commodity chain

Economic Systems and Activities

- ☐ Adaptive strategies
- ☐ Farm crisis
- ☐ Fair trade

Agriculture and Gender

- ☐ Specialization

Agriculture in the United States

- ☐ Metes and bounds
- ☐ Township and range
- ☐ Survey pattern

- ☐ Long lots
- ☐ Desertification
- ☐ Soil erosion

- ☐ Aquaculture
- ☐ Fishing
- ☐ Forestry

Agriculture and the Environment

- ☐ Sustainable yield

World Crop Regions

- ☐ Planned economy
- ☐ Collective farm

Next Steps

Step 1: Tally your correct answers from Part A, and review the quiz explanations at the end of this chapter.

1. B	6. A
2. B	7. D
3. D	8. E
4. D	9. A
5. B	10. C

____ out of 10 questions

Step 2: Count the number of key terms you checked off in Part B.

____ out of 62 key terms

Step 3: Compare your Test What You Already Know results to these Test What You Learned results to see how exam-ready you are for this topic.

For More Practice:

- Read (or reread) the comprehensive review for this topic in Chapter 14.
- Go to kaptest.com to complete the online quiz questions for Agriculture and Rural Land-Use Patterns and Processes.
  - Haven't registered your book yet? Go to **kaptest.com/moreonline** to begin.

CHAPTER 7 ANSWERS AND EXPLANATIONS

Test What You Already Know

1. C

The agricultural hearths for seed agriculture include southern Mexico, northeastern Africa, northern China, and northeastern India. Thus, **(C)** is correct. Vegetative planting hearths include southeast Asia, West Africa, and Central America and northwestern South America. (A), (B), (D), and (E) are incorrect.

2. B

Shifting cultivation is seen in the tropical forested areas of southeast Asia and central Africa, as well as the Amazon Rainforest in Brazil. Natural vegetation in this area keeps the soil from eroding due to its root structure. When the natural vegetation is removed, soil is more susceptible to erosion, enabling thousands of tons of silt to get washed into rivers and eventually the oceans. Thus, **(B)** is correct. (A) is incorrect because crop rotation involves the use of the same field year after year, but the planting of different crops on that same field. Pastoral nomadism and transhumance are usually practiced in arid climates, making (C) and (E) incorrect. Mediterranean agriculture must be practiced in a climate that has a dry summer and a cool, moist winter; (D) is incorrect.

3. C

Hunting and gathering was most likely the first form of agriculture in the world, although it is not "farming" as we tend to think of it today. It involved the hunting of game species and the gathering of natural plant products. **(C)** is correct. Slash-and-burn only became needed once farming was an established practice, making (A) incorrect. Seed agriculture didn't develop until the First Agricultural Revolution; (B) is incorrect. Pastoral nomadism involves domesticated animals; before domestication, humans still relied on animals for food and other resources, but they traveled naturally in their herds instead of being herded by humans. Shifting cultivation developed only after the soil of the first farm fields became exhausted. (D) and (E) are incorrect.

4. E

The Tuareg are a nomadic people who live in the southern Saharan. They seasonally take their herds to the highlands during the hot, dry season and bring them down to the valley during the cool, moist season. Transhumance refers to this type of seasonal migration, so **(E)** is correct. Pastoral nomadism is a close second choice, but it describes the overall type of agriculture and lifestyle, not the specific practice of moving herds seasonally; (A) is incorrect. Livestock fattening and livestock ranching deal with commercial agriculture and do not involve herd migration at all, making (B) and (C) incorrect. Dairy farming involves livestock roaming in fixed pastures rather than any seasonal migration; (D) is incorrect.

5. A

Looking at the corn-growing regions on the map, you can see that they are primarily located in the central northern U.S. region. Knowing that most of the corn in the United States is used for animal consumption of some sort, you can infer that this region is linked with the livestock-fattening region. Thus, **(A)** is correct. Corn is not a high-bulk food but rather a commercial grain and, according to von Thünen, can be grown farther from large urban centers. (B) is incorrect. Even though Americans eat a large amount of corn in their daily diets, the majority of this crop goes toward livestock fattening, making (C) and (D) incorrect. The production of corn for ethanol has led to higher prices for corn, increasing farmers' profits, so (E) is incorrect.

6. C

There are a number of trends in modern agriculture in the United States; one is that a small number of large corporate farms accounts for an increasingly large share of agricultural revenue. Therefore, **(C)** is correct. The average size of farms is actually increasing as small farms are bought out by larger corporate farms or go out of business; (A) and (B) are incorrect. The process to convert a conventional farm into a sustainable or organic farm is a lengthy and involved one, making (D) incorrect. Presently, revenue from sustainable farms makes up a fraction of total agricultural revenue, but their numbers are growing at a rapid rate; (E) is also incorrect.

7

7. B

Plantation agriculture drives an export economy in many formerly colonized areas, employing people who normally would be involved in subsistence farming. **(B)** is correct. Slash-and-burn farming is more associated with subsistence farming than exporting crops to more developed countries. (A), (C), and (D) are all forms of subsistence agriculture, and are thus incorrect. Commercial agriculture involves the sale of products, but plantation agriculture more accurately encompasses the aspect of growing goods for the express purpose of selling them to developed countries; (E) is incorrect.

8. C

Desertification is the expansion of deserts; in other words, dry, dusty land that is not agriculturally productive. This is the process that occurred in the arid Great Plains region, and thus, **(C)** is correct. (A) is incorrect because while soil erosion was a major factor in the Dust Bowl, it was just one factor, and the term does not describe the entire process cited in the question. Climate change is believed to contribute to desertification, but it does not describe the specific circumstances surrounding the Dust Bowl; (B) is incorrect. Food deserts are areas, often in cities, where people have little access to affordable, healthy food such as fresh vegetables; (D) is incorrect. Lastly, (E) is incorrect because a farm crisis occurs when farmers are too productive, causing a surplus of crops, which lowers the prices for those crops.

9. E

This question offers choices that are all examples of commercial farming except for one. Unlike the other choices, slash-and-burn farming is a subsistence agricultural practice, not a commercial one. Thus, **(E)** is correct and (A)–(D) are incorrect.

10. B

The discovery of agriculture was most likely made by women gatherers, as they would be best positioned to observe seasonal patterns in the growth of wild plants. While (C) describes the gathering activities women did prior to the First Agricultural Revolution, **(B)** is correct because it specifically describes how that activity led to the First Agricultural Revolution. Job specialization only followed the development of agriculture, and labor-saving agricultural devices did not become popularized until the Second Industrial Revolution; (A), (D), and (E) are incorrect.

Test What You Learned

1. B

Only three of these survey patterns are found in the United States: metes and bounds, township and range, and long lots. The picture shows the grid-like pattern of the township and range system, which is predominantly used in much of the Midwest owing to the vast expanse of fairly flat land. Therefore, **(B)** is correct and (A) and (E) are incorrect. The long lots system uses narrow strips of land that abut a river and extend back for up to a mile. The metes and bounds system forms fields that are irregularly shaped, often conforming to the natural ebb and flow of the landscape. Thus, (C) and (D) are incorrect.

2. B

Overgrazing has led to arid regions becoming deserts, a process known as desertification. When herds of animals graze on land that does not receive enough rainfall, the land becomes barren and desert-like. Thus, **(B)** is correct. (A), (C), (D), and (E) are incorrect because they do not describe processes that lead to desertification.

3. D

Livestock ranching requires much more space than livestock fattening, which is usually done in a feedlot or small pasture. Livestock ranching is practiced in large areas, where technology is used to track the animals. Therefore, **(D)** is correct and (A) is incorrect. Fattening is more profitable than ranching due to the cattle being confined in a small area, making (B) incorrect. Livestock fattening actually requires more food because livestock graze on naturally occurring vegetation during ranching, so (C) is incorrect. Ranching does not require greater capital investment for feed, as the cattle feed themselves by grazing on pasture; (E) is also incorrect.

4. D

The majority of the world's agricultural workforce is involved in subsistence farming, using the land to sustain its immediate inhabitants; **(D)** is correct. Pastoral nomadism takes place in arid areas where few people reside. Mediterranean agriculture is done in only a few areas of the world, where the climate is conducive for the growing of olives, dates, and grapes. Thus, (A) and (B) are incorrect. Shifting cultivation is done in tropical areas, as is plantation agriculture; however, both of these forms of agriculture involve relatively few laborers, making (C) and (E) incorrect.

5. B

The Second Agricultural Revolution coincided with the Industrial Revolution. Mechanization and improved transportation helped farmers by expanding the market area for their agricultural commodities. Thus, **(B)** is correct. The First Agricultural Revolution introduced seed agriculture; (A) is incorrect. The Green Revolution involved the development of new crops through hybridization, and later, genetic engineering; (C) and (D) are incorrect. The rise of large-scale corporate farms and the global streamlining of the agricultural industry are also characteristics of the Green Revolution, not the Second Agricultural Revolution. Thus, (E) is also incorrect.

6. A

The trend in the second half of the twentieth century in U.S. agriculture was toward the industrialization of agriculture and food production. The food chain has been made more productive and efficient through this process, lowering the price of food. **(A)** is correct. A debt-for-nature swap is practiced in less developed countries, but the United States is a developed country, making (B) incorrect. The "tragedy of the commons" refers to individual self-interest resulting in the collective loss of a common resource; because agricultural land in the United States is mostly privately owned, (C) is incorrect. Organic products, the result of more sustainable yields, are a vital niche in U.S. agriculture and are becoming more popular today, but they were not the main trend in the later twentieth century; (D) is incorrect. Intertillage refers to the use of manual equipment to clear rows in fields. Manual labor has been on the decline in U.S. farming since the Second Agricultural Revolution, making (E) incorrect.

7. D

One hallmark of the Green Revolution is the advent of double-cropping: planting and harvesting two crops in the same field with the aid of irrigation systems, chemical fertilizers and pesticides, and/or hybridized seeds. This practice increases yields by altering natural processes, so **(D)** is correct and (C) is incorrect. Subsistence farmers, by definition, grow only enough food to feed themselves and their families, leaving little surplus for trade to others; (A) is incorrect. Double-cropping involves growing more crops during the year than would naturally be possible, but it does not necessarily lead to more choices in the market; (B) is incorrect. While double-cropping can help commercial farmers meet business demands, it is also practiced by family farmers without investors; (E) is incorrect.

8. E

Von Thünen's model must be applied to commercial farming, given its focus on markets. If applied to subsistence farming, it would lose its characteristic concentric rings around the market area because subsistence farming is not focused primarily on selling goods. Therefore, **(E)** is correct and (D) is incorrect. According to the von Thünen model, conditions in each of the different zones are consistent (i.e., climate conditions, soil fertility, and transportation would be the same from the market-gardening area to the livestock-ranching areas). Therefore, (A)–(C) are incorrect.

9. A

Fruit production would best fit the market-gardening zone. Fruits are bulky products that cost a lot to transport to the market. Based on their weight and fast rate of spoilage, fruit production farming would be best suited near the market. Therefore, **(A)** is correct. The remaining zones would not be suitable for fruit production, based on von Thünen's model, due to their distance from the market. (B)–(E) are incorrect.

10. C

Von Thünen suggested that dairy regions must be close to large urban areas. The three largest U.S. dairy-producing regions are all close to major urban centers. Thus, **(C)** is correct. Transportation systems are roughly the same throughout the United States, with road systems developed enough to provide adequate transportation. The climate is also suitable for dairy farming in regions like Oregon, but that region lacks the population to support a major dairying industry on par with the three regions listed. (A) and (B) are incorrect. Likewise, crops produced elsewhere could support a dairy industry, but the greatest population of dairy consumers is not located in these areas. Milk and milk products are a common feature of diets throughout the United States. (D) and (E) are incorrect.

CHAPTER 8

Cities and Urban Land-Use Patterns and Processes

LEARNING OBJECTIVES

- Explain the driving factors behind urbanization and suburbanization.

- Describe city infrastructures.

- Define city populations using quantitative and qualitative data.

- Analyze urban settlements and development using geographic models.

- Identify housing, urban planning, and political organization factors unique to cities.

- Evaluate problems and solutions unique to urban areas.

TEST WHAT YOU ALREADY KNOW

Part A: Quiz

Questions 1–2 refer to the image below.

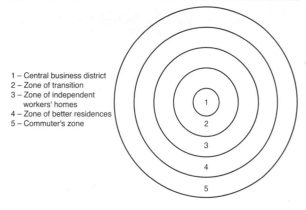

1 – Central business district
2 – Zone of transition
3 – Zone of independent
      workers' homes
4 – Zone of better residences
5 – Commuter's zone

1. Which of the following best describes the concentric zone model, pictured above?

   (A) It suggests that the lower classes live closest to the central business district, while the upper classes live farther out.

   (B) It is based primarily on transportation systems.

   (C) It suggests that urban growth is independent of the central business district.

   (D) It is a representation of a post-industrial North America.

   (E) It is based on Los Angeles and suggests that areas are zoned off from other zones in the city.

2. Which of the following describes a problem with the concentric zone model?

   (A) It was modeled on Chicago, which never had concentric zones.

   (B) Most cities today are no longer organized in clear zones.

   (C) Wealthy residents actually prefer to live far from the central business district.

   (D) It applies well to European cities but not to other cities.

   (E) It incorporates globalization too heavily.

3. Queenstown has a population of 2.2 million. The next largest city in the country is Kingsville with a population of 850,000. Based on this information, Queenstown is an example of which type of city?

   (A) Edge city

   (B) European city

   (C) Boomburb

   (D) Gateway city

   (E) Primate city

4. Which of the following lists the urban hierarchy of settlements in order from smallest to largest?

   (A) Town, hamlet, village, metropolis, megalopolis

   (B) Village, town, hamlet, metropolis, megalopolis

   (C) Megalopolis, metropolis, village, town, hamlet

   (D) Hamlet, town, city, megalopolis, metropolis

   (E) Hamlet, village, town, city, metropolis

5. Which of the following best explains why Ullman and Harris developed the multiple nuclei model?

   (A) To demonstrate the effects of decreased car ownership

   (B) To support the concentric zone model

   (C) To describe the complex development of urban areas

   (D) To standardize urban studies terminology

   (E) To explain the consolidation of cities' central business districts

8

6. Which of the following statements is NOT true regarding world cities?

    (A) These cities are the financial capitals of their regions.

    (B) These cities have double the population of the next largest city in their countries.

    (C) Large financial institutions are located in these cities.

    (D) Large publishing companies and transnational corporations are located in these cities.

    (E) These cities define their own countries and countries throughout their regions.

7. Which of the following statements best explains the bid-rent theory?

    (A) Land value is highest in the central business district, and land value decreases with distance from the CBD.

    (B) Land value is highest in the suburbs, resulting in larger houses.

    (C) More space is available in the urban core because most growth is upward.

    (D) Land value is higher in the suburbs due to a greater demand for land there.

    (E) Land value is constant throughout the metropolitan area due to the high demand for residential space in general.

8. Which of the following statements best describes the Latin American city model?

    (A) Many of the streets in Latin American cities are in a dendritic pattern.

    (B) Squatter settlements extend outward from the central business direct.

    (C) The majority of Latin American city districts have become gentrified.

    (D) Middle-class residential areas extend out from the central business district.

    (E) High-income residential areas extend out from the central business district.

9. Which of the following is an example of a basic industry?

    (A) A hotel in San Francisco

    (B) A restaurant in Atlanta

    (C) A car factory in Detroit

    (D) A convenience store in Dallas

    (E) A movie theater in Tampa

10. Gateway cities are associated with which of the following population trends?

    (A) Counterurbanization

    (B) Suburbanization

    (C) Gentrification

    (D) Immigration

    (E) Industrialization

Part B: Key Terms

The following is a list of the major concepts for the AP Human Geography topic of Cities and Urban Land-Use Patterns and Processes. You will likely see many of these on the official AP exam.

For each key term, ask yourself the following questions:

- Can I define this key term and use it in a sentence?
- Can I provide an example related to this key term?
- Could I correctly answer a multiple-choice question about this key term?
- Could I correctly answer a free-response question about this key term?

Check off the key terms if you can answer "yes" to at least three of these questions.

Defining Urbanization

- ☐ Urbanized population
- ☐ Urbanization
- ☐ Quantitative data
- ☐ Qualitative data

Urban Economies

- ☐ Commercialization
- ☐ Employment structure
- ☐ Underemployment

Urban Hierarchies

- ☐ Unincorporated areas
- ☐ Hamlets
- ☐ Villages
- ☐ Towns
- ☐ Cities
- ☐ Metropolises
- ☐ Megalopolis
- ☐ Megacities
- ☐ Metacities
- ☐ World cities
- ☐ Urban hierarchy
- ☐ Emerging cities
- ☐ Gateway cities
- ☐ Festival landscape

Characteristics of Cities

- ☐ Central business district
- ☐ Bid-rent theory
- ☐ Boomburbs
- ☐ Suburbs
- ☐ Utility infrastructure
- ☐ Zoning laws
- ☐ Greenbelts
- ☐ Urban growth rates
- ☐ Squatter settlements
- ☐ Latin American city model
- ☐ Southeast Asian city model
- ☐ Office parks
- ☐ High-tech corridors
- ☐ African city model

Models of U.S. Cities

- ☐ Class
- ☐ Concentric zone model
- ☐ Peak land value intersection
- ☐ Zone in transition
- ☐ Invasion and succession
- ☐ Sector model

- ☐ Multiple nuclei model
- ☐ Edge cities
- ☐ Multiplier effect
- ☐ Galactic city model
- ☐ Keno-capitalism model
- ☐ Ethnoburbs

- ☐ Central place theory
- ☐ Market area
- ☐ Census tracts
- ☐ Gravity model
- ☐ Rank-size rule
- ☐ Primate cities
- ☐ Symbolic landscape

Suburbanization in the United States

- ☐ Suburbanization
- ☐ Urban sprawl

- ☐ Planned community
- ☐ New Urbanism

- ☐ Brownfields

Urban Issues

- ☐ Counterurbanization
- ☐ Decentralization
- ☐ Centralization
- ☐ Urban hydrology
- ☐ Urban morphology

- ☐ Gentrification
- ☐ Urban renewal
- ☐ Blockbusting
- ☐ Racial steering
- ☐ Segregation

- ☐ Redlining
- ☐ Zones of abandonment
- ☐ Disamenities
- ☐ Walkable city

8

Next Steps

Step 1: Tally your correct answers from Part A and review the quiz explanations at the end of this chapter.

1.	A	6.	B
2.	B	7.	A
3.	E	8.	E
4.	E	9.	C
5.	C	10.	D

_____ out of 10 questions

Step 2: Count the number of key terms you checked off in Part B.

_____ out of 73 key terms

Step 3: Read the Key Takeaways in this chapter.

Step 4: Consult the table below, and follow the instructions based on your performance.

If You Got...	Do This
80% or more of the Test What You Already Know assessment correct (8 or more questions from Part A and 59 or more key terms from Part B)	• Read the definitions in this chapter for all the key terms you didn't check off. • Complete the Test What You Learned assessment in this chapter.
50% or less of the Test What You Already Know assessment correct (5 or fewer questions from Part A and 36 or fewer key terms from Part B)	• Read the comprehensive review for this topic in Chapter 15. ○ If you are short on time, read only the High-Yield sections. • Read through all of the key term definitions in this chapter. • Complete the Test What You Learned assessment in this chapter.
Any other result	• Read the High-Yield sections in the comprehensive review of this topic in Chapter 15. • Read the definitions in this chapter for all the key terms you didn't check off. • Complete the Test What You Learned assessment in this chapter.

8

ESSENTIAL CONTENT

Key Takeaways: Cities and Urban Land-Use Patterns and Processes

1. Cities often have economic, cultural, and political importance in the areas they serve. Different continents have cities with different characteristics.

2. The hierarchy of cities from smallest to largest is hamlet, village, town, city, metropolis, and megalopolis.

3. There are many models of urban structure in the United States. Some of these include the concentric zone model, the sector model, the multiple nuclei model, the galactic city model, and the Keno-capitalism model.

4. All cities fit within Christaller's central place theory, but some cities have greater ranges and need bigger thresholds. Range is the maximum distance people are willing to travel to get a product or service. Threshold is the minimum number of people needed for a business to operate.

5. Cities have problems such as traffic, water delivery, pollution, and urban sprawl that can negatively affect their inhabitants unless handled appropriately by local government.

8

Key Terms: Cities and Urban Land-Use Patterns and Processes

Defining Urbanization

Urbanized population: The number of people living in cities.

Urbanization: The process by which people live and are employed in a city.

Quantitative data: Information that can be expressed numerically (e.g., census surveys, statistical analysis, etc.).

Qualitative data: Information that consists of narratives and words (e.g., field studies, personal interviews, etc.).

Urban Economies

Commercialization: The selling of goods and services for profit.

Employment structure: The way in which most workers are employed within a city.

Underemployment: A situation that occurs when too many employees are hired, and there is not enough work for all of them.

Urban Hierarchies

Unincorporated areas: Areas that exist on the fringes of suburbs with only a few families living there today, even though they were once considered urban areas.

Hamlets: Areas that may only include a few dozen people and offer limited services.

Villages: Areas that are larger than hamlets and offer more services.

Towns: Areas that consist of 50 to a few thousand people and are considered to be urban areas with a defined boundary.

Cities: Large, densely populated areas that may include tens of thousands of people.

Metropolises: Areas that have large populations that are usually focused around one large city.

Megalopolis: An area that links together several metropolitan areas to form one huge urban area.

Megacities: Cities that have populations of over 10 million people.

Metacities: Cities with large populations that don't have a distinct business center, but are instead a collection of cities and industrial hubs.

World cities: The most important cities, also called global cities, as defined by Saskia Sassen; this categorization is based on their economic, cultural, and political importance. As of 2018, the two most important cities are New York City and London. Other global cities are classified in tiers of descending importance: alpha, beta, and gamma.

Urban hierarchy: A hierarchy that puts cities in ranks from small, first-order cities to large, fourth-order cities. The higher the order of the city, the greater the sphere of influence that city possesses on a global scale.

Emerging cities: Cities that are experiencing population growth and increasing economic and political clout within their regions.

Gateway cities: Cities that connect two areas and serve as an entry point between them.

Festival landscape: A space within an urban environment that can accommodate a large number of people.

8

Characteristics of Cities

Central business district: The commercial center of an urban area.

Bid-rent theory: A theory suggesting that the closer to the central business district, the higher the value of the land and that only commercial enterprises can afford the land within the central business district.

Boomburbs: Cities located around major metropolitan areas that see massive growth.

Suburbs: Residential areas located on the outskirts of a central city that may possess numerous commercial and industrial enterprises.

Utility infrastructure: A system set in place by the government for delivery of electricity, sewer services, and Internet connectivity.

Zoning laws: Laws that determine how land and buildings can be used. Residential zoning is for housing; commercial zoning is for business or retail types of structures; industrial zoning is for manufacturing plants; and institutional zoning is for government structures such as schools, courtrooms, and government offices.

Greenbelts: Rural areas that are set aside to prevent development from extending too far outward. Another purpose of greenbelts is to prevent in-filling, the process by which cities that are close to each other merge.

Urban growth rates: The rates at which individual cities increase their populations.

Squatter settlements: Areas of extreme poverty in developing countries; these often occur due to rapid urbanization and the inability of city infrastructure to keep up.

Latin American city model: A model that shows the characteristics of many cities in Central and South America; many of the high-income residences that extend out from the central business district are gated communities, designed to protect the residents from the crime bred by widespread urban poverty.

Southeast Asian city model: A model illustrating the typical structure of Southeast Asian cities that shows the importance of the port zone; growth extends outward from the port.

Office parks: Agglomerations with shared phone and Internet services and transportation infrastructure. Office parks allow businesses of similar structure and production to locate near each other and experience the benefits of the area's infrastructure.

High-tech corridors: Places where microchips can be produced cheaply that use the principle of agglomeration to their benefit. High-tech corridors are instrumental in providing the world with the computer chip equipment needed to run its operations on a daily basis.

African city model: A model depicting three distinct CBDs (colonial, traditional, and market) with ethnic neighborhoods extending outward from them. Beyond the ethnic neighborhoods are the mining and manufacturing zones, as well as informal towns (squatter settlements).

8

Models of U.S. Cities

Class: Demographic category based on economic, social, and cultural factors (e.g., lower, middle, or upper class).

Concentric zone model: A city model established by Robert Park, Ernest Burgess, and Roderick McKenzie suggesting that the lower classes live closest to the central business district, while the upper classes live farther out because they can afford the commute into the city to work.

Peak land value intersection: The area with the greatest land value and commercial value.

Zone in transition: A city zone that is just outside of the central business district and usually contains areas of substandard housing.

Invasion and succession: Burgess's idea that the central business district would continually expand and push beyond the zones.

Sector model: A city model established by Homer Hoyt in 1939 that is based on class and describes social structure based on transportation systems.

Multiple nuclei model: A city model established by Chauncy Harris and Edward Ullman, in 1945, suggesting that urban growth is independent of the central business district.

Edge cities: Large commercial centers that offer entertainment and shopping in the suburbs. Such cities may approach 100,000 in population.

Multiplier effect: The principle that development spurs more development.

Galactic city model: A city model representing a post-industrial city in North America in which a city with growth independent of the central business district is traditionally connected to the central city by means of an arterial highway or interstate.

Keno-capitalism model: A city model based on Los Angeles that suggests that areas are zoned off or even gated off from other zones in the city.

Ethnoburbs: Neighborhoods dominated by a specific ethnic group.

Central place theory: A theory established by Walter Christaller that is based on assumptions of uniform topography, equal transportation systems, and the notion that people will travel the least distance possible to meet their service needs.

Market area: The area in which a product, urban area, or commercial outlet has influence.

Census tracts: Geographic areas, with about 5,000 people on average, used to determine population for business purposes.

Gravity model: A model that suggests that the greater the sphere of influence a city has, the greater its impact on other cities around it. To determine the degree to which two cities are related, multiply the populations and divide by the square of the distance between the cities.

Rank-size rule: A rule that states that the size of cities within a country will be in proportion to one another.

Primate cities: Cities that have more than twice the population of any other urban area in that country. A primate city is the most important urban area economically, politically, and culturally in its country.

Symbolic landscape: An urban landscape that reflects the city's history and has become synonymous with the city.

Suburbanization in the United States

Suburbanization: A process by which a population expands from the city center to surrounding, less dense areas.

Urban sprawl: The process of growth in which the second-ring suburbs grow and infringe on the surrounding rural areas.

Planned community: An area in which a developer plots out each house and builds an entire development from scratch.

New Urbanism: The movement to plan communities that are more walkable, rather than automobile dependent, with a diversity of jobs.

Brownfields: Former industrial sites that cities are now attempting to redevelop.

Urban Issues

Counterurbanization: The process in which problems of an urban area become so great that people leave.

Decentralization: The distribution of authority from a central figure or point to other sectors in the city.

Centralization: The focusing of power into one authority, usually a mayor or city manager.

Urban hydrology: The way in which a city provides clean water to its citizens, removes dirty water, and purifies water before it is distributed back into the world's rivers and oceans.

Urban morphology: The street patterns, structures, and the physical form of the city, which combine to cause the urban heat island effect.

Gentrification: The process of wealthy people moving into inner-city neighborhoods.

Urban renewal: The process of cities buying properties in order to redevelop the area to encourage economic investment.

Blockbusting: A situation that occurs when real estate agents try to induce people of a certain race to sell their homes because of a perception that a different race is moving into the neighborhood.

Racial steering: A situation that occurs when real estate agents show homes only in certain neighborhoods based on the race of the buyers.

Segregation: The separation of races.

Redlining: The refusal of lending institutions to give loans to those in areas associated with a high risk of default; legally used in neighborhoods subject to natural disasters but historically associated with racial discrimination.

Zones of abandonment: Areas that no longer have police or fire protection because the city has decided the tax revenue cannot sustain public services to those areas.

Disamenities: Factors that cause people to not want to live in the city.

Walkable city: A city that has options, such as grocery stores, bakeries, butchers, and other services, within walking distance of residences to reduce the need for automobiles, thus reducing pollution and traffic congestion.

8

TEST WHAT YOU LEARNED

Part A: Quiz

1. Which of the following is an example of block-busting?

   (A) A lending institution refuses to give loans to those in neighborhoods that have a high default rate on mortgages.

   (B) A lending institution refuses to give loans to those in high-risk areas.

   (C) A real estate agent tries to induce people to sell their homes by appealing to a perception that a different race is moving into the neighborhood.

   (D) A real estate agent shows homes only in certain neighborhoods based on the race of the buyers.

   (E) A real estate agent and a financial institution make it very difficult for people of different races to live in the same area of town.

2. Which of the following statements best describes a major difference between U.S. and European cities?

   (A) U.S. cities have zones that are often inter-mixed, with commercial establishments and residences in the same building.

   (B) Traditional European cities were not designed to accommodate automobiles.

   (C) U.S. cities have a dendritic street pattern, whereas European cities have a grid street pattern.

   (D) European cities were constructed in accordance with religious beliefs.

   (E) Skyscrapers in U.S. cities are located far from the center of the city.

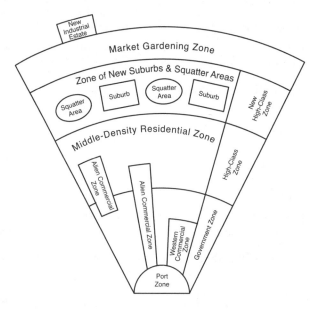

3. Based on the image above, which of the following statements is NOT true regarding Asian cities?

   (A) Many of the high-income residences are designed to protect residents from the crime bred by widespread urban poverty.

   (B) Asian cities have no formalized central business districts.

   (C) Growth occurs throughout the cities, in part owing to few zoning laws and almost laissez-faire economics.

   (D) Growth extends outward from the port.

   (E) Asian cities usually include a market-gardening zone because of a cultural preference for fresh food.

8

4. Which of the following would likely result from deindustrialization?

   (A) A walkable city

   (B) Decentralization

   (C) In-filling

   (D) Urbanization

   (E) Zones of abandonment

5. In which of the following ways has suburbanization impacted cities?

   (A) Cities are becoming dominated by the elderly and younger couples with either no children or very young children.

   (B) Cities are losing nightclubs, theaters, and sports facilities as more people move to the suburbs.

   (C) Cities are losing workers as they find new jobs closer to their suburban homes.

   (D) Many couples move to suburbs once their grown-up children move away.

   (E) Many people are being pushed away from the suburbs by their negative perceptions of them.

6. *Favelas* are symptoms of which problem in Latin American cities?

   (A) Pollution

   (B) Gentrification

   (C) Colonialism

   (D) Wealth inequality

   (E) Underpopulation

7. Greenbelts are primarily created to prevent which of the following?

   (A) Entrepots

   (B) Urban sprawl

   (C) Commercialization

   (D) Squatter settlements

   (E) Redlining

8. Which of the following best describes the multiple nuclei model?

   (A) Areas are zoned off or even gated off from other zones in the city.

   (B) Growth may begin in commercial, industrial, and even residential suburbs outside the central business district.

   (C) A city's size, including its hinterlands, determines the size of its range.

   (D) Urban zones extend along transportation routes.

   (E) The lower classes live closest to the central business district.

9. Which of the following best explains the basis for Walter Christaller's central place theory?

   (A) Social structure is based on transportation systems rather than on the distance from the central business district.

   (B) Growth independent of the central business district is connected to the central city by a highway or an interstate.

   (C) People will travel the least distance possible to meet their service needs.

   (D) Zones are randomly placed in the city and are separated from each other by walls.

   (E) Lower classes will likely live closest to the central business district, while the upper classes will likely live farther out.

10. New York City's Central Park is a public outdoor space that offers activities, events, concerts, and other attractions. Central Park is an example of which of the following?

    (A) A greenbelt

    (B) A festival landscape

    (C) A catacomb

    (D) A bazaar

    (E) A core area

8

Part B: Key Terms

This key terms list is the same as the list in the Test What You Already Know section earlier in this chapter. Based on what you have now learned, again ask yourself the following questions:

- Can I define this key term and use it in a sentence?
- Can I provide an example related to this key term?
- Could I correctly answer a multiple-choice question about this key term?
- Could I correctly answer a free-response question about this key term?

Check off the key terms if you can answer "yes" to at least three of these questions.

Defining Urbanization

- ☐ Urbanized population
- ☐ Urbanization
- ☐ Quantitative data
- ☐ Qualitative data

Urban Economies

- ☐ Commercialization
- ☐ Employment structure
- ☐ Underemployment

Urban Hierarchies

- ☐ Unincorporated areas
- ☐ Hamlets
- ☐ Villages
- ☐ Towns
- ☐ Cities
- ☐ Metropolises
- ☐ Megalopolis
- ☐ Megacities
- ☐ Metacities
- ☐ World Cities
- ☐ Urban hierarchy
- ☐ Emerging cities
- ☐ Gateway cities
- ☐ Festival landscape

Characteristics of Cities

- ☐ Central business district
- ☐ Bid-rent theory
- ☐ Boomburbs
- ☐ Suburbs
- ☐ Utility infrastructure
- ☐ Zoning laws
- ☐ Greenbelts
- ☐ Urban growth rates
- ☐ Squatter settlements
- ☐ Latin American city model
- ☐ Southeast Asian city model
- ☐ Office parks
- ☐ High-tech corridors
- ☐ African city model

8

Models of U.S. Cities

- ☐ Class
- ☐ Concentric zone model
- ☐ Peak land value intersection
- ☐ Zone in transition
- ☐ Invasion and succession

- ☐ Sector model
- ☐ Multiple nuclei model
- ☐ Edge cities
- ☐ Multiplier effect
- ☐ Galactic city model
- ☐ Keno-capitalism model

- ☐ Ethnoburbs
- ☐ Central place theory
- ☐ Market area
- ☐ Census tracts
- ☐ Gravity model
- ☐ Rank-size rule
- ☐ Primate cities
- ☐ Symbolic landscape

Suburbanization in the United States

- ☐ Suburbanization
- ☐ Urban sprawl

- ☐ Planned community
- ☐ New Urbanism

- ☐ Brownfields

Urban Issues

- ☐ Counterurbanization
- ☐ Decentralization
- ☐ Centralization
- ☐ Urban hydrology
- ☐ Urban morphology

- ☐ Gentrification
- ☐ Urban renewal
- ☐ Blockbusting
- ☐ Racial steering
- ☐ Segregation

- ☐ Redlining
- ☐ Zones of abandonment
- ☐ Disamenities
- ☐ Walkable city

8

Next Steps

Step 1: Tally your correct answers from Part A, and review the quiz explanations at the end of this chapter.

1.	C	6.	D
2.	B	7.	B
3.	A	8.	B
4.	E	9.	C
5.	A	10.	B

_____ out of 10 questions

Step 2: Count the number of key terms you checked off in Part B.

_____ out of 73 key terms

Step 3: Compare your Test What You Already Know results to these Test What You Learned results to see how exam-ready you are for this topic.

For More Practice:

- Read (or reread) the comprehensive review for this topic in Chapter 15.
- Go to kaptest.com to complete the online quiz questions for Cities and Urban Land-Use Patterns and Processes.
  - Haven't registered your book yet? Go to **kaptest.com/moreonline** to begin.

CHAPTER 8 ANSWERS AND EXPLANATIONS

Test What You Already Know

1. A

The concentric zone model suggests that the lower classes live closest to the central business district, while the upper classes live farther out because they can afford the commute into the city to work; thus, **(A)** is correct. The sector model, not the concentric zone model, is based on transportation systems, with zones extending along transportation routes; (B) is incorrect. (C) is incorrect because this statement describes the multiple nuclei model. The galactic city model, not the concentric zone model, is a representation of a post-industrial North America, eliminating (D). The Keno-capitalism model is based on Los Angeles and suggests that areas are zoned off from other zones in the city; (E) is incorrect.

2. B

The concentric zone model suggests that there are five areas in a city: the central business district, a transition zone, working-class residences, middle-class residences, and commuter residences. However, this model is generally considered outdated, as cities today have expanded in ways that cannot be categorized by simple concentric zones; **(B)** is correct. This model was based on Chicago of the early 1900s because the city had concentric zones at the time, eliminating (A). (C) is incorrect because this fact is not at odds with the model, which suggests that upper classes live farther from the central business district because they can afford to commute into the city to work. In European cities, the wealthy live close to the central business district, which does not fit the concentric zone model; (D) is incorrect. This model of development applies to a single city, not businesses or organizations that begin operating on a global scale, eliminating (E).

3. E

Cities with both the largest population and a population at least double the size of the next largest city are called primate cities; **(E)** is correct. The other choices are incorrect because these types of cities cannot be determined based on population data alone. Edge cities, also called boomburbs, are rapidly growing cities located in suburban areas; (A) and (C) are incorrect. There is no evidence that Queenstown is a European city, making (B) incorrect. Lastly, a gateway city is one that serves as an entry point to the country; (D) is incorrect.

4. E

The urban hierarchy is determined by the population of the urban area. Hamlets may only have a dozen or so people, villages may contain up to about a hundred people, towns may consist of several thousand people, cities have tens of thousands of people, metropolises have more than 50,000 people, and a megalopolis is made of several metropolises. Thus, **(E)** is correct. (A), (B), (C), and (D) are incorrect because they list the urban areas out of order.

5. C

Ullman and Harris's multiple nuclei model describes the complexity of urban areas in which several satellite business districts often develop; **(C)** is correct. Multiple business districts result from increased, not decreased, car ownership, eliminating (A). (B) is incorrect because the multiple nuclei model challenges the concentric zone model. Though Ullman and Harris's model entered urban studies terminology, standardization was not the express purpose of developing the model, eliminating (D). The multiple nuclei model describes the formation of multiple business districts, not the consolidation of one single district; (E) is incorrect.

6. B

Primate cities, not world cities, have the highest population and at least double the population of the next largest city in their countries; **(B)** is correct. As of 2018, both London and New York City are world cities, but only London qualifies as a primate city. World cities are the financial capitals of their regions and have large financial institutions, publishing companies, and transnational corporations; this eliminates (A), (C), and (D), because the question is asking for what is *not* true. In addition, world cities not only define their own countries, but also other countries in the region, making (E) incorrect.

8

7. A

The bid-rent theory suggests that land value closest to the central business district (CBD) is high due to the limited availability of land; thus, **(A)** is correct and (C) is incorrect. According to the bid-rent theory, land value in the suburbs is low due to a lower demand for land, making (B) and (D) incorrect. Land value directly correlates to its proximity to amenities and is not constant throughout a metropolitan area, eliminating (E).

8. E

In Larry Ford's model, high-income residential areas extend out from the central business district; **(E)** is correct. Latin American streets resemble the hub and spoke of a bicycle wheel with all roads leading to the center of the city, while many of the streets in Europe are in a dendritic pattern, which looks like the root system of trees. Thus, (A) is incorrect. (B) is incorrect because squatter settlements are located around the edge of the city and extend out from the market district, rather than extending outward from the central business district. Only a small sliver within the Latin American city model represents gentrification, making (C) incorrect. (D) is incorrect because the middle-class residential areas are in the outermost area of the city model and do not extend outward from the central business district.

9. C

A basic industry is one that is city forming, such as steel in Pittsburgh, automobiles in Detroit, and computer chips in San Jose, California. Thus, **(C)** is correct. (A), (B), (D), and (E) are incorrect because these are non-basic industries; they provide services to residents of established cities.

10. D

A gateway city is an area that serves as an immigration entry point for a country or another large area; **(D)** is correct. Counterurbanization occurs when the problems of an urban area become so great that people move from urban to rural areas, which is associated with sub-urbanization, or the growth of outlying areas known as suburbs; neither counterurbanization or suburbanization are associated with gateway cities in particular, making (A) and (B) incorrect. Gentrification, which is the process of wealthy people moving into inner-city neighborhoods, is a population trend that is not linked to gateway cities; (C) is incorrect. Industrialization is the development of industries in a country or a region on a large scale, and it is also not directly connected to gateway cities; (E) is incorrect.

Test What You Learned

1. C

Blockbusting is when real estate agents use a perception that people of a different race are moving into a neighborhood, and that their presence is likely due to lower property values, to induce current residents to sell their homes; **(C)** is correct. Redlining is the refusal of lending institutions to give loans on properties where data indicates a relatively high default rate on mortgages; (A) and (B) are incorrect. Racial steering is when real estate agents show homes only in certain neighborhoods based on the race of the buyers, eliminating (D). (E) is incorrect because, while blockbusting is associated with residential segregation, financial institutions are not involved in blockbusting.

2. B

Traditional European cities were built long before the invention of the automobile, resulting in streets that are difficult for modern driving; **(B)** is correct. European cities often intermix zones, while structures in the United States are often zoned for a single use, eliminating (A). (C) is incorrect since European cities have a dendritic street pattern, while U.S. cities usually have a grid street pattern. Islamic cities, not European cities, are built to reflect religious beliefs, making (D) incorrect. U.S. cities have skyscrapers that are located in the central business district; (E) is incorrect.

3. A

It is in Latin American cities, not Asian cities, where many of the high-income residences that extend out from the central business district are gated communities, designed to protect the residents from the crime bred by wide-spread urban poverty. Thus, **(A)** is correct. (B), (C), (D), and (E) accurately describe Asian cities; these choices are therefore incorrect because the question is asking for the statement that is *not* true.

4. E

When a city goes through deindustrialization, factories are shut down and the old infrastructure is often left to rot or rust. This can lead to zones of abandonment, areas where public services are no longer funded, making **(E)** correct. (A), (B), and (C) are incorrect because these terms are unrelated to an economic shift away from industry. A walkable city, (A), is created when grocery stores, bakeries, butchers, and other services are within walking distance of residences to reduce the need for automobiles. Decentralization, (B), refers to power shifting away from a central authority. (C), in-filling, is the process of geographically close cities merging into each other. (D) is incorrect because urbanization, the growth of cities, historically occurred in conjunction with the increase, not the decline, of industry.

5. A

Suburbanization is changing the demographics of cities, resulting in a core city that is dominated by the elderly and younger couples with either no children or very young children; thus, **(A)** is correct. Nightclubs, theaters, and sports facilities remain more present in the core city than in the suburbs, eliminating (B). (C) is incorrect because people often commute from the suburbs into the city for work. When grown-up children move away to go to college or develop families of their own, many older couples move back into the city because they no longer wish to keep up a large house and yard, making (D) incorrect. (E) is incorrect because people are being pushed away from the core city, not the suburbs, by their negative perceptions, which involve issues of crime, race relations, gentrification, pollution, and more.

6. D

Favela is a term for a squatter settlement, which is an area of squalor and extreme poverty located at the edge of a large Latin American city; **(D)** is correct. Where pollution is a problem, it affects entire cities, making (A) incorrect. Gentrification is the process in which wealthy residents move into inner-city areas, while *favelas* are on the outskirts of large cities; (B) is incorrect. (C) is incorrect because colonialism is the practice of acquiring control over a different area, which does not necessarily cause squatter settlements to form. Overpopulation, not under-population, of a city drives poorer residents to squatter settlements, making (E) incorrect.

7. B

Greenbelts are rural areas that are set aside to prevent in-filling and development from extending too far outward, which is a process called urban sprawl; **(B)** is correct. (A) is incorrect because entrepots are not related to development; rather, these are locations that reexport goods around the globe. Greenbelts tend not to have a significant effect on commercialization, which generally is not regarded as a problem, making (C)

incorrect. Squatter settlements are areas of extreme poverty, but these economic conditions could not be prevented solely by the creation of a greenbelt; (D) is incorrect. Redlining is a discriminatory practice regarding mortgage loans and is unrelated to the development of greenbelts, eliminating (E).

8. B

The multiple nuclei model suggests that urban growth is independent of the central business district and may begin in commercial, industrial, and even residential suburbs outside the central business district. Thus, **(B)** is correct. (A) is incorrect because this describes the Keno-capitalism model. The central place theory, not the multiple nuclei model, describes the relationships between urban areas, including their hinterlands and the range that individual cities need to maintain their size; (C) is incorrect. (D) is incorrect because the sector model, not the multiple nuclei model, suggests that zones extend along transportation routes. The concentric zone model is the one that suggests lower classes live closest to the central business district, making (E) incorrect.

9. C

Christaller based his central place theory on assumptions of uniform topography, equal transportation systems, and that people will travel the least distance possible to meet their service needs. Thus, **(C)** is correct. (A), (B), (D), and (E) are incorrect because these describe other models: (A) suggests the sector model, (B) represents the galactic city model, (D) describes the Keno-capitalism model, and (E) depicts the concentric zone model.

10. B

Central Park is a public outdoor space designed to accommodate a large number of people, which fits the definition of a festival landscape. Thus, **(B)** is correct. A greenbelt is a rural area used to prevent urban sprawl, while Central Park is at the center of a large urban area, making (A) incorrect. Catacombs are underground areas where the dead were buried for centuries beneath European cities, eliminating (C). A bazaar is an open-air street market common in Middle Eastern and South Asian cities; (D) is incorrect. A core area is the center of development, whereas Central Park is a designated outdoor space, making (E) incorrect.

8

CHAPTER 9

Industrial and Economic Development Patterns and Processes

LEARNING OBJECTIVES

- List major economic sectors.

- Describe the Industrial Revolution's effects.

- Explain industrial location using Weber's model.

- Analyze the causes and effects of the global economy.

- Analyze the intersection of gender and economic development.

- Analyze measures of social and economic development, particularly corresponding spatial patterns.

- Describe the economic consequences of recent industrialization and development.

TEST WHAT YOU ALREADY KNOW

Part A: Quiz

1. Which of the following best describes a significant position in Weber's least cost theory?

    (A) People will travel the least possible distance for services.

    (B) The greater influence a city has, the more migration to that city.

    (C) The cost to transport raw materials is more important than the cost of the raw materials themselves.

    (D) Birth rate, death rate, and total population are the only factors relevant to population growth.

    (E) Farmers sell all of their agricultural harvest.

2. Which of the following is an example of a weight-gaining industry?

    (A) Automobile manufacturing

    (B) Potato chip making

    (C) Sugar processing

    (D) Pharmaceutical manufacturing

    (E) Fresh produce shipping

3. Which of the following best describes the economic relationship between less developed countries in Africa and more developed countries in Western Europe?

    (A) Western European countries have no economic relationship to African countries because they have gained economic independence.

    (B) Western European countries continue to remain economically separated from less developed African countries.

    (C) Western European countries procure raw materials and inexpensive, unskilled labor from less developed African countries.

    (D) Western European countries own much of the land in less developed African countries through private owners.

    (E) Western European countries have a declining economic relationship with less developed African countries due to an unfavorable market orientation.

4. Which of the following statements concerning the Human Development Index (HDI) is most accurate?

    (A) The HDI of a country correlates with the level of commitment to democracy by its citizens.

    (B) The HDI of a country decreases with the level of gender inequities maintained by the country.

    (C) The HDI of a country decreases when students study abroad without returning.

    (D) The HDI of a country increases with a high literacy score.

    (E) The HDI of a country increases when its birth rate is at least two.

9

5. Which of the following most directly influenced the economic success of the Four Asian Tigers?

    (A) Raw materials

    (B) International trade

    (C) Cheap immigrant labor

    (D) Low transportation costs

    (E) Low land costs

6. The transfer of a shipment of blue jeans from a train to a truck at a distribution point is an example of

    (A) gross domestic product

    (B) a growth pole

    (C) outsourcing

    (D) a break-of-bulk point

    (E) carrier efficiency

7. Which of the following exemplifies why Shanghai is considered one of China's special economic zones (SEZs)?

    (A) The workforce in Shanghai equates personal and professional value with how the company performs.

    (B) Foreign car makers including Ford, General Motors, and Volkswagen have located plants near Shanghai.

    (C) The Huang River serves as a major transportation route for the manufacturing industries in Shanghai.

    (D) Shanghai is a treaty port that efficiently exports goods made in China.

    (E) Kaohsiung, one of the busiest ports in the world, is an exportation hub that has given rise to Shanghai's rapid economic growth.

8. Which of the following concepts describes the benefits companies receive due to clustering together in the same location?

    (A) Variable costs

    (B) Fixed costs

    (C) Carrier efficiency

    (D) Agglomeration

    (E) Substitution principle

9. Which of the following portions of the economy processes raw materials in order to manufacture goods?

    (A) Primary sector

    (B) Secondary sector

    (C) Tertiary sector

    (D) Quaternary sector

    (E) Quinary sector

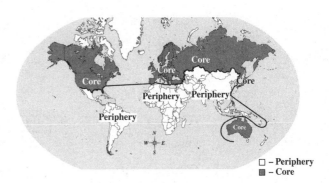

10. According to the core-periphery model, as shown in the map above, the Canadian northern territories would be classified as

    (A) an industrial core

    (B) an upward transition

    (C) a downward transition

    (D) a semi-periphery

    (E) a resource frontier

9

Part B: Key Terms

The following is a list of the major concepts for the AP Human Geography topic of Industrial and Economic Development Patterns and Processes. You will likely see many of these on the official AP exam.

For each key term, ask yourself the following questions:

- Can I define this key term and use it in a sentence?
- Can I provide an example related to this key term?
- Could I correctly answer a multiple-choice question about this key term?
- Could I correctly answer a free-response question about this key term?

Check off the key terms if you can answer "yes" to at least three of these questions.

Keys to Economic and Industrial Development

- ☐ Economic geography
- ☐ Capitalism
- ☐ Neoliberalism
- ☐ Socialism

- ☐ Communism
- ☐ Site factors
- ☐ Situation factors
- ☐ Basic industry
- ☐ Non-basic industry

- ☐ Multiplier effect
- ☐ Variable cost
- ☐ Fixed cost
- ☐ Time-space compression

Location of Industry

- ☐ Industrial Revolution
- ☐ Cottage industry
- ☐ Agglomeration
- ☐ Cumulative causation
- ☐ Deglomeration

- ☐ Weber's least cost theory
- ☐ Weight-gaining industry
- ☐ Weight-reducing industry
- ☐ Maquiladoras

- ☐ Outsourcing
- ☐ Footloose industry
- ☐ Multinational corporations
- ☐ Sweatshops
- ☐ Manufacturing exports

Global Industrial Zones

- ☐ Rust Belt
- ☐ Treaty ports
- ☐ Export processing zones

- ☐ Special economic zones (SEZs)
- ☐ Four Asian Tigers

- ☐ Newly industrialized countries (NICs)
- ☐ BRIC

Ways to Describe Development

- ☐ Development
- ☐ Developed country
- ☐ Developing country
- ☐ Gross domestic product (GDP)
- ☐ Human Development Index (HDI)
- ☐ Brain drain
- ☐ Brain gain

- ☐ Gross national income (GNI)
- ☐ Physical Quality of Life Index (PQLI)
- ☐ Economic sector
- ☐ Primary sector
- ☐ Secondary sector
- ☐ Tertiary sector
- ☐ Quaternary sector
- ☐ Quinary sector

- ☐ Technology gap
- ☐ Technology transfer process
- ☐ Neocolonialism
- ☐ Gender balance
- ☐ Gender Development Index (GDI)
- ☐ Sustainable Development Goals (SDGs)

Development Theories

- ☐ World systems theory
- ☐ Core areas
- ☐ Periphery areas
- ☐ Dependency model

- ☐ Semi-periphery areas
- ☐ Core-periphery model
- ☐ Industrial core
- ☐ Upward transition

- ☐ Sun Belt
- ☐ Downward transition
- ☐ Resource frontier
- ☐ Rostow's stages of growth model

Land Use and Resources

- ☐ Topocide
- ☐ Sustainable development
- ☐ Conservation
- ☐ Ecotourism
- ☐ Debt-for-nature swap

- ☐ Tragedy of the commons
- ☐ Renewable resources
- ☐ Nonrenewable resources

- ☐ Organization of Petroleum Exporting Countries (OPEC)
- ☐ Biomass

9

Next Steps

Step 1: Tally your correct answers from Part A and review the quiz explanations at the end of this chapter.

1.	C	6.	D
2.	A	7.	B
3.	C	8.	D
4.	C	9.	B
5.	B	10.	E

_____ out of 10 questions

Step 2: Count the number of key terms you checked off in Part B.

_____ out of 77 key terms

Step 3: Read the Key Takeaways in this chapter.

Step 4: Consult the table below, and follow the instructions based on your performance.

If You Got...	Do This
80% or more of the Test What You Already Know assessment correct (8 or more questions from Part A and 62 or more key terms from Part B)	• Read the definitions in this chapter for all the key terms you didn't check off. • Complete the Test What You Learned assessment in this chapter.
50% or less of the Test What You Already Know assessment correct (5 or fewer questions from Part A and 38 or fewer key terms from Part B)	• Read the comprehensive review for this topic in Chapter 16. ○ If you are short on time, read only the High-Yield sections. • Read through all of the key term definitions in this chapter. • Complete the Test What You Learned assessment in this chapter.
Any other result	• Read the High-Yield sections in the comprehensive review of this topic in Chapter 16. • Read the definitions in this chapter for all the key terms you didn't check off. • Complete the Test What You Learned assessment in this chapter.

9

ESSENTIAL CONTENT

Key Takeaways: Industrial and Economic Development Patterns and Processes

1. Industry is based on transportation and labor costs. Weber's least cost theory suggests that a production point must be located within a "triangle," with raw materials coming from at least two sources. Weight-gaining industries must have their production point closer to the market. Weight-reducing industries must have their production point closer to the source of raw materials.

2. Basic industries are city-forming industries, whereas non-basic industries are city-serving industries. Basic industries are often the main business for which a city is known.

3. The five main means of industrial transportation are truck, train, airplane, pipeline, and ship. Each has advantages and disadvantages for hauling raw materials or finished products to production points and markets around the globe.

4. A common statistic used to measure an area's development is the Human Development Index (HDI), which measures average life expectancy, amount of education, and per capita income. Since 1990, the United Nations has used the HDI as a way to rank all of the countries in the world in terms of their development.

5. The core-periphery model describes regions as core, semi-periphery, and periphery areas. It also describes four areas: the industrial core, upward transition, downward transition, and resource frontier. The model can be used from a worldwide scale down to a city scale.

Key Terms: Industrial and Economic Development Patterns and Processes

Keys to Economic and Industrial Development

Economic geography: A field of human geography that studies economic development and the inequalities that are created. The main goal is to find out why the world is divided into relatively rich and relatively poor countries.

Capitalism: An economic system in which businesses are owned by private individuals and companies who are free to decide what to produce and how much to charge.

Neoliberalism: Political and economic ideology that favors free-market capitalism. Typically advocates for free trade, free movement of labor, globalization, and minimal government oversight of the economy.

Socialism: An economic and political system in which the government regulates private business and basic industries and controls the means of production (e.g., factories, resources, machinery, and technology).

Communism: An economic and political system in which the central government holds the means of production in common for all of the citizens.

Site factors: A place's physical features related to the costs of business production, such as land, labor, and capital.

Situation factors: The features of a location's surrounding area, especially as related to the cost of transporting raw materials and finished goods.

Basic industry: An industry that is the main focus of an area's economy (e.g., the automobile industry was historically the basic industry of Detroit).

Non-basic industry: Industry that supports the work of the basic industry; created due to the economic growth brought about by the area's basic industry.

Multiplier effect: Describes the expansion of an area's economic base as a result of the basic and non-basic industries located there.

Variable cost: A cost that changes based on the level of output that a business produces.

Fixed cost: A cost that does not change based on the level of output that a business produces.

Time-space compression: Describes a company's effort to increase efficiency in the delivery process by diminishing distance obstacles.

Location of Industry

Industrial Revolution: A period of rapid development of industry that started in Great Britain in the late eighteenth and nineteenth centuries. It was brought about by the introduction of machinery and technology, such as steam power, which resulted in the growth of factories and the mass production of goods.

Cottage industry: A form of industry where products are made by an individual, family, or small group of workers.

Agglomeration: A localized economy in which a large number of companies and industries cluster together and benefit from the cost reductions and gains in efficiency that result from this proximity.

Cumulative causation: Describes the continued growth due to the positive aspects of agglomeration.

Deglomeration: The process of industrial deconcentration in response to technological advances or increasing costs due to competition.

Weber's least cost theory: A theory that suggests a company building an industrial plant will take into consideration the location of both the raw materials and the market for the product.

Weight-gaining industry: An industry where the finished product weighs more than the raw materials.

Weight-reducing industry: An industry where the raw materials weigh more than the finished product.

Maquiladoras: Industrial plants located in Mexico that produce goods using relatively inexpensive labor and then sell the products in the United States.

Outsourcing: A business practice used by companies to reduce costs or improve efficiency by shifting tasks, operations, jobs, or processes to another country.

Footloose industry: An industry that does not have a strong locational preference because the resources, production skills, and consumers on which it depends can be found in numerous places.

Multinational corporations: Large companies that have offices or divisions around the world.

Sweatshops: Factories in which the workers make very little money and work long hours in poor working conditions.

Manufacturing exports: Products shipped out of the country to a foreign market.

Global Industrial Zones

Rust Belt: An area including parts of the northeastern and midwestern United States that is characterized by declining industry, aging factories, and a shrinking population. Steel-producing cities in Pennsylvania and Ohio are at its center.

Treaty ports: International ports that must be kept open for international trade because of the signing of a treaty.

Export processing zones: Zones designed to efficiently ship out goods to other seaports.

Special economic zones (SEZs): Business areas, found mostly in China and India, designated specifically for foreign companies to locate their headquarters.

Four Asian Tigers: Four countries in East Asia that have undergone rapid economic expansion over the past few decades; they are Hong Kong, South Korea, Taiwan, and Singapore.

Newly industrialized countries (NICs): Countries whose economies do not yet meet the criteria to be considered developed, but have grown much more rapidly than those of other developing countries.

BRIC: An acronym representing the countries of Brazil, Russia, India, and China, all of which have significant wealth and industrialization but, due to other factors, do not necessarily qualify as developed countries.

9

Ways to Describe Development

Development: The process of improving the material conditions of people through the creation of a modern economy and the distribution of knowledge and technology.

Developed country: A country that has progressed relatively far along a continuum of development and has a stable modern economy.

Developing country: A country that is still in an early stage of development and does not yet have a strong, modern economy. Also referred to as a less developed country (LDC).

Gross domestic product (GDP): The value of the total output of goods and services produced in a country during one year.

Human Development Index (HDI): A United Nations–created indicator that measures a country's development based on three factors: average life expectancy, amount of education, and per capita income.

Brain drain: When a large number of young people move to a different country for school or other opportunities and do not return to work in their home country.

Brain gain: When less developed countries send their top students to colleges and universities in more developed countries, then see their investment return as former students return to their home countries and initiate development.

Gross national income (GNI): The total income earned by a country's residents both in the country and abroad.

Physical Quality of Life Index (PQLI): A statistic that is used to measure a country's development. Unlike the Human Development Index, the PQLI directly factors in a country's literacy rate and does not include per capita income.

Economic sector: A large segment of the economy that is characterized by a distinct type of production or service.

Primary sector: Basic economic activities that include agriculture, forestry, fishing, and the extraction and harvesting of natural resources from the Earth.

Secondary sector: Manufacturing-based economic activities that include the processing of raw materials and natural resources obtained through the primary sector.

Tertiary sector: Service-based economic activities that include the selling of goods and services as well as transportation.

Quaternary sector: Economic activities that include industries concerned with the creation and distribution of knowledge.

Quinary sector: Economic activities that involve upper-level management decisions for governments, businesses, and other organizations.

Technology gap: The difference between the high level of technology in the developed world and the low level of technology in the less developed world.

Technology transfer process: The amount of time that it takes a new technology to leave the manufacturer and be available for people to use.

Neocolonialism: The continued influence that certain European countries have over countries that were formerly European colonies.

Gender balance: A measure of the opportunities available to women compared to those available to men within a given country.

9

Gender Development Index (GDI): Uses the same statistics as the HDI but also factors in gender differences and imbalances.

Sustainable Development Goals (SDGs): A collection of 17 global goals adopted by the United Nations in 2015; the SDGs build on the successes of the Millennium Development Goals, which existed from 2000 to 2015. The SDGs represent a universal call to action to end poverty, protect the planet, and ensure that all people enjoy peace and prosperity.

Development Theories

World systems theory: The view that there is a three-level hierarchy to the world's countries: periphery, semi-periphery, and core. The theory holds that core countries are dominant capitalist countries that exploit peripheral countries for labor and raw materials.

Core areas: Areas where the more developed countries are located, including much of North America and Europe, Japan, Australia, and New Zealand.

Periphery areas: Areas where the less developed countries are located.

Dependency model: Represents the idea that countries do not exist in isolation but are part of an interconnected global economy within which countries are dependent on each other.

Semi-periphery areas: Areas that are gaining in development but are still lacking the political importance associated with the core countries.

Core-periphery model: Development model that builds on the world systems theory by looking at four distinct spatial factors: industrial core, upward transition, downward transition, and resource frontier.

Industrial core: Location where the majority of the industrial activities are located within a country.

Upward transition: Describes an area that is gaining jobs and attracting industry.

Sun Belt: Consists of states in the Southeast and extends into areas of the Southwest; it is associated with growing productivity, government incentives, tax breaks, lower cost of living, and milder climate.

Downward transition: Refers to areas where a lot of companies are leaving and unemployment rates are high.

Resource frontier: An area that provides the majority of the resources for the industrial core.

Rostow's stages of growth model: Model developed by Walt Whitman Rostow which explains the five stages that a country progresses through in its development: traditional society, preconditions to takeoff, takeoff, drive to maturity, and age of mass consumption. Also known as the takeoff model.

Land Use and Resources

Topocide: The destruction of a landscape to extract resources or to build a development.

Sustainable development: Development that meets the needs of the present without compromising the ability of future generations to meet their own needs.

Conservation: The sustainable use and management of a natural resource; the resource can be replaced at the same or a higher rate than it is consumed.

Ecotourism: A type of tourism in which people visit a natural landscape, such as a rainforest or wildlife refuge.

Debt-for-nature swap: The forgiveness of debts in exchange for the setting aside of land for conservation or preservation.

Tragedy of the commons: A theory that suggests humans will inevitably do what is best for themselves despite what is the best for the public good. This theory attempts to describe the cause of environmental damage.

Renewable resources: Resources that can be used again or replenish themselves naturally (e.g., sunlight, wind, water, geothermal energy sources).

Nonrenewable resources: Resources such as fossil fuels that are gone forever once they are used.

Organization of Petroleum Exporting Countries (OPEC): Group of oil-producing countries that determine the level of oil production and oil prices.

Biomass: The use of agricultural products, natural vegetation, or urban waste to produce a type of fuel that automobiles or other engines can use.

TEST WHAT YOU LEARNED

Part A: Quiz

1. A large corporation looking to lower labor costs would most likely seek which of the following?

    (A) Outsourcing

    (B) Agglomeration

    (C) Carrier efficiency

    (D) Basic industries

    (E) Sustainable development

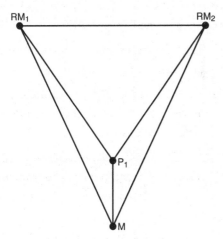

2. According to Weber's least cost theory, which of the following types of industry is depicted in the image?

    (A) Weight-reducing

    (B) Weight-gaining

    (C) "Brick bunny"

    (D) Production point

    (E) Market

3. Which of the following industries is most likely to produce goods in a sweatshop?

    (A) Garment manufacturing

    (B) Poultry processing

    (C) Commercial agriculture

    (D) Consumer electronics manufacturing

    (E) Oil refining

4. Which of the following would most likely be undertaken by a corporation engaging in sustainable development?

    (A) Producing goods in a maquiladora to avoid high tariffs

    (B) Slowing production to avoid oversaturating the market

    (C) Raising workers' wages to ensure lower rates of turnover

    (D) Adopting assembly-line manufacturing techniques to maximize efficiency

    (E) Pursuing alternative energy sources to reduce pollution

5. Which of the following best matches the rationale for the most used method of industrial transportation?

   (A) Automobiles are efficient vehicles that are also cost effective due to the relatively low cost of fuel.

   (B) Trains are able to carry large amounts of goods over long distances to any location.

   (C) Airplanes are the fastest way to disseminate goods, reaching even remote locations at low costs.

   (D) Ships are the most energy-efficient means of transportation.

   (E) Trucks are extremely mobile, efficient, and flexible as they can move large amounts of cargo long distances relatively quickly.

6. Which of the following best exemplifies the practices of a multinational corporation?

   (A) Company X prides itself on limiting the amount of mass production of its products by including artisanal designs.

   (B) Company X has facilities in multiple states and territories in the United States, including Puerto Rico.

   (C) Company X negotiates trade with countries that offer high tariffs.

   (D) Company X invested in equipment that allows for mass production of most of their products.

   (E) Company X produces some of its goods internationally, but the bulk of its manufacturing is done locally.

7. The adoption of the North American Free Trade Agreement (NAFTA) in 1994 resulted in which of the following?

   (A) Entry into the Trans-Pacific Partnership

   (B) More strictly regulated trade between member countries

   (C) A modest increase in the United States' GDP

   (D) A substantial decrease in trade between Mexico and Canada

   (E) Decreased access to large export markets

8. Why was the Gender Development Index (GDI) developed by the United Nations?

   (A) The GDI was created to measure the ratio of female to male children.

   (B) The GDI was created to measure the percentage of women employed in manufacturing industries.

   (C) The GDI was created to determine the disparities between men's and women's relative overall human development.

   (D) The GDI was created to measure the three dimensions of human development.

   (E) The GDI was created to determine the differences in educational attainment for men and women.

9. Which of the following best describes gross domestic product (GDP)?

    (A) The total market value of goods exported to other countries

    (B) The total market value of the goods and services produced in a country within a given year

    (C) The total income earned by a country's residents both in the country and abroad

    (D) A large segment of the economy that is characterized by a distinct type of product or service

    (E) The difference in value of a country's exports and imports

10. Which of the following industry-region pairs is NOT an example of a basic industry?

    (A) Steel—Pittsburgh

    (B) Automobiles—Detroit

    (C) Healthcare—Los Angeles

    (D) Computer chips—Silicon Valley

    (E) Oil refining—Texas Gulf Coast

9

Part B: Key Terms

This key terms list is the same as the list in the Test What You Already Know section earlier in this chapter. Based on what you have now learned, again ask yourself the following questions:

- Can I define this key term and use it in a sentence?
- Can I provide an example related to this key term?
- Could I correctly answer a multiple-choice question about this key term?
- Could I correctly answer a free-response question about this key term?

Check off the key terms if you can answer "yes" to at least three of these questions.

Keys to Economic and Industrial Development

- ☐ Economic geography
- ☐ Capitalism
- ☐ Neoliberalism
- ☐ Socialism
- ☐ Communism
- ☐ Site factors
- ☐ Situation factors
- ☐ Basic industry
- ☐ Non-basic industry
- ☐ Multiplier effect
- ☐ Variable cost
- ☐ Fixed cost
- ☐ Time-space compression

Location of Industry

- ☐ Industrial Revolution
- ☐ Cottage industry
- ☐ Agglomeration
- ☐ Cumulative causation
- ☐ Deglomeration
- ☐ Weber's least cost theory
- ☐ Weight-gaining industry
- ☐ Weight-reducing industry
- ☐ Maquiladoras
- ☐ Outsourcing
- ☐ Footloose industry
- ☐ Multinational corporations
- ☐ Sweatshops
- ☐ Manufacturing exports

Global Industrial Zones

- ☐ Rust Belt
- ☐ Treaty ports
- ☐ Export processing zones
- ☐ Special economic zones (SEZs)
- ☐ Four Asian Tigers
- ☐ Newly industrialized countries (NICs)
- ☐ BRIC

Ways to Describe Development

- ☐ Development
- ☐ Developed country
- ☐ Developing country
- ☐ Gross domestic product (GDP)
- ☐ Human Development Index (HDI)
- ☐ Brain drain
- ☐ Brain gain

- ☐ Gross national income (GNI)
- ☐ Physical Quality of Life Index (PQLI)
- ☐ Economic sector
- ☐ Primary sector
- ☐ Secondary sector
- ☐ Tertiary sector
- ☐ Quaternary sector
- ☐ Quinary sector

- ☐ Technology gap
- ☐ Technology transfer process
- ☐ Neocolonialism
- ☐ Gender balance
- ☐ Gender Development Index (GDI)
- ☐ Sustainable Development Goals (SDGs)

Development Theories

- ☐ World systems theory
- ☐ Core areas
- ☐ Periphery areas
- ☐ Dependency model

- ☐ Semi-periphery areas
- ☐ Core-periphery model
- ☐ Industrial core
- ☐ Upward transition

- ☐ Sun Belt
- ☐ Downward transition
- ☐ Resource frontier
- ☐ Rostow's stages of growth model

Land Use and Resources

- ☐ Topocide
- ☐ Sustainable development
- ☐ Conservation
- ☐ Ecotourism

- ☐ Debt-for-nature swap
- ☐ Tragedy of the commons
- ☐ Renewable resources

- ☐ Nonrenewable resources
- ☐ Organization of Petroleum Exporting Countries (OPEC)
- ☐ Biomass

9

Next Steps

Step 1: Tally your correct answers from Part A, and review the quiz explanations at the end of this chapter.

1.	A	6.	D
2.	B	7.	C
3.	A	8.	C
4.	E	9.	B
5.	E	10.	C

_____ out of 10 questions

Step 2: Count the number of key terms you checked off in Part B.

_____ out of 77 key terms

Step 3: Compare your Test What You Already Know results to these Test What You Learned results to see how exam-ready you are for this topic.

For More Practice:

- Read (or reread) the comprehensive review for this topic in Chapter 16.
- Go to kaptest.com to complete the online quiz questions for Industrial and Economic Development Patterns and Processes.
    - Haven't registered your book yet? Go to **kaptest.com/moreonline** to begin.

CHAPTER 9 ANSWERS AND EXPLANATIONS

Test What You Already Know

1. C

Alfred Weber's least cost theory is concerned with the ideal location of a factory. Weber's theory asserts that because an industrial plant should take into consideration the source of the raw materials needed for the product, the factory should be located wherever the cost of raw materials and their transportation will be the least amount. Therefore, **(C)** is correct. (A) is incorrect because Weber's theory is not concerned with the transportation of people, but goods. (B) is incorrect because this is a staple of the gravity model, not Weber's least cost theory. (D) is incorrect because the factors described are for the demographic transition model. (E) is incorrect as the assumption of farmers selling their entire agricultural output is a basis for von Thünen's model, not Weber's theory.

2. A

The raw materials that go into automobile manufacturing (rubber, steel, etc.) weigh less than the finished product, so **(A)** is correct. In contrast, potato chip making, sugar processing, and pharmaceutical manufacturing are all examples of weight-reducing industries, in which the finished product weighs less than the raw materials. Therefore, (B), (C), and (D) are incorrect. (E) is incorrect because fresh produce remains approximately the same weight from when it is harvested to when it is sold to consumers.

3. C

In procuring raw materials and cheap, unskilled labor from less developed countries, developed countries engage in a form of economic dominance best described as neocolonialism. In neocolonialism, the less developed country is dependent on, and often exploited by, the more developed country, mirroring prior colonial relationships. This term is often used to describe the relationship between Western European countries and the less developed African states that were former colonies of Europe. Therefore, **(C)** is correct. A status that describes countries that are no longer under the control of an outside power is postcolonialism, making (A) incorrect. No economic dependence or interplay between countries describes precolonialism, or regions before they were absorbed into imperial territories, making (B) incorrect. (D) is incorrect because private ownership is a component of capitalism, which refers to a system of economics in which businesses and industries are privately owned in order to make a profit. Less developed African countries are not privately owned by Western Europeans. Finally, market orientation refers to an industry locating itself close to its market, which has not changed, making (E) incorrect.

4. C

Created by the United Nations in 1990, the Human Development Index (HDI) measures a country's development based on three factors: life expectancy, amount of education, and per capita income. Therefore, **(C)** is correct because the country described experienced a decrease in amount of education held by its citizens. While many democracies have a high HDI score, the HDI does not directly consider a country's commitment to democracy, making (A) incorrect. Though gender inequities influence a society, this is not factored into the HDI, making (B) incorrect. (D) is incorrect because, while the HDI is concerned with education level, it does not directly measure literacy. Instead, literacy scores are used for measures of the Physical Quality of Life Index (PQLI). Although the HDI relies on life expectancy, it is not explicitly based on birth rate, making (E) incorrect.

5. B

The Four Asian Tigers (Hong Kong, Singapore, South Korea, and Taiwan) are countries that underwent rapid industrialization, and a subsequent increase in wealth, in the latter half of the twentieth century. Their success is largely due to international trade, making **(B)** correct. These countries do not have significant access to raw materials or cheap immigrant labor, making (A) and (C) incorrect. Transportation and land costs are very high due to the geography of the region, making (D) and (E) incorrect.

6. D

Transferring goods from one transportation method to another occurs at a break-of-bulk point; **(D)** is correct. Gross domestic product (GDP) is the total market value of goods produced within a country's borders, making (A) incorrect. A growth pole is an urban area that stimulates growth in its hinterland; (B) is incorrect. Outsourcing is the practice of using cheap foreign labor in manufacturing, so (C) is incorrect. Finally, carrier efficiency is the ratio of capacity to cost for a method of transportation, making (E) incorrect.

7. B

Special economic zones (SEZs) are regions in China where foreign and transnational companies and industries can operate using Chinese labor while avoiding tax burdens. Because of several foreign companies establishing headquarters in Shanghai, resulting in the production and sale of more than a million cars per year, as well as major migration from other cities in China due to an increase in manufacturing jobs available, Shanghai is one of China's SEZs. Therefore, **(B)** is correct. (A) is incorrect because it's a reason for the economic success in Japan, not Shanghai. Although the Huang River does act as a major transportation route for manufactured materials, this river is in northeastern China and supports the economic zone centered around Beijing. Thus, (C) is incorrect. (D) describes an export processing zone that would apply to Hong Kong, not Shanghai. (E) is incorrect because Kaohsiung is the major port in Taiwan, not Shanghai.

8. D

An agglomeration is a clustering of businesses in the same location. Companies in the agglomeration can share infrastructure and utility services (e.g., electricity, water, sanitation), hire workers from the same labor pool, and use the same suppliers for their raw materials. Because of this relationship, companies often reduce costs substantially. **(D)** is correct. Variable costs, (A), are costs that change based on how many units of a product a company makes; (A) is incorrect. (B) is incorrect because fixed costs are the costs that stay the same within a certain period of time (usually one year). Examples of fixed costs include warehouse rent and insurance premiums. Carrier efficiency refers to transportation, making (C) incorrect. Finally, the substitution principle holds that the best geographic location for a business is the one which is most profitable, making (E) incorrect.

9. B

The part of the economy that processes raw materials in order to manufacture goods is known as the secondary sector, making **(B)** correct. The rest of the choices are incorrect because these sectors of the economy serve other functions. Because natural resources are needed before goods can be manufactured, resource extraction (e.g., mining and timbering) is referred to as the primary sector. Tertiary-sector activities are service-based economic activities that include the selling of goods and services. The quaternary sector involves creating and distributing knowledge (e.g., research and development, financial consulting, and marketing). Quinary-sector activities include high-level decision making by top business executives, government officials, and other professionals.

10. E

The northern territories of Nunavut, Northwest Territories, and Yukon Territory are quite remote and removed from industrial development. Therefore, these regions represent Canada's resource frontier, making **(E)** correct. Canada's industrial core is located in southeast Canada, making (A) incorrect. Canada's upward transition zone is in the western section of the country, and the Atlantic Maritime Provinces on the east coast comprise Canada's downward transition zone; (B) and (C) are incorrect. Finally, the northern territories are too remote to be considered semi-periphery, making (D) incorrect.

9

Test What You Learned

1. A

Outsourcing labor to foreign countries results in lower labor costs for large corporations. Customer support call centers, factories, and farming are all examples of types of labor that can be outsourced. Therefore, **(A)** is correct. Agglomeration refers to the geographic concentration of other industries, which would not impact labor costs, making (B) incorrect. High carrier efficiency would result in lower transportation costs, not labor costs; thus, (C) is incorrect. (D) is incorrect because the concept of basic industry is unrelated to a corporation lowering its labor costs. Sustainable development could raise all costs associated with business, so (E) is incorrect.

2. B

Weber's least cost theory posits that the weight of the raw materials and the finished product will determine the location of the production facility for a given industrial company. If the good being produced is in a weight-gaining industry (an industry where the finished product weighs more than the raw materials), then the production point should be located closer to the market to minimize the transportation costs associated with a relatively heavy product. The image shows what Weber's triangle diagram would look like for a weight-gaining industry; therefore, **(B)** is correct. A weight-reducing industry would have the production point closer to the raw materials, not the market, making (A) incorrect. (C) is incorrect because the "brick bunny" is a fictional product made of bricks and feathers; the company producing this bunny would need to put the production point closer to the heavier raw materials (bricks) than to the lighter raw materials (feathers). The production point and the market are key elements of Weber's least cost theory, not types of industry; (D) and (E) are incorrect.

3. A

A sweatshop is an assembly-line-style factory with poor working conditions and low wages. Sweatshops are typically associated with garment manufacturing, making **(A)** correct. Though poultry, agriculture, electronics, and oil are all industries in which exploitation of workers is possible, these industries are not specifically associated with sweatshops.

4. E

Sustainable development as a business model acknowledges a corporation's negative environmental impact and seeks to lessen it. Therefore, **(E)** is correct. Avoiding tariffs, oversaturation, turnover, and inefficiency are not directly related to sustainable business practices, making (A)–(D) incorrect.

5. E

There are five primary means of industrial transport: truck, rail, airplane, ship, and pipeline. Due to the combination of mobility, efficiency, and flexibility with relatively low cost and disadvantages, trucks are the most used method of industry transport. Therefore, **(E)** is correct. Due to the relatively small size of automobiles, they are not used for industrial transport, making (A) incorrect. Although trains are able to carry massive amounts of goods over large distances, this method can be very cumbersome and slow given the need to load and unload across several different stations. Further, given the lack of tracks, trains cannot travel to every industrial location, making (B) incorrect. While airplanes are indeed the fastest method to transport goods and a major advantage is its reach to isolated areas, its primary disadvantage is the high cost to transport these goods. Thus, (C) is incorrect. Like trains (which are actually the most efficient form of transport), ships have break-of-bulk points because not all industrial plants have access to waterways. Moreover, ships are also the slowest method of transportation. So, (D) is incorrect.

6. D

Multinational corporations that are involved in manufacturing can mass-produce goods cheaply and quickly. By contrast, a company that is engaged in artisanal manufacturing relies on a small number of highly skilled workers to do hands-on manufacturing. Therefore, **(D)** is correct and (A) is incorrect. Multinational companies, by definition, are located in multiple countries, not multiple states of a country, making (B) incorrect. All multinational companies seek lower tariffs (taxes on imports and exports) and rely on foreign labor, so (C) and (E) are incorrect.

7. C

Adoption of the North American Free Trade Agreement (NAFTA) in 1994 resulted in a generally positive economic outcome for the member countries, including an increase in the United States' GDP. Therefore, **(C)** is correct. (A) is incorrect because the Trans-Pacific Partnership (TPP) was not signed until 2016 and is not directly related to NAFTA. NAFTA reduced trade barriers between member countries and increased U.S. access to export markets; therefore, (B) and (E) are both incorrect. With the creation of NAFTA, trade barriers between Mexico and Canada were reduced, leading to an increase in trade between the two countries; (D) is also incorrect.

8. C

The Gender Development Index (GDI) was created by the United Nations to measure a country's disparities in opportunities for men and women. The formula compares the Human Development Index for women and the Human Development Index for men. Therefore, **(C)** is correct. (D) and (E) are related to the GDI, but they do not provide the reason why the GDI was created and are therefore incorrect. (A) is incorrect because it is referring to sex ratio, not the GDI. (B) is incorrect because employment in a manufacturing industry is not in itself a significant marker of gender equality.

9. B

Gross domestic product (GDP) is a leading economic indicator used to analyze a country's level of development. GDP is defined as the total market value of the goods and services produced in a country. This includes the value generated by both residents and foreigners, but does not include value earned outside the country. Thus, **(B)** is correct. (A) is incorrect because this represents the total value of exports, not GDP. (C) is incorrect because it represents another important development statistic called gross national income (GNI). A large segment of the economy characterized by a distinct product or service is called an economic sector, making (D) incorrect. The difference in value of a country's exports and imports is referred to as a trade deficit, not GDP; (E) is also incorrect.

10. C

Though there are certainly plenty of hospitals in Los Angeles, healthcare is not a basic industry there because it is not the focal point of that city. (A better example of a basic industry in Los Angeles would be the entertainment industry.) Therefore, **(C)** is correct. The other regions listed are paired correctly with their historic basic industries.

PART 3

Comprehensive Review

CHAPTER 10

Thinking Geographically

LEARNING OBJECTIVES

After studying this chapter, you will be able to:

- Define major geographical concepts and geography's importance.

- Interpret map data.

- Analyze data across different scales.

- Interpret quantitative, qualitative, and geospatial geographic data.

- Explain the nature of regions and the regionalization process, and give examples of regions.

- Describe the human organization of space using landscape analysis and spatial thinking.

- Describe how people interact and exchange resources differently over time.

- Interpret geographic concepts using mathematical formulas and graphs.

- Apply major geographic models to specific topics and questions.

10

HISTORICAL FOUNDATIONS OF GEOGRAPHY

Since their beginning, humans have sought to acquire and define their space. It is an innate aspect of human nature to wonder: Who are we? How did we get here? What is the world's true nature?

Geography is the description of the Earth's surface and the people and processes that shape its landscapes. Some people mistakenly believe that geography is merely memorization of place names and facts. In reality, geography is a nuanced social science. It touches upon every aspect of human existence. It is also a way of thinking about the world and humanity's place within it.

This discussion of geography will begin with its historical foundations. You will find throughout the AP Human Geography course that other fields, like history, sociology, and anthropology, offer complementary perspectives. Remember: *Human* geography is a field that lives up to its name.

The Ancient World

The Greeks first classified the study of geography as a science. Greek philosophers wrote about the Earth being a sphere and established mathematical principles for the world around them. Greek explorers sailed the Mediterranean Sea around 800 B.C.E. and, in many instances, left behind fascinating firsthand geographical accounts. These accounts are an invaluable resource; for example, sailors arriving and departing at the port of Miletus, in present-day Turkey, gave the Greeks a practical base for their study of geography as they established knowledge of three primary continents in the world: Europe, Asia, and Africa.

Greek explorers had detailed descriptions of areas around the eastern Mediterranean, but information beyond that realm remained a mystery. Details were few. Myths abounded. This mystery led to creative ideas as to what lay beyond the horizon.

Anaximander is the first person credited with making a map of the known world, which he did in part by using information from sailors' accounts. Although Anaximander's map was a fairly accurate large-scale rendering of the eastern Mediterranean, it was inaccurate concerning the rest of the world owing to the lack of available information.

Eratosthenes is credited with first using the term *geography* to describe this new area of scientific study. Using two points on the Earth's surface, he measured the angle of the sun, and from his calculations, he was able to determine the Earth's circumference with great accuracy. The classic Greek philosophers, Aristotle, Socrates, and Plato, furthered the belief that the Earth was round. Their evidence, along with mathematical and scientific work by Pythagoras and Posidonius, seemed to prove the Earth's roundness.

The Modern Period

In 1830, the Royal Geographical Society was founded in London. In 1888, its American counterpart, the National Geographic Society, was formed. These institutions formed the bedrock for the field of geography in the English-speaking world. As geography developed as a science, many debates followed. A key controversy was that of determinism versus possibilism.

In the early twentieth century, an important school of thought in the field began to develop around the theory of **environmental determinism**, which proposes that cultures are a direct result of where they exist. This school of thought was led by geographers such as Carl Ritter, Ellen Churchill Semple, and Ellsworth Huntington. They concluded that warmer climates tend to cause inhabitants to have a more relaxed attitude toward work and progress. This philosophy also led some people to believe that Europeans and those from more temperate climates were more motivated, intelligent, and culturally advanced than those from warmer climates.

During the 1930s, environmental determinism was criticized as a prejudicial tool of Western colonialism. However, in the late 1990s, it underwent a revival in the form of neo-environmental determinism. Led by geographers like Jared Diamond, this variation placed emphasis on how natural resources and ecology affect the development, expansion, and potential collapse of cultures. Fierce debate continues to this day over the theory's merits.

Most contemporary geographers favor **possibilism**, which is an approach to geographic study first promoted in the United States by Carl Sauer in the 1920s. The possibilist approach suggests that humans are not a product of their environment but, rather, that they possess the skills necessary to modify their environment to fit human needs. In other words, people can determine their own outcomes without regard to location.

Today and Beyond

Today, technologies like **global positioning systems (GPS)** and **geographic information systems (GIS)** are providing geographers with new means to describe the world. Prior to computer technology, cartographers were limited in the maps that they could produce. With current technology, we are seeing more advanced geography entering our daily lives, and the field of geography is being profoundly affected.

10

GPS uses latitude and longitude coordinates to determine an exact location on the Earth. GPS technology can be incorporated into handheld devices such as smartphones that pick up signals broadcast by satellites circling the Earth. The GPS unit interprets these signals to give you an absolute location. In recent years, a Russian competitor has entered the market. It is known as GLONASS (Global Navigation Satellite System).

GIS uses geographic information and layers it into an interactive map showing specific types of geographic data. Watersheds, population density, highways, and agricultural data are just a few of the geographic features that can be used as layers of data. In many ways, GIS is the new geography, allowing geographers to analyze new data in ways never before imagined, revealing previously overlooked interrelationships.

Aerial photography also allows geographers to see land use changing over time by comparing pictures of places from years past to current photographs. Other technologies, such as Google Earth, are revolutionizing the way that we look at the world. Satellite imagery and remote sensing can study an object or location without making physical contact with it, vastly expanding the areas geographers can study. For example, satellites have mapped the ocean floor by studying gravity waves. These technologies are also bringing places from around the world onto our computer screens at home, work, and school.

> ✔ **AP Expert Note**
>
> **Be able to apply outside concepts to geography**
>
> GPS works through triangulation, so if you understand a bit of geometry, you understand GPS. In geography, you often need to connect with concepts learned in other disciplines, like math or social studies. Don't forget to draw on that information even though you may be studying for a different subject.

MAPS: AN INTRODUCTION

Maps are the basic tools that geographers use to convey information. Although there are many different types and projections of maps, they generally represent the Earth's surface in some fashion. The ability to interpret data from maps is an important skill in determining the meaning of location and place within the study of geography. Traditional maps have a fundamental problem, however: distortion. When you attempt to convey a three-dimensional object, such as the spherical planet Earth, onto a two-dimensional, rectangular piece of paper, the object is not presented in a way that is completely true to life.

Scale

High-Yield

Scale is the relationship of the size of the map to the amount of area it represents on the planet. In other words, scale is the abstract dimension into which one renders the real world. A map the size of your desk that shows an area the size of your desk is at 1:1 scale. Small-scale maps show more area in less detail. Large-scale maps show a smaller area but in greater detail.

An easy way to distinguish between the two types is to think of your school. The larger the school would appear on the map, the larger the scale. A map of a town or city would have a larger scale than a map of a continent. The smallest scale map is of the world. Distortion is greatest on small-scale maps.

Remember: The larger the scale, the less the distortion. Local maps, such as maps of cities, have very little distortion. Regional maps have more distortion, and national maps have even more distortion. The world map features the most distortion, often warping the shape and size of continents. For example, consider world maps that depict Greenland as being roughly equal in size to the whole of Africa, despite Greenland actually being a mere 1/14th Africa's size.

There are three ways to depict scale on a map. The first way is to write the scale in words. "One inch equals 100 miles" is an example of a word scale. The second way is to use a line to measure the distance on a map. The line may be drawn out to one inch or two inches. The unit of measure will then be located along the line to represent the scale of the map. The third way to write a scale on a map is to use a ratio. An example of a map ratio is 1:24,000. This means that for each unit of measure on the map, it would take 24,000 of those same units to cover the same amount of ground in the real world. Thus, 1:24,000 would mean that 1 inch on the map equals 24,000 inches on the planet.

Distortion

Cartographers are always concerned with the concept of distortion. With many map types, the farther that one goes from the equator, the greater the distortion on the map. Different types of maps result in different presentations of that distortion. There are maps that try to space out the distortion equally throughout the map, which is called **equal-area projection**. They keep the size (or amount of area) intact but distort shapes. An example of an equal-area map would be the Goode homolosine projection, which breaks up the globe into continents and separates the oceans.

Alternatively, maps that distort area but keep shapes intact are called **conformal maps**. An example of a conformal map would be the Lambert conic projection. On this projection, the distance between latitude lines increases the farther one moves away from the common line of latitude. This type of distortion is evident on a Mercator map. While useful for determining distance on the surface of the Earth, it greatly exaggerates the land forms around the polar regions. On a Mercator map, all lines of latitude and longitude meet at right angles. These right angles force the top and bottom of the globe to stretch out, creating more distortion of the polar regions. This is why Greenland looks as though it is the size of Africa on a Mercator map projection. The distortion is especially severe on small-scale maps using the Mercator projection. In reality, Greenland is only a fraction of the size of Africa.

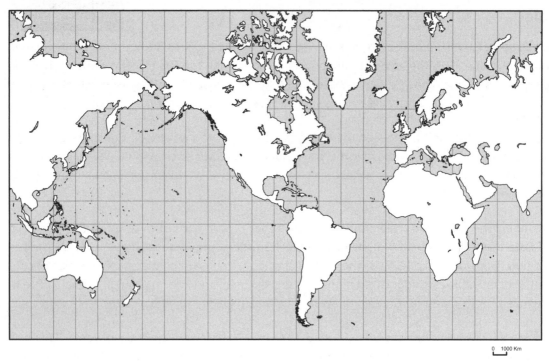

Mercator Map Projection

Map Classes and Types

High-Yield

Cartographers can use one of four map classes to determine how best to construct their maps. A **cylindrical** map shows true direction but loses distance. The Mercator map projection is an example of a cylindrical class. Another map class is a **planar** projection. An azimuthal map shows true direction and examines the Earth from one point—usually a pole or polar projection—and is an example of a planar class. All points go either north from the South Pole point or south from the North Pole point. The third type of map class is a **conic** projection. Conic projection puts a cone over the Earth and tries to keep distance intact but loses directional qualities. The fourth map class is an **oval** projection, which is a combination of the cylindrical and conic projections. The Molleweide projection is an oval projection. In addition to showing areas, maps may also be used to represent some types of geographic phenomena. **Thematic maps** can represent information in a variety of ways. Area class maps, area symbol maps, cartograms, choropleth maps, digital images, dot maps, flow-line maps, **isoline maps**, point symbol maps, and proportional symbol maps are all used to show geographic properties such as elevation. Geographers and map readers need to be familiar with different types of maps to determine meaning.

Flow-line maps are good for representing movement such as migration. **Choropleth maps** put data into a spatial format and are useful for representing demographic data such as infant mortality rates by assigning colors or patterns to areas. **Cartograms** chart and assign data by size. World population by country is often shown in a cartogram; countries with a larger population appear larger on the map. The country with the largest population on Earth is China; therefore, it is the largest country on a cartogram map, followed by India, the United States, Indonesia, Pakistan, and Brazil.

The Misuse of Maps

Maps can also be used to mislead readers. Because maps are a form of communication, maps can intentionally or unintentionally cause confusion or provide misinformation in several ways.

One way a map can be used to mislead a reader is by using colors. Bolder colors usually indicate strength in a factor or a place name on the map. Conversely, lighter colors often represent weakness. German maps during World War II showed Germany in a bold color while showing the Allied powers in a light color; these maps were distributed to the German citizens to promote the perception that the Allied powers were weak.

The size of an item on a map usually indicates strength as well. The bigger the item appears, the greater its perceived strength and importance. Conversely, the smaller the item, the less important it seems to be. U.S. military maps that are made public often show U.S. bases with spheres of influence that appear greater than they actually are.

Maps can also mislead a reader by intentionally deleting information. By not putting something on a map, the cartographer is making a statement about the importance of the item. For example, some of the maps from the former Soviet Union omitted information, such as military and government buildings, possibly for political or strategic reasons.

Focus is another issue. Most Western world maps center on the prime meridian. This line runs through the Royal Observatory in Greenwich, London. Why? That site was chosen at an international conference in 1884, in large part due to the British Empire's naval dominance at the time. One result is that the prime meridian gives Europe a position of prominence while pushing East Asia off to the side. Some alternate maps favor a Pacific-centered view, or a South-up orientation.

THEMES OF GEOGRAPHY

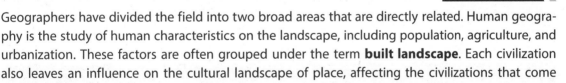
High-Yield

Geographers have divided the field into two broad areas that are directly related. Human geography is the study of human characteristics on the landscape, including population, agriculture, and urbanization. These factors are often grouped under the term **built landscape**. Each civilization also leaves an influence on the cultural landscape of place, affecting the civilizations that come after it. For example, British colonialism spread the use of the English language around the world, making it a common tongue for business and trade. This is termed **sequent occupance**.

The other field is **physical geography**, which examines the physical features of the Earth and tries to define how they work. Physical geographers analyze wind, water, and weather patterns. When geographers try to explain a place, they cannot separate the two fields. Physical processes affect human activities, and human activities affect some physical processes.

10

To further define geography, five distinct themes have emerged:

1. Place

2. Region

3. Location

4. Human-environment interaction

5. Spatial interaction or movement

The five themes of geography are a good way to analyze a particular location or region on Earth's surface. Geographers from the American Association of Geographers and the National Council for Geographic Education arrived at the five themes in 1981.

Place

To classify what we observe on the surface of the Earth, geographers have assigned attributes to assist in the description of one of the major themes of geography: place. Describing the individuality of place can be as simple as showing cell phone video of your latest vacation, or as complex as presenting a detailed analysis of agricultural practices in Bangladesh. Let's look at some examples that highlight the importance of place as a concept.

It has been said that Shanghai is one of the fastest-growing cities in the world, but what exactly does that mean? What does the phrase *fastest-growing* mean? Does it mean the city is the fastest growing in terms of population or in terms of economic growth? More description is needed. This type of description is at the core of place.

Shanghai sits at the junction of the Huangpu River and the Yangtze delta, making it a major trading port for Asia and the rest of the world. By describing Shanghai's economic growth rate and continued advancement in a worldwide economy, we clarify what the phrase *fastest-growing* means. By giving Shanghai these unique descriptions, we are shaping the view of Shanghai and further refining its characteristics.

✔ **AP Expert Note**

Be sure to hone your critical thinking skills

College-level thinking about human geography requires that you always dig a bit deeper. For example: If Shanghai is one of the fastest-growing cities in the world, what creates that growth and why? What is Shanghai's role within China, within Asia, and within the world? This kind of critical thinking, and the answers that accompany it, is what you'll be expected to demonstrate on the official exam, especially in the free-response section.

New York City has the largest population of any city in the United States. New York City has been called "the city that never sleeps." Home to millions of people, it has been mentioned as the cultural capital of the United States. The culture of New York is different from the culture of Shanghai. The differences between the two cities help to define the concept of place for both locations and make each city unique.

Descriptions of place are often based upon the cultural attributes or the cultural landscape of the area. By describing the area in this way, we place our subjective attributes on the landscape itself. Office buildings, theaters, places of worship, and so forth can define the cultural landscape, all of which comprise a person's view of a place.

When describing the physical environment of a place, descriptions of natural landscapes are often used. Natural landscapes include mountains, rivers, valleys, or anything within the landscape that is physical. This physical landscape affects the people of the area greatly.

> ✔ **AP Expert Note**
>
> **Be able to describe the layered meaning of terms like *place***
>
> The AP exam will expect you to not only be able to define a term but also to know its more nuanced meaning and context. **Place** is not just an objective description of what a location is like. It is the description of what we as humans see and how we experience a certain aspect of the Earth's surface. Place defines and refines what we are. *Hot* and *cold* as well as *busy* and *calm* can all be used when describing a certain place.

Region

While all places are unique, common threads in the landscape can be used to pull different places together. The concept of **region** links places together using any parameter the geographer chooses.

The Midwestern portion of the United States is characterized by its dependence on agriculture, especially corn farming. By looking at agricultural productivity and commodity charts, at either a state or county level, we can determine the location of corn-growing regions in the United States. These regions are sometimes called "belts." The Corn Belt region of the United States overlaps with the Midwest region.

Another example of a region or belt would be the presence of evangelical Christians in the southern United States. The term *Bible Belt* is often used to describe the prevalence of the Southern Baptist religion there. Many areas in the South have evangelical churches that take up city blocks. The importance of these churches in the landscape is vital in determining what the South is like, and the attitudes of evangelicals in the South are important in determining the overall culture of the region.

A region can range in size from a single location up to a global area. There are three main types of regions: formal, functional, and perceptual (or vernacular) regions. **Formal regions** are regions where everything inside has the same characteristic or phenomenon. This characteristic might include a political zone, language, or other cultural trait. Germany is a formal region. Germany has a defined political boundary with sovereignty. People who are inside of Germany share the characteristic of being subject to the laws and regulations of the country of Germany. The people who reside there legally have either been born there or entered the country through a customs office. Whether in Hamburg, Munich, or Berlin, people share the characteristic of being inside the country of Germany. When a person steps into a bordering country, that individual no longer shares the common characteristic of being in the sovereign country of Germany.

The Corn Belt is also defined as a formal region. Even though many of the places within the Corn Belt grow other crops, corn is the predominant crop. A person may not know that they have stepped out of the Corn Belt unless agricultural commodity data is analyzed.

Functional regions can be defined around a certain point or node. These functional regions are the most intense around the center but lose their characteristics the farther the distance from the focal point. Distance decay, the lessening of a feature as distance is increased from the hearth, is an indication of a functional region. An example is accessing the Internet through a WiFi network. The farther you go from the access point, or hotspot, the weaker the Internet connection becomes. A functional region could be described as the range of the WiFi signal.

A shopping mall trade area is another example of a functional region. Shoppers who live in close proximity to a particular mall will frequent that mall more often than other shoppers who live farther away. Shoppers who live farther from that mall are likely to live closer to another mall whose influence is greater on them. The trade area is strongest near the mall and decreases with the distance. The sphere of influence is reduced as the distance increases. This is an example of distance decay. It is also an example of friction of distance, where longer distances require increasing amounts of energy or money to traverse. This often means that people will resist going someplace far away.

The third type of region is known as a **perceptual/vernacular region**. These regions exist primarily in an individual's perception or feelings. If you were to ask a person from the East Coast of the United States where the Midwest is, you will likely get a different response than from someone who resides in Nebraska. Some people from the East Coast perceive that the Midwest starts in western Pennsylvania and ends around Illinois. While a person from Nebraska may feel strongly that his or her home is located in the Midwest, a person from the East may feel that the person from Nebraska is located in the Great Plains or the North Central region rather than the Midwest.

Another example of a vernacular region, within the United States, is the concept of *the South*. The South means different things to different people. Where does the South begin? While most can agree that Alabama is located within the Deep South, some may feel that Kentucky may not be Southern enough. Others may use climate as a criterion. Still, others may use the Southern dialect to determine where "Dixie" is.

It is also important to note that a person may be in several regions simultaneously. A person may be in the state of Florida (formal region), reading a New York City newspaper (functional region), while dreaming of a skiing trip to the Rocky Mountains in the West, which this person perceives as a winter wonderland of snow (perceptual region). Regions can overlap depending upon their characteristics. By using the concept of region, geographers organize data to assist in describing information. Geographers then render this information into maps.

✔ **AP Expert Note**

Be careful about similar-sounding terms

Make sure you watch for differences in terminology. *Site* and *situation* are both related to the concept of location, but each has a distinct meaning. Likewise, *longitude* and *latitude* are easily confused. Mistaking one term for the other is a mistake that you'll want to avoid on the AP exam.

Location

Another theme that geographers use in their analysis of the Earth is location. "Where am I?" is a question often asked. There are two ways to answer that fundamental question. People may use **relative location**, which means giving their location in reference to another feature on the Earth's surface. People may also use **absolute location**, which means using latitude and longitude coordinates.

Site refers to the intrinsic, physical characteristics of a place. For example, New Orleans is a very poor site for human habitation. Being eight feet below sea level makes it prone to flooding during times of heavy rainfall. Its **situation**, however, at the base of the Mississippi River, has enabled its growth. New Orleans is a city with a poor site but an excellent situation. Anchorage, Alaska, is another city with a good situation but a poor site. Located right on fault lines, it is prone to earthquakes, as demonstrated during the Alaskan Earthquake of 1964; registering 9.2 on the Richter scale; it leveled the city.

A person may have a mental map of an area when he or she is driving to a familiar location. This mental map may be very accurate or significantly inaccurate. Mental maps are important because most people possess them, and they can prove useful tools in communication. For example, when you give directions to your friend to come over to your house, you are probably giving him or her a relative location. Telling your friend to "turn left at the gas station and then right at the firehouse" is using reference points (gas station and firehouse) to assist in determining the location of a place.

However, problems can arise when using relative location. You assume that your friend knows where the firehouse or the gas station is, but what if your friend doesn't know these reference points? There needs to be another way to define exactly where you are located. Geographers use latitude and longitude for this.

The grid system that geographers set up uses latitude and longitude, which are the fictional lines that divide the Earth's surface to assist people in determining an exact location. **Latitudes** are parallel lines that run east/west on the surface of the Earth. For this reason, latitudes are also called parallels. The latitude line that runs in the middle of the Earth is the **equator**. This is 0 degrees latitude. Anything to the north of the equator is in the northern hemisphere, and anything to the south of the equator is in the southern hemisphere. The highest degree of latitude is 90 degrees. This is the angle where the equator meets the lines of longitude. Thus, 90 degrees north would be the North Pole, whereas 90 degrees south would be the South Pole. **Longitudes**, or meridians, are the fictional lines that run north and south. The 0 degree longitude line, or **prime meridian**, runs through Greenwich, in southeast London, England. Here, visitors can stand with one foot in the eastern hemisphere and one foot in the western hemisphere.

The globe is a sphere made up of circles, all with the same center point. All circles possess 360 degrees. A day is 24 hours long, and dividing 360 by 24 equals 15. Therefore, for every 15 degrees longitude traveled east or west, a person will theoretically enter a new **time zone**. Time zones are based largely on that 15-degree principle, although the exact location of the line may vary to take into account other factors such as political boundaries and domestic political policy. For example, China has one time zone, despite being comparable in size to the continental United States, which has four time zones. Another example of this is the **International Date Line**. The farthest that one can go on the longitude scale is 180 degrees, and that longitude roughly represents the International Date Line. Yet the International Date Line zigzags its way through the Pacific Ocean owing to the location of countries there.

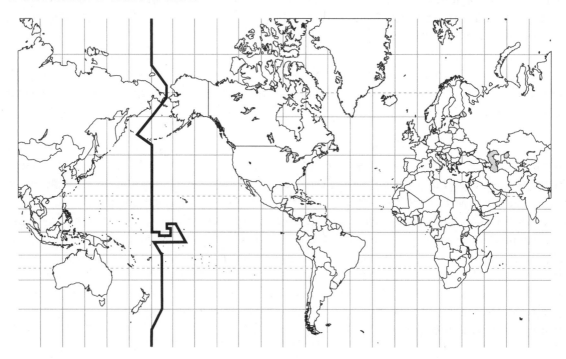

International Date Line

Human-Environment Interaction

The fourth theme in geography is the concept of **human-environment interaction**. This theme describes how people modify or alter the environment to fit individual or societal needs.

The city of Las Vegas, Nevada, is built in the middle of a desert. Humans have modified the environment around Las Vegas to provide enough water to meet the needs of the city. Water management is a critical issue in areas like Las Vegas. The Hoover Dam creates one of the largest human-made lakes in the world, Lake Mead, and provides electricity to much of the desert Southwest. The flooding of the backwaters directly changed the environment behind the dam and made life livable in areas such as Las Vegas. The dam's electrical power, recreational opportunities, and water management capability have sustained a large and growing population in the desert.

Humans cannot live in climates that are too hot, too cold, too wet, too dry, or too hilly. Any of these environmental conditions taken to the extreme makes land uninhabitable. As human engineering and invention continue to improve, however, humans can adjust to survive in conditions that they previously could not. An example is the Ice Hotel in Sweden, which has made it posh to take a vacation surrounded by frozen water. Guests are welcomed into an igloo and spend their evenings resting within a block of ice. By modifying their environments, humans have enabled habitation of areas that previously were off-limits.

Spatial Interaction/Movement

The last theme of geography is the idea of **spatial interaction/movement**. How linked is a place to the outside world? The answer to this question determines much about an area. How well an area is connected to the world determines its importance. Without transportation systems, it is considered a remote area and, hence, less important, regardless of its geographical distance from a destination point. The remote location's spatial interaction is poor owing to its lack of transportation connections.

International airports are a good example of the movement theme. Thanks to international air travel, it is now possible to fly directly from Singapore to New York. New York's John F. Kennedy (JFK) Airport receives direct, daily flights from around the world. Looking at the flight board at JFK, one notices the proximity of New York City to other cities in the world. Within one day, a person can fly from New York City and land almost anywhere in the world. Thus, the spatial interaction of New York City is high owing to its transportation systems such as the international airport. In contrast, Devil's Lake, North Dakota, has a small airport. Although it is serviced by daily flights, they must go through a hub in Denver to get anyplace else. This limits transportation into and out of Devil's Lake. The flight board at Devil's Lake looks much different from the flight board at New York's JFK airport.

Many of the cities on the Great Plains, in the United States, are built 13 miles apart. Railroads determined that this was the distance that farmers could bring their agricultural commodities to town and still make a reasonable profit while limiting the railroads' investment in infrastructure. Towns missed by the railroad line quickly died, while populations increased in cities where the railroad was located. Trains were the lifeline of these agricultural communities. They brought settlement into areas and agricultural products out of these areas. The spatial interactions of these communities were based on the railroad during their settlement days; today, spatial interactions are based on both railroad and highway systems as well as airplane travel.

Spatial interaction often deals with the concept of situation. Situation is how well connected a place is with the outside world. Different places have a better situation than others. As previously mentioned, New Orleans has a wonderful situation. Located at the base of the Mississippi River, all of the goods that come down the river go through ports located around New Orleans. This situation once enabled New Orleans to become one of the richest cities in North America. Chicago's situation is very good because of its position in the central region of the United States, making it a regional hub for transportation. O'Hare Airport is one of the busiest in the world, and railroad and interstate systems converge in Chicago. Chicago's situation has enabled it to become the third-largest city in the United States.

By looking through a geographic lens, people can spot the traits of a place and begin to describe it. Since humanity's beginnings, the Earth has been searched, explored, and defined. Geographers can identify unique characteristics and define areas with some specificity using the five themes: place, region, location, human-environment interaction, and spatial interaction or movement.

ESSENTIAL ELEMENTS OF GEOGRAPHY

About a decade after the five themes of geography were introduced to classrooms around the world, the National Geography Standards were introduced to the classrooms in the United States. These National Geography Standards fall in line with the following six essential elements of geography instruction.

> ✔ **AP Expert Note**
>
> **Think like a geographer**
>
> The six elements are crucial to understanding what AP Human Geography is about. These fundamental concepts of geography are not a part of the curriculum itself, but, together with the five themes of geography, they make up a foundational way of thinking that gives a greater understanding of the AP Human Geography course. Remember, the official AP exam is much more about thinking like a geographer than it is about recalling facts.

The Spatial World

No place is alone. Certain places are lonelier than others, but all places are linked by some common factors. These factors can include population, agriculture, or industrial and economic bases. Culture, too, can link locations based on colonialism and other factors. Each of these elements links places or assists in defining places.

Places and Regions

By describing places and regions, we assign characteristics to particular locations and link them by means of their commonalities. As previously mentioned, a particular place may be linked by almost any factor one wishes to consider. Level of urban development, language spoken, and religion practiced are merely three examples of traits geographers use to define a particular location and link it to other locations.

Physical Systems

Physical systems are not among the major five themes of geography, but they would most likely overlap with the human-environment interaction theme. The physical systems of the Earth are intricately related to the human systems on the Earth. Physical barriers (such as mountain ranges and deserts) prevent the movement of people across landscapes. Volcanoes, earthquakes, and floods all prevent people from living in certain locations.

Human Systems

Human systems are anything that humans have done to modify the Earth's surface. Human systems can include anything from agriculture to hydroelectric construction to homes and office structures, and they all affect the natural systems of the Earth in some way. The Earth has limited some of these activities due to its topography. The interaction between the physical environment and human systems has had a profound impact on place.

Environment and Society

Another of the essential elements is the relationship between the environment and society. The chapter on Agriculture, Food Production, and Rural Land Use describes four primary ways of using land or perceiving land use: economic, sustainable, environmental, and preservationist. Each of these determines how humans can use the land to their advantage economically or otherwise.

Uses of Geography in Today's Society

The last of the essential elements in geography instruction is how geography is used in today's society. The profession of geographer is often in high demand. Geography allows us to think spatially about the Earth as a whole as well as to analyze it on progressively smaller scales, down to levels as small as our interactions with a single person, within a particular location. As previously mentioned, technological advancements, including GIS and GPS, have greatly altered business technology. Marketing and distribution patterns across the globe are constantly being affected by the new technology that geography has to offer.

It is important to remember that these six essential elements are, in a way, in flux. While the *physical* geography of a place does not change, its *human* geography can. For example, cell phones and satellite communication can allow people to hold a face-to-face conversation from opposite ends of the planet. This phenomenon is termed time-space compression. It is the increasing nature of interconnectedness that human civilization enjoys despite physical distance being fixed.

Each of the essential elements in geography assists geographers in defining place, determining characteristics of a particular space, and describing the surface of the Earth in rich and meaningful detail. Thus, geography is a multidisciplinary approach to studying the world around us.

> ✔ **AP Expert Note**
>
> **Be able to analyze data and draw conclusions**
>
> Part of thinking like a geographer is analyzing information that comes in both qualitative and quantitative forms. On the AP exam, you will need to be able to analyze various sets of data and make conclusions based on that data.

DIFFUSION

Diffusion is the movement of any characteristic, such as disease or migration, over time. Diffusion relates to the spatial interaction theme. The more easily accessible something is, the more quickly it can be moved from one culture to another. Because the world is constantly changing, the Earth can be difficult to examine. The place where a given characteristic began is known as a **hearth**, and diffusion is the process by which it is spread. For example, the hearth of the game of basketball is Springfield, Massachusetts. From this point, the game of basketball diffused to become a world-wide phenomenon.

Relocation Diffusion

Relocation diffusion is the physical spread of cultures, ideas, and people. When people migrate, they often bring with them various aspects of their culture such as language. For example, when the Hmong refugees came to the United States from Laos, they brought with them their language, religion, and customs, particularly to California, Minnesota, Wisconsin, and North Carolina. The physical spread of these people, or their movement from one place to another, is another aspect of relocation diffusion.

Expansion Diffusion

Another type of diffusion is **expansion diffusion**. Expansion diffusion is the spread of a characteristic from a central node, or hearth, through various means. Expansion diffusion can be further broken down into hierarchical, contagious, and stimulus diffusion.

Hierarchical diffusion is the idea that a phenomenon spreads as a result of a group, usually the social elite, spreading ideas or patterns in a society. The social elite may be political leaders, entertainment leaders, or sports stars. For example, elite members of society often start clothing trends. When an entertainment leader wears a particular hat that becomes a fashion, it is an example of hierarchical diffusion. Not all trends are started by the social elite. Rap music and the hip-hop culture were started by urban African Americans. This clothing, language, and music culture has moved from urban streets to suburban homes. Much of the language from the urban culture has become part of suburban and rural culture as well, especially among youth.

Contagious diffusion is usually associated with the spread of disease. Contagious diseases, such as influenza, spread without regard to race, social status, or family status. Contagious diffusion is often rapid. There are, however, examples of contagious diffusion other than disease. The Internet has led to many ideas spreading through rapid contact. People can observe items on the Internet with relative ease and can get information instantaneously. Live events on the Internet, where people can directly experience something happening, are mediums of contagious diffusion. Viral videos are a great example of contagious diffusion.

Stimulus diffusion takes a part of an idea and spreads that idea to create an innovative product. For example, in the 1980s, two dominant computer systems were being used: Apple's icon-based interface and IBM-based DOS systems. Then, IBM used Apple's idea of clicking on an icon to open a program in all its products. Prior to this diffusion, IBM computer users were forced to open programs by typing in the prompt for the program that they wanted to open, a process that was often time-consuming and confusing. It is also important to note that technology has increased the speed of diffusion. Computers, airplanes, and other forms of transportation allow the rapid transformation and distribution of a diffused feature.

DISTRIBUTION

Everything on the Earth's surface has a physical location and is organized in space, in some fashion. This is called distribution and may involve anything from buildings, to people, to desks in a classroom. There are three aspects of distribution: density, concentration, and pattern.

Density is how often an object occurs within a given area or space. Density is most often used with respect to population density. When calculating arithmetic population density, the number of people is divided by the amount of land of a certain area, usually in miles or kilometers. This calculation results in the number of people per square mile or kilometer. Population density can be expressed in other ways as well. **Physiologic density** is a more accurate way to measure a country's population density. Physiologic density only takes into account the land that is being used by humans, whether as pasture, as an urban center, or in some other way. **Arithmetic density** divides the entire population of a country by the total land area to come up with a population density for the country as a whole. Arithmetic density is important when looking at a country's population trends, but it doesn't tell the whole story. **Agricultural density** represents a basic calculation: the number of farmers per unit area of arable land (potential and utilized farmland).

A country may have a high population density yet a low total population. For example, Singapore's population density is far greater than India's population density, even though India has a much greater total population than the city-state of Singapore. India has much more land than Singapore, making its density much lower.

Concentration refers to the density of a particular phenomenon over the area in which it is spread. In the area of concentration, the objects are considered clustered or agglomerated if they are close together. If the objects are spread out, they are considered dispersed or scattered.

Pattern relates to how objects are organized in their space. Patterns may be anything from triangular, to linear, or even three-dimensional. Geometric shapes are used to describe how the phenomena are laid out. If the items are laid out on a singular line, the pattern is linear. If they're clustered together, the pattern is centralized. The lack of a pattern on the landscape is called a random distribution. These patterns are distributed across the Earth, and geographers interpret them for meaning, working to establish models to explain the patterns. These models are in almost every unit of this book. Models examine behavior and attempt to infer meaning and predict future occurrences. They are important in examining location and other features on the landscape.

MATHEMATICAL PRINCIPLES AND GEOGRAPHIC MODELS

Geographers often analyze data, which comes in both qualitative and quantitative forms, in order to draw conclusions about the world. Geographers must interpret this data on a variety of scales, while avoiding the ecological fallacy. An **ecological fallacy** is an assumption made at one scale and then applied to a variety of different scales. An example of an ecological fallacy would be assuming that relationships that exist at the group level also apply to individuals. Keep in mind that the "ecological" in "ecological fallacy" refers to broad systems, not just the environment.

Consider the following example: "Indianapolis has the most award-winning teachers of any city in the country. Miss Bliss teaches in Indianapolis. Therefore, Miss Bliss is an award-winning teacher." Do you see the leap in logic? Just because Miss Bliss teaches in that city does not mean she is necessarily an award-winning teacher. That is an example of the ecological fallacy.

Over the centuries, geographers have discovered certain mathematical principles underlying our world. One example is the **rank-size rule**, which describes the pattern of urban settlement in a country. The rule says that the population of a country's second-largest city will be approximately half the population of the largest city. The country's third-largest city will have approximately one-third the largest city's population. In general terms, the *nth* largest city will have 1/*nth* the population of the largest city.

According to the 2016 census, New York City had a population of a little over 8,500,000. The second-largest U.S. city, Los Angeles, had a population of nearly 4,000,000. The third largest, Chicago, had a population of just under 2,700,000. These examples illustrate the rank-size rule.

The gravity model is another mathematical concept used in geography. This model suggests that the greater the sphere of influence a city has, the greater its impact on other cities around it. This means that there will be more migration between these cities, regardless of the distance between them. The gravity model takes into account not only migration between cities but also travel between them, telephone calls between them, and trade between them. To determine the degree to which two cities are related, the populations must be multiplied by and then divided by the square of the distance between the cities.

There are many other models that geographers use to analyze and understand the world. The demographic transition model, for example, is a good yardstick for how population growth changes over time. The demographic transition model typically has four stages. It is based on three primary factors: the birth rate, the death rate, and the total population. Every society or country must go through these stages, and once a country moves from one stage to another, it does not go backward unless it suffers a nuclear attack or other cataclysmic event, like a plague or a genocide. The end result is zero population growth; the society neither grows nor shrinks but instead maintains a stable number of people within it.

Another established model is von Thünen's agricultural land use model, which states that the productivity of the land (the farmer's net profit) can be calculated ahead of time. The formula considers the potential yield of a given crop, the market price per unit of that commodity, and how expensive it is to ship the commodity to market. If a farmer grows products that don't fit the model, that farmer will go bankrupt from the increased costs of production and transportation.

Alfred Weber's least cost theory is also centered on economics, but it concerns the ideal location of a factory. The least cost theory suggests that a company building an industrial plant needs to take into consideration the source of raw materials and the market for the product. An industrial factory will be located wherever the cost of raw materials and transportation will be smallest.

Geography is a multidisciplinary approach, and logic, data, and models are all important tools. The examples discussed in this section are just a sampling of the ways geographers use multiple sources of information to analyze and understand the world around us.

✔ **AP Expert Note**

Revisit chapters as you study

Many ideas in human geography interconnect. Concepts introduced in one chapter will be referenced later on in a different chapter. All of that information can be overwhelming at first. Yet, you can make things easier on yourself by occasionally returning to other chapters to refresh your memory as you study. This practice will reinforce key concepts and the interconnection of big ideas.

NEXT STEP: PRACTICE

Go to Rapid Review and Practice Chapter 3 or to your online quizzes on kaptest.com for exam-like practice on this topic.

Haven't registered your book yet? Go to kaptest.com/moreonline to begin.

CHAPTER 11

Population and Migration Patterns and Processes

LEARNING OBJECTIVES

After studying this chapter, you will be able to:

- Identify factors influencing population distribution.

- Describe human interaction with the environment in regard to population distribution and density.

- List factors affecting population composition.

- Explain causes and effects of changes in population policies, fertility rates, and aging.

- Analyze historical and modern-day examples of migrations.

- Explain population trends using growth and decline theories.

- Evaluate the effect of push and pull factors on migration.

- Explain the ways migration affects culture, politics, economics, and the environment.

FACTORS AFFECTING POPULATION

When most people think of human geography, they usually think about population. With a world population of around 7.5 billion people and rising, population and the burden of overpopulation are certainly issues that many areas will be forced to deal with.

The study of population characteristics is called **demography**. Demography is the scientific analysis of population trends, and it predicts future occurrences based on present statistics. A country's population growth and demographics are important in setting political policy and allocating scarce resources. Two major factors in demographics are the birth rate and the death rate. **Birth rate** refers to the number of births per 1,000 people in the population. The **death rate** is the number of deaths per 1,000 people.

It is important to consider scale when analyzing population trends, as factors will be weighted differently depending on what subject is being studied. For example, the demography of a small town (local scale) may be heavily influenced by the health of one particular industry. If a coal mine runs out of coal, the town supporting that mine will likely wither away as the population emigrates to seek job opportunities elsewhere in their region. But when studying the demography of a whole country, the coal output of one mine likely will not even register at that scale. Instead, factors such as the overall fertility rate and immigration will take on greater importance when determining demographic trends.

Population has been increasing for as long as humans have been on this planet. For the majority of this time, population increase has been slow, but over the past 200 years, the global population has exploded. Most population growth is taking place in areas, particularly in less developed countries, that are ill-prepared to handle growing numbers of people, leading to a population crisis for the world. This crisis is sometimes called a population explosion.

When looking at population, it is important to note that not all areas of the world are overpopulated. People cannot live in large populations in five distinct areas: where it is too hot, too cold, too hilly, too wet, or too dry. Thus, humans are able to thrive on just a small percentage of the planet.

Some areas of the world experience **underpopulation**, a situation where resources cannot be optimally utilized because of an insufficient number of residents in an area. Sometimes this is due to climatic conditions and sometimes due to other factors, like politics or economics. The Great Plains of the United States is a good example of an underpopulated region. Although the Great Plains has been called the breadbasket of the United States, this area is sparsely populated and is dominated by agriculture. The food availability is good, and the water levels are somewhat sparse but acceptable, yet still very little population is located there.

Japan is a good example of a country living on a small percentage of its land. The country of Japan has approximately 127.5 million people in an area about the size of California. However, only 16 percent of the physical layout of Japan can support any population; the rest of the topography of Japan is too hilly. This terrain means that Japan is very densely populated. Space is at a premium in Japan, especially in Japanese urban areas, making property very expensive in larger cities such as Tokyo, Kyoto, and Osaka.

11

Overpopulation is defined as the lack of necessary resources to meet the needs of the population of a defined area. These resources include food, water, and shelter. In a desert, the carrying capacity of the environment is far less than that of an agriculturally productive area. **Carrying capacity** is the ability of the land to sustain a certain number of people. The more people inhabit an area, the more likely they will reach the carrying capacity of the environment. Once the carrying capacity is reached, the problems of overpopulation become apparent. People begin to starve, and many deaths occur due to a lack of resources. Certain factors can alter an environment's carrying capacity such as technological innovations that can increase food productivity (e.g., the Green Revolution).

As more and more humans inhabit a specific area, the strain on the resources of the environment becomes greater and greater. This causes a form of **environmental degradation** (the harming of the environment). Environmental degradation may take on several forms. Water may become polluted, or water rights and water use issues may become prominent. Watering restrictions are common in most places in the United States during the summer months. In addition to water use, food supplies may become diminished, a factor that will be discussed in the agriculture unit. The issue is usually less one of food production (unless a natural disaster takes out much of the food source) than one of food distribution.

Another result of rapid population growth could be a loss of biodiversity. As human populations grow, they require more land to sustain them, often resulting in habitat loss for plants and animals. Air pollution may also result from the overuse of natural resources due to overpopulation.

Natural disasters can have a dramatic impact on population growth. Population pyramids become skewed due to natural disasters when a segment of the population dies off due to a catastrophe such as a tornado, flood, or earthquake. For instance, the tsunami that hit coastal areas of Thailand and other parts of Southeast Asia in 2004 wiped out entire populations of children in some communities. When a large segment of the population is lost, a government is hard-pressed to find a taxable income, further straining its ability to provide a community's basic needs.

POPULATION DISTRIBUTION AND DENSITY

Population density can be expressed in many ways. As discussed in the previous chapter, physiological density refers to the total number of people divided by the arable land (land that can be farmed). This is a more accurate measure of population density than simple arithmetic density, which calculates the density using all the land in a given area. For example, while Canada is the second-largest country in the world by area, much of the country is too cold to support farming. Most Canadians live in the southernmost regions of the country, within a hundred miles of the U.S.-Canadian border. Agricultural density represents a basic calculation: the number of farmers per unit area of arable land (potential and utilized farmland). There are five main areas of population density (or population concentrations) in the world.

11

The first major area of population density is East Asia. The East Asia region contains the countries of China, South Korea, North Korea, and Japan. This region of the world is home to over 1.5 billion people. China alone has over 1.3 billion people, most of whom live within the eastern third of the country, along the Pacific Ocean. This area has favorable climatic conditions for food growth and transportation routes.

The second major region of population density is South Asia. In this region, which includes the countries of India, Pakistan, Sri Lanka, and Bangladesh, population growth is still outpacing policies to reduce growth. Within the next decade, India is anticipated to surpass China as the world's most populated country. Pakistan and Bangladesh are also within the top 10 most populous countries in the world.

The third major area of population density is located in Southeast Asia, which includes Vietnam, the Philippines, Malaysia, Indonesia, and Thailand. Vietnam is quickly becoming one of the fastest-growing countries in the world.

The fourth major area of population density is located in Western and Central Europe and extends eastward into Ukraine. Large cities such as London, Moscow, and Paris dominate this section of the world. Europe is mostly urbanized, as opposed to the East Asia and South Asia regions, which are still dominated by agriculture and rural economies.

The fifth major area of population density is located in the northeastern section of the United States and southeastern Canada. In the megalopolis of the East Coast of the United States, the urban area extends all the way from Boston, Massachusetts, to Washington, D.C. This area, along Interstate 95, still contains a large proportion of the population of the United States, although outward migration in recent decades has diminished its population. The southeastern section of Canada, including the cities of Toronto, Ottawa, and Montreal, contains the majority of Canada's population. This area extends southward into the U.S. megalopolis region.

Each of these five areas has a high population density that is conducive for economic growth, and climate and access to agriculture are the major factors. If adequate climate conditions no longer existed, or if food could not be produced fast enough to support the populations, these populations could eventually die out.

POPULATION AND GROWTH

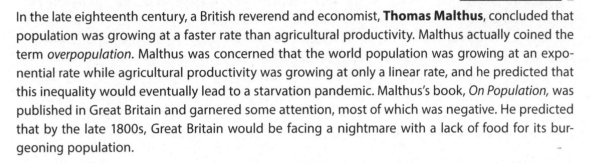

In the late eighteenth century, a British reverend and economist, **Thomas Malthus**, concluded that population was growing at a faster rate than agricultural productivity. Malthus actually coined the term *overpopulation*. Malthus was concerned that the world population was growing at an exponential rate while agricultural productivity was growing at only a linear rate, and he predicted that this inequality would eventually lead to a starvation pandemic. Malthus's book, *On Population,* was published in Great Britain and garnered some attention, most of which was negative. He predicted that by the late 1800s, Great Britain would be facing a nightmare with a lack of food for its burgeoning population.

Malthus is considered to be the first person to publicly foresee such a population crisis. He was correct in his assumptions that the world population would grow exponentially (as shown in the graph below), but his theory foundered on the agricultural side. Malthus never could have predicted the inventions that would mechanize farming and modify crops, hence greatly increasing productivity. In the twentieth century, Ester Boserup, a Danish economist, countered Malthusian theory with her own findings, which were published in her book, *The Conditions of Agricultural Growth*. Her theory, known as Qays's theory, posited that population change directly affects levels of agricultural production. In other words, Boserup believed that the more human population increased, the more people would figure out new ways to produce enough food.

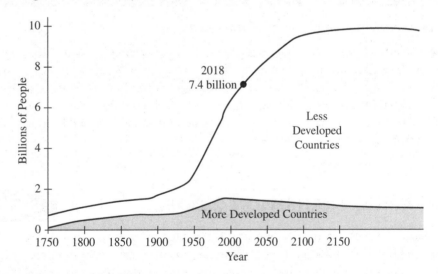

Linear growth is simply growth that occurs evenly across each unit of time. For example, a village with 100 people and a linear growth rate of 10 people per year would see an increase of 10 people after the first year, which would bring its population to 110. During the second year, the population would grow by 10 again to reach 120, and so on. After 10 years, the population of that village would be about 200 people.

11

Exponential growth looks at growth as a percentage of the total population. In the aforementioned village, a 10 percent exponential growth rate would mean that there would be 110 people after the first year. But then in the second year, population would grow by 110 × 10% = 11 new people; the base population of 110 plus the 11 new people equals 121. After 10 years, the population would be 234. The difference between the linear and exponential growth rates over a 10-year span, in a village that starts with 100 people and experiences 10 percent growth each year, is 34. Exponential growth is how the world's population growth has been expanding since the early twentieth century. As population continues to expand in the twenty-first century, we can predict which areas of the world will see the greatest growth.

The **neo-Malthusian** viewpoint is critical of Malthusian projections. According to neo-Malthusians, if there are multiple minority groups and no majority group within a population set, the growth rate will eventually resemble the rate of growth of the fastest-growing group within that set, regardless of the country's economic development. For example, the neo-Malthusians believe that the United States is ripe for a return to exponential population growth because of its immigrant communities. Proponents point to the large divide in the United States between its high crude birth rate and its low crude death rate, despite the fact that the U.S. economy is well into the tertiary (service-based) and quaternary (information-based) sectors.

✔ **AP Expert Note**

Be ready to explain multiple sides of the same issue

Because human geography is a multidisciplinary and ever-changing field, issues are often complex. In the free-response section of the AP exam, you may be asked to discuss multiple perspectives on a given issue. You just saw an example of this in this chapter's treatment of population growth, specifically Malthusian theory and the theories that counter it. As you study, look for other examples of issues that have a more nuanced approach, and lock these away in your memory for use on the official exam.

DEMOGRAPHIC TRANSITION MODEL   High-Yield

The **demographic transition model** is a good indicator of what will happen to a society or country's population. It is based on three primary factors: the birth rate, the death rate, and the total population. Furthermore, most demographic transition models have four stages. Every society or country must go through these stages. Once a country moves from one stage to another, it does not go backward unless it suffers a nuclear attack or a cataclysmic event such as a war or widespread epidemic.

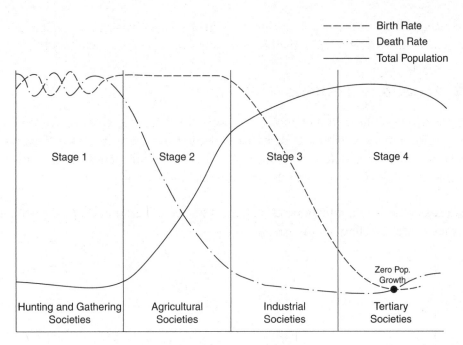

Demographic Transition Model

Stage 1: Hunting and Gathering Societies

A hunting and gathering society characterizes stage 1 of the demographic transition model. During this stage, a society has a low total population, with fluctuations in both the birth and death rates. When the birth rate is high, the death rate is low, and vice versa.

These variances in the birth and death rates occur naturally and still take place today. When food sources are plentiful and economic times are good, people have more children. When parents are more optimistic about the future, the result is an increase in the birth rate. The reverse is also true. When economic times are poor, parents are more pessimistic about the future and have fewer children. Baby booms and busts are heavily dependent upon economic conditions. Because food sources are sporadic in hunting and gathering societies, which depend upon herd animals for food, people generally will not have many children for fear of starvation. Thus, population levels during stage 1 remain low.

No countries are in stage 1 of the demographic transition model today. However, some societies, such as the Aborigines of Australia and the Bushmen of Namibia, still practice hunting and gathering. Both of these populations have remained low for centuries, owing to their unstable food sources.

As humans developed agriculture, food sources changed. Instead of relying on wild animals or seasonal vegetation for food, people began experimenting with farming. This process became known as the First Agricultural Revolution. Although the revolution took time to begin and accelerate, it was quite significant to the human population. Once people began planting crops and raising animals, they had some consistency in food production. This change helped to stabilize populations, an essential factor in the transition of people from nomadic hunters to sedentary farmers.

Stage 2: Agricultural Societies

Stage 2 of the demographic transition model, the agricultural society, sees unprecedented population growth. Birth rates stay high, but death rates decline sharply in this stage because of more stable food sources and the diffusion of modern medicine. This imbalance between the birth and death rates leads to a sharp increase in the total population of a society.

As you can see in the graph, total population begins to increase around stage 2, eventually stabilizing in stage 4, thus creating an S-shaped curve.

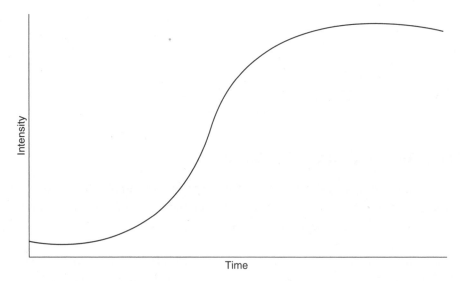

World Population Growth: S-Shaped Curve

As a country moves into stage 2, the majority of people are involved in farming. These are usually subsistence farmers who are simply trying to feed their families. Stage 2 economies are very basic and use very little technology. Within stage 2 countries, a traditional family structure is valued. Men usually work in the fields, while women stay at home and raise the children. Having many children serves an agricultural society's primary purpose of possessing a sufficient labor force on the farmsteads. In agricultural societies, it is not uncommon for families to have 10 or more children. As the children get older, they become workers on the farm, dramatically increasing productivity.

Another reason for having so many children is that they are often seen as a source of security. As people age, they become more dependent upon others, but government structures in stage 2 countries are not set up to provide public welfare. The elderly often have no form of support outside of individual wealth. Many people work simply to eat.

The overall death rate continues to fall during stage 2. One of the reasons for this is that a more stable food source allows people to live longer. In addition, advances in medical technology as well as the increased effectiveness and availability of medicines allow more people to live healthier and longer. Such advances and medicines cure many of the ailments that devastated populations in prior generations.

Many African countries south of the Sahara Desert are in stage 2 today. You can tell that a country is in stage 2 of the demographic transition model by comparing its birth and death rates with the current world average birth rate (20) and death rate (8). In a stage 2 country, both the birth rate and death rate are higher than the world averages. For example, Angola, located in Central Africa, had a 2013 birth rate of 47 and a death rate of 15, both well above the world averages. Liberia is another good example of a stage 2 country, with a birth rate of 36 and a death rate of 10.

In both Liberia and Angola, the majority of the population is involved in agriculture. In addition, life expectancy is generally very low in these countries. Only 2 percent of Angola's population is above the age of 65. Sanitation and education are rarely provided, especially in rural areas. In stage 2 countries, women often have more babies to offset the high number of babies who die before their first birthday. Total fertility rate is the number of babies that an average woman delivers during her childbearing years. In many developing countries, the total fertility rate is high and may exceed eight children.

It is also important to note that some countries may enter and exit a stage in the model relatively quickly, while other countries remain in a stage for a long time. Some countries, like the more developed European countries, were in stage 2 for 50 to 100 years before moving into stage 3.

Stage 3: Industrial Societies

A stage 3 country is characterized by a more industrial society. Initially, the Industrial Revolution, which began in the mid-1700s in Europe, spurred many European countries to adopt a more mechanized system of farming. As a result, these countries experienced an improved quality of life and dramatic population growth (stage 2). This move from an agricultural to an industrial society dramatically changes many aspects of a country, including its demographics.

Mass production begins in factories located in urban areas. Key reasons for declining birth rates in this stage are that the reliance on children for labor decreases and that children become more of a liability than an asset. The assembly line method of production takes hold, and government restrictions on child labor often prevent children from participating in the labor force as they did in the past. In addition, women enter the workforce in greater numbers, gaining career opportunities that often motivate them to delay having children for several years. This reduces the fertility rate of a country.

As an economy enters stage 3, more people are involved in the production of goods. The number of factories increases, meaning that more and more people move off the farm and into urban areas for manufacturing jobs. Increased pay for factory jobs and less reliance on the unpredictable whims of nature that affect farmers also support a more stable economy.

During stage 3, a country's birth rates and death rates will be close to the world averages. In a stage 3 country, the birth rate starts out high, persisting from stage 2, but then begins to drop sharply. At the same time, the death rate continues to fall (although the death rates can increase at the very end of stage 3 due to the increased percentage of the elderly population). There are several reasons for this, including continuing improvements in medicine and inoculations becoming more common. In addition, the quantity and quality of food increase, as food is now being produced by a more mechanized system of farming. Countries at the end of stage 3 will have average to low birth rates and average death rates.

During the early 1900s, much of Europe and the United States entered stage 3. Many of the countries in Central and South America are currently in stage 3. A country like Bolivia, with a birth rate of 24 and a death rate of 7, is at the beginning of stage 3. The high birth rate indicates that the country has just entered stage 3. The low to average death rate indicates some development within the country. In comparison, a country like Argentina, with a birth rate of 18 and a death rate of 8, is well established in stage 3. The low birth rate indicates a relatively urbanized and industrialized society, where dependence upon farming for primary employment has become less important.

Stage 4: Tertiary Societies

Conditions permitting, countries will eventually move into stage 4 of the model, which is characterized by a more tertiary or service-based economy. The birth rates and death rates become almost equal in stage 4. When the birth rate equals the death rate, the phenomenon is called **zero population growth**, or ZPG.

During stage 4, a country moves away from its reliance on industry to a more service-based economy. More people are involved in selling products than in production. For example, more people are selling or fixing automobiles than producing them. Countries in stage 4 do not always have successful economies. There are other factors that determine the success of an economy.

Many European countries have entered into stage 4 of the demographic transition model. Countries like Belarus, for instance, have a birth rate of 11 and a death rate of 14. In many Eastern European countries, the death rate is relatively high because of the lack of environmental standards during the communist era in the mid-1900s; pollution on a massive scale led to increased health problems in many areas.

Total fertility rates in a stage 4 country are at or below two, which is the natural increase rate (the rate required to replace the two parents). When the total fertility rate is below two, then the country experiences a loss of population. Several countries are trying to offset this lack of population growth by offering incentives for having children. For example, the Korean government has established several national policies aimed at increasing the fertility rate. These policies include starting kindergarten at the age of five instead of age six and giving tax breaks to families with more than one child. During stage 4, children become even more of an economic liability. In addition, women have more access to birth control options, also limiting the number of children being born. Although the population level is high, its growth has flattened out.

Stage 5

While the demographic transition model used to have only four stages, a fifth stage has become increasingly accepted by human geographers. Stage 5 is when low birth and death rates lead to a drawn-out overall population decrease. Poland is getting close to becoming a stage 5 country, since it has both a birth rate and a death rate of 10, leading to zero population growth. Modern-day Japan has also been suggested as an example of a stage 5 country, as its aging population shrunk by nearly one million people between 2010 and 2015.

Epidemiological Transition Model

The Epidemiological Transition Model deals with the changing causes of death in a society. It was developed by Abdel Omran in 1971 and has three stages. In stage 1, death is typically caused by famine and infectious diseases; the average life expectancy is low. In stage 2, life expectancy increases. Plagues and infectious diseases become less common, and improved agricultural practices lower the frequency of famine. Population also massively increases. In stage 3, the death rate levels off and population growth depends mainly on the fertility rate. People increasingly die from degenerative diseases such as heart attacks and cancer as well from certain behaviors such as substance abuse.

POPULATION STRUCTURE

Demography is not only concerned with population growth but also with the characteristics of the population itself. How old are the people? What is the gender breakdown of the population? Demographers study all the characteristics of populations all around the world.

One important characteristic of a country's population is its breakdown by age and gender. The sex ratio is the number of males compared to females in a population. One of the easiest ways to identify a population's sex ratio is by analyzing a **population pyramid**, a tool that geographers and demographers use. Population pyramids, sometimes called age/sex structures, chart populations on a graph. These graphs break down the population based on both gender and age, and it can then be analyzed in terms of the demographic transition model to determine in which stage a society is grouped. Age distribution is also presented in population pyramids, with individual brackets demonstrating age groupings.

Population pyramids are also a good way to analyze population projections. A **population projection** uses demographic data to determine future population. By analyzing birth and death rates, one can reliably determine what the population of an area will be 30, 50, or even 100 years into the future, assuming that the governmental structure and cultural customs remain the same.

Population pyramids of less developed countries (LDCs) have a wide base, because the majority of the population of an LDC is under the age of 15. There are also few elderly people owing to the lack of sanitation and medical care.

The following population pyramid represents the population in Angola. The center numbers are the age groupings of the population. The numbers on the bottom are the population totals of each age group. In a stage 2 country, the base is very wide and the top very narrow. A large part of Angola's population is under 15. These children are dependent upon those older than 15, who can enter the workforce. When the number of people in the workforce (ages 15 to 64) is low, very few people are available to support the younger population, putting an extra burden on an already strained government. The **dependency ratio** tracks how many people are dependents (the very young and the elderly) compared to how many people can contribute to the workforce.

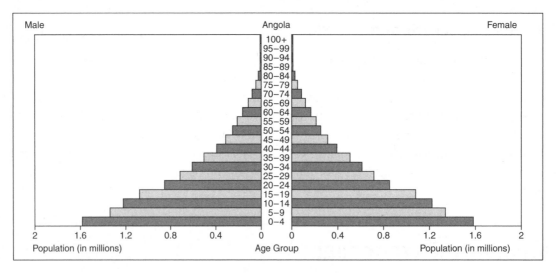

Population Pyramid: Angola

Countries that are in stage 2 have what is called demographic momentum. **Demographic momentum** is a continued population increase as a result of a large segment of the population being young. These young people, as a group, will eventually produce more offspring than their parents' generation because there are so many of them, thus continuing the demographic momentum. These countries are likely to see monumental population growth for a minimum of 50 years and likely longer.

In a stage 3 country, like Argentina (shown in the following figure), there are more adults and elderly in the population and fewer children as compared to a stage 2 country. This makes the pyramid look less bottom heavy, and the population is distributed by age a little more evenly. There are more older people because of improvements in medical care. As the stage 3 society becomes more industrialized, it becomes more urban and offers more access to health care.

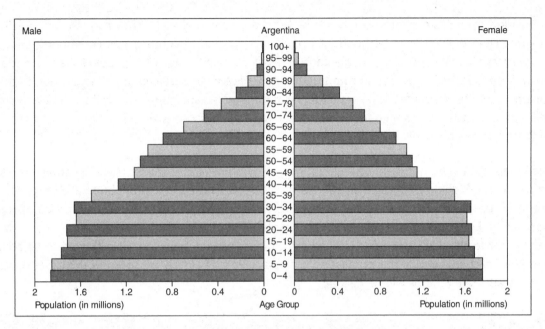

Population Pyramid: Argentina

In a stage 4 country, the percentage of children decreases dramatically, and the workforce segment of the population actually bulges, with 20- to 50-year-old adults becoming the majority of the population. There are more parents than children. In stage 5, the population begins to see a decrease in total population growth. When the natural increase rate falls below zero, the country begins to lose population, a process called **negative growth**.

A large percentage of the United Kingdom's population, shown in the following figure, is of child-bearing years, yet people are choosing not to have many children for various reasons. Children are becoming more and more expensive, and the majority of the population lives in urbanized areas. Furthermore, people are living longer as a result of continued improvements in medical care.

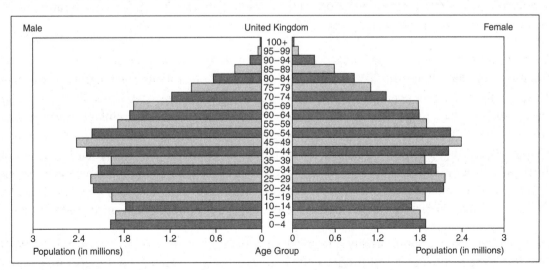

Population Pyramid: United Kingdom

11

Population pyramids do not only have to be used on a national scale. They can also be used to describe cities or even neighborhoods. A population pyramid for a retirement community, which has very few children and a large percentage of residents over the age of 65, would have an upside-down look to it. Mining or fishing communities may have a large percentage of males due to the job opportunities they offer. Areas where many of the workers are immigrants will often have more males than females. Areas hit hard by war may have an imbalance toward females because many of the men have been killed in combat.

Assuming that the numbers are correct, population pyramids accurately represent a nation's, city's, or community's demographics in an easy-to-read picture. Having this information allows governments to develop policies and allocate resources to meet the current and future needs of the population. For example, communities with a higher percentage of children ages four and under will see those children soon move into the educational system. New schools will need to be built and new teachers hired. If the population consists mainly of elderly persons, on the other hand, more health care options will be needed.

✔ **AP Expert Note**

Be able to visualize and explain population pyramids

Take a moment to visualize or to sketch each of these population pyramids so that if you were to see similar examples on the AP exam, you could recognize them immediately. Additionally, the exam will expect you to be able to discuss the factors that lead to different population pyramid shapes, including in what stage of growth a region is.

Birth and Death Rates

The average world birth rate is 20 per 1,000 people, and the average death rate is 8 per 1,000 people. The **demographic equation** is global births minus global deaths, and it determines the population growth rate for the world. Currently, the inequity between birth and death rates means the global population is growing by about 80–100 million people per year.

Another statistic that affects a country's population is the **infant mortality rate**. This is the number of babies who die within their first year of life. Like birth and death rates, the infant mortality rate is usually given as a rate per 1,000 people. More developed countries have lower infant mortality rates than less developed countries. A more developed country may see an infant mortality rate below 10 per 1,000, while in less developed countries, the infant mortality rate may approach 150 per 1,000. A high infant mortality rate is a huge hindrance to a population. When 15 percent of the population is dying before the age of 1, it is indicative of other social and developmental problems. Women in these circumstances often have more children, uncertain of how many infants will survive and knowing that children will largely determine the family's financial stability as the parents age.

The opposite of the infant mortality rate is the natality rate, which is another term for the birth rate. This is the number of live births per 1,000 people in the population. The natality rate and the infant mortality rate are always given per 1,000.

A major population problem in the world is that the birth rate in many less developed countries is far outpacing the death rate. The result is a world population that has grown extremely fast within less developed countries for the past half century. One of the main reasons for this is that people in these countries tend to lack birth control due to low income, religious beliefs, lack of social status, inadequate education, or poor transportation.

Many people in the less developed world live in rural villages, which are generally the poorest areas of the world, and simply do not have access to birth control measures. Traveling to an urban area may take a week or longer, and to be away from the children and the work that the farm requires is an opportunity cost that families cannot afford. In more developed countries, people have greater access to birth control options and are more likely to use them, reducing the number of births.

Change is slowly occurring. There has been a diffusion of fertility control in recent years. Much of the developed world, which has transitioned into stages 3 and 4, has the access and the resources to purchase birth control and is spreading it to a larger number of women and men across the world. Although there are still many obstacles to overcome, such as distance and money, more people today have access to birth control options than ever before in human history.

✔ **AP Expert Note**

Be able to identify patterns within population structures

Note how the discussion in the next three paragraphs links gender to population, economic development, politics, and culture. Being able to recognize such patterns allows you to anticipate exam questions and see themes that connect various geography topics.

Various governments around the world have adopted measures to control the birth and death rates in their countries. Some have been more successful than others. One of the most successful measures of governmental birth control was enacted in China. In 1979, China adopted its one-child policy to curb its population growth. Since then, China has seen a drop in its natural increase rate, total fertility rate, and birth rate. However, despite its successes, a problem with the one-child policy was that it was not adopted by all minority groups evenly across the country. In western China, where subsistence agriculture is practiced, minority groups are still having more children out of economic necessity.

Another issue that concerns many human rights activists is the treatment of female infants. Chinese families are very motivated to have a male child due to China's societal emphasis on passing down the family name and heritage through a son. Infanticide and abortions, particularly of female children and fetuses, increased since China's policy was enacted in 1979. In 2016, China rescinded its one-child policy for a number of reasons including laborer shortages and skewed sex ratios.

Other countries have tried to control their populations, sometimes through extreme measures. Some countries, for example, have attempted the forced sterilization of their citizens, often of their minority groups. Because this has only been done on a small scale, it has had very little impact on the population as a whole. Measures must be applied to an entire country for them to be effective.

11

Depending upon what stage the country is in within the demographic transition model, it may attempt to impose either pro-natal or anti-natal policies. China's one-child policy was an example of an anti-natal policy. An anti-natal policy tries to slow down the population growth of a society, while pro-natal policies try to encourage people to have more children. Several countries, including Japan, South Korea, and Germany, have implemented policies encouraging their citizens to have more children. Incentives vary from beginning kindergarten at an earlier age to offering tax incentives and early retirement for parents who have more children.

POPULATION EQUATIONS AND SCIENTIFIC METHODS

Doubling time is the number of years that it takes for a country to double its population. The lower the number, the faster that country will double its population. Countries with a high natural increase rate will double their populations faster than countries with a low natural increase rate.

An equation for approximating doubling time is doubling time = 70 ÷ growth rate. Thus, if a country has a natural increase rate of 7 percent, its doubling time will be approximately 70 ÷ 7 = 10 years. If a country has a 3.5 percent growth rate, its doubling time is about 20 years, and a 1.75 percent growth rate gives a doubling time of about 40 years. Even a country that has a 1.75 percent growth rate is considered to be increasing its population very rapidly.

If you are given the natural increase rate of any population, you can determine its doubling time to within a couple of years. Morocco, a country located in northwestern Africa, is 57 percent urbanized. Its birth rate is 19, and its death rate is 5. It is a stage 3 country, in part owing to regulations established by the Islamic religion. Its natural increase rate is 1.4 percent, and the doubling time is around 50 years for Morocco.

This can be done for any country that has a natural increase rate. If the country is losing population, like many of the countries in Eastern Europe and Japan, there is obviously no doubling time because a country cannot double its population when the population is declining. Many countries in Europe are experiencing doubling times approaching 700 years with a 0.1 percent natural increase rate.

✔ **AP Expert Note**

Be able to apply basic geographic math principles

Geography is a field that borrows from many other areas, including math. For example, understanding how demographers calculate and predict population increases is key to answering such questions correctly on the AP exam. The test makers may ask you to calculate a population's doubling time, but they will not supply you with the formula. Be sure to memorize formulas like the one for doubling time (doubling time = 70 ÷ growth rate), so you can confidently apply these mathematical principles on the exam.

Demographers use the mathematical relationship between doubling time and natural increase rates to calculate growth rates and expected increases in the total population, usually with a high degree of accuracy, assuming that governmental structure and cultural practices of the country do not change. If these factors change, they can dramatically alter the natural increase rates. To slow down its demographic momentum, a country can slow its growth rate in one of three ways. Each of these three methods—imposing government laws, decreasing the birth rate, and increasing the death rate—has its pros and cons.

By decreasing their birth rates, countries can slow down their population growth and natural increase rate. This can be done by law, as it is in China. It can also be done through the distribution of birth control. The United States has tried making birth control accessible to the masses through free distribution. Also, U.S. high schools teach birth control methods, including abstinence, as a means to reduce the birth rate among teenage girls. Critics of reducing the birth rate say that making birth control available in this way is not working. Although the pregnancy rate in the United States has been decreasing since its high point in 1990, teenage pregnancy rates are still high. In fact, despite these significant declines, the United States still has the highest teenage pregnancy rate among developed Western countries.

Another means of controlling population is to increase the death rate. By increasing the death rate, population control would be achieved. Increasing the death rate does not mean the killing of innocent civilians. Rather, it suggests that those with terminal diseases not be given the care they need to sustain their lives. This morbid approach goes against many doctors' codes of ethics. Doctors take the Hippocratic oath, vowing never to do harm to anyone.

Proponents of this method, however, suggest that we are spending countless billions on medicines for the clearly terminal that could be used to assist others with manageable diseases, like malaria. Every person is mortal. This mortality principle has led some to this question: If the Earth has a limited number of resources, why are we spending them on people with no hope of survival? Proponents argue that it makes more sense to let one person die today than to let the natural increase rate continue, see the environment reach its carrying capacity, and experience mass starvation.

Recent studies have suggested that this next generation is the first generation that will live fewer years than their parents. The bottom line is that the world must find some means of sustainability for the population. **Sustainability** is the responsible use of resources so that future generations will be able to live at the same or higher standard of living than the population today.

HISTORICAL AND GLOBAL PERSPECTIVES

Until recently, governments have seen an increase in population as a positive event. A greater population means a higher tax base, increased military capability, and more workers for either farming or industrial jobs. Only in recent decades have some areas of the world tried to reduce their overall growth rates. The population growth of a country can follow one of two broad patterns, depending on environmental conditions: exponential growth (the J-curve) or logistic growth (the S-curve).

The J-curve occurs in ideal environments. Food, water, and living space are plentiful. Small populations can quickly fill up a region. Exponential growth is often seen when an invasive species is introduced to a new region. As the species has no natural predators in its new environment, it can reproduce at an explosive rate that drives local species to extinction.

The S-curve occurs in environments with a strict carrying capacity; this is when there is only so much food, water, and living space available. When the population nears the carrying capacity, these natural restrictions limit growth, and eventually, the population stabilizes at a certain level. Consider the arid American Southwest. Until the advent of dams, air-conditioning, and modern transportation systems, that region was unable to support (or "carry") the million-plus residents of cities like Phoenix, Arizona.

The majority of the world's most populous countries are in Asia. Almost 60 percent of the world's population, or three out of every five persons, is of Asian descent. Many of the available world demographic statistics are given in terms of *with* and *without China*. Because of heavy government influence, China doesn't really follow the demographic transition model. Because one out of every six persons on Earth is Chinese, including or excluding China can obviously vary the statistical accuracy of any set of world demographic data.

For much of the world, including today's more developed countries, the population was growing at a constant rate until the mid to late 1800s. Once many countries in Europe reached stage 3, the population began to level off. However, the less developed world is now seeing the highest growth rates and natural increase rates. To give an example, the doubling time of Nigeria, as of 2012, was 35 years. This country will see its population of 166 million double within the next 30 to 40 years. Countries like Nigeria face the greatest population growth problems. Because the carrying capacity of Nigeria may not be able to support its population, it will either need to increase its agricultural productivity exponentially or import more food.

Bangladesh is another country that is seeing a population crisis. Bangladesh is the size of the state of Iowa. As of 2012, its population was over 152 million. In comparison, Iowa's population is around four million. Bangladesh's natural increase rate is 1.8 percent. At a growth rate of 2 percent, Bangladesh's population will double in 35 years. With more and more countries facing critical problems due to population growth, many people feel the world needs to reassess its role in reducing overpopulation.

Why do some countries stay in stage 2 or stage 3 of the demographic transition model, while others move beyond that to tertiary or even quaternary economies? The answer ties into some of the most fundamental aspects of geography: economic systems. When economies change their basic functions, demographics within the country change in response.

The United States was in stage 2 of the demographic transition model for all of the nineteenth century. It was not until the early 1900s that the United States entered stage 3. This is when the Industrial Revolution and mass industrialization took hold in the United States. Henry Ford's assembly line method of producing automobiles had a ripple effect on almost every other industry in North America, moving people off the farms and toward better and more reliable incomes.

Great Britain entered stage 3 in the 1800s. The Industrial Revolution began in the mid-1700s, and by the 1800s, Great Britain had come into the modern age. After World War II, industry took a backseat to tertiary activities in Great Britain. Even today, some cities in Great Britain are reeling from the closing of the mega-factories that used to employ thousands of people. Many of these workers have ended up on government assistance due to a lack of industrial jobs. Major urban areas, such as London, have relied more on financial or tertiary economic pursuits than on industrial enterprises. Most demographers can agree that the United Kingdom is in stage 4. The United Kingdom has a very low population growth rate, and the majority of its people are working in some type of tertiary or quaternary sector of the economy. Having a low disparity between the birth rate (13) and death rate (9) is evidence of being a stage 4 country.

FACTORS AFFECTING POPULATION GROWTH AND DECLINE

High-Yield

Causes of Population Increase

Four primary factors lead to an increase in population: medical advances, quantity and quality of food, ethnic and religious issues, and economic issues.

Medical Advances

Medical advances are one of the biggest reasons for an increase in population because they directly affect the death rate. By decreasing the death rate, a country automatically sees its population increase as long as birth rates are constant. Because birth and death rates determine natural increase rates, changing one of the rates affects the overall population growth of a country.

New medicines and inoculations have allowed millions around the world to live longer and healthier lives than ever before in human history. For hundreds of years, explorers were afraid to enter the inner reaches of Africa and South America for fear of malaria. Today, new medication keeps people from catching the disease, and new treatments allow people to live productively for many years after having the disease. Disease diffusion, which is simply the spread of disease, does not occur as widely as it used to. Although some viruses, such as HIV, SARS, and avian flu, still dominate the news, medicine has eliminated smallpox from the map and has made progress against polio, malaria, and the plague.

Quantity and Quality of Food

Increased food quantity and quality have had a dramatic effect on the population as well. Advances in agricultural technology have helped to feed billions of people around the world. The advancements in the technology of growing rice, for example, have allowed triple-cropping and increased production in Asia. The importance of rice in the Asian diet cannot be overstated. Rice is a high-calorie food that provides energy for millions on a daily basis. Rice is eaten in all three meals of the day and is an essential staple crop for billions of people around the world.

11

Ethnic and Religious Issues

Ethnic and religious issues also play a major role in population growth around the world. Many patriarchal cultures forbid the use of any form of birth control. In countries where the gender gap (the gap between men and women in terms of status and education) is high, women are more likely to lack certain rights that men are possess such as the right to vote. In these societies, women are usually subjugated to men, are treated as second-class citizens, and have less control over their birth control options. This leads to an abundance of children, sometimes despite the wishes of the women.

Economic Issues

Economic issues are a good indicator of a society's population growth rate. If the economy of the country is fundamentally based on agriculture, the odds are high that the country has a high growth rate. If the economy is based on industry or services, chances are high that the population growth is minimal or even nonexistent.

Causes of Population Decline

Just as there are reasons for population growth, there are also factors that contribute to population decline. The three major factors that contribute to population decline are natural hazards and disasters, war or political turmoil, and economic issues.

Natural Hazards and Disasters

Natural hazards become disasters when loss of life and property are involved. From a population distribution perspective, millions of people live in areas that are subject to natural hazards. Many earthquake-prone areas, such as California, Japan, Turkey, and Pakistan, have large populations. Many natural hazards easily become disasters because of population growth, density, and distribution.

Natural disasters can kill thousands of people at a time. Recent earthquakes around the world have killed tens of thousands of people at a time. Many of the deadliest earthquakes occur in less developed countries because of the lack of building codes that would require structures to withstand tremors. Tsunamis, tornadoes, blizzards, and other natural disasters kill thousands of people every year.

Famines and plagues can lead to mass starvation and disease. Famines are usually caused by some type of natural disaster (such as a drought) that affects the food supply. When transportation systems are unable to bring in sufficient food, populations starve. Famine has killed tens of thousands of people in places such as Ethiopia and Sudan. Poverty and lack of health care can lead to plagues, which can also cause a lack of food production in a region.

War or Political Turmoil

Other factors that negatively affect population growth are war and political turmoil. In Cambodia during the 1970s, for example, the Khmer Rouge forced millions to leave the country or be killed. This exodus greatly affected Cambodia's population during this time. The Killing Fields of Cambodia have been well documented, and the effects of the political situation of the 1970s are still being felt in that country.

War leads to refugees, who flee for fear of persecution or death if they remain in the country. The ethnic conflict in Rwanda and Uganda resulted in a refugee crisis in central Africa that led to the deaths of millions of people on both sides of the conflict. The battles were so intense that some people say the rivers and creeks ran red with blood. World War II directly affected the lives of millions of people around the world.

Losing a spouse to war affects the entire family structure. In societies afflicted by war, the male section of many population pyramids is often greatly diminished.

Economic Issues

Various economic issues contribute to population decline as well. The number one reason people move is for economic concerns. If there are no employment opportunities available in a certain area, people tend to go where jobs are available. Such out-migration leads to a decrease in the population of certain areas. Much of the Great Plains region of the United States is experiencing out-migration as a result of a lack of job opportunities. It is important to note, however, that migration does not affect population on a worldwide level. Greater education and employment opportunities for women in the developed world have led to a decline in fertility, as couples delay marriage and having children, reducing their window for producing offspring.

Natalist Policies

The government management of population growth is referred to as natalist policies. Pro-natalist policies encourage fertility and the production of children. For example, maternity and paternity leave encourage working parents to have more children as they do not need to fear the loss of employment when taking time off to care for a newborn. Anti-natalist policies discourage fertility and population growth. For example, free access to birth control reduces the birth rate.

THEORIES OF MIGRATION

Migration is the movement of people. People may move across town or across the world, again for a variety of reasons. As a whole, the percentage of people who move a long way from their place of origin is relatively low. People who move into a country or region are called **immigrants**. People who leave a region or country are called **emigrants**. An easy way to distinguish between "immigrant" and "emigrant" is to think about "into" and "exit." Immigration is the influx of people into a particular region or location, whereas emigration is the outflow of people from a particular region or location. **Net migration** is the number of immigrants minus the number of emigrants.

Most people move at least once in their lifetimes. These moves are generally short in distance and rarely involve leaving the country. When migration does involve moving to another country, the destination is usually one of the major urban centers of the new country. For example, if people are moving to Egypt, they are probably moving to Cairo. If people are moving to China, they are probably moving to Shanghai, Hong Kong, or Beijing. New York is known for its immigrant neighborhoods. It is important to note that movement does not affect the world's population. Once a person is alive, their movement on the Earth affects only a certain area's population.

Push and Pull Factors

High-Yield

A **push factor** is a negative perception about a location that induces a person to move away from that location. A **pull factor** is a positive perception about a location that induces a person to move there.

Both push and pull factors are based on an individual's perceptions of the area. A pull factor for one person may be a push factor for another. A good example of what could be considered both a push and a pull factor is climate. One person is tired of the cold weather. She does not like the major snowstorms that hit her area. She is tired of getting her automobile stuck in the snow. She decides to move to a warmer climate where it does not snow. For this person, the cold weather is an environmental push factor. For another person, the cold weather is a pull factor. He loves to ice skate and sled with his children in the winter. He also loves to downhill ski. This person is willing to put up with the inconveniences of the snow so as to enjoy the amenities of the climate. For this individual, the cold weather is a pull factor.

There are four different types of push and pull factors: economic, political, environmental, and social. These factors are all reasons why people would want to move to, or away, from a certain location. Each can be so strong that people are willing to sacrifice in the short term for monetary, environmental, or political gain in the long term. They are willing to undertake the journey, sometimes thousands of miles, for the opportunity for freedom, employment, safety, or some other positive aspect of another location.

> **✔ AP Expert Note**
>
> **Be able to differentiate between various push and pull factors**
>
> In preparation for the exam, familiarize yourself with the push and pull factors (economic, political, environmental, and social) that affect migration. Be ready to identify and even discuss in detail specific examples that illustrate each factor. This chapter gives you some scenarios to consider, but it will help your study to come up with even more examples on your own.

Economic Factors

Economic pull factors are the number-one reason people move. Often, they relocate for new employment opportunities. If an area opens a new factory, or is in need of more employees, more people may move to the area to fill those available jobs. If the jobs are high paying, people may be willing to relocate at a considerable expense.

Economics can also be a push factor. Downturns in the economy frequently lead to business layoffs and shutdowns. Without jobs, people cannot support themselves or their families, so they must go where there are enough jobs. In this case, the economy forces the person to leave an area in search of new employment. Economics has now become a push factor.

Economic factors rely on the idea of human capital, the idea that an individual has certain skills that are valuable to a society or a company. Many companies will conduct worldwide searches for top positions and then pay for those employees to move to their location. These people have some skill or experience that makes them of value to the organization; hence, the costs that go into the search and moving processes are outweighed by the benefits the individual will bring to the organization.

Political Factors

Other push and pull factors can be political. Sometimes, people are forced to leave a country for fear of persecution or even death. **Refugees** are people who are forced to flee their homeland for such reasons to seek some type of asylum in another country. Sometimes refugee movements occur on a massive scale, with tens of thousands of people forced to flee their homelands.

The migration movement of the Hmong population into the United States is an example of such a refugee movement. The Hmong fought alongside U.S. soldiers during the Vietnam conflict. When the United States left, the Hmong were forced out of the country for fear of persecution by the new, anti-U.S. government. Thus, the Hmong became a refugee group, and the stories of the Hmong crossing the Mekong River are heroic. Many of the migrations were done under cover of darkness for fear of being shot by enemy soldiers, and many of the recent immigrants to the United States lost close family members in the move away from their homelands.

Scale is important when discussing the issue of internally displaced people. An internally displaced person is a person who has been removed from their home but has not left their country. This has been the case in Colombia, the Democratic Republic of the Congo, and other countries when governments forced individuals to move from their homes. Rebel movements in many of these countries are the reason for the government movement of its citizens. Oftentimes, noncombatants are the ones who are internally displaced.

The Jews who emigrated during World War II were refugees. Jews from around Europe fled the Nazis for fear of death. Many countries refused to take the Jews. Other countries, like Denmark and Sweden, were havens for Jews as they tried to escape imprisonment and torture.

There have been dozens of refugee crises around the world during the past 50 years. One of the largest refugee movements occurred in Rwanda and Uganda during the 1990s. The conflict between the Hutus and the Tutsis caused the deaths of hundreds of thousands of people on both sides. Brutal retaliation led to further conflicts. Refugees of this war fled to the Democratic Republic of the Congo and other neighboring countries to escape the bloodshed, putting social and economic pressure on these countries and spreading political instability. The same type of refugee movement occurred in the former Yugoslavia during the 1990s. The breakup of the former Yugoslav Republic led to increased refugee movement into neighboring countries, such as Albania.

This type of refugee movement occurs on a daily basis in many locations around the world. People leave their homelands fearing persecution and death. In addition, some people leave to search for freedom, opportunity, and a new life. They want to enter new countries for the opportunity to better their economic situation and to have the political freedom to say and do things that they only dreamed of in their homeland.

Environmental Factors

The third push and pull factors are environmental. Environmental factors are often associated with voluntary migration, in which people choose to move. For example, people may move to a warmer climate or a climate that better suits their lifestyles. Many retirees in the United States have voluntarily moved to Florida for the warmer climate and amenities that Florida can offer them.

The southern portion of the United States has seen a large in-migration during the previous four decades. This area, known as the Sun Belt, includes states extending from North Carolina to Southern California. It has seen dramatic growth during the latter half of the twentieth century. The invention and mass use of air conditioning has made warmer areas more livable in the summer. Many new residents are retirees, but many have moved for economic opportunities as well.

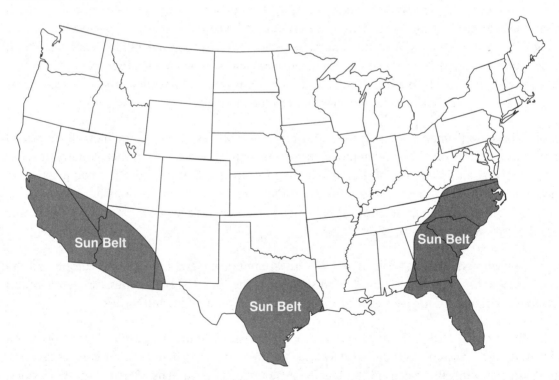

Sun Belt Areas in the United States

Many see North Carolina, South Carolina, and areas extending into Georgia as positive places to move. Citizens of these states can participate in summer activities practically year-round. For example, golf in Florida is a year-round industry.

Many job seekers moved from the Rust Belt to the Sun Belt during the 1980s and 1990s. This movement was caused by factory closings in the Northeast and Great Lakes regions. These workers moved to where the new factories were being built. Honda and other car manufacturers have huge industrial plants in the Sun Belt; Honda builds many of its cars in Alabama, and BMW builds some of its cars in South Carolina.

This Sun Belt phenomenon has skipped several locations. Mississippi, Louisiana, and Alabama have not seen the immense growth of other southern areas. Other areas that have been skipped in the Sun Belt include sections of western Texas and eastern portions of New Mexico. Part of this is due to poor economic situations. Also, the relative lack of education of the population has negatively impacted these areas' economic growth.

Many communities in the South have offered incentives for people to move to their areas. By offering tax breaks for companies and increased recreational opportunities (parks, sports arenas, etc.), these towns and cities in the Sun Belt have marketed themselves to other areas around the country. This concept is referred to as **place utility**. Several commercials about specific communities have run nationally around the United States. In the north, Sioux Falls, South Dakota, has run advertisements throughout the Upper Midwest, presenting itself as the ideal place for a business to be located. This marketing has attracted hundreds of new employment opportunities to a town that is growing already.

Another area in the United States that has seen growth due to its environmental amenities is the mountain state region in the western portion of the country. States like Utah, Colorado, Montana, and New Mexico have seen populations in some of their small towns double over the past several decades. People like the views and the recreational opportunities offered in these areas.

People have left specific areas owing to environmental factors. Natural disasters are one environmental push factor that moves people away from where they live. Hurricane Katrina, which hit the Gulf Coast of the United States, was one of the costliest natural disasters in the country's history. The storm wiped out communities and forced people out of their homes and into temporary shelters, sometimes located in cities hundreds of miles away. Residents of New Orleans were put on buses and sent to Houston, Texas, and other cities around the United States. Many of the people who left New Orleans have decided to make Houston their permanent home. In the Midwest, Americans also face natural disasters, such as tornadoes and floods.

Another example of an environmental push factor was the Dust Bowl, which occurred during the 1930s in the Central Plains. At one time, this region was heavily cultivated, but when the drought of the 1930s occurred, many farmers experienced economic ruin and were forced to leave their homesteads. The Dust Bowl resulted in a significant migration in American history; in fact, the migration of people from Oklahoma was the backdrop for John Steinbeck's *The Grapes of Wrath*.

Outside the United States, the tsunami that hit the Indian Ocean in late 2005 devastated coastal communities and forced tens of thousands of people out of their homes and into shelters. After the earthquake, tsunami, and nuclear disaster of 2011, tens of thousands of Japanese were forced to move away from their homes. Many of these people cannot move back due to the radiation from the power plant.

Social Factors

The fourth push and pull factor is social. Social factors could include healthcare, education, or even religious freedom. These can be both push and pull factors: push factors would be lack of health care, lack of opportunities in education, or policies restricting religious practices, and pull factors would be advances in any of these three areas.

Ravenstein's Laws of Migration

E. G. Ravenstein studied migration trends and came up with 10 laws of migration in 1885:

1. Most migration is over a short distance.
2. Migration occurs in a series of steps.
3. Long-distance migrants usually move to centers of economic opportunity (urban areas).
4. Each migration produces a movement in the opposite direction (although not necessarily of the same volume).
5. People in rural areas migrate more than people in cities.
6. Men migrate over longer distances than women.
7. Most migrants are young adult males.
8. Cities grow more by migration than by natural increase.
9. Migration increases with economic development.
10. Migration is mostly due to economic causes.

Many of these generalizations are still valid today; however, women are now migrating internationally in larger numbers than men in some cases. In considering these rules, it is important to think of examples for each law and to determine how valid the trend is now.

Migration Transition

Wilbur Zelinsky put forth the idea that a migration transition occurs in conjunction with a demographic transition. For instance, when a country is in stage 2 (high growth) of the demographic transition, the excessive population growth encourages people to move to another country where there is more economic opportunity. Countries in stage 4 tend to have more economic opportunities because their economies are growing faster than their stable population. When a country is in stage 3 (moderate growth) or stage 4 (stable growth) people tend to move internally (internal migration) for job opportunities. Examples of **internal migration** include people in the United States moving from the Midwest or northeastern areas to the South for economic and environmental reasons. An example of this would be the Great Migration in the early twentieth century wherein African Americans moved from the South to the Midwest, Northeast, and West to find jobs in industrial cities. Other forms of migration, especially in the United States, include rural to urban, urban to suburban, and suburban to exurban or urban.

Human Capital

The **human capital model** of migration, developed by Larry Sjaastad in 1962, attempts to explain the major reasons why people migrate. This model basically states that people seek to improve their incomes over the course of their lives; therefore, people weigh the costs against the benefits of migrating. William A. V. Clark contributed to the explanation in 1986 with two observations. First, migration rates drop as people age since personal wealth is accumulated over time, and the potential benefit of moving decreases with increased age. Second, Clark observed that psychological and economic costs and benefits are considered before people make a major move, something Sjaastad overlooked in his initial model.

Life Course

The **life course theory**, first put forward in the 1960s, posits that people make major decisions early on in life that directly affect their life in the future. This theory sees people's lives as a timeline but evaluates their lives by looking at their social and cultural perspectives and situations. These decisions may dictate migration preferences and opportunities in the future.

Major turning points in a person's life include college, employment, marriage, having children, and retirement. Each of these events helps determine the decisions a person makes with respect to migration. For example, the larger the household, the less likely it is the household will relocate. Single people are the most likely to move, followed by couples, families with fewer children, and then families with more children or older dependents. However, larger families can encourage certain types of migration. When couples have children, they tend to move in order to obtain more space for their growing family. The most frequent example of this in North America is urban-to-suburban migration within the same metropolitan area. Finally, many people in North America move when they retire from work. Warm and sunny states with limited tax burdens on retirees, like Florida and Arizona, have traditionally been favorite spots.

Socioeconomic Consequences of Migration

Migration impacts both the areas receiving migrants and the areas that the migrants left. Large numbers of migrants can change the socioeconomic nature of an area. Two examples of this in the United States are Miami, Florida, and Dearborn, Michigan. The culture of Miami and the surrounding area of south Florida changed significantly after the Cuban Revolution when many Cuban refugees immigrated to the area. Dearborn, Michigan, is home to one of the largest Muslim populations in the United States because many immigrants from the Middle East came to the area in the 1920s to work in the automobile industry. As a result, Dearborn and its surrounding communities form a unique cultural landscape.

On the other hand, large-scale emigration can have a dramatic effect on the area that the migrants leave. For instance, a large percentage of men from rural Mexican villages migrate to the United States for work, creating a dearth of men in those villages. The effect is a change in the general workforce and culture of the villages, with women becoming the heads of households. The long-term consequences have not been well studied; however, this situation is a change to the traditional Mexican way of life.

Additional Types of Migration

Intercontinental Migration

Intercontinental migration is the movement of people across an ocean or continent, such as the movement of the Hmong people from Laos and Thailand to the United States. This type of migration usually involves a large sum of money for the migrant, including the cost of the trip as well as establishing oneself in the new location.

Some type of **distance decay** of the former culture typically follows intercontinental migration as people begin to assimilate into the culture in which they are presently living. Although they may still hold on to their native language or religion, the influence of their native culture is not as strong as it was in their original country. This transfer of cultures is called **acculturation**, and it typically occurs over three generations in a given family. The first generation that comes over speaks very little or none of the new country's language. Their children, however, are educated in the new country's educational system and speak two languages. The native tongue is still spoken in the home, but when the children leave for school, they are immersed in the new country's language. The third generation primarily speaks the new country's language and usually knows very little of the primary language. Most German settlers in the United States were assimilated into U.S. culture through this three-step process. The same process continues today with the Hmong migration, among others.

Churches in the United States first began sponsoring Hmong families in the 1970s. These churches would welcome a family into the United States and provide them with their basic needs until they could provide for themselves. Once the families had established themselves in the United States, they sent money back home to Laos and Thailand so that other family members could come to the United States. Eventually, cultural mini-centers developed in cities such as Sacramento, California, and Saint Paul, Minnesota. This is an example of **chain migration**. This type of migration is usually voluntary in nature and functions to reunite families and cultures. It can take many years to bring over a large number of people through chain migration. The first immigrants must establish themselves financially and earn enough money to send back to other family members.

Much of the United States was built on chain migration. Different ethnic groups around the United States, in large and small cities alike, have seen the results of chain migration. Immigrants from countries like Italy and China developed distinctive communities in New York City; Little Italy and Chinatown have become famous among New York City's ethnic neighborhoods. Italians entered the United States at ports in Boston or New York and established themselves in these cultural neighborhoods. Irish people settled in Boston, and Koreans in Los Angeles. It was easier for immigrants to adjust to the United States in areas where people already spoke their language and practiced their religion. Chain migrations continue today all over the world.

Interregional Migration

Another type of migration is **interregional migration,** which is just what it sounds like. This type of migration is usually done within a country's borders, from region to region. This type of migration is usually voluntary as well. Interregional migration should not be confused with **international migration**, which is movement between countries.

Intraregional Migration

Intraregional migration is the movement of people within the same region. The most common example of this form of migration is the move from rural to urban areas. This migration is usually done for economic reasons. People move off the farm and into cities in the hope of finding jobs. Rural-to-urban migration usually takes place in less developed countries, where the fastest rate of urbanization is taking place.

Rural-to-urban migration occurred at a great rate in the United States during the second half of the twentieth century and still continues today. Farmers who cannot make enough to pay their bills are forced to look for employment in urban areas. According to the United States Department of Agriculture Census, the number of U.S. farmers has continued to decline significantly.

However, there has been an urban-to-rural movement recently within sections of more developed countries due to the high living costs in cities. People are moving away from urban areas, into the suburbs and exurbs, to avoid the high costs and property taxes associated with the urban lifestyle.

Cyclic Migration

People also move seasonally, usually for agricultural reasons; this is called **cyclic migration**. Societies that practice pastoral nomadism also practice **transhumance**, the seasonal migration of livestock to areas where food is more available; this sometimes involves moving livestock to higher elevations during the summer to escape the heat in the valleys and to lower elevations during the winter to escape the severe cold of the mountains. Cyclical movement ties in closely with the demographic transition model. As a country moves from an agricultural to an industrial base, urbanization spreads, and reliance on agricultural practices such as transhumance decreases.

Intervening Obstacles

An **intervening obstacle** can adversely affect trade and migration between areas. An intervening obstacle forces individuals to halt and abort their migration plans due to some negative factor, which can range from cultural to physical.

One of the factors that limits migration is the physical environment. Inhospitable weather and unfavorable agricultural conditions have caused people to change their destinations.

Another factor that greatly influences migration success is the distance of travel and the costs associated with it. The most expensive trips today are the ones that cross an ocean, and the same was true during the peak migration period in U.S. history. Despite being a wonderful opportunity to achieve success, the transatlantic journey came at a considerable financial expense.

Other factors that can hinder migration are cultural factors, such as language. During migration to the United States, Eastern Europeans first traveled to the port cities in Western Europe and encountered many scams. They were often talked into paying for their journey by a person who barely spoke their own language and, after doing so, were taken for a ride and dropped off at a foreign port with promise that they were in the United States. This scam made thousands of dollars illegally and cost many immigrants their opportunity to reach the United States.

Additionally, not every person who wants to come into a country is allowed access. Many countries have laws and policies around immigration; one example is quotas, which are limits that governments put on the number of immigrants they allow into their countries. The issue of immigration can be very politically charged, and many governments are in active debates over how to handle the inflow of people who want to move to their countries.

Intervening Opportunities

An **intervening opportunity** is the opposite of an intervening obstacle. An intervening opportunity occurs when a migrant stops and decides to stay at a location along his or her journey because he or she encounters favorable economic opportunities or environmental amenities along the way. An example of an intervening opportunity would be in the case of a person who is moving from Boston and wants to end up in Miami. Along the journey, he sees the coast of North Carolina and enjoys the area so much that he decides to purchase a home there. Although the opportunities available in Florida are good, this person underestimated his enjoyment of the area around North Carolina. Economic opportunities are also available in North Carolina; thus, he decides to make the stay permanent.

Forced Migration

Not all migration is positive or voluntary. Aside from the negative push factors previously discussed, **forced migration** has had a dramatic impact on the western hemisphere. The forced migration of over 15 million Africans to the Americas was one of the most significant components of the Columbian Exchange. By the mid-1600s, thousands of enslaved Africans had been brought across the ocean. The death toll en route was considerable, with as many as half the captives on any one ship dying from disease or brutal mistreatment. Several African societies experienced severe population loss and a drastic change in male-female ratio. The impact of the slave trade on the demographics and ethnicity of the Caribbean and other countries in the western hemisphere cannot be underestimated. Millions of people of African descent are in the United States, the Caribbean, and South America today as a result of slavery. Although many of the enslaved Africans were Christianized or otherwise assimilated by the Europeans, they retained parts of their language and culture. A unique cultural synthesis occurred, as African music, dress, and mannerisms mixed with Spanish and indigenous cultures in the Americas.

Population transfers are another form of involuntary migration; these involve the mass movement of a large group of people from one region to another. It is often a forced process, typically done on the basis of ethnicity or religion. The loss of land, property, and life during population transfers is substantial. One of the most well-known examples in the United States is the forced transfer of the Cherokee Nation along the Trail of Tears from Georgia to Oklahoma; many died along the way from exposure, illness, and starvation. Another example involves ethnic Germans in Europe, after World War II. Ethnic Germans were expelled from many European countries out of fear of them being potential traitors.

Transmigration is the removal of people from one place and their relocation to somewhere else within a country. This is not always done voluntarily. Indonesia is the fourth most populated country in the world. A large percentage of its people live on the island of Java. To ease the resource strain on Java, the government of Indonesia put some of its population on other islands. Opponents of the transmigration argued that the government put minority groups in the fringes of the country to quell separatist movements.

U.S. IMMIGRATION: A CASE STUDY

A case study of immigration throughout U.S. history shows distinct patterns. Historically, the two major entry points into the United States were the ports of Boston and Ellis Island. The port of Ellis Island has been turned into a national park in New York Harbor.

A census, which is a detailed counting of the population, has occurred in the United States every 10 years since 1790. Census results show that the center of population in the United States has shifted from Maryland in 1790 to southern Missouri in 2010. This shift is a direct result of the country's international and interregional migration trends.

Eras of U.S. Immigration

1607 to Early Nineteenth Century

During the early history of the United States, the primary reasons for coming to this country were religious and economic freedom. After the United States gained independence from Great Britain, more and more immigrants came here.

1820s to 1880s

In the late 1800s, immigrants continued to come from Europe, and many immigrants, specifically Chinese, arrived on the West Coast of the United States. They took jobs completing the first transcontinental railroad, working in the difficult, mountainous terrain of the western United States. The railroad eventually united the U.S. coasts for the first time (linking in Promontory Summit, Utah, in 1869).

End of the Nineteenth Century to the Beginning of the Twentieth Century

Immigration into the United States saw one of its peaks during 1900 to 1920. These immigrants came primarily from southern Europe, including Italy, Spain, and Greece, which saw millions of their residents emigrate to the United States.

A major migration within the United States, which often goes unmentioned, is the migration of African Americans from the South to major urban centers in the North during the 1900s. Tens of thousands of African Americans moved into northern cities, such as Chicago and Cleveland. They also moved to the Northeast for employment opportunities in industrial centers.

During the 1930s, immigration declined dramatically, going from almost 1 million people per year to less than 50,000. During World War II, immigration into the United States almost ceased. However, some Jews escaped Europe and came to the United States.

1960s to Present

Since the mid-1960s, immigration to the United States has continued to rise. Whereas during the 1800s, the majority of immigrants came from countries in northern Europe, now immigrants come around the world, especially Latin America but increasingly from Asia. The second peak in immigration occurred at the end of the last century. The greatest number of international immigrants into the United States came from 1980 to 2000.

The issue of immigration continues to be debated and becomes an issue during every major national election. Future trends in immigration will depend heavily upon the policies of the U.S. government.

 **NEXT STEP: PRACTICE**

Go to Rapid Review and Practice Chapter 4 or to your online quizzes on kaptest.com for exam-like practice on this topic.

Haven't registered your book yet? Go to kaptest.com/moreonline to begin.

CHAPTER 12

Cultural Patterns and Processes

LEARNING OBJECTIVES

After studying this chapter, you will be able to:

- Define culture and cultural traits.

- Explain the geographic patterns associated with different expressions of cultural identity.

- Explain how the five themes of geography (region, place, location, human-environment interaction, and movement) influence cultural patterns.

- Describe globalization's impact on cultural interaction.

- Discuss the causes and effects of cultural diffusion over time.

- Explain how geographers use maps and spatial thinking to analyze cultural groups.

THE MEANING OF CULTURE

Culture is often defined as the way of life of a particular people, including their language, religion, food, and music. Although no two cultures are exactly alike, geographers can establish links between cultures and combine them into regions. They can then assess the foundations of culture in the context of individual cultures and compare and contrast these individual cultures. Geographers also look at trends over time to analyze cultural distinctiveness (stability or change) and to determine whether cultures are dying out. Sometimes cultures are threatened by globalization.

Trying to define a specific culture can be difficult. Broad generalizations about a group of people are required to discuss their culture, but not everybody in the group has the same values. Ethnicity and culture are intertwined because much of a particular group's culture is defined by ethnicity, and much of ethnicity embodies the main attributes of a culture. The term *culture*, in and of itself, can take on different meanings. When someone suggests that another person is "cultured," they are not referring to their cultural identity but, rather, to their appreciation of the arts and sciences. Thus, a cultured person may attend symphonies and art festivals. Another use of the term *culture* is to identify a particular group of people defined by demographics (e.g., "teen culture").

Material culture encompasses anything that can be seen on the landscape, including such things as houses, furniture, and musical instruments. The material culture produces what is called the **built environment**, the tangible impact of human beings on the area. **Nonmaterial culture** is anything that makes up culture that cannot be touched. This category includes language, religion, folklore, philosophies, and superstitions. Regionalization is the process by which regions within the same country develop different cultural characteristics. This can range from accents, to food, to such things as folk culture.

Folk culture is the practice of a particular custom by a relatively small group of people in a focused area. The practice of folk customs is part of what makes each area unique and distinguishes peoples. Most folk culture is passed from generation to generation by means of oral history. In some cultures, for example, fathers teach their sons how to harvest crops the way farming has been done for hundreds of years, and mothers teach their daughters how to sew as their mothers taught them.

Stories that are passed from generation to generation are known as folklore. These stories are an important part of a group's overall culture, as they pass on a group's shared values. Folklore can also maintain feelings of nationalism within a group. Bedtime stories are good examples of folklore; they usually involve lessons on how children should behave, and they also express the group's cultural perspective on life.

Sometimes, folklore takes on a life of its own, creating heroes. William Wallace is a heroic figure to the Scottish people. His resistance to the King of England is legendary. Today, William Wallace is memorialized by a statue in Stirling, Scotland, and his story is told in the movie *Braveheart*, with Mel Gibson portraying William Wallace. Although he died in 1305, he is still known as one of the greatest patriots of Scottish history, and his legend has passed from generation to generation for over 700 years.

In the Appalachian Mountain regions of Kentucky and West Virginia, "Jack tales" are often passed from older to younger generations. As their name suggests, Jack tales involve the character Jack and his adventures. A couple of the more famous Jack tales are "Jack and the Three Steers" and "Jack and the Beanstalk."

The opposite of folk culture is popular culture. **Popular culture** is the practice of customs that span several different cultures and may even have a global focus. A folk culture, however, may become part of the popular culture through its own popularity. For example, as Tex-Mex music, also called Tejano music, becomes more common in the United States, it eventually will no longer be considered folk music but will become part of popular culture.

Much of the difference between folk culture and popular culture is determined by the areas in which a culture has influence. Folk culture is practiced in a relatively small area, whereas popular culture may be practiced in a wider area. An example of folk culture is Cajun people in southwestern Louisiana listening to Cajun music. This particular style of music is heard in many areas of the country, yet it is not as prevalent in those areas as in southwestern Louisiana. On the other hand, the continued trend toward a global culture of business attire, involving the wearing of Western-style business suits, is an example of popular culture.

When cultures mingle, a **multicultural** society develops. The United States is a multicultural society due to the influence of migration. Other forces can also spur the creation of a multicultural society. Innovations in transportation and other technologies have allowed products to be shipped to areas around the globe within hours, rather than weeks or months. These developments have increased the opportunity for cultural mingling for millions worldwide.

The study of culture has two contrasting approaches. **Cultural relativism** is the concept that social practices, morality, and ethics are not universal; instead, different cultures have different concepts of right and wrong. This is in contrast to **ethnocentrism**, in which one's own culture is considered paramount and is used as the lens through which to study the rest of the world.

THE CULTURAL LANDSCAPE

In the words of Carl Sauer: "A cultural landscape is fashioned from a natural landscape by a culture group. Culture is the agent, the natural area is the medium. The cultural landscape the result." Sauer, a preeminent human geographer in the late twentieth century, coined the term **cultural landscape** as, first, the interactions of a group in relation to their own cultural practices and, second, the values of a society as reflected through artifacts and architecture. A cultural landscape is different from the **natural landscape**, which deals with the physical Earth and is often associated with the field of physical geography.

One of the best places to observe the cultural landscape is in a city park. City parks exhibit traits of the surrounding landscape and culture. By looking at parks, a person can assess the cultural values of the society.

When analyzing a park, observe the different statues. Whom do the statues represent? What are they made of? Usually, statues provide a look into the history and geography of the area, indicating the past heroes of the community. In many larger cities, the ethnicity of the area will be evident through the public artwork on display in the park. Also, the area around a park will have commercial activities that cater to a specific ethnicity. For example, in the southwestern United States, many grocery stores sell items familiar to most Latin American immigrants, and the parks showcase Latin American artwork.

How the land is used is important as well. Are there large areas for socializing? How many park benches are there? How many trails are located within the park, and are they walkways, bike paths, or horse trails? Some parks allow motorized vehicle access, while others ban all vehicles from the property.

Culture is one of the most fascinating units in geography. Each place is distinct and interesting in its own way. People move for economic, environmental, and political reasons and find themselves in new locations, which have different cultures. How a person adapts to a new culture is called an **adaptive strategy**. In a way, this is how a human adapting to a new cultural landscape they find themselves in.

MUSIC AND CULTURE

Musical styles and lyrics express characteristics of particular cultures. For example, the culture of the U.S. South and Bible Belt values are often expressed in country music, which is centered in Nashville, Tennessee. Another example is folk music, which most geographers can agree is born from oral tradition. Folk songs are passed down from generation to generation, modified as they go. Their lyrics center on a group of people and reflect the values and cycles of their daily lives. Woody Guthrie and Pete Seeger are two examples of artists who sang American folk songs.

One of the best ways to study the listening habits of a group of people is to analyze the radio stations that they listen to. Radio stations often play a particular format of music, anything from hip-hop to country to jazz. A researcher can describe a region based on the number of stations of each type of music within it. Because radio stations are private enterprises, they need to play a style of music that will appeal to the region's populace. If nobody is listening, the radio station will not be able to sell advertising and will quickly go out of business.

> ✔ **AP Expert Note**
>
> **Be able to explain how music is affected by regional characteristics and population movement**
>
> Music genres are affected by the people that live in or move to a region. Polka music reflects areas of notable German immigration. Bluegrass music grew out of the mix of Irish, Scottish, and African American people in the American South. So, music genre and regional populations impact one another. The AP exam will expect you to make connections like this, so be ready to discuss specific subjects like music in relation to broader geography topics.

Country Music

Country music has its roots in the Southern United States. Country music uses guitars and violins, instruments that were brought over from other countries, but the style of music is distinctly American. It has roots in both European folk music and African American blues and jazz. Its pioneers include such folk heroes as Hank Williams and Marty Robbins. This style of music has had a dramatic impact on several regions in the United States.

The foundations of country music are the spiritual songs sung in many Southern churches. Kentucky, Tennessee, West Virginia, and Texas are believed to be the hearths of country music—hence the location of the Grand Ole Opry in Nashville, Tennessee. Deep religious values are often expressed in the old-time country songs and even in many current songs. For example, a fundamental element of the Baptist religion, a belief in being saved through faith, is prevalent in many older country songs.

The term *hillbilly* was once used to describe this new style of music. Because the term was associated with people from Appalachia, where a large percentage of the population lived in poverty, this term quickly acquired a negative connotation. The term *hillbilly music* was replaced with *country music* in the 1940s. Hank Williams is credited with the movement of country music from the South to more national prominence.

Listening to the legends of country music, one begins to appreciate the complexity of the music and its reflection of Southern culture. Hank Williams, Johnny Cash, Merle Haggard, Patsy Cline, Tammy Wynette, and Loretta Lynn all notably contributed to country music. These artists diffused country music to all parts of the world. Huge stars, such as Johnny Cash, frequently sold out shows throughout Europe and in other regions.

The Grand Ole Opry, a legendary country music hall, has seen the greats (including Elvis Presley) play. WSM, one of the pioneering music stations of country music, first broadcast the Grand Ole Opry in 1927. On clear evenings, WSM can be heard in many parts of the United States. The Country Music Hall of Fame is located in Nashville, Tennessee, in part because the Grand Ole Opry is located there.

Bluegrass Music

Bluegrass is a musical style closely associated with country music. It is characterized by such musical instruments as washboards, fiddles, banjos, and even spoons. This style of music has Irish and Scottish roots as well as African American influences. Bluegrass originated in the Appalachian highland regions and extended west to the Ozark Mountains located in southern Missouri and northern Arkansas.

During the 1940s, it first gained popularity in Kentucky thanks to Bill Monroe and his band, the Blue Grass Boys. Kentucky is credited with being one of the hearths of bluegrass music. Two of the most important bluegrass musicians are the banjo players Lester Flatt and Earl Scruggs. Both Flatt and Scruggs have made numerous recordings of bluegrass music, including some with Bill Monroe. Although radio stations that play this style of music are located throughout the United States, they are concentrated in the Appalachian and Ozark Mountains.

Blues Music

Another genre of music that is distinctly American is the blues. Developed from African American roots, it can be traced back to West Africa. It has since been modified by American musicians specializing in different forms of American blues music. The exact origins of American blues are difficult to pin down, as it was transmitted through an oral tradition. However, it can be traced to the Mississippi Delta region, where spirituals and working chants were sung in the cotton fields by sharecroppers. In the 1940s and 1950s, this style of music began to come into its own in the region.

The king of the Delta blues is Robert Johnson, a recluse, about whom very little is known. Johnson recorded several records before dying in 1938 at the young age of 27. He was inducted into the Rock and Roll Hall of Fame in Cleveland, Ohio, and many musicians consider him the grandfather of rock-and-roll music.

Tejano Music

Yet another style of music heard around the country today is called Tex-Mex or Tejano music. It is found primarily in the Southwest. (*Tejano* is Spanish for Texan.) The Tex-Mex culture has a distinctive style of music and food. Neither American nor Mexican, it is a blend of both.

The Tejano musical style uses guitars and mariachi-style bands to play upbeat tunes. The result is high-energy music that has many fans stomping their feet all across the United States. It became more mainstream in the late twentieth century owing in part to the popularity of Selena Quintanilla-Pérez. Known as Selena, she modernized and captured the essence of Tejano music, putting it on the cultural map before her 1995 murder at the age of 23. One of the greatest legends in Tex-Mex music is Flaco Jimenez. Originally from San Antonio, Texas, Jimenez learned to play the accordion from his father. Flaco Jimenez has appeared on both stage and screen.

The increase in number of Spanish-speaking Americans has led to a surge of interest in Latino culture in many areas. Spanish-speaking regions include the Cuban settlements in the Little Havana community in southern Miami, the Mexican neighborhoods in southern California, and many communities in between. *Time* magazine felt that this region was so important, it devoted almost an entire issue to "Amexica." As Latinos continue to increase in number, so will the popularity of Tejano music.

Cajun and Creole Music

Cajun and Creole music stem from south-central Louisiana. Baton Rouge, Lafayette, and other towns in Louisiana are famous for their French heritage. This is because the Acadians (French Canadians) migrated there from southeastern Canada; they developed Cajun music, which was influenced by African American music and other traditions. Creole music was developed by African Americans and was influenced by European musical traditions, among others. Despite their different roots, today the two genres are closely associated. This music is often played by Cajuns and Francophone Creoles in Louisiana.

The instruments used in this music include the accordion, fiddle, and even the washboard. The music is usually upbeat and easy to dance to. People sing in Cajun, which is a dialect of French. Cajun and creole music have influenced the closely related zydeco style of music.

Dewey Balfa is credited with the resurgence of popularity of Cajun music. Balfa played at Cajun music festivals around the country. His music brought attention to the Cajun people and their culture. Also prominent is the group BeauSoleil, which comprises of five artists who have been playing cajun, creole, and zydeco music for more than 30 years.

Polka Music

Another style of music that is associated with a distinct culture is polka music, found in the upper Midwest, especially in North Dakota, South Dakota, Minnesota, Wisconsin, and Michigan. This style of music was brought by immigrants from Scandinavia, Poland, and Germany. A form of dance is associated with polka music. The dance usually involves a two-step pattern that accompanies the upbeat music.

There are different styles of polka music. Traditional polka music began in what is now the Czech Republic, but different versions of it originated in other areas, including Poland and Sweden. The U.S. style of polka evolved thanks to Polish immigrants, especially in Chicago. This music has been called the Chicago push style of polka. The Polka Hall of Fame is located in Chicago, Illinois.

Radio stations tend not to play polka music as their primary format but, rather, in addition to their usual playlists. Most radio stations that play polka are in the north and central United States, correlating with the immigration patterns of Eastern and Northern Europeans. Another major region of polka music is in southern Texas, correlating to German settlement in areas around New Braunfels, just north of San Antonio.

Motown Music

Motown is a style of music named after the city in which it originated. Detroit is often called the "motor city," a name which was shortened to become Motown. This forerunner of modern rock and roll has been credited with a revitalization of urban music in the 1950s and 1960s. Motown is not only the name for a style of music, but also the name of the Detroit-based record label that recorded many musicians. Berry Gordy Jr. established the record label in 1959, and it was an instant success. Gordy sold the Motown record label to Universal Music in 1988.

Motown has been associated not only with music, but also with the integration of cultures in the United States. During the 1950s and early 1960s, the civil rights movement was a major force in American politics and civic life. The music played by African Americans in Detroit caught on in many neighborhoods that were not African American. The appeal of Motown music to all types of people even encouraged an openness to racial integration.

Gordy's first superstar act was a group called the Matadors, who later changed their name to the Miracles. Their lead singer was Smokey Robinson. The Miracles were soon joined by groups like Diana Ross and the Supremes, The Jackson 5, and The Temptations. These groups produced numerous number-one hits on the Billboard charts during the 1960s. Other artists, including Stevie Wonder and Marvin Gaye, got their start with the new record label. Later additions to the Motown label include the group Boyz II Men. The success of the music along with the label has made Motown synonymous with American culture. Along with the antiwar protests of the 1960s, this music is iconic of the decade.

Music of all types has a profound effect on many people, not only in the United States, but around the world. African music is much different from Indian music, which is different from South American music. Many cultures use art and music to describe who they are and where they would like to be in the near and distant future.

FOOD AND CULTURE

Food is a terrific way to understand the concept of folk culture because certain areas have dishes that are distinct to their cuisine. *National Geographic* magazine did a study on food preferences around the world. Many foods from the United States ranked high on the food preference list that was compiled for this study. Hamburgers, hot dogs, fried chicken, french fries, and pizza scored the highest on the food preference list. Just as important were the foods that were not selected. The least popular foods included such delicacies as smoked black whale meat, rappie pie, pinchberry tart jelly, and fried cod tongues. Very few people who took the survey had tried these international foods before, nor were they even willing to.

International Food Cultures

Different food preferences from around the world say a lot about a particular culture. The location of a restaurant relative to a food source may determine the dishes on its menu. For example, China has a geographic "noodle line." North of the noodle line, where more wheat products are grown, noodles are produced and are a daily part of the diet. To the south of the noodle line, where the climate is warmer, rice is grown. Rice served with a sauce and vegetables forms the basic meal.

Much of the world's diet depends upon the agricultural products grown in a certain region. Rice is a staple crop in Asia. Millet is a staple crop in many parts of Africa. Manioc is grown in South America and is used in many dishes in Brazil. However, many cultures have distinct national dishes.

The United Kingdom recently made fish and chips its national dish. In the United Kingdom, the word *chips* refers to fried potatoes. In the United States, fried potatoes are called french fries, and *chips* are potato chips.

In Denmark, sandwiches called smørrebrød are eaten open-faced on one slice of bread. Sandwiches are eaten with forks and knives in Denmark. It is often considered rude to eat a sandwich with your hands.

In Scandinavian countries, fish is a primary food source. Lutefisk is dried codfish soaked in lye and then baked. Many Scandinavians love lutefisk with mashed potatoes and white gravy. Many towns in North Dakota, Minnesota, and Wisconsin still have lutefisk bakes in country churches, and the fish is still served on holidays in the region.

Iceland has many distinctive delicacies, due in part to its location. Fishing is a major industry, and shark is eaten on special occasions. The shark is kept outside to rot. Once the shark is "ripe" enough, it is cut down and served to the waiting diners, who love the taste.

In many parts of East Asia, including China, snake is eaten. The consumption of snake is said to give the human body spirit and energy as well as warming the heart. Szechuan food comes from the Sichuan region in south-central China. This food is known for its spiciness, due to the Szechuan peppercorn plant. One of the most commonly eaten Szechuan dishes in the United States is kung pao chicken.

The blowfish, or *fugu*, is a high-priced delicacy in Japan. Chefs need to take a special course in how to prepare the deadly fish. If cut the wrong way, its toxins will be released into the flesh, killing the eater. The cost of a fugu dish can run as high as $200 per plate.

In the Andes of South America, guinea pigs are considered a delicacy. The guinea pig, called a *cuy*, is fried whole and brought to the consumer in a lifelike stance. *Cuy* is usually consumed for special celebrations such as anniversaries or birthday parties.

In parts of Tanzania, mopane worms are mixed with peanut butter to provide a nutritious, tasty snack. Ants are eaten in Brazil in the Amazon Rainforest. In Australia, many Aborigines eat raw worms for their liquid content in arid regions.

All of the aforementioned dishes are part of folk food. A folk food is attributed to a particular people or a culture. Each of these folk foods is concentrated around a particular hearth or a nodal region. Popular culture, as expressed by food, does not necessarily have a hearth, or it has become so common that the hearth has either been forgotten or become relatively unimportant. For example, the hearth of McDonald's is in Des Plaines, Illinois, but the widespread diffusion of McDonald's has minimized the importance of its hearth. Many people today could not name the hearths of popular fast-food brands because of the pervasiveness of fast food on the landscape.

U.S. Food Cultures

In the United States, there are distinct food regions. This is an example of regionalization, as these cuisines came about thanks to the specific environmental factors and ingredients common to the regions. New England is known for clam chowder. Lobster from Maine southward to Cape Cod is another New England delicacy. The fishing industry was historically vital to both regions. Southern food features fried chicken along with collard greens and peach or cherry cobbler.

One cannot talk about Southern food without mentioning barbecue. In the South, it is considered an art form. Barbecue can be mustard based, ketchup or tomato based, or vinegar based. How the barbecue is served ranges from wet to dry. In wet barbecue, the cook puts sauce directly onto the meat, while dry barbecue calls for rubbing spices into the meat before cooking, rather than using sauce. People swear by one or the other method, and loyalties to a particular style run deep. Also, some places specialize in pork while others specialize in beef barbecue. Smoked barbecue involves smoking the meat in cooking houses for upward of 24 hours.

Barbecue arose from Southern states relying heavily on pigs for meat during the eighteenth century. Pigs were allowed to roam free in the woods because it was a cheap, low-maintenance way for the animals to fatten themselves. Cattle ranching did not make economic sense in the South and took far longer to produce meat.

To suggest that any particular area has the greatest barbecue would be blasphemy to many barbecue connoisseurs. Texas and South Carolina each claim to have the best barbecue of any U.S. region. People will drive for many miles to get the taste of specific styles of barbecue in the Hill Country, Dallas, and western sections of Texas. The upper Midwestern regions also have barbecue establishments. Many of these establishments were started by immigrants from the South. Barbecue festivals are held around the United States throughout the year. During these festivals, many establishments enter their barbecue sauces for prizes and compete for buyers. The secret recipes of barbecue sauces are jealously protected.

Barbecue is also popular around the world, from Mongolia to Australia to South Africa. Each area has its own methods of preparing the meat, and the types of meat vary greatly. In Central Asia, sheep, also known as mutton, is often eaten. Many regions around the world even barbecue seafood products.

SPORTS AND CULTURE

The spread of the U.S. sports baseball and basketball around the world is a form of hierarchical diffusion. Many Americans have become dismayed at the lack of success of U.S. teams in international play. Some suggest that the play of the United States has not gotten worse; rather, the play of the rest of the world has improved. The Dominican Republic and Venezuela have a proud tradition of producing many Major League Baseball players. Children in these regions grow up playing the sport from a very young age. Japan and Korea have also created a culture of baseball. In fact, while many Japanese players have come to the United States to play, many major league players have left the United States to play professional baseball in Japan and Korea.

The world's most popular sport is soccer. Called *football* in most areas of the world, it attracts the fervent loyalty of its fans. The history of soccer dates back over 2,000 years in China and Europe, when people began to play games that involved kicking a sphere with their feet. Soccer diffused from the United Kingdom eastward, into mainland Europe, as far as Russia. Most historians credit the British with the modern rules of the game. The size of the field as we know it today, with one goal on each side, was established in the sixteenth century.

Today, one of the governing bodies of soccer is FIFA (Federation Internationale de Football Association), which oversees the World Cup. The World Cup is played every four years in a different part of the world. The tournament brings together countries in one of the most-watched televised sporting events on the planet.

Soccer has a sensational following in many countries. The United Kingdom, in particular, is known for its violent soccer hooligans: fans who incite violence at soccer matches, often through hurling racial or religious epithets against opposing players and fans. FIFA has forced games to be played in empty stadiums as a punishment for hooliganism. Many fans' devotion to soccer cannot be overstated. Some stadiums in Latin America can seat over 100,000 fans. Many people around the world live and breathe the results of their local club teams as well as their national teams.

ARCHITECTURE AND CULTURE

The architecture of residential, commercial, and spiritual structures varies greatly around the world. Houses are the dominant structures in many areas and are built in many different shapes and sizes. Houses are the primary structure for the family unit on which societies are based, and the home can be considered the foundation of culture.

Most folk housing is constructed with local materials, which are in large part determined by the climate of the area. Many traditional huts in Africa are constructed with the grasses and the wood that are available nearby. Adobe, bricks made out of mud, is used in many Latin American countries where lumber-quality wood is scarce. Many U.S. houses are built with wood, which is abundantly available.

In Mongolia, *gers* (also called yurts) are the primary form of housing for nomadic hunters. *Gers* are easily mobile. They are frequently round and measure 20 to 30 feet in diameter. Camels and other pack animals haul the *gers* from location to location as the nomads move their herds across the plains.

In the American Indian cultures of the Great Plains, the teepee was the predominant style of housing. Because these tribes had a mobile culture, they needed a housing style that could be moved readily. A frame of sticks was used to support the covering, which was made of stitched hides. An opening at the top of the teepee allowed for smoke from a fire to escape. Early European settlers on the Great Plains built houses from sod because of a lack of wood. Many of these structures were below the surface of the earth. Dirt would be piled into a mound and grass planted or sod placed on top of the mound to protect the structure from erosion and to prevent leaks. Evidence of these sod houses is still preserved in the Great Plains region.

Different regions emphasize different parts of the house. In Islamic households, Muslims have a special wall that faces Mecca. Islam requires them to pray facing Mecca five times a day. In many other cultures, doors into the house must face certain directions for either religious or other cultural reasons. In many homes in China, feng shui properties are extremely important. These include a front door facing East, a curved walkway leading up to the house, and a backyard larger than the front yard, among other factors.

Noted geographer Fred Kniffen has identified three distinct regions of folk housing types in the United States today. The three styles include the New England–style house, the Middle Atlantic–style house, and the Lower Chesapeake–style house. Within the New England style, Kniffen identified four major housing types: the saltbox, the two-chimney, the Cape Cod, and the front gable and wing styles. All four of these homes can be seen in New England today as well as in the north and central United States owing to migration. The Middle Atlantic housing style is distinguished by what is called an "I" house. The "I" house is characterized by a two-story structure with gables on either end. From the Middle Atlantic region, this housing style moved southward along the Appalachian Mountains and then westward into the south-central states. The lower Chesapeake style of house usually has two stories with chimneys located on both sides. From the lower Chesapeake Bay, this housing type diffused south along the Atlantic coast.

The township and range patterns established by early settlers dominate the landscape in the Midwest and Great Plains regions, and this is still evident when one flies over the United States. Long rows of roads are laid out on the flat landscape in square or rectangular patterns. This, along with the housing styles based on British and early American influences, is called the Anglo-American landscape.

A folk landscape is what people perceive the landscape to be based on their cultural notions of an area. One of the great folk landscapes in the United States is the Wild West, perceived as a rugged environment where settlers took the law into their own hands. The image of cowboys herding cattle and sleeping beneath the stars has a quality of Americana to it. In reality, the landscape of the Western frontier was anything but romantic, requiring long hours of hard work every day. When reality clashed with perception, many settlers turned around and went back to the urban areas on the East Coast.

In much of the United States, architecture is relatively new in comparison to that of the rest of the world. Part of the U.S. culture is to replace the old with the new. In European culture, on the other hand, tradition is prized, and buildings are on average much older. In areas of Copenhagen, for instance, some houses are over 500 years old. The traditional architecture of an area is the style of building that was typical when that area was being established.

Today, housing styles are often very similar around the United States. The increase of housing developments means that construction companies usually build similar types and styles of houses, letting buyers make minor choices about the room layout and finishing touches of new homes. This means a more uniform landscape around the United States.

LANGUAGE AND CULTURE

High-Yield

Language is one of the most important aspects of culture. Very few things tie a group together quite like a common language. Language can unify or divide whole nations. But what exactly is language? It is the ability to communicate with others orally and/or in writing when both parties agree on comprehension.

There is a saying that language is a dialect with an army behind it. In some cases, this is true. The majority of a country's population can wield its political power to ensure the widespread adoption of its language. The imposition of a dominant language has been used to enforce political unity. For example, the people of France did not always speak French as their primary language. Likewise, many independence movements have been fueled partially by a group's desire to use its own language rather than the tongue of its conqueror.

A **monolingual country** has only one official language, in which all government business is conducted. A **multilingual country** has more than one official language. Switzerland is an example of a multilingual country with four official languages: German, French, Italian, and Romansh.

Current estimates are that over 7,000 languages are spoken in the world today. Most of these are spoken by remote tribes, many by only a few dozen people. The majority of these languages diffused through colonization or relocation diffusion. Another way in which these languages were diffused was through trade.

Language makes traveling internationally all the more interesting; it is challenging to communicate with somebody who does not speak your language, but it can be exhilarating. The United States is notorious for teaching students only one language in school, although some colleges require students to have taken a foreign language while in high school. In contrast, European countries sometimes teach students four or more languages. This is an example of geography at work. Many European countries are about the size of a U.S. state, and there is far more language diversity in Europe than in the whole of the Americas, where English, French, and Spanish dominate as the major national languages.

Lingua Franca

Although the United States does not have an official language, the overwhelming majority of its citizens speak English. English has become the most widespread lingua franca in the world thanks to the United States and the former British Empire. A **lingua franca** is a language used as a common tongue, often to smoothly conduct business, among people who speak various languages.

For example, all airline pilots in the world must communicate in English. If an Angolan pilot is flying into a Bangladesh airport, that pilot must communicate in English, as must the control tower staff. In addition, many international industries prefer to use English as the language of business, publishing their professional brochures in English and insisting that their employees speak English.

The more influential a country's economy is, the more its language is used in worldwide commerce. As China is gaining a greater foothold in the global economy, the importance of learning Mandarin Chinese has increased. In many parts of Southeast Asia, Mandarin Chinese is becoming a lingua franca. In many areas of East Africa, Swahili is the lingua franca. Because business culture is becoming more global, the ability to communicate in another language is gaining increasing status and importance. Learning a new language is an important step in what is called an adaptive strategy. It makes the communication process much easier when entering another language region. Spanish and, increasingly, Mandarin Chinese are commonly taught in U.S. schools today.

The acquisition of a language involves several different skills. The first skill is the ability to speak and sound out the words. For many Westerners, the acquisition of Asian languages is difficult. In Mandarin Chinese, for example, the sound intonations are different than in English. The second skill is the ability to write the symbols that are associated with each sound or meaning. The third major skill is comprehension, mostly through vocabulary acquisition. Much of the culture of a non-oral society is expressed in its literature, which plays an important part in the transfer of culture to future generations.

Linguistic Divisions within States

Several countries are divided by language barriers. Belgium is less united than it might be because people in the Flanders region in the north speak Flemish while people in the south speak French. The demarcation lies on an east/west axis near the capital of Brussels. Over 800 languages are spoken within the borders of India, posing a barrier to developing unity. The island of Papua New Guinea is said to have over 1,000 languages; many of these are spoken by indigenous groups who have rarely, if ever, seen people from outside their villages.

A country that has seen conflict over linguistic identity is Canada, where the French-speaking province of Québec has tried to secede several times. Canada is officially bilingual; both French and English are languages of business and government. French Canadians have an accent that is different from that of people in France. By law, products sold in Canada must include directions or instructions in both English and French.

Dialects

A **dialect** is a form of a language that is unique in sound, speed, syntax (the grammatical arrangement of a language), and vocabulary. Dialects can often be difficult to understand, depending on how far they've diverged from the listener's speech. Dialects in the United States include the northeastern accent, the Southern accent, the Midwestern accent, the Cajun accent, and accents that are based on age. Modern mass communication has led to a flattening of accents and some dialects, as television and movies offer a model for a standardized way of speaking.

An **isogloss** is the boundary of a dialect. Isoglosses can be difficult to determine because patterns of speech vary among members of the same groups of people. Geographers or linguistic experts interview people of different regions to determine speech patterns, including listening to how people pronounce different words. In the North, *you guys* is often used to mean "a group of people." In Appalachia, *you'uns* is used in the same way; in the South, the word is *y'all*. The boundary lines for each of these units of speech are established through an isogloss.

The Northeastern dialect is evident in the city of Boston as well as other parts of New England. One of its major characteristics is the elimination of the sound of the letter *r* when a short *a* precedes it. The letter *a* is held out with an "aaah" sound, so for example, *party* becomes "*pahty*." The Southern dialect involves sustaining vowels. It can be broken down further by various regions of the South; it is different in Mississippi, Texas, and North and South Carolina. The Upper Midwestern accent or dialect seems to love the letter *o*. The long *o* sound is sustained in many words and pronounced very distinctly. Some Minnesotans pronounce their state with a *d* instead of a *t*: *Minnesoda*. Also, the *o* syllable is held longer and stressed more than any other part of the word.

Dialects can also be computer generated. New technologies, such as global positioning systems in automobiles, have the ability to talk, taking the driver to a destination one turn at a time. The programming of these voices has a lot of research behind it. The voice needs to be clear, and its inflection and tone need to be soothing, not irritating. These computer-generated dialects have their speed, vocabulary, spelling, pronunciation, and syntax programmed for the ease of the listener.

There are also different dialects of English around the world. "BBC British" pronunciation (spoken by announcers on British Broadcasting Corporation television and radio news programs) is the most recognized in the world. Many Europeans, Africans, and Asians who study English are taught the British style of English. However, Australia and South Africa have distinct dialects of English, as does the United States.

There are several reasons for the differences between the American and the British versions of the language. One is the distance between the two countries, which caused the two versions of the language to evolve separately over the centuries. New words were created in the new location to describe things not encountered in the old area (e.g., *canoe* and *chipmunk*). Also, an important event in regard to the development of American English was the creation of an American dictionary by Noah Webster in 1828. This helped standardize different spellings and word choices.

In Britain, the word *mom* is spelled *mum*. A *loo* refers to a bathroom. You wait in a *queue*, not a line. You would take the *lift* to your hotel room instead of the elevator. *Pants* refers to underwear in many parts of the United Kingdom, whereas in the United States, it simply refers to clothes that you wear on your legs. Even within the United Kingdom, there are different dialects. For example, in George Bernard Shaw's *Pygmalion* (filmed as *My Fair Lady*), Eliza Doolittle demonstrates the Cockney accent of eastern London. This section of London has long been considered one of the poorer areas of the city, and thus the accent has a low-status connotation. There are also Scottish, Irish, and Welsh dialects.

English itself has changed over the centuries. Shakespeare's plays and the King James Bible may be difficult for modern readers to decipher. New words are constantly being added because of new inventions and innovations.

Pidgin, Trade, and Creole Languages

In many cases, when cultures collide, languages mix. A mixture of languages is known as a **pidgin language**. Pidgin languages are often very elementary in grammar and vocabulary but are none-theless useful, allowing trade to occur. Sometimes a pidgin language becomes a new language altogether.

When the first European settlers came to North America, they encountered American Indian soci-eties, and the result was the creation of a **trade language**. A trade language is a made-up language that is used by people who want to trade. Each party learns the modified language to communicate with the other and conduct trade. Instead of learning the dialects of the multiple American Indian languages, the Europeans could learn the modified trade language. Likewise, American Indians did not have to learn English, French, Spanish, and Portuguese.

The Cajun language was created by mixing English and French. The traditional Cajun dialect may be incomprehensible to either an English speaker or a French speaker. Likewise, Spanglish often uses Spanish and English words within the same sentence.

A **creole language** is a stable language resulting from the blend of two or more languages that often does not include features of either. In Haiti, people speak a creole language that is a blend of African languages with French. The result is a broader vocabulary as well as a language that is native to Haiti.

> ✔ **AP Expert Note**
>
> **Be sure to review language key terms**
>
> Key terms such as *dialect, syntax, isogloss, pidgin,* and *creole* can be confusing at first glance. However, they and other key terms listed in this section will be important on the AP Human Geography exam. Being able to clearly define what each key term means, including examples related to that term, will help set you up for success.

Official Languages

An **official language** is a language in which all government business is conducted. Some countries have more than one official language. Official languages are hotly debated in many countries. If your language is not one of your country's official languages, you may fear that your language will go extinct, meaning that you will lose an irreplaceable part of your cultural heritage.

There has been a lot of talk in the United States about making English the official language. Pro-ponents suggest that having an official language will save money because government forms, ballots, and so on will need to be printed in only one language instead of the dozens of languages currently used. Proponents also say that they are trying to preserve the American culture. The proponents of having an official language argue that anybody has the right to speak any language they want at home, but when dealing with federal, state, and local governments, communication should be done in English. Some individual states in the United States have adopted English as their official language.

Opponents of establishing an official language suggest that by having an official language, the United States would lose an integral part of its culture. They argue that the United States was built upon diversity of language and culture. Also, by mandating the use of a particular language, opponents suggest that we are discriminating against those who cannot speak English.

In the 2001 Supreme Court case of *Sandoval v. Alabama*, Sandoval sued the state of Alabama, insisting that she had the right to take her driver's license test in Spanish. The court, by a five-to-four margin, voted that Sandoval did not have the right to take the test in Spanish. Even though the United States does not have an official language, this court case set a precedent for enforcing homogeneity of language and, therefore, culture.

This type of debate over issues such as an official language can cause cultural conflicts within a community. While some people see a policy as preserving culture and national unity, others see it as stifling diversity within a region.

Linguistic Diversity and Extinction

Having everyone speak the same language is important to maintaining a unified identity within a state's borders. However, learning more than one language gives an individual more opportunity for cultural and economic success. The learning of more languages is known as **linguistic diversity**. Linguistic diversity can operate on both a large and a small scale. When a society speaks more than one language, linguistic diversity can be seen as a problem because it can hinder unification. However, when a person speaks more than one language, she has linguistic diversity, making her more marketable in the global economy and giving her access to a wider range of cultural experiences.

On a global scale, there is a gradual decline of linguistic diversity. Within the next century, the number of languages, currently about 7,000, is expected to decrease by between 50 and 90 percent. Young people usually leave isolated villages to obtain work in urban areas, where the dominant language is spoken. Eventually, only the elderly speak a language, and when they die, they take the language with them. This process is called language extinction. Recent languages that have gone extinct include Livonian (Latvia), Pazeh, (Taiwan) and Eyak (Alaska). The result will be a world that is dominated by megalanguages, such as Mandarin Chinese, English, Spanish, and Hindi. The growth of the Internet is one factor accelerating language extinction. Because megalanguages like English are used by hundreds of millions of Internet users, people wishing to access most online content are required to use it. The more time users spend partaking of English-language online content, the less time and attention they will devote to content created in their own language, further decreasing its prominence.

Language Families

Language families are groups of languages organized by their common heritage. The result is the language tree, which demonstrates how different languages and linguistic groups are related to each other. Language subfamilies are smaller groups of languages within a language family. The subfamily of West Germanic languages includes present-day German as well as English. The Northern Germanic language subfamily includes the Scandinavian languages of Danish, Swedish, Norwegian, and Icelandic. It also includes the Gothic language, now extinct, spoken by the Goths in Germany during the fourth through sixth centuries. Danes and Swedes, along with other Scandinavians, can generally understand each other because they are in the same language subfamily.

The term *Romance language* comes from the word *Roman*. These languages descended from the Latin spoken in the Roman Empire and spread by Roman soldiers across much of southern Europe. Italian, Spanish, French, Catalan, Romanian, and Portuguese are all Romance languages spoken today. They form a subfamily branch within the Indo-European language family.

Language groups are people whose languages are descended from a common tongue. For example, most people in France and Spain belong to the same language group, because both French and Spanish are Romance languages. In Scandinavia, the populations can understand each other with relative ease because their languages are all part of the Northern Germanic subfamily. Swedish, Danish, Norwegian, and, to a lesser extent, Icelandic people can comprehend each other relatively well. The word structure, vocabulary, and pronunciation are similar enough to allow people to decipher meaning from ordinary sentences.

The Indo-European Language Family

The Indo-European language family, which includes English, is the largest language family in the world. It includes the Greek languages of Aeolic, Ionic, and Doric as well as the Asian languages of Farsi, Bengali, and Hindi. Farsi is spoken primarily in Iran, Hindi is the dominant language of India, and Bengali is the language of Bangladesh. Of the top 10 languages spoken in the world today, 7 are descendants of the Indo-European language family. Some of these languages are used throughout most of the world because of colonialism.

The Sino-Tibetan Language Family

One of the other major language families is the Sino-Tibetan language family. Upward of 20 percent of the world's population speaks a Sino-Tibetan language. The Sino-Tibetan language family includes the most widely spoken language in the world: Mandarin Chinese. Sometimes called Han Chinese, it is spoken by just over a billion people. Although the majority of the people who speak Mandarin Chinese are located in mainland China, Singapore has large areas where Mandarin Chinese is spoken. Other languages in the Sino-Tibetan language family include Thai, Cantonese, and Burmese.

Like the United States, China possesses numerous dialects. About 75 percent of Chinese people speak Mandarin Chinese. Cantonese is another form of Chinese. Cantonese and Mandarin Chinese are like the Scandinavian languages; speakers of one can sometimes understand speakers of the other, but different words and sounds make comprehension difficult.

Language can become a political, hot-button issue. The issue of mutual comprehension can be difficult to determine. Even though Danish, Swedish, and Norwegian are somewhat mutually intelligible, they are considered different languages because of nationalist forces in each country.

There are even different dialects within the urban areas of China. For example, people in Shanghai speak a unique dialect. Many minority groups in the western sections of the country speak other Sino-Tibetan languages, such as Hakka, Min, Wu, and Xiang. Most of these minority groups are nomadic herders, and their populations are relatively small. Some Muslims in the remote western regions speak Arabic, which is not a Sino-Tibetan language. The national government of China is now embracing Mandarin as the official language to unify the country.

The Afro-Asiatic Language Family

Another language family with many language groups is the Afro-Asiatic family. Many of these languages are spoken in northern Africa. Its most common language is Arabic, which is found in North Africa and the Middle East. Arabic is part of the Semitic language subgroup. Other languages within the Afro-Asiatic language family are Hebrew, Somali, and Berber. The Berber languages are spoken primarily in Morocco and Algeria.

The Niger-Congo Language Family

The Niger-Congo language family consists of the languages found in southern Africa, including one of the dominant languages in the area, Swahili. Zulu, spoken in South Africa, is also a part of the Niger-Congo language family. Many of the Niger-Congo languages are spoken by only a small part of the population. Over 10 million people speak Zulu as their primary language, and 5 million people speak Swahili as their primary language. However, Swahili is a lingua franca in East Africa.

Origins of Language Families

Most historians and geographers agree that the hearth of human settlement was in present-day Iraq. The Babylonian Empire began in the Middle East and moved outward. Today's language families originated from prehistoric language families, including the Sino-Caucasian, Nostratic, and Austric language families. The Sino-Caucasian language family was the forerunner to today's Sino-Tibetan language family. From the Nostratic language family come today's Dravidian, Altaic, Uralic, Afro-Asiatic, and Indo-European families. From the Austric language family came the Austronesian language family, spoken today on many islands in the South Pacific. Also, the Austro-Asiatic languages, of which the largest is Vietnamese, descended from the Austric language family.

The Indo-European language family descends from something known as the Proto-Indo-European (PIE) language. The most widely accepted theory is that a steppe people who lived north of the Black Sea spread Proto-Indo-European as their population diffused throughout Europe and Asia. The domestication of the horse, which occurred in the same area as PIE, is believed to have helped spread Proto-Indo-European.

Languages and the Landscape

Languages are a distinguishing feature on the landscape. Different place names are often indicative of the people or cultures that live there. When looking at a map of Québec, one immediately sees the impact of French colonization in the toponyms. The same holds true of areas around the border between the United States and Mexico and throughout California, which reflect Spanish influence. For example, *Los Angeles* means "the angels."

In Tennessee, the term *knob* is used to refer to a hill. Several towns, such as Pilot Knob and Orchard Knob, are named after hills. *Hollow* is another regional topographic term. A hollow is a small valley. Sleepy Hollow in New York was made famous by Washington Irving's 1819 short story "The Legend of Sleepy Hollow." The word *bayou* refers to swamp-like wetlands in Louisiana and Texas. Phelps Bayou and Routh Bayou are just two place names that include this term.

In northern areas of the United States, there is a tendency, inherited from New England migrants, to name places relative to a previous settlement point. The four cardinal directions (east, north, west, and south) are put in front of town names to describe their location with respect to a larger urban area. South Saint Paul and West Saint Paul are two suburbs of Saint Paul, Minnesota. Interestingly enough, West Saint Paul is located south of Saint Paul. The term *west* was given to describe the river traffic on the Mississippi River. Anything on the left of a boat traveling northward was "west," and anything to the right of the boat was "east." In Saint Paul, the river turns, and the left side of the river for a boat traveling upriver is to the south; however, the term *west* stuck.

Many U.S. places are named after the American Indian tribes that were located in the area prior to European settlement. Almost half of the 50 states have names derived from American Indian words. For example, Kentucky is named after the Iroquois word for "land of tomorrow." Minnesota comes from Lakota and means "sky-tinted water." Utah is named after the Ute tribe, with *Ute* meaning "people of the mountains."

RELIGION AND CULTURE

Religion is a value system based on belief in a spiritual or divine aspect of the world. The variety of religions and religious practices across the globe is a major aspect of cultural geography. Geographers have a particular interest in the distribution of different religions around the world throughout history, as religion influences people's architecture, beliefs, traditions, and actions. Major religions have a daily impact on the lives of billions of people, whether or not they are religious; for example, religious architecture affects the landscape.

Religion often determines behavioral constraints in a society. Societies set up laws and courts that may have historical connections to religion but may or may not be separate from any established faith. Most countries, however, have a cultural set of morals that people agree to, regardless of religion, which determines acceptable behavior.

Religious Structure

High-Yield

In all religions, faith is present. **Faith** is the belief in things that cannot be seen or be proven. **Fundamentalism** is based on a literal interpretation of the basic principles of a religion. It urges strict behavioral guidelines to comply with those principles. According to many fundamentalist traditions, failure to follow such rules usually means less likelihood one will enjoy the benefits of the afterlife.

Two main characteristics are used to classify religions. The first is whether the religion is monotheistic or polytheistic. Followers of **monotheistic** religions believe in only one god, while those of **polytheistic** religions believe in multiple gods. The second characteristic concerns how worshipers enter the faith. In **ethnic religions**, a person is born into the faith, and little to no effort is put forth to convert others to the religion. This is the opposite of a **universalizing religion**, whose members actively try to convert others. Another name for a universalizing religion is a proselytic faith.

Usually, but not always, universalizing religions are larger than ethnic religions because of their proselytizing activity. Judaism is an ethnic religion with around 14 million followers. The largest universalizing religions are far more widespread. Christianity has around 2.3 billion followers, which is about a third of the global population. Islam has about 1.8 billion followers and is the fastest growing religion globally. However, Hinduism is a notable exception; this ethnic religion has over a billion followers, mainly located on the Indian subcontinent.

People who do not believe in any god or god-like figure are called **atheists**. Sometimes atheists go by the term *secularist*, even though it is a distinct term with its own meaning. Properly speaking, a **secularist** is a person who wants to separate religion from all other aspects of society, including government and other social institutions such as marriage. **Jainism** is a religion that is sometimes considered a form of atheism, as it disavows the existence of god or gods, but followers do venerate enlightened individuals who have escaped from the cycle of death and rebirth.

There are five primary religions in the world today. These religions have their foundations in one of two places. Both Buddhism and Hinduism began in India. Christianity and Islam trace many fundamental tenets to Judaism, and all three of these faiths began in the Middle East or Southwest Asia.

✔ **AP Expert Note**

Be able to compare and contrast world religions

Is the religion monotheistic or polytheistic? Is it an ethnic or universalizing faith? Does it have roots in other religions? Is it still widely practiced? For the AP exam, be prepared to compare and contrast various religions based on these types of fundamental principles.

Christianity

Christianity is the world's largest religion, with well over two billion followers. There are three main branches of Christianity: Roman Catholic, Protestant, and Eastern Orthodox. Roman Catholicism is mainly found throughout Western and Southern Europe, the Americas, and parts of Central and East Africa. Various Protestant denominations are found in northern Europe, the United States, Southern Africa, and parts of East Asia. Eastern Orthodox Christianity is practiced mainly in Eastern Europe, Russia, Central Asia, and parts of the Middle East.

Architecture

The religious architecture of Christianity is centers on the cross, which is usually located somewhere within the primary structure of worship, the church. The steeple of the church extends to the heavens to symbolize a reaching toward God. The cross is often located at the top of the steeple to signify God in the heavens.

In the Middle Ages in Europe, churches were built with great splendor, and at great expense. Many of these churches are still standing today; England's Canterbury Cathedral is one such, and the Cathedral of Notre Dame in Paris, under reconstruction after a serious fire, is another. Throughout Europe, the church was built in the center of town, and homes were built around it. Communities saw the church not only as their religious center but also as a social center. Likewise, in many communities today in the United States, churches are as much social spaces as places of religious significance.

Who leads the church varies by denomination. The head of the Roman Catholic Church is the pope; this hierarchy also includes cardinals, bishops, and priests. The Orthodox Church is governed by regional patriarchs. For Protestants, the church is run in a more decentralized manner; in faiths with many followers a conference of clergy similar to a legislature typically makes decisions for the church as a whole.

Foundational Beliefs

The foundation of the Christian religion is the life of Jesus Christ, who, according to the Bible, was crucified on a cross for the sake of humanity. He took on the sins of humanity (or all Christians, or Christians who meet certain criteria; different denominations offer different interpretations) when he died and was subsequently resurrected. In some denominations, all humans are created evil and their only hope of salvation is a belief in Jesus Christ. Other denominations believe that new-born babies are without sin and offer hope of salvation through good works and repentance in this life.

The holy book of Christianity is the Bible. The Bible is composed of two distinct sections: the Old Testament and the New Testament. The Old Testament is based on the experiences of the Israelites and follows the lives of Moses, Abraham, David, and other leaders prophesying the coming of the Savior, whom Christians believe to be Jesus Christ. The New Testament describes the life of Jesus Christ and the foundations of the new faith.

Most Christians believe in the existence of the Holy Trinity: God the Father, Jesus the Son, and the Holy Spirit. These three distinct aspects share a common essence, forming a singular God. However, some groups, such as Jehovah's Witnesses and Mormons, disagree on this issue.

Distribution and Diffusion

One justification for colonialism was the opportunity to convert "unsaved" populations outside of Europe. In almost all of the areas that Europeans colonized, they brought their religion with them. Christian missionaries from a variety of denominations are still found all over the world today, in areas both urban and remote. Because of these missionaries, Christianity is now growing fastest in Africa and Asia.

In the first century C.E., many evangelists migrated (relocation diffusion) throughout the Roman Empire, spreading the teachings of Christ. During early Christian times, people would often spread the teachings from neighbor to neighbor (contagious diffusion). In the early fourth century C.E., the Roman emperor Constantine supposedly converted to Christianity on his deathbed. This allowed for the diffusion of the religion throughout the empire (hierarchical diffusion). During the age of exploration (early 1400s through 1600s), many Christian missionaries spread the religion and converted indigenous populations all over the world. Through the combination of these different forms of diffusion, Christianity has become the most widely distributed religion on Earth.

Denominations

Denominations are branches of a religion that differ on specific aspects of the principles of the religion. The largest denomination of Christianity is the Roman Catholic Church. Over 1.2 billion people are professed Roman Catholics, making this the largest denomination of any religion in the world. It is also Christianity's oldest denomination. It is based in Vatican City, where the Pope resides. Catholics believe that Jesus Christ founded their denomination in an event known as the Pentecost. Their tradition holds that Saint Peter was the first Pope.

Eastern Orthodox Christianity and Roman Catholicism broke off from one another in the Great Schism of 1054. The split reflected a growing cultural division between Latin-speaking Western Europe and the Greek-speaking East. Eastern Orthodoxy is the third-largest Christian denomination with over a quarter billion followers. It has no single authority figure. Instead, a council of high-ranking bishops (patriarchs) responds to issues. Eastern Orthodox churches hold that they maintain an unbroken tradition dating back to the founding of Christianity by Jesus Christ.

During the Protestant Reformation, Martin Luther developed the idea of having a personal relationship with Jesus Christ, instead of communicating with God through priests and the hierarchy of the Roman Catholic Church. He posted his *95 Theses* upon a church door in Germany in 1517, launching the Protestant movement (named for "protesting" against the Catholic Church). Luther created the Lutheran Church in northern Europe. Other Protestant denominations have since branched off: there are Baptists, Presbyterians, Methodists, and many more. Today, just over 900 million people are professed Protestants.

However, not every denomination of Christianity falls cleanly into one of those three branches. Mormonism, also known as the Church of Jesus Christ of Latter-day Saints, is a nontrinitarian denomination, which means that followers disagree with the doctrine of the Holy Trinity. Founded by Joseph Smith in 1830, Mormonism is the dominant religion in Utah and other parts of the American West. The Book of Mormon is the fundamental book in the religion. Mormons believe that the Book of Mormon, in addition to the Old and New Testaments, contains the teachings of God. The Book of Mormon is considered sacred to Mormons but not to other Christians.

All this has made an indelible mark on the U.S. landscape. The South is dominated by the Southern Baptists, Methodists are most prevalent in the midsections of the country, and Lutherans dominate the northern sections. The Roman Catholic Church has a strong foothold in New England, southern Louisiana, and the Southwest. Eastern Orthodox churches are a small and scattered U.S. minority but have a notable presence in Alaska. Utah and other parts of the West are heavily Mormon.

Islam

The second-largest religion in the world today is **Islam**. The followers of Islam are called Muslims. The Muslim population is approaching two billion people, and the majority live in an arc stretching from North Africa to the Middle East, through Central Asia and into Southeast Asia. Members can also be found in East Africa thanks to Islam's spread there via trade routes.

Islam is a universalizing, monotheistic religion. It shares a common heritage with the Jewish and Christian religions. For Muslims, Abraham holds spiritual significance, and Jesus Christ was another prophet but not the Son of God. Their primary prophet is Muhammad, who lived in the sixth century C.E. According to Islamic tradition, he received divine revelations from Allah (God). These revelations were later written down by his followers and compiled into the Koran (Quran).

Architecture

Islamic religious architecture centers on the mosque, which is also the community's focal point. Many mosques have several minarets, which extend from the mosque's sides and reach up to Allah. The minaret is usually one of the tallest structures in an Islamic community. The vertical nature of the minaret represents the relationship between Heaven and Earth. The leader of the mosque is called an imam. The imam leads prayers and is in charge of an individual mosque.

Foundational Beliefs

There are five fundamental principles in Islam, sometimes called the five pillars of Islam.

1. There is no god but Allah. Muhammad is the messenger of God (shahadah).
2. Prayer must be done five times daily facing the city of Mecca (salah).
3. Taxes must be paid directly to the poor and needy or to the mosque (zakat).
4. One must fast during Ramadan (sawm).
5. One must make a pilgrimage to Mecca once during one's life (hajj).

The profession of Allah as being the one and true god is taken by all Muslims upon acceptance of the faith. It means more to devout Muslims than anything else in life. A Muslim's passion for religion should dominate every aspect of life. When one accepts the creed of Allah, or the shahadah, one has officially become a Muslim and then needs to follow the other four pillars of Islam.

The salah must be prayed five times daily: at dawn, in the early afternoon, in the late afternoon, just after the sun has set, and during the nighttime hours. These prayers must face the Ka'aba, which is the stone in the center of the primary mosque in Mecca. Praying five times a day helps Muslims focus on Allah throughout the day, no matter how busy their lives may be. Prayer is such an essential part of Muslim life that it affects even nonreligious architecture; for example, hotels in Southwest Asia will have arrows pointing toward Mecca so Muslims can orient themselves properly during prayer.

The zakat is the giving of alms to the poor or needy. It is given to the mosque once a year. In Christianity, the traditional tithing amount is 10 percent. In the Islamic religion, the amount varies depending upon one's income and savings. The zakat is considered a form of worship and is required of all Muslims. Through the giving of money, one purifies one's own heart and maintains the purity and holiness of one's family. The recipients of the zakat are the poor, the needy, and converts to Islam. Travelers may also receive some of the zakat funds to assist them in their hajj to Mecca.

Muslims must fast, or perform the sawm, during the holy month of Ramadan. Ramadan, the ninth month of the Islamic calendar, occurs at different times of the year in the United States. (In the Islamic world, calendars are based upon the lunar cycle, while in the Western calendar, months are based on the solar cycle.) During Ramadan, Muslims fast during the day; once the sun sets, they are allowed to eat. It is thought that fasting focuses one's thoughts on Allah as well as on the poor.

The pilgrimage to Mecca is called the hajj. If one can afford the journey, one should make a trip to Mecca and attend the ceremonies around the Ka'aba. Mecca is the holiest city in Islam. Medina and Jerusalem also have religious significance to Muslims.

Distribution and Diffusion

Islam began in present-day Saudi Arabia and extended its influence quickly. It diffused in a matter of centuries throughout North Africa, the Middle East, Southeastern Europe, Central Asia, and northern India from its heart in the Arabian Peninsula. Today, Indonesia is the country with the largest population of Muslims, with close to a quarter billion followers.

The religion initially spread through a combination of expansion and armed conquest by armies (relocation and hierarchical diffusion). Later, Islam spread to various ports throughout the Indian Ocean region to parts of East Africa and Southeast Asia via trade networks (relocation and contagious diffusion). Today, Islam is also spreading to Europe and North America via migration (relocation diffusion).

12

Denominations

Islam has two basic branches. Shiites (or Shiahs) comprise about 10 to 15 percent of all of Muslims. Almost all of the remainder are Sunnis. Shiite Muslims live predominantly in Azerbaijan, Bahrain, Iran, and Iraq. They also form small minorities in Sunni-dominated countries. Sunni Muslims live in the rest of the Middle East, Northern Africa, and Southeast Asia. Many of the governments in these areas are theocracies. A **theocracy** is a state that is ruled by religious leaders; religious laws and principles play a vital role in the institutional laws of the society. Islamic theocracies are ruled by Shariah Law. Shariah Law does not separate church and state. It is based on the Koran and the teachings of Muhammad.

Judaism

One of the oldest religions in the world is **Judaism**. It's important to note that Jews may follow the Jewish religion, but the Jewish population also includes people who are born into Jewish families or have Jewish ancestry but are not religious. Most geographers would agree that the Jewish people are a nation. In 1980, the U.S. Supreme Court ruled in a discrimination case that being Jewish could be classified as a "race." However, the idea of being identified as a race frightens many Jewish people, owing to the devastating application of that term during the Holocaust. Most would agree that the Jewish population is an ethnicity.

In 1900, the total Jewish population worldwide was a little over 11 million. By 2010, the population had risen to roughly 13.5 million. In the same period, the Earth's population rose from 1.6 billion to almost 7 billion. The small total increase in the Jewish population over that same period reflects the genocide perpetrated by Nazi Germany and its allies. Over a third of the Jewish people were murdered during the Holocaust.

Architecture

The Jewish symbol is the Star of David, and it is significant because David was one of the patriarchs of the Jewish religion. It is displayed on synagogues, and it is incorporated into the Israeli flag. Some scholars suggest that the six sides of the star represent the days of the week. Other scholars suggest that the six sides of the star represent the astrological chart at the time of David's anointment as king.

Foundational Beliefs

Judaism is an ethnic religion and a monotheistic religion. The name for the Jewish god figure is sacred, with many Jews using the term G-d. When a specific name is used, the common Hebrew name is HaShem; less common are Adonai and Elohim. The Jewish holy book is called the Tanakh (or, more commonly, the Hebrew Bible) and consists of three parts: the Torah, the Nevi'im, and the Ketuvim. The Torah consists of the five books that were written by Moses according to Jewish tradition. The Nevi'im is composed of the writings of various prophets. The Ketuvim is an anthology of 11 books containing poetry, prophecy, and history. Jewish worship is led by a rabbi in the synagogue on Saturday, the faith's holy day.

The foundations of the Jewish faith are also fundamental tenets of Christianity and Islam as well as the Bahá'í faith. Religious Jews believe that G-d is an omnipotent yet loving deity. In the Jewish tradition, the faith began when G-d made a covenant with the patriarch Abraham. The faith's tenets are embodied through Moses in the Ten Commandments, which are recorded in the Talmud.

Distribution and Diffusion

Roughly half of the world's Jewish population lives in the United States, and the majority of Jews in the United States live in larger urban areas on the East Coast, such as New York City. The place most associated with Judaism is Israel, which was founded in 1948 as a homeland for Jewish populations after World War II.

Denominations

Like Christianity and Islam, Judaism has different branches. The most traditional branch is sometimes known as Haredi Judaism. This strictly orthodox denomination follows traditional customs and Jewish law, and most Haredi Jews live in communities comprised mostly of others of the same denomination.

Orthodox Jews are similar to Haredi Jews in that they believe that God gave the Ten Commandments to Moses and these laws must be accepted and practiced. However, Orthodox Jews can live within modern society, whereas the Haredi Jews see modern society as sinful and try to avoid its temptations. The Orthodox branch feels that the Torah came from God but that humans have had a profound impact on it. They believe it is open to interpretation and can change with the times. Religious practices may accommodate modern culture if adaptation is deemed necessary. However, even modified traditions cannot depart from fundamental religious tenets.

Another branch is Reform Judaism. Reformists feel strongly that the Torah is open to continuous interpretation. In fact, in America, many Reform Jews would not consider themselves religious, in the sense of believing in a supernatural higher power. They partake in the religious traditions as part of a preservation of their heritage and culture.

Holidays

The Jewish calendar is significant to the faith. One of the most widely known holidays is Passover, which always occurs on the fifteenth day of the Jewish month of Nissan. Over 80 percent of all Jews have attended a Passover seder (holy service).

Rosh Hashanah is the Jewish new year celebration that occurs in the month of Tishri. During Rosh Hashanah, Jewish people look back at the previous year, analyze their sins or mistakes, and try to amend those sins by resolving to live a better life during the upcoming year. No work is done for 24 hours. Worshipers spend most of the day at the synagogue in introspective thought.

One of the most important holidays of the year is Yom Kippur, which is the holiday of atonement. It occurs on the tenth day of Tishri. Jewish followers practice fasting, taking in no food or water, and try to make up for the sins between man and God. The only people who are exempt from fasting are children under the age of nine and pregnant women. The requirement to fast may also be lifted when someone is at risk of death. This day of atonement is deemed especially significant because once sins are made known, they are sealed in a book forever until the Day of Judgment.

Religious Conflict in the Middle East

Both Christianity and Judaism have deep roots in the land that is the site of modern-day Israel and Jordan. Jerusalem is the holiest city in the Christian faith, because it is where Jesus Christ performed much of his ministry and was eventually crucified. It is also one of the holiest places in the Jewish religion, because the Second Temple was located there. It stood from 516 B.C.E. to 70 C.E., when the Romans destroyed the city. The retaining wall supporting the Temple Mount, called the Western Wall or Wailing Wall, is all that is left to remember the Second Temple. Jerusalem also holds some significance for Muslims, as the Al-Haram al-Qudsi al-Sharif (the Noble Sanctuary) is located there. Islamic tradition holds that Muhammad ascended into heaven at this site to speak with several prophets and saw Allah.

Numerous conflicts have occurred in Jerusalem during the past two millennia. During the Crusades, for example, Christians wanted to take back their Holy Land from the Muslims, who had taken it over in the eleventh century. The Christian kings and queens of Europe sent thousands of soldiers but only took control of the land for a short period.

The issue of ownership of the Holy Land remains contentious. Jews and Muslims have been in conflict since the establishment of Israel as a state in 1948. Many Palestinians feel that they were treated unfairly when the boundaries were established, and they object to the Israeli state's claim on property where Palestinians had resided for over 1,000 years. Israelis point to the devastation of the Holocaust as necessitating a refuge for the Jewish people as well as to the Biblical promise of land to their ancestors. All this and more has led to over half a century of conflict, which has often turned violent.

While religion frames the ongoing tension and debate over Jerusalem, many geographers feel that the conflict between Palestinians and Jews is a political conflict rather than a religious one. Indeed, the political ramifications can be seen in modern-day diplomatic relations, conflicts, and alliances between countries.

Monotheism and Polytheism: West and East

Christianity, Islam, and Judaism are all monotheistic, with followers believing that there is an almighty, omnipotent god that reigns over humans. This god figure can be loving yet judgmental. Nonbelievers will find themselves in hell after they die, while the faithful will go to heaven.

Many scholars trace these three religions' roots back to Zoroastrianism, one of the oldest religions still practiced. **Zoroastrianism** is the belief in Zarathustra as the father of religion. It includes a concept of monotheism, heaven and hell, and a messiah who will resurrect the dead and bring everlasting life. These principles are at the heart of all three Western faiths. However, Zoroastrianism is dying out. Fewer than 150,000 people still practice it. Today the religion is primarily found in Iran and India.

As opposed to the Western religions, whose hearths are in the Middle East, the two major religions of Asia have their hearths in India. Although India today is primarily Hindu, the foundations of Buddhism began there. From India, it spread into East Asia and is now one of the main religions of East and Southeast Asia.

Hinduism

Many geographers consider **Hinduism** the oldest religion on Earth, with origins dating back over 3,000 years. The majority of the world's Hindus live in India. Hinduism is the world's third-largest religion, in part because India's population is so large. As with Judaism, the diffusion of Hinduism, an ethnic religion, is almost nonexistent except for cases of relocation diffusion, when Hindus migrate to other parts of the world.

Architecture

Over 80 percent of the population of India professes to be Hindu, and over 90 percent of the population of Nepal professes to be Hindu. Therefore, many of the Hindu temples in the world are located in the Indian subcontinent. However, more Hindu temples are being built in the United States due to the immigration of more people from India.

Foundational Beliefs

The foundations of the Hindu faith are built on a legal code of behavior in addition to the principles of the deities themselves. There are three primary deities in the Hindu faith: Brahma, Shiva, and Vishnu. Brahma created the universe, Shiva destroys the universe, and Vishnu is the preserver of not only the Earth but also the universe. These three deities keep the universe in balance and are called the triumvirate. They are considered manifestations of a universal god (but this is not considered a single god).

Hinduism deals with the individual's spiritual placement in life as well as in previous lives. Reincarnation is the belief that one has lived a previous life and will continue to live another life after death. The good deeds that one does in this life count toward a higher standing in a future life. Conversely, negative deeds count against a person, causing him or her to lose standing in the hierarchy of the afterlife.

One of the highest forms one can achieve is that of a cow. Cows are seen as life builders. They provide milk for the sustenance of people, and dairy products are staples in the Indian diet. Their droppings are often used as insulation in houses in rural areas of India. The killing of a cow is a terrible crime in the Hindu religion, because Vishnu was a cattle herder. To upset a cow would bring the wrath of Vishnu on you or your family. Because of this belief, cows roam the country. Traffic may come to a standstill in huge cities such as Calcutta, Mumbai, and Delhi when a cow crosses the road.

Sects

In India, thousands of temples are devoted to the worship of Shiva and Vishnu, while only two temples are devoted to Brahma. Vishnu and Shiva each have their different sects of the religion. Over 70 percent of all Hindus worship Vishnu, and 25 percent worship Shiva. The third main sect of the religion belongs to the goddess Shakti. Shakti is the female personification of God, and the word *shakti* means energy. Shakti also represents the power of femininity.

Vishnu worshipers are called Vaishnava. They believe that Vishnu is the true god in the religion and that the other gods exist but are not as powerful. Vishnu has been reincarnated nine times in the history of the world. Vishnu worshipers feel that when he is reincarnated again, the end of the world will be near. Most Hindus believe that Vishnu is represented by a human-looking figure with blue skin and four arms extending from the main body.

Shiva is the destroyer of the universe. However, Shiva is not necessarily seen as a negative deity. For something to be rebuilt, it must be destroyed first. The role of Shiva is to destroy what is wrong with the world to create something new. However, Shiva can be conceived of as evil, too. Therefore, Shiva is in constant conflict between good and evil. Shiva is married to Parvati, who keeps Shiva in balance. When Shiva is represented as a person, his face and throat are blue.

The last of the triumvirate is Brahma. Brahma is the creator of the world and the universe. Because Brahma created the universe, he is considered the first god in the triumvirate. Brahma consists of four heads facing in all the directions. These four heads are thought to represent the Vedas, which are holy texts in Hinduism. India's caste system has four categories, which are also thought to have originated from Brahma.

There are also thousands of other gods, which may be represented by different symbols of the life cycle. The worship of these gods can be done in many different ways.

Buddhism

Another of the Eastern religions, **Buddhism** focuses on the elimination of unwanted desires from the human soul through meditation. Therefore, the worship of a god is not a part of Buddhism; instead, it focuses on the personal devotion of the individual follower. The majority of the world's Buddhists live in East Asia, and Buddhism extends from Northeast to Southeast Asia.

Buddhism is a universalizing religion. However, many Buddhists would consider their practices as part of a social code rather than a strict religion. To this end, one can be a Buddhist as well as an animist or a follower of any other faith, as long as that other faith allows it. When a person combines two or more faiths into one belief system, the result is known as a **syncretic religion**. In many cases, followers of Buddhism also follow Shintoism or Confucianism.

Architecture

Buddhists do not have churches or mosques but, rather, pagodas. Pagodas are tall buildings of ornate design. They often extend high into the sky and are the focal point of many Asian communities. Pagodas are made more for individual worship than congregational worship and, unlike many Western places of worship, do not serve as a social space. Individuals will enter a pagoda and burn incense to release the spirits of their ancestors and contemplate or meditate on the principles of becoming a better person. Buddhist monks live in monasteries, usually separated from urban areas so the monks can focus on meditation. They often leave their monasteries only to ask for food; the villagers in the surrounding region will often donate food to the traveling monks.

Foundational Beliefs

The foundation of the Buddhist religion focuses on Siddhartha Gautama. Siddhartha was a prince who lived in Nepal during the fifth century B.C.E. His father was the king of a large empire and tried to shield his son from the poverty of the time. The prince lived a life of luxury until his teen years. He left the confines of his palace and saw abject poverty. He felt this was unjust, and from that moment on, he began living a life focused on getting rid of material possessions to obtain a state of nirvana. Tradition holds that Siddhartha received his enlightenment at the Bodhi tree in northeastern India, which is still a holy site in the Buddhist religion.

In Buddhism, the Four Noble Truths form the faith's cornerstone.

1. All living beings experience and endure suffering (dukkha).
2. The cause of suffering is craving and attachment (samudaya).
3. The goal is to leave the suffering perpetuated by reincarnation (nirhodha).
4. Nirvana can be achieved through practicing the following eight steps: rightness of belief, resolve, speech, action, livelihood, effort, mindfulness, and meditation (magga).

Distribution and Diffusion

Since its founding, Buddhism has spread from Nepal and India across East Asia. Like Islam, Buddhism was spread along trade routes. Most of East Asia professes to be Buddhist, even if they also practice other belief systems like Confucianism or Shintoism.

Ashoka, emperor of the Mauryan dynasty in India, converted to Buddhism around 263 B.C.E. He sent missionaries (relocation, hierarchical, and contagious diffusion) to Sri Lanka, Myanmar, and Tibet and throughout India. A few hundred years later, missionaries traveling on the Silk Road spread Buddhism to China, and eventually the religion spread to Korea and Japan. Today, Buddhism is well represented throughout most of East and Southeast Asia and Sri Lanka.

Sects

As with other religions, there are different branches of Buddhism. The largest is the Mahayanist, which includes approximately 56 percent of all Buddhists. Japan, Korea, and eastern China, for the most part, practice the Mahayanist branch. Theravada is the second-largest branch of Buddhism. It is practiced in Mongolia, Nepal, and the Tibet region of China. Southeast Asia is the home of the Theravadist branch.

✔ AP Expert Note

Be sure not to neglect the study of regional religions

The religions discussed so far in this chapter have either been major world religions or influences upon those religions. However, there are other faiths, discussed below, that you may also encounter on the AP Human Geography exam. Their ideas and histories are often interwoven with those of the major faiths, or they reflect particular regional cultures.

Other Religions

The five primary religions do not encompass all the belief systems of the world. Many smaller religions are practiced by millions of people, and some play major roles in the regions where they dominate.

Sikhism

Sikhism is a belief in one god that formed as a rejection of India's caste system. Founded by Guru Nanak, Sikhs believe that all people are created equal. Therefore, different communities are established where people of different caste systems can congregate and eat together. Individual responsibility is crucial in this faith. Sikhs are located primarily in the Punjab region of India as well as in Pakistan; Sikhism has approximately 30 million followers. Sikhs wear turbans on their heads as part of their faith. Many Sikhs also do not cut their hair as a sign of their devotion.

Bahá'í

The **Bahá'í** faith is practiced in many parts of Africa and Asia. Founded in Iran in the mid-1800s by Sayyed 'Ali Muhammad Shirāzi, the Bahá'í faith is similar to the Sikh faith in that Bahá'í followers believe that there should be no class distinctions. The Bahá'í faith extends this philosophy to race and religious differences too.

12

Animism

Animism is a belief that all things, including places and objects as well as plants and animals, possess a spirit or soul. Spirits can be either positive or negative. When one of the negative spirits enters your house, field, or animals, it must be removed by a shaman. A shaman has the ability to mediate between the supernatural and natural worlds. The shaman can remove evil spirits by performing ritualistic ceremonies.

Animism takes on many forms, and although the names of the gods and the practices may be different, the same themes are consistent across societies that practice animism. Animism exists in many remote locations of Southeast Asia, including the islands of Indonesia and Papua New Guinea. Other areas where animism is widely practiced are rural Africa and the Amazon Basin of South America. Also, many American Indians hold animistic beliefs.

Confucianism

Confucianism is based on the teachings of Confucius, who lived in China about the same time as Siddhartha Gautama lived in Nepal, during the fifth century B.C.E. Confucianism focuses on relationships. Many of the teachings of Confucius are still fundamental to Chinese society and can be linked with the philosophy of feng shui. This geomancy (feng shui) concerns maintaining proper relationships in life through the positioning of items to keep the flow of energy in harmony. The principles of yin and yang come from Confucianism. For every good there is an evil; for every positive there is a negative.

Taoism

Taoism (Daoism), like Confucianism, is based on the release of personal desires. Adherents practice simplicity and patience. Started by Lao Tzu, a Chinese philosopher who was a contemporary of Confucius, Taoism is based on the philosophy that the world operates according to universal laws and people should seek to live in harmony with it. While Confucianism focuses on how people engage with society, Taoism focuses on nature.

Shinto

Shinto, practiced mainly in Japan, has characteristics of both polytheism and monotheism. Shintoists believe that nature is divine. The forces of nature—including rivers, mountains, and other natural features—have kami (spirits) associated with them. A person's ancestors are revered. Shinto became Japan's official religion in the early twentieth century but lost that status after World War II.

Sacred Spaces in Religions

In many religions, certain locations hold spiritual significance for the faithful. These places, called **sacred spaces**, are reserved and preserved for their holiness. In many cases, these sites attract millions of visitors and much-needed tourist dollars to economies that need the income. The largest hotel in the world, the Abraj Kudia, is set to open in Mecca to serve the needs of Muslims performing the hajj.

What is interesting about the sacred places in various religions is how they are used. During the hajj, millions of pilgrims follow the path to the Ka'aba in Mecca; the pilgrimage has become part of the culture and economy there. Other places are feared and are not visited by the followers of the religion. Many of the sacred burial sites in American Indian religions are treated this way. To walk in these sacred places will bring followers bad luck.

Many faiths consider the death of an individual a sacred occurrence. Because of this, the process of handling the physical body is an important custom for faiths around the world. In many cases, how the body is handled after death determines the fate of the individual in the afterlife.

The Christian tradition usually involves the burial of a dead body in a cemetery. Large areas of land in the middle of urban centers are used for this purpose. These areas could be developed very profitably. However, the treatment of the dead is important in Christianity. In many areas of the United States, laws stipulate that land that was once a cemetery cannot be used for any other purpose for upward of 50 or even 100 years after the cemetery has shut its doors. Muslims and Jews also bury their dead in cemeteries.

In the Hindu religion, the dead are not buried but rather are cremated on a pyre to purify the soul before reincarnation can occur. The ashes are often scattered in the Ganges River to ensure the deceased has a better next life. For Hindus, the Ganges River is the holiest river in the world because of its association with Shiva, one of the main deities of the Hindu faith.

Some religions, such as the Zoroastrian faith, simply leave the body in the open air. Burying the dead would upset the balance of the Earth. Buddhists often use this method as well.

The impact of religion on the landscape is profound. Religious toponyms (place names) mark many landscapes. Québec is renowned for its Catholic toponyms. Many areas in California and the Southwest are dotted with cities named after Catholic missions. For example, Mission Viejo, California, was named after the mission started by Spanish priests hundreds of years ago.

Religion and Conflict

Many battles have been fought and much blood has been shed in the name of religion. Religious conflicts are occurring throughout the world as you read this book. Almost all religions have fought with another culture for control of interfaith boundaries, the boundaries between people of different faiths.

12

Christians fought against Muslims, and sometimes against Christians of different sects, over several centuries in a series of Crusades. In another example, conflict between India and Pakistan is ongoing. Pakistan is a Muslim country, whereas India is predominantly Hindu. Much of the rhetoric is about control of the land in Kashmir, a majority Muslim area, but a fundamental disagreement over religion also underlies the long-running tensions.

Religion often bleeds into issues of ethnic or nationalist conflict, sometimes resulting in terrorist acts against civilians of an opposing group. In Sri Lanka, Buddhists and Hindus were engaged in a civil war from 1983 until 2009. The Tamil Tigers led a separatist movement against the formal government of Sri Lanka. The Tamils, primarily Hindu, forced Muslims out of their region and have led attacks against Buddhist monasteries until their defeat in the late 2000s.

As in political geography, many religious enclaves and exclaves exist. An **enclave** is a group of people with a particular religion surrounded by people of a different religion. In some cases, this can cause turmoil. An **exclave** is a group of people who are physically separated from their religious hearth. For example, many missionaries practice in exclave environments in the remote areas of the South Pacific or Asia. If the community has an outlet to an ocean, then it is not considered an exclave.

12

CULTURAL DIFFUSION

As discussed earlier, diffusion is the movement of any characteristic over time; therefore, cultural diffusion is the movement or spread of any characteristic of a culture. To give an example, if a political ruler dictates the spread of a certain religion, this could lead to hierarchical diffusion. The proliferation of popular memes is a type of contagious diffusion. Also, when people move to different areas or countries, they bring parts of their culture with them, which often results in relocation diffusion. Or, as is the case with stimulus diffusion, a popular concept could be incorporated into another culture but in a different way, such as the American pizza, which was borrowed from Italian food culture. Cultural diffusion can take many shapes and forms, and has multiple effects throughout the world.

 ## NEXT STEP: PRACTICE

Go to Rapid Review and Practice Chapter 5 or to your online quizzes on kaptest.com for exam-like practice on this topic.

Haven't registered your book yet? Go to kaptest.com/moreonline to begin.

CHAPTER 13

Political Patterns and Processes

LEARNING OBJECTIVES

After studying this chapter, you will be able to:

- Describe the contemporary political map and its changes over time.

- Explain the power of politics and territoriality, particularly with regard to boundaries.

- Analyze globalization's impact on a state's economy, politics, culture, and technology.

- Compare and contrast forms and patterns of governance.

- Explain how geopolitical changes impact the contemporary political map.

- Explain national centripetal and centrifugal forces.

- Evaluate the intersection of politics, culture, and economy.

UNDERSTANDING POLITICAL GEOGRAPHY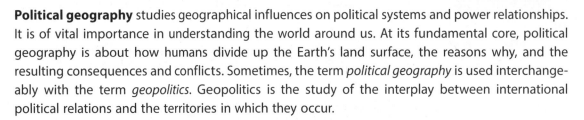

Political geography studies geographical influences on political systems and power relationships. It is of vital importance in understanding the world around us. At its fundamental core, political geography is about how humans divide up the Earth's land surface, the reasons why, and the resulting consequences and conflicts. Sometimes, the term *political geography* is used interchangeably with the term *geopolitics*. Geopolitics is the study of the interplay between international political relations and the territories in which they occur.

Political geographers look at how the size, shape, and boundaries of a country impact its economy and international relations. They contrast patterns of development and trade in core countries (those that are wealthy and highly developed) and periphery countries (those that are poor and less developed). Political geographers also look at how natural resources are distributed both globally and locally. They want to determine why some countries have more political influence and larger economies than others and why some areas are more prone to war than others.

Political geographers are concerned with how the Earth's land surface is divided up among different people and power groups. In everyday conversation, and often in the media, two important terms are commonly misused: *state* and *nation*. A **state** is an area controlled by an established government that has authority over its internal affairs and foreign policy. A **nation**, however, is a group of people who share a common culture and history. For example, the country of India is a state, not a nation. The Indian state is maintained through a system of governance. Within India, however, there are many different nations of people including the Bengalis, Gujaratis, Kashmiris, and Punjabis.

States

Our world is divided into political units called states or countries. The terms "country" and "state" are synonymous and are used interchangeably. The political authority of a state to govern itself is called **sovereignty**. A state generally has a well-defined political boundary that is agreed on by most of the international community. Most states also maintain relatively permanent populations. Currently, there are just under 200 countries in the world.

Over the past century, political boundaries have shifted significantly. Many larger states dissolved and were broken up into smaller states, while new states were created after gaining independence from other states. In fact, there are approximately 100 more states now than there were a century ago. What drove this breakup of the old colonial empires was the growth of self-determination, a cardinal principle that the people of a given culture and/or region have the right to determine their own system of government and system of law. However, conflicts exist when the desires for self-determination of two or more groups come into disagreement. These disagreements can span from conflicts over territory and resources to whether a given ethnicity or tribe even exists (and thus, whether or not that group merits self-determination at all).

States differ widely in geographical size. The five largest states are Russia, Canada, the United States, China, and Brazil. At the other extreme, there are several tiny states called microstates. Examples of microstates include Monaco, Malta, Singapore, and Vatican City. These four states are also referred to as city-states. A **city-state** is a small sovereign state that is made up of a town or city and the surrounding area. Multistate nations also exist but are rare. North Korea and South Korea are an example of a multistate nation; both are constituted from the Korean people.

Nearly all habitable land currently belongs to a state. The only significantly large landmass that is not part of a state is Antarctica. Several states such as Australia, New Zealand, Argentina, Norway, France, and the United Kingdom have some control over Antarctica.

Nations

A nation is a group of people bound together by some sense of a common culture: ethnicity, language, shared history, and attachment to a homeland. In most cases, a nation has a country that it considers its home country. For example, most members of the Thai nation live in the state of Thailand. Some nations, however, do not necessarily belong—or feel as if they belong—to a particular state. The Basque nation is an example of a **stateless nation**. The Basque nation is located in a region referred to as Basque Country, which straddles parts of Spain and France in the western end of the Pyrenees Mountains. Basques are an indigenous ethnic group with a shared language, culture, and ancestry. Basque Country is not an independent state, however. A contentious issue facing Western Europe today is the future status of the Basque nation and whether this nation will form its own independent state.

Nation-States

The **nation-state** is a state in which the cultural borders of a nation correspond with the state borders of a country. In a textbook nation-state, there would only be one ethnicity. As such, every person would speak the same language, practice the same religion, and generally share the same cultural characteristics. While there is no such nation-state in existence, examples of countries that are considered nation-states include Japan, Iceland, and Denmark. Of those examples, Japan is often described as the country closest to being a true nation-state. Japan consists of approximately 127 million people, of which 98.5 percent are considered ethnic Japanese. Approximately 80 percent of ethnic Japanese practice the same religion, which is Shinto. Given its nearly monolithic culture, Japan is very nationalistic, and its culture encourages loyalty to the state over individual gain.

Sovereignty

An independent state has the power to regulate its own internal and external affairs. Once a country has sovereignty, it can determine its own political, legal, and economic systems. It can decide whether or not to get involved with foreign affairs, maintain a military force, or join international organizations such as the United Nations.

A state cannot obtain sovereignty simply by declaring that it has sovereignty. Instead, a state is sovereign based on its recognition by other states and international groups. The Southeast Asian state of East Timor is an example of a country that obtained sovereignty relatively recently. Prior to gaining sovereignty, East Timor spent decades seeking independence. Most other countries, however, did not recognize its call for sovereignty until May 2002. East Timor has the distinction of becoming the first country to gain independence in the twenty-first century.

Sometimes, a group of people are considered **semiautonomous**. This is the case with the American Indian nations within the United States. Federally recognized American Indian nations possess their own sovereignty over tribal land and affairs. Several Supreme Court rulings have concluded that American Indians can abide by their own laws and customs, separate and apart from the laws of the federal government. Different American Indian tribes, such as the Navajo, have created their own constitutions and have tribal councils to determine laws and government rulings.

Throughout history, there have been times when a state's sovereignty is questioned or even over-thrown. States generally take these situations seriously, as such acts threaten the very existence of the state itself. In 2010, major threats to sovereignty unfolded in North Africa and the Middle East. Known as the Arab Spring, a series of major revolts occurred in Tunisia, Egypt, Libya, Syria, Yemen, and Bahrain. These political uprisings led to many regimes in the region being toppled and replaced. While much of the intensity of the Arab Spring has subsided, its results are still being felt. The governing authorities in the region are still quite concerned about additional threats to their sovereignty.

> ✔ **AP Expert Note**
>
> **Be able to distinguish among important political geography terms**
>
> There are many similar-sounding terms within political geography (e.g., *state, nation, nation-state*). On top of this, some of these terms are often misused by the general public. Therefore, make sure you study the terms and examples identified in this section so that you can correctly identify and discuss them on the official exam.

BOUNDARIES

Satellite images from space can show detailed images of the Earth's bodies of water, mountains, deserts, cities, forests, and farmlands. With great clarity, these images provide geographers plenty to study. One feature that these images cannot show, however, is a political boundary. A **political boundary** is an invisible line that marks the outer limits of a state's territory. While political boundaries do sometimes coincide with natural boundaries such as rivers and mountains, most boundaries are determined by other factors including political negotiation, war, or international recognition.

Historically, states and territories were separated not by political boundaries but by frontiers. A **frontier** is a zone of territory where no state has governing authority. While a political boundary is an invisible line that brings two neighboring states into direct contact, a frontier is a geographic area that provides separation. Antarctica is the world's only remaining large, remote frontier. Of great interest to political geographers is how frontiers disappeared and how political boundaries have developed and changed over time.

Geometric Boundaries

Geometric boundaries are created by using lines of latitude and longitude and their associated arcs. These lines are visible only on maps. Many of the state boundaries in the western United States, such as those of Colorado, Wyoming, and Utah, are geometric boundaries. Much of the boundary between the United States and Canada is drawn according to latitude: the border follows the 49th north latitude for about 1,300 miles. The United States and Canada share another extensive geometric boundary between Alaska and the Yukon Territory.

Other areas of the world are drawn with geometric boundaries. Iraq's borders with Saudi Arabia were drawn using geometric boundaries, as were the borders of many African countries. Using latitude and longitude to set up boundaries has some significant advantages. The lines are easy to determine with a global positioning system (GPS). Likewise, they are highly visible on political maps and tend to be more permanent than borders that are not as well-defined. However, problems between countries often emerge when geometric boundaries are created without consideration of cultural and ethnic factors. If a nation is separated by such a boundary, people may be reluctant to accept the division, hampering the country's ability to unify the population.

Physical Boundaries

While geometric boundaries are based on lines of latitude and longitude, **physical boundaries** are based on the geographical features of the Earth's surface. The three main types of physical boundaries include bodies of water, mountain ranges, and desert regions.

The Rio Grande is an example of a water boundary. Flowing through the southwestern United States and across northern Mexico, this magnificent river provides a natural border between parts of Mexico and the United States. Over the years, the two countries have signed international agreements to govern river access and water usage.

Within the United States, the Ohio River and the Mississippi River separate dozens of states along their paths across North America. For example, the state of Kentucky is separated from West Virginia, Ohio, Indiana, and Illinois by the Ohio River. The Mississippi River separates many states, including Arkansas from Tennessee and Louisiana from Mississippi.

Water boundaries are also common in East Africa. Boundaries that separate Kenya, Uganda, and Tanzania run through Lake Victoria. The boundary between Mozambique and Malawi goes through Lake Malawi. One major benefit of having a water boundary is that the body of water is highly visible on the map. Another benefit is that the body of water can serve as a natural border defense between the two countries.

13

The Andes mountain range, sometimes called "the spine of South America," is an example of a mountain boundary. The Andes fall between Chile and Argentina as well as between Ecuador and Brazil. Another major mountain boundary is the Himalayas. This mountain range, including several of highest mountains in the world, provides a natural boundary between the Tibetan plateau region and India. The boundary is so massive that it has caused India to be called a "subcontinent."

Deserts can also separate countries. Africa, Egypt, Libya, and Algeria are separated from Sudan, Chad, Mauritania, Niger, and Mali by the expansive Sahara. Like other types of physical boundaries, desert boundaries can offer some level of natural defense between countries because these areas can be hard to travel across.

Using physical features to establish boundaries does have some disadvantages. For example, if a river serves as a boundary, any project involving the river, such as building a bridge or dam, involves working with two different governments. This often requires a lot of communication, cooperation, and negotiation. Another disadvantage is that some physical boundaries can actually move. Rivers, for example, can change course. The boundary between Mississippi and Louisiana has altered slightly over the years because the Mississippi River has shifted. The Rio Grande between the United States and Mexico has also shifted a little, making the precise definition of the Mexican-U.S. boundary somewhat unclear at times.

Ethnographic or Cultural Boundaries

Not all boundaries are based on geometric or physical features. In some instances, ethnographic and cultural considerations such as language and religion have influenced the creation of **ethnographic/cultural boundaries**. These boundaries are in many cases the hardest to agree upon and are the most ambiguous and fluid.

One notable example of an ethnographic boundary is the divide between Ireland and Northern Ireland. In the early twentieth century, the two regions split up. Ireland (or the Republic of Ireland) formed its own independent state, and Northern Ireland became part of the United Kingdom. Motivating factors for the breakup were religion and politics. Another example of a cultural boundary, based to some degree on religious differences, is the boundary between Pakistan and India. When both countries were colonies of Great Britain, the British wanted to separate the Muslim majority in Pakistan from the Hindu majority in India.

After World War I, the victorious Allied Powers met at the Versailles Peace Conference in France to redraw the borders of Europe. The boundaries of Poland, Hungary, Bulgaria, and Romania were partly based on language considerations. The Allied Powers believed that grouping people who share a common language would promote peace and unity.

The Creation of Boundaries

The process of creating boundaries can range from being a peaceful negotiation to being a highly contentious and violent affair. In most cases, drawing a boundary involves representatives of two or more countries meeting to work out the location and conditions of the boundary. When the boundary is in dispute, a mediator from another country or an international political group may be used to negotiate the boundary location.

The term *boundary evolution* refers to the technical wording of a treaty that legally defines where a boundary should be located. Once the boundary evolution becomes part of the official document, cartographers (mapmakers) must accurately represent it. This representation or translation of the boundary evolution is called **delimitation**. After the process of delimitation has been established, the two countries place physical markings on the landscape, such as border crossings, fences, walls, etc., to show where the boundary is located.

The process of physically representing a boundary on the landscape is known as **demarcation**. The zone on both sides of the boundary is referred to as the **border landscape**. The border landscape can be inclusionary or exclusionary. An inclusionary border has fewer barriers between the two states, facilitating travel and trade. The border between the United States and Canada is inclusionary. An exclusionary border landscape is designed to inhibit movement. For example, the border between the United States and Mexico is exclusionary.

Boundary Origins

There are four main types of boundary origins: antecedent boundaries, subsequent boundaries, superimposed boundaries, and relic boundaries.

An **antecedent boundary** is one that existed either before humans settled an area or very early during the settlement history. Future settlement is then determined by the antecedent boundary. The 49th parallel is a good example of an antecedent boundary. People who wanted to live in the United States settled south of the 49th parallel, and people who wanted to be in Canada settled north of it. Much of the boundary between Canada and the United States is unguarded, making it one of the longest undefended borders in the world. Another example of an antecedent boundary is the division between Indonesia and Malaysia on the island of Borneo. Most of this border passes through sparsely inhabited tropical rain forest, providing a natural split between the two populations that would eventually form independent states.

Subsequent boundaries develop along with the development of the cultural landscape. A good example of a subsequent boundary is the border between Ireland and Northern Ireland. As the cultural landscape developed, the border was drawn to accommodate religious, cultural, and economic differences. Another example of a subsequent boundary is the boundary between China and Vietnam. This boundary has been in dispute on many occasions.

A **superimposed boundary** is a political boundary that ignores the existing cultural organization on the landscape. It is usually forced in place by a superpower or a delegation of superpowers. The boundary between North Korea and South Korea is a superimposed boundary. A demilitarized zone was placed along the 38th parallel to resolve the conflict between the communists in the north and non-communists in the south. The irony is that the demilitarized zone is one of the most militarized zones in the world. In 1884, several European countries attended the Conference of Berlin in order to divide up much of the African continent. France, Great Britain, Portugal, and Germany were the major participants. Instead of drawing borders according to the different nations in Africa, they superimposed boundaries that didn't always fit the cultural boundaries. Ethnic groups that had been in conflict for centuries were now supposed to live together under the umbrella of one state. When superimposed boundaries split up an ethnic group into two different countries, the ethnic group often seeks to reunite its population. This situation is referred to as **irredentism**. The end result of the Conference of Berlin was a jumble of poorly designed countries, many of which are still dealing with major boundary issues.

A **relic boundary** is, just as the term implies, a relic on the landscape. The term "relic" refers to a surviving object from the past. These boundaries are no longer used for separation, but their impact is still felt and seen on the landscape. Perhaps the most famous example of a relic boundary is the Great Wall of China, which was built during the third century B.C.E. as a defensive barrier to keep out the invading Mongols from the north. The old boundary between East Germany and West Germany is also a good example of a relic boundary. Economic development in West Germany was far greater than in East Germany. Upon the **reunification** (the reuniting of two regions that were previously a single state) of Germany in the early 1990s, the difference in development between the communist East and the capitalist West was quite stark. For example, the East Germans had built basic concrete buildings and apartments, and their country suffered from crumbling infrastructure, whereas the West Germans had built attractive residences and a modern infrastructure.

Boundary Disputes

Areas such as Rwanda, Uganda, and Sudan have experienced some of the greatest mass atrocities and refugee movements the world has ever seen. Millions of people have died as the result of violence arising from the poorly designed boundaries created at the Conference of Berlin. Ethnic conflicts involving the Hutus and Tutsis have created one of the largest refugee movements in the last 30 years. Ethnic conflicts are disagreements that usually result in military action or violence of one ethnic group against another. Religious conflicts, on the other hand, involve violence between members of different religious groups. Such conflicts are currently occurring in Syria between the Sunni and Shiite Muslims. Also, violence has periodically erupted in India and Pakistan as Hindus and Muslims have disagreed over boundary location.

In the former country Yugoslavia, mass ethnic unrest and violence occurred during the 1980s and 1990s. After World War II, Yugoslavia was controlled by a dictator named Josip Tito. When Tito died in 1980, the country began to unravel, and a civil war ended with the breakup of Yugoslavia into multiple states, including Bosnia and Herzegovina, Macedonia, Serbia, Montenegro, Croatia, and Slovenia. Another, Kosovo is still only a partially recognized state. The breaking up of Yugoslavia

13

has been described as a **balkanization** due to the region's location on the Balkan Peninsula. The term "balkanization" originated in the early twentieth century to describe a contentious process of a state fragmenting into smaller states, which are often hostile or uncooperative with one another. Balkanization is often fueled by ethnic separatism, when an ethnic minority seeks independence from a majority group.

The opposite of balkanization is **annexation**, which is the process of adding territory to an already existing state. For instance, when the United States purchased the Alaska territory from Russia in 1867, it annexed the land as a territory, even though Alaska didn't officially become a U.S. state until 1959.

A boundary issue that many countries face today concerns the question of who controls particular territories. One example is the case of the Senkaku Islands (also called the Diaoyu or Diaoyutai Islands) located in the East China Sea. Japan, China and Taiwan all claim ownership of the small islands, which are under 200 miles from the coastal areas of each of the three countries. Another boundary dispute is the Takeshima/Dokdo Island dispute in the East Sea/Sea of Japan. Both Japan and Korea claim the island, and Koreans exhibit fierce nationalism, asserting that the island is strictly Korean.

There are four types of boundary disputes: definitional boundary disputes, locational boundary disputes, operational boundary disputes, and allocational boundary disputes.

Definitional boundary disputes arise from the legal language of a treaty's definition of the boundary. A common remedy involves one of the countries suing the other country in the International Court of Justice (the World Court), which will try to determine what was intended when the boundaries were initially described.

Locational boundary disputes arise when the definition of the border is not questioned but the interpretation of the border is. In these cases, the border has shifted, and the original intention of the boundary is called into question. For example, geographical areas located in the state of Mississippi have shifted to the state of Louisiana due to the river shifting its course.

Operational boundary disputes occur when two countries next to each other disagree on a major issue involving the border. For example, the United States and Mexico disagree over the issue of illegal immigration into the United States. Both sides agree where the border is but cannot agree on how to handle border crossing. Currently, there is a political dispute between the United States and Mexico over how to patrol the border landscape. Some U.S. political groups want to erect more physical barriers and add more armed guards along the border. Other groups believe such measures are not needed to regulate border activity.

Like operational boundary disputes, **allocational boundary disputes** do not question the boundary itself but, rather, the use of it. Allocational boundary disputes usually involve some type of natural resource, often in the open ocean and/or underground. For example, when an aquifer extends across a boundary, each side may lay a claim to it.

The United Nations held a conference in 1958 to try to establish the United Nations Convention on the Law of the Sea (UNCLOS). When finally adopted as international law in 1983, the International Law of the Sea held two important points: foreign countries could not have their military or other ships travel within 12 miles of the coast of any other country, and countries have access to **exclusive economic zones** (EEZs). Within the EEZs, countries have the right to explore for resources up to 200 miles off their shores. For example, the United States can drill for oil and natural gas in the Gulf of Mexico out to 200 miles.

The International Law of the Sea doesn't always work. Sometimes the 200-mile barriers conflict with those of other countries. In these cases, sometimes the median-line principle is used. A line is drawn in the water equidistant from each competing party. However, the median-line principle does not necessarily give all parties equal access to the resources. In the Caspian Sea, Iran is contesting the median-line principle because other countries such as Turkmenistan, Azerbaijan, and Kazakhstan would receive a greater percentage of the resources than Iran.

In some areas, called the **global commons**, countries do not have the right to search for natural resources. One of the largest global commons areas is Antarctica, shown in the following map. No country is allowed to exploit Antarctica for natural resources, although several countries have claimed segments of territory on the continent. Australia claims the largest amount of land, followed by Norway, France, Chile, Argentina, and the United Kingdom. However, it has been globally accepted that the land in Antarctica will be used solely for scientific research and not for military purposes or resource exploration. Boundary disputes persist between the United Kingdom, Argentina, and Chile, which explains the overlap shown in the figure.

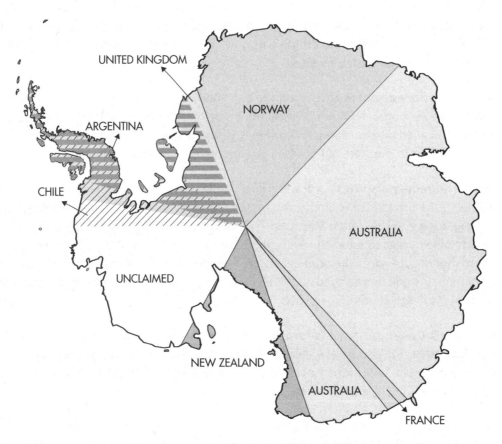

Map of Antarctica, Divided by Land Claimed by Various Countries

COLONIALISM AND IMPERIALISM

Very few geopolitical practices have had as profound an impact on the world as we know it as colonialism. **Colonialism** is the practice of establishing political dominance over a people for economic, political, and territorial gain. **Imperialism**, on the other hand, is the practice of taking control of an area that is already politically organized. There is a fine line between the two terms, and sometimes controversies emerge over which definition applies to a given situation. Colonialism began with the Ancient Greeks and their exploration of the Mediterranean Sea. Later, the Europeans colonized the western hemisphere and Africa. Today, the practice of colonialism has mostly ended, but the impact of the era of colonialism is still being felt in many parts of the world.

The political geographer Friedrich Ratzel, who coined the term *geopolitics*, developed a theory about the growth of states that is called the organic theory. Ratzel argued that the state was like a living entity that constantly needed to grow in order to thrive. According to Ratzel's theory, states constantly need new territory to meet the demands of their ever-growing populations. This partly explains the motives behind Europe's historical desire for expansion. To increase their countries' economic and military power, Europeans colonized different parts of the world to gain natural resources, raw materials, and territory.

Motives for Colonialism

Spreading Christianity was an often stated motive, especially by the Spanish, for colonialism. A fundamental tenet of the Christian faith is that one should seek to convert others to Christianity. All of the European colonizers participated in some form of conversion. The Spanish largely forced Christianity upon the indigenous peoples of South and Central America; if they did not convert, they were often killed. The Spanish also set up missions in what is now the southwestern United States. The French and English set up missions in the New World, many of which still exist today. Montréal was first established as a mission and trading post on the St. Lawrence Seaway by the French.

While colonizers used religion as a justification for colonizing indigenous lands, the primary motivation was an economic one—the quest for wealth and resources. Spanish explorers were looking for the instant wealth that gold could bring. For example, the myth of El Dorado, a city where the streets were supposedly made of gold, persisted until the nineteenth century. A great many Spanish explorers uprooted their lives to search for this fabled city paradise.

Less enticed by fabled cities of gold, the French sought animal furs and skins to produce hats and coats for the upper classes in France. A fur hat cost the yearly wage of an average worker in Paris during the seventeenth century. The French established working relationships with the American Indians along the borders of the present-day United States and Canada. These relationships were invaluable for trade and survival in the wilderness.

Colonies were expected to provide resources that the home country needed to sustain itself. For many years, the Spanish brought back ships filled with gold and jewels. The Spanish used this newfound wealth to build castles and palaces. The British used its resources to modernize the military. Smaller countries such as Denmark and the Netherlands also played an important role in the colonization of the West and Africa. Denmark controlled Greenland and the Faroe Islands. Seeking spices, the Netherlands became an important player in East Asia. Until the mid-twentieth century, Indonesia was called Dutch Indonesia. Dutch cities became some of the wealthiest in the world because of the spice trade.

It was important for the prestige of the kings and queens of Europe to have colonies around the world. The saying "the sun never sets on the British Empire" was once a common utterance because the sun was indeed always shining in a British-controlled territory somewhere in the world. Britain held the east coast of what is now the United States until the American Revolution, South Africa until the early twentieth century, India until the mid-twentieth century, and Hong Kong until 1997. Canada and various points in Africa, including the Straits of Gibraltar and the areas around the present-day Suez Canal, were under British control. The British controlled New Zealand and Australia, which was originally established as a penal colony for offenders in Great Britain. Several ports in the Middle East were under the control of the British. The British provided them with military protection, and in return the colonies provided Great Britain with valuable resources for its industrial base.

Self-Determination

One of the most widely known stories of British colonialism is the story of the independence of India. Mohandas Gandhi led the independence movement through nonviolent protests. By controlling trade and manufacturing, rebel forces crippled British control in the region. Losing the ability to govern, the British were ultimately forced out. Eventually the countries of Pakistan, Bangladesh, and India emerged as independent states.

Self-determination is the power of a people to establish their own government the way that they see fit. Many former colonies would rather see less-than-ideal conditions managed by their own country than have more stable conditions under the rule of a colonial power. Along with self-determination, many people want suffrage, which is the power to vote. One of the key factors leading to the American Revolution was the colonists' lack of voting power, especially given that they were being heavily taxed by the British. The colonists were expected to pay British taxes and adhere to all British laws without having a voice in deciding those taxes and laws. Thus, the phrase "taxation without representation" was one of the rallying cries of the American colonists.

Patterns and Impacts of Colonialism and Imperialism

When the British defeated the French in the French and Indian War, the French were forced to retreat to the Québec region. French is still spoken in Québec today. The Acadians migrated from the French-speaking regions of Canada to the southern Louisiana region, beginning the Cajun culture. The French dominated some islands in the Caribbean as well as French Guiana in South America. The French were integral players in Southeast Asia. A few elderly people in Vietnam today can still speak French as a result of the French control of Indochina.

The Spanish colonized the southwestern part of the United States as well as the majority of the land to the south. This area extends through Central America down the west coast of South

America. Portugal controlled present-day Brazil. Because Spain and Portugal, two countries on the Iberian Peninsula, were both Roman Catholic countries, they decided to let the Catholic Church determine the ownership of the South American continent. The Pope declared that anything to the east of the 70° west longitude line would be controlled by Portugal, and any land to the west of the 70° west longitude line would belong to Spain. Today, countries such as Colombia, Venezuela, Chile, and Ecuador all speak Spanish as their primary language, and Brazilians speak Portuguese.

Denmark owned Greenland, and still does to this day. However, Denmark has given Greenland more autonomy in making decisions concerning its own welfare.

The Netherlands owned Suriname, which still has Dutch as its official language. The Netherlands also owns several islands in the Caribbean, such as Aruba. The Netherlands owned the Dutch East Indies until 1949, when the territory became independent and renamed itself Indonesia.

Belgium colonized much of central Africa, establishing the Belgian Congo. The Belgians were known for their ruthless King, Leopold III, who killed more than half the native population in the Congo. World opinion quickly turned against the king, and he gave control over the area to the Belgian parliament, which ruled it more benignly until the Congo gained its independence in 1960.

Italy took over sections of northeastern Africa. Italian East Africa, including present-day Ethiopia and part of Somalia, only existed from 1936 to 1941. Although the Italians use the word *colonization*, many consider their presence a brief occupation. After World War II, the Allied powers established an ineffective boundary between Somalia and Ethiopia. Tension still exists today as both countries have mounted attacks on the other.

13

✔ AP Expert Note

Be able to discuss the multiple impacts of colonialism

European states established colonies throughout the world for three main reasons: to seek wealth, to increase their land holdings, and to promote Christianity. The impacts of this colonialism have been varied and far-reaching. On the AP exam, you'll be expected to have an understanding of how colonialism has changed the physical and cultural landscape of the world. Some examples include the following: the exchange of ideas and goods, the drawing of new boundaries, conflicts and wars, changes in land ownership and government, and struggles for sovereignty.

Democratization

Democratization is the transition from a form of government not based on rule by elected political authorities to one that is. For example, if a country replaces an authoritarian regime with a popularly elected leader, then the country has undergone a form of democratization.

There have been three major waves of democratization over the past three centuries. The first wave took place in the late eighteenth and nineteenth centuries in North America and Western Europe. This wave was highlighted by revolutions in America and in France. The second wave occurred immediately after World War II with the defeat of Germany, Italy, and Japan. The world underwent a major political realignment, which resulted in several former colonies in Africa and Latin America gaining independence. We are still experiencing the third wave of democratization, which started in 1974 with the end of dictatorships in Portugal and Spain. In the 1990s, with the collapse of the Soviet Union and the breakup of Yugoslavia, the progress of democratization in Europe and Asia saw a surge.

A major example of democratization in Africa coincided with the end of apartheid in South Africa in the early 1990s. In 1948, South Africa adopted its infamous apartheid policy, which segregated blacks and other non-whites and revoked their voting rights. After decades of struggle and world-wide condemnation, the South African government could no longer enforce its discriminatory policy. In 1994, famed leader Nelson Mandela, who had previously been imprisoned as a political opponent, was elected the country's leader in a free election. Mandela's election represented one of the most monumental moves towards democratization during the twentieth century.

There is a great deal of debate regarding the conditions that must be present for democratization to take hold and then ultimately become successful. Democratization has been more likely to take root in countries with relatively high income levels, a strong educational system, mobility between social classes, a homogeneous population, a long cultural history, and a stable older population. Some political scientists speculate that globalization and the widening access to the Internet will usher in a new era of democratization throughout the world. They believe that authoritarian regimes will find it difficult to operate in an increasingly transparent environment in which the masses can share information nearly instantly through social media.

SHAPES OF COUNTRIES

Countries come in different sizes and shapes. One feature of a state's political boundary is that it gives a country a particular shape. There are five basic shapes that countries take: compact, elongated, fragmented, perforated, and prorupted.

Compact Countries

When the distance from the center of a state to any of its outer boundaries is roughly the same length, the state's shape is classified as a **compact shape**. Most compact states are relatively small and feature state governments located near the country's center. In theory, compact states have several advantages. First, travel and communication are often easier than in more spread-out states. Second, political boundaries can be more easily monitored and protected, in most cases. Lastly, governmental programs and economic resources should be more accessible in a logistical sense.

Because a compact country is usually small and uniform, one of the most common disadvantages is a lack of natural resources. Poland is often named as an example of a nearly perfect compact state. Other examples include Rwanda, Kenya, and Uganda. The following is a basic map of Rwanda, illustrating the typical shape of a compact state.

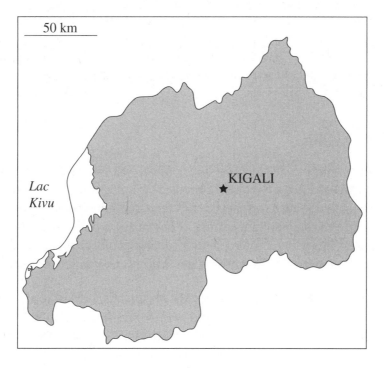

Map of Rwanda

Elongated Countries

A state with an **elongated shape** is long and narrow; an excellent example is Italy. One characteristic of an elongated state is diversity. The physical geography, culture, and economy can greatly vary throughout a state that is very long and narrow.

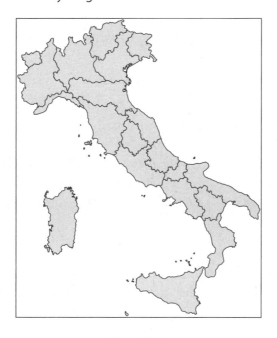

Map of Italy

13

Challenges related to communications, accessibility to the capital, and transportation of resources are potential problems that elongated countries face. An ideal example of an elongated state is the South American country of Chile. Wedged between the Andes Mountains to the east and the Pacific Ocean to the west, Chile extends approximately 2,500 miles north-to-south but only about 90 miles east-to-west.

Fragmented Countries

Technically, any country that has offshore islands is considered a fragmented state. A state is defined as having a **fragmented shape** if it has discontinuous pieces of territory. Like with elongated states, governments of fragmented states can have a hard time delivering services. Maintaining political boundaries, traveling, and communication are also potentially problematic. Often it is more challenging for fragmented countries to foster a sense of national unity given that people are physically separated. One big advantage of fragmented states is access to a variety of natural resources.

Examples of fragmented states include Indonesia, the Philippines, and Denmark. Indonesia consists of more than 13,000 islands, of which about 900 are permanently inhabited. The Philippines has more than 7,000 islands, while Denmark has more than 400. The United States is also considered a fragmented country given that Alaska and Hawaii are physically separated from the U.S. mainland.

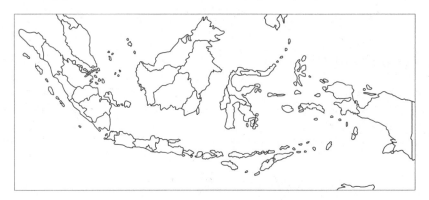

Map of Indonesia

Perforated Countries

A **perforated** country has an entire state completely inside of its borders. There are only two perforated states in the world: South Africa and Italy. South Africa contains the country of Lesotho completely inside of its borders. Italy contains two countries completely inside of its borders, San Marino and Vatican City.

An **exclave** is a portion of a state that is geographically separated from the mainland by another country or countries. Alaska is an example of an exclave. An **enclave** is a country that is completely surrounded by another political state, such as Lesotho, Vatican City, and San Marino.

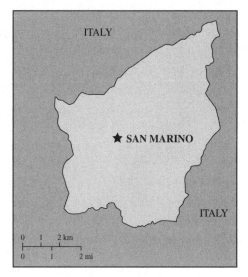

Map of San Marino

In addition to being physically surrounded by another state, countries such as Lesotho, Vatican City, and San Marino are considered landlocked states. A **landlocked state** is any country that does not have direct access to the sea due to being surrounded by neighboring states. In Africa, there are several landlocked states, including Botswana, Rwanda, Zambia, and Zimbabwe. In South America, Bolivia and Paraguay are landlocked states. Without access to the sea, these states have to ship goods and resources through neighboring states in order to engage in international trade. For example, Botswana ships approximately 90 percent of its exports through South Africa.

Prorupted Countries

A country with a **prorupted shape** is characterized by having a compact portion with a large projecting extension. Usually, the land extension has to do with resource access. Namibia, a state in the southwestern part of Africa, is an example of a prorupted country. While the main part of Namibia has a compact shape, there is a nearly 300-mile protrusion called the Caprivi Strip that extends eastward, giving Namibia crucial access to the Zambezi River and trading routes to the East. Other examples of prorupted countries include Thailand and Myanmar. Both have extensive protrusions that run several hundred miles south along the Malay Peninsula.

In North America, both Mexico and the United States have extending protrusions. In the United States, Florida is an extensive peninsula that projects off the southeastern U.S. mainland. In the northwestern part of Mexico, the Baja region extends more than 750 miles southward. The Baja protrusion is famous for its natural pristine beauty and ecotourism.

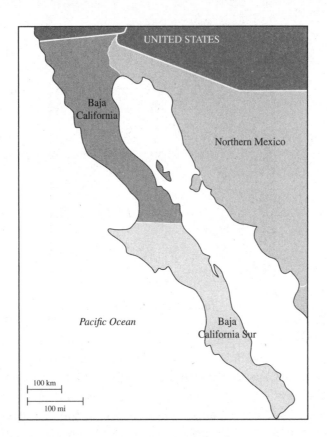

Partial Map of Mexico

THE POLITICAL ORGANIZATION OF SPACE

People have long had different ways of dividing up and governing the Earth's surface. These differences can cause harmony or dissension within and between countries. Each day, newspapers are filled with stories of conflicts between states, ethno-national conflicts, regional issues, and issues over political representation. To understand any of these issues, one needs a basic knowledge of the political organization of space.

The Modern State

In earlier sections, we discussed the concept of the state. A state is a bounded territory that is officially controlled by a people and their governing authority. It generally has the power to decide its own domestic, economic, legal, military, and foreign policy. In the course of recorded history, the concept of the state is relatively new. The idea of the state didn't begin to take shape until the sixteenth and seventeenth centuries in Europe. The practice of dividing up territory into states and the recognition of states' sovereign authority led to the doctrine of **nationalism**. This doctrine is based on the idea that each ethno-cultural group, or nation, has the power to control its own affairs.

13

As the modern political map has emerged over the past several centuries, different forms of state governance have developed. The United States has a **federal government** system, meaning that it shares power with the 50 U.S. states. The term "state" typically refers to a country, not a regional subdivision of a country. So unless otherwise specified, the term "state" will refer to an independent country rather than a subdivision of a country.

If a state has a central government that maintains control over the full country, the state's government is classified as **unitary**. France and the United Kingdom are examples of unitary states.

To interact with other countries, state governments create formal offices of diplomats called **embassies**, which are set up in other states. In the United States, for example, the Department of State operates embassies in most countries around the world. An embassy's function is to represent the nation's interests in the other country. The top official representing a country in another state is called an **ambassador**. Embassies are usually located in the capital of a country, while secondary offices called **consulates** are located throughout the host country. Like embassies, consulates can issue official documents such as passports and visas and promote economic interests and trade relations. More than 175 countries have embassies located in the United States' capital, which is Washington, D.C. Consulates are usually located in large regional cities. For example, there are more than 100 foreign consulates located in New York City.

Supranational Organizations

Diplomatic relations between countries are vital for maintaining international harmony. Still, many political, economic, military, and social issues lead to disagreements. Often, these disagreements cannot be worked out between two states. In the early part of the twentieth century, the inability of states to settle differences through diplomacy led to the two biggest wars that the world had ever seen—World War I and World War II. Following War World I, leaders in the West created an international organization called the League of Nations, which had the mission of preventing another global conflict. Two decades later, however, World War II broke out.

Since the founding of the League of Nations, a multitude of international and regional organizations have been formed. These groups are referred to as **supranational organizations**, which are bodies formed by three or more states to promote shared objectives.

The United Nations

Following the end of World War II, world leaders set up the most important international organization: the United Nations (UN). The UN was established in 1945 and originally consisted of 49 states. Today, nearly 200 states belong to the UN. The UN plays an important role in trying to bring peace to conflict-prone areas such as the Middle East and sub-Saharan Africa. Although the UN has failed to maintain peace in many instances, it does represent a global forum in which the states of the world can meet to discuss and vote on international issues.

NATO, the Warsaw Pact, and the Iron Curtain

During the Cold War, world politics were dominated by two superpowers: the United States and the Soviet Union. American foreign policy was dominated by attempts to reduce the spread of communism and spread democracy. The United States fought wars in Korea and Vietnam and aided troops in Central America and Central Asia to oppose communism. Large military bases were established around the world, including in Korea, Taiwan, the Philippines, Turkey, Germany, and Iceland. When the Soviet Union started building missile bases on Cuba in 1962, the world came close to a nuclear war. Ultimately, the missile bases were removed.

To counter the Soviet Union, the United States and the West created the North Atlantic Treaty Organization (NATO) after World War II. NATO, which still exists today, was formed as a military alliance of 16 states, consisting of the United States, Canada, and 14 European countries. To oppose NATO and protect Eastern Europe, the Soviet Union created its own military alliance called the Warsaw Pact. Formed in 1955, the Warsaw Pact included the Soviet Union and the satellite states of Bulgaria, East Germany, Poland, Hungary, Romania, and Czechoslovakia. The term **satellite state** describes a country that is technically independent but is under heavy political, economic, and military influence from another country. The Soviets sought to control Eastern European states partly so that these states would serve as a buffer zone between the East and West. A **buffer zone** is a region or state that provides territorial separation, or a "cushion," between rivals. As buffer states, the Soviet satellites formed what was called the Iron Curtain. The Iron Curtain divided democratic, capitalist Western Europe from totalitarian, communist Eastern Europe. The following map shows Europe during the Cold War.

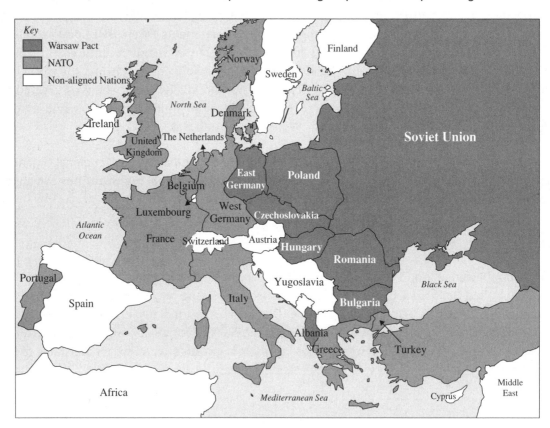

Europe During the Cold War

For many years, the two superpowers battled indirectly by using other countries as pawns. Regions caught up in a conflict between two superpowers are called **shatterbelt regions**. Their boundaries are often changed as a result of the conflict. East Asia was a shatterbelt region during the Korean and Vietnam wars. The Middle East was a shatterbelt region as the superpowers vied for access to petroleum. During the 1980s, the shatterbelt region was in Central America, with conflicts in Nicaragua and El Salvador.

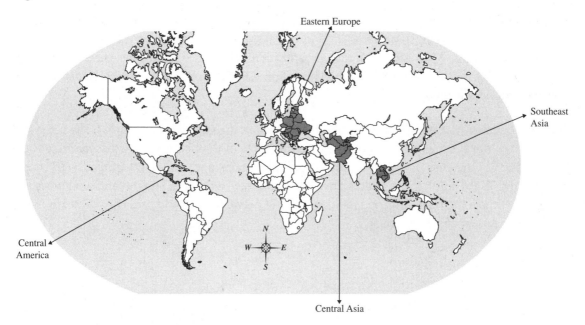

Shatterbelts Around the World During the Cold War Era

Political Geography Theories

The Heartland Theory

In 1904, Halford Mackinder, a British political geographer, wrote a thesis and presented it before the Royal Geographical Society in London. In his article, titled "The Geographical Pivot of History," he outlined his heartland theory. The **heartland theory** suggested that whoever controlled Eastern Europe and Western Asia would have the political power and capital to rule the world. Mackinder based his theory on the fact that Eastern Europe contained one of the richest agricultural regions in the world. The Ukraine region could produce enough wheat and other agricultural products to sustain a large population—and feed its armies. Also, abundant raw materials such as coal, essential to develop a military and industrial base, are available in this region.

Adolf Hitler believed in the heartland theory, which is why he invaded Eastern Europe. Hitler, however, underestimated the Soviet citizens' resolve and the severity of the Russian winter and eventually had to retreat ignominiously. After World War II, the Soviet Union exerted control over Eastern Europe, greatly concerning Western Europe, the United States, and other non-communist countries.

The Rimland Theory

Nicholas Spykman, another political geographer, used Mackinder's ideas when he wrote his own theory on world domination and politics. Spykman was originally from the Netherlands and came to the United States to teach at Yale University. He originated the rimland theory of containment and is known as the "godfather of containment."

The **rimland theory** claimed that forming alliances is necessary to keep the heartland in check. Because the heartland was so powerful, no individual country could contain it by itself. Hence the establishment of the North Atlantic Treaty Organization (NATO), the Southeast Asian Treaty Organization (SEATO), and the Central Treaty Organization (CENTO) in response to the spread of communism around the world.

Spykman believed that the alliances should seek to control the sea and coastal areas. The heartland is, in a sense, trapped by its own geography. To the north of the heartland is an ocean that is icebound much of the year. To the east are the Ural Mountains and vast tracts of land with sparse populations. To the south is the Middle East with its immense deserts. The rimland would use the oceans to contain the heartland, engaging in a battle between land and sea. The following figure shows the heartland and the rimland.

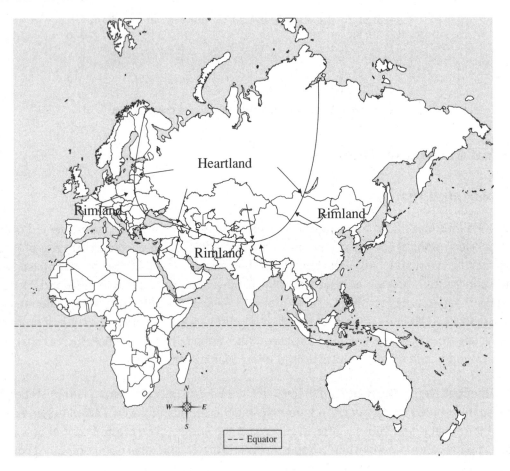

Heartland/Rimland Map

The Domino Theory

The domino theory was adopted by the United States in the 1960s and 1970s. The Central Intelligence Agency (CIA) developed this theory, which suggested that when one country experiences rebellion or political disunity, other countries around it will also experience turmoil as a result, leading to a domino effect of political instability in the region. The domino theory was established in response to the communist incursions that had been occurring around the world. It justified U.S. military involvement in Southeast Asia during the 1960s and 1970s and in Central America during the 1980s.

During the Cold War era, opponents of the domino theory pointed out that the United States was able to maintain political stability despite the political instability of Mexico at the time. Supporters of the domino theory countered that Mexico was not as vulnerable to communism as were areas such as Vietnam.

> ✔ **AP Expert Note**
>
> **Be able to explain how different states interact**
>
> The United States is a superpower, which gives its citizens a different perspective on how states interact, as the U.S. government is often the driver of global events. However, for the AP exam, you must keep in mind that most states rely on international organizations and on balancing ties with various countries to maintain their sovereignty. Be sure to review the key terms and concepts in this chapter so that you understand how everything in the world order ties together.

13

The European Union

During the Cold War, Western European states came together to build stronger relations. In the 1950s, France, Belgium, Italy, Luxembourg, the Netherlands, and West Germany signed a treaty to create the European Economic Community (EEC). After decades of cooperation and organization, the European Union (EU) was officially established in 1993. With nearly 30 member-states and a population of over 510 million, the EU's aims are to promote the free movement of people, goods, service, and economic capital; to enact legislation and administer justice for all members; and to maintain common policies in important areas like trade, development, and agriculture.

Other International Organizations

While organizations such as the United Nations, NATO, and the European Union capture daily headlines in world newspapers, there are other important international organizations that play a role in political geography. A few of those are summarized in the following chart.

Organization of American States (OAS)	Consisting of 35 states in the western hemisphere, the OAS promotes regional solidarity and cooperation.
African Union (AU)	Consisting of 55 African states, the AU defends its members' sovereignty and promotes peace, security, economic development, and solidarity among member states.
Association of Southeast Asian Nations (ASEAN)	Formed by 10 states, ASEAN's goal is to facilitate trade and improve economic and political relations between Southeast Asian member states.
Arab League (AL)	Consisting of 22 members, including Palestine, the AL aims to strengthen ties and coordinate foreign and domestic policies in the Middle East and North Africa on a state and local level.
Organization of the Petroleum Exporting Countries (OPEC)	Currently consisting of 14 states, OPEC members control almost half the world's oil production and more than 70 percent of the known oil reserves. Its mission is to coordinate and unify its members' petroleum policies and to provide a regular supply of oil to maintain a stable, healthy oil market.

CENTRIPETAL AND CENTRIFUGAL FORCES

A concern of every state is how to maintain its sovereignty in the face of forces that may divide its citizens. The theory of centripetal and centrifugal forces is associated with political geographer Richard Hartshorne. He stated that the integration of a state's geographical area involved two competing forces: **centripetal forces** that bring people together and **centrifugal forces** that pull people apart.

Centripetal Forces

Centripetal forces might be symbolized through art such as a flag or a painting. These symbols of nationalism are sometimes called national iconography. For many people, their country's flag inspires patriotism, as does the national anthem. During the Olympics, national iconographies are very evident.

Centripetal forces can also occur on an economic level. A state needs to have sufficient resources to support the long-term economic well-being of its citizens. Also, the state needs a relatively equitable method of administering its resources. If all such benefits go to the upper classes, then this could be a centrifugal force that spreads animosity among the classes. Strong infrastructure, such as roads and bridges, and a good transportation system are additional examples of centripetal forces on the economic level. The Netherlands, Germany, Japan, Singapore, and the United Arab Emirates are examples of countries with world-class infrastructure systems serving as centripetal forces.

Perhaps the most powerful centripetal forces are on the cultural level. Having a common language and a common religion can foster a stronger feeling of national pride and work to keep the state together. Hinduism in India, Islam in Jordan, and Judaism in Israel are examples of centripetal forces.

Ethnonationalism is another expression of centripetal force. Japan offers an example of ethnonationalism, as the Japanese people view their common cultural, linguistic, and historical heritage as a unifying force.

Centrifugal Forces

In contrast, centrifugal forces divide a state's citizens. Differences in political views, economic status, and culture are all centrifugal forces. These forces can prevent interaction and create dissimilarity among the country's people. This in turn can lead to **regionalism**. In extreme forms of regionalism, a certain area of a country may seek to create its own **autonomous region**, which is a segment of a country that has some degree of self-governing authority granted to it by the state. To stop a country from breaking apart, a country must have centripetal forces of greater magnitude than the centrifugal forces. When the centripetal forces are stronger than centrifugal forces, the country will be better able to handle both global and internal domestic challenges. When centrifugal forces are dominant, the national government can lose control and even fail.

A religious or linguistic factor may be both a centrifugal and a centripetal factor at the same time. In countries that are **theocracies**, where one particular religion is intertwined with the political structure, religion is a unifying force. Many of the laws of the country are based on the principles of the official religion. In the Muslim world, Saudi Arabia, Iran, and Pakistan have many social laws that are based on Islam. Vatican City is an example of a Christian theocracy. In the Vatican, Christianity is a very strong centripetal force. In other countries, religion can be a centrifugal force. Earlier in the chapter, we discussed Ireland and Northern Ireland and how religion was a major dividing force. Conflicts between Sunni Muslims and Shiite Muslims in Iraq and Syria are also examples of religion serving as a centrifugal force within a state.

13

> **✔ AP Expert Note**
>
> **Be able to give examples of countries experiencing centripetal and centrifugal forces**
>
> Centripetal and centrifugal forces are multifaceted and fairly common. Most states of the world face issues that threaten to pull apart their citizens. Differences in religion, language, culture, economic status, and political affiliation can be causes for unrest and even hostility. But there are also forces that help countries unite their citizens. Loyalty and love of country are unifying forces. On the AP exam, you should be able to identify and give your own examples of these centripetal and centrifugal forces as well as explain their impact on various countries.

The Former Soviet Union

The Soviet Union experienced strong centrifugal forces, which intensified greatly during the 1980s. Trying to rule a country as large and as diverse as the former Soviet Union proved to be an impossible task. A poor economy contributed to the breakup of the Soviet Union. Shelves in grocery stores were empty, causing unrest. As a result, Soviet leader Mikhail Gorbachev started *perestroika*, a major restructuring of the economy.

As the Cold War came to a close, the process of breaking up the Soviet bloc was termed "devolution." **Devolution** is when the central or federal government gives up power to the different regions of the country. Latvia, Lithuania, Estonia, Belarus, and Ukraine in the West formed their own countries based on their individual ethnicities and languages. In the Central Asian region, Kazakhstan, Uzbekistan, Kyrgyzstan, Turkmenistan, and Tajikistan seceded to create their own independent states. The states around the Caspian Sea—Georgia, Armenia, and Azerbaijan—also broke off.

The Russian state, largely under the leadership of Vladimir Putin, has squelched further secession attempts. Russia is still the largest country in the world by area and possesses vast natural resources. In the 1990s, however, the economy of Russia was in peril. The black market thrived, and the Russian federal government had very little control over pricing structures. Putin's leadership restabilized the country but did so at the expense of personal and political freedom, causing many NATO countries to fear another cold war.

Earlier in the chapter there was a discussion on the breakup of Yugoslavia, which underwent a process referred to as balkanization. In Yugoslavia, there were a myriad of centrifugal forces. There were many different ethnic groups within the same country. Certain areas were dominated by certain Christian denominations, and other areas included large populations of Muslims. There were a variety of languages spoken in various swaths of Yugoslavia. Some areas were more capitalistic and pro-Western, and other areas were more anti-West. These forces reached a critical level, and war broke out across the Balkan Peninsula. The end result was a balkanization of the former Yugoslavia, producing multiple independent states. Today, the area that was once Yugoslavia consists of Serbia, Croatia, Bosnia and Herzegovina, Montenegro, Slovenia, Macedonia, and Kosovo. Kosovo is still struggling to gain full international recognition as a country, aptly illustrating the long-term and complicated nature of centrifugal forces in the Balkans.

Syria

One of the most profound ongoing examples of how centrifugal forces have threatened a country's existence is in Syria. Civil war broke out in Syria in 2011. But long before the fighting started, many Syrians were concerned about the lack of employment, widespread political and business corruption, and a lack of political rights under President Bashar al-Assad, who took power in 2000. In early 2011, pro-democracy demonstrations inspired by the Arab Spring erupted in Syria. The government immediately deployed armed forces to crush the resistance. This triggered further protests, which were soon followed by open warfare across Syria.

The two sides of the civil war have some very significant differences in terms of politics and religion. President al-Assad and his supporters are members of a minority Shiite Muslim sect, while the opposing forces are mostly part of Syria's Sunni majority. As of 2018, the death toll in Syria was estimated to be around 500,000. More than five million Syrians have fled the country to seek refuge in Lebanon, Jordan, and throughout the rest of the Middle East and Europe. The centripetal forces in Syria were woefully inadequate to balance the centrifugal forces that have ripped the country apart.

THE HISTORICAL GEOGRAPHY OF THE UNITED STATES

A subset of geography called **historical geography** analyzes geographical patterns through history. As a large landmass with varied physical features, the United States has an interesting geographical pattern. Because the United States was settled by multiple peoples over multiple centuries, the United States is considered an immigrant state. An immigrant state is comprised primarily of immigrants and their descendants. Settlement of the United States by the Europeans began in the early 1600s and continues today as people come in from around the world. The United States was a colony of Great Britain until the Revolutionary War in the late 1700s. After gaining independence, the first U.S. government was a confederation, or a loose grouping of states for a common purpose. However, the Articles of Confederation didn't work very well because the states had too much power and the federal government didn't have enough. Without adequate authority, the national government was unable to collect enough tax revenue and provide a national defense. Ultimately, the federal government could not support itself financially.

To remedy the power imbalance, a Constitutional Convention was convened in Philadelphia, where political leaders developed the U.S. Constitution, which granted more power to the federal government. The U.S. political system is considered a federal system, where the ultimate power rests in the hands of the national government. The state governments can establish laws but cannot supersede the authority of the national government. This form of government is in between a confederation, where power lies in the hands of the individual states, and a unitary style of government, where all decisions are made by the national government. Great Britain is an example of a state with a unitary government.

The U.S. government is a representative form of government. Leaders are elected from the individual states to be representatives and senators in two houses of Congress. Today, the United States has 100 senators and 435 representatives. U.S. senators serve an entire state for six-year terms, while U.S. representatives serve their districts for two-year terms. Senators and representatives can be reelected to multiple terms with no limitation on the number of times they can serve. These districts are **reapportioned** every 10 years based on the results of the census so that each district has about the same number of people. Therefore, urban areas with a higher population density have smaller districts, while rural districts are larger. Due to population changes, political boundaries must be redrawn so that the districts are more representative of the new population numbers. Because the redistricting is controlled by each state's legislature, the political party with the majority vote can control the redistricting. As such, this process has become a contentious and often manipulative one. In fact, one type of political redistricting has been given a negative nickname, "gerrymandering." **Gerrymandering** is a process in which a political party manipulates the drawing of political boundaries for political gain. In recent years, the states of North Carolina and California have been criticized for engaging in blatant gerrymandering.

After gaining its independence, the United States expanded steadily west into its frontier area, a term for territory not under the control of a state. The Louisiana Territory was a large purchase of land by the U.S. government in 1803, encompassing land up the Mississippi river and westward to the Rocky Mountains. Famed explorers Lewis and Clark were sent out on an expedition by President Thomas Jefferson to explore and bring back reports of what the new territory encompassed.

Expansionism continued in the 1840s, when the phrase "manifest destiny" was introduced into the American political discourse. Manifest destiny was the belief that the U.S. government should rule all lands from the Atlantic Ocean to the Pacific Ocean. Manifest destiny was used to justify the acquisition of new lands by any means.

Early in the nineteenth century, the United States was growing rapidly, and white settlers in the South faced what they considered to be an obstacle: the area was home to the Cherokee, Creek, Choctaw, and Seminole nations. These nations, in the view of the settlers and many other white Americans, were standing in the way of progress. Eager for land, the white settlers pressured the federal government to acquire American Indian territory. The U.S. government sided with the white settlers and in the 1830s began the long process of forcibly relocating large populations of American Indians. They were made to travel to designated tracts of land known as reservations, located hundreds of miles from their original homelands. These migrations are collectively called the Trail of Tears because thousands of American Indians died due to the harshness of the journey or clashes with the U.S. military.

Expansion continued in the twentieth century as the United States granted statehood to Alaska and Hawaii (the 49th and 50th states respectively) in 1959. A lingering question is whether or not the United States will ever add more states. Puerto Rico is a territory of the United States, and its citizens enjoy all of the privileges of being U.S. citizens except for representation in Congress and the right to vote for the president. Puerto Ricans do not have to pay U.S. taxes. Of all of the U.S. territories, Puerto Rico is the most likely to someday become a U.S. state.

Canada, by contrast, has recently incorporated new territory into its state. The recently created territory of Nunavut was established as a homeland for American Indians. Created out of the Northwest Territories in 1999, Nunavut encompasses the traditional lands of the Inuit people, the indigenous people of Arctic Canada. Nunavut's admission to the Canadian state represented the first major change to Canada's political map since the incorporation of Newfoundland in 1949.

Map of Canada

ISSUES OF GEOPOLITICS

As discussed in the previous section on boundaries, there are many boundary disputes in the world today. Sometimes these disputes are decided diplomatically and sometimes by military action. Self-interest and economic well-being often play a major role in the creation of boundaries instead of the population's ethnic and cultural characteristics.

Currently, land is in dispute in several areas. One is the Kashmir region of India, Pakistan, and China. In this territory, there are both ethnic and religious differences. Since Indian independence in 1947, India has fought four wars over the territory, three with Pakistan and one with China. Also crucial in this region are the rivers. Because Kashmir is high in the Himalayan Mountains, it is the source of many rivers that flow into both India and Pakistan. The control of these rivers means the control of transportation and water resources.

Early in the settlement of Canada and the United States, there was some conflict over the interpretation of where the border lay. The Aroostook War was fought over the boundary between Maine and New Brunswick. An 1842 treaty permanently established the border between the United States and Canada.

If you look at a map of the Middle East today, you'll see a small region near the border of Iraq and Kuwait that some suggest is still in dispute today. The claim was settled by the United Nations in 1994, and the boundaries on current maps show that decision. A very pressing issue in the Middle East is the dispute between the Israelis and the Palestinians over territory claims.

Ethnicity and Culture: Concepts and Issues

High-Yield

The concept of ethnicity is a difficult one for geographers to deal with because the definition of ethnicity is a controversial one. **Ethnicity** is connected to the cultural traditions of a group of people. It is different from **race**, which encompasses the perceived physical characteristics of a group of people. Ethnicity tends to emphasize nationalism more than race and often corresponds with nationhood. To many, ethnic groups are comprised of a number of different characteristics. Some say that religion and language determine ethnicity, while others suggest that country of origin or nationality are more important. Another perspective maintains that skin color and other racial characteristics indicate ethnicity. While there is no widespread agreement about what precisely ethnicity consists of, all of these characteristics can play a role when identifying ethnic groups.

Globalization and Cultural Shatterbelts

Globalization is the expansion of economic, political, and cultural processes to the point that they become global in scale and impact. Globalization can refer to the interconnections of ideas, goods, and information around the Earth. As communication increases, globalization increases. Popular culture is spread quickly in today's world. While many cultural trends further the process of globalization, the celebration of ethnic identities can serve as a counterpoint, separating different groups of people and keeping individual differences alive.

A **cultural shatterbelt** is an area where people are caught between the globalization or modernization of their culture and their traditional cultural identity. This term can be applied to any area where different cultural elements come into contact and create instability. In Vietnam, for example, modernization is taking hold in the larger urban areas of Hanoi and Ho Chi Minh City, but the old culture persists in most rural areas. Another example is when a population conflicts with the majority religion; in 2006, Lebanese Christians were stuck in the middle of a conflict between Lebanon's Hezbollah militia and Israel. Such cultural battles are driving away much-needed tourism income and are dividing the Lebanese state.

Because of globalization, English has become the world's lingua franca. Most world business is done in English. All airline pilots in the world communicate in English. It can be argued that this process of cultural adaptation, the transition of a varied cultural environment into one culture, means that local traditions are fading out and new ones are emerging. For example, the use of cell phones and text messaging has created its own form of cultural communication among today's youth.

Immigration

Because the United States is an immigrant state, the ethnicities and cultures in the United States are varied. One can find Americans with ancestors who are Italian, Swedish, Chinese, Vietnamese, Colombian, and so on. Sometimes, the United States is called a "melting pot" of cultures.

Many of today's U.S. immigrants arrive through the process of chain migration. In this process, immigrants who already live in a given country gain access to visas for close relatives and provide a support network for them to also enter the country. Sometimes, chain migration involves money that immigrants send to family members; for example, many of the Hmong in the United States send a large percentage of their incomes back to Laos and Thailand so family members can someday join them. One of the most contentious political issues in the United States is whether or not to continue allowing chain migration, as there are many who feel this practice should be prohibited.

Upon entering a new country, most immigrants exercise voluntary segregation owing to the language barrier. Newly arrived immigrants who do not speak the language often choose to live in an area where they can communicate and feel comfortable culturally. This voluntary segregation leads to the creation of ethnic neighborhoods. Ethnic neighborhoods share the same language and sometimes a dominant religion. Ethnic neighborhoods may have restaurants, clothing stores, music stores, and other retail shops that cater to that culture's needs.

New York City, a key immigrant entry point, is known for its ethnic neighborhoods. Little Italy in the Lower East Side of Manhattan was once known for its distinctive restaurants and shops catering to the Italian immigrants who lived there. Likewise, many recent immigrants from China have established commercial activities in Chinatown, and their cultural imprint has given this neighborhood a distinctive flair. A McDonald's located in Chinatown has its menu printed in Chinese, and tai chi classes are held at dawn in the parks there. Similarly, a strong Puerto Rican community is concentrated in the Spanish Harlem area.

Brazilians, Poles, Jamaicans, and Greeks all have concentrated in different areas of New York City from Queens to the Bronx. These ethnic neighborhoods have left a distinct impression on the ethnic landscape. The **ethnic landscape** is the evidence of an ethnicity on the features of the landscape. This may include murals on public buildings and the nature of the commercial businesses in an area. In many large urban centers, a plural society has developed. A plural society is characterized by two or more ethnicities living in the same area, but each keeping their own identity and characteristics. The diversity of food, architecture, language, religions, and other cultural traits is a positive characteristic of large urban areas in the United States, creating a wonderful cultural experience.

Oppression of Minorities

Forced segregation is the separation of a group of people by law. In the United States, the old Jim Crow laws in the South that designated separate drinking fountains for black people and white people offer a classic example of forced segregation. In addition, different bathrooms, schools, and legal statuses all were in effect for blacks and whites.

As discussed earlier in the chapter, in South Africa the policy of apartheid, a system of segregation on the grounds of race, separated the country's whites and blacks from 1948 to 1991. Under pressure from Nelson Mandela and activists abroad, the policy of apartheid was finally abolished. Nevertheless, the country still feels the legacy of apartheid and continues to engage in a national healing process.

In one of the most severe cases of forced segregation, Germans during World War II segregated and executed millions of Jews, Romany (Gypsies), homosexuals, and people with disabilities during the Holocaust. Some Jewish people were rounded up and put into ghettos. Ghettos were essentially walled holding pens within cities where minorities were kept before eventually being taken to concentration camps. Ghettos are an example of an ethnic enclave. Just as a political enclave is a country that is entirely surrounded by another country, an **ethnic enclave** is an ethnic neighborhood that is surrounded by people of a different ethnicity; usually the surrounding ethnicity is hostile to the group in the enclave.

When two different ethnic groups vie for the same territory, the result is an ethnic conflict. In extreme cases, a dominant ethnicity will try to eliminate the less powerful group. This is sometimes called ethnic cleansing, a benign-sounding term for genocide. Millions have been killed due to genocide around the globe. For example, under Slobodan Milošević, Bosnian Serbs killed thousands of Bosnian Muslims. Genocide has also occurred in Sudan and with the Hutu and Tutsi tribes in Rwanda.

Ethnic Diversity in the United States

The two largest minority ethnicities in the United States are Latinos and African Americans. There are approximately 58 million Latinos in the United States, accounting for more than 17 percent of the total population. With a population of about 47 million, African Americans comprise approximately 13 percent of the total U.S. population. Asian Americans account for just over 5 percent of the population. The evidence of an increasing Latino population is evident on the cultural landscape, especially in the Southwest and in large cities. Latino communities are common in most American cities, and restaurants serving Latino food and bilingual street signs and advertisements are common in many areas.

 ## NEXT STEP: PRACTICE

Go to Rapid Review and Practice Chapter 6 or to your online quizzes on kaptest.com for exam-like practice on this topic.

Haven't registered your book yet? Go to kaptest.com/moreonline to begin.

CHAPTER 14

Agriculture and Rural Land-Use Patterns and Processes

LEARNING OBJECTIVES

After studying this chapter, you will be able to:

- Describe the impacts of the First and Second Agricultural Revolutions.

- Evaluate the Green Revolution's positive and negative effects.

- Explain how agricultural practices shape the surrounding environment.

- Define real-world applications of von Thünen's land use model.

- Describe the interrelationship of agribusiness and economic factors.

- Analyze the intersection of gender and food production and consumption.

- List pertinent issues of modern-day agriculture and food production.

- Explain the global nature of food supply chains, particularly in terms of production and consumption.

- Define the major bioclimatic zones' impact on agricultural production regions.

A HISTORICAL PERSPECTIVE

An old joke suggests that all farmers are "out standing" in their fields. Yet, this pun carries a deeper meaning. Today's farmers grow more agricultural products on less land than ever before in human history. How? Through a mastery of the increasingly advanced technology, transportation, and techniques of **farming**.

Today's farmers compete with one another in a global market. They also need to be aware of crop prices and policies practiced, not just in their own communities but around the world. In the United States, only 2 percent of the population is involved with farming as a full-time occupation; this is a far cry from the mid-nineteenth century, when half the U.S. workforce was involved in farming. However, millions of people are still involved in the transportation, production, and distribution of agricultural products. In many Midwestern states, this multi-billion-dollar industry is the states' largest employer.

Farming hasn't always been a common source of food, however. The first way humans obtained food was by **hunting and gathering**. Nomadic tribes around the world depended on migratory animals for sustenance; these societies also sustained themselves on wild fruits and berries. However, during periods of environmental stress, like drought, the supply of fruits and berries was limited, causing starvation. Because of this, an alternative was needed.

First Agricultural Revolution

High-Yield

Agriculture is the raising of animals or the growing of crops to obtain food for primary consumption by the farm family or for sale. Systems of agriculture developed around the ancient world, in several different locations; these systems developed independently of one another. The shift from societies' hunting and gathering to planting crops for food took many years and changed human history. This **First Agricultural Revolution**, also called the Neolithic Agricultural Revolution, allowed humans to form settled societies and create a more reliable source of food.

To understand how truly revolutionary this event was, consider the nature of human life before agriculture. Imagine that humans don't know how to grow crops. The idea of planting seeds and watering them to produce a plant has not yet been thought of. People depend on picking wild fruits and roots and hunting animals for food, making for a precarious existence. Eventually, people realized that some of the berries that were dropped the previous year left seeds on the ground. If given enough water, sunlight, and the right temperature, those seeds grew into plants and produced more berries.

This revelation came after hundreds, if not thousands, of years. Migrating people had to make the association between the dropped berry and the new bush, and in order to do that, they had to return to the same location year after year. When humans began to figure out how to cultivate seeds, they started to plant and sustain crops themselves. Many failed attempts preceded what we know as today's agriculture. At first, humans could plant crops only on a relatively small scale; these societies could not support large urban areas. Agriculture was also very labor intensive at this point.

Once people developed a better understanding of the process of planting crops, they became more successful. With a more stable food source, the global population began to grow. More people needed more food, causing a cycle of increased farming production and increasing populations. As societies grew more complex, so too did labor; job specialization arose along class and gender lines. Societies also became organized around the growing season.

In addition to **plant domestication**, the cultivation and breeding of plants for human benefit, animal domestication became more common, changing the diets of people around the world. **Animal domestication** is the process of taming and raising wild animals for human benefit. Cows, pigs, and chickens were each domesticated in different parts of the world and remain staples of our diet today.

Animal domestication also had dramatic social effects. For example, taming the horse allowed the formation of large-scale Eurasian steppe nomad societies such as the Mongol Empire, which loomed over settled agricultural societies as a potential military threat. This dynamic between settled and nomadic societies spanned centuries, until the eighteenth century, when horse cavalry declined in usefulness thanks to advancements in gunpowder weapons.

Second Agricultural Revolution

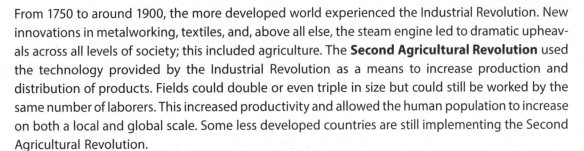
High-Yield

From 1750 to around 1900, the more developed world experienced the Industrial Revolution. New innovations in metalworking, textiles, and, above all else, the steam engine led to dramatic upheavals across all levels of society; this included agriculture. The **Second Agricultural Revolution** used the technology provided by the Industrial Revolution as a means to increase production and distribution of products. Fields could double or even triple in size but could still be worked by the same number of laborers. This increased productivity and allowed the human population to increase on both a local and global scale. Some less developed countries are still implementing the Second Agricultural Revolution.

Consider the cotton gin; Eli Whitney invented it in 1793. Removing the cotton fiber from the stalk and the pods of the cotton plant was extremely labor-intensive to do by hand and, therefore, expensive. A single cotton "engine" automated this process; it did the work of dozens of people more quickly. This greatly increased agricultural production in the American South, which had a climate conducive for growing cotton. It was vital for the development of new textile industries that employed thousands. However, the cotton gin also made slavery a far more lucrative practice in the South, ensuring decades of further slavery for African Americans.

For all its consequences, the cotton gin was merely one invention of the Second Agricultural Revolution. Wheat was being harvested by machines instead of by hand, corn farmers began using a technological forerunner to the modern combine, and dozens of other inventions increased the productivity of agriculture in general, creating multiple social effects. Factories to build these farming devices sprouted up. Railroads, faster ships, and new canals were needed to transport these agricultural products to market; this was important because if the agricultural products couldn't make it to market in time, they would spoil. Markets also expanded farther outward. Economic

14

systems in the United States and across Europe grew increasingly complex in order to manage this new environment. The concentration of the vast wealth produced by farming led to significant economic inequality and labor strife.

The Second Agricultural Revolution had a dramatic effect on rural areas. More people left the farms because less manual work was available. They moved to urban areas to fulfill industries' demands for workers. The share of the U.S. population that lived in urban areas ballooned from roughly 15 percent in 1850 to nearly 40 percent by 1900. As transportation continued to improve, productivity increased, which had a profound effect on agricultural methods and crops. This increase in food production corresponded with the first wave of human population growth.

The Green Revolution

High-Yield

During the latter half of the twentieth century, the **Third Agricultural Revolution** began. It is commonly referred to as the Green Revolution. This revolution corresponded with the exponential population growth occurring around the world, a direct result of the Second Agricultural Revolution and innovations in medicine that led to longer, healthier lives. This revolution involved the rise of industrial farming, which is the mass production of agricultural products. Family-owned farms had largely become a thing of the past with the rise of corporate agribusiness.

The Green Revolution began in the early 1940s, but did not truly take off until the 1960s. Many argue that the Green Revolution started with Norman Borlaug, an agricultural specialist at the University of Minnesota. His work with wheat production in Mexico transformed the country from an importer to an exporter of wheat within a few years. Borlaug's work spread to other less developed world regions and to other crops. Borlaug is often credited with saving a billion people from mass starvation, thanks to his research. Universities around the world now specialize in agricultural science as a result.

The Green Revolution's key innovation was the hybridization of crops and animals as well as the increased use of chemical fertilizers. Both hybridization and an increased use of fertilizers had a revolutionary impact on food production. Through selective breeding, scientists created many hybrids of plants and animals that survived in conditions where they previously couldn't. The Green Revolution also involved the increased use of chemical fertilizers to enhance productivity and the continued benefit from mechanization. (Note that hybridization is a separate issue from GMOs and their effects on agriculture, as that issue emerged in the 1990s.)

In the United States, the Green Revolution began on a massive scale in the 1960s. Scientists crossbred different varieties of wheat, corn, and other agricultural products to change their characteristics. For example, wheat traditionally needed to be grown in a dry climate; too much moisture meant that the crop would spoil in the fields. As a result of hybridization, modern wheat strains can resist spoilage in the field. Corn, soybeans, cotton, and dozens of other products underwent similar hybridization.

Another hallmark of the Green Revolution was double-cropping, which is planting and harvesting two crops in the same field. In the past, a field could only support one crop per season because there is typically just one rainy season. With the advent of irrigation systems, along with hybridized seeds and chemical fertilizers and pesticides, double-cropping and even triple-cropping became possible.

14

Environmental modification is the introduction of human-made chemicals and practices to an area. At times, it has had drastic effects on the native soil and vegetation. It is an important aspect of the Green Revolution. The use of pesticides on farm products and the practice of double-cropping have led to increased crop yields; however, this also means altering the natural environment, including introducing more chemicals to food and land. Organic farming has become more popular in direct response to the use of pesticides.

Social Effects of the Green Revolution

The Green Revolution was also vital in the evolution of the modern supermarket. With the increased efficiency in transportation, **globalized agriculture** arose. Today, farmers in the Great Plains monitor the prices of wheat and corn in Asia and Europe, which directly affect their profits. Farmers in western North Dakota ship their wheat via train to Seattle, where it is then loaded onto ships and sent to Asia. Much of the Upper Midwest sends products down the Mississippi River to ports around New Orleans, where it is then sent to South America.

Because of the mechanization and mass production of farm products during the Green Revolution, most food is now coming from highly industrialized, automated operations that produce millions of dollars in profit each year instead of small mom-and-pop farms in the Midwest. This has led to the development of what is known as **agribusiness**. These industrialized farmers contract out with big processing facilities and manufacturers to generate profit for both the farmer and the manufacturer.

Agribusiness practices have concerned some animal rights activists, who feel that the quality of an animal's life is adversely affected when it isn't living in natural conditions. For example, hundreds of thousands of chickens are forced to live in cramped conditions on large production farms. Producers respond by saying that they are simply trying to satisfy the demand of a population that increasingly prefers chicken in their diet. Growth hormones and antibiotics are also given to chickens to increase breast size as well as reduce the spread of diseases, which can wipe out entire farms. Chicken has become a staple food in the Western diet, and the industrial-scale raising of chickens is an important aspect of the Green Revolution.

Another aspect of agribusiness is a preference for fields that grow corn, soybeans, wheat, and other high-yield crops as opposed to a range of produce. This approach creates something known as a **monoculture**. While it can maximize profits, monocultures also increase vulnerability to pests, blights, and other diseases.

The Green Revolution has meant that farming productivity has never been higher in human history, feeding more people than ever. People around the world still have trouble accessing stable food supplies, but this is mostly due to inadequate distribution systems to get products to hungry people, not to a lack of food production. Political systems and policies around the globe are more of an obstacle to feeding people than agricultural production.

14

Genetically Modified Organisms (GMOs)

The Green Revolution continues today, and we may have only begun to see its effects. Researchers across the world are looking for new ways to grow crops better and faster. The abundant, varied supply of foodstuffs at your local grocery store is proof. An important way that these new crops are being produced is through the use of **biotechnology**. Also known as genetic engineering, biotechnology is the altering of DNA in plants and animals to create **genetically modified organisms**, or GMOs.

Genetic engineering is distinct from hybridization, which merely applies selective breeding and other traditional agricultural practices in a laboratory setting. Biotechnology can create new or altered species that were previously difficult, if not impossible, to achieve. Some examples of genetic modification include altering chickens to produce more meat, altering rice to produce extra vitamins, or even just changing the cosmetic features of the plant, like its color. GMOs first entered the market in 1994 but are now commonplace. This technological revolution is ongoing and is having a dramatic impact on the food quality in more developed countries. The future of GMOs may have profound effects on the productivity of agriculture as a whole.

One of the greatest feats in agricultural engineering took place with the genetic modification of rice. Rice was first modified in the Philippines and then diffused to other areas of Asia. Even today, new hybrids are constantly being produced in laboratories all over the world. Rice is now heartier and can be grown more quickly. This helps feed more people in some of the poorest regions of Asia.

Some scientists and environmentalists argue against the use of GMOs. They make the case that the resulting food is unsafe and causes problems in humans such as more allergies in children. This has led to the mandatory labeling of GMO products in several countries. Some accuse GMO critics of being against progress and innovation. Others criticize the business dimension of GMOs, such as agribusiness companies suing farmers for copyright infringement if the GMO crops accidentally cross-pollinate with non-GMO strains in neighboring fields. Legal action is initiated as cross-pollinating violates the patent that the agribusiness has on the DNA of the GMO seed stock it developed.

Organic farming has grown tremendously over the past two decades. It uses natural processes and seeds that are not genetically altered by any means. To be certified as organic in the United States, farmers must demonstrate organic methods on a number of different measures.

✔ **AP Expert Note**

Be sure to know the timing and differences of the three agricultural revolutions

It is easy to mistakenly attribute facts about one agricultural revolution to another. Make sure you have their timing, major innovations, and consequences nailed down. Do not be led astray by wrong answer choices on the exam that mix up their key facts.

Fourth Agricultural Revolution

The **Fourth Agricultural Revolution** was, in part, a response to the trade-offs of the Green Revolution; rather than being geared toward the global marketplace, food is both grown and sold locally, reducing transportation costs. Chemical fertilizers and pesticides are minimized, when not eliminated, in favor of pure, organic farming. Heirloom plant seeds are often used instead of modern hybrids. Heirloom plants can result in a diversity of flavor and texture at the cost of a lower crop yield.

While it only truly blossomed in the twenty-first century, the seeds of the Fourth Agricultural Revolution date back millennia. Small urban gardens have been present in cities since Ancient Egypt. In the United States, the first government-sponsored urban farming effort occurred during World War I; Americans were encouraged to grow "victory gardens" in their window boxes, backyards, and rooftops as a way to reduce pressure on the food supply during wartime rationing.

Vertical farms are another key aspect in the Fourth Agricultural Revolution. Crops are grown indoors, in vertically stacked layers, in farms that can fill a whole skyscraper. They often rely on hydroponics, where plants are grown in water rather than soil. When actual sunlight is not practical for such a farm, artificial sunlight can be generated using LED lights.

The Fourth Agricultural Revolution is not without its own drawbacks, however. Urban land is far more expensive than rural land. Thus, urban farming often takes advantage of otherwise unused space like rooftops and back lots. However, the soil in urban areas can be contaminated with toxins, like lead from old construction materials. Air pollution from vehicles can affect plants as well. Vertical farming faces questions of economic and environmental sustainability, as heating and lighting an indoor vertical farm requires more energy than traditional urban farms.

The Next Agricultural Revolution?

The continuing debate over GMOs has not stopped biotechnology research. The techniques that created the original GMOs seem primitive in comparison to modern tools. This has some scientists predicting an impending biorevolution. Plants, animals, and even human beings may be re-engineered in ways that might once have seemed like wild flights of science fiction.

For example, the refinement of genome-editing techniques allows for a kind of "molecular scissors." Imagine the DNA of a plant, animal, or even a human as a book. In a few short years, genome editing has gone from being able to target specific paragraphs for deletion or insertion to being able to alter single words. Animals are being modified in new ways as well. In 2017, Chinese researchers created leaner pigs that can survive better at lower temperatures, saving on heating costs for farmers and offering consumers the possibility of healthier pork.

Precision genetic engineering has the potential to allow the almost limitless modification of agricultural products, sparking a Fifth Agricultural Revolution. What effects it will have on farming and global society remain to be seen.

AGRICULTURAL HEARTHS

One of the most distinguished cultural geographers in the history of agriculture was Carl Sauer. A professor of geography at the University of California–Berkeley, Sauer was one of the most vehement critics of the philosophy of environmental determinism. He started the field of cultural ecology due to his belief that humans had power over their environment and weren't simply the product of it. Finally, Sauer mapped out the **agricultural origins** of both vegetative planting and seed agriculture.

Hearths of Vegetative and Seed Planting and Animal Domestication

Sauer suggested that there are two distinct types of agriculture: vegetative planting and seed agriculture. **Vegetative planting** means removing part of a plant and putting it in the ground to grow a new plant. For example, consider the hosta plant. A person can cut a hosta in half vertically and replant each side to form two independent plants. The replanted halves will grow just like the original plant. **Seed agriculture** means taking seeds from existing plants and planting them to produce new plants. The vast majority of farmers use this method today.

It is believed that vegetative agriculture developed in three areas: Central America and northwestern South America, West Africa, and Southeast Asia. These were all tropical regions, meaning their climates were conducive to growing agricultural products. They also had relatively large populations to provide the workforce to domesticate regional plants and animals.

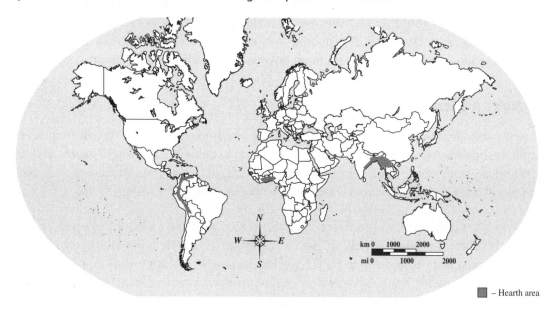

— Hearth area

Vegetative Planting Hearths

Central America and Northwestern South America

According to Sauer, one of the earliest agricultural regions was Central America and northwestern South America; both regions are in close proximity to each other, so they are considered a single primary agricultural region. They also domesticated many of the same animals at the same time. The peoples of these areas were the Aztecs, Mayans, and Incas.

The first major hearth of vegetative planting was this area. Here, they grew manioc, sweet potato, and arrowroot. Manioc, sometimes called cassava, is a root crop that is still a staple food source in much of Brazil. It is poisonous if not fully cooked, but cooking the manioc denatures its toxins, making it safe to eat.

The animals first domesticated in this area were turkeys, llamas, and alpacas. The llama and alpaca are indigenous to the Andes Mountains and are still very common along this "spine" of South America. Llamas and alpacas are important for their wool, used in the production of clothing. Turkeys became famous as a meat source; many U.S. families cook them as a centerpiece of the traditional Thanksgiving meal. These products and animals later diffused from Central America and northwestern South America northward into the present-day United States and Canada and southward to the tip of Patagonia in Argentina.

West Africa

The second major hearth of vegetative planting was West Africa. The major agricultural products that were first domesticated in this region were yams and palm oil. West Africa also domesticated livestock such as cattle, sheep, and goats. These animals were later diffused throughout the Old World. Later, European explorers and settlers brought them to the New World, Australia, and New Zealand. Raising cattle became, and still is, a major agricultural industry in the United States. Our dairy supply depends upon cattle, which are also a major source of meat.

Southeast Asia

The third major vegetative planting hearth region was Southeast Asia. The plants that were first domesticated in this area were root crops, such as taro (now a staple in Pacific Island nations), bananas, and palm trees. The animals first domesticated here were dogs, pigs, and chickens. Today, chicken is a staple meat source in Europe and the western hemisphere.

Hearths of Seed Agriculture

In addition to the hearths of vegetative planting, there are also hearths of seed agriculture. The vast majority of modern farmers use this method. The four main hearths of seed agriculture are Central America, northeastern Africa, northern China, and northeastern India. These hearths were important because seed agriculture diffused into neighboring areas that still predominantly practice this type of farming today.

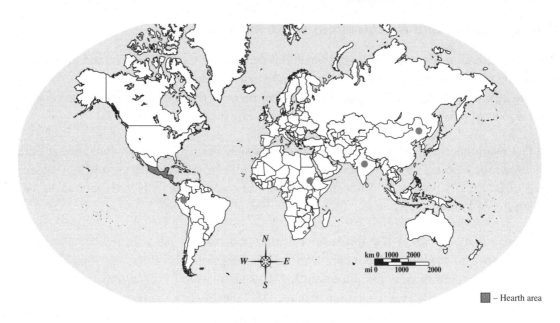

Seed Agriculture Hearths

Central America

The first major area of seed agriculture was in Central America, in southern portions of Mexico. Squash, beans, and cotton were the major seed crops domesticated here. Over time, these crops spread throughout the rest of North America and Central America as well as South America. Once European colonizers realized the importance of cotton, they sold it back to European markets for major profits. Cotton is a highly labor-intensive crop, and prior to the invention of the cotton gin, it had to be harvested by hand. Cotton was one of the crops that fueled the slave trade, the source of agricultural labor in the southern United States.

Northeastern Africa

The second major hearth of seed agriculture was in northeastern Africa, around the present-day country of Ethiopia. One of the major crops domesticated here was coffee. Coffee dates back approximately 1,200 years and is still a major source of Ethiopian national pride. Coffee production then spread to West Africa and consequently to South America along with the slave trade. Northern countries in South America, such as Colombia and Venezuela, have prospered from the production of coffee.

Northern China

In the northern China region, millet was domesticated. Millet is a grain crop that possesses more calories than the average wheat plant. Millet is oftentimes used as a substitute in the diets of people who have allergies to wheat.

14

Northeastern India

Rice may have first been domesticated in northern India after arriving via trade routes from southwest Africa, but the precise origins of rice are as yet unknown. Some geographers have given the nod to Southeast Asia as a forerunner in the development of rice because of its climatic conditions. Rice then spread throughout southern China and the remainder of South Asia and into the Pacific regions. Most geographers agree that wheat may have been domesticated in northern India. Others suggest wheat may have first been domesticated in Turkey. Today, wheat is one of the staple crops of the United States; as a main ingredient in bread and other food products, it is an essential part of the American daily diet.

The Importance of Trade Routes

Trade routes helped to spread many of the agricultural products that we use today. The Colombian Exchange saw many plant and animal species traded between the Old and New Worlds, primarily as a result of European colonialism. This movement was all part of the First Agricultural Revolution and initiated many of the vegetative and seed planting techniques still used today in the less developed world. The diffusion of various products led to different styles of farming around the world. Climate dictates what crops can be grown where. For example, lemons and oranges do not grow well in New England and wheat does not grow well in Florida. These differences led to a wide variety of styles of farming and types of farm products.

AGRICULTURAL REGIONS AND PATTERNS OF CHANGE

In a discussion of nations or large areas, **cultivation regions** are those that specifically deal with agriculture production. You would rarely find a farm or cattle inside an urban area, for example. Agricultural regions are typically areas of **rural settlement**. These settlements can be dispersed (spread over a large area) or nucleated (clustered in a tightly packed area). They typically use building materials common in their region, which can include brick, bush, grass, wattle, and/or wood.

Village form refers to the layout of the rural settlement. There are several variations of the village form:

- Cluster: The dwellings are nucleated.

- Grid: The dwellings are sorted along a rectangular street grid.

- Linear: The dwellings are tightly grouped along a straight line, such as a river or railroad.

- Round: The dwellings surround an area for animals, acting as a pen.

- Walled: The settlement is fortified for protection against attacks.

The land people choose to farm and what products they choose to farm are known collectively as the **agricultural landscape**. The following sections will discuss different types of agricultural landscapes.

14

Subsistence Farming

In today's world, there are two predominant styles of farming. The first type is **subsistence farming**. Subsistence farmers produce the food that they need to survive on a daily basis. Their daily sustenance depends on the crops that they grow and the animals they raise. Milk, not only from cows, but also from goats and camels, provides an important source of daily nutrition for millions around the world. Other animal products include wool for textiles and meat for protein.

Most of the world still practices subsistence agriculture in one form or another, depending on the climate and the economic conditions of the country. In less developed countries, upward of 80 percent of the farming population may be involved in this type of farming. However, subsistence farming as a primary means of food attainment is decreasing, even in less developed countries. In more developed countries, the percentage of subsistence farming may be in the single digits.

Shifting Cultivation

One of the main types of subsistence farming is **shifting cultivation**. It involves the moving of crops to a new field after several years of depleting the nutrients in the original field. Shifting cultivation takes place in the forested tropical areas of Southeast Asia and Central Africa as well as in the Amazon rainforest in Brazil where the soil is fertile but porous and shallow. Because moisture and precipitation are plentiful, the soil erodes rather quickly. Natural vegetation in this area keeps the soil from eroding due to its root structure. When the natural vegetation is removed, however, soil is more susceptible to erosion, so thousands of tons of silt get washed into rivers and eventually the oceans.

Instead of using crop rotation techniques to mend damaged soil, the farmer practicing shifting cultivation actually leaves barren soil behind. The farmer moves on to the next area and clears the land of vegetation, usually by burning it. This burning of the land, called **slash-and-burn agriculture**, puts nitrogen into the soil, which is a nutrient needed by plants. This cycle repeats with each shift in cultivation. The scars on the landscape indicate areas with little soil due to erosion. The soil that is left behind can take decades to be replenished with nutrients. With farmers constantly moving on to clear more land for agriculture, rainforests and other native ecosystems are at risk. Unfortunately, the alternative for the farmers in these areas is often poverty or starvation.

Crop Rotation

Crop rotation is the planting of different types of crops each season to replenish the soil with nutrients used by the previous crop. Crop rotation is different from shifting agriculture; it involves using the same field year after year but planting different crops on that same field. An example of crop rotation would be a farmer planting corn in a field one year, soybeans the next, and then corn again. Soybeans replace the nutrients that corn takes out of the soil and vice versa. This practice maintains the health of the soil over time. In addition, by planting other nitrogen-rich crops such as clover, the farmer can further replenish the soil and improve agricultural productivity.

14

Pastoral Nomadism

Another type of subsistence farming is **pastoral nomadism**, which involves herding domesticated animals, including moving animals to areas that have the necessary resources to meet the needs of the herd. In a seasonal practice known as **transhumance**, nomads move their herds on a seasonal basis, relocating to higher elevations in the summer to protect them from the lowland heat, and bringing the animals back down to the valley floor in the winter.

Pastoral nomadism is usually practiced in arid climates. One of the best examples of pastoral nomadism is in the Sahara Desert in northern Africa, which has some of the harshest environmental conditions in the world; nomads have been taking their herds along trade routes in the region for thousands of years. The Gobi Desert region in Mongolia and northern China also has many nomadic tribes. The Mongols based their dominance of the region on the use of horses in war. The Middle East is also populated by a large number of nomads. The common characteristic of all of these regions is their lack of precipitation.

The herds of pastoral nomads include camels, sheep, and goats, among others. Cattle are not suited for nomadism since they eat too much, move slowly, and don't thrive on arid land. A typical family can survive with 10 camels and approximately 50 to 100 sheep and goats. These animals provide many useful products, including milk from the camels and meat from the sheep. Mutton (sheep meat) is a common item in the central Asian region. In much of central Asia, such as in Turkmenistan and Kyrgyzstan, the government keeps track of the number of sheep that each nomad possesses, and each sheep must be accounted for when it is killed. Even if the sheep is killed by a wolf or for a cultural celebration, it must be recorded. Pastoral nomads often trade their animal products for crops such as wheat, sorghum, or barley.

Both pastoral nomadism and shifting cultivation are a farming type known as **extensive subsistence agriculture**, which uses more land than other types of subsistence farming and which has been criticized for causing soil erosion, water degradation, and other environmental problems. However, it is often more productive than other types of subsistence farming since it requires less labor than intensive subsistence agriculture.

14

Intensive Subsistence Agriculture

The third type of subsistence agriculture is called intensive subsistence agriculture. As its name suggests, **intensive subsistence agriculture** is a more intense style of subsistence farming. More work is needed to obtain the same level of production in this type of farming. The number-one crop that geographers associate with intensive subsistence agriculture is wet rice. Grown in rice sawahs (flooded fields), it requires the planting and harvesting of each stalk by hand. Because the fields cannot be left alone, this type of farming is very time-consuming and labor intensive. Many of the rice paddies are terraced so that water flows gently over the edges of each paddy into the next one below. This flow keeps the water from becoming stagnant. Carp often swim within the sawahs and both eat insects that could ruin the rice crop and fertilize the crop with their waste. This rice is a crucial part of the daily diet of the fast-growing populations of Asia.

Other crops involved in intensive subsistence agriculture include wheat and barley. Like wet rice, they require a large amount of human and animal labor for production; the fields are tended on a daily basis. Oxen may pull the plows that break up the soil, and farmers are aided by a few manual tools, including hoes and rakes, but the majority of the work is done by hand, consuming most of a farmer's time each day. Many farmers store their food over the winter and will use it to trade for other goods. Some farmers will save up for years to earn enough money for an animal to assist with production. In many parts of Southeast Asia and Africa, intensive subsistence agriculture is the predominant method of farming.

Often, intertillage is used in subsistence agriculture. **Intertillage** is the clearing of rows in the field through the use of hoes, rakes, and other manual equipment. Because machinery is too expensive for subsistence farmers, they use manual labor to clear the fields of weeds and rocks.

✔ **AP Expert Note**

Be able to describe the various types of farming

Agriculture is a wide-ranging topic in AP Human Geography. The AP exam will expect you to know the various types of farming, but there are so many, it can be easy to mistake one for the other. A good way to check your knowledge level is to quiz yourself. You should be able to give a definition and an example for each type of farming as well as provide a region where that farming method is prevalent.

Commercial Farming

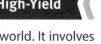

Commercial farming is the second predominant style of farming in the modern world. It involves the mass production of specialty crops for sale off the farm. It requires the use of machinery. Commercial farming is practiced in the United States, Europe, and Japan as well as in areas like northern China. For example, the United States is one of the leaders in world crop production, especially in corn and soybeans, which are mainly used to feed Midwestern livestock.

Commercial farming produces crops at relatively low cost and sells them at a variable price, depending on demand. Farms involved with commercial agriculture tend to be large, sometimes consisting of tens of thousands of acres. Wheat fields in Kansas and the Dakotas are examples of large-scale farms measured in acres. Ranches in the western United States are not measured by the acre but by the square mile. Machines and technology must be used to farm such large areas successfully. Ranchers may put radio collars on their cattle and fly over in a helicopter to find them. The farmer can also track cattle on a computer to determine their location. Because of the size of ranches, fencing in the animals is not cost-effective. Cattle are allowed to roam free; there are even road signs that limit the liability of the farmer if drivers run into their cattle.

Although commercial farming is largely dependent upon climate, genetic engineering has led to increased production regardless of weather. For example, new hybrids and GMOs may be more tolerant of drought, so farmers can experience the same productivity even if rainfall is lackluster.

14

Mediterranean Agriculture

There are many different types of commercial farming. One is **Mediterranean agriculture**, which must be practiced in a climate that has a dry summer and a cool, moist winter. The crops associated with the Mediterranean Sea region consist of grapes, dates, and olives. Parts of California and some of the southern portions of Australia have a Mediterranean-type climate and are known for their wine production.

Dairy Farming

Another style of commercial farming is **dairy farming**, also known as dairying, which has become highly mechanized in recent years. The old idea that the farmer milks the cows early in the morning and again in the afternoon is no longer the case. Most dairy farms in the Midwest are highly mechanized; cows are brought into the milking barn and hooked up to mechanical milkers. The machines pump the milk and store it in a large, cooled container that is picked up by a specialized milk truck. The farmer typically has a contract with a milk or dairy company to provide a certain number of gallons of milk every month or year. Safety precautions tightly control the dairy industry to ensure that consumers and customers receive milk or other dairy products that are of high quality. For example, cows cannot be given certain antibiotics.

Dairy farming usually needs to be done relatively close to a major market. For years, Wisconsin, which is close to large urban areas such as Chicago, Detroit, Milwaukee, and Minneapolis-Saint Paul, held the title of "America's Dairyland." Because of its short expiration date, milk is quickly sent to these urban areas and put on store shelves.

In the twenty-first century, the title of "America's Dairyland" has become a matter of contention. With the increase in California's population, milk must be produced in the vicinity of that state's urban areas. As a result, California now produces more milk than Wisconsin, creating a highly profitable industry. California's dairy farms are located in the state's Central Valley, which is ideal for the cows. However, Wisconsin still holds the title of "the cheese state." Cheese, which has a longer shelf life than milk, can be produced in Wisconsin, sent to all areas of the country, and still have enough shelf life so as not to spoil.

The region from New England through the Great Lakes, including a large section of the Midwest, still produces a large percentage of the milk and dairy products in the United States. Another large area of dairy production is in northern Europe, including Great Britain.

Mixed Livestock with Crop Production

A third type of commercial farming is **mixed livestock with crop production**. In this type of farming, cows grown for meat and other products are fed with crops (including corn and soybeans) grown on the same farm. These animals require a large amount of food, and the majority of the corn and soybeans that are grown in the United States are not meant for human consumption but, rather, as feed for livestock. Cows are fed in the barn and led out to a pasture area where they can eat grass and get fattened up before they are sold to the slaughterhouse. The cows are sold by the pound, so the plumper they are, the more money the farmer gets. Cows are not the only livestock raised in this fashion; hogs are increasingly being raised due to America's appetite for pork.

This type of farming occurs in the American Midwest region around Iowa and extends east into the Carolinas and south to Arkansas. In Europe, the mixed livestock and crop region lies in the center of the continent. The Manchurian region of China also has a large number of farms devoted to this method of farming.

Livestock Ranching

Livestock ranching is another form of commercial farming; it almost always appears in more developed countries. **Livestock ranching** is done on the fringes of productive land. Because the feeding of livestock is done by allowing the animals to roam the fields without the assistance of the farmer, huge areas of land are needed. Much of the western portion of the United States, west of the Great Plains and east of California, is dedicated to livestock ranching. Other areas with a large percentage of agriculture devoted to livestock ranching include the interior of southern Brazil (extending into Argentina), the interior of Australia, and parts of Central Asia.

Much of the livestock ranching in the United States and other developed regions is done in remote, arid to semiarid regions where the land is relatively inexpensive due to its remoteness from major urban areas.

Specialized Fruit Production

Another style of commercial farming is **specialized fruit production**. The orchards in the southwestern and southeastern portions of the United States as well as those along the Atlantic coast engage in this type of farming. In the dry regions of Arizona, **irrigation** provides crops with much-needed water. Around the world, specialized fruit production is found in scattered portions of southern South America and small portions of Eastern Europe. The climate is warm and humid in these areas, ideal for growing these crops. Large orchards produce most of the fruit crops in the United States, including oranges, lemons, limes, peaches, berries, and apples.

Plantation Agriculture

Specialized fruit production is not to be confused with plantation agriculture. **Plantation agriculture** often occurs in less developed countries and usually involves the production of one crop, which is sold in more developed countries. Banana, sugarcane, coffee, and cotton plantations are common in many tropical areas. Originally, these plantations were set up by colonial governments to provide agricultural products for their home countries, but they have persisted despite the end of colonialism because of their profitability. Many plantation owners are located in more developed countries, and their operations provide low-paying employment to workers where jobs are in relatively short supply.

14

Plantation agriculture involves interaction between core countries and periphery countries. Core countries often rely on periphery countries for their raw materials or agricultural products. For example, much of Europe depends on Africa for citrus crops during the winter. Much of the fruit crops in the United States are flown in from Chile and other South American countries during the winter.

Truck farms are a key aspect of fruit farming. The term *truck farm* refers to a farm where farmers use mechanization to produce large quantities of fruits and vegetables that are sold to processors. For example, many of the Jolly Green Giant plants in Minnesota receive their products from truck farms. These farms specialize in the production of beans or other vegetables and then sell them to the processor, which distributes them after either canning or freezing them. Many truck farms use migrant labor to keep costs low. This industrialization of farming has created a new source of income for farmers.

Suitcase farms are farms on which no one resides permanently. Suitcase farms go against the grain of traditional farming in the United States. Migrant workers provide a cheap, abundant labor source; they work on the farm during the day and leave the farm at night. In some cases, work will be done during the evening, but there is no residence on the property. Many suitcase farms are in the business of market-gardening products.

The development of commercial farming has led to the rise of agribusiness. Agribusiness is the mass production of agricultural products. Mass producers of food, such as Cargill, are in the agribusiness industry, and they are constantly trying to find better ways to grow crops and improve their distribution systems to increase profits. Agribusiness is a form of **large-scale commercial agriculture** that has seen the expansion of cropland and production.

Mass production has led to the rise of **agricultural industrialization**. It is the increased mechanization of the farming process to boost profits and productivity. Farming is less and less an industry of individual proprietors; instead, farms are becoming larger and more geared toward the large-scale production of specific food products. For example, instead of 100 head of cattle, farms today often have 5,000 head. And instead of a single farmer owning a farm, a group of people runs the operation like a business with a chain of command.

Grain Farming

One final method of commercial farming likely to appear on the exam is grain farming. **Grain farming** is the mass planting and harvesting of grain crops, such as wheat, barley, and millet. These fields take up an enormous amount of space because of the increasing demand for abundant production to meet the dietary preferences of more developed countries. Grain farming is often done in drier climates, and wheat is the predominant crop. The Great Plains is one of the largest regions in the world that specializes in the production of grain. Other regions include Ukraine and Russia in Eastern Europe, some of the world leaders in the production of wheat. These regions are often termed bread baskets. Also, some small regions of grain agriculture are seen in South America and Australia.

The grains that are produced in commercial grain-farming regions are sometimes known as staple grains. Staple grains include wheat, barley, millet, and other grain products that a large percentage of the world population depends on for survival. Check your kitchen cabinets for the food products that you own. You will find that many of the products in your kitchen have some type of grain in them; in the United States, many products contain wheat.

VON THÜNEN'S MODEL OF AGRICULTURAL LAND USE

In 1826, Johann Heinrich von Thünen developed his **model of agricultural land use** or, as it is sometimes called, the agricultural location model.

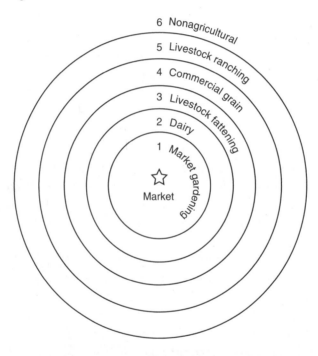

Von Thünen Model of Agricultural Land Use

Von Thünen's model states that the productivity of the land (the farmer's net profit) can be calculated ahead of time. The formula considers the potential yield of a given crop, the market price per unit of that commodity, and how expensive it is to ship the commodity to market. If a farmer grows products that don't fit the model, that farmer will lose out on profit opportunities due to the increased costs of production and transportation.

Von Thünen's model revolves around specific agricultural markets and only applies to commercial agriculture. The model assumes that farmers sell all of their agricultural harvest. It describes six concentric rings around the market. The products' weight determines where farmers must be in relation to the market.

14

Market-Gardening Activities

The first zone in von Thünen's model is reserved for market-gardening activities, which include various heavy and bulky products such as melons and vegetables. These products need to be close to the market for two primary reasons. First, if they are too far away, they will take too long to get to market and spoil. Second, the cost of transporting these bulky items is relatively large because of their weight and mass. A truckload of watermelons is much more expensive to haul than a truckload of wheat. The agricultural areas around urban areas are devoted to such items as fruits and vegetables. Because the cost of producing these products is usually high, owing to the high cost of land near the urban center, cheap transportation is needed to offset this expense.

Dairy Farming

The second zone in von Thünen's model is devoted to dairy farming. Dairy trucks must cool the milk, cheese, or other dairy product while in transit, adding to the cost of transportation. Also, because milk spoils more rapidly than the dairy products that are produced from it, milk production must be relatively close to the market in large urban areas. This explains the rise of the California dairy industry in response to population increases on the West Coast.

Livestock Fattening

The third zone in von Thünen's model is devoted to livestock fattening. Livestock fattening is the deliberate adding of weight to animals, such as cows and hogs, to increase their sale price. Cows and hogs are brought to the barn to be fed in a small space. Pastures are used, but they are small in comparison to livestock ranching pastureland. The cost of transporting livestock or poultry to urban areas for sale is high because of the weight of the animals. However, farmers don't need to do this on a daily basis. Farmers may only bring livestock to the slaughterhouse to sell several times per year.

Today, many livestock fattening areas are large feedlots. Feedlots are farms that specialize in cattle or hogs, and they may have thousands of head. One downside to feedlots is the runoff of waste products from them; these often infiltrate and contaminate local watersheds. Another downside to feedlots is the smell. The stench from a large feedlot can be overpowering for the surrounding countryside. The foul odor, along with potential groundwater contamination, has many people questioning the increased usage of feedlots. Feedlots are also critiqued based on animal welfare concerns.

Commercial Grain Farming

The fourth major zone in von Thünen's model is commercial grain farming. Commercial grain farming is the selling of wheat, corn, millet, and other grains. The transfer process from ground to market area can be done rather quickly with the assistance of combines and semitrailers. Farmers simply need to harvest the field and put the seed in the truck. Large machines, called combines, separate the seed from the shaft of the plant, eliminating the need to do so manually. Because combines are expensive pieces of machinery, farmers often purchase one jointly and share the machine during harvest. One new combine can cost upward of $600,000.

After harvesting, commercial grain is sent to the market area, usually in semitrailers, where it is sold to a producer that makes a product, such as bread, with the grain. The product is then sold to a wholesaler, who resells it to a grocery store, where individual customers can buy it. This process is called the **food chain**. Similarly, the **commodity chain** is the process that food goes through to get from the primary (resource-based) sector of the economy to the tertiary (service-based) sector. The in-between players include the transportation systems and two, three, or more different sellers before the consumer has the opportunity to purchase the item. Each time the commodity is sold, the transaction adds to the consumer price of the product.

Livestock Ranching

The fifth zone in von Thünen's model is devoted to livestock ranching. Livestock ranching uses the most land per farm of any of the zones in the model. Farmers can often afford the extra land because of their distance from the urban market area. Farmers let cattle graze freely, branding them so people know to whom they belong. Transportation to the market area occurs sporadically throughout the year.

The romantic vision of the cowboy on the range lingers as part of the image of U.S. livestock ranching, but the farmer on horseback has been replaced with high-end technology such as RFID tags and drones, helping the rancher's productivity and profit. Sometimes, farmers don't have fences around their property because their farms are so large, and cattle are often allowed to roam on neighboring government-controlled land. Although the cattle roam freely, they are tracked with GPS units to ensure their safety and monitor their location.

Nonagricultural Land Use

The last part of von Thünen's model is devoted to nonagricultural land use and isn't really a zone at all. The distance to market is so vast that a farmer cannot productively or profitably sell agricultural products.

Discussion of von Thünen's Model

Within all zones, costs of products are carefully balanced to account for both distance and weight. The cost of transporting items from any zone to market is the same. Therefore, the cost of sending wheat to market would be identical to the cost of sending milk to market. Because milk needs to be cooled during its journey, the cost of refrigeration is offset by the shorter distance traveled, and since grain is easy to take to the market due to mechanization, the cost of the longer distance it travels is offset.

Von Thünen had to make several assumptions in his model. The model assumes that all of the land has the same quality soil. Inadequate soil would mean that farmers would have to plant different crops to achieve profitability. The model also assumes that farmers have equal access to

14

transportation across all zones of the ring. This means that if a trucking company operates in zone 1, then it must also operate in zone 5. The land areas must be physically similar across the model. Mountains, rivers, or other obstructions would mean an increase in transportation prices. Von Thünen's model also assumes an equal climate in all areas of the model and an equal political structure as well. An international boundary in the middle of the area could affect transportation routes because of tariffs on products as they crossed the border.

Although models are representations of human behavior and activity on a mass scale, no model works perfectly in the real world. However, some patterns in real life support this model on a variety of scales. Consider the United States in relation to the von Thünen model, as shown in the following image. Assuming that populous New York City is the market, would the model hold up? The answer is yes and no.

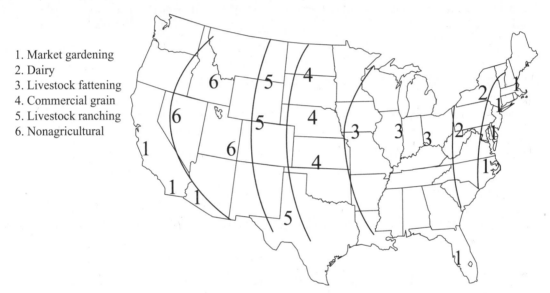

1. Market gardening
2. Dairy
3. Livestock fattening
4. Commercial grain
5. Livestock ranching
6. Nonagricultural

Von Thünen's United States Map

The area around New York City, including New England and upstate New York, is dotted with orchards and other farms that fit the bill for the market-gardening area. The next area is dairy farming. Dairy extends westward into Pennsylvania and upstate New York. The third area, a bit farther away than the dairy sections, is livestock fattening. By analyzing crop patterns in the United States, we see that corn and soybeans, intended mostly for livestock consumption, are grown in the Midwest. The fourth area, commercial grain, extends out to the Great Plains. Wheat and barley fields cover that region's landscape. The next area, livestock ranching, is in the Rocky Mountain states, mostly because of the relatively dry climate in the region. The last area is that of non-agricultural land use. Vast sections of land in the western United States are unused, again an effect of the climate and mountainous terrain of the area. They serve no agricultural purpose and could be classified as non-agricultural.

Then we get to California, Oregon, and Washington, which confound the model. California is dominated by fruit farming and dairy products. Oregon and California are renowned for their wine production thanks to their temperate Mediterranean climates. Washington is known for its apples. These products, along with the market-gardening areas in Arizona, tend to skew the model. However, if the heavily populated West Coast were considered the market, its market-gardening classification would make sense, but then the nonagricultural zone of the mountain states would not conform to the model.

> ✔ **AP Expert Note**
>
> **Have an in-depth understanding of von Thünen's model**
>
> The AP exam will very likely have one or more questions about von Thünen's model for agricultural land use. Your knowledge of this model should include not only its premises and its various zones but also a complex understanding of how it applies (or does not apply) to real-life scenarios.

ECONOMIC SYSTEMS AND ACTIVITIES

The type of economic system in which a farmer operates directly affects the farming system's degree of technology and mechanization. In less developed countries, farmers are usually practicing some type of subsistence agriculture, which typically involves more manual labor and less mechanization. If plantation agriculture is practiced, the profits usually flow back to the plantations' owners in a developed country.

The physical environment of a society influences its economic activities. Alaska would not be able to support citrus fruit orchards, for example. However, the Alaskan weather would spur the sales of heavy jackets, and the long distances between small settlements would make snowmobiles a thriving industry. The **adaptive strategies** that humans adopt to thrive in a given region thus influence a society's economic activities.

Farming today is much different than it was, even in the 1970s. Previously, farmers would sell their products to the elevator, often a cooperative (or "co-op") whose members were the farmers of that small town or village. The elevator then sold the harvest to a processor, who transported it to a plant where the commodity was turned into some type of food product.

Today, advances in technology and mechanization allow farmers to grow more food than ever before in human history. The mass production of food products is hurting the small farmer, who must either conglomerate or face extinction. This has led to the **farm crisis**: farmers are productive enough that supply exceeds demand for many products, meaning lower prices and less revenue for farmers. Thousands of small farmers have been forced to leave the land that they have owned for generations. In addition, increased revenue has not kept up with rising operating costs, leaving many farmers bankrupt.

On the opposite end of the spectrum are the farmers who live or have lived close to urban areas. As suburban and urban areas expand and encroach on neighboring farmland, developers often pay premium sums to farmers for their land. Thus, land that might have been bought for dollars

14

on the acre may be sold for tens of thousands of dollars per acre. This land is so valuable that many farmers feel they have no reasonable choice but to sell the land, and some farmers are walking away with millions of dollars.

What this leaves is an agricultural industry that continues to become more mechanized and industrialized. Farmers may broker deals with processing plants to produce a certain amount of product each year. Such contracts assure farmers a guaranteed income, usually more than what they would have earned had they continued to farm the land on their own.

Commercial farming is quite different from the subsistence farming in less developed countries, where the food is eaten in the rural villages that produce it. A quarter of the world's population depends on subsistence agriculture. Such rural settlements are dispersed, making trade with other villages infrequent. Many of the villages in Southeast Asia employ intensive subsistence agriculture in the production of rice. Because rice is such a labor-intensive crop, villagers may all work together during the harvest season so that the whole crop can be brought into storage for the non-growing season. Many societies that practice subsistence agriculture hold cultural festivals to celebrate the completion of the harvest.

In recent decades, a new social movement, known as **fair trade**, advocates for what it describes as a more ethical approach to trade. Fair trade goods must be produced in a way that protects the rights of workers and the environment. Sometimes, but not always, businesses in developed countries purchase fair trade goods directly from their producers abroad rather than buying the goods from a third-party.

AGRICULTURE AND GENDER

For tens of thousands of years, early humans lived by hunting animals and gathering roots and plants. Beginning about 10,000 years ago, the Earth's climate began to warm as the last Ice Age ended. Possibly as a result of this climatic change, permanent agricultural villages began emerging, signaling the start of the First Agricultural Revolution.

14

Women in the First Agricultural Revolution

Women played a key role in the First Agricultural Revolution. As men were off hunting prey for meat, women often helped secure food by gathering roots and plants. The discovery of agriculture was most likely made by women gatherers, as they would be the ones best positioned to observe seasonal patterns in plant growth and how plants might be cultivated.

The development of agriculture radically altered human society. The average hunter and gatherer worked only four hours a day to find food. Even though farming required vastly more work than hunting and gathering, it offered a much more stable food supply. Before, humans lived in small bands of 20 to 60 people. Now large-scale societies could form.

As farmers began to develop a surplus of food, job **specialization** followed. Men worked in the fields and herded animals, which required them to be outside the home. Women, on the other hand, performed jobs such as caring for the children, weaving cloth, and making cheese from milk, all of which required them to be in the home. Over time, the work outside the home became perceived as more important, and men began to take a more dominant role in the gender relationship. This led to a patriarchy, with men holding power over the family, government, and economy.

The exact details of this patriarchy varied, even among ancient civilizations, as did the legal rights of women. With the beginning of privately owned land, such as rich farmland, a wealthier class emerged. Land ownership equaled economic power. This land was passed down from generation to generation within a family, which furthered the rise of patriarchy. Because the mother of a child was always certain, but the father was not necessarily so, laws and social customs increasing control over women developed to reduce uncertainty over parentage and to ensure that ownership of land and private property stayed within a man's lineage.

Women in the Second Agricultural Revolution

The Second Agricultural Revolution used the technology provided by the Industrial Revolution as a means to increase production and distribution of products. In many places, new labor-saving devices freed up women from regular toil in the fields. Many moved to the cities in search of work in factories, contributing to urbanization and the development of the labor movement in places such as the United States and Britain. Some turned to the religious and social movements of the era, such as temperance, anti-slavery, and eventually women's suffrage.

In the United States, no agricultural invention was arguably more important than the cotton gin. Removing the cotton fiber from the stalk and the pods of the cotton plant was extremely labor-intensive to do by hand, and thus expensive. The cotton gin ("engine") automated this process. Each one did the work of dozens of people. This greatly increased agricultural production in the South, which had a climate conducive for growing cotton, but it also further solidified the practice of slavery. The cotton gin was also vital for the development of new textile industries in the North that employed thousands of women.

Women in the Green Revolution

Again, the pattern of technological innovation freeing people from the toil of agricultural labor continued. In many places in India as well as in Southeast and East Asia, the social effects were especially dramatic. Again, there were trade-offs. Rural women were disproportionately affected by the job losses created by automation. Indigenous agricultural seed stocks and knowledge, often overseen by women, were replaced by the Western techniques, technologies, and hybrid crops of the Green Revolution.

Women in the Fourth Agricultural Revolution

With the rise of urban farming, many new business opportunities have arisen for women in cities. They might own or operate the farm itself. Local markets and restaurants need salespeople to connect them to these farms. Women at nonprofits can supervise and sponsor urban gardening nonprofits, helping foster the growth of local communities.

AGRICULTURE IN THE UNITED STATES

Like most countries, the United States has relied on agriculture for its success, yet its agricultural practices have changed considerably over time.

Early European Settlements

The first successful English settlement in what became the United States was at Jamestown, Virginia, in 1607. Poor agricultural practices nearly doomed this colony. The colonists arrived in August and tried planting crops at this time, but the growing season was far too short. Without enough food to eat, most of the colonists died of starvation. It took forced labor and irregular resupply from overseas before the colony was able to feed itself. Tobacco cultivation soon gave Jamestown the lucrative economic base it needed to thrive and expand.

Another wave of settlers came to Plymouth, Massachusetts, in 1621. Instead of alienating themselves from the American Indian population, these settlers initially befriended them. American Indians assisted them with their agricultural practices, teaching them how to grow maize and other native vegetables. This assistance from American Indians was vital to the success of the Massachusetts colony, although relations between the settlers and the American Indians would later sour.

More Europeans began arriving in North America, and with them came their cattle. Cattle were a source of milk and food for the growing populations. Horses also were used to assist in plowing the land. The soil in New England was very rocky, so many people of European descent moved west, where the soil was richer and much more productive.

Early in the settlement process, the Erie Canal, connecting Lake Erie with the Hudson River, was built to bypass the formidable barrier of the Appalachian Mountains. The canal linked the fertile Midwest regions with the markets on the East Coast. Pennsylvania tried to construct something similar, but it was never as successful as the state of New York's. This is one of the reasons why New York City is still the dominant U.S. urban center.

Westward Migration

Europeans used traditional seed agriculture and began planting their crops in typical northern European style on the American landscape. The **metes and bounds** system, already used in Great Britain for many centuries, was used in many areas of New England during the 1700s. The metes and bounds system of measuring uses the land's physical features to describe ownership claims. The bounds system uses more generalized features, such as a boundary created by a river or adjoining roadway, while the metes system uses traditional distance measurements, such as a compass bearing.

Westward settlement in the United States was motivated largely by agricultural opportunities on some of the richest soil in the world. Indeed, the American Revolutionary War was, in part, motivated by the British Crown legally prohibiting the Thirteen Colonies from expanding past the Appalachian Mountains. This ban was meant to protect the British fur trade with American Indian tribes.

In English culture, however, owning land was the path to gaining political representation and amassing wealth. Thus, the ban angered colonists who wanted to own farmland, as the coastal regions of North America had largely been divvied up already.

Railroads brought new immigrants to the Midwest and West. The U.S. government sold land to the railroads, which then gave the land to immigrants if they promised to farm it for five years. The railroads, in return for giving up land, earned profits from the farmers' transportation of agricultural products to markets in the East. The Homestead Act, passed by Congress in 1862, was one of the most successful laws intended to promote white settlement on the Great Plains. It allowed citizens to claim up to 160 acres of surveyed but unclaimed public land, after making improvements and residing there for five years.

As settlers continued to move west, they began using the **township and range** system. This broke up much of the Midwest into square-mile tracts known as sections, and settlements were often dispersed around the township. Farms were dispersed, but commercial enterprises needed larger residential areas as markets and to supply labor. Therefore, markets were usually located in the community center or town.

Evidence of the township and range land-use pattern can be seen when flying over the central portions of the United States. You can see tiles of land almost one square mile across in sections of Missouri, Iowa, and Nebraska. This was done both for ease of settlement and so that the railroads, which originally owned most of this land, could bring in settlers and help export agricultural products to larger markets in the East.

Township and Range Land-Use Pattern

14

Farmers would receive huge profits from the productive use of the soil in the 1800s, in the American West. Settlements began to fill in the central portions of the United States as well, inhabiting areas that had been labeled the "Great American Desert" by the early Spanish explorers. They had seen the Great Sand Dunes off the Platte River in Nebraska, and the name stuck until the mid-1800s. However, settlers had technology the Spanish explorers did not, and they were able to tap the vast Ogallala Aquifer underneath the Great Plains. They used its water to grow wheat and other commodities.

Another type of **survey pattern** that is still evident on the landscape came from the French settlers, who used the **long lots** system along the rivers in Louisiana. Because the French used rivers as a primary form of transportation, the lots extended back from the river as far as one-half mile or more. The farmers would farm the land away from the river and use the river to haul their agricultural products to market, either up- or downstream. This system also ensured that everyone in an area received equal measures of soil of the same quality.

Each system made a lasting imprint on the landscape: the metes and bounds system in New England, the township and range system in the Midwest and Great Plains, and the long lot system in Louisiana.

✔ **AP Expert Note**

Be able to explain how settlement patterns reflect the development of U.S. agriculture

New England used the metes and bounds system, as it was initially settled by English people. The French-descended settlers of Louisiana used a long lots system to divide the land. The Midwest and Great Plains, meanwhile, used a township and range system that reflects the more methodical settlement efforts after the American Revolutionary War. All of these settlement patterns reflect how those groups of people used the land in different ways.

U.S. Agriculture Throughout the Twentieth Century

Agrarianism, or agrarian politics, was an important political movement throughout U.S. history until the second half of the twentieth century. Agrarians support policies that advance the needs and interests of farmers. However, after World War II, as the country increasingly urbanized, farmers gradually lost their political power. Today, one of the few notable aspects of agrarian interests is the ethanol industry. Due to Iowa holding its caucus early in the presidential nomination process for both major U.S. political parties, Iowan farmers can make support for ethanol production a make-or-break issue for would-be presidential nominees.

In 1910, a geographer at the American Association of Geographers (AAG) conference in Chicago by the name of Fredrick Jackson Turner wrote a paper declaring that the West was now closed. There were still spots of settlement to fill in, but he argued that the United States had reached its Manifest Destiny to settle the land from the East Coast (Atlantic Ocean) to the West Coast (Pacific Ocean). Agriculture had provided a means and a reason for people to leave the East Coast in search of riches found in the dark, rich soil of the Midwest.

The idea that humans could influence nature was prevalent in the United States in the late nineteenth century. There was a saying on the Great Plains that the "rain followed the plow," meaning that the more land was plowed and used for agriculture, the more rain would fall. Logically, it followed that more farmers were needed to plow the drier areas to increase precipitation and agricultural yields. During the 1870s and 1880s, the Great Plains saw a time of abnormally high precipitation, seemingly verifying the theory. However, this was a fluke. Many homesteaders were soon left out to dry when the Great Plains reverted to its arid norm. Yet the groundwork had been laid for future disaster.

In 1929, the United States spiraled into the Great Depression. This economic downturn coincided with the Great Plains region suffering the worst droughts in American history. The early to mid-1930s saw portions of Texas, New Mexico, Colorado, Kansas, and, most famously, Oklahoma endure what became known as the Dust Bowl. Storms on the Great Plains produced no rain, just scouring whirlwinds of dirt and dust that stretched as far as the East Coast.

The Dust Bowl was created by a combination of drought, overgrazing by cattle, and farming practices that overtaxed the soil. Native grasses had helped maintain the integrity of the soil during droughts, but they had since been cleared or disturbed by plows. Trees that once served as windbreaks had been cleared or chopped down for firewood. Millions of settlers moved away or emigrated from the Great Plains as banks foreclosed on farms that could not turn a profit.

The "rain follows the plow" philosophy was largely discredited. In fact, the direct opposite is known today. The more natural vegetation that a region possesses, the more likely it is that precipitation will increase. Unsustainable agricultural practices resulted in millions of tons of fertile, productive Great Plains soil literally vanishing into the air as a result of wind erosion. American society also suffered widespread disruption.

Yet the Great Plains were not the westernmost lands settled by Americans. People found the continent got drier the farther west they went, until they reached the California coast. California's climate was perfect for fruit production. Just as in Florida, river water could be channeled to orchards and fields to produce crops unlike those of any other area. Production of lemons, oranges, and pineapples boomed in these areas of California as well as in Arizona. Even today, market gardening or fruit farming produces the most cash crop receipts in the country, more than any other method of farming.

The West depends on irrigation for its water needs. The Ogallala Aquifer, a large body of water found under the surface of the Earth in the Great Plains, is being depleted at a rapid rate. Rainfall is not enough to replace the water that the farmers use to irrigate their crops. If conservation of remaining water resources and innovations in drought-resistant GMO crops are not enough, then the Great Plains may regain its old label of the "Great American Desert."

The United States is not alone in experiencing the effects of unsustainable farming practices. They are felt around the globe. Overgrazing has led to arid regions becoming deserts, a process known as **desertification**. When herds of animals graze on land that does not receive enough rainfall, the land becomes barren and desert-like. Southern Saharan regions have experienced significant **soil erosion** and loss of farmland to the expanding desert.

14

The Future of U.S Agriculture

Agriculture is ever changing. New farms may hardly resemble the farms of the past. For example, new farms may be involved in **aquaculture**, the farming of aquatic organisms for sale off the farm. Fish may be raised in pools and then sold for food or to stock lakes for the tourism industry. Aquaculture is intended as a substitute for traditional **fishing** because the ocean's finfish and shellfish populations are increasingly depleted or contaminated with harmful pollutants.

Some don't consider **forestry** to be farming but, rather, the harvesting of a natural resource. Forestry will be discussed in more detail in the chapter on Industrialization and Economic Development. Ideally, timber companies will replant millions of trees to ensure a sustainable yield; that is, to produce a crop for many years to come.

The Business of Farming

In recent decades, the focus of U.S. agriculture has shifted away from small farmers selling their products or commodities to processors. The processors of livestock, such as poultry and cattle, have been complaining for many years that the quality and the quantity of the meat has been variable because many different small producers or farmers have been providing the animals. Processors would rather buy from one mass producer or farmer to achieve more uniform quality and also so that the processing plants do not have to shut down while waiting for another small batch of animals. One mass producer can ensure consistent quality and guaranteed quantity.

This preference has led to the rise of huge feedlot operations in the poultry, hog, and cattle industries. Huge feedlots can handle tens of thousands of chickens or turkeys at a time, feeding them in an industrial process that fattens them up before they are taken to plants for processing. Cattle were late arrivals to the feedlot game, but in recent decades, huge feedlots for cattle have been popping up, primarily in the western areas of the country. The poultry industry has been dominated by the South; North Carolina is one of the leading producers of turkeys in the United States, and Arkansas is one of the leading producers of chickens, primarily because national brands have located their processing plants in these states.

What this method of farming has produced is a "just-in-time" method of delivery, where products arrive at the grocery store just before consumers purchase them. U.S. processors have become so efficient that they can process the commodity, usually in a plant close to the farmers who raised the livestock, then ship the product directly to the store just in time to fill an empty shelf so customers can buy it.

The development of mass production forces small farmers into a decision. Do they contract out with the processor or continue to go it alone? If they do contract out with the food processors, they will almost always receive a guaranteed income, but they must invest in new barns and holding areas for the hogs, chickens, turkeys, or cattle—a prohibitive cost for many farmers. The days when farmers produced all of their products for sale in the local grocery store have almost vanished. The raising of livestock in the Corn Belt has diminished greatly. Now, those farmers who used to raise cattle as well as crops are being forced out of the cattle industry to focus on growing corn for sale to the huge feedlots.

14

Large corporate farms and feedlots have come under pressure from the public and press to clean up their operations because of environmental concerns. Large conventional farms use large quantities of pesticides and herbicides that impact wildlife and water systems. Massive feedlots have serious issues dealing with processing livestock waste, which can pollute local air and water.

The Future of Small Farms

Small family farmers have resorted to a number of methods to stay profitable and keep their businesses. First, many farmers have started to incorporate sustainable farming techniques such as ridge tillage, integrated pest management, limited use of pesticides and herbicides, and using a mixed crop and livestock operation. These methods help reduce costs for the farmer in an era of declining incomes. This type of agriculture is riskier, but once farmers have made the move to sustainable agriculture, they can get more money per pound for their crops than if the same crop were grown conventionally. Farmers can earn even more if their crops are certified organically grown by the USDA, although this is often a lengthy and involved process.

Another strategy that small farmers have used is to take advantage of the "local food" movement. Many people feel that it is important to support local farmers because the food is fresher, does less harm to the environment (fewer "food miles" traveled), and helps the local economy. Grocery stores and restaurants have also used this angle to market their products and increase customer loyalty. All these efforts also contribute to reducing food deserts, which are common in urban areas. Food deserts are areas with little to no access to affordable, healthy food, such as fresh vegetables, instead relying on preserved or canned goods.

This idea of just-in-time production has produced a movement of consumers known as **locavores**, people who consume products grown or raised close to them. Locavore cafes have popped up around the United States and Europe, serving locally produced items on their menus. Consumers like the idea of fast, fresh food that aids people in their local community rather than corporations located hundreds or thousands of miles away.

AGRICULTURE AND THE ENVIRONMENT

Agriculture has often been criticized in past decades for not being environmentally friendly in its practices. Pesticides, for example, have improved crop yields at the cost of disrupting the wider food chain. Bees that helpfully pollinated both wild vegetation and farm crops can become sickened and die from exposure to certain pesticides. This criticism illustrates a shift in the central question of agriculture from how society can produce enough food to avoid famine to how society can produce that food in such a way that ensures an environmentally friendly, **sustainable yield** in the long term.

Even basic agricultural practices, such as irrigation, contain long-term costs. Almost all water, including rainfall, contains some degree of dissolved salt. Over time, these salts are deposited in soil, increasing the soil salinity. This is ordinarily not a problem, but irrigation for crops over time artificially increases the amount of salt deposited into the soil. Eventually, this can turn arable land into

14

something that cannot be farmed. One example of this is the Fertile Crescent in the Middle East; as ancient irrigation systems gradually increased its soil salinity over millennia, the land became far less fertile.

Farm land is also increasingly lost to growing cities. The global trend toward urbanization is only accelerating, with cities and their suburbs gradually overtaking land that was used for farming. While this loss of arable land is compensated for with global trade and productivity increases, this interconnected system creates new vulnerabilities. For example, drought in Mexico can affect corn and beef prices throughout North America.

Agriculture has a role to play in the area of alternative energy sources that are renewable. Corn grown in states like Iowa can be converted to ethanol, a gasoline substitute. However, ethanol also illustrates the complexity of applying environmentalism to agriculture. Farmers can make the most profit from corn through ethanol production, and so they funnel roughly 40 percent of U.S. corn into it. Yet there is only a finite amount of arable land in the world, and corn used for ethanol does not feed cattle or people. Therefore, in a global marketplace, everyone ends up paying more for food, even when the poorest may not be able to afford food at all.

Environmental issues within a single region or country are sometimes less complex in nature. For example, in many places in the Midwest, runoff from animals and fertilizer from fields goes into rivers and streams where children swim only a few miles downstream. Efforts are now being made to protect these ecosystems from pollution by providing buffer zones between fields or pastures and the streams. These buffer zones may simply be an area of grass extending from both sides of the stream by only 20 to 30 feet. However, during times of excessive water runoff from rains or snowmelt, the grassy area provides a buffer for the stream, keeping it cleaner.

WORLD CROP REGIONS

High-Yield

When looking at world crop regions, the number-one factor to examine in terms of productivity is climate. If one compares a map of world agriculture regions with a map of world climate regions, it is obvious how climate determines what type of agriculture is practiced. For example, shifting cultivation dominates in the tropical rain forests, and pastoral nomadism is prevalent throughout most semi-arid regions of the developing world.

Moving down the scale of analysis to the regional level, one can analyze the complexity of agricultural systems within a more developed country. Two factors must be considered within each system: the level of wealth, and the incorporation of technology.

If the country is a less developed one, its people are usually involved in subsistence agriculture, which means a dependence on animals in more arid climates and a dependence on crops in more moist climates. For a more developed region, consider California. Many different types of agriculture are practiced there, in a relatively small area. In contrast to many less developed regions, California farms will use technology to improve food production. Tractors might be automated, with their on-board computers guided by GPS coordinates and satellite maps.

In a **planned economy**, or government-controlled economy, the government dictates to farmers the quantity and type of agricultural products they can produce. Planned economies were a notable aspect of communist governments during the twentieth century. They resulted in decidedly poor agriculture. Almost no traditional planned economies remain today, with North Korea being the most noteworthy exception.

One aspect of agriculture linked with the planned economy is the **collective farm**. However, these farms can, and do, exist in both free-market and mixed economies. On a collective farm, workers are not paid with money. Instead, they receive a share of the crop. This arrangement may come about because the farmers have a common religious or political ideal, or because they are forced to accept it by their rulers.

A Global Rundown

The United States is the world leader in the production of corn, which is used to raise livestock and also as a food source for humans. The United States is also a large producer of soybeans, which are seen as a healthier alternative to many available meat products. Soy products are part of many Americans' diets.

As the demand for fuel continues to rise in the United States, corn is increasingly being used to produce ethanol. Roughly 40 percent of U.S. corn goes into ethanol production. Many states now require that a certain percentage of the gasoline sold within their state be made of ethanol. As the demand for ethanol increases, so does the demand for corn. As the demand for corn continues to climb, the price of corn continues to rise. This rise in price motivates more farmers to plant corn as their primary crop.

In South America, some ethanol is made from corn, but the majority is made from sugarcane. Brazil is one of the largest producers of ethanol. This ethanol is mainly sold to more developed countries, though some is used in Brazil because transporting ethanol can be a challenge.

In Eastern Europe, wheat is a major product. Bread is a building block in most diets around the world, and Europe is no exception. The European Union has set strict policies regarding the growing of food across portions of Europe. Environmental regulations and soil conservation techniques have had a huge impact on European agriculture, as have regulations on the use of pesticides and GMOs. As a result, almost half of the European supermarkets are filled with organic produce of some type. This market far exceeds that of the United States, where organic foods, although increasingly popular, still make up a small fraction of the total food sold.

In Africa, the crop of choice is sorghum or millet. Both are high-calorie energy sources. As Africa's population continues to rapidly increase, the importance of agriculture to feed people continues to increase. Much of Africa is working with Western or Chinese universities and research institutions to increase food production.

Rice is the staple food source in most of Asia; areas from the Middle East to the Far East depend on it. Rice is often traded to people in drier climates for their animal products. Areas such as Southeast Asia, where rainfall is plentiful, can grow rice on terraced mountainsides. This terrain and the warm, moist climate there are ideal for the production of rice.

As mentioned previously about China, there is a so-called "noodle line," a difference in regional climate that dictates the type of crops grown. To the north of the noodle line, where wheat is grown, the primary food is noodles. To the south of the noodle line, rice is grown; here, it is the staple food.

 # NEXT STEP: PRACTICE

Go to Rapid Review and Practice Chapter 7 or to your online quizzes on kaptest.com for exam-like practice on this topic.

Haven't registered your book yet? Go to kaptest.com/moreonline to begin.

14

CHAPTER 15

Cities and Urban Land-Use Patterns and Processes

LEARNING OBJECTIVES

After studying this chapter, you will be able to:

- Explain the driving factors behind urbanization and suburbanization.

- Describe city infrastructures.

- Define city populations using quantitative and qualitative data.

- Analyze urban settlements and development using geographic models.

- Identify housing, urban planning, and political organization factors unique to cities.

- Evaluate problems and solutions unique to urban areas.

DEFINING URBANIZATION

In the United States, almost 98 percent of the population lives in an urban environment. People are moving to urban areas every day. Today, the world's **urbanized population**, the number of people living in cities, is higher than ever in human history. Cities serve and entertain. They harbor culture and keep history. Cities mold people as much as people mold them. Cities define their inhabitants.

Urban areas can be as small as two families or as huge as megalopolises. An example of the latter is Tokyo, Japan, which has over 37 million people within its metropolitan area. The larger the city, the more purposes it fulfills and the more needs it serves. Large urban areas provide employment to millions, and their influence extends far beyond their borders.

Urbanization is the process by which people live and are employed in a city. People are drawn to urban areas for a variety of reasons. Cities provide products and services for their populations. Also, employment is usually quite accessible, with more jobs available in larger cities than in smaller towns or rural areas; this attracts job seekers. The increased labor force then creates a larger consumer base that purchases goods and services. Thus, industries in cities have a ready market for their products and a ready labor force to produce them.

Urban areas have a nucleated form of settlement, which means that they have a center area of development, known as a core area. This is different from a dispersed form of settlement, which is usually found in rural areas where houses are far apart.

Site and situation factors determine where cities form. Site factors concern the physical location of the city. Some cities are built on swampland, and others are built on highpoints for strategic locational advantage. Situation factors are the external characteristics of a place relating to the connections between cities. New Orleans has a great situation due to the city being located near the delta of the Mississippi River.

Cities offer many amenities, which may include professional sports teams, professional dance companies, and art museums. Large sports franchises, such as the National Football League (NFL), Major League Baseball (MLB), the National Basketball Association (NBA), and the National Hockey League (NHL), have teams in major metropolitan areas. These teams have high thresholds, so generally only the largest cities gain professional franchises. (A threshold is the minimum number of people needed to meet the needs of the industry.) Some cities, such as New York, Los Angeles, and Chicago, are large enough for two professional teams playing the same sport.

There are many factors surrounding urbanization, leading urban geographers to pose a variety of questions. Why do some cities grow more than others? What are the characteristics of different world cities, and are these characteristics beneficial or not? How do world cities change over time? What effects do transportation systems have on cities? How do American cities reflect their regions?

Studying urbanization

Broadly speaking, there are two types of data used to analyze cities and urban land use patterns: **quantitative data** and **qualitative data**.

Quantitative data is information that can be expressed numerically. For example, census surveys provide quantitative data about the population of a city. What is the total population and how has it changed over time? How many members of various ethnicities live there? How many students are enrolled in local schools? What is the average class size? These questions can be answered with concrete numbers.

Qualitative data is information that consists of narratives and words. Field studies and personal interviews reveal individual attitudes about cities. For example, a city government might survey students about their attitudes toward their school. Are they happy with their teachers and class options? What changes would they like to see in the operation of their school? Answers to questions like these cannot be expressed numerically, but must be analyzed more holistically.

URBAN ECONOMIES

Cities serve an economic function, which depends on what type of economy the country possesses. The following chapter on Industrial and Economic Development discusses the different types of economies, ranging from primary services (agriculture, forestry, etc.) to secondary (manufacturing) to tertiary (selling goods and services). **Commercialization** is the selling of goods and services for profit. Cities begin as bartering or market centers, but they can grow to have global economic impact.

When one large industry moves into a city, it is known as a basic industry. A basic industry is a city-forming industry. Basic industries in the United States historically include steel in Pittsburgh, automobiles in Detroit, and computer chips in San Jose, California. After the establishment of a basic industry, non-basic industries are established. These are the city-serving industries and may include anything from construction to industrial equipment. Together, basic and non-basic industries form the economic base of cities, generating tax revenue and employment and spurring the development of infrastructure.

Cities tend to move in their **employment structure** from industrial to tertiary to quaternary activities. First, most workers are employed in producing goods; then, most become employed in selling and servicing goods manufactured elsewhere. Eventually, a city may become a post-industrial city, specializing in information-based work. This shift toward more specialized economic activities is called the deindustrialization of a city. When a city goes through deindustrialization, factories are shut down, but new jobs appear in customer service, professional services, and management.

Occasionally, a city will go through an underemployment situation. **Underemployment** occurs when too many employees are hired and there is not enough work for all of them to do. When this occurs, layoffs usually ensue. Cities with good educational systems can assist workers in developing new skills to meet an ever-changing job market.

URBAN HIERARCHIES

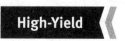

Hierarchy by Size

Urban areas are classified in a hierarchy depending on their population. **Unincorporated areas** were once considered urban areas, even though only two or three families live there today. Unincorporated areas are often found in the western United States. They might have once been a town or hamlet but have lost people over the years. Unincorporated areas also exist on the fringes of suburbs. They are rural areas that may someday incorporate once their populations rise.

Hamlets may only include a dozen or two people and often offer very limited services. The people in the hamlet are clustered around an urban center, which may consist only of a gas station or a general store.

Villages are larger than hamlets and offer more services. Instead of just a general store, there may be stores specializing in the sale of food, clothing, furniture, and so on.

Towns may consist of anywhere from 50 to a few thousand people. A town is considered to be an urban area with a defined boundary, but a town is smaller than a city in terms of its population and area. Surrounding farms are often the hinterland of towns. A hinterland is the area in which an urban area, a product, or a commercial outlet has influence. Local towns may serve area farmers, providing stores such as a supermarket. Towns typically have schools and libraries as well.

Cities are large, densely populated areas that may include tens of thousands of people. **Metropolises** have large populations, incorporate large areas, and are usually focused around one large city. According to the U.S. government, a metropolitan area must have over 50,000 people. Metropolitan areas usually include suburbs (and exurbs) from which people commute to their jobs in the urban core or in other suburbs. The central city and its suburbs usually border each other, and the suburbs are usually socially and economically dependent upon the urban core. Many of the larger cities around the world are centers of metropolitan areas.

The biggest urban area is called a **megalopolis**, where several metropolitan areas are linked together to form one huge urban area. A good example of a megalopolis is the East Coast of the United States. The area that extends from Boston, Massachusetts, to Washington, D.C., along the Interstate 95 corridor, is one large urban area. Besides Boston and Washington, it includes Providence, Rhode Island; Hartford, Connecticut; New York City, New York; Newark, New Jersey; Philadelphia, Pennsylvania; Dover, Delaware; and Baltimore, Maryland. This area contains the largest concentration of population within the United States.

Another megalopolis is the southeastern region of Canada. The area extending from Hamilton, through Toronto, up to Ottawa in Ontario, and east to Québec is also considered a megalopolis. Even though these cities have far fewer people than the East Coast megalopolis of the United States, together they form the heart of Canada's population as well as its industrial core.

Megacities are cities that have a population over 10 million people. Currently, there are 35 cities that could be placed in the megacity category, including New York City and Los Angeles. Tokyo is considered the largest megacity in the world, with a population of over 37 million in its metropolitan area.

15

Metacities are distinct from megacities in terms of layout. Where a megacity like New York or Tokyo has a distinct business center and fully integrated system of infrastructure, such as a sewer network and electrical grid, metacities are essentially a collection of cities and industrial hubs. They are heterogenous in nature, with overlapping infrastructure systems, and often display less urban planning than a megacity.

> ✔ **AP Expert Note**
>
> **Be sure to use precise language for urban areas**
>
> In everyday speech, you probably do not distinguish between a town and a village. Both words seem interchangeable. Another example is a city and a metropolis, which are not the same thing despite having a degree of overlap. AP Human Geography has distinct meanings for these terms, and you will be expected to use them all precisely and correctly on the exam.

Saskia Sassen wrote that certain cities possess more authority in terms of cultural outreach and political influence than others. These cities define, not only their own countries, but also other countries in the region. As of 2018, New York and London are considered **world cities** (also called global cities). These cities are the financial capitals of their regions because they are the locations of the major stock markets for their respective continents. Large financial institutions as well as large publishing companies and transnational corporations are located in these cities.

These cities are also characterized by their familiarity; they often appear on the news and as settings for films and literature. These cities have world-class international airports. Their infrastructures include some form of mass transportation in addition to well-maintained freeways. New York and London have vibrant ethnic communities, and they have large expatriate communities—that is, many people from other countries live there for business or personal reasons. They have hosted global events, such as the Olympics or the World's Fair. For these reasons and more, these cities are considered dominant over their counterparts in terms of cultural and economic influence over an extended area.

Hierarchy by Influence

Cities are given rankings based on their amenities as well as their importance in global commerce. This **urban hierarchy** puts cities in ranks from small, first-order cities to fourth-order cities, which are large, world-class cities. The higher the order of the city, the greater the sphere of influence that city possesses on a global scale. Fourth-order cities have a larger hinterland than first-order cities. On a regional scale, the terms for urban development are (in ascending order from smallest to largest) hamlet, village, town, city, metropolis, and megalopolis.

One can also use the urban hierarchy on a smaller scale, such as at the individual U.S. state level. The state of New York would have New York City as its most important city, owing to its financial and cultural importance. Albany would be next, along with Buffalo, Rochester, and possibly Syracuse. In 2004, Ithaca, New York, was voted the top emerging city in the United States according to *USA Today*. Smaller urban areas in the state would be ranked as first order, those being the smallest, least influential urban areas.

15

Another way that geographers organize cities is by ranking them using the Greek alphabet. Major cities are sorted into alpha, beta, and gamma cities. Alpha cities include the world cities, which are New York City and London. Some geographers also consider Tokyo and Paris to be part of this order. Other geographers insist that Shanghai should be included in this first tier of alpha cities because of China's economic importance in the world market.

Cities in the second tier of the alpha world cities are still impressive in their economic and political clout. These alpha cities include Buenos Aires, Chicago, Dubai, Hong Kong, Istanbul, Kuala Lumpur, Mexico City, Miami, Paris, Seoul, Taipei, and Warsaw.

The next order of cities, sometimes called the beta world cities, includes Bangalore, Beirut, Berlin, Boston, Cairo, Calgary, Cape Town, Hangzhou, Kiev, Kuwait City, Lyon, Manchester, Nairobi, Perth, Seattle, and Vancouver. Each of these beta cities has a unique feature (e.g., being a financial, fashion, or governmental center) that makes it important within its region.

The next order, called gamma world cities, includes Austin, Belfast, Cologne, Detroit, Minsk, Ottawa, Phoenix, Rotterdam, St. Louis, Tirana, Turin, and Zhengzhou.

Other City Types

Emerging cities are experiencing population growth as well as increasing economic and political clout throughout their regions. Shanghai, China, is quickly developing, trying to compete for financial dominance not only in Asia but also around the world. Its exports of commodities and its attraction of foreign investment have led to growth that could not have been imagined 30 years ago.

Other cities are gaining importance in the world economy. Many of these emerging cities are located in Asia. Hanoi in Vietnam, Bangkok in Thailand, and Dubai in the United Arab Emirates are all trying to establish their place as world cities. Dubai is becoming a destination city, with amenities that attract travelers; many flights from the United States and Europe to the Middle East stop over in the Dubai airport. Dubai's influence in the region is growing by the year.

Many emerging cities are in less developed countries. Not only are many of these cities gaining more importance politically and economically, but they are also becoming extremely populated. In 1950, only seven of the world's 20 largest cities were in the developing world, compared to 16 by the year 2000.

Another type of city is a gateway city. **Gateway cities** serve as a connection point between two areas. Often, gateway cities connect two cultures and serve as a cultural point of entry. For example, Boston and New York City were the two primary entry points for European immigrants to the United States. Ellis Island, which is in New York Harbor, is now a national park, commemorating its role as an entry point.

Likewise, San Francisco is considered a gateway city. Millions of Chinese have entered the United States through San Francisco since the mid-nineteenth century. San Francisco's Chinatown is not only a tourist destination but also an important cultural center for thousands of Chinese and Chinese Americans.

15

Another gateway city in the United States is St. Louis, Missouri. St. Louis is so proud of its gateway heritage that it built a monument known as the Gateway Arch. The Gateway Arch symbolizes migration to the western United States, especially the important psychological step of crossing the Mississippi River. To many pioneers, this river represented entry into the vast expanses of the plains.

Gateway cities can be found all around the world. In Australia, Sydney is considered a gateway city because it is where immigrants often enter Australia. One of the world's great gateway cities is Istanbul. Istanbul is the only city in the world located on two continents, with Europe on the west side of the Bosporus Strait and Asia on the east side. Istanbul, known formerly as Constantinople, has always been considered the gateway between the West and the East.

Many cities have what is known as a festival landscape. A **festival landscape** is a space within an urban environment that can accommodate a large number of people. It may be decorated and used for celebrations. One of the most famous festival landscapes is Central Park in New York City. Central Park was built specifically for the citizens of New York City to have a place to play and enjoy some semblance of nature within densely populated Manhattan. Today, Central Park holds concerts for tens of thousands of people on summer evenings. Hyde Park in London is similar to Central Park. Hyde Park has a small lake where people can rent boats and ride trails on horseback. Shanghai has the People's Park, which can hold thousands of people. Flying kites is a popular activity in this park.

CHARACTERISTICS OF CITIES

High-Yield

U.S. Cities

The **central business district (CBD)** is the commercial center of an urban area. The CBD is the downtown region of a city. In the United States, many buildings in the CBDs are skyscrapers, which maximize the occupancy on very expensive land because they are tall. The **bid-rent theory** suggests that only commercial landlords can afford the land within the central business district. As a person moves farther from the central business district, the value of the land decreases. Therefore, the suburbs have more land per residence, on average, because the land is cheaper than in the inner city. Homes in the inner city usually have smaller lots because the land is more expensive. Residential properties in the central business district are usually apartment buildings or condominiums.

U.S. shopping malls exemplify the principle of agglomeration. A shopping mall is a group of retail outlets that either share a roof or are connected by a set of walkways. Shopping malls attract more customers than a single store would. People shopping for one item may find themselves purchasing several items from several stores. Agglomeration is advantageous for every store in the mall. Sometimes shopping centers are located along a major transportation route, such as the Magnificent Mile on Michigan Avenue in Chicago. The agglomeration of retail outlets in this highly visible area, where thousands of tourists and customers walk by daily, presents an attractive business opportunity.

15

The United States is undergoing a revival in urban design and function. Edge cities are popping up around major metropolitan areas. One example is Crystal City in Arlington, Virginia, which is an edge city of Washington, D.C. These areas can see expansive growth and are sometimes called **boomburbs**. Other zones in the city are also seeing a revival. The area to the east of the United States Capitol, known as Eastern Market, is becoming a high-profile, chic place to reside. New restaurants, hotels, and shops are filling in areas that were previously abandoned. These areas, with entertainment options including restaurants, theaters, and commercial shopping, are known as uptowns. These uptown areas are usually within city limits, yet a mile or more away from city centers.

Greenfields are zones where there is little development. Oftentimes the owner will simply donate the land to the city to avoid paying taxes. This land is then developed into some sort of commercial development in the hopes that the area will turn into another uptown region.

Eastern U.S. Cities

Eastern cities in the United States were built before the invention of the automobile, so their streets tend to be narrow, and parking is usually done in the alleys. The residential areas are tightly packed, making for a dense population. Homes usually face the street with little or no yard in front; yards are in the back of the house.

Many eastern cities have some type of mass transportation, such as trains or subways. The density of the population on Manhattan Island would make travel by car difficult, if not impossible, without some form of train service. Subways run fairly regularly and are relatively easy to use. They provide a good way to get around the city without dealing with traffic-congested streets.

Traffic in eastern cities is heavy at most times of day but especially during rush hours. Rush hours are when people travel to work in the morning, usually between 6 and 9 a.m. and then home again between 3:30 and 6:30 p.m. Commutes to work can often be measured in hours due to both distance traveled and traffic congestion. Many suburban residents drive as far as the outskirts of the city and then take mass transportation into the core downtown where they work. Washington, D.C., was built so that invading armies would have difficulty finding and taking over the city. This complex pattern has also made it a nightmare for people trying to drive in the city. Washington's subway system allows people to travel without dealing with its roads and traffic.

Western U.S. Cities

Cities in the western United States share some characteristics with eastern cities but are also profoundly different. As in East Coast cities, the central business districts contain skyscrapers. However, cities in the western United States are much more spread out, and the homes are often more widely spaced as well. Also, both front yards and backyards are common in western cities. These cities rely on the automobile, rather than mass transit, as the primary means of transportation.

Because these cities were built for the automobile, and many were built on relatively flat land, many use the grid street system. Streets run east/west and north/south, creating a grid pattern on the landscape. In many cases, these streets are named first, second, third, and so forth. North/south streets may be called avenues and may be numbered or given names that proceed alphabetically. This logical progression of street names is common in western cities because their grid layout allows it. Such street naming conventions allow for ease of navigation.

Many of these cities depend upon the interstate highway system for transportation, and interstates with eight lanes in each direction are not uncommon in the larger West Coast cities, such as Los Angeles and San Diego. In an effort to curb congestion of the interstates, some highway lanes are reserved for "multiple-occupancy vehicles" (MOVs) to encourage people to carpool. Others are toll roads, and people must pay to use them. Also, sometimes lanes will be open only one way, into the city, during the morning rush hour and again one way, out of the city, during the afternoon rush hour. Another characteristic of western cities is the private residential garage. Garages, either attached to the houses or unattached, are common because space is so plentiful. On the East Coast, cars are generally parked in the alley in back or in multilevel commercial parking garages for a monthly fee.

Suburbs are key to any western city. **Suburbs**, located on the outskirts of a central city, are usually residential but can possess numerous commercial and industrial enterprises. Hundreds of thousands of people work in the suburbs of the western United States. The suburbs combined often have more people than the central city. The Minneapolis-Saint Paul metropolitan area is a good example of this. Minneapolis and Saint Paul combined have approximately 700,000 people, but the entire metropolitan area has close to 3.8 million people. Only one out of every four people in the metropolis lives within the Minneapolis or Saint Paul city limits. In many eastern cities, the primary city still contains more people than the suburbs.

Seattle, Washington, is one of the few major cities in the northern United States with a high growth rate. Its port plays a vital role in the economy, making it one of the major ports of entry for Asian goods.

Utility infrastructure is becoming more important in city design and development. **Utility infrastructure** is the system set in place by the local government for delivery of electricity, sewer services, and even Internet connectivity. Locations outside of the utility infrastructure may have to subcontract these services independent of city planning. Some cities do this intentionally to prevent urban sprawl.

15

> ✔ **AP Expert Note**
>
> **Be able to explain the major differences between cities in various regions**
>
> More often than not, a city's structure and characteristics depend on where it is located. Understanding the major differences between eastern and western U.S. cities will be an important step in succeeding on the AP exam. The exam will likely include questions about the differences between cities in U.S. regions and even between cities around the world. As you continue reading, be sure to note such differences.

Stages of U.S. Cities

In 1967, John Borchert suggested that American cities have gone through five distinct stages.

- Stage 1: The sail-wagon period extended from around 1790 to 1830. The only means of international trade was sailing ships. Once goods were on land, they were hauled by wagon to their final destinations.

- Stage 2: The railroad transported goods and people in the iron-horse period, which lasted from 1830 to 1870.

- Stage 3: The steel-rail period occurred from 1870 to 1920, when steel was the primary building material in the United States. Mining its raw materials and manufacturing and transporting it provided many jobs.

- Stage 4: The auto-air-amenity period extended from 1920 through 1970, when the engine transformed the American landscape via the automobile. People could commute farther to work and live farther outside the central urban area. The airplane meant that goods could be exported and imported much more quickly.

- Stage 5: The high-technology stage started in 1970 and continues into the present day. This stage focuses on the expansion of the service and information sectors of the economy.

European Cities

European cities are very different from American cities. European cities are much older and thus have a different structure. Rome and Athens date as far back as 3,000 years; London and Paris date back 2,000 years; and even the newer cities in Europe had their beginnings before the Americas were settled by Europeans.

Europeans zone their cities differently than Americans. **Zoning laws** determine how land and buildings can be used. There are four different types of zoning: residential, commercial, industrial, and institutional. Residential zoning is for housing, commercial zoning is for business or retail types of structures, industrial zoning is for manufacturing plants, and institutional zoning is for government structures such as schools, courtrooms, and government offices. In Europe, zones are often intermixed; an example would be allowing commercial establishments on the ground floor of a building and apartments on the upper floors. Structures in the United States are often zoned only for commercial use, and the entire building is an office complex.

In the United States, if something is old, it is often torn down and replaced. Europeans, however, have a philosophy that what is old should be preserved. The preservation of historic buildings means that some districts in European cities are hundreds or even thousands of years old.

Many of the streets are in a dendritic pattern, which looks like the root system of trees, with streets that curve and meander through the city. Unlike with the grid system, which is relatively easy to navigate, people traversing European cities can easily get lost if they do not know their way. European cities were built when the automobile was still hundreds of years in the future. Designed primarily for foot traffic, city streets tend to be narrow. Some streets in Copenhagen, Paris, and London are only a few meters wide.

Copenhagen, Denmark, has one of the largest outdoor shopping malls in Europe. It was not always a mall but, rather, used for transportation until recently. Such rezoning for commercial land use has revitalized many urban districts. Like Copenhagen, Neuss in Germany contains an outdoor shopping mall. However, the narrow city streets show that this part of the urban area was built before the invention of the automobile. Trains move people around the densely populated interior.

The Industrial Revolution spurred major changes in European cities. Agricultural products could be sent farther, and markets grew with the increase in urban populations. Fewer people were needed on farms, and more people migrated to cities searching for employment. Cities began to feel crowded. Subways were built in London in the late nineteenth century, and these tracks are still in use today by the Tube, London's subway system. Despite the impact of the Industrial Revolution, cities in Europe are usually smaller than cities in the United States. London, Paris, Berlin, and Moscow are obviously very large cities. However, cities such as Copenhagen, which consists of only 1 million people, are considered a moderate size compared to cities in the United States.

Another difference between the United States and Europe is in the distribution of people by social class. In the United States, the perception is that the lower classes live relatively close to the urban center in apartment complexes, while the upper classes live outside the city and commute to work. The opposite is true of European cities; the wealthy live in the central city and the lower classes live on the outskirts. Lower-income people cannot afford to live in the inner neighborhoods of many European cities; housing costs are too prohibitive. Many of the wealthy escape to rural homes on weekends to enjoy fresh air and space not available in the core urban environment. City parks in European cities are very crowded on weekends, especially when the weather is nice.

Because European cities were built before the technology existed for skyscrapers, many of the structures within the central, older part of the city are only five or six stories tall. By the time skyscrapers could be built, many European cities had already established their downtown regions. Therefore, skyscrapers in European cities are built on the outskirts of town.

In London, the tallest buildings are located in the Canary Wharf area. The Docklands development is located just to the east of downtown London. What used to be desolate, low-income, industrial style housing has now become one of the most fashionable residential areas in all of Europe. The high rises in the Canary Wharf area were built very recently. New development and investment in the area has meant more infrastructure and new buildings. In a neighborhood that used to be devoted to industrial activities around a port, expensive lofts and other apartment complexes are sprouting up.

In Europe, when the buildings of the central business districts were built, the wealthy lived in the bottom floors because elevators had not yet been invented. Less affluent people lived on upper floors and walked up and down stairs every time they left their apartments. Once elevators were invented, however, the upper classes wanted the views that the top floors provided, so upper-floor apartments became more valuable.

15

European cities may feel claustrophobic to people accustomed to the spaciousness of U.S. cities. The buildings in the inner city are all the same height and extend as far as the eye can see. There are no yards; instead, parks provide some open space. The density of these cities also causes some problems for the residents, such as pollution. To prevent urban sprawl, urban planners established greenbelts. **Greenbelts** are rural areas that are set aside to prevent development from extending too far outward as well as to reduce overall pollution. Greenbelts are prevalent in the United Kingdom. The metropolitan area of London has a greenbelt that is over 5,000 square kilometers. Another purpose of greenbelts is to prevent in-filling, the process of cities that are close to each other merging together. In-filling has occurred with U.S. cities such as Dallas-Fort Worth and Minneapolis-Saint Paul. The cities are politically separate and have distinctive cultures, but together they form one giant metropolitan area.

When walking in European cities, one notices buildings that are hundreds of years old next to modern buildings erected within the past couple of decades. In World War II, urban areas in some countries were bombed, demolishing some buildings but sparing others. The result is 500-year-old stone buildings next to 50-year-old buildings constructed of glass and concrete.

Eastern European cities are a little different from many of the cities in Western Europe owing to Soviet dominance during the Cold War. Communist planners built apartments of concrete. For example, in Bucharest, Romania, rows of rectangular concrete apartment buildings were constructed. They were designed to be useful, not interesting or attractive. Eastern European cities have no high-rises in their central business districts. The money simply was not available, and commercial enterprises did not thrive under communism. Also, environmental damage caused by decades of Soviet rule will take decades to clean up.

Since the fall of communism, the urban dwellers of Eastern Europe and its tourists are beginning to experience a reinvigorated urban lifestyle. Prague, with its historic districts, rivals the beauty of Paris. Berlin is now a shopper's paradise. Cities in the former Baltic republics of Latvia, Lithuania, and Estonia are attracting tourism dollars because of their beauty as well as the distinctive cultural experiences they offer.

Latin American Cities

Cities in Latin American countries often integrate their native pasts into their design. This area is experiencing one of the world's fastest urban growth rates. **Urban growth rates** are the rates at which individual cities increase their populations. Cities are growing rapidly, owing to the poverty of the countryside. Many farmers are being forced off rented land for not producing enough profit, or they are leaving their own land because they cannot make a good enough living. The result is an influx of migrants looking for employment.

Latin American cities are distinctive in that their urban structure includes a "spine" of high-income residential areas. This spine extends outward from the central business district, while squatter settlements are located on the edges of the city. **Squatter settlements** are areas of extreme poverty. They often occur due to rapid urbanization and the inability of city infrastructure to keep up with growth within certain developing countries.

The **Latin American city model** developed by Larry Ford, who was a professor of geography at San Diego State University, shows the characteristics of many cities in Central and South America. Many of the high-income residences that extend out from the central business district are gated communities designed to protect the residents from the crime bred by widespread urban poverty.

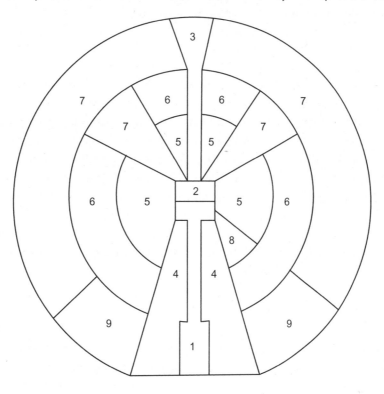

1 – Commercial business district
2 – Market district
3 – Industrial district
4 – Elite residential sector
5 – Zone of maturity
6 – Zone of in situ accession
7 – Zone of peripheral squatter settlements
8 – Gentrification
9 – Middle-class residential

Latin American City Model

In Brazil, many of the squatter settlements are located in the large cities of Rio de Janeiro and São Paulo. Here, the squatter settlements are called *favelas*. In São Paulo, many of the *favelas* are located on the periphery of the city settlements. In Rio de Janeiro, the *favelas* are located throughout the city but are concentrated primarily in the northern sections. In many cases, anarchy rules within the *favelas*. Child gangs dominate the drug trade, and other crimes are rampant in these poverty-stricken areas. Police try to impose order, sometimes brutally, but the sheer number of people living in the *favelas* and the extreme poverty make control difficult.

Another characteristic of Latin American cities is a focus on the central business district. Cities are laid out like the hub and spoke of a bicycle wheel. All roads lead to the center of the city, where commuters must hook up with another road or other transportation system to get to another section of town. Because of this hub-and-spoke pattern of transportation, the central business district is the focus of employment, entertainment, and economic activity. Roads, trains, and buses are fairly reliable in many of these cities.

Mexico City now has a population of over 20 million people. The constant influx of migrants is causing massive urban growth, a high unemployment rate, and an abundance of homeless, abandoned children. Much of the western section of the city is *barriadas*. Mexico City was built on a former lake bed that has been filled in with dirt. As a result of urban structures resting on unstable soil, the city is sinking a few centimeters per year, posing a predicament that must be dealt with in the upcoming decades. Also, Mexico City is located on a fault line and suffers from many earthquakes. A 1985 earthquake had a magnitude of 7.4 on the Richter scale; over 9,000 people lost their lives, over 30,000 people were injured, and over 100,000 people were left homeless. Another problem is that Mexico City is built in a mountain valley with mountains in all directions. Therefore, the city's pollution has little outlet. Warnings for air pollution are constantly being issued. To reduce emissions and improve public health, automobile license plates are color-coded so that certain colors may drive only on certain days.

Asian Cities

Many Asian cities are some of the most prosperous cities on Earth. Their economic development of the past four decades has been extraordinary in terms of both infrastructure and economic importance. For the most part, Asian cities are located on coasts and have been built for trade, with ports playing an important economic role. Much of their growth is due to trading goods to more developed countries, such as the United States and Japan. Investment of capital from more developed countries has also promoted growth.

Many of these cities have specific zones that have been established for western companies to locate within their borders. These zones provide tens of thousands of jobs in cities such as Shanghai, China, and Mumbai (Bombay), India. The result is an infrastructure that is ultramodern in its appearance and financial capital measured in billions of U.S. dollars. Automobile companies, such as Volkswagen and Ford, have established production facilities in Shanghai, and Chinese demand for cars is increasing sharply as the middle class expands. Coca-Cola (the most recognized brand name in the world) and Pepsi have also seen opportunities in many Asian markets.

The **Southeast Asian city model**, developed by Terry McGee, shows the importance of the port zone; growth extends outward from the port. The specific areas designated as western commercial zones are usually located near the port to easily export their products. Suburbs and squatter developments as well as market-gardening zones still exist.

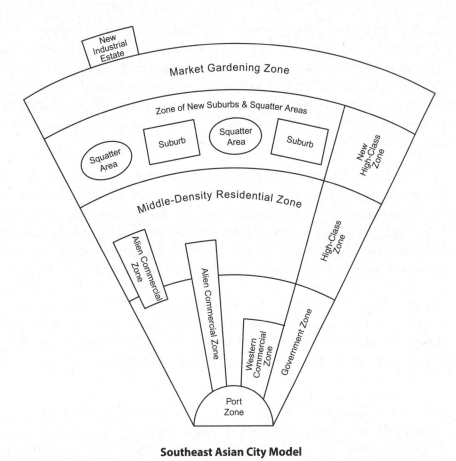

Southeast Asian City Model

Seoul, South Korea; Singapore, a city-state; and Hong Kong, China, have seen tremendous growth rates due to their ports. These areas reexport goods, sending them to all areas of the globe. Singapore and Hong Kong are magnets for foreign investment, which has generated much wealth in these cities. In Singapore, many foreign companies like its strict laws, which ensure low crime rates.

Shanghai has seen growth rates near 30 percent each year for the past decade, making it one of the world's largest ports. Huge industrial and office parks measure in the square miles. **Office parks** are agglomerations with shared phone and Internet services and transportation infrastructure. Office parks have situation advantages, such as freeway access and port facilities, which allow companies to prosper. They also offer site advantages, such as low labor and infrastructure costs. One of these large office and industrial parks is located just outside of Shanghai in Suzhou. Suzhou was traditionally known for its imperial gardens and silk production. Today, this area is becoming known as the "Silicon Valley" of China.

Asian cities have established many shopping malls like the kind that are familiar to Americans. For example, the Lotus shopping mall, located within Shanghai, has characteristics similar to those of the larger malls in the United States; it houses movie theaters, restaurants, and retail outlets. As Southeast Asian consumers earn more expendable income, shopping malls will likely become more common across China and other Southeast Asian countries.

15

Because many Asian cities have grown within the past decade, their modernity is evident. Newly designed and architecturally creative skyscrapers grace many Asian cities. In Shanghai alone, there are over 6,000 skyscrapers. The Taipei 101 building, constructed in 2004, reaches a height of nearly 1,700 feet and has 101 floors. The Petronas Towers in Kuala Lumpur, Malaysia, rise nearly 1,500 feet and are 88 stories high. The Jin Mao Tower in Shanghai is just under 1,400 feet and 88 stories. The Grand Hyatt Shanghai, which claims to be the tallest hotel in the world, is located on the upper stories of the tower and provides views of the city's skyline.

Asian cities have no formalized central business districts. Instead, growth occurs throughout the city, partially due to few zoning laws and almost laissez-faire economics. The result is an incredible number of megacities. Megacities are cities with over 10 million people within their metropolitan areas. Tokyo and Osaka in Japan; Beijing and Shanghai in China; Delhi, Mumbai, and Calcutta in India; Karachi in Pakistan; Jakarta in Indonesia; Dhaka in Bangladesh; and Manila in the Philippines are all megacities and exercise a strong sphere of influence over their surrounding areas.

Asian cities usually include a market-gardening zone because of a cultural preference for fresh food. In some Asian cities, farmers grow vegetables next to skyscrapers. Many of the farmers are poor peasants, while the urban dwellers are middle and upper class. This inequity in wealth leads many rural people to migrate to urban areas looking for employment and dreaming of joining the middle and upper classes.

The workforce in many Asian cities is in high demand from transnational corporations, which can make a substantial profit from employing low-cost labor. Some of the profits are reinvested in the infrastructure of these cities, which will continue to grow and build skyscrapers. This is a prime example of the new international division of labor.

In Asian cities, along with cities around the world, high-tech corridors are also popping up. Like office and industrial parks, **high-tech corridors** use the principle of agglomeration to their benefit. These high-tech corridors are instrumental in providing the world with the computer equipment needed to run its operations on a daily basis. Computer chips are key components of computers, and computers facilitate much of the world's business and personal activity. In high-tech corridors, microchips can be produced cheaply.

Islamic Cities

Islamic cities are found in the Middle East and in parts of Indonesia, which is the country with the most Muslims in the world. Islamic cities are also located in North Africa. The largest Islamic cities in the world include Cairo, Tehran, Dubai, Karachi, Jakarta, Dhaka, and Lagos. Islamic cities located in hot, desert regions have twisted streets because the more twisted the street, the greater the opportunity for shade. Also, personal privacy and space for common gatherings are valued in many of these cities. Like many other large cities, large Muslim cities have squatter settlements.

What distinguishes Islamic cities from other cities is the religion itself. Much of the city layout is based on Islamic principles found in the Koran. The most important physical feature of an Islamic city is the mosque. The principle mosque, located in the center of the city, dominates the landscape and is usually the city's focal point. The call to prayer is heard from mosques five times daily. Much of the traditional city is walled, just like many medieval European cities, for defense.

Because the perceived purity of women is important in Muslim culture, structures are built to protect them. In residential areas, windows are generally small, and to ensure privacy, doors or windows do not face each other on opposite sides of the street. Although Islamic cities are densely compacted, they preserve the privacy of their citizens. Buildings are often connected, but homes are built so that it is impossible to look inside a neighbor's house. Cul-de-sacs are treasured in many Islamic cities because of the privacy they offer. While these impede efficient travel across a city, they protect residents from quickly moving traffic.

Another commonality among many Islamic cities is the bazaar, particularly in North Africa. The bazaar is a street market sometimes called a *suq*. These *suqs* can be enormous, taking up several city blocks and selling anything from produce to carpets and clothing. Each alley is organized by what the market stalls are selling.

Modern Islamic cities, such as Dubai in the United Arab Emirates, are some of the most impressive cities on the planet. The tallest building in the world is in Dubai. The Burj Khalifa is over 2,700 feet tall. The building has 160 floors and is being promoted as the centerpiece of the Middle East's most prestigious development. As the number of Muslims continues to grow, the importance of Islamic cities, such as Dubai, will grow as well.

African Cities

African cities are the fastest-growing urban areas in the world today. The economic conditions in most of Africa motivate many people to migrate to urban areas to look for work. Unemployment rates in some countries are as high as 30 percent. Cities in Muslim-dominated northern Africa have high growth rates but not as high as cities south of the Sahara Desert (called the sub-Saharan region). Although urbanization is proceeding rapidly here, the region still has the lowest urban population in the world, based on percentage. More people are occupied by rural activities in Africa than on any other continent.

Because colonialism ended only as recently as four decades ago, a strong colonial imprint is still visible in the structures and functions of African cities. Many were trade centers for the exportation of resources to colonial powers. Because of colonialism, African cities have three distinct central business districts. The headquarters of the colonial government were found in the colonial CBD (central business district). The architecture in this area often resembles that of the colonizers' country. In much of West Africa, the French style of architecture is evident in cities, such as in Abidjan in Côte d'Ivoire. In other areas, such as in South Africa, Dutch architecture is prevalent.

The traditional CBD holds the distinction of being the current commercial center of these cities. Many of the financial institutions in the country are located in these sections of the city. They align closely in purpose with CBDs in U.S. cities.

15

The market CBD, or market zone, plays a vital role in many African cities. The market, or bazaar, sells anything from rugs and vegetables to animals, within a setting that can best be described as a farmers market in the United States. Taxes are difficult to collect on transactions conducted in the bazaar because they are not easily monitored. Often these bazaars are huge, taking up city blocks, and people have been known to get lost in them. Thousands of people show up for the commerce and excitement that is associated with these CBDs. Cities such as Addis Ababa in Ethiopia and Mogadishu in Somalia possess large market areas.

The **African city model** shows the three CBDs with ethnic neighborhoods extending outward from them. Beyond the ethnic neighborhoods are the mining and manufacturing zones as well as informal towns (squatter settlements).

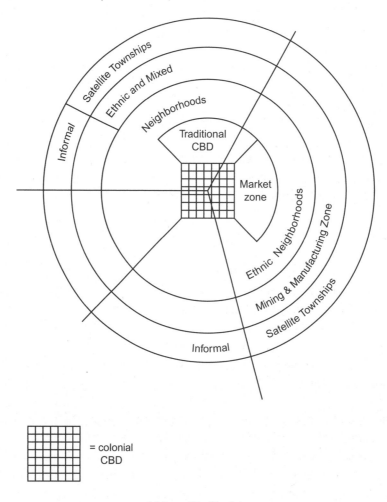

African City Model

For the most part, African cities lack the efficient transportation systems that many cities in other parts of the world enjoy. Either the governments do not have the money to build transportation infrastructure or the money has been misappropriated. Because of this, transportation is difficult in many sub-Saharan African cities. Many roads are unpaved. In addition, many African cities are afflicted by high rates of HIV infection and have large numbers of orphaned and homeless children.

There are exceptions to the picture of poor African urban areas. Most of the cities in South Africa, for example, are modern in their appearance and demonstrate characteristics common to many European, U.S., and Asian cities. Skyscrapers dominate the landscape, efficient transportation systems are in place, and suburbs are growing.

Cairo, Egypt, is quickly becoming a modern city. However, traffic is often at a standstill, and space is at such a premium that development is currently taking place on cemeteries. Cairo's long history on the banks of the Nile River has been important in determining its place in Egypt. The Nile is the life source of Egypt since it provides water for crops and for the urban population. The great pyramids were built in nearby Giza by ancient pharaohs. (Along with Kalyobia, the cities of Cairo and Giza compose the urban metropolitan area of Cairo.) The city is rich in history and contains one of the world's great museums, the Egyptian Museum, which has relics dating back to the ancient Egyptian empire.

MODELS OF U.S. CITIES

Geographers have suggested many different models to describe cities in the United States. No one model accurately predicts or portrays every city in the United States. All of these models deal with social structure, or **class** structure. Lower class, middle class, and upper class are the three classes most often associated with these models. However, these classes can be broken up further.

Concentric Zone Model

The **concentric zone model** was established by urban geographers Robert Park, Ernest Burgess, and Roderick McKenzie in the early 1920s. The model suggests that the lower classes live closest to the central business district (CBD), while the upper classes live farther out because they can afford the commute into the city to work.

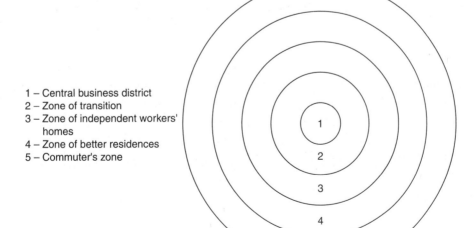

1 – Central business district
2 – Zone of transition
3 – Zone of independent workers' homes
4 – Zone of better residences
5 – Commuter's zone

Concentric Zone Model

In the concentric zone model, the central business district is the commercial center of the city and contains the **peak land value intersection**, the area with the greatest land value and commercial value. Outside of the central business district is the **zone in transition**, which usually contains high-density areas of lower-class citizens who live in substandard housing. Most residences are apartments; these are intermixed with industrial zones. Because very few people want to live next to industrial zones and their noise and pollution, the value of the housing is usually very low. Many of the apartments in these areas are tenements: rundown apartment buildings that are minimally kept up by landlords because their value is so low. Landlords either barely comply with housing codes or do not comply at all.

Next out from the CBD is lower-class housing. These are typically older, well-established neighborhoods. Working-class families and singles alike tend to purchase homes in this region. The fourth zone is an area of middle-class housing. Homes get larger as the income of their inhabitants rises. The fifth zone is an upper-class residential area. In some cases, this zone is called a commuter zone because of the number of people who commute either into the city or to other suburbs for work.

Burgess elaborated on the concentric zone model to include the ideas of invasion and succession. **Invasion and succession** refer to the continued expansion of the central business district and the continual push outward of the zones. This pushing-out process causes the zones to rebuild their infrastructures. Areas that were once low-income residences and older working-class neighborhoods are converted into apartment buildings. The upper class continually needs to commute farther and at a greater expense to maintain the lifestyle of the fifth zone. This is the opposite of the situation in European cities, as mentioned earlier.

The concentric zone model was based on early 1900s Chicago. The problem with this model is that it reflects a perception about American cities but not the reality. The concentric zone model really does not exist in the United States today. Many upper-class and upper-middle-class residents are moving back into the city, creating wealthy areas relatively close to the urban center. Stretches of upper-class residences usually follow transportation routes outward from the central business district rather than occupying zones in concentric circles outward from the city center.

Sector Model

The **sector model** was established by Homer Hoyt in 1939. It is also based on class but describes social structure based on the transportation systems rather than on distance from the central business district. Zones extend along transportation routes.

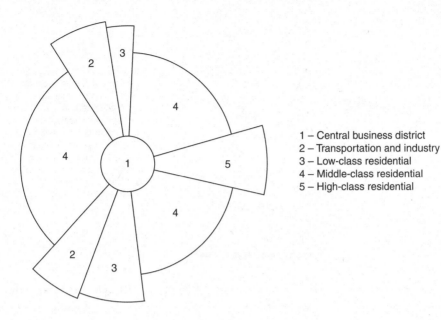

1 – Central business district
2 – Transportation and industry
3 – Low-class residential
4 – Middle-class residential
5 – High-class residential

Sector Model

The sector model is similar to the concentric zone model in that it uses social structure to determine neighborhoods. It should be noted that many other characteristics could be used to define zones, including ethnicity and physical features.

Interestingly enough, Hoyt based his model on Chicago as well. He argued that Chicago showed growth extending outward, especially on the north side of the city where upper-income residences were being built. These residences were closer to the central business district than the concentric zone model would predict. Likewise, Hoyt argued that if the concentric zone model were true, high-income housing would be built on the outskirts of the south side of Chicago and the north side, but it was not. Hoyt also showed that industrial zones in Chicago extended along the major transportation routes. At the time, trains were the primary means of industrial transportation, and industries extended outward along the railroad tracks.

Multiple Nuclei Model

The **multiple nuclei model** was established by Chauncy Harris and Edward Ullman in 1945. It differed from the previous two models by suggesting that urban growth is independent of the central business district. Growth may begin in commercial, industrial, and even residential suburbs outside the central business district. Different industries spring up wherever there are opportunities for growth. According to the multiple nuclei model, growth may occur haphazardly and extend more in one direction than in another. The different zones are still based on class, but more emphasis is placed on the extent and type of economic development.

15

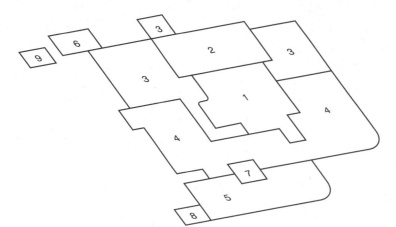

Multiple Nuclei Model

1 – Central business district
2 – Wholesale, light
    manufacturing
3 – Low-class residential
4 – Medium-class residential
5 – High-class residential
6 – Heavy manufacturing
7 – Outlying business district
8 – Residential suburb
9 – Industrial suburb

One of the best examples of this model involves airports. Airports are usually located on the outskirts of the city for reasons of space and to limit noise and air pollution. However, around the airport is usually substantial development of hotels, restaurants, and entertainment facilities. This development does not arise from the central business district. Rather, an economic opportunity allows certain companies to prosper around the airport. Likewise, in this model, industrial development may occur around a port.

The multiple nuclei model also takes into account the economic effects of universities. Around college campuses, there are usually more fast-food restaurants, coffee shops, and bookstores. Again, development is independent of the central business district.

Although the central business district is still the commercial hub of the city, and much development takes place there because of the economic activity, commercial and industrial enterprises may place a higher priority on being close to an airport or seaport. However, in these areas of growth, one would not likely find high-income housing. That tends to be built in its own area, based on the idea that the wealthy like to live next to the extremely wealthy and so on.

Many American cities follow the multiple nuclei model. Growth occurs where it is needed and where developers can maximize profits. **Edge cities**, large commercial centers that offer entertainment and shopping in the suburbs, often result. Edge cities may approach 100,000 in population.

The **multiplier effect** is the principle that development spurs more development. When development occurs in a city, more services are needed to meet the needs of the growing population. When more infrastructure is needed, more tradespeople are needed. These tradespeople need more grocery stores, gas stations, and so forth, and more services attract more people. The city's tax base increases, supporting even more development through increased amenities, such as parks, sports facilities, and better schools.

Galactic city model

The **galactic city model** is a relatively new urban model developed in the late twentieth century as a representation of a post-industrial city in North America. Chauncy Harris developed this model as a revision to the multiple nuclei model. The galactic city model represents a city with growth independent of the central business district (CBD) that is traditionally connected to the central city by means of an arterial highway or interstate.

Some geographers argue that the galactic city is simply an extension of the multiple nuclei model. The Los Angeles metropolitan area shows extensive edge cities around the core city of Los Angeles. Cities such as Santa Ana, Burbank, and other smaller metropolitan areas have high-rise areas within the urban core of the larger system.

Other cities have commercial areas located outside of the city proper, such as the King of Prussia region within the Philadelphia metropolitan area. This large shopping area has attracted other amenities, such as restaurants and hotels, providing employment opportunities in the area. The King of Prussia area has seen near double-digit population growth, with the population now surpassing 20,000 people. Because most people do not want to live next to the noise and environmental pollution of industry, heavy industry is often nonexistent in such areas.

Oftentimes, these areas of greater growth (edge cities) are located along major arteries of transportation routes. Interstates or rail lines will connect these areas to the core city, but they are not solely dependent on the core city for their economic success. Many larger metropolitan areas have some type of growth outside of the downtown districts. Atlanta, Baltimore, and Minneapolis-Saint Paul all have large areas of growth in the suburbs.

Keno-Capitalism Model

Michael Dear and Steven Flusty, geographers from the University of California, Los Angeles (UCLA) and the University of Southern California (USC), created a somewhat controversial model in the 1990s. The **Keno-capitalism model** is based on Los Angeles and suggests that areas are randomly placed and are zoned or gated off from other zones in the city.

Using the city of Los Angeles, not Chicago (as was often the case with traditional U.S. urban models), different areas of the city are described by such diverse features as street warfare and amusement parks. Other areas set aside for shopping malls are called consumption opportunities. Yet other areas are designated as **ethnoburbs**, or neighborhoods dominated by a specific ethnic group, such as Chinatown or Little Saigon in Los Angeles. Through a haphazard approach to management, these zones are adjacent, yet may have little contact with each other. The city almost resembles a scrambled Rubik's cube.

15

Central Place Theory

Walter Christaller established the **central place theory** in 1933, based on his study of southern Germany. Like von Thünen, Christaller based his central place theory on assumptions of uniform topography, equal transportation systems, and that people will travel the least distance possible to meet their service needs.

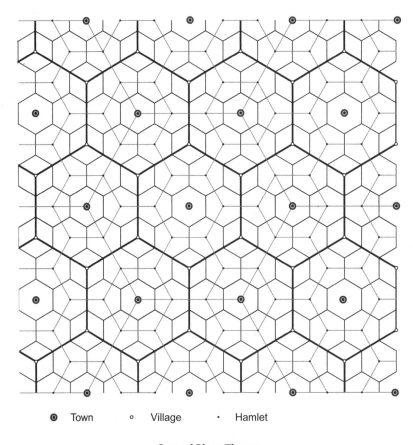

◉ Town   ○ Village   · Hamlet

Central Place Theory

The central place theory shows the relationships between urban areas, including their hinterlands, and the range that individual cities need to maintain their size. Larger cities need larger ranges and hinterlands.

Range is the maximum distance that people are willing to travel to purchase a product or partake in a service; it may vary depending upon the product. Let's say that you are craving a bottle of soda. You own a car and are willing to travel about a mile to a local convenience store to purchase your soda. The range for the soda is limited because it is a low-cost item and commonly available. People go to the nearest store selling soda rather than travel to a store farther away if the price is about the same. Now, say you want to purchase a Rolls-Royce. Rolls-Royces are not sold in every metropolitan area. You must travel, sometimes hundreds or even thousands of miles to purchase one. The range is greater for a Rolls-Royce Phantom than for, say, a Ford Focus. In general, people are willing to travel farther to enjoy goods and services that are rarer. People are also willing to travel extended distances for concerts or sporting events.

The threshold of a product is the minimum number of customers needed for it to succeed. The threshold for a bottle of soda is much lower than a threshold for a waterbed. Less range is needed to find customers for the bottle of soda than for a waterbed. However, more soda needs to be sold to make the same amount of profit as one waterbed. Usually, waterbed stores are located in larger urban areas because they need a greater range to meet the customer base threshold to survive.

The hinterland is sometimes called the **market area** of the product. The hinterland is what makes the central place theory hexagonal in shape. It is equidistant along all edges from the product center or urban area. An entity's sphere of influence remains strongest near its source or center, but people in the hinterland may still be willing to travel some distance to purchase or enjoy it.

Smart new business owners find out the threshold for their business before they even open their doors. They must also try to find the range of their customers once the doors have opened. Finding the range can be done simply by asking customers where they are from. This is sometimes accomplished by collecting zip codes at the cash register. To assist business people, census tracts are used to determine population. **Census tracts** are geographic areas with about 5,000 people on average, though they can vary from 2,500 up to approximately 8,000 inhabitants. From this, businesses can use geographic information system (GIS) technology to figure out the best location for their business.

The Gravity Model

The gravity model relates to central place theory because the mathematical formula can determine where the breaking point (BP) is between two cities. The BP determines the market area for each city. If a person lives somewhere between two cities, the gravity model will predict which city has more retail pulling power.

The increasing dominance of cities ties in with a fundamental principle of urbanization. The **gravity model** suggests that the greater the sphere of influence a city has, the greater its impact on other cities around it. This means that there will be more migration between these points, regardless of the distance between them. The gravity model takes into account not only migration between cities but also travel between them, telephone calls between them, trade between them, etc. To determine the degree to which two cities are related, the populations must be multiplied and then divided by the square of the distance between the cities. The gravity model is an effective way to determine the relationship between two urban areas. World-class cities, such as New York City and Tokyo, will have a high relationship even though the distance between them is far.

$$\frac{\text{Population 1} \times \text{Population 2}}{\text{Distance}^2}$$

The gravity model

Let's assume that a city called Geograville, with a population of 10 million, and another city, Geotown, with a population of 8 million, are being analyzed for their relationship. The distance between Geograville and Geotown is 1,200 miles. Take the population of Geograville and multiply it by the population of Geotown. Ten million people multiplied by 8 million people

15

gives 80,000,000,000,000. This number must be divided by the distance between the cities squared: 1,200 squared is 1,440,000. By expressing all the numbers in millions, we get $10 \times 8 = 80$. Then $80 \div 1.44 = 55.5$, which means that Geograville and Geotown have a relatively strong relationship with each other.

By looking at another example of smaller towns that are closer together, we can compare the results. Demograville has a population of 1,000, and Migrationton has a population of 500. The distance between these two cities is 500 miles. We calculate as follows: $1,000 \times 500 = 500,000$; $500^2 = 250,000$; and $500,000 \div 250,000 = 2$.

These results mean that the relationship between Geograville and Geotown is stronger than the relationship between Demograville and Migrationton. Thus, there would likely be more trade between Geograville and Geotown, even though they are farther apart. The cities of Migrationton and Demograville do not hold the same amount of sway over each other, even though they are closer together. Instead, other trade areas or urban locations closer to them will dominate their migration, trade, and other patterns.

> ### ✔ AP Expert Note
>
> **Be able to explain the different models of U.S. cities**
>
> As you can see, there are many different models for U.S. cities. It's important for you to be able to describe the key points of each and, if applicable, how one might relate to another. The AP exam will likely test you on identifying what is true of a certain model or even on predicting human behavior based on a set of data.

The Rank-Size Rule

The **rank-size rule** states that the size of cities within a country will be in proportion to each other. The second-largest city should have half the population of the largest city, the third-largest city should have one-third the population of the largest city, and so on.

Primate cities have more than twice the population of any other urban area in that country. Primate cities are the most important urban areas economically, politically, and culturally in their countries. London is a good example of a primate city. London's population, depending upon how you measure it, exceeds 7 million. The next-largest city in the United Kingdom is Birmingham, with 2.25 million people. Likewise in France, Paris' population approaches 10 million, while the next-largest city, Marseille, has 1.5 million people. In Argentina, Buenos Aires is the largest city, with a population approaching 14 million, while the second-largest city is Córdoba, with a little over 3 million people. Thailand's largest city is Bangkok with a population of 7.5 million, while the next-largest city is Nonthaburi with just over 1 million.

Having a primate city does not make a country more or less developed. Great Britain and France, with London and Paris, respectively, are more developed countries. Thailand, with Bangkok, is considered less developed. Many countries do not have a primate city, including the United States. New York City is the largest U.S. urban area with over 18 million people, and the next largest is

Los Angeles with about 13 million, more than half of the population of New York City. Even though New York is considered the cultural and financial capital, it is not the primate city in the United States. China also does not have a primate city. Shanghai, Beijing, and Hong Kong are all large and function as financial centers for their respective areas, but they are not more than twice the size of the next largest city. India also does not have a primate city.

Proponents of the rank-size rule suggest that if a country does have a primate city, it lacks an effective distribution of goods and services throughout the country. Therefore, less developed countries would tend to have primate cities, while more developed countries would not. For the most part, this is true, with the notable exceptions of London and Paris.

Opponents of the rank-size rule suggest that the United Kingdom, France, and many other countries in Europe contain primate cities, even though they are developed, because most European cities simply do not tend to be very large.

Built Environment and Social Space

All cities revolve around their central business districts. In the United States, CBDs are characterized by the tallest buildings of the urban landscape. In Europe, the CBDs do not contain the tallest buildings because many of those areas were already fully developed before skyscrapers became technologically feasible. Building skyscrapers in cities, such as Paris and parts of Rome, is made even more difficult by the expanse of underground catacombs. For centuries, the dead were buried beneath the city, creating a labyrinth of pockmarks in the soil and making the ground too unstable to support the weight of skyscrapers. However, the core of European cities frequently contains beautiful old architecture, including churches and other landmarks, that is as distinctive as skyscrapers.

When cities are painted or imagined, usually their central business districts are pictured. Artwork that shows a city is called a cityscape. Many cityscapes are recognizable around the world. When people think of Paris, they picture the Eiffel Tower; London, the Parliament building with Big Ben watching over it; and New York, the Manhattan skyline. Many cities around the world are trying to create a memorable cityscape. Seattle built the Space Needle, and Beijing has its Forbidden City.

A **symbolic landscape** is an urban landscape that reflects the city's history and has become synonymous with the city. The symbolic landscape is not the economic foundation of a city but, rather, the imprint of its historical foundation. In Athens and Rome, for example, the ruins from the great Greek and Roman civilizations are still evident. The Seven Hills of Rome and the ancient temples of Athens have drawn millions of tourists to these urban areas. In each of these examples, the symbolic landscape has become an icon for another cultural or political phenomenon.

One of the world's best-known symbolic landscapes was the World Trade Center Towers in New York City. They represented a particular aspect of Western culture in their grandiose splendor, which is why they were targeted for the 9/11 terrorist attack that destroyed them. The Pentagon, which symbolizes the U.S. military presence around the world, was also struck. The terrorists were not only attacking these physical buildings but also the psyche of the citizens of the United States. A third potential target was the Capitol Building in Washington, D.C., which represents the U.S. government.

15

SUBURBANIZATION IN THE UNITED STATES

In many cities around the world, **suburbanization** is a source of growth. Suburbs are usually outside of the primary city, yet their economic and cultural focus lies within the city. Suburbs may have residential, commercial, and industrial zones. Often, commuters are not commuting from suburbs to the city but, rather, from suburbs to different suburbs. Some suburbs possess more than 100,000 inhabitants. Outlying suburbs, which are newer, usually have modern buildings and bigger houses. First-ring suburbs usually have smaller, older homes.

Much suburbanization is centered around push and pull factors. American culture favors wanting something that is new. Therefore, many people prefer new houses, which are more abundant in the suburbs. At the same time, people are being pushed away from the core city by their negative perceptions of it.

Suburbanization is changing the demographics of cities, resulting in a core city that is dominated by the elderly and younger couples with either no children or very young children. As families leave the core city in the hopes of finding homes with more bedrooms and larger yards, better schools, and more amenities, they are often replaced by new immigrants from other countries and couples with two incomes and no kids, who like living close to the amenities that the core city offers. More nightclubs, theaters, and sports facilities are present in the core city than in the suburbs.

However, when suburban children move away to go to college or develop families of their own, many older couples move back into the city. They no longer want to keep up a large house and yard, and they are at a stage in life where they value the conveniences of the city. This move back can spark a gentrification initiative in many core city neighborhoods.

Characteristics of U.S. Suburbs

The suburbs have more children per capita than urban areas. The suburbs also tend to have more parents between the ages of 30 and 50; on the other hand, the inner city has more 20- to 30-year-olds and elderly people. Both areas offer different amenities to different demographic segments.

The first ring of suburbs includes older neighborhoods that abut directly with the primary city. These suburbs saw their primary growth take place decades ago, and the result is a community with all of its available space filled with residential and commercial activities. The neighborhoods at one time may have been considered upper class or middle class but now may be considered lower class. This is not to suggest that many of these first-ring suburbs are not nice communities. Many of these suburbs possess amenities that make them desirable places to live.

The second-ring suburbs are growing and infringing on the surrounding rural areas. This process of growth is called **urban sprawl**. Urban sprawl puts a strain on the resources of the core city. Sewer lines, utility hookups, water treatment plants, and transportation systems are often designed with a certain reach in mind. When the urban area continues to expand, they suffer strain. Second-ring suburbs may be two or three decades old.

Some communities even have third-ring suburbs. Third-ring suburbs abut and encroach on rural areas. In some states, real estate developers are offering farmers top dollar for their land. Some farmers resist this easy money because they love the agricultural lifestyle despite its difficulties, but many take the offer and retire comfortably for the remainder of their lives.

Many third-ring suburbs are adopting the trend of planned communities. A **planned community** is an area where the developer can plot out each house and can build the entire development from scratch. Many newer planned communities have multimillion-dollar homes with community pools, golf courses, and parks and playgrounds. In some cases, these communities are gated to ensure that only the residents and their guests are allowed to enter; aptly, such communities are called gated communities.

This process of **New Urbanism** is evident in many of the newer suburban developments in the United States. New Urbanism is the movement to plan communities that are more walkable, rather than automobile dependent, with a diversity of jobs. By establishing diversity in economic structure, the community is less susceptible to economic downturns or recessions in the economy. The walk-ability factor also promotes a healthier population. Sidewalks and bike paths are built into the plans to ensure both recreational opportunities and transportation routes.

> **✔ AP Expert Note**
>
> **Be able to describe New Urbanism and its impact on a community**
>
> With any city, there are pros and cons to living in a certain area, and the same is true of suburbs. Prior to the AP exam, review the different types of suburbs and how New Urbanism could improve residential life within a suburban development. You will likely see a couple of questions on the AP exam that ask you to identify, describe, or explain how suburban lifestyles are shifting.

Many of the first-ring suburbs—those bordering the central core city—are seeing an increase in the number of brownfields. **Brownfields** are former industrial sites that cities are now attempting to redevelop. The success of the development oftentimes is relative to the level of pollution left from the previous tenants. If there is little pollution, brownfields may even be converted to residential housing. If the soil has been contaminated and can be cleaned, big-box stores such as Walmart, Target, or Home Depot may convert the area into a store. These will be tied to railroad zones once used for hauling industrial products and may now even be used as passenger rail lines.

URBAN ISSUES High-Yield

Cities suffer from the problems that arise when large numbers of people are concentrated together. These include crime, pollution, traffic congestion, housing costs, race relations, and many other problems. Some cities handle these issues better than others. When the problems of an urban area become so great that people leave, the process is called **counterurbanization**.

Different management structures can have either negative or positive effects on any urban problem. **Decentralization** is the distribution of authority from a central figure or point to other sectors in the city. **Centralization** is the opposite of decentralization; it is the focusing of power into one authority, usually the command of a mayor or city manager.

Crime and Pollution

In terms of raw numbers, crime is higher in cities than in suburbs, and there is more crime in larger urban areas. However, there are also more people in larger cities. On a per capita basis, urban areas may be no different than suburban or even rural areas in the incidence of crime.

Pollution is another difficulty plaguing larger urban areas. With the "greening" of cities, pollution has been curbed in the more developed countries. However, in the less developed countries, many of the larger urban areas are still health hazards for their residents. Rivers are polluted by industry, and local, state, or federal government agencies have few resources and little power to fight the polluting companies. Air pollution in many of these cities makes seeing the horizon a rarity. Waste management is another problem; indoor plumbing is nonexistent for many people in less developed countries.

Urban hydrology is how a city manages distributing clean water to its citizens and then removing dirty water and cleaning it before it is released back into the world's rivers and oceans. Many cities in less developed countries do not have the infrastructure or the resources to build water mains and sewage lines into every residence. In some cases, millions of structures need hook-ups. Improper sewage treatment leads to endemic disease and occasional epidemics. Sickness in large urban areas can kill hundreds quickly. Recently, severe acute respiratory syndrome (SARS) and the bird flu have become concerns in Asia. Many doctors fear a pandemic due to a lack of safe drinking water and inaccessible health care. Some argue that the cause of disease is not urban areas but rather poverty.

Another effect of pollution and congestion is that cities create their own heat. This process is known as the urban heat island effect. Usually cities are warmer by several degrees than their suburban areas. This can affect weather patterns around cities, even moving storms around a city. The urban heat island effect is due to **urban morphology**—that is, all of the street patterns, structures, and the physical form of the city. For example, all the blacktop and concentrated brick, stone, and metal in buildings hold the heat much longer than a natural landscape does.

Traffic Congestion

Traffic congestion is another problem often associated with cities. Traffic can be a nightmare in many larger urban areas. There are simply not enough roads to meet the needs of the population. Cities have tried solving this problem in several ways. Mass transit moves tens of thousands of people around cities on a daily basis. Larger cities usually build trains or subways, which are expensive to construct, while smaller cities usually establish bus systems.

15

One might think that a way to relieve traffic congestion is simply to build more roads. However, the situation is more complex than it first seems. Many traffic studies have suggested that the more roads that are built or lanes that are added to a freeway, the more traffic is created. More road space makes traveling by car appear more desirable, thus resulting in the congestion that the construction was intended to reduce. For example, thousands of people in the Dallas-Fort Worth area commute between the cities. Although the cities are connected by Interstate 30, many drivers do not use this road because it gets too crowded during rush hours. If developers added lanes to I-30, some commuters would leave the back roads and attempt to use the freeway. Now, instead of congestion on four lanes, there would be congestion on six lanes. As cities continue to expand, the issue of how to move people around the city becomes more pressing. The issue of mass transportation versus more roads is constantly fought in the political arena.

✔ **AP Expert Note**

Be ready to discuss issues within urban areas

Urban areas have many people, and with so many people, they have a variety of issues, such as pollution, crime, gentrification, and more. The AP exam will ask you to explain how each of these problems impacts city life and how urban areas try to minimize such issues. As you read through this section, consider which issues have the greatest impact on your nearest city and how that urban area acts to resolve those issues.

Gentrification

Housing costs can be prohibitive in many larger urban areas. Gentrification is both a problem and an advantage in inner-city neighborhoods. **Gentrification** is the process of wealthy people moving into inner-city neighborhoods and rebuilding older homes. The improvements create more demand for housing in the neighborhood. The result is a gradual increase of property value and then taxes. Landlords see an economic opportunity and raise rent costs, even without making improvements that would justify such increases, based on the sheer demand for city housing. Eventually, the original inhabitants of the neighborhood can no longer afford to live there and have to move; this is true for small businesses in the area as well. Many people who have lived and worked in these neighborhoods for decades are being forced out.

On the positive side, the result of gentrification is a beautiful urban neighborhood with expensive homes. The wealthy urbanites who have moved in have made the neighborhood prosperous, and the city enjoys much higher tax revenue. Often, the city uses the expanded tax revenue to build parks, repair sidewalks, and provide amenities that make the area a very pleasant place to live.

Because gentrification can be a high-risk investment, it is often undertaken by a developer who razes old buildings to build high-end townhomes or condominiums in the hopes of attracting affluent residents. Much gentrification uses the postmodern architecture that is trendy today. Postmodern architecture blends historical foundations with modern touches. Postmodernism is a reaction to the modern architecture that prevailed in the twentieth century in the United States. Modern architecture emphasized boxy structures, usually made from concrete and glass.

15

To prevent the economic decline of newly gentrified areas, restrictive covenants are enforced. For example, it may not be illegal to park your car outside at night, but your development may fine you for doing so. Garbage cans must be kept inside the garage, and, in some cases, garage doors must be kept closed at all times.

In Portland, Oregon, the city council has restricted the expansion of the city limits. By restricting outward growth, the city has forced growth inward, creating a high demand for housing within the urban area. Outlined by mountains on many sides, Portland has a site advantage to limit growth. The downside to this urban planning approach is that housing costs have skyrocketed. First-time home-buyers are being forced either to buy outside of the city and face long commutes or to make excessive mortgage payments on homes within the city limits. Many urban planners have praised Portland's attempt at trying to halt urban sprawl. Opponents suggest that this strategy makes it nearly impossible for a lower-class or even a middle-class resident to purchase a home within the city boundaries.

Race Relations

Yet another problem that cities around the world face is how to deal with race relations in the urban framework. Race riots have occurred in Los Angeles and in other cities around the world. In some cases, illegal activities, such as blockbusting, have occurred. **Blockbusting** is when real estate agents try to induce people to sell their homes because of a perception that a different race is moving into the neighborhood. Real estate agents may claim that property values are about to fall, playing on the perception that the more minorities who move into a neighborhood, the lower property values will be. In fact, just the opposite may be true.

Racial steering also takes place in some areas today. **Racial steering** occurs when real estate agents show homes only in certain neighborhoods based on the race of the buyers. Racial steering was often used in the South prior to the civil rights movement. **Segregation**—the enforced separation of races—was practiced in many urban areas in the South and in some northern cities. In some cases, the institutions of the city were involved in the segregation process. These institutions not only included the real estate agents but also financial institutions that lent money to home buyers. **Redlining** is the refusal of lending institutions to give loans to those in high-risk areas; it was often employed in neighborhoods that had high default rates on mortgages, many of which were in traditionally ethnic communities.

The Abandonment of Cities

As the United States continues to deindustrialize, the old infrastructure of cities is often left to rot or rust. Detroit, Michigan—once a bastion of industry and production—is experiencing a problem that other cities will soon begin to experience unless some significant changes take place. Detroit is facing **zones of abandonment**, which are areas that no longer have police or fire protection because the city has decided the tax revenue cannot sustain public services to those areas. Large areas of Detroit have no buildings on city blocks, to the point where the idea of urban agriculture has even been discussed. As a result of these **disamenities**, people do not want to live in the city and often move away, exacerbating the problems of the inner city. In many cases, these areas have a high rate of house foreclosures, resulting in abandoned neighborhoods that once thrived with children.

Urban Renewal

As cities age, sections of them become blighted with urban decay, such as when deindustrialization leaves factories shuttered and undermines local and neighborhood economies. This creates a vicious cycle: as property values in an area decline, residents begin to move out of the area for fear that their property will further decrease in value, but so many people moving out creates a glut in the market, lowering property values for the area, and thus the urban decay spreads outward. One solution to urban decay is the process of **urban renewal**, where cities buy properties in order to redevelop the area to encourage economic investment.

Urban renewal has pros and cons. On the positive side, it has often spurred economic prosperity for downtown areas, encouraging new people to move into the city center. On the negative side, urban renewal is often dependent on city governments seizing the land and property of poor and minority groups. In the United States, for example, African Americans have had homes, businesses, and public housing projects seized under eminent domain, only to be priced out of the resulting housing market despite the financial compensation they received for their property.

The Walkable City

The **walkable city** has options, such as grocery stores, bakeries, butchers, and other services, within walking distance of residences to reduce the need for automobiles, thus reducing pollution and traffic congestion. By becoming more walkable, urban areas can allow more people access to grocery or food stores. When there is a lack of fresh food available, less healthy options fill the gap. Though some grocery stores have attempted to locate in cities and give people more options for fresher food, people without cars are less likely to shop at a store when it is more than a couple of miles away.

Changing Employment Mix

Because of the rapid suburbanization of many American metropolitan areas, the employment mix and opportunities have changed according to location. Prior to World War II, there were many industrial and manufacturing jobs located in cities. With the construction of the interstate highway system, many industries moved to the suburbs and rural towns to take advantage of inexpensive land and good access to highways.

In addition, the central business district (CBD) of cities used to have the most retail and office space of anywhere in a metro area. Prior to the 1950s, there were plenty of service and secondary jobs in urban areas. Suburbanization over the last 50 years has been accompanied by the movement of retail business, office parks, and industry to the suburban fringe. As a result, many low-paying service jobs in suburbia are difficult to fill. A larger percentage of low-wage workers live in the inner cities, and they often do not own automobiles or have access to mass transit systems that could take them where the jobs are.

15

Recent census data has revealed that American suburbs have become increasingly ethnically and economically diverse in the last decade. By analyzing the changing employment mix, one could have anticipated the demographic changes that have taken place.

The Ongoing Evolution of Cities

Cities, like people, are constantly evolving. Sometimes this change is for the better, sometimes for the worse. Development brings in new buildings at the expense of older and sometimes historic buildings. The result is a new landscape that may be visually stimulating or aesthetically ugly. The one constant among cities is that they are vital to understanding human nature. Humans need cities for trade, services, and cultural amenities. As cities around the world have larger populations, their status will change. The city's responsibility to its citizens is to plan for the growth and to develop according to need.

 NEXT STEP: PRACTICE

Go to Rapid Review and Practice Chapter 8 or to your online quizzes on kaptest.com for exam-like practice on this topic.

Haven't registered your book yet? Go to kaptest.com/moreonline to begin.

CHAPTER 16

Industrial and Economic Development Patterns and Processes

LEARNING OBJECTIVES

After studying this chapter, you will be able to:

- List major economic sectors.

- Describe the Industrial Revolution's effects.

- Explain industrial location using Weber's model.

- Analyze the causes and effects of the global economy.

- Analyze the intersection of gender and economic development.

- Analyze measures of social and economic development, particularly corresponding spatial patterns.

- Describe the economic consequences of recent industrialization and development.

KEYS TO ECONOMIC AND INDUSTRIAL DEVELOPMENT

When discussing economic development and industrialization, it's important to note that some countries develop faster than others. Likewise, some urban areas develop faster than others. Over the past 150 years, patterns of development around the world have been uneven on many different geographic scales. The field of **economic geography**, a subfield of human geography, studies economic development and the inequalities that are created. The main goal is to find out why the world is divided into relatively more developed and less developed countries. Economic geography also analyzes the same questions on a country level, asking why certain parts of a country are better or worse off than others, and exploring how economic development of a country influences other major areas such as agriculture and urbanization.

There are several reasons for the economic success or failure of a country or region. The level of industrialization, access to resources, stability of the government, and quality of political leadership are all important factors for development. Industrialization is one of the main components of economic success. Nearly all underdeveloped countries seek to industrialize their economies. They believe doing so will enable their countries to obtain the material conveniences, goods, and services that modern, developed countries have. Before considering the factors that lead to industrialization, we must first consider the different types of economic systems in the world.

Economic Systems

There are three main types of economic systems in the world: capitalism, socialism, and communism. These economic systems exist on a spectrum with different levels of economic freedom.

Capitalism

Capitalism, in a broad sense, is an economic system in which businesses are owned by private individuals and companies, who are free to decide what to produce and how much to charge. By letting the market decide prices, people have the freedom to choose their own outcomes, constrained only by their ability and willingness to pay. Capitalism is the most common economic system in the world; it is the system in the United States, Canada, most of Europe, and many parts of Asia.

One notable manifestation of capitalism in the twenty-first century is **neoliberalism**, a political and economic ideology that favors free-market capitalism. Neoliberalism broadly advocates for free trade, free movement of labor, globalization, and minimal government oversight of the economy. Organizations and agreements that transcend national boundaries, such as the European Union and World Trade Organization, are expressions of neoliberalism.

Socialism

Socialism is an economic and political system in which the government regulates private business and basic industries and controls the means of production (e.g., factories, resources, machinery,

16

and technology). This effectively limits how much a business can grow. As such, socialist countries generally have less inequality among the social classes. Also, individual tax rates are usually higher so the government can pay for such things as transportation, education, and health care. The return for paying higher taxes is that people generally enjoy services at little or no expense besides their taxes.

It has been suggested that socialism provides less incentive for people to work because the government provides social security for its citizens. Others reject that criticism, arguing that socialist countries have a higher quality of life. Germany is an example of a country that has effectively blended both socialistic and capitalistic policies, resulting in the largest economy in Europe.

Communism

Communism is an economic and political system in which the central government holds the means of production in common for all of the citizens. The central government makes all decisions concerning production and consumption. Various countries have experimented with communistic economies over the past hundred years or so, but they have not worked out very well. The most notable example of communism was in the former Soviet Union between 1917 and 1991. Producers in the Soviet Union were frequently unable to produce enough basic goods because they did not have the necessary raw materials. At other times, they produced goods that nobody wanted. Being unable to adequately provide basic necessities to the population, the Soviet Union's economic system collapsed in 1991.

According to many economists, the heart of the problem with communism is a lack of incentives, which are rewards or consequences that motivate particular choices. In capitalism, producers are allowed to charge higher prices when there is a shortage of something and keep the resulting profits. Thus, higher profits provide incentives for producers to make more of the most-demanded goods and services. Such supply and demand decisions are not freely made in a communist economy, thereby limiting producers' motivation to produce what is most needed.

Economic Success Factors

The following economic factors are vital in determining the success of the industry base of a country: political support, societal acceptance, and a strong economic support base, including trained, experienced workers as well as investment capital.

An important factor in a company's ability to succeed is having political support. In many countries, local governmental bodies create zoning laws and approve construction plans. Without political support from these bodies, a business usually has little chance to get started.

Society's acceptance is also critical. A company will only succeed if it is selling goods and services that the local citizens need or want. Most companies avoid selling products that violate cultural standards. For example, in the United States, liquor stores are not allowed to be located near schools. In some Muslim countries, such as Kuwait, the sale of alcohol is forbidden altogether.

16

Another key factor for economic development is having an economic base of support. Companies tend to locate in regions that have adequate infrastructure (e.g., roads, airports, utilities), good educational systems that can train workers, and access to banking and financial institutes.

Geographic Factors

Two major types of geographic factors, site and situation, contribute to the industrial development of some countries. **Site factors** refer to a place's physical features that are related to the cost of business production. Areas with favorable site factors tend to attract new businesses. Favorable site factors may include access to plentiful clean water, raw materials, and varied energy sources. Having a nice climate or a climate suitable for a company's business needs is also a site factor.

Situation factors refer to the features of a location's surrounding area, especially as related to the cost of transporting raw materials and finished goods. Pittsburgh has an ideal situation for its production of steel. Iron ore, an essential component for the production of steel, comes from the Great Lakes region, including Minnesota, Wisconsin, and Michigan. The high-quality coal needed for steel production is found nearby in western Pennsylvania and West Virginia. Another city with an ideal situation is Detroit, which became famous for its production of cars. The city could export the cars by means of the Great Lakes and through the St. Lawrence Seaway with access to the Atlantic Ocean. Railroads could send the automobiles throughout the United States.

Both Pittsburgh and Detroit have, at least historically, established basic industries. A **basic industry** is an industry that is the main focus of an area's economy. For Pittsburgh, the basic industry is steel. For Detroit, the basic industry is automobiles. For Silicon Valley in California, it is the production of computer chips and equipment. An urban area's site and situation determine which basic industry will work there. Basic industry products are usually made for export around the country or world.

Non-basic industries support the work of the basic industry. These businesses are created due to the economic growth brought about by the area's basic industry. Non-basic industries are city-serving industries whose products are usually for sale in the local area. Examples of non-basic industries include restaurants, retailers, construction, and finance.

All of these businesses together contribute to the multiplier effect. The **multiplier effect** describes the expansion of an area's economic base as a result of the basic and non-basic industries located there. For example, the steel industry in Pittsburgh led to the expansion of the area's construction industries, which led to the expansion of raw material supply companies. The multiplier effect is especially important in terms of employment; when a basic industry grows, employment in both the basic and non-basic sectors tends to increase.

✔ **AP Expert Note**

Be sure to consider how human geography and physical geography interact to form the economy

Economic and industrial development has to do with both physical and human types of geography. For example, Florida has a climate suitable for plantation agriculture, but U.S. labor and environmental protection laws make that practice far less profitable than in developing nations. Likewise, an abundance of a certain natural resource may skew a nation's economic development. Foreign powers may seek to control that resource through colonialism or neocolonialism, resulting in domestic political corruption. Knowing and being able to explain complex factors such as these will serve you well on the official AP exam.

A variety of factors contribute to a country's industrial success or failure, which impacts overall economic success. Industrial costs are a major consideration for every company. Industrial costs are either fixed or variable. The **variable cost** of producing a good is based on how many units are produced. **Fixed costs**, on the other hand, do not fluctuate based on how many units are produced. For example, if a company is making wooden tables, the cost of the wood and materials to build the table make up the variable cost. The costs associated with the factory and utilities (e.g., electricity and water) are generally considered fixed.

When a business decides whether to move into an area, the owners will analyze the variable and fixed costs. If obtaining raw materials in an area is too expensive, increasing its variable costs, then the business may choose to locate elsewhere. Likewise, if fixed costs, such as rent and electricity, are too high, it may choose not to locate in the area.

Transportation Systems

Transportation is one of the more prominent expenses for most industries. Labor is usually the most expensive factor, but labor costs are somewhat fixed costs. Transportation costs are variable, which means they are often one of the most important factors in determining industrial location.

A company needs to use a low-cost form of transportation that will get its products to market quickly. Transportation occurs throughout the industrial business process. Raw materials are transported to the production point. Finished products are transported to the wholesaler, perhaps traveling via several modes of transportation. Then the products are transported to the retailer, who sells them to consumers. Each of these steps in the industrial process involves a means of transportation.

When delivering products, speed and efficiency are key. The term **time-space compression** describes a company's effort to increase the efficiency in the delivery process by diminishing distance obstacles. One of the best ways to increase time efficiency is through the use of modern technologies such as the Internet. With the Internet, orders can be placed in seconds. By reducing the time used in the communication process, the overall process becomes more efficient.

16

A general rule in transportation is the greater the distance traveled and the weight of the products, the greater the cost to transport them. As distance and weight decrease, so does the transportation cost. Distance is a major factor in the transportation costs of both raw materials and finished products. The five primary means of industrial transportation are truck, train, airplane, pipeline, and ship.

Trucks are a highly mobile and efficient form of transportation that can go almost anywhere there are roads, and they are flexible in the routes they can take. Trucks are the most used method of industrial transportation, hauling large amounts of cargo long distances relatively quickly. Such efficiency helps keep prices low. In fact, most of the items that you purchase are delivered by truck. Some disadvantages of truck transportation include traffic, increasing fuel costs, and high maintenance costs.

Trains are one of the most efficient and cost-effective forms of transportation. They can haul an enormous amount of freight for long distances. Trains have become more and more fuel efficient over the past few decades.

Trains have some disadvantages. One is that train tracks don't go to every industrial location. Second, many trains must travel to multiple stations, where the cargo must be unloaded and reloaded. These transfer points are called break-of-bulk points. Cargo is usually shifted from the train to another train or from a train to a truck, which can then carry it the rest of the way. However, some larger factories, like the huge automotive plants in Detroit, have access to cargo trains right at their facilities, greatly minimizing transportation costs. Other disadvantages of train transportation include high operating and maintenance costs. It is quite expensive to operate trains and to build and maintain railroad tracks.

Airplanes are often the fastest way to get products to market. In many isolated areas, such as northern Alaska and the interior regions of Africa, planes are the only means of accessing supplies. Airplanes can deliver products to nearly every major urban area in the world. Most freight hauled by airplane must go through a break-of-bulk point, usually to some type of truck, in order to reach the final delivery point. Much of the produce consumed in the United States comes from Central and South America, and airplanes are essential in the transport process. Shipping the produce by other means would take too long and increase the risk of spoilage.

The most significant disadvantage is cost. Of the major types of transportation, air transport is typically the most expensive due to rising fuel costs. Many airlines in the United States, for example, have suffered financially because of increases in fuel prices. Airlines have tried to offset this cost by charging shippers more.

Pipelines are a highly efficient way of moving gas or liquid products from one region to another, often carrying the product hundreds or even thousands of miles. Pipelines are also one of the safest means of hauling these products. One of the most famous pipelines in the world is the Alaskan Pipeline, which extends over 800 miles through some of the highest mountains in North America. Its primary purpose is to get petroleum from the production point in the North Slope to the transportation point near Valdez, Alaska. The amount of oil in the North Slope of Alaska greatly eases the burden of importing foreign oil.

As with all means of industrial transportation, pipelines have some drawbacks. First, pipelines are limited to gas and liquid products. Second, they're very expensive to build, and once a pipeline is built, moving it becomes extremely difficult or even impossible. Also, it can take a long time to get approval to build a pipeline due to the necessary environmental impact studies that need to be done before construction can begin.

There are thousands of ships on the world's oceans at any given time. All different types of products are shipped by water. Many are hauled in cargo containers and shipped to and from massive seaports, such as those in Hong Kong and Singapore. Ships are the most energy-efficient means of transportation, even more so than trains. The average cost per distance traveled is the lowest among the five means of transportation.

However, ships are also the slowest method of delivering industrial products to either production points or markets, so they work best when speed is not a necessity. Athletic shoes and clothing coming from China and South Asia to the United States are usually transported by ship. Another downside to using ships is that many industrial plants lack access to waterways, so a break-of-bulk point is needed to get products from the warehouse or production facility to the port, where the cargo must be loaded. This break-of-bulk point adds to shipping costs. So while the actual ship transportation cost is generally low, the overall transportation costs per product can still be high.

LOCATION OF INDUSTRY

The **Industrial Revolution** started in the mid-1700s and was an extension of the Enlightenment period in Europe. One major invention of the Industrial Revolution was the steam engine, which enabled farther and faster travel than ever before in human history. The steam engine could be used to power trains as well as ships. As a result, both agricultural and industrial products had access to bigger markets, and more products had to be manufactured to meet the increased demand. Mass production methods and technologies allowed industries to take advantage of the new business environment.

The Industrial Revolution allowed for more mechanization, speeding up the production process and allowing the quantity and sometimes the quality of the product to improve. Prior to the Industrial Revolution, most industry was conducted in the form of **cottage industry**, where products are produced in an individual's home. After the Industrial Revolution, most industry transferred to the assembly-line method of production, in which workers specialize in one facet of production.

> ✔ **AP Expert Note**
>
> **Be able to describe the economic impacts of the three agricultural revolutions**
>
> Innovations in transportation and industry have often gone hand-in-hand with new developments in agriculture. This is especially true of the Second Agricultural Revolution, which is closely tied to the advances of the Industrial Revolution. For example, the cotton gin spurred the growth of slave plantation agriculture in the American South as well as the rise of textile factories in the North. On the AP exam, you'll be expected to know details, regarding how each agricultural revolution affected the economy in various parts of the world.

The importance of location

Agglomeration is the clustering of similar or related firms in close proximity to one another. Factories, for example, that are clustered near each other can share roads, utilities systems, and access to resources. They can also draw on the same labor supply, which is especially important for skill-based industries.

The agglomeration principle has worked very well in Detroit, where companies like General Motors and Ford have benefited from being near each other. Secondary or non-basic industries provide products and services to all three. The unions provide the quality labor that is essential in the production of cars. Tires are made in nearby Ohio and sent to Detroit. When companies locate themselves around these major industrial centers, their production costs actually decrease, because raw materials don't have to be shipped as far to the assembly plants. Industrial parks often provide companies with tax breaks to locate their manufacturing plants in the industrial park. Shared services, such as the construction of railroad tracks for train transportation, can greatly reduce costs.

The term **cumulative causation** describes the continued growth due to the positive aspects of agglomeration. For example, if agglomeration is successful, more agglomeration occurs. Cumulative causation can also lead to a disadvantage due to the same agglomeration principle. **Deglomeration** occurs when a market becomes saturated by too many companies in a particular industry. This creates too much competition, forcing some of the businesses within that industry either to relocate or close down.

Weber's Least Cost Theory   `High-Yield` ◀

One of the developers of economic geography was Alfred Weber. Weber was a German economist and socialist who in the twentieth century developed a theory to describe the industrial location decisions made by certain industries; this became known as the least cost theory. **Weber's least cost theory** suggests that a company building an industrial plant will take into consideration the location of both the raw materials and the market for the product. The weight of the raw materials and the finished product will determine the location of the production facility for that company.

16

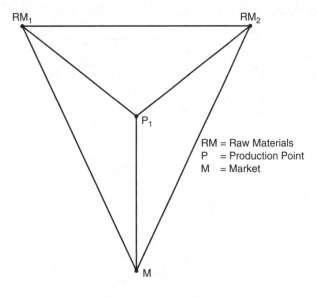

Weber's Least Cost Theory

Weber's theory describes transportation using a triangular model. The base of the triangle consists of the raw materials necessary for the production of the product. If the good being produced is in a **weight-gaining industry** (an industry where the finished product weighs more than the raw materials), then the production point should be located closer to the market to minimize the transportation costs associated with a relatively heavy product. If the industry is a **weight-reducing industry** (an industry where the raw materials weigh more than the finished product), the production point should be located closer to the raw materials.

Many of the resource-extraction industries are weight-reducing industries. The weight-reducing industries try to minimize the costs of hauling heavy materials, such as ore, long distances by placing their industrial production points closer to where the resources are located, such as mines. The production of potato chips is an example of a weight-reducing industry. For our purposes here, let's assume that there are two primary raw materials: salt and potatoes. Because the potatoes and the salt are heavier than the finished product—the bags of potato chips—the production point should be located closer to the potato farms and the salt plant.

Automobiles are an example of a weight-gaining industry. The plastic, rubber, and engines all add to the overall weight of the finished product. The materials and components that go into manufacturing automobiles may be shipped in from distant places, including other countries. Automobile manufacturers prefer to build cars closer to the market, given the weight gain.

Another example of Weber's least cost theory is the fictional "brick bunny." The brick bunny is built with two primary products: bricks and feathers. Because the bricks weigh more than the feathers, the producer puts the production point closer to the bricks to minimize their transport cost. The production point is skewed toward the side of the triangle where the raw material that is the heaviest (bricks) comes from.

16

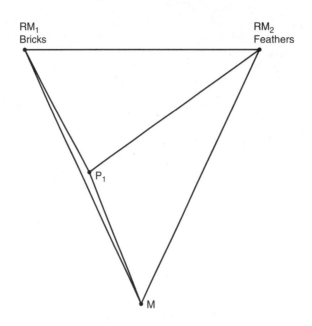

Weber's Least Cost Theory: Brick Bunny

The three primary factors that Weber included in his model were raw materials, labor, and transportation. The most expensive is labor; however, transportation is usually the easiest of the three to control through the location of the new industrial facility. Still, all three factors are vital in determining the success of a business or industry.

Least Cost Theory Assumptions

For Weber's theory to work, he had to make some assumptions. First, the industrial production point must be located somewhere within the triangle. Otherwise, excessive transportation costs will make the product too expensive, and the consumer will be able to purchase the same product more cheaply from another manufacturer that is located within the triangle. Second, all parts of the triangle must be uniform in topography. Everything inside the triangle must have the same landscape characteristics so that transportation costs are the same everywhere in the triangle. Third, the areas inside of the triangle are assumed to have the same political, cultural, and economic values. Every person within the triangle must have the same opportunity to purchase the product and the same desire for it. Fourth, Weber assumed that the availability of transportation is equal in all parts of the triangle. The items must be shipped via the shortest and/or cheapest available method. Last, he assumed that labor is infinitely available within the triangle, but that labor is unwilling to work outside of the triangle.

Weber's theory can be used on different, typically macro-level scales, from national to state or city levels. Weber's assumptions suggest that all of the industry occurs within the same national boundaries. However, industrialization is becoming more global. With free-trade agreements, such as the North American Free Trade Agreement (NAFTA), the ability to produce goods in one country and sell them in another is becoming much more common. NAFTA and other such agreements reduce or eliminate trade barriers between countries.

Foreign Production of Goods

Maquiladoras are industrial plants located in Mexico that produce goods using relatively inexpensive labor and then sell the products in the United States and other countries. Currently, there is a lot of debate over the **outsourcing** of jobs from the United States to less developed countries, where companies can pay employees far less than American workers. Unions and supporters of American labor are strongly opposed to the loss of American jobs to less developed countries. However, U.S. consumers benefit from buying foreign-made products because they are generally cheaper than American-made products. With the increased efficiency of transportation systems, companies can produce their goods around the world and ship them to the markets in the more developed countries with relative ease and lower expenses.

A **footloose industry** is an industry that does not have a strong location preference because the resources, production skills, and consumers on which it depends can be found in numerous places. Such a company may therefore be more prone to relocation, hence the term *footloose*. Footloose industries often locate in pleasant environments and close to transport routes and markets. An example of a footloose industry would be a high-tech industry such as computing.

Multinational Corporations

Multinational corporations are large companies that have offices or divisions around the world. Large companies open up in different countries in order to expand their market reach, to take advantage of incentives provided by the host countries, and to reduce transportation costs. Profits of these multinational corporations are measured in billions of U.S. dollars. Coca-Cola is an example of a multinational corporation with offices on six continents. Another example is McDonald's. A person can eat at a McDonald's in nearly every major city in the world.

Division of Labor and Mass Production

When an industry's workers specialize in doing individual tasks, their speed, efficiency, and quality increase, thereby reducing costs. Henry Ford was one of the first to apply labor specialization to mass production. He did this through the assembly line method, which he used to produce automobiles. Each person on Ford's assembly line did a specific task, thus allowing the person to develop an expertise. Ford's workers were paid well for their skills and could then afford to purchase the cars that they were making. Prior to the assembly line method, most manufacturing was done by individuals making the entire product. This process was very slow and, therefore, expensive.

Soon after Ford, the assembly line method and the division of labor became standard in almost every industry, increasing industrial profitability. Some industries are better suited than others to mass production. In the automobile industry, new mechanization techniques have allowed many manual jobs to be taken over by machines. However, other industries, such as certain types of agriculture, are more labor intensive.

16

The textile industry is another labor-intensive industry. Most of the clothes sold by American retailers were produced in a factory in a less developed country. Because of the labor-intensive nature of some of these factories, these factories have become known as sweatshops. **Sweatshops** are factories in which the workers make very little money and work long hours in poor working conditions.

The growth of **manufacturing exports** (products shipped out of the country to a foreign market) has led to a global economy of commerce. As production costs have continued to increase in the United States and Europe, more products are being imported from Asia and less developed countries around the world.

GLOBAL INDUSTRIAL ZONES

Where is the world's industry located? There are four primary industrial zones in the world today: the northeastern portion of the United States and the southeastern portion of Canada; Western Russia and Ukraine; Central and Western Europe; and East Asia, including China and Japan. Some areas have site and situation advantages that have contributed to their economic success. Each of these locations employs a large percentage of its workforce in industry.

United States and Southeastern Canada

New England

Early on in its modern development, New England benefited from the cheap labor provided by immigrants who used Boston as their entry point into the United States. One of the largest industries in the Boston region was textiles. Much of this industry has moved to the South in recent decades because of the lack of unionized labor in the South, but New England used to be famous for its clothing manufacturing. Much of the cloth was made from cotton, which was imported from the South.

Large factories were set up in towns such as Lowell, Massachusetts. Life for workers was difficult, but the pay was relatively good. Life in the factory was often strictly controlled by the owners. The owners of the factory set up bunks within the factory itself, and the workers stayed on the factory campus. Even religious worship was located in the factory, and the factory developed its own culture. The large textile machines created a very loud, unhealthy working environment. Children were often used to clean the textile machines while they were still operating, resulting in a high number of injuries and even deaths. Child labor laws in the United States arose partially due to the textile operations in New England.

The Middle Atlantic

The Middle Atlantic region of the United States is known today as "the megalopolis." This area includes the large urban areas of New York City; Philadelphia, Pennsylvania; Wilmington, Delaware; Baltimore, Maryland; and Washington, D.C. This region had a large pool of available labor to work in factories. It also had a large market to purchase manufactured products. This area also was known for its major ports. Today, New York City is still one of the largest and busiest ports in the United States.

The Eastern Great Lakes

The Eastern Great Lakes region includes the southeastern portions of Canada, the city of Pittsburgh, and the upstate New York region. The majority of these areas received hydroelectric power from the Great Lakes and Niagara Falls. The situation of Pittsburgh was ideal for the production of steel. Barges and ships hauled iron ore from the Great Lakes to the port of Erie, Pennsylvania. From there, the ore was put on trains and hauled to Pittsburgh. Steel was then hauled to market via barges on the Ohio River and by train.

The southeastern portion of Canada, which extends along the St. Lawrence Seaway and includes Hamilton, Toronto, and Montréal, represents the heart of Canadian industrial production. With more than 5.5 million people, Toronto is Canada's largest metropolitan area. This area supplies both a large workforce and thriving market to support the area's industries. Since the North American Free Trade Agreement (NAFTA) was enacted in the early 1990s, goods can be freely shipped across the U.S. border. The St. Lawrence Seaway exports products to the Atlantic Ocean for transport to markets around the world, helping to make Canada one of the most developed countries in the world.

The Western Great Lakes

The Western Great Lakes region includes the cities of Detroit, Chicago, and Milwaukee. Chicago is the largest city between the East Coast and the West Coast. As such, Chicago serves as a major transportation hub linking the country. It contains O'Hare Airport, one of the busiest airports in the world. Dozens of railroad lines converge in Chicago, as do many interstate highways. Because of this unique location, Chicago is a huge market for the transportation and resale of products, as well as a major labor source for factories. As mentioned previously, Detroit has become a major automobile manufacturing region. All of the major automobile makers in the United States have huge factories there. This includes what are called the "Big Three": General Motors, Ford, and Fiat Chrysler.

Due to globalization, many factories in the Western Great Lakes region have relocated to other areas of the country or to foreign countries to take advantage of cheaper labor as well as tax and other financial benefits. As such, this region has become known as the **Rust Belt**. It is called the Rust Belt because of the crumbling infrastructure that remains in the area. The Rust Belt contains the greatest amount of industrial area in the United States.

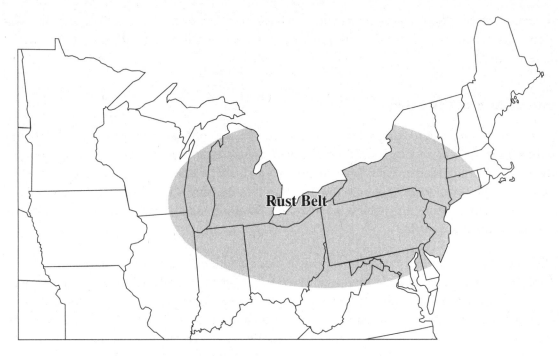

Rust Belt Area in the United States

The South

Today, there is a new industrial realm in the United States. Many Southern states, such as Georgia, North Carolina, and South Carolina, are attracting manufacturing industries to their cities by offering tax breaks. Wages in the South are generally lower than in other parts of the country, so this is also very attractive to companies.

Silicon Valley

Silicon Valley is the nickname for the southern portion of California's San Francisco Bay Area. In the 1950s and 1960s, it was the home to early innovators in silicon transistors and microchips, such as Intel. This fostered the growth of the computer industry in the area and, from the 1990s onward, modern Internet companies such as Google have set up headquarters in the Silicon Valley. Nearby Stanford University has been a magnet for attracting and training talent for Silicon Valley companies.

Ukraine and Russia

Russia and Ukraine have high levels of manufacturing due to the enormous amounts of natural resources located in the area. For most of the twentieth century, Ukraine was part of the Soviet Union. It provided the Soviet Union with both manufactured goods and agricultural products. Ukraine gained independence in 1991 and has further diversified its economy. It has a very large heavy industry sector, especially in the production of aerospace and industrial equipment. In addition to heavy industry, Ukraine is known for its fertile farmlands and agricultural production. Referred to as the region's "bread basket," Ukraine is one of the world's largest grain exporters. Much of Russia's industrial base is in the west of the country, around Moscow and St. Petersburg. In addition to the major urban centers of Russia, the Siberian region contains a large amount of industry due to its vast natural resources. In this heavily forested region, the production of paper and packaging materials is prevalent. The Siberian region has a very small population, and transportation, mostly by rail, is limited. The creation of the Trans-Siberian Railroad, one of the great wonders of the transportation world, led to industrial cities growing up along its routes during the Soviet era.

Central and Western Europe

The core area of development in Central and Western Europe includes Germany, northeastern France, northern Italy, Switzerland, Scandinavia, Great Britain, Belgium, the Netherlands, and Luxembourg. In the post–World War II era, Central and Western Europe advanced economically at a break-neck pace. By forming the European Union, this region has reduced or eliminated many of the obstacles to trade, travel, and economic cooperation. The European Union rivals the United States and China in terms of economic activity and market size.

Great Britain

Large industrial areas in Great Britain include London, Manchester, Leeds, and Newcastle. These areas depend largely on the coal industry. Great Britain has large deposits of coal within its borders. Coal production was instrumental in developing the industrial base for many of Great Britain's large urban centers.

Germany

In Germany, the steel industry depends on the coal that is mined within its borders. Germany has the advantage of having many rivers to transport goods, including the Rhine and the Ruhr rivers. Because the population of Germany is spread out among many different cities, inland transportation via rivers and highways is very important. Today, Germany is the leader in industrial production in Europe. Abundant raw materials combined with an educated workforce and a close market with good transportation systems have enabled Germany to continue its industrial success.

France

Today, many other portions of Europe have become more industrialized. The production of automobiles in France and Germany as well as airplanes in France has provided many jobs. Airbus, with its headquarters located in Toulouse, France, competes with Seattle-based Boeing to be the world's largest manufacturer of airplanes. With the aircraft market in Asia growing, both Boeing and Airbus have completed projects on new airliners, which can haul people farther, faster, and for less cost by using less fossil fuels.

Ireland

Since the 1980s, Ireland has transformed its economy from being predominantly agricultural to a modern knowledge-based economy focused on high-technology industries and services. Ireland

16

has benefited greatly from investments made by foreign companies, such as Microsoft and Google. Ireland has become one of the world's largest exporters of medical equipment, software-related goods and services, and mineral resources.

East Asia

China, Hong Kong (an autonomous region of China), South Korea, Taiwan, and Singapore dominate a large part of the global marketplace. Many of the ports in China, Japan, and Korea are designated treaty ports. **Treaty ports** are international ports that must be kept open for international trade because of the signing of a treaty. These ports facilitate international trade. Many of the ports in eastern China are **export processing zones**. These zones are designed to efficiently export goods made in China. Most of these products go to Japan, Europe, and the United States.

Over the last few decades, China has become an industrial powerhouse in Asia. The Chinese market includes more than 1.4 billion people and a growing middle class. China's gross domestic product has increased around 10 to 12 percent annually in recent years. China's population is very well educated, enabling China to compete in a global marketplace. China has had some growing pains as it struggles to keep up with the infrastructure requirements of such a rapid growth rate. The following map shows China's major industrial regions.

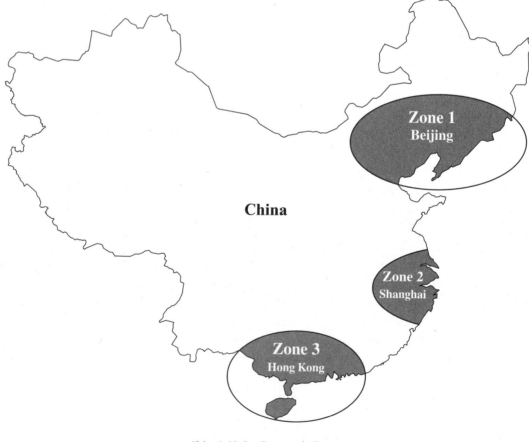

China's Major Economic Zones

Shanghai

Probably no city represents the immense growth in industrialization and urban development in China better than Shanghai. Shanghai is the largest city in China in terms of population. Located at the mouth of the Yangtze River, it has seen tremendous investment in its infrastructure and industrial zones in recent years. The port of Shanghai, once a seldom-used facility, is now one of the busiest ports in the world. Goods made in China are produced relatively cheaply and then sent around the world. The textile industry in China employs tens of thousands of Chinese workers. Walmart and other large retailers receive many of their products from Chinese manufacturers, which keeps the cost of the products low. Shanghai's industrial park is one of the largest in the world. The area known as Pudong has been one of the most successful economic initiatives in history. Pudong has seen the development of a new international airport and a world-renowned convention center.

The Chinese have set up **special economic zones (SEZs)**, designated specifically for foreign companies to locate their headquarters. Areas like Shanghai have seen enormous investment from foreign companies trying to get into the Chinese market. American car makers Ford and General Motors have located plants near Shanghai. German car maker Volkswagen is also now in Shanghai, where it produces and sells more than a million cars per year. Shanghai's population has grown as many people migrate from the rural areas to Shanghai to look for work in manufacturing. Shanghai is now one of the most important economic centers in East Asia and competes with areas like Hong Kong, Singapore, and even Tokyo for financial supremacy in all of Asia.

Northeastern China

Northeastern China, or Manchuria, includes the city of Beijing as well as the majority of China's natural resources. Coal manufacturing has dominated industrial activity in the region. Because of the coal, steel is produced here. Much of the industrial activity in northeastern China has developed around the Huang He River (also known as the Yellow River), which serves as a major transportation route for manufactured materials. Steel, iron, agricultural equipment, and food processing have developed here. Like the U.S. Rust Belt, this area has experienced factories shutting down or leaving for other sections of the country.

Japan

Japan's modern economic success can be traced back to World War II; the treaty that ended the war forbade Japan from building up its military. Without the expense of an army, Japan could invest in industrial development. Japan has very few natural resources yet is one of the world leaders in industry. Japan has used trade to increase its share of world industry. Japan's influence on the world has been especially pronounced in the automotive and electronics industries. Japan's well-educated workforce is extremely loyal to its companies, and workers equate personal and professional value with how the company performs. Areas around Tokyo, Yokohama, and Osaka have seen enormous increases in industrial productivity. The transportation systems, including highways, shipping ports, and rail transport, are world renowned.

16

The Four Asian Tigers

The **Four Asian Tigers** are Hong Kong, South Korea, Taiwan, and Singapore. Each has experienced rapid economic growth over the last few decades due to its industrial base and the export of items to the United States and Europe. All of the Four Asian Tigers have access to world-class seaports. They also have well-educated workers who are trained to do highly skilled labor. Manufacturing in all of the Four Tigers mainly includes electronics, technology, and other higher-end goods.

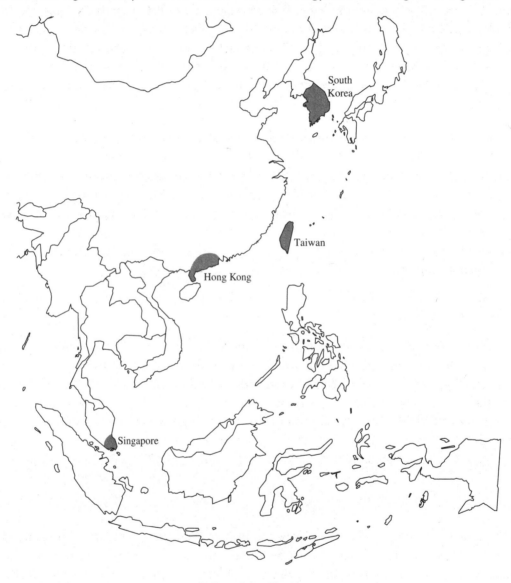

Four Asian Tigers

Hong Kong

In 1997, Great Britain relinquished its control of the port of Hong Kong, which it had gained from China in the Opium War in the late 1800s. For most of the twentieth century, capitalist Hong Kong was a symbol of economic success and stood in stark contrast to communist China. Due to China's success in recent decades, that stark contrast no longer holds true. Still, Hong Kong is a major trading post for all of Asia. Areas that neighbor Hong Kong have benefited from its reintegration into China. Cities along the border, such as Guangzhou, are now well developed. Many of the factories in this region, including a Nike factory, specialize in clothing and other textiles.

The port of Hong Kong is one of the busiest in the world. Exporting Chinese goods is Hong Kong's main industry. Hong Kong is known as a major area where trade goods are brought to be reloaded onto other forms of transportation. Many of the textiles that are manufactured in China are loaded onto ships and sent to Hong Kong, where they are reloaded onto other ships to go elsewhere for resale.

South Korea

South Korea's economic center is located in its capital city, Seoul. Seoul is the largest city in South Korea with a population of more than 25 million people in the greater metropolitan area. South Korea has a high-quality educational system and a highly skilled workforce. South Korea exports automobiles and electronics. Port facilities are available in cities such as Busan and Kwangju, allowing access to worldwide markets. The port of Incheon, west of Seoul, exports South Korean goods all over the world. Some of the world's largest companies, including Hyundai, Samsung, and LG, are located in and export from South Korea.

Taiwan

Another of the four Asian Tigers is Taiwan. After Mao Zedong took control of China in 1949, nationalist forces, led by Chiang Kai-shek, retreated to the island of Taiwan. A topic subject to debate is whether Taiwan is an independent country or a territory of the People's Republic of China. China holds the latter view. The United States maintains unofficial diplomatic relations with Taiwan because of its economic and military ties to the United States while officially paying lip service to the position that Taiwan is part of China to avoid damaging U.S. relations with this powerful country. Taiwan has seen rapid economic growth in response to exports. In Taiwan, the main port of Kaohsiung facilitates the majority of exports.

Singapore

Singapore is a city-state located at the tip of the Malay Peninsula. While Singapore's growth has slowed somewhat in the last few years, it had many years of astonishing growth in terms of its gross domestic product (GDP). Singapore, like Hong Kong, takes in goods and re-exports them to the rest of the world. The port in Singapore is one of the busiest ports in the world. Massive cargo containers put thousands of freight boxes onto ocean liners for export to Japan, Europe, and the United States.

Other Areas of Industrialization

Other areas of the world are experiencing rapid industrialization and, hence, rapid development in their economies. Mexico and Chile have greatly increased their exports in the past decade. In the Middle East region, Saudi Arabia, Qatar, the United Arab Emirates, and Kuwait have increased their level of global trade substantially since the 1970s. Much of this trade has been based on the exportation of oil.

Some countries such as South Africa, Turkey, Indonesia, Malaysia, and Mexico have recently become known as **newly industrialized countries (NICs)**. NICs are countries whose economies have not yet reached a developed country's status but have grown much more rapidly than those of other developing countries. BRIC is another term commonly used by economic geographers. **BRIC** is an acronym standing for the countries of Brazil, Russia, India, and China, all of which have significant wealth and industrialization but are still not classified as developed countries.

WAYS TO DESCRIBE DEVELOPMENT

There are several different ways to describe development. Development does not necessarily mean wealth. In fact, it's much more than wealth. A society may even deem too much individual wealth a hindrance to its development, especially if a few people gain wealth at the expense of the majority of citizens.

In a general sense, **development** is the process of improving the material conditions of people through the creation of a modern economy and the distribution of knowledge and technology. Development is a continuous, never-ending process with the goal of improving the health and prosperity of a place's people. Countries are generally classified as either developed countries or developing countries. A **developed country** has an advanced level of development. Examples of developed countries include the United States, Canada, most countries in Western Europe, Australia, New Zealand, Singapore, Japan, and South Korea. **Developing countries** (also referred to as less developed countries, or LDCs) are still in an early stage of development. Most of the world's countries are classified as developing; examples include Brazil, Mexico, Nigeria, India, and Vietnam.

Measures of Development

There are a number of measures of development that economic geographers consider when studying a country's level of development or when comparing and contrasting the development of multiple countries. Some of these measures include gross domestic product (GDP), the Human Development Index (HDI), the Physical Quality of Life Index, economic sector type, level of technology, access to natural resources, and various demographic factors.

Gross Domestic Product (GDP)

One economic indicator that economic geographers look at is gross domestic product. **Gross domestic product (GDP)** is the value of the total output of goods and services produced in a country during one year. As of 2016, the gross domestic product for the United States was over $18.6 trillion, which is the largest GDP in the world. China ranked second with a GDP of approximately $11.2 trillion. All of the European Union countries combined had a GDP of nearly $16.4 trillion.

Dividing a country's GDP by the total population gives per capita GDP. The United States has a per capita GDP of approximately $59,500. The two countries with the highest per capita GDP are Liechtenstein at $139,100 and Qatar at $124,900. Like many measures, per capita GDP is far from being a perfect measure of development. One problem is with income distribution. If the income of a country goes only to a small percentage of people, per capita GDP may still be high while most people receive very small incomes. Therefore, a country's overall standard of living may be low despite its high per capita GDP.

Human Development Index

Another indicator of development is the Human Development Index (HDI). Created by the United Nations in 1990, the **Human Development Index (HDI)** measures a country's development based on three factors: average life expectancy, amount of education, and per capita income. A country's HDI value is calculated by a formula that produces a score ranging from zero to one, where zero is the lowest level of development and one is the highest. While there are a number of other ways to measure development, the HDI is the one most commonly used by economic geographers.

Life Expectancy

Countries with a relatively high life expectancy can expect their citizens to live 70 or more years. According to the Centers for Disease Control and Prevention (CDC), the average life expectancy in the United States is 78.7 years. The average life expectancy for U.S. women is 81.1 years, and for U.S. men it is 76.1 years. Many developing countries have a lower life expectancy. For example, the life expectancy for South Africa is only about 62.9 years.

In both developed and less developed countries, the average life expectancy is a little higher for women than for men. There are multiple theories as to why this is the case. One is that women are biologically stronger than men because they must be able to give birth. Another is that men are often involved in more dangerous professions, including fishing, mining, drilling, construction, and firefighting, which may be physically damaging to the body. Over the past several decades, this theory has become increasingly outdated. Women in many countries have jobs that are just as physically demanding and stressful as the jobs men have, and yet females still have a higher average life expectancy.

In developed countries, people can expect to live longer due to better access to healthcare and modern medicine. In less developed countries, people still die from diseases directly related to unclean water, malnutrition, and poor sanitation. The life expectancy may only be as high as 50 years in some of the world's poorest countries.

Education

Education is a measure of economic development. When workers are better educated, they are generally more productive, thereby increasing the productivity of the whole society. In addition to having few educational facilities or teachers, many less developed countries are experiencing what's referred to as brain drain. **Brain drain** occurs when a large number of young people move to a different country for school or other opportunities and do not return to work in their home country. Trained professionals, such as nurses, doctors, and engineers, also leave for better living conditions in more developed countries. Brain drain is the opposite of **brain gain,** which happens when a country sends its top students to universities in other countries, then sees its investment pay off

16

as the graduating students return to home to work. When computing the HDI in terms of education, the United Nations analyzes the average years of education obtained by the country's students and gives the country an education score. This score goes into the overall HDI calculation.

Per Capita Income

Per capita income is the third component of calculating a country's HDI score. The United Nations uses a measure called the gross national income. **Gross national income (GNI)** is the value of income earned by the country's citizens both in the country and abroad. The United States, for example, determines its GNI by including all of the income earned by American residents working in the United States and in foreign countries. It does not, however, include the income earned by foreigners working in the United States. Gross domestic product (GDP), on the other hand, is the value of all goods and services produced in a country, including the value generated by foreigners.

Physical Quality of Life Index

The **Physical Quality of Life Index (PQLI)** is another statistic that is used to measure a country's development. Unlike the Human Development Index, the PQLI directly factors in a country's literacy rate and does not include per capita income. To calculate the PQLI, experts consider the literacy rate, infant mortality rate, and life expectancy of a country. The PQLI of the United States is 99.5, putting the United States at the high end of the development spectrum.

> ✔ **AP Expert Note**
>
> **Know your acronyms**
>
> The various measures of development can feel like information overload at first. That's okay! Take your time to memorize what their acronyms stand for and what ideas they embody. A little time spent on review will save you from confusion on exam day.

Economic Sectors

`High-Yield`

Another way to analyze development is by looking at where the majority of people work in their economy. According to the demographic transition model (see Chapter 11 on Population and Migration), when the majority of the people in a society are employed in the agricultural sectors of an economy, the society is at an early stage of development. As more people begin to be employed in the industrial sectors, development increases. As a society moves into a service-based and knowledge-based economy, development reaches an advanced level.

An **economic sector** is a large segment of the economy that is characterized by a distinct type of production or service. There are five different economic sectors: primary, secondary, tertiary, quaternary, and quinary.

- **Primary sector** activities include agriculture, forestry, fishing, and the extraction and harvesting of natural resources from the Earth. In less developed countries, a majority of workers are typically employed in the primary sector.

16

- **Secondary sector** activities include the processing of the raw materials and natural resources obtained through the primary sector. The result is the creation of manufactured goods. An example of a secondary sector industry is furniture making. The furniture maker depends on the wood that comes from the primary sector.

- **Tertiary sector** activities are service-based economic activities that include the selling of goods and services as well as transportation. For example, the retail activities of a shopping mall would be classified as tertiary. In highly developed economies, often 70 percent or more of the workers are involved in the tertiary sector.

- **Quaternary sector** activities include industries that are concerned with the creation and distribution of knowledge. Examples include research and development, finance, banking, marketing, and business consulting.

- **Quinary sector** activities involve the management decisions of a society. Examples include the work done by top executives in business, government, science, education, nonprofit organizations, and healthcare.

Technology

Another development indicator is a country's level of technological advancement. Developed countries are characterized by advanced technology that has generally improved its citizens' quality of life. Developing advanced technology is also essential for a country to compete in the global marketplace. The **technology gap** describes the contrast between the high level of technology in the developed world and the lower level of technology in much of the less developed world.

The technology gap is at its starkest contrast in many parts of sub-Saharan Africa. Without modern technology, these countries are having a hard time industrializing their economies, educating their people, and providing healthcare. The technology gap in the less-developed world has proven hard to close. One reason is that developed countries have a faster technology transfer process. The **technology transfer process** is the amount of time that it takes a new technology to leave the manufacturer and be available for people to use.

Natural Resources

It would seem likely that if a country had more natural resources than others, then it would be more developed. While this is true in many cases, it is not always true. If the natural resources are controlled by a small number of people or by the government, and if they are not used for the benefit of the overall country and economy, then development may be slowed.

For example, many oil-rich countries in the world have immense wealth due to oil extraction. However, this wealth is often concentrated in the hands of a small elite, hindering the overall development of these countries' economies. Many African countries have access to natural resources but are still stuck in poverty due to neocolonialism. **Neocolonialism** refers to the continued influence that certain European countries have over the African countries that were formerly European colonies.

16

Most developed countries have sufficient access to the natural resources they need for industrial production. The countries may not actually extract the natural resources themselves, but they are able to get them from other countries. For example, the Four Asian Tigers—Singapore, Taiwan, South Korea, and Hong Kong—do not have a lot of natural resources. Instead, they trade manufactured goods for natural resources. Likewise, Japan has few natural resources but has become one of the most productive and advanced economies in the world, thanks in part to its vibrant trade with other countries.

Demographic Factors

Economic geographers also consider demographic factors when analyzing the development of a country. One of these factors, **gender balance**, is a measure of the opportunities available to women compared to those available to men within a given country. Gender balance in many developed countries, especially in Western Europe, has improved markedly over the past 100 years. Gender inequality does not always improve as countries become wealthier. For example, gender inequality is a big issue in some wealthy Middle Eastern countries, such as Saudi Arabia, where women have restricted rights in terms of traveling, voting, and working.

Another key demographic factor of development is birth rate. Birth rate is defined as the number of births per 1,000 people in the population. Less developed countries tend to have much higher birth rates than more developed countries. As a country moves from an early stage of development (e.g., primary or secondary sector) to a higher level (e.g., tertiary), an increasing number of women participate in the workforce; this leads to women having fewer children. When a country is still in a primary sector, children are often seen as economic assets; they can provide labor for agriculture, mining, fishing, etc.

Gender Development Index (GDI)

The main drawback to the Human Development Index is the fact that it does not directly consider gender balance issues. The **Gender Development Index (GDI)** was created to give a clearer picture of what life is like for women throughout the world. The GDI uses the same statistics as the HDI but factors in gender differences. The GDI shows that women in Western Europe face the fewest gender imbalances, whereas women in sub-Saharan Africa face the biggest challenges. The top 10 gender-balanced countries, according to the 2015 GDI, are Norway, Australia, Switzerland, Germany, Denmark, Singapore, Netherlands, Ireland, Iceland, and Canada.

One recently developed tool to bolster women's entrepreneurship is the microloan (also known as microcredit). The microloan is a very small loan given to a borrower who could not ordinarily afford a traditional bank loan due to their poor credit history, lack of collateral, lack of steady employment, or other factors. The effectiveness of microloans is a matter of some debate. Advocates champion them as a way to reduce poverty and help women escape from welfare programs. Critics argue that microloans are essentially a neoliberal replacement for welfare, and they are ineffective at helping impoverished women start new businesses.

Sustainable Development Goals

When discussing economic development, perhaps no issue is more central than the unequal distribution of resources. Economic geographers and other experts differ on how to consider global inequality. The United Nations and other international organizations have worked for decades to help bring about a more level playing field for countries to develop.

The **Sustainable Development Goals (SDGs)** are a collection of 17 global goals adopted by the United Nations in 2015. The SDGs represent a universal call to action to end poverty, protect the planet, and ensure that all people enjoy peace and prosperity. These 17 goals build on the successes of the Millennium Development Goals, which existed from 2000 to 2015. The SDGs focus strongly on areas such as climate change, economic inequality, innovation, sustainable consumption, and peace and justice. The SDGs provide guidelines and targets for all countries to adopt in accordance with their own priorities and the environmental challenges.

According to the United Nations, achieving the SDGs will require the partnership of governments, private businesses, nongovernmental organizations, and citizens alike to make sure the planet is left a better place for future generations.

The 17 Sustainable Development Goals	
1.	End poverty in all its forms everywhere
2.	End hunger, achieve food security and improved nutrition, and promote sustainable agriculture
3.	Ensure healthy lives and promote well-being for all at all ages
4.	Ensure inclusive and equitable quality education and promote lifelong learning opportunities for all
5.	Achieve gender equality and empower all women and girls
6.	Ensure availability and sustainable management of water and sanitation for all
7.	Ensure access to affordable, reliable, sustainable, and modern energy for all
8.	Promote sustained, inclusive, and sustainable economic growth, full and productive employment, and decent work for all
9.	Build resilient infrastructure, promote inclusive and sustainable industrialization, and foster innovation
10.	Reduce inequality within and among countries
11.	Make cities and human settlements inclusive, safe, resilient, and sustainable
12.	Ensure sustainable consumption and production patterns
13.	Take urgent action to combat climate change and its impacts
14.	Conserve and sustainably use the oceans, seas, and marine resources for sustainable development
15.	Sustainably use terrestrial ecosystems, combat desertification, halt and reverse land degradation, and halt biodiversity loss
16.	Promote peaceful and inclusive societies for sustainable development; provide access to justice for all; and build effective, accountable, and inclusive institutions at all levels
17.	Strengthen the means of implementation and revitalize the global partnership for sustainable development

16

DEVELOPMENT THEORIES

High-Yield

World Systems Theory

Economic geographers have tried to analyze world development in spatial, or locational, terms. Immanuel Wallerstein did this with his world systems theory. The **world systems theory** is the view that there is a three-level hierarchy to the world's countries. These levels are called the core, periphery, and semi-periphery.

The **core areas** are the more developed countries (MDCs). These are located primarily in North America and Western Europe as well as Japan, Australia, and New Zealand. The **periphery areas** are the less developed countries (LDCs). Wallerstein noted that the core areas take advantage of the natural resources and labor supply located in the periphery, furthering the success of the core. The periphery also lacks foreign investment from developed countries, thereby keeping the peripheral countries in a state of underdevelopment. The world systems theory is a **dependency model**, meaning that countries do not exist in isolation but are part of an interconnected global economy within which countries trade and work together on international issues. An important aspect of the dependency model is commodity dependence, which occurs when a country's economy is largely dependent on the export of a primary sector good (oil, minerals, agriculture).

The following map shows the core and periphery countries. Wallerstein concluded that a line ran roughly at 30 degrees north latitude that separated the core from the periphery, with the exception of Australia and New Zealand.

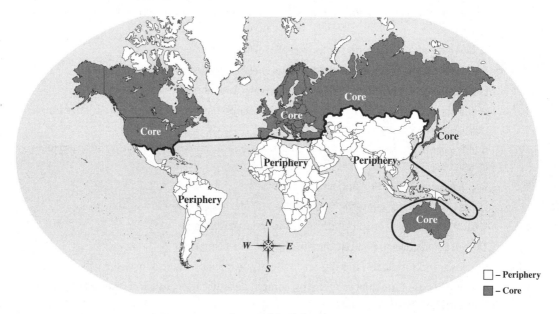

Core and Periphery

In recent years, the **semi-periphery** has been added to the model. The semi-periphery are the countries, such as the Four Asian Tigers, that are gaining in development and have some of the benchmarks of economic success but are still lacking the political importance associated with the core countries.

The Core-Periphery Model

The **core-periphery model** of development builds on the world systems theory by looking at four distinct spatial factors: industrial core, upward transition, downward transition, and resource frontier. Each of these can be seen on a global scale down to a national or even city scale.

The **industrial core** is where the majority of the industrial activities are located within a country. These areas are usually within or near large urban areas, which provide both a market for the products and a workforce to produce them. In the United States, the largest industrial core extends from the Northeast to the Midwest, including the cities of Pittsburgh, Cleveland, Milwaukee, and Chicago.

The next major area in the core-periphery model is the upward transition area. **Upward transition** describes an area that is gaining jobs and attracting industry; the economy grows rapidly, which leads to further development. Upward transition areas generally experience improvements in transportation, education, environmental conditions, and healthcare. In the United States, the upward transition area is the South. This area is experiencing rapid population growth due to the relocation of industrial activities from the Northeast and Midwest. The **Sun Belt** is a region generally considered to stretch across the United States from the Southeast to the Southwest (with the exception of certain rural, less developed areas in Alabama, Mississippi, New Mexico, and Texas).

The third area in the core-periphery model is the downward transition area. **Downward transition** means that companies are leaving and unemployment rates are high. As people leave an area, the tax base is reduced, and just as the upward transition area is in a self-perpetuating cycle upward, the downward transition area is in a downward cycle. In the United States, the Great Plains region is experiencing a downward cycle, with the exception of western North Dakota. At the beginning of the twentieth century, the Great Plains area was in an upward transition due to the rich farmland and immigrants settling there. Today, companies are moving out of the Great Plains partly because of the region's small population. Without companies to provide jobs, people leave to seek opportunities in other areas. This is especially true for young people.

The last section of the core-periphery model is the resource frontier. The **resource frontier** areas provide the majority of the resources for the industrial core. Many of these resources are used for energy production or manufacturing. The remote north section of Alaska, with crude oil resources, is the largest resource frontier in the United States. The Appalachian region—in particular West Virginia, Kentucky, and parts of Pennsylvania—has also served as a resource frontier, providing a large share of the country's coal supply.

On a city scale, different zones in the city may occupy different places in the core-periphery model. For example, certain areas of a large urban center are devoted to industry and manufacturing, thus forming the industrial core. Other areas, where people want to move, are classified as upward transition areas. In contrast, certain neighborhoods experience higher unemployment rates and are less attractive; these are downward transition areas. The resource frontier is where natural resources are located. For example, sand and gravel, a base product used in many roads and driveways, is often found near large urban areas to reduce transportation costs (recall Weber's least cost theory).

16

Rostow's Model of Development

As countries advance from a primary or secondary economic sector to a higher one, they go through different stages of development. **Rostow's stages of growth model** (also sometimes called the takeoff model) suggests five stages that a country progresses through in its development:

1. Traditional society
2. Preconditions to takeoff
3. Takeoff
4. Drive to maturity
5. Age of mass consumption

In the traditional society, the majority of the workforce is involved in the primary sector of the economy. Most people farm and gather food. Any trade involves farmers and their agricultural products. Mass production is not yet developed. The second phase of Rostow's model is the preconditions to takeoff, sometimes called the transitional phase. In this phase, a country starts to develop an infrastructure, educational system, and trade relations. Business developers emerge and begin to undertake money-making activities. As this happens, the economy starts shifting from a primary to secondary sector. During the takeoff stage, more companies become involved in the manufacturing sectors of the economy. Agriculture becomes a large-scale activity, and food is processed for resale. In this stage, growth is generally limited to large urban areas and only a few industries. During the drive to maturity, the technology that was available to only a few companies during the takeoff stage is now being diffused and integrated into all areas of industry. Technology advances and workers become more skilled. The final phase of Rostow's model is the age of mass consumption. Workers have become highly skilled and the economy is stable. Productivity, earnings, and savings are at all-time highs. While manufacturing is still important, the society has moved into a higher economic sector focused on service- and knowledge-based activities.

Rostow's model is based on the assumption that consumers will save and invest personal wealth, stimulating the economy and allowing industry to develop. The development of industry further fuels economic growth, advancing the economy and development of the society. Some economic geographers criticize Rostow's stages of growth model as being unrealistic. They suggest that the model does not explain Africa's lack of development, for example. The critics argue that the model does not consider the political and governmental corruption, the vast income inequality, or the lack of investment in underdeveloped countries.

LAND USE AND RESOURCES

Land-Use Models

Thinking about land according to the different land-use models helps developers determine how to use natural resources for the world's industrial activity and how to best use the land. There are four basic land-use models that economic geographers and business developers use to think about land-use issues. These are the economic, sustainability, environmental, and preservationist land-use models.

Economic Land-Use Model

The economic land-use model posits that business developers should develop an area and its resources for immediate use. This model looks at land use for current development. Thus, this model suggests that resources should be extracted from the environment right away and used for the society's economic benefit. Likewise, idle land should be developed for some type of economic activity. Doing so stimulates the economy and provides additional jobs for the area.

Critics of this model believe that following this model is damaging to the geography of an area. They use a term called **topocide** to describe the destruction of a landscape to extract resources or to build a development.

Sustainability Land-Use Model

The sustainability land-use model suggests that people should use resources or develop an area only if they can replace what is taken. In other words, this model calls for **sustainable development**, which is a type of development that meets the needs of the present without compromising the ability of future generations to meet their own needs. A good example of a sustainable industry is the current U.S. forestry industry. In many cases, when timber companies cut down trees, they are required to replant new trees. In the next 50 to 100 years, those trees will mature and be ready for harvest. This sustainable approach ensures a future for the forestry industry well into the next century.

Some types of farming also employ sustainable development in their use of the land. When farmers use crop rotation techniques, they are practicing sustainability. By planting soybeans one year and corn the next, the farmer replaces the nutrients that the other crop removed from the soil, thus ensuring the fertility of the soil for decades to come.

Environmental Land-Use Model

The environmental land-use model suggests that if developers use the land, they should not alter the overall natural state of the landscape. For example, if a park is built on a green space, then any structures such as shelters, walking paths, or recreational facilities should be designed and built in a way that does not fundamentally change the natural landscape. The U.S. National Park System uses this model. The proponents of this model are conservationists. **Conservation** is the preservation or sustainable use of a natural resource. Conservationists, for example, would not want an area developed if the development damaged the area's water systems or cut down a large tract of forest.

16

Preservationist Land-Use Model

The preservationist land-use model sees the landscape as worth more in its natural state than in any type of developed state. Therefore, this model does not want to alter the landscape at all. Many American Indians believe in the preservationist land-use model because of their spiritual heritage. Devil's Tower in Wyoming is an example of preservationist land use. Many of the local American Indian tribes view this site as sacred, and therefore the U.S. National Park Service restricts land access and use by tourists. The Arctic National Wildlife Refuge (ANWR) in Alaska is another area that preservationists want to protect, especially against oil and mineral extraction.

Land developers often criticize this model, since it does not help an area generate any economic activity. One compromise that developers and preservationists have come up with is ecotourism. **Ecotourism** is the practice of letting visitors come into a natural landscape and enjoy it but not damage it. This allows the developers to generate economic activity while preserving the landscape.

Land-Use Issues

Less developed countries are usually not as free as developed countries in deciding how to use their land. Many of the less developed countries are faced with enormous debt. As a result, there is pressure either to repay the debt or enact policies to protect the environment. This pressure sometimes results in a solution called a **debt-for-nature swap**. This occurs when an international agency (usually the World Bank) makes a deal with a country to cancel its debt if the country sets aside a large tract of land for preservation. This is less than ideal for many countries because they are then prohibited from extracting the natural resources on the preserved land. In the 1980s, Bolivia received a debt-for-nature swap from the World Bank. In exchange for debt forgiveness, it had to set aside millions of acres of rainforest for preservation.

In 1833, British economist William Forster Lloyd developed an idea called the tragedy of the commons. Later, American ecologist Garrett Hardin modernized the idea to relate to natural resources. The **tragedy of the commons** is a theory that suggests humans will inevitably do what is best for themselves despite what is the best for the public good. When the best use of limited resources in a community comes up for debate, society must dictate the best uses of those natural resources. The political pressure on both sides of the spectrum makes choices difficult, and often one's position in the debate depends on which land-use model one believes in.

Types of Natural Resources

There are two distinct types of natural resources: renewable and nonrenewable. **Renewable resources** can either be used again or regrow themselves relatively quickly. The sun and wind are resources that can be used again, and water and trees are resources that can replenish themselves relatively quickly. The sun and wind are the most abundant examples of renewable resources.

16

Nonrenewable resources, on the other hand, are gone forever once they are used. The best examples of nonrenewable resources are fossil fuels (e.g., coal, oil, natural gas). These resources come from the breakdown of carbon-based sediment over long periods of time under great pressure. Reserves are the amount of the resource left in the ground yet to be used. Production or extraction is the removal of the resource. Fossil fuels are finite resources, and so they will eventually run out. Those who embrace the environmental land-use model warn of the likelihood of fossil fuels running out fairly soon. They believe society should develop and use alternative fuel sources such as wind and solar.

Oil

Oil is the lifeblood of modern industrialized economies in both the developed and less developed world. The majority of the oil in the United States comes from three major sources: states on the Gulf of Mexico, including Texas and Louisiana; the Northern Great Plains, including the Bakken basin in North Dakota; and California. Alaska and Oklahoma also produce some of the nation's oil.

Oil comes from deep inside the Earth. Often, these oil reserves are located beneath the ocean, and oil rig platforms are used for their extraction. Miles of pipes tunnel deep under the Earth's surface to extract the oil located there. The different products that are made from oil come from the refining process. These include gasoline, methane, propane, butane, kerosene, diesel fuels, and jet fuel. Oil refineries produce these different products by extracting the resource at different points during the heating process. Most of the easily recoverable oil in the world has already been discovered. As oil becomes harder and harder to extract, it is likely that prices for gasoline will increase. At some point in the future, it could become cheaper to operate a vehicle using an alternative fuel than with gasoline.

Currently, the United States is one of the top oil-producing countries, extracting more than 10.5 million barrels per day. Russia and Saudi Arabia are the top two producers, each extracting about 12 million barrels per day. China, Canada, Iraq, and the United Arab Emirates are other top oil-producing countries.

The United States, by far, consumes more oil than any other country. Currently, the United States consumes about 19.5 million barrels of oil per day. China is the second-largest consumer, using 12 million barrels per day. India is the third-largest consumer, using about 4 million barrels per day. Together, the United States and China consume more oil per day than the next top 10 countries combined.

Producing oil and having oil are two different considerations. While the United States currently extracts the most oil per day, it does not have the vast oil reserves that other countries have. In fact, the United States is not even in the top 10 countries in terms of available oil reserves. The top 10 oil reserve countries are Venezuela, Saudi Arabia, Canada, Iran, Iraq, Kuwait, the United Arab Emirates, Russia, Libya, and Nigeria.

16

Oil Reserves of the World

OPEC

The countries in the world that have large reserves of oil have organized themselves into a cartel called the **Organization of Petroleum Exporting Countries (OPEC)**. This cartel was established in 1960, primarily with Middle Eastern member countries. However, in recent years, countries from Africa and South America have been included. The full list of OPEC countries includes Algeria, Angola, Ecuador, Equatorial Guinea, Gabon, Iran, Iraq, Kuwait, Libya, Nigeria, Qatar, Saudi Arabia, United Arab Emirates, and Venezuela. OPEC determines the price of crude petroleum by setting the numbers of barrels each member country will produce. The more barrels that are pumped, the lower the price, and vice versa.

OPEC's relationship with the United States has sometimes been rocky. During the 1970s, OPEC decided to refuse to sell petroleum to the United States. Gasoline prices in the United States sky-rocketed almost overnight. The price of gas more than doubled, and long gas lines were common. Many gas stations sold out within hours and then shut down until they could get more gasoline. The price of a barrel of crude oil rose more than 1,000 percent in a matter of months. As a result of this crisis, the United States set up the U.S. Petroleum Reserve, to be used only in an emergency situation.

Natural Gas

Natural gas is an odorless, colorless gas from inside the Earth. When burned, it provides abundant heat to homes and businesses in the United States and around the world. The majority of the homes in the United States are heated with natural gas. In 2016, natural gas surpassed coal as the leading source for U.S.-produced electricity. Natural gas accounts for about 34 percent of all U.S.-produced electricity, whereas coal represents only 30 percent. As of 2017, the top natural gas–producing states in the United States are Texas, Pennsylvania, Oklahoma, Louisiana, and Wyoming.

In terms of world production, no other country comes close to Russia in regard to its reserves of natural gas. Russia contains one-third of all of the natural gas reserves in the world. Iran has the second-largest reserves, with about 16 percent of the total, and the United States has about 10 percent of the world's natural gas. These three countries together possess just under 60 percent of all of the natural gas in the world.

Coal

Historically, the United States has had abundant reserves of coal. Coal is extracted and produced mainly to generate electricity. Currently, the United States depends on coal for about 30 percent of its electricity production.

There are different forms of coal. The majority of the coal mined in the western United States is lignite coal. The majority of the coal found in the Appalachian region is bituminous coal. The purest form of coal, anthracite, is found in large quantities in Pennsylvania. Anthracite coal has the highest value of any coal because of its high heat output. This is the type of coal used most often to heat homes. All of these forms of coal are useful in creating electricity. As of 2017, the top five coal-producing states in the United States were Wyoming, West Virginia, Pennsylvania, Illinois, and Kentucky.

Despite the growth in natural gas production and renewable energy sources, coal is still an important part of the overall U.S. energy production. In terms of worldwide coal production, China is the top producer, and the United States is second. Other large producers of coal include Australia, Russia, and India.

The safety records of Chinese coal mines have recently come under intense scrutiny. A number of coal mines have exploded or caved in due to poor safety standards. China is also one of the leaders in coal consumption, which causes air pollution in many urban areas. Russia's coal mining industry has seen tremendous changes, which accompanied the political changes in the former Soviet Union. The privatization of the coal mining industry has brought about an improvement in safety standards. The majority of coal mining takes place in Siberia.

In Europe, coal production has declined much faster and further than the United States. Great Britain was once a worldwide leader in coal production, but it has embraced renewable energy sources and weaned itself off its coal dependency. In fact, in April of 2017, Great Britain's electricity system ran a full day without any coal-powered electricity.

16

Forestry and Fishing

Forestry is a huge industry in North America. Forests are some of the most treasured national resources in the United States. The redwood forests in California are older than the first European settlements in the United States, and some trees have been alive for many centuries. Despite this, society needs the products, such as paper and furniture, that can be made from these trees. Furthermore, the efficiency of the timber industry has generated significant profits. According to the U.S. government, the number of forested acres is projected to increase over the next two decades.

Often, a timber company owns a certain parcel of land, harvests the wood, and then replaces the trees that it cut down. Once the land has been replanted, it is left alone for several decades so that the trees can mature and then be cut down again. Sustainable practices ensure the profitability and productivity of the industry for both the near and distant future. Sometimes, the timber companies sign contracts with local and state governments to harvest timber on government-controlled land.

North America, with its large areas of virgin forest, is the world leader in the production of timber. Billions of trees have been harvested on the continent since humans have lived there. Brazil is another area in which forestry and the timber business is of vital importance. Because of its location and climate, Brazil possesses many different species of trees. Some of the trees that grow in tropical areas are highly prized around the world.

Many environmentalists and preservationists feel that the pristine timber lands of Brazil, much of them located in the interior of the country, should be preserved. However, Brazil needs resources and employment opportunities. The national and local governments of Brazil have tried to strike a balance between the need for the timber industry and the need to preserve the environment. Still, the Brazilian forests are being depleted, and their future is in doubt.

When it comes to the fishing industry, there continues to be a very high demand for fish products. Environmentalists, however, argue that the increased demand has outpaced the ability of the fish to reproduce, leading to dramatic decreases in much of the world's fish population.

In the United States, one of the largest fished areas is off of the coast of New England. Cool waters from Canada and warm waters from the Gulf Stream produce ideal conditions for the capture of fish. However, overfishing in these areas has contributed to what some now consider a biological crisis. The cod off the coast of New England and the maritime provinces of Canada have been severely depleted. Another area known for its fishing production is the Pacific Northwest region, including the coasts of Oregon and Washington. Unfortunately, the salmon, for which the region is famous, have been depleted. In addition, Alaska is one of the leading sources in the United States for crab and fish harvests.

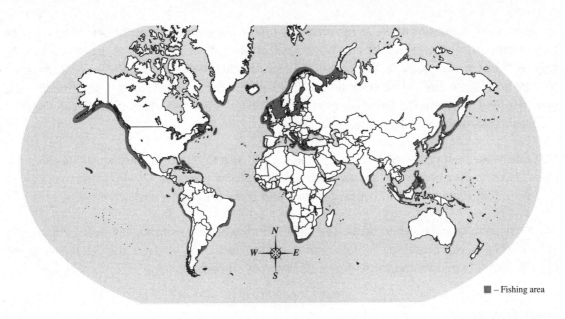

Key Fishing Areas of the World

⬛ – Fishing area

Alternative Energy

Over the past couple of decades, tremendous progress has been made in developing alternative energy sources. This progress has greatly reduced the consumption of fossil fuels in the developed world. Because of this progress, more and more energy developers have made investments in the alternative energy industry. Currently, there are six large-scale forms of alternative energy: hydro-electric, solar, wind, nuclear, biomass, and geothermal.

Hydroelectric Power

Hydroelectric energy is electrical power generated from the use of water. The power of falling water has been used in industry for thousands of years. Before electricity was distributed on a mass scale, factories had to rely on water as their primary source of power.

Huge dams have been built around the world to harness the power of moving water. The largest dam in the world is the Three Gorges Dam in China. At more than a mile wide, the Three Gorges Dam is the largest public works project that China, or the world, has ever attempted. It harnesses water from the Yangtze River to provide power for the population centers in the eastern portions of the country. Finished in 2009, the dam is thought to be capable of meeting more than 10 percent of China's future power needs.

Major dams in the United States include the Hoover Dam on the Arizona-Nevada border, the Grand Coulee Dam in Washington state, and the Oroville Dam in California. The United States uses many of its dams as recreation areas. The Lake Mead area near Las Vegas was turned into a National Recreational Area when the Hoover Dam was completed. The damming of the Columbia River by the Grand Coulee Dam formed Franklin D. Roosevelt Lake.

16

There are some major downsides to hydroelectric power. Dams can create a lot of energy, but they are expensive to build and must be on a waterway that can provide the necessary power to produce large amounts of energy. Major rivers are prime sites for dams, but damming the river affects many people, both upstream and downstream. By blocking the river, a reservoir is created behind the dam, flooding that area. The Three Gorges Dam in China has flooded villages and forced the relocation of upward of one million Chinese citizens.

Many dams are built on rivers that fish, such as salmon, use to migrate upstream. By blocking the rivers, dams create a barrier for the fish, halting their reproductive cycle. Newer dams are built with diversions that allow the fish to bypass the dam and complete their reproductive cycle.

Dams have also been known to break. The 1889 Johnstown flood, which killed over 2,200 people in Pennsylvania, was caused by the failure of the South Fork Dam. In Idaho, the Teton Dam broke in 1976, killing 14 people and causing over $1 billion in property damage.

Solar Energy

Another major source of alternative energy is solar energy. Solar energy is power created from the heat of the sun. Solar energy is one of the best renewable energy sources available as well as one of the cleanest. Solar energy systems use solar panels to absorb the heat of the sun and store it. The panels are relatively small, but when enough are placed together to create a significant amount of electricity, they can be quite visible features of a structure. Newer technology has enabled solar panels to become smaller and more efficient. Solar panels can now be placed directly on the rooftops of homes and businesses. When people use these panels, they are using an active solar energy system. An active solar energy system soaks up light and converts it through special cells to produce electricity.

Solar farms are being built near urban areas, both to meet electric demands and to satisfy demands on utility companies to utilize alternative energy. When solar plants are large enough, there can be negative effects on the environment, such as the clearing of land for construction or the use of large amounts of ground water to clean and cool equipment.

Proponents of solar power feel that the benefits outweigh the potential downsides. Solar power also will likely become more cost-effective in the future due to advancements in solar technology. It may become common practice for new homes and businesses to be built with solar energy systems.

Wind Energy

One of the cleanest methods of producing energy involves the use of wind. Wind energy is a form of power that is harnessed from the movement of wind. Huge wind turbines are located in windmill parks, also called wind farms. As the windmill blades turn, they spin the turbines, which in turn produces electricity.

Along with hydroelectric power, wind is one of the oldest sources of alternative power. Farmers have been using windmills for over a century. Prior to the electricity boom in the 1930s and 1940s, many rural areas in the United States did not have power. In fact, some areas were not connected to the country's power grid until the 1960s and 1970s. Such people had their own power sources, usually from the wind. They also used the wind to pump water for irrigation.

Wind farms are usually located in areas that experience more wind than other areas. The Great Plains is a good example of an area that has ideal wind conditions, and so there are many wind farms there. Many farmers build large windmills on their farms and then sell their excess power to utility companies in larger urban areas, like Chicago.

The worldwide use of wind energy has seen major growth during the last decade. This growth is expected to continue, as many countries have mandated that larger percentages of total energy production come from wind energy in the coming decades. Currently, the United States is second in the world in wind power production—only China produces more.

Critics of wind power note that birds fly into the turbines and are killed. Another concern about wind energy is the blight on the landscape that wind farms create. Dozens of large wind turbines are needed to produce significant energy. Some people find them unattractive, and the noise can be a nuisance for those who live near them.

Nuclear Power

Another form of alternative energy comes from nuclear power. Nuclear energy is the energy that holds together the nucleus of an atom. Nuclear power is generated by nuclear power plants that capture the energy released from the nucleus of an atom during nuclear fission. Nuclear fission is a process in which the nucleus of an atom is split into smaller parts; this process generates the energy that is harvested and converted into a useful form, such as electricity.

Nuclear power is one of the most controversial yet productive power sources in the world. Some people suggest that nuclear power shouldn't even be considered an alternative energy source because it needs uranium or plutonium (nonrenewable resources) for its production.

The power of nuclear energy cannot be overstated. The amount of energy produced from nuclear energy far outweighs the amount of energy from any other power source, including fossil fuels. Currently, the United States receives about 15 percent of its total power from nuclear energy. Some countries in Europe, such as France, receive over 70 percent of their power from nuclear energy.

One of the biggest drawbacks to nuclear energy is plant safety and the potential for nuclear meltdowns. The largest accident in the history of nuclear power occurred in Ukraine with the meltdown of Chernobyl in 1986. It was the result of inadequate safety measures and poor supervision of the nuclear fission process. The accident sent clouds of radioactive dust throughout northern Ukraine. Exposure to a radioactive cloud can have severe health impacts. Following the disaster, rates of cancer and birth defects have been high. Decades later, radioactivity is still high in the Chernobyl region.

16

Another nuclear meltdown occurred north of Tokyo in March of 2011, when the Fukushima Daiichi nuclear power plant suffered a meltdown as a result of a tsunami hitting the power plant. The meltdown sent radiation into the atmosphere, contaminating the ground and water for dozens of kilometers around the nuclear site.

The closest thing to a disaster in the United States occurred at the Three Mile Island nuclear power plant in central Pennsylvania in 1979. A partial meltdown of one of the reactors began. The reaction was brought under control within a few days, but the potential disaster has had a profound impact on the U.S. perception of nuclear power ever since.

The other major drawback to nuclear power is the storage of waste. The spent rods of uranium are radioactive. These radioactive rods must be disposed of somewhere. The question is where? Nobody wants to have radioactive waste near their homes. An acronym, NIMBY, has been coined; it stands for "Not In My Back Yard." Currently, the United States sends its radioactive waste to a storage facility in Nevada. However, this is intended to be only a temporary solution.

Biomass

Another form of alternative energy in use today is biomass. Biomass is a form of fuel energy created from agricultural products, natural vegetation, or urban waste. Biomass is used to create fuels such as biodiesel and ethanol, which can be used to operate automobiles and other machines.

Ethanol-based fuel is much cleaner than pure gasoline. When ethanol is burned in the combustion engine, the by-product is carbon dioxide, which plants can use for photosynthesis. A by-product of the combustion of normal gasoline is carbon monoxide, which is dangerous to animals and humans. As biomass technologies improve and as concern for environmental impact increases, it is likely that the United States and the rest of the world will increase its use of biomass as an alternative to fossil fuels.

The United States and Brazil are the two leaders in biomass production. In Brazil, sugarcane is the chief source for biomass, and in the United States, corn is the main source. Many states provide subsidies for farmers to produce corn, which is then sold to produce ethanol. Ethanol can be added to gasoline to make it burn cleaner. Ethanol plants are dotted throughout the Midwest, corresponding to the Corn Belt. In some parts of the world, though, forests and large areas of natural vegetation have been cleared to grow crops for the production of biodiesel. This creates concern that the negative effects of this practice may outweigh the environmental benefits of biodiesel.

Geothermal Energy

Geothermal power is derived from the heat in the interior of the Earth. This power can be used to heat and cool homes and buildings. Areas with high amounts of volcanic activity are ideal for geothermal energy production. The Earth's magma is relatively close to the surface of the Earth in these areas. For example, magma is only two miles below the surface in Yellowstone National Park, located primarily in Wyoming. Most of the western United States has relatively large amounts of geothermal activity, allowing more energy to be generated from this source. Due to California's location on the Pacific's "ring of fire" and because of its tectonic plate conjunctions, California contains the largest amount of geothermal electric generation capacity in the United States. In 2016, geothermal energy produced nearly 6 percent of the state's total system power. This was the most of any state in the United States.

Not all places can use geothermal energy. To use geothermal energy effectively, a location must have close proximity to the Earth's magma or interior heat. In such locations, many buildings are now being equipped with heating and cooling systems that use geothermal energy.

Geothermal power and all of the other alternative energy systems hold tremendous promise. As the world's supply of fossil fuels dwindles, alternative energy will be essential for the world's energy needs. Huge investments in infrastructure and advanced technology will be necessary. Many businesses and governments are already committed to making the investments necessary to transform societies' traditional energy systems to alternative energy systems.

Pollution

Because fossil fuels must be burned to make energy, the result is a relatively large amount of air pollution. Air pollution is the occurrence of hazardous products in the atmosphere, most often as a result of human activities. Some fossil fuels produce more air pollution than others when they are mined and/or burned to create energy.

There are different kinds of pollution. Carbon monoxide is one of the more common types of air pollution. It is a byproduct of incomplete combustion when burning coal, gas, and oil. Carbon monoxide poisoning is the most common type of fatal air poisoning in many countries. Carbon monoxide is a colorless, odorless, and tasteless but highly toxic gas.

According to the World Health Organization (WHO), air pollution kills more than three million people globally each year. In fact, the WHO says that air pollution is the greatest environmental risk to health. Poor air quality can lead to an increased risk of heart disease, lung cancer, and asthma. Today, no country is at greater risk than India, which is home to 22 of the 50 most polluted cities in the world. The city of Zabol in Iran currently has the worst air pollution of any city on the planet.

Historically, the coal industry has been one of the biggest air polluters, especially in United States. In recent decades, however, the coal industry has greatly reduced the amount of air pollution by using carbon-capturing technology and better filtering systems. Also, the Environmental Protection Agency has recently required energy producers to reduce the emissions of coal-burning plants. Perhaps most significantly, the amount of coal burned in the United States has fallen over the past 20 years, thereby reducing the amount of air pollution due to coal.

Air pollution has also resulted in acid rain. Acid rain is a form of precipitation with an unusually low pH value. It is the result of pollutants, such as sulfur dioxide and nitrogen oxides, that chemically alter water droplets. The burning of fossil fuels releases sulfur dioxide and nitrogen oxides. The Rust Belt in the United States has a lot of heavy industry, with smokestacks billowing pollutants

16

into the atmosphere. Acid rain expedites the decay process of buildings, bridges, and other structures. Forested areas have seen increases in soil acidity levels, creating unhealthy conditions for the native plant species.

Climate change occurs when carbon dioxide and other air pollutants collect in the atmosphere and absorb sunlight and solar radiation. Normally, this radiation would escape into space—but these pollutants, which can last for years to centuries in the atmosphere, trap the heat and cause the planet to get hotter. This is what is known as the greenhouse effect. In the United States, the burning of fossil fuels to make electricity is the largest source of heat-trapping pollution, producing billions of tons of carbon dioxide each year. The second-largest source of carbon pollution is the transportation sector, which generates nearly two billion tons of carbon dioxide emissions a year.

Over the past 50 years, the average global temperature has increased at the fastest rate in recorded history. And experts see the trend is accelerating. Scientists point to the retreating glaciers in both the Arctic and the Antarctic regions as evidence of the devastating effects of global temperature change. Some glaciers that were once huge have been reduced to relatively small chunks of ice. The melting of the polar ice caps would result in massive flooding of coastal regions around the world. Many scientists say that unless we curb global-warming emissions, average global temperatures will continue to rise over the next century.

 NEXT STEP: PRACTICE

Go to Rapid Review and Practice Chapter 9 or to your online quizzes on kaptest.com for exam-like practice on this topic.

Haven't registered your book yet? Go to kaptest.com/moreonline to begin.

CHAPTER 17

The Free-Response Section

FREE-RESPONSE STRATEGY

Overview

Together, the three free-response questions are worth 50 percent of your total exam score. You have 75 minutes to answer the three questions in Section II of the exam, which gives you about 25 minutes to plan and write each question.

> ✔ **AP Expert Note**
>
> **Treat Section II as a marathon (and train accordingly)**
>
> Although 75 minutes can feel like no time at all when you have to write three free-response questions, it is actually a long time for your brain to maintain sharp focus—especially after you have already spent 60 minutes on the multiple-choice questions in Section I. However, if you practice writing, including sticking to the timing and pacing required for Section II, you will build up the necessary stamina and feel much more prepared and confident on the official exam.

Readers will score each individual question according to a rubric: each prompt requires you to complete seven tasks, all related to a geographic scenario, and you can earn one point for successfully completing each task, for a total of seven points for each question.

The three free-response questions will always follow the same pattern:

1. **Question 1** has no source stimulus. A short paragraph will introduce a geographic scenario, and the seven tasks, (A)–(G), that follow will require you to analyze that geographic scenario.

2. **Question 2** is based on one source stimulus, which could be a map, image, table, or graph. Some, or all, of the seven tasks, (A)–(G), will ask you to respond based on information provided in the source stimulus.

3. **Question 3** is based on two related source stimuli. The seven tasks, (A)–(G), may ask you to respond based on information provided in one, or both sources, so pay careful attention to which tasks refer to which sources.

You may answer the questions in any order, as long as you write your responses on the corresponding pages of your response booklet. Begin with whichever question you feel most confident about—and be sure you give about a third of your time to each question, since each is weighted the same in your score.

The Kaplan Method for Free-Response Questions

You can and should approach every prompt using the same Kaplan Method. Employing a methodical, strategic approach will help ensure that you effectively address every part of every question. Just follow these four steps (which spell out AP-AP)!

1. **Analyze the prompt.**
2. **Plan your response.**
3. **Action! Write your response.**
4. **Proofread.**

Let's look at the Kaplan Method steps in more detail.

Step 1: Analyze the Prompt

Take the time to understand each and every part of every prompt—or what the question asks you to do. If you don't answer each of the prompt's required tasks, it will be impossible to earn a high score for that question! Analyzing the prompt means thinking carefully about the following components.

- **The introductory paragraph.** Most questions include an introductory paragraph before the tasks (A)–(G). Read this paragraph carefully, since it often identifies the topic and important details that will be asked about in the tasks.

- **The source stimulus.** Two of the three free-response questions contain source stimuli, such as a map, image, table, or graph. Because your response must incorporate the information from the source, you must analyze it just as thoroughly as the wording of the prompt itself. Review each source thoroughly, noting components such as title, topic, and data trends. Ask yourself what information each source provides about the question topic.

- **The content of the question**. Consider exactly what each task, (A)–(G), asks you to do. Underline key terms and requirements.

- **The action words.** Finally, make sure you know exactly what you have to do with the content: *describe, explain,* etc. Consider circling the action words so you make sure you do the correct required action. While we often use these action words somewhat interchangeably when speaking, consider carefully how each one calls for a slightly different treatment of the content. The following are some example action words, from simple to more complex.

    - *Identify*: point out a trend or piece of information; this task does *not* require providing an explanation

    - *Define*: provide the meaning of a term

    - *Describe*: fully lay out the details of something

    - *Explain*: analyze the *why* or *how* of something (e.g., what causes it, why it's important) using reasoning and/or evidence

    - *Compare*: describe or explain how two concepts are similar and different

Step 2: Plan Your Response

This is the *most important* factor in writing a quality response. Planning is never a waste of time; rather, it is a crucial step to creating an effective response that addresses every part of every prompt. The test makers expect you to take at least 5 minutes to plan your response to each question—that means at least 15 minutes of planning time have been built into the exam timing, so take advantage of it. Ultimately, planning saves you time by helping you write a focused response. You only have time to write each response once, so make it count!

Here are some tips to help you make your plan:

- Think about what you will write for each part of a prompt. Jot down brief notes—phrases and/or examples—for each part.

- Whenever possible, see if you can come up with specific examples to help support your response.

- Check that your notes reflect the action word for each part of the prompt: for instance, your notes should include more details for parts that ask you to *describe* than for parts that ask you to *identify*.

- Double-check the prompt to make sure you didn't skip any required tasks.

✔ AP Expert Note

Be strategic with the information you provide

Don't just write as much as you know about the topic of a prompt; rather, respond with information that satisfies each specific requirement. For example, if a part of a free-response prompt asks you to "Describe a population characteristic typical of stage four countries in the demographic transition model," don't waste time writing out *every* population characteristic. Instead, use details to describe one significant characteristic, such as low birth rates. Focus your writing on what the question asks for, and move on!

Step 3: Action! Write Your Response

After thoroughly completing the pre-writing steps, actually writing the response should be relatively easy: just use the notes you jotted down in Step 2 to write your response to each task, (A)–(G). Although you may be able to respond to a task that asks you to *identify* by simply writing a word or phrase, you should use full sentences, even if it's just one short sentence. Tasks that ask you to *define*, *describe*, *explain*, or *compare* entail more complex ideas that are best communicated in several complete sentences, or even a couple small paragraphs.

As you write, keep in mind that your responses should clearly focus on the required tasks. Time is limited, so every word you write should help you earn points. Avoid "filler" and "fluff." The length of your response has nothing to do with your score; you earn points based on the quality of the content and how well it addresses the prompt.

Finally, make sure you write neatly. Readers can't award points if they can't read what you wrote. Keep in mind that actual people will be reading every word you write, so make them happy by making your responses as easy as possible to read.

Step 4: Proofread

Try to leave a minute or two to briskly proofread. Your responses need not be perfect, but you should quickly correct any glaring errors that might distract your readers from your content. If you catch a mistake, just neatly cross it out and write the correction above. There's no time for a complete overhaul of the response, but if you made a plan, there won't be any need for one!

✔ AP Expert Note

Remember to "AP-AP"

Recall that the steps of the Kaplan Method for Free-Response Questions spell out AP-AP. Follow all of the steps of this easy-to-remember acronym every time you encounter a free-response prompt, both in practice and on Test Day. By making the Kaplan Method second nature, you won't have to think about what you're doing and can instead focus on the quality of the content you're writing.

SAMPLE QUESTIONS

Now that we've established the Kaplan Method (AP-AP) to apply to every free-response question, let's review a couple sample prompts. The following sections provide step-by-step walk-throughs of two sample questions, one with no source stimulus and one with two source stimuli.

Prompt with No Source Stimulus

Regionalization and globalization are two powerful, and sometimes opposing, trends occurring in today's world.

A. Define the concept of regionalization.

B. Define the concept of globalization.

C. Describe a specific example of regionalization.

D. Describe a specific example of globalization.

E. Describe a factor that has enabled globalization.

F. Explain the conflict that can exist between regionalization and globalization.

G. Explain a benefit that can result from globalization.

Step 1: Analyze the Prompt

Since this sample question has no source stimulus, it would appear as Question 1 on the exam. Although there is no source to analyze, pay attention to the introductory paragraph, the content of the question, and the action words of each task.

- **The introductory paragraph** designates that the overall topic of this question concerns regionalization and globalization. The paragraph provides the details that these trends are powerful and sometimes may conflict with each other.

- **The content of the question** asks for definitions and examples of both terms, a factor that enables globalization, and explanations of the conflict between the trends and a benefit of globalization. Underline or circle the key terms that the tasks require.

- **The action words** include *define*, *describe*, and *explain*. Circle each action word so you can be sure to respond in a way that fulfills what each action word requires.

Step 2: Plan Your Response

The paragraphs below describe what a high-scoring writer might notice and think about when planning a response. Samples of what that high-scoring writer might write as notes are provided for each part of the prompt.

For Part (A), the prompt directs you to define *regionalization*. Since the action word is *define*, a response only needs to provide the meaning of the term.

Part A: classifying an area by its unique characteristics.

For Part (B), the prompt directs you to define *globalization*. Once again, only the meaning of the term is required.

Part B: world interactions that contribute to shared global culture.

Parts (C) and (D) ask for descriptions of specific examples of both terms. Since the action word is *describe*, the response should use details to indicate how each example demonstrates the term. While multiple examples would apply for each term, what the writer of this sample chose is shown below.

Part C: regional languages (Spanglish)

Part D: popular television ("Pop Idol")

Part (E) asks for a description of a factor that enabled globalization. Since the action word is *describe*, the response should use details to describe the factor and how it enabled globalization. The high-scoring writer will brainstorm possible factors and choose the one for which he or she can provide the best description.

Part E: communication tech (Internet, television)—ideas and trends spread almost instantly

Part (F) asks for an explanation of the conflict between regionalization and globalization. Since the action word is *explain*, the response should use evidence and/or reasoning to explain *how* the two trends can be in conflict. The high-scoring writer will brainstorm possible sources of conflict and choose one for which she can write a reasoned explanation and/or provide specific evidence.

Part F: regional identity could be difficult to maintain due to pull of globalization (evidence: pressure to conform to English)

Part (G) asks for an explanation of a benefit of globalization. Since the action word is *explain*, the response should use evidence and/or reasoning to identify a possible benefit and explain *why* it is a benefit. The high-scoring writer will brainstorm possible benefits and choose one for which she can write a reasoned explanation and/or provide specific evidence.

Part G: more innovations when sharing ideas (evidence: Internet discussion boards for computer programming)

Step 3: Action! Write Your Response

Just write out the information, using your planning notes. As you write, remember to label each part of your response (A, B, C, etc.) and to keep your writing legible. Refer back to the question's action words to make sure you're doing the correct tasks.

Step 4: Proofread

Leave a minute or so for a quick proofread, neatly correcting any errors you catch.

Sample High-Scoring Response and Scoring Explanation

The following is a sample high-scoring response and scoring explanation. One of the best ways to improve your own free-response answers is to read sample responses, thinking carefully about what makes the responses effective and what features you can mimic in your own writing.

Sample Response

(A) Regionalization refers to describing an area in terms of its individual characteristics, such as a shared language or cultural identity, that make that place unique.

(B) Globalization is the spread of a cultural factor among many populations due to interactions throughout the world, resulting in a shared global culture.

(C) An example of regionalization can be found in regions that commonly use Spanglish, which is a hybrid of words and phrases from both English and Spanish in locations where there are many speakers of both languages. Regions that use Spanglish are common along the United States-Mexico border due to the interactions and migrations of speakers of both languages. There are even smaller pockets of particular dialects of Spanglish, creating even smaller regions within the Spanglish-speaking area.

(D) An example of globalization is "Pop Idol." This TV show aired in the United Kingdom as a means for ordinary people to showcase their singing ability. This phenomenon diffused to North America, and the American version became one of the most popular television shows of all time in the United States. Today, many other countries around the world have used this idea and developed their own musical competition programs, creating a factor of cultural homogeneity that defines a globalized phenomenon.

(E) One factor that enables globalization is the development of improved communication technology that has enabled the almost instant spread of ideas throughout the world. Whereas trends in one region once took months or years to spread across boundaries or oceans, the Internet and television enable the rapid diffusion of images, videos, and trends at a worldwide scale—for instance, a dance style can be viewed in social media and video-sharing sites and become a worldwide trend in mere hours.

(F) Regional identity could be difficult to maintain due to the forces of globalization. For instance, speakers of Spanglish might be pressured to conform to the primary language spoken in their country, whether English in the United States or Spanish in Mexico, and find it difficult to maintain their regional language identity and traditional heritage. Additionally, regional dialects of English became less distinct as more Americans watched nationally broadcast television. Some people might embrace this common culture, while others might lament the loss of their traditional and unique ways of speech.

(G) A benefit of globalization is that more innovations are possible when ideas can easily be shared throughout the world. For instance, through Internet discussion boards and shared programming code, developers throughout the world can use the Internet to collaborate about the creation of computer programs. Rather than individuals working independently and starting programs from scratch, programmers can share their codes and tips, building off of each other's work and developing new programs at a more rapid pace.

Sample Response Explanation and Scoring: 7 points (1 for each task)

The following is information about how a free-response question would be scored. A successful short-answer response accomplishes all seven tasks set forth by the prompt. Each part of the prompt is worth 1 point, for a total of 7 possible points.

Part A (1 point)

To earn the point, the response must define the concept of regionalization as classifying a geographic area according to its unique characteristics.

Part B (1 point)

To earn the point, the response must define the concept of globalization as the processes of growing interconnectedness throughout the world, resulting in an increasingly worldwide culture.

Part C (1 point)

To earn the point, the response must use details to describe, not merely identify, a specific example of regionalization. The writer of the sample response effectively describes details about Spanglish that show how it is an example of regionalization.

Part D (1 point)

To earn the point, the response must use details to describe, not merely identify, a specific example of globalization. The writer of the sample response effectively describes details about a television show and its diffusion that show how it is an example of globalization.

Part E (1 point)

To earn the point, the response must use details to describe a factor that has enabled globalization. The writer of the sample response effectively describes details about improvements in communication that show how this development enabled globalization.

Part F (1 point)

To earn the point, the response must use reasoning and/or examples to explain the potential conflict between regionalization and globalization. The writer of the sample response effectively uses the evidence of the conflict between regional languages and dialects and national languages in the United States and Mexico to explain how regionalization and globalization can conflict.

Part G (1 point)

To earn the point, the response must use reasoning and/or examples to explain a benefit that can result from globalization. The writer of the sample response effectively uses the evidence of sharing computer programming information over the Internet to explain why ease of innovation is a benefit of globalization.

Prompt with Two Source Stimuli

WHEAT CROP YIELDS IN BUSHELS PER ACRE, ENGLAND, SELECTED YEARS

Year	Bushels Per Acre
1400–1449	5.89
1550–1559	7.88
1600–1649	10.45
1700–1749	13.79
1750–1799	17.26
1800–1849	23.16
1850–1899	26.69

WHEAT PRODUCTION IN METRIC TONS, MEXICO

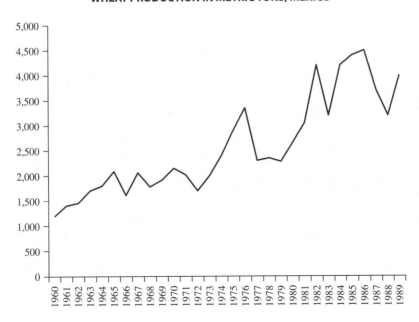

Developments in farming, over time, have revolutionized agricultural practices and impacted crop yields.

A. Identify the type of farming most likely practiced during the years 1400–1449 as shown in the data table.

B. Describe a development that impacted crop yields as shown in the data table.

C. Describe an impact of the increase in crop yields as shown in the data table.

D. Describe a development that impacted crop yields as shown in the graph.

E. Describe a way in which the Green Revolution was successful.

F. Describe a way in which the Green Revolution did not meet expectations or brought about criticism.

G. Explain the significance of the Green Revolution in light of population trends in less developed countries.

Step 1: Analyze the Prompt

Since this sample response has two source stimuli, it would appear as Question 3 on the exam. A high-scoring response writer would begin by carefully analyzing both sources, the introductory paragraph, the content of the question, and the action words of each task.

- **The introductory paragraph** designates that the overall topic of this question concerns developments in agriculture. The paragraph provides the details that these developments impacted both farming practices and crop yields.

- **The source stimuli** include a table and a graph. Analyze each source individually.

  - The title of the table indicates it contains data about wheat crop yields in England. The data in the table shows a trend of steadily increasing crop yields, in bushels of wheat per acre, from the years 1400 to 1899. A high-scoring writer might note that this time span encompasses the Second Agricultural Revolution.

  - The title of the graph indicates it contains data about wheat production in Mexico. The data in the graph shows a trend of generally increasing wheat production, in metric tons, from the years 1960 to 1989. A high-scoring writer might note that this time span encompasses the Green Revolution.

- **The content of the question** asks for descriptions of causes and effects of increased crop yields, as shown in the sources and descriptions, and an explanation of the results and significance of the Green Revolution. Underline or circle the key terms that the tasks ask about.

- **The action words** include *identify*, *describe*, and *explain*. Circle each action word so you can be sure to respond in a way that fulfills what each action word requires.

Step 2: Plan Your Response

The paragraphs below describe what a high-scoring writer might notice and think about when planning a response. Samples of what that high-scoring writer might write as notes are provided for each part of the prompt.

For Part (A), the prompt directs you to identify the type of farming most likely practiced in the years 1400 to 1449, as shown in the data table. The high-scoring response writer would focus only on the data table and identify that wheat yields were lowest in the years 1400 to 1449. Since the action word is *identify*, the writer only needs to supply the type of farming practiced.

Part A: family, subsistence

For Part (B), the prompt directs you to describe a development that impacted crop yields shown in the data table. During Step 1, a high-scoring response writer would have identified the years and yields in the table as reflecting changes during the Second Agricultural Revolution in England. Since the action word is *describe*, the response will need to use details to indicate how a development in the Second Agricultural Revolution impacted crop yields.

Part B: 2nd Agr. Rev.—crop rotation increased yields

For Part (C), the prompt directs you to describe an impact of the increase in crop yields as shown in the data table. Since the table shows increases in yields during the Second Agricultural Revolution, and the action word in the question stem is *describe*, the response will need to use details to indicate an impact of the Second Agricultural Revolution in England.

Part C: excess food supply for urban/industry workers

For Part (D), the prompt directs you to describe a development that impacted crop yields shown in the graph. During Step 1, a high-scoring response writer would have identified the years and yields in the table as reflecting changes during the Green Revolution in Mexico. Since the action word is *describe*, the response will need to use details to indicate how a development in the Green Revolution impacted crop yields.

Part D: development of new crops (high-yield, resist disease, grow in less favorable locations)

For Part (E), the prompt directs you to describe a way in which the Green Revolution succeeded. Since the action word is *describe*, the response will need to include details that indicate a result of the Green Revolution that could be considered a success. Describing a specific country would be an effective approach.

Part E:

- Mexico before Green Rev.: hacienda agriculture & land redistribution
- After: better economy and less food shortage when Mexican government set up irrigation systems & new seeds
- Results: benefited large-scale farms, more food produced, crops for export

For Part (F), the prompt directs you to describe a way in which the Green Revolution did not meet expectations or drew criticism. Since the action word is *describe*, the response should include details that indicate a result of the Green Revolution that could be criticized. Describing an example of a specific country would be an effective approach.

Part F: did not give nutritious diet in Philippines: high-yield rice increased dependence on one crop, pesticides destroyed other traditional crops

For Part (G), the prompt directs you to explain the significance of the Green Revolution in light of population trends in less developed countries. Since the action word is *explain*, the response should use reasoning and/or examples to explain how the Green Revolution relates to population trends in less developed countries. The high-scoring response writer would first identify population trends in less developed countries, such as growing populations, high birth rates, or relatively young populations. Then the high-scoring response writer would brainstorm ways to use evidence and/ or reasoning to relate these trends to the Green Revolution's work to increase crop yields.

Part G:

- Trends: high birth rates/lower death rates led to population growth
- Significance of Green Rev.: subsistence agr. would strain food supply; irrigation and pesticides increased staple crops (wheat & rice) in Americas & Asia

Step 3: Action! Write Your Response &

Step 4: Proofread

Use your plan to write each part of the response, and briskly skim for errors when finished.

See the following high-scoring response, and be sure to read the scoring explanation to help you identify what makes this response effective. Think about what features you can incorporate into your own free-response answers.

Sample High-Scoring Response and Scoring Explanation

Sample Response

(A) As indicated by the relatively low crop yields, subsistence agriculture was most likely practiced in 1400–1449.

(B) During the Second Agricultural Revolution of the 1600s to 1800s, crop yields increased over time, as shown in the data table. One factor that increased yields was the development of more effective methods of crop rotation. The use of 4-crop rotation systems in England eliminated the need to leave land empty for a growing period. This practice also more effectively replaced nutrients in the soil, increasing the overall productivity of farmland.

(C) As crop yields increased and land became more productive in England, the agricultural work did not require as many laborers. These former farm workers often moved to urban areas in search of work. Coupled with the increase in food production that could support a growing non-agricultural population, this migration led to urban growth. This time period also saw the Industrial Revolution, which was possible in England partly due to the available labor freed up by more productive agriculture.

(D) The increase in crop yields shown in the graph occurred during the Green Revolution. Scientists had developed new seed varieties containing qualities that increased crop yields. For instance, the new wheat seeds used in Mexico during this period were disease-resistant, high-yield, and could grow in a wider variety of environments.

(E) At the end of the Second World War, Mexico faced economic hardships due to the continuing impacts of its traditional hacienda system of agriculture and the mixed results of previous attempts at land redistribution. Facing food shortages, the Mexican government actively pursued methods to improve agricultural production, including the creation of irrigation infrastructure and the development of higher-yield varieties of wheat and other crops. While these changes could be said to benefit large-scale agribusinesses at the expense of small farmers, the overall impact increased food production and supplied profitable bumper crops for export.

(F) The Green Revolution did not meet expectations in providing a nutritious diet in other world areas, such as the Philippines. Although high-yield rice varieties increased rice production, one result was a high dependence on this one cereal crop in the diet, which can lead to malnutrition. Additionally, the use of many chemical pesticides, some of which destroyed fish and traditional crops, further deteriorated the health of the population.

(G) Modern medicine brought down death rates in many less developed countries, while birth rates remained high. The difference between these two rates led to rapid population growth. Many developing countries had large populations still employed in traditional subsistence agriculture. With a growing population to support, the food supplies of these countries would be strained. Therefore, the countries worked to implement agricultural practices, including techniques such as irrigation and use of pesticides that could make formerly unsuitable land useful for agriculture, to help increase food production. In particular, the increase of staple crops such as wheat and rice in Central/South America and Asia helped ensure the food stability of these countries.

Sample Response Explanation and Scoring: 7 points (1 point for each task)

The following is information about how a free-response question would be scored. A successful short-answer response accomplishes all seven tasks set forth by the prompt. Each part of the prompt is worth 1 point, for a total of 7 possible points.

Part A (1 point)

To earn the point, the response must identify that the type of farming most likely practiced in England from 1400 to 1449 was subsistence, family, or small-scale farming.

Part B (1 point)

To earn the point, the response must use details to describe a development that increased crop yields in England during the years shown in the table. The writer of the sample response effectively describes details about how crop rotation increased crop yields during the Second Agricultural Revolution.

Part C (1 point)

To earn the point, the response must use details to describe an impact of increased crop yields in England during the years shown in the table. The writer of the sample response effectively describes details about how increased crop yields impacted internal migrations of laborers and contributed to urbanization.

Part D (1 point)

To earn the point, the response must use details to describe a development that increased crop yields in Mexico during the years shown in the chart. The writer of the sample response effectively describes details about how new seed varieties increased crop yields during the Green Revolution.

Part E (1 point)

To earn the point, the response must use details to describe a way in which the Green Revolution succeeded. The writer of the sample response effectively uses a specific example that shows a success by describing details about agriculture before and after the Green Revolution in Mexico.

Part F (1 point)

To earn the point, the response must use details to describe a way in which the Green Revolution did not meet expectations or drew criticism. The writer of the sample response effectively uses a specific example that shows a criticism by describing details of the Green Revolution's impact on nutrition in the Philippines.

Part G (1 point)

To earn the point, the response must use reasoning and/or examples to explain how the Green Revolution is significant in relation to population trends in less developed countries. The writer of the sample response effectively uses reasoning to explain how increasing food yields due to the Green Revolution would be important in less developed countries with growing populations and subsistence agriculture. The writer also effectively includes the specific examples of crops in Central America, South America, and Asia to support this reasoning.

PART 4

Practice Exams

How to Take the Practice Exams

The next section of this book consists of three full-length practice exams. Taking a practice AP exam gives you an idea of what it's like to answer AP questions under conditions that approximate those of the real exam. You'll find out which areas you're strong in and where additional review may be required. Any mistakes you make now are ones you won't make on the actual exam, as long as you take the time to learn where you went wrong.

Our full-length practice exams, like the official AP exam, each include 60 multiple-choice questions and 3 free-response questions. Before taking a practice exam, find a quiet place where you can work uninterrupted, and bring blank, lined paper for the free-response questions. (The proctor will provide lined paper when you take the official exam.) Time yourself according to the time limit given at the beginning of each section: 60 minutes for the multiple-choice questions and 75 minutes for the free-response questions. It's okay to take a short break between sections, but for the most accurate results, you should approximate real test conditions as much as possible.

As you take the practice exams, remember to pace yourself. Train yourself to be aware of the time you are spending on each problem. Try to be aware of the general types of questions you encounter, as well as being alert to certain strategies or approaches that help you to handle the various question types more effectively.

After taking each practice exam, complete the following steps.

1. Self-score your multiple-choice section using the answer key immediately following each exam.
2. Read the answers and explanations for the relevant exam, located in the back of your book. These detailed explanations will help you identify areas that could use additional study. Even when you have answered a question correctly, you can learn additional information by looking at the explanation.
3. Self-score your free-response questions using the information in the answers and explanations section.
4. Navigate to the scoring section of your online resources (kaptest.com/moreonline) to input all of these raw scores and see what your overall score would be with a similar performance on Test Day.

Finally, it's important to approach the exam with the right attitude. You're going to get a great score because you've reviewed the material and learned the strategies in this book.

Good luck!

Practice Exam 1

Practice Exam 1 Answer Grid

1. Ⓐ Ⓑ Ⓒ Ⓓ Ⓔ
2. Ⓐ Ⓑ Ⓒ Ⓓ Ⓔ
3. Ⓐ Ⓑ Ⓒ Ⓓ Ⓔ
4. Ⓐ Ⓑ Ⓒ Ⓓ Ⓔ
5. Ⓐ Ⓑ Ⓒ Ⓓ Ⓔ
6. Ⓐ Ⓑ Ⓒ Ⓓ Ⓔ
7. Ⓐ Ⓑ Ⓒ Ⓓ Ⓔ
8. Ⓐ Ⓑ Ⓒ Ⓓ Ⓔ
9. Ⓐ Ⓑ Ⓒ Ⓓ Ⓔ
10. Ⓐ Ⓑ Ⓒ Ⓓ Ⓔ
11. Ⓐ Ⓑ Ⓒ Ⓓ Ⓔ
12. Ⓐ Ⓑ Ⓒ Ⓓ Ⓔ
13. Ⓐ Ⓑ Ⓒ Ⓓ Ⓔ
14. Ⓐ Ⓑ Ⓒ Ⓓ Ⓔ
15. Ⓐ Ⓑ Ⓒ Ⓓ Ⓔ

16. Ⓐ Ⓑ Ⓒ Ⓓ Ⓔ
17. Ⓐ Ⓑ Ⓒ Ⓓ Ⓔ
18. Ⓐ Ⓑ Ⓒ Ⓓ Ⓔ
19. Ⓐ Ⓑ Ⓒ Ⓓ Ⓔ
20. Ⓐ Ⓑ Ⓒ Ⓓ Ⓔ
21. Ⓐ Ⓑ Ⓒ Ⓓ Ⓔ
22. Ⓐ Ⓑ Ⓒ Ⓓ Ⓔ
23. Ⓐ Ⓑ Ⓒ Ⓓ Ⓔ
24. Ⓐ Ⓑ Ⓒ Ⓓ Ⓔ
25. Ⓐ Ⓑ Ⓒ Ⓓ Ⓔ
26. Ⓐ Ⓑ Ⓒ Ⓓ Ⓔ
27. Ⓐ Ⓑ Ⓒ Ⓓ Ⓔ
28. Ⓐ Ⓑ Ⓒ Ⓓ Ⓔ
29. Ⓐ Ⓑ Ⓒ Ⓓ Ⓔ
30. Ⓐ Ⓑ Ⓒ Ⓓ Ⓔ

31. Ⓐ Ⓑ Ⓒ Ⓓ Ⓔ
32. Ⓐ Ⓑ Ⓒ Ⓓ Ⓔ
33. Ⓐ Ⓑ Ⓒ Ⓓ Ⓔ
34. Ⓐ Ⓑ Ⓒ Ⓓ Ⓔ
35. Ⓐ Ⓑ Ⓒ Ⓓ Ⓔ
36. Ⓐ Ⓑ Ⓒ Ⓓ Ⓔ
37. Ⓐ Ⓑ Ⓒ Ⓓ Ⓔ
38. Ⓐ Ⓑ Ⓒ Ⓓ Ⓔ
39. Ⓐ Ⓑ Ⓒ Ⓓ Ⓔ
40. Ⓐ Ⓑ Ⓒ Ⓓ Ⓔ
41. Ⓐ Ⓑ Ⓒ Ⓓ Ⓔ
42. Ⓐ Ⓑ Ⓒ Ⓓ Ⓔ
43. Ⓐ Ⓑ Ⓒ Ⓓ Ⓔ
44. Ⓐ Ⓑ Ⓒ Ⓓ Ⓔ
45. Ⓐ Ⓑ Ⓒ Ⓓ Ⓔ

46. Ⓐ Ⓑ Ⓒ Ⓓ Ⓔ
47. Ⓐ Ⓑ Ⓒ Ⓓ Ⓔ
48. Ⓐ Ⓑ Ⓒ Ⓓ Ⓔ
49. Ⓐ Ⓑ Ⓒ Ⓓ Ⓔ
50. Ⓐ Ⓑ Ⓒ Ⓓ Ⓔ
51. Ⓐ Ⓑ Ⓒ Ⓓ Ⓔ
52. Ⓐ Ⓑ Ⓒ Ⓓ Ⓔ
53. Ⓐ Ⓑ Ⓒ Ⓓ Ⓔ
54. Ⓐ Ⓑ Ⓒ Ⓓ Ⓔ
55. Ⓐ Ⓑ Ⓒ Ⓓ Ⓔ
56. Ⓐ Ⓑ Ⓒ Ⓓ Ⓔ
57. Ⓐ Ⓑ Ⓒ Ⓓ Ⓔ
58. Ⓐ Ⓑ Ⓒ Ⓓ Ⓔ
59. Ⓐ Ⓑ Ⓒ Ⓓ Ⓔ
60. Ⓐ Ⓑ Ⓒ Ⓓ Ⓔ

SECTION I

Time—60 Minutes

60 Questions

You have 60 minutes to answer the following 60 multiple-choice questions. Each of the questions or incomplete statements is accompanied by five possible answers or completions. Select the one that best answers the question or completes the statement.

Questions 1–3 refer to the graphs below.

Boserup's Theory

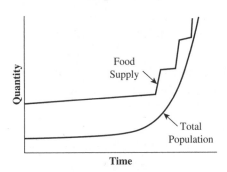

Malthus's Theory

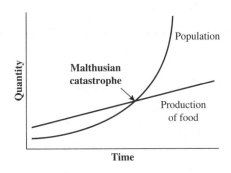

1. According to the graphs, how does Boserup's theory differ from Malthus's theory regarding the relationship between food and population?

   (A) Malthus's theory shows that food production is never higher than the population.

   (B) Malthus's theory shows the rate of population growth is always greater than the rate of food production.

   (C) Boserup's theory shows that population grows at an exponential rate.

   (D) Boserup's theory shows that food production increases exponentially.

   (E) Boserup's theory shows that the rate curves of food production and population growth never cross.

2. In the early 1800s, Thomas Malthus predicted that population would soon be in which of the following stages of growth?

   (A) Exponential

   (B) Negative

   (C) Static

   (D) Proportional

   (E) Linear

GO ON TO THE NEXT PAGE

3. Which of the following events contradicted Malthus's prediction?

   (A) The First Agricultural Revolution

   (B) Pastoral nomadism

   (C) Plant domestication

   (D) The Second Agricultural Revolution

   (E) The Fourth Agricultural Revolution

4. Weber's least cost theory is based on what primary cost?

   (A) Labor

   (B) Infrastructure

   (C) Transportation

   (D) Government taxes

   (E) Land costs

5. Which country has created special economic zones (SEZs) to attract investment?

   (A) Japan

   (B) Vietnam

   (C) South Korea

   (D) China

   (E) Laos

6. Almost 99 percent of the people in Denmark are Danes, follow the Lutheran religion, and speak Danish. Denmark is thus an exemplar of which of the following?

   (A) City-state

   (B) Microstate

   (C) Stateless nation

   (D) Political boundary

   (E) Nation-state

Questions 7–8 refer to the image below.

Demographic Transition Model

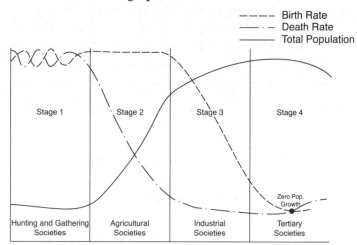

7. According to the demographic transition model, a country enters stage 3 when

   (A) the birth rate sharply increases

   (B) the birth rate decreases

   (C) the birth and death rates are nearly equal, stabilizing the population

   (D) the fertility rate falls below two children per family

   (E) the introduction of medicine causes the death rate to decrease

8. What stage in the demographic transition model has exponential growth rates?

   (A) Stage 1

   (B) Stage 2

   (C) Stage 3

   (D) Stage 4

   (E) Stage 5

GO ON TO THE NEXT PAGE

9. In the 1930s, many low-income regions of the city of Baltimore, Maryland, were designated as "hazardous," resulting in a reduction in the availability of mortgage lending and an increase in lending costs when mortgages were available. Which of the following terms best describes this phenomenon?

   (A) Blockbusting

   (B) White flight

   (C) Segregation

   (D) Ghettoization

   (E) Redlining

Questions 10–12 refer to the graphs below.

World Coal Consumption

Quadrillion Btu (British thermal unit)

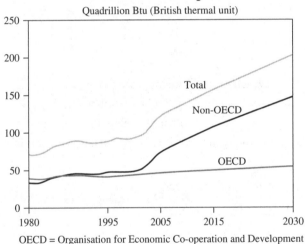

OECD = Organisation for Economic Co-operation and Development

Potential Impact of Nuclear Power Plant (NPP) Retirement on Carbon Emissions

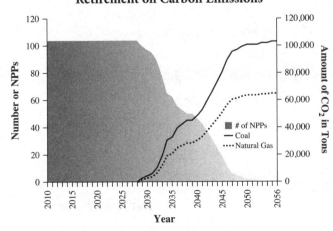

10. Which of the following best explains the trend of total coal consumption depicted in the first graph?

    (A) Despite the availability of renewable energy sources, non-OECD countries opt to burn coal instead.

    (B) The increasing industrialization of developing nations depends on coal as its primary energy source.

    (C) The growing use of alternative energy sources in non-OECD countries has displaced the consumption of coal.

    (D) The primary energy produced in OECD countries is petroleum.

    (E) The world's coal reserves are decreasing, resulting in a decline of coal consumption in OECD countries.

11. Which of the following statements about energy sources and pollution is best supported by the second graph?

    (A) Nuclear power does not create any pollution.

    (B) Natural gas is a safer form of renewable energy compared to coal.

    (C) Natural gas causes less pollution than either coal or nuclear power.

    (D) Nuclear power plants do not directly produce polluting carbon emissions.

    (E) Nuclear power is the safest energy source available.

12. Which of the following continents uses nuclear power for a greater percentage of its total power output than any other continent?

    (A) North America

    (B) South America

    (C) Europe

    (D) Asia

    (E) Africa

GO ON TO THE NEXT PAGE

United States Population Change (2010–2017)

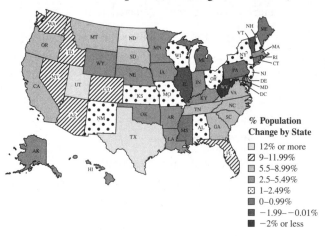

% Population
Change by State
□ 12% or more
▨ 9–11.99%
▢ 5.5–8.99%
▨ 2.5–5.49%
▨ 1–2.49%
■ 0–0.99%
■ −1.99–−0.01%
■ −2% or less

13. A retired couple moves from Chicago, Illinois to Lakeland, Florida. According to the map above, this is most likely an example of what geographic factor?

    (A) Economic pull factor

    (B) Economic push factor

    (C) Environmental pull factor

    (D) Political pull factor

    (E) Political push factor

14. A family plans to move from Los Angeles, California, to New Orleans, Louisiana, but stops and stays in Albuquerque, New Mexico, because of the positive amenities. This is an example of

    (A) distance decay

    (B) an environmental pull factor

    (C) an environmental push factor

    (D) intervening opportunity

    (E) intervening obstacle

15. During the process of acculturation, how many generations, on average, does it take for an immigrant family to lose its primary language?

    (A) One generation

    (B) Two generations

    (C) Three generations

    (D) Four generations

    (E) They never lose their primary language.

16. Which of the following theories, pictured above, suggests that whoever owns the Eastern European region could control the world based on the agricultural and industrial production of the region?

    (A) Rimland theory

    (B) Heartland theory

    (C) Domino theory

    (D) Transnational theory

    (E) Organic theory

17. The delivery area of the *Pittsburgh Post-Gazette* is an example of

    (A) a functional region

    (B) a formal region

    (C) a vernacular region

    (D) a statistical region

    (E) an urban region

GO ON TO THE NEXT PAGE

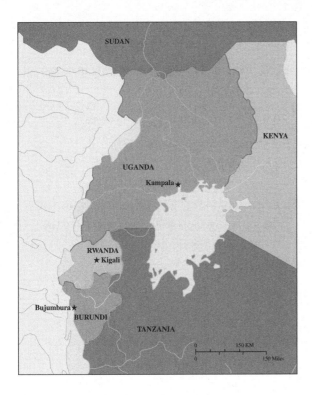

Country	City	Population (millions)
Colombia	Bogotá	7.2
	Medellín	2.5
Denmark	Copenhagen	0.60
	Aarhus	0.34
Germany	Berlin	3.6
	Frankfurt	0.74
Italy	Rome	2.9
	Venice	0.26
United Kingdom	London	8.1
	Birmingham	1.1

Cities listed are the two largest cities in that country.

18. The conflict in Rwanda and Uganda in the mid-1990s is an example of

(A) a religious conflict

(B) an ethnic conflict

(C) a transnational conflict

(D) an ethnic enclave conflict

(E) a border conflict

19. Based on the information in the table above, which of the following cities is a primate city in its country?

(A) London, United Kingdom

(B) Venice, Italy

(C) Frankfurt, Germany

(D) Aarhus, Denmark

(E) Medellín, Colombia

20. Which of the following countries would be considered an enclave?

(A) United States

(B) Indonesia

(C) Lesotho

(D) Egypt

(E) Morocco

GO ON TO THE NEXT PAGE

21. Prior to the First Agricultural Revolution, how did humans primarily obtain food?

    (A) Fishing

    (B) Planting crops

    (C) Hunting and gathering

    (D) Genetically engineering food for mass production

    (E) Purchasing crops in small, food-specific establishments

Wheat Harvested (1919–1929)

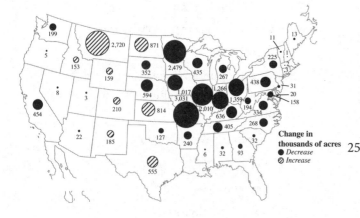

22. Farming in the United States is in a transition period best characterized by

    (A) the increase in farms located in the Midwest

    (B) the movement toward industrial farming

    (C) the movement from hunting and gathering to planting and sustaining

    (D) the movement of population to rural areas

    (E) the use of less genetic engineering to modify plants and animals

23. The Second Agricultural Revolution coincided with

    (A) increased genetic engineering of crops

    (B) the Industrial Revolution

    (C) the transition to planting crops

    (D) the Green Revolution

    (E) the Enlightenment in Europe

24. In terms of today's global economy, which of the following areas would be considered the resource frontier of the world?

    (A) East Asia

    (B) The Middle East

    (C) Sub-Saharan Africa

    (D) Central and Western Europe

    (E) Eastern South America

25. Which of the following areas of the world is currently experiencing the most rapid population growth?

    (A) North America

    (B) Western Europe

    (C) Sub-Saharan Africa

    (D) South Asia

    (E) South America

GO ON TO THE NEXT PAGE

26. A lack of economic development in developing regions of the world is predominantly attributed to a lack of

    (A) infrastructure

    (B) physical features, such as rivers

    (C) labor availability

    (D) foreign investment

    (E) modern technology

Settlement of the Mississippi River Basin

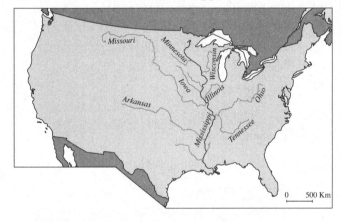

27. According to the map above, the Mississippi River is a prime example of which of the following types of political boundaries?

    (A) Relic

    (B) Subsequent

    (C) Antecedent

    (D) Geometric

    (E) Superimposed

Questions 28–29 refer to the map below.

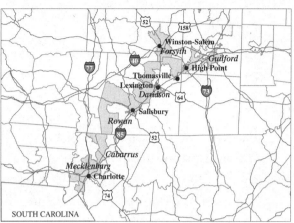

28. Which of the following political tactics was allegedly used when the boundaries of North Carolina's Twelfth Congressional District were drawn?

    (A) Gerrymandering

    (B) Reapportionment

    (C) Sundown towns

    (D) Blockbusting

    (E) Redlining

29. Which of the following describes the spread of religion as a result of Bhutanese refugees migrating to North Carolina?

    (A) Expansion diffusion

    (B) Stimulus diffusion

    (C) Sun Belt migration

    (D) Relocation diffusion

    (E) Distribution

GO ON TO THE NEXT PAGE

30. What is the primary type of farming used in the rain forests of Brazil?

    (A) Commercial agriculture

    (B) Slash-and-burn agriculture

    (C) Intensive subsistence agriculture

    (D) Truck farming

    (E) Irrigated fruit farming

31. Which of the following most accurately describes typical Southeast Asian cities?

    (A) Cities are laid out like the hub and spoke of a bicycle wheel, with all roads leading to the center of the city.

    (B) High-income residences that extend out from the central business district are gated communities.

    (C) Growth extends outward from the port, and commercial zones are near ports.

    (D) Cities include three central business districts with ethnic neighborhoods extending outward from them.

    (E) Bazaars and markets play significant roles in propelling the economy in cities.

32. Sub-Saharan agricultural regions, as depicted in dark gray on the map, are primarily adversely affected by which of the following environmental factors?

    (A) Climate change

    (B) Desertification

    (C) El Niño

    (D) Increased earthquake activity

    (E) Transhumance

GO ON TO THE NEXT PAGE

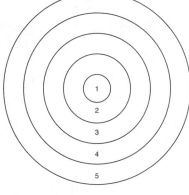

Questions 33–35 refer to the images below.

1 – Central business district
2 – Zone of transition
3 – Zone of independent workers' homes
4 – Zone of better residences
5 – Commuter's zone

1 – Central business district
2 – Transportation and industry
3 – Low-class residential
4 – Middle-class residential
5 – High-class residential

33. Which of the following example best fits the city structure depicted in the first image?

(A) Commuting to work from the suburbs in Atlanta

(B) Living on campus at a local university in Texas

(C) Living and working within an edge city in New York

(D) Migrating from New York to Los Angeles

(E) Living and working in the downtown area of Tampa

34. Which of the following is the city model depicted in the second image?

(A) Galactic city model

(B) Multiple nuclei model

(C) Gravity model

(D) Concentric zone model

(E) Sector model

35. Which of the following models suggests that in an urban setting, the farther a neighborhood is from the central business district, the greater its wealth is?

(A) Sector model

(B) Keno-capitalism model

(C) Multiple nuclei model

(D) Concentric zone model

(E) Urban periphery model

GO ON TO THE NEXT PAGE

36. Languages that are in danger of extinction are typically used in isolated regions around the world. Which of the following regions has the fewest languages that are under threat of extinction?

    (A) Europe

    (B) The Americas

    (C) The Pacific islands

    (D) Asia

    (E) Sub-Saharan Africa

37. What is the primary form of agriculture found in desert regions, such as the Gobi Desert regions of Mongolia?

    (A) Truck farming

    (B) Slash-and-burn farming

    (C) Plantation agriculture

    (D) Commercial agriculture

    (E) Pastoral nomadism

38. Central Park in New York City is a public recreation space that hosts outdoor events. This is a good example of which of the following features?

    (A) A central business district

    (B) A greenbelt

    (C) A festival landscape

    (D) Urban development

    (E) An ethnic landscape

39. The prevalence of corn production in the United States correlates with which of the following practices that is normally classified as an extensive agricultural activity?

    (A) Cattle production

    (B) Irrigated farmland

    (C) Dairying

    (D) Market-gardening activities

    (E) Pastoral nomadism

Questions 40–41 refer to the map below.

World Religions*

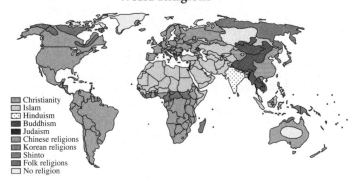

Christianity
Islam
Hinduism
Buddhism
Judaism
Chinese religions
Korean religions
Shinto
Folk religions
No religion

*Self-identified by majority of population

40. According to the map, which of the following is the universalizing religion that is most prevalent in the world today?

    (A) Christianity

    (B) Islam

    (C) Buddhism

    (D) Judaism

    (E) Hinduism

41. Based on the map and your knowledge of human geography, which of following represents the world's fastest-growing religion?

    (A) Shintoism

    (B) Islam

    (C) Judaism

    (D) Folk religions

    (E) Hinduism

GO ON TO THE NEXT PAGE

42. Which religions are most prominent today in the regions that were the hearths of the world's five major religions?

    (A) Christianity and Buddhism

    (B) Christianity and Hinduism

    (C) Buddhism and Islam

    (D) Hinduism and Islam

    (E) Hinduism and Buddhism

43. The 38th parallel was created to form the border between North and South Korea after World War II. This line is an example of a(n)

    (A) relic boundary

    (B) antecedent boundary

    (C) superimposed boundary

    (D) maritime boundary

    (E) subsequent boundary

Questions 44–45 refer to the chart below.

Projected Population of Japan, 2050

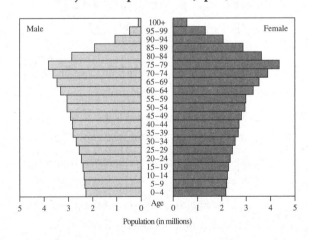

44. Based on the population pyramid, the population of Japan in 2050 is projected to have a large percentage of which of the following groups?

    (A) Immigrants

    (B) Parents

    (C) Youth

    (D) Women

    (E) Elderly people

45. An increase in which of the following would most likely broaden the base of the population pyramid?

    (A) Birth rate

    (B) Literacy rate

    (C) Per capita gross domestic product

    (D) Immigration rate

    (E) Life expectancy

46. A television personality starts a fad of wearing shorts with a shirt and tie. The trend gradually spreads throughout the United States. This is an example of which of the following types of diffusion?

    (A) Acculturation

    (B) Contagious

    (C) Stimulus

    (D) Relocation

    (E) Hierarchical

47. Which of the following religions is a monotheistic religion?

    (A) Hinduism

    (B) Shintoism

    (C) Animism

    (D) Judaism

    (E) Buddhism

GO ON TO THE NEXT PAGE

48. Which of the following cities would be classified by Saskia Sassen as a global city?

    (A) Prague

    (B) Madrid

    (C) London

    (D) Los Angeles

    (E) Buenos Aires

49. A city is located on a river that is prone to flooding yet provides trade advantages that bring measurable wealth to the city. Based on this information, which of the following statements would best fit that city?

    (A) The city has a good site yet a poor situation.

    (B) The city has a good situation yet a poor site.

    (C) The city has a good situation and a good site.

    (D) The city has flood disadvantages that outweigh the trade advantages.

    (E) The city has trade advantages that outweigh the flood disadvantages

50. According to the Latin American city model, Latin American cities are typically centered around which of the following?

    (A) Industrial district

    (B) Market district

    (C) Squatter settlements

    (D) Zone of maturity

    (E) Elite residential sector

Questions 51–52 refer to the image below.

The von Thünen Model of Agricultural Land Use

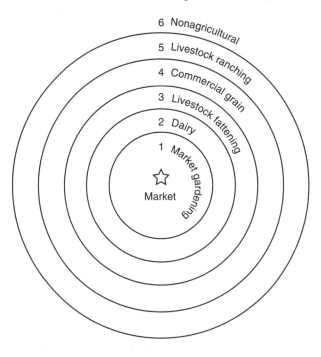

51. Which of the following is presupposed in von Thünen's model of agricultural land use?

    (A) The farmers sell all of their farm production to a market.

    (B) The higher-end commodities are located farther from the market.

    (C) The lighter commodities are closer to the market to ensure profitability.

    (D) The heavier commodities are around the market because they need irrigation.

    (E) The market is based on subsistence farming practices in less developed countries.

GO ON TO THE NEXT PAGE

52. Which of the following best explains an aspect of von Thünen's model of agricultural land use?

    (A) The cost of transportation from livestock fattening is more than the cost of livestock ranching.

    (B) While the cost of transporting vegetables is low, they belong in the first zone because the cost of spoilage is very high.

    (C) Although dairy byproducts do not spoil easily, the dairy industry is close to the market because milk does spoil easily.

    (D) Livestock ranching is a higher zone because the animals weigh much less compared to those raised by livestock fattening.

    (E) Because the cost to produce and transport grain is low, commercial grain farming can be far from the market.

53. Which of the following distinguishes Islamic cities from other city models?

    (A) The role religion plays in city infrastructure

    (B) The way the city layout features bazaars

    (C) The proliferation of squatter areas

    (D) The existence of multiple central business districts

    (E) The lack of population growth

54. Which of the following types of industries best applies to the production of potato chips?

    (A) Variable-cost industry

    (B) Fixed-cost industry

    (C) Weight-gaining industry

    (D) Weight-reducing industry

    (E) Market-dependent industry

55. Which is the world's primary lingua franca language?

    (A) Mandarin Chinese

    (B) Russian

    (C) English

    (D) Spanish

    (E) Hindi

56. Which of the following accurately identifies the urban hierarchy of settlements from least populous to most populous?

    (A) Hamlet, village, town, city, metropolis

    (B) Hamlet, town, city, megalopolis, metropolis

    (C) Megalopolis, metropolis, village, town, hamlet

    (D) Village, town, hamlet, metropolis, megalopolis

    (E) Town, hamlet, village, metropolis, megalopolis

57. Los Angeles receives goods from Asia via ships. In the ports, the goods are put on trains for distribution around the United States. Which of the following terms best describes Los Angeles in this scenario?

    (A) Break-of-bulk point

    (B) Variable-cost provider

    (C) Fixed-cost provider

    (D) Basic industry site

    (E) Trade alternative partner

GO ON TO THE NEXT PAGE

Questions 58–60 refer to the map below.

Agricultural Hearths and Crops

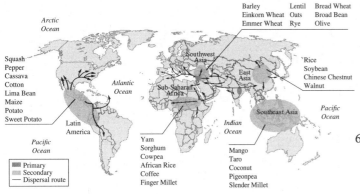

58. Which of the following world regions did not serve a historic role in the spread of agriculture as shown in the map?

    (A) Southeast Asia

    (B) Peruvian Highlands

    (C) Indus River Valley

    (D) Latin America

    (E) Europe

59. The hybridization and spread of which of the following crops most significantly increased crop production in Asia in the twentieth century?

    (A) Corn

    (B) Rice

    (C) Potatoes

    (D) Sorghum

    (E) Barley

60. Which of the following types of agriculture is practiced by the greatest number of people in the world today?

    (A) Subsistence agriculture

    (B) Highly mechanized commercial farming

    (C) Pastoral nomadism

    (D) Shifting cultivation

    (E) Slash-and-burn agriculture

END OF SECTION I

**IF YOU FINISH BEFORE TIME IS CALLED,
YOU MAY CHECK YOUR WORK ON SECTION I ONLY.
DO NOT GO ON TO SECTION II UNTIL INSTRUCTED TO DO SO.**

SECTION II

Time—75 Minutes

3 Questions

You have 75 minutes to answer ALL THREE of the following questions. You should devote about 25 minutes to each question, including 5 minutes to plan each answer. While a formal essay is not required, it is not enough to answer a question by simply listing facts. Be sure that you number your answers, including each individual part.

1. Models created to help explain urban settlement patterns in the United States include the concentric zone model, the sector model, the multiple nuclei model, and the galactic city model.

   (A) Describe the features that characterize urban central business districts.

   (B) Describe the difference between city growth in relation to the central business district in the concentric zone model and in the multiple nuclei model.

   (C) Describe a demographic similarity between populations living in close proximity to central business districts in U.S. cities and those living near such districts in European cities.

   (D) Describe a socioeconomic difference between populations living in close proximity to central business districts in U.S. cities and those living near such districts in European cities.

   (E) Explain the extent to which the concentric zone model reflects the socioeconomic characteristics of populations living in close proximity to central business districts identified in Part D.

   (F) Describe a current issue of urban development in U.S. or European cities.

   (G) Explain a possible solution to a current issue of urban development in U.S. or European cities.

GO ON TO THE NEXT PAGE

Country	2018 Median Age in Years	Country	2018 Median Age in Years
Niger	15.4	Colombia	30
Mali	15.8	Vietnam	30.5
Kenya	19.7	Costa Rica	31.3
Swaziland	21.7	Argentina	31.7
Guatemala	22.1	Brazil	32
Laos	23	Chile	34.4
Egypt	23.9	Uruguay	35
Botswana	24.5	China	37.4
Cambodia	25.3	United States	38.1
Guyana	26.2	United Kingdom	40.5
Bangladesh	26.7	France	41.4
South Africa	27.1	Canada	42.2
Bhutan	27.6	Netherlands	42.6
India	27.9	Spain	42.7
Venezuela	28.3	Austria	44
Mexico	28.3	Italy	45.5
Malaysia	28.5	Germany	47.1

2. Demographic trends, such as the median age of a population increasing or decreasing over time, have both socioeconomic and demographic impacts.

(A) Identify a trend in the data in the table for less developed countries.

(B) Compare the trends in the data in the table for more developed and less developed countries.

(C) Describe the shapes of the population pyramids of Germany and Mali, based on the data in the table.

(D) Explain a factor that impacts birth rates in more developed countries.

(E) Explain a factor that impacts birth rates in less developed countries.

(F) Explain an impact of the demographic trends occurring within more developed countries.

(G) Explain an impact of the demographic trends occurring within less developed countries.

GO ON TO THE NEXT PAGE

Member States Added to the United Nations in the 1960s

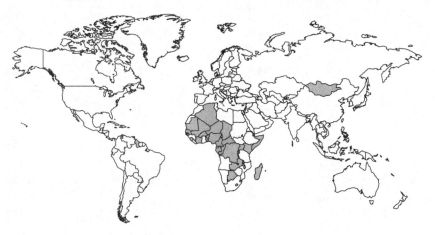

Member States Added to the United Nations in the 1990s

Andorra (93)	Armenia (92)	Azerbaijan (92)	Bosnia & Herz. (92)
Croatia (92)	S. Korea (91)	Eritrea (93)	Estonia (91)
Georgia (92)	Kazakhstan (92)	Kiribati (99)	Kyrgyzstan (92)
Latvia (91)	Liechtenstein (90)	Lithuania (91)	Macedonia (93)
Micronesia (91)	Moldova (92)	Monaco (93)	Marshall Isl. (91)
Nauru (99)	Palau (94)	N. Korea (91)	Namibia (90)
Slovakia (93)	Slovenia (92)	Tajikistan (92)	San Marino (92)
Tonga (99)	Turkmenistan (92)	Uzbekistan (92)	

3. A state can be added to the United Nations if it is considered sovereign, accepts the United Nations' Charter, and is approved by the Security Council and General Assembly.

   (A) Identify a state that was added to the United Nations in the 1960s.

   (B) Explain how a geopolitical circumstance led to states being created or added to the United Nations during the 1960s.

   (C) Identify a world region from which states were added to the United Nations in the 1990s.

   (D) Explain how a geopolitical circumstance led to states being created or added to the United Nations during the 1990s.

   (E) Describe an example of a historic political boundary that followed cultural or national divisions.

   (F) Describe an example of a historic political boundary that was imposed without regard to cultural unity or divisions.

   (G) Explain a possible economic or cultural impact of political boundaries.

END OF SECTION II

ANSWER KEY

Section I

1. E	13. C	25. C	37. E	49. B
2. A	14. D	26. D	38. C	50. B
3. D	15. C	27. C	39. A	51. A
4. C	16. B	28. A	40. A	52. C
5. D	17. A	29. D	41. B	53. A
6. E	18. B	30. B	42. D	54. D
7. B	19. A	31. C	43. C	55. C
8. B	20. C	32. B	44. E	56. A
9. E	21. C	33. A	45. A	57. A
10. B	22. B	34. E	46. E	58. E
11. D	23. B	35. D	47. D	59. B
12. C	24. B	36. A	48. C	60. A

Section II

See Answers and Explanations and self-score your responses.

Section I Number Correct: _____

Section II Points Earned: _____

Sign into your online account at kaptest.com and enter your results in the scoring section to see your 1–5 score.

Haven't registered your book yet? Go to kaptest.com/moreonline to begin.

ANSWERS AND EXPLANATIONS

Section I

1.   E

The main difference between Malthus's theory and Boserup's theory is that Malthus predicted a time when population growth will outpace the production of food (the Malthusian catastrophe, shown above). Unlike Malthus, Boserup predicted that as the human population increased, so would food production because humans would find new ways to increase production. Therefore, **(E)** is correct. (A) is incorrect because Malthus said that food production is greater than the population's demand for food prior to the Malthusian catastrophe. (B) is incorrect because the rate of population growth is lower than the rate of food production at the beginning of the graph, or early in time. Both Malthus's theory and Boserup's theory show that population growth is exponential, so this is not a difference, making (C) incorrect. Finally, (D) is incorrect because Boserup's theory does not show an exponential increase in food production (which would make it look like the curve for population growth), but instead, a series of linear increases with differing slopes.

2.   A

Thomas Malthus coined the term "overpopulation," which originally meant that the human population was growing exponentially while agricultural production was only growing linearly. The larger the gap between population growth and food production, the greater the possibility of starvation. Therefore, **(A)** is correct. Negative population growth would mean that there were fewer people each year who needed to be fed, leading to a decreasing risk of starvation within the population; (B) is incorrect. Static population growth would likewise decrease the risk of starvation, as the number of people would remain the same while agricultural production continued to increase. Thus, (C) is incorrect. Both proportional and linear population growth would mean that linear agricultural production kept pace with population growth, so (D) and (E) are incorrect.

3.   D

Thomas Malthus was concerned that because agricultural activity was only growing linearly while the population was growing exponentially, the world was heading for a starvation pandemic. However, Malthus failed to predict that inventions would mechanize farming, dramatically increasing the production and distribution of agricultural products. Thus **(D)** is correct. The First Agricultural Revolution was the shift from hunting and gathering practices to planting crops for food; this occurred long before Malthus's work on population growth, making (A) incorrect. Pastoral nomadism usually occurs in arid climates when animals are moved to areas that have the necessary resources to meet the needs of the herd. This does not impact the relationship between agricultural production and population growth on a large scale, so (A) is incorrect. Plant domestication occurs when wild plants are cultivated into productive crops that typically have more desirable traits for agriculture. As this was a primary aspect of the First Agricultural Revolution, which proceeded Malthus's theory, (C) is incorrect. The Fourth Agricultural Revolution involves local food movements in which food is both grown and sold locally; also, fertilizers and pesticides are minimized or eliminated in favor of organic farming. This movement has been partially in response to the many innovations of the Green Revolution, but it has not affected food production on a large scale. Thus (E) is incorrect.

4.   C

Alfred Weber's least cost theory is about the ideal location for a factory. It states that a factory will be located wherever the cost of raw materials and transportation will be the lowest. Therefore, **(C)** is correct. Labor is considered while calculating transportation expense, but it is not the primary cost, so (A) is incorrect. Infrastructure can affect transportation cost; for example, whether a railroad exists in an area would affect the cost of transporting raw materials and finished products. However, infrastructure is not itself the primary cost, so (B) is incorrect. Government taxes and land costs would affect the price of the factory's product, but these would not be considered primary costs, so (D) and (E) are incorrect.

5.   D

Shanghai, Hong Kong, and many other large Chinese cities possess special economic zones (SEZs), where foreign companies can establish bases of operations. SEZs have different business and trade laws from the rest of China. These special laws encourage foreign investment. The result is a greater tax base and increased employment through the creation of office parks and production centers for both exporting goods and internal Chinese consumption. Thus, **(D)** is correct. None of the other countries listed have created SEZs, so (A), (B), (C), and (E) are incorrect.

6. E

A nation-state is traditionally defined as an entity where the entire population of the country is the same ethnicity, practice the same religion, and speak the same language. Unlike many countries that have one or more minority groups that encompass at least a small segment of their total population, Denmark does not. Thus, Denmark is a close example of a nation-state, making **(E)** correct. A city-state is a small sovereign state that is made up of a town or city and the surrounding area. Since Denmark is a much larger area, (A) is incorrect. Although Denmark is not known for its size, it is by no means a microstate, such as tiny states like Monaco and Vatican City, making (B) incorrect. A stateless nation is a nation of people without a state that they consider home. Since Denmark is a country, it cannot be a nation of people without a state, making (C) incorrect. A political boundary is an invisible line that marks the outer limits of a state's territory and does not describe Denmark, making (D) incorrect.

7. B

As countries enter stage 3, characterized by moderate economic growth, many people decide to reduce the size of their families. This is normally due to factors such as improved economic conditions and increased access to healthcare. Thus, **(B)** is correct and (A) is incorrect. In stage 4, the birth and death rates are nearly equal, stabilizing the population, so (C) is incorrect. Fertility rates typically do not fall below two children per family until late in stage 4, making (D) incorrect. (E) is incorrect because the introduction of medicine normally occurs in stage 2.

8. B

The demographic transition model explains both population growth and economic development within a society. Exponential growth rates are found in stage 2 of the model: the agricultural stage. Therefore, **(B)** is correct. The death rate decreases sharply in stage 2 because of the availability of more reliable food sources as well as the improved availability and quality of healthcare; these changes lead to rapid population growth. This is a marked departure from stage 1, making (A) incorrect. Multiple children are seen as a liability in stages 3 and 4, so neither is characterized by high population growth; (C) and (D) are incorrect. Stage 5 is a hypothetical stage wherein low birth and death rates lead to a drawn-out population decrease. Modern-day Japan has been suggested as an example of stage 5. Thus, (E) is incorrect.

9. E

Redlining is the refusal to give reasonably priced mortgage loans to people living in certain areas of a city. Historically, banks and other financial institutions used redlining ostensibly to protect themselves from high default rates on loans in certain areas, but this practice had an adverse impact on minority communities. Today, lenders can legally use redlining to protect themselves from a high risk to the property from natural disaster, such as a flood or earthquake. In either case, the end result is an area where few people can get a loan to purchase a residential property; those who can get a loan pay higher rates of interest than they would in other areas. This situation describes 1930s Baltimore, so **(E)** is correct. While redlining is often associated with discriminatory lending practices toward nonwhite populations in U.S. cities, the definition of *redlining* does not include a motive of racial bias. To protect against racial discrimination, modern banks are encouraged to use a person's lending history, rather than geographic area, in their decisions to grant mortgages and other loans. Blockbusting and white flight both deal with white property owners selling their real estate to avoid association with nonwhites; refusal of loans to those property owners is not a factor. Thus, (A) and (B) are incorrect. While restrictive mortgage-lending practices may be used as tools in segregation and ghettoization, these terms do not fit with the specific situation described in the question stem; (C) and (D) are incorrect.

10. B

The first graph shows an increasing total consumption of coal from 1980 to 2005 and projected increases through 2030. Because coal is widely available in many developing countries, and is relatively inexpensive, it remains a competitive energy source for consumption. Therefore, **(B)** is correct. Although the graph shows that non-OECD countries are increasingly consuming coal, this is not in lieu of other energy resources. Instead, it makes up a larger portion of the energy portfolio; thus (A) is incorrect. While many countries are decreasing the use of fossil fuels by using alternative energy sources, the graph shows that this trend is more likely true of OECD countries than non-OECD countries, making (C) incorrect. The type of energy produced in OECD countries, being different than coal sourced energy, does not explain the total increasing consumption of coal. Further, several member countries of the OECD do not produce petroleum. (D) is incorrect. Though fossil fuels are nonrenewable resources, the world's coal reserves remain high. Also, the first graph does not show a decline in OECD countries' consumption of coal, making (E) incorrect.

11. D

One of the primary benefits to nuclear power is that, unlike the use of fossil fuels, nuclear power plants do not directly create harmful carbon emissions. The graph supports this by showing the rise of carbon emission pollution due to the use of coal or natural gas in lieu of current nuclear power plants. **(D)** is correct. Although nuclear power plants do not emit carbon gases, nuclear power does create pollution through nuclear waste and the energy it takes to produce nuclear power. Thus, (A) is incorrect. While natural gas does not produce as many carbon emissions as coal, neither is a renewable energy source, so (B) is incorrect. (C) is incorrect because, even though natural gas produces less carbon emissions than coal, it causes more pollution than nuclear power. Natural gas also causes approximately 40 times more deaths per unit of electric energy produced. Although nuclear power plants create less deadly air pollution in carbon emissions, compared to coal and natural gas, it can be a dangerous form of energy production. Further, renewable energy sources, such as solar and wind, are the safest energy sources; therefore, (E) is incorrect.

12. C

Over the past few decades, Europe has increased the amount of nuclear energy that it uses. France, for example, receives over 70 percent of its total energy from nuclear power, and Belgium and Hungary get more than half of their energy from nuclear power. **(C)** is correct. Nuclear power remains a small percentage of North America's total power output; (A) is incorrect. In South America and Africa, nuclear energy is nearly nonexistent, making (B) and (E) incorrect. In China and South Korea, the use of

nuclear energy is increasing, but nuclear power comprises a small percentage of total power output in Asia; thus, (D) is also incorrect.

13. C

When retirees move, the relocation is usually voluntary and is often influenced by environmental factors, such as being drawn to a warm climate. This accurately describes a move from Illinois to Florida, so **(C)** is correct. Economic pull factors involve better jobs and higher wages, which would be non-factors for the retired. Economic push factors are related to scarcity of jobs and low wages, which again do not generally affect the retired. Thus, (A) and (B) are incorrect. Examples of political push factors are governmental instability and war. Political pull factors include freedom from persecution and greater safety. These are unlikely reasons for a retired couple to move from one state to another. Thus, (D) and (E) are incorrect.

14. D

An intervening opportunity is a positive experience along the migration route that induces a person to stop migrating and reside somewhere along the way instead; this matches **(D)** and eliminates (E). (A) is incorrect; distance decay describes the decrease in influence of a person's native culture as he or she assimilates into a new culture. The family's decision to halt their migration and stay in the Albuquerque area is due to positive amenities rather than environmental factors, eliminating (B) and (C).

15. C

The process of acculturation usually takes three generations to complete; **(C)** is correct, and (A), (B), (D), and (E) are incorrect. The first generation to arrive in the new country speaks very little of the new language. The second generation is usually bilingual, speaking the new language at school and at work while speaking the original language at home. The third generation speaks very little of the original language and uses the new language in most situations.

16. B

The heartland theory, established by Halford Mackinder, suggests that whoever controls the Eastern European region will have the necessary food production and natural resources to rule the world; **(B)** is correct. The rimland theory, developed by Nicholas Spykman in reaction to the heartland theory, suggests that sea power is more important than the land power of the heartland, eliminating (A). (C) is incorrect because the domino theory suggests that when one country falls, others around it will experience the same political instability. The transnational theory argues that there is a direct linkage among nations and states that facilitates the sharing of information, eliminating (D). With his organic theory, Friedrich Ratzel argued that the state was like a living entity that constantly needed to grow in order to thrive; (E) is incorrect.

17. A

Functional regions revolve around a node. Newspaper delivery is an example of a functional region because the delivery areas revolve around the newspaper production facility; **(A)** is correct. A formal region has defining characteristics, such as state or country borders, eliminating (B). A vernacular region exists primarily in an individual's perception or feelings, making (C) incorrect. (D) and (E) are incorrect because statistical and urban regions do not describe the transitory nature of newspaper delivery.

18. B

The conflict in Rwanda and Uganda is an example of an ethnic conflict. The Hutus and the Tutsis have been in conflict for decades. However, during the 1990s, hundreds of thousands of Hutus and Tutsis were killed in clashes based on ethnocentrism. In other words, each side felt that its ethnic group was superior to the other. Therefore, **(B)** is correct. This was not a religious conflict because it did not involve violence between members of different religious groups; rather, the conflict was between the peoples of two ethnic groups, making (A) incorrect. A transnational conflict is between two or more countries, but this conflict occurred within the countries, not between them; (C) is incorrect. (D) is incorrect because an ethnic enclave refers to a neighborhood or district that retains some cultural distinction from a larger neighboring area, but Rwanda and Uganda are two separate countries. The border was not in dispute between the authorities of the two countries, eliminating (E).

19. A

A primate city describes the largest city in a country when it has more than twice as many people as the second-largest city. Because London has more than double the population of the next largest city in the United Kingdom,

(A) is correct. (B), (C), (D), and (E) are incorrect because they are not the most populated cities in their respective countries, as is clear from the table.

20. C

An enclave is an area completely surrounded by another state. Lesotho is completely surrounded by the country of South Africa, so **(C)** is correct. Two other states are land-locked completely within another country: San Marino and Vatican City. While both of these small states are located within the borders of Italy, each has sovereign control over its foreign and internal affairs. The United States is not inside another country; (A) is incorrect. Indonesia is broken up into over 13,000 islands, so (B) is incorrect. Egypt borders several countries in northern Africa, and Morocco borders the ocean as well as other countries in the northwest corner of Africa, making (D) and (E) incorrect.

21. C

Prior to the First Agricultural Revolution, which involved the process of planting and sustaining crops over an extended period of time, humans hunted and gathered their food, which matches **(C)**. While fishing is included in hunting and gathering, this does not encompass all human methods for obtaining food prior to the First Agricultural Revolution, making (A) incorrect. (B) is incorrect because the First Agricultural Revolution marked the first time humans began planting crops. The genetic engineering of crops happened much later, in the Third Agricultural Revolution (also called the Green Revolution), making (D) incorrect. Humans did not purchase food until the Second Agricultural Revolution, which included access to market areas through better transportation; (E) is incorrect.

22. B

Farming in more developed countries, such as the United States, has seen an increase in use of mechanization and industrial methods over the past 100 years. This change has contributed to the movement of people away from rural areas and toward growing urban centers. Therefore, **(B)** is correct and (D) is incorrect. The map does not indicate an increase in farms located in the Midwest and, in fact, the decrease of wheat yields in those areas suggests that the opposite could be true; (A) is incorrect. The movement from hunting and gathering took place during the First Agricultural Revolution, also known as the Neolithic Revolution, not present day; (C) is incorrect. The map does not indicate anything about genetic engineering, so (E) is incorrect.

23. B

The Industrial Revolution coincided with the Second Agricultural Revolution; **(B)** is correct. The Industrial Revolution provided the technology and the mechanization for agricultural practices to become much more efficient. This also increased transportation efficiency, allowing agricultural products to be sent farther and faster than before and allowed farmers to till more land, increase profits, and produce crops for export to other countries. The Green Revolution introduced the genetic engineering of products significantly after the Second Agricultural Revolution, eliminating both (A) and (D). The First Agricultural Revolution, not the Second Agricultural Revolution, marked the transition from hunting and gathering to planting and sustaining, making (C) incorrect. (E) is incorrect because the Enlightenment in Europe occurred before the Second Agricultural Revolution. The Industrial Revolution, which coincided with the Second Agricultural Revolution, was a later consequence of the Enlightenment in Europe.

24. B

A resource frontier is an area that provides the majority of resources for an industrial core. A resource that today's global economy depends on is petroleum, and the area with the largest deposits of petroleum is the Middle East, making **(B)** correct. (A), (C), (D), and (E) are incorrect because these areas do not produce a resource that is as high-impact as petroleum. Other areas of the world depend on many different natural resources for their energy needs, but almost all of the more developed world, or the core countries, depends upon petroleum for its energy production.

25. C

The most rapid population growth is occurring in sub-Saharan Africa. This is evidenced by the high birth rates of countries such as Nigeria, Ethiopia, and Uganda. **(C)** is correct. There is only modest population growth in North America, making (A) incorrect. There is very little population growth in Western Europe; in fact, many countries in this area are experiencing a decline in population, making (B) incorrect. While the population of South Asia is very large, especially in India, Bangladesh, and Pakistan,

growth rates are lower than in sub-Saharan Africa, so (D) is incorrect. Growth rates have also declined in South America, making (E) incorrect.

26. D

Developing into a strong, self-sufficient economy requires foreign investment to begin the process; **(D)** is correct. A lack of foreign investment is the root cause of a lack of infrastructure and a lack of modern technology, making both (A) and (E) incorrect. Though physical features, such as rivers, can aid transportation and shipping, a region's physical features are not entirely responsible for a lack of economic development, so (B) is incorrect. Finally, many developing regions have a large labor force available for employment; however, there are often few opportunities for gainful employment, making (C) incorrect.

27. C

The Mississippi River system provides a good example of antecedent boundaries. The map depicts how regions of the United States were settled and politically divided into territories (and eventually states) based on the natural boundaries created by the Mississippi River basin. **(C)** is correct. A relic boundary is no longer used but can still be seen on the landscape, such as the Great Wall of China. Since the Mississippi River is not a relic, (A) is incorrect. Because the settlement of the territories along the Mississippi River basin was not due to cultural differences between populations, it is not an example of a subsequent boundary; (B) is incorrect. (D) is incorrect as the lines of latitude and longitude were not used to determine boundaries around the Mississippi River basin. Superimposed boundaries are political boundaries that ignore the existing cultural organization of people across the landscape. As with (B), culture was not a part of the Mississippi River basin boundaries, which were determined prior to cultural establishment, making (E) incorrect.

28. A

Gerrymandering is the establishment of congressional districts for political gain rather than for accurate representation of the population. The Twelfth Congressional District of North Carolina is a notable example, as is clear from its shape on the map; therefore **(A)** is correct. The terms in (B), (C), (D), and (E) do not primarily describe the situation depicted in the map. Reapportionment is the process by which representatives are allocated to accurately represent the population. Sundown towns were all-white areas that enforced racial segregation with laws prohibiting people of color from living in the town. Blockbusting is the process of invoking racial fear of incoming minority residents in white property owners to convince them to sell their homes at low prices. Finally, redlining is the process of directly or indirectly denying services (such as banking, insurance, and healthcare) to populations living in certain areas.

29. D

Relocation diffusion is the physical spread of cultures, ideas, and people. Because this has occurred upon the immigration of the Bhutanese people to North Carolina, **(D)** is correct. Expansion diffusion is the spread of a characteristic from a central point outward. As this is not characteristic of immigration, (A) is incorrect. (B) is incorrect because stimulus diffusion is a type of expansion diffusion. In particular, stimulus diffusion refers to a process in which ideas or trends spread to a new location and change in their new location or context. Sun Belt migration is the phenomenon of in-migration in the United States to southern areas. As this is a voluntary migration, (C) is incorrect. (E) is incorrect because distribution does not necessarily describe the spread of religion that can occur as a result of immigration; instead, it can mean the physical distribution of people or things.

30. B

Slash-and-burn farming is a traditional method of clearing the land and is used in subsistence agriculture in tropical regions of Brazil, making **(B)** correct. Commercial agriculture, wherein large amounts of crops are sold for profit, is the opposite of the type of subsistence farming that uses slash-and-burn practices, making (A) incorrect. Intensive subsistence agriculture, in which farmers maximize crop production in a small area, is associated with densely populated regions such as the Philippines, not Brazil; therefore, (C) is incorrect. Truck farming uses mechanization to produce large quantities of fruit, a practice which is not conducted in the tropical regions of Brazil, making (D) incorrect. Finally, large amounts of rainfall in tropical regions of Brazil render irrigated fruit farming, which utilizes outside water sources, unnecessary, making (E) incorrect.

31. C

The Southeast Asian city model, developed by Terry McGee, shows the importance of the port zone; growth extends outward from the port. The specific areas designated as commercial zones are usually located near the port to easily export their products, making **(C)** correct. (A), (B), (D), and (E) are incorrect because these describe other city models. (A) and (B) represent Latin American cities, while (D) and (E) are typical of African cities.

32. B

Sub-Saharan Africa is increasingly encroached upon by the Sahara Desert, making **(B)** correct. Desertification can be caused by a number of factors, including inefficient irrigation, an increasing population, and farmers who allow their animals to eat the vegetation at the edges of the desert, allowing the desert to expand into previously productive farmland. Though climate change is certainly a contributing factor, it is not the primary factor negatively impacting the sub-Saharan region, so (A) is incorrect. El Niño refers to a system of weather created by seasonally warm ocean waters and primarily affects regions surrounding the Pacific Ocean, making (C) incorrect. Increased earthquake activity does not impact the climate of sub-Saharan Africa, making (D) incorrect. Transhumance, the herding practice of moving livestock with the seasons, has a significantly lower impact on the environment than desertification; therefore, (E) is incorrect.

33. A

The sector model and the concentric zone model are based on the idea that many who can afford the daily commute will choose to live in the suburbs and travel to work in the central business district; **(A)** is correct. (B) and (C) are incorrect because these are associated with the multiple nuclei model, which suggests that development occurs within areas of need in a city independent of the central business district. For example, a local university campus typically has restaurants and bookstores built around it to accommodate students. The gravity model was created to anticipate migrations and the interactions between two cities; thus, migrating from New York to Los Angeles would represent the gravity model, not the sector model, making (D) incorrect. Living and working in the downtown area of Tampa only represents life within the central business district and does not serve as an example of the sector model; (E) is incorrect.

34. E

The second image depicts growth extending along transportation routes, which is the sector model; **(E)** is correct. (A), (B), (C), and (D) are incorrect because these models are not represented in the second image. The galactic city model represents a city with growth independent of the central business district, traditionally connected to the central city by means of an arterial highway or interstate. The multiple nuclei model, developed by Ullman and Harris, suggests that growth is independent of the central business district. The gravity model does not illustrate a city structure; instead, it explains the interactions between two cities. The first image, not the second one, represents the concentric zone model, which is composed of concentric rings separated by class.

35. D

The concentric zone model suggests that economic structure is dependent upon an area's distance from the central business district (CBD). Think of it as a bull's-eye with the CBD as the centermost circle. Moving outward, the order of the rings is as follows: the industrial zone, the working-class residences, the middle-class residences, and the commuter zone with high-end residences. The wealthy can afford the commute into the city on a daily basis and, therefore, can afford a large suburban home. Thus, **(D)** is correct. The models in (A), (B), (C), and (E) organize the CBD and residential areas differently, so they are incorrect. The sector model maintains the CBD nucleus but uses pie slices instead of circles, with the high-end residences located furthest from the industrial zone rather than the CBD. The Keno-capitalism model favors a chessboard-like patchwork of random zones. The multiple nuclei model suggests that growth is independent of the central business district. The urban periphery model reverses the concentric zone model. A core urban living area is ringed by suburbs. Business and industry exist on the outside, ringing both those zones, and everything is tied together by belts of roads.

36. A

Given the history of Europe as a crossroads between the East and West, as well as its early modern development, languages there have been well codified for many years. Therefore, Europe has the fewest languages under threat of extinction; **(A)** is correct. Languages that are in danger of going extinct are typically in isolated regions. In these locations, the populations are aging and shrinking. Young people often migrate to cities and tend not to maintain their language heritage. In the Americas, many American Indian languages are vanishing; (B) is incorrect. Locations in the Pacific, such as island nations in Polynesia and Melanesia, as well as in Asia and sub-Saharan Africa face similar problems of languages not being maintained, making (C), (D), and (E) incorrect.

37. E

Pastoral nomadism is a form of subsistence agriculture that is animal based. It involves moving herds to different pastures or tracts of land due to a lack of rainfall and vegetative growth. Pastoral nomadism is commonly found in desert areas, including the Gobi Desert in Mongolia. **(E)** is correct. Truck farming involves growing crops, usually on a large scale, and then transporting them to the market; this is not common in desert areas, so (A) is incorrect. Slash-and-burn farming is used to clear away the natural vegetation in order to plant crops and would not be used in a desert environment, making (B) incorrect. Both plantation and commercial agriculture depend on access to abundant fresh water or rainfall, making (C) and (D) incorrect.

38. C

A festival landscape is an area that is set aside for leisure activities. Many festivals, concerts, and holiday activities are held in these large open spaces. Parks are common types of festival landscapes, and Central Park in New York City is a prime example; **(C)** is correct. (A) is incorrect because a central business district is the primary location for businesses, such as retail shops, offices, and banks, which Central Park does not offer. (B) is incorrect because a greenbelt is an area that a city, state, or other government body sets aside for preservation purposes or to prevent urban sprawl; Central Park is not an example of a greenbelt since these areas are typically preserved in their natural states, and Central Park was heavily modified by its designers. Central Park is not considered an area of urban development or an ethnic landscape, so (D) and (E) are also incorrect.

39. A

Cattle production correlates with corn production in the United States because the majority of corn in the United States is used for cattle feed; **(A)** is correct. Whether a farmland is irrigated or not depends on the amount of available fresh water and rainfall; irrigation does not correlate with corn production, making (B) incorrect. Dairying and market gardening operate independently of U.S. corn production, making (C) and (D) incorrect. Pastoral nomadism is common in less fertile, arid areas of the world, making (E) incorrect.

40. A

With about 2.3 billion followers, the largest universalizing religion in the world today is Christianity. Therefore, **(A)** is correct. The second-largest religion in the world is (B), Islam, with about 1.8 billion followers. Hinduism, (E), has approximately 1.1 billion followers and is an ethnic religion confined primarily to India. Buddhism, (C), has around 500 million followers. At about 14 million followers, Judaism, (D), is by far the smallest of the world's five primary religions in terms of headcount.

41. B

The fastest-growing religion in the world is Islam. Much of this has to do with where the religion is spreading; northern Africa, the Middle East, and Southeast Asia, including Indonesia, are some of the fastest-growing areas in the world based on their population growth and other demographic characteristics. Islam is also a universalizing religion, meaning that followers try to convert people to their faith. Therefore, **(B)** is correct. (A), (C), (D), and (E) are incorrect because Shintoism, Judaism, folk religions, and Hinduism are ethnic religions, which are limited to a specific ethnic group or national scope.

42. D

The two main hearths of the five world religions are southwest Asia, including Saudi Arabia and Israel, and northern India. Today, these areas are dominated by Islam and Hinduism, respectively; **(D)** is correct. None of the other choices correctly identify the most prominent religions in both hearth regions. Christianity, Islam, and Judaism all began in southwest Asia, and Buddhism and Hinduism began in northern India.

43. C

A superimposed boundary is placed by outsiders on a landscape that has already been developed, and it often ignores the cultural landscape imprinted on the land. In the case of the 38th parallel boundary in Korea, outside governments negotiated the boundary, splitting up the Korean peninsula into two countries: North Korea and South Korea. Thus, **(C)** is correct. A relic boundary is a boundary that is nonfunctional but still in existence, which is not true of the 38th parallel, making (A) incorrect. (B) is incorrect because an antecedent boundary is one that exists in an area before human settlement. (D) is incorrect because a maritime boundary divides water surface area. The 38th parallel boundary creation was not primarily based on the cultural landscape, making (E) incorrect.

44. E

Population pyramids are demographic tools to determine the sex and age demographics of a specific population. The younger cohorts are at the bottom of the population pyramid, whereas the older cohorts are at the top. Therefore, if a population pyramid looks like an upside-down triangle, it has a high percentage of elderly people. An example of this would be many of the retirement communities in Florida and Arizona. **(E)** is correct. Population pyramids do not depict the number of immigrants within a country, making (A) incorrect. If (B), (C), or (D) represented a large percentage of the population, the pyramid would have a different shape. A high percentage of parents would cause the pyramid to bulge in the middle, a high percentage of youth would cause the pyramid to bulge at the bottom, and a high percentage of women would cause the pyramid to extend outward to the right, making these choices incorrect.

45. A

Broadening the base of the population pyramid would signal an increase in population growth. The number-one factor in determining a population's growth rate is its birth rate, which matches **(A)**. The birth rate is the number of births per 1,000 people, and the higher the birth rate, the greater the population growth. The literacy rate has an inverse correlation with population growth; demographic data shows that the higher the literacy rate, the lower the population growth rate, eliminating (B). Per capita gross domestic product is an economic indicator (generally the higher the wealth, the slower the population growth), making (C) incorrect. Immigration involves people of all ages, but most typically is undertaken by young adults, and so would not broaden the base of the pyramid, which represents children; (D) is incorrect. The countries with the highest life expectancies have some of the lowest birth rates and the lowest growth rates, eliminating (E).

46. E

Hierarchical diffusion occurs when an idea or some sort of information is spread by someone in a well-known group, usually the social elite. A fad, for example, may start due to the influence of a celebrity, sports star, or figure of authority. This reflects the situation described in the question stem, so **(E)** is correct. (A) is incorrect because acculturation is not a type of diffusion; instead, acculturation is the process of assimilation into a new culture. Contagious diffusion occurs when an idea rapidly spreads throughout society; an example is when an idea goes "viral" on social media. (B) is incorrect because the stem does not indicate this fad spread in this way. (C) is incorrect because stimulus diffusion occurs when an idea spreads to other places and gets incorporated into something new. Relocation diffusion occurs through the physical movement of people, such as when migrants introduce an element of their culture into a new society; (D) is also incorrect.

47. D

Monotheism is the belief that there is only one god. Of the choices provided, only Judaism is considered a monotheistic religion; other major monotheistic world religions are Christianity and Islam. **(D)** is correct. Hinduism, Shintoism, Animism, and Buddhism lack a singular deity that adherents believe in, making (A), (B), (C) and (E) incorrect.

48. C

According to Saskia Sassen, as of 2018, there are two major global cities: London and New York City. **(C)** is correct. Global cities, or world cities, are defined by their importance to the areas surrounding them. There are also alpha cities, beta cities, and gamma cities. Cities are placed in these categories based on name recognition, economic activity, and other criteria that make them more or less important. Prague is considered a gamma world city, Madrid is considered a beta world city, Los Angeles is defined as an alpha world city, and Buenos Aires is a primate city; because none of these are also classified as global cities, (A), (B), (D), and (E) are incorrect.

49. B

Site refers to the characteristics of a place's physical location, and situation refers to how easily connected the place is to other places around it. Because this city provides trade advantages that bring measurable wealth to the city, it has a good situation. However, because this city is located on a river prone to flooding, it has a poor site. Therefore, **(B)** is correct and (A) and (C) are incorrect. (D) and (E) are incorrect because there is no indication that certain advantages or disadvantages outweigh the other.

50. B

The Latin American city model, which was developed by Larry Ford, includes the market district and the central business district at the center; thus, **(B)** is correct. (A), (D), and (E) are incorrect because these areas extend outward from the market district or the central business district; the industrial district extends outward from the market district, the zone of maturity extends outward from both districts, and the elite residential sector surrounds the central business district, extending outward. (C) is incorrect because squatter settlements are the outermost areas of the model.

51. A

In commercial farming, all of a farm's agricultural products are sold at market. The productivity of the land (the farmer's net profit) can be calculated ahead of time with a formula that considers the potential yield of a given crop, the market price per unit of that commodity, and how expensive it is to ship the commodity to market. This calculation is known as von Thünen's model of agricultural land use. Therefore, **(A)** is correct. While it is true that higher-end commodities can be located farther from the market due to their higher price per unit when sold, it is not necessary according to von Thünen's model. Thus (B) is incorrect. Lighter commodities are less expensive to transport to market, so they do not need to be closer to the market to ensure profitability; (C) is incorrect. Heavier commodities may or may not require irrigation, depending on the crop in question, but von Thünen's model would primarily consider a commodity's weight when calculating transportation expense. Thus, (D) is incorrect. The von Thünen model of agricultural land use was developed in the preindustrial era. It does not consider the distinction between more and less developed countries, as those terms did not exist in that era, making (E) incorrect.

52. C

The cost of dairy is largely due to the high spoilage of milk that must be transported in refrigerated trucks. While cheese and other byproducts do not spoil as easily, the high costs of transporting milk itself requires dairy farming to be in the second zone of von Thünen's model;

thus **(C)** is correct. (A) is incorrect because livestock is not usually shipped on a daily basis. The cost is primarily due to the heavy weight of the animals. It is true that one of the reasons market-gardening activities, such as the production of vegetables, are costly is due to the possibility the food could spoil before getting to market. However, a more important factor is that the products are bulky and thus costly to transport, making (B) incorrect. Although the animals shipped from livestock-ranching pastures likely weigh less than those raised through livestock fattening, the reason livestock ranching is a higher zone is because of the large amount of land these farmers need. Livestock ranching uses more land per farm than any of the other models, which is more cost effective farther from the urban market, making (D) incorrect. (E) is incorrect because while the cost to transport grain is relatively low, compared to shipping the heavy produce associated with zone 1, the cost to produce the grain is relatively high. This is due in part to costly pieces of farm equipment.

53. A

What distinguishes Islamic cities from other cities is the religion itself. Much of the city layout is based on Islamic principles found in the Koran. The most important physical feature of an Islamic city is the mosque; **(A)** is correct. Bazaars are a feature of the African city model, not the Islamic city model, making (B) incorrect. Islamic cities are not the only city model with squatter settlements; the Latin American and Southeast Asian city models also have squatter areas, for example. Thus, (C) is incorrect. African cities, not Islamic cities, have multiple central business districts, eliminating (D). (E) is incorrect because many Islamic cities are rapidly gaining in population. For example, Cairo, Istanbul, and Jakarta are all among the most populous cities in the world.

54. D

The production of potato chips is an example of a weight-reducing industry, which matches **(D)**. The primary inputs in the production of potato chips are potatoes, salt, and oil, and the end product weighs less than the raw materials that were delivered to the production factory. (A) and (B) refer to the types of costs, not the types of industries; therefore, (A) and (B) are incorrect. If the end product weighs more than the raw materials, then its production is a weight-gaining industry, making (C) incorrect. All industries are market-dependent industries, eliminating (E).

55. C

A lingua franca is a language that is mutually understood by two people and is usually used in some type of business transaction. The world's largest lingua franca is English, which matches **(C)**. English is the global business language because of the dominance in economic activity of the United States and United Kingdom. Many people in other countries are trying to learn English to compete in a world economy. Mandarin Chinese is quickly becoming a lingua franca in parts of Southeast Asia, but this is not the world's primary lingua franca; (A) is incorrect. (B), (D), and (E) are incorrect because these languages are not considered a global business language.

56. A

The correct urban hierarchy, from smallest to largest population, is: hamlet, village, town, city, and then metropolis. **(A)** is correct. The rankings are based on the population of the urban area, as well as its importance to the surrounding area. Hamlets may include only a few dozen people and offer very limited services; villages are larger than hamlets and offer more services; towns may consist of 50 to a few thousand people; cities are large, densely populated areas with tens of thousands of people; metropolises have large populations, incorporate large areas, and are usually focused around one large city; and a megalopolis is the biggest urban area. (B), (C), (D), and (E) are incorrect because the settlements are not ordered from smallest to largest.

57. A

A break-of-bulk point is a location where goods are transferred from one mode of transportation to another mode of transportation, which matches **(A)**. (B) and (C) are incorrect because they refer to whether a provider's costs fluctuate based on the volume of an order; the scenario does not specify Los Angeles's costs. Basic industries are the focal point of the economy for a city, like steel was for Pittsburgh; this concept does not apply to the situation described, making (D) incorrect. To be a trade alternative partner, Los Angeles would need to produce goods for export; instead, Asia is producing the goods in this example, eliminating (E).

58. E

Europe did not have a significant agricultural hearth; instead, agriculture diffused into Europe from Southwest Asia. **(E)** is correct. Seed agricultural hearths included

East Asia, East Africa, the Indus River Valley in South Asia, Middle America, and the Peruvian Highlands. Vegetative planting hearths were located in South America, West Africa, Southeast Asia, and the Ganges River delta area. Therefore, (A), (B), (C), and (D) are incorrect.

59. B

As part of the Green Revolution, rice was first modified in the Philippines and then diffused to other areas of Asia. The hybridization and spread of rice has significantly increased crop production, feeding people in some of Asia's poorest regions; **(B)** is correct. While corn, potatoes, sorghum, and barley are genetically modified, the hybridization of these crops has not increased crop production in Asia as dramatically as rice, making (A), (C), (D), and (E) incorrect.

60. A

Most farmers in the world practice subsistence agriculture to meet the food needs of their families; **(A)** is correct. This type of farming is labor intensive and is the full-time occupation of many rural inhabitants of less developed countries. Highly mechanized commercial farming is practiced in more developed countries, such as the United States and many places within Europe, eliminating (B). Pastoral nomadism is primarily practiced in the drier regions of the world; (C) is incorrect. Shifting cultivation involves abandoning fields after several years in search of more productive soil after depleting the nutrients in the original field; this type of agriculture is practiced in the tropical forests of Southeast Asia, Central Africa, and the Amazon, eliminating (D). Slash-and-burn agriculture is a form of subsistence agriculture that is primarily practiced in tropical regions, making (E) incorrect.

Section II

1. A successful response to the free-response question accomplishes all tasks set forth by the prompt. Each part of the prompt is worth 1 point, for a total of 7 possible points.

(a) To earn the point, the response must describe two or more features that characterize a central business district (CBD). Examples include that they are commercial centers of cities, contain a concentration of shopping and other commercial activities, typically experience traffic congestion, contain historical districts, have an abundance of expensive real estate, and are structured around mass transit.

(b) To earn the point, the response must describe the difference in city growth in relation to the CBD by identifying the characteristics of city growth in both models. In the concentric zone model, the CBD is located in the center of the model and city growth extends in predictable, concentric rings of type of development outward from the center. In the multiple nuclei model, the CBD may still be centrally located, but growth occurs independent of the CBD wherever there is need or economic opportunity.

(c) To earn the point, the response must describe a demographic similarity in populations that live near the CBD in both U.S. and European cities. Examples of populations near the CBD in both locations include the elderly and young adults (ages 20 to 30).

(d) To earn the point, the response must describe a socioeconomic difference in populations that live near the CBD in U.S. and European cities by identifying a characteristic of both populations. Examples include that lower-income citizens tend to live near the CBD in the United States, that higher-income citizens are beginning to move to gentrified areas near CBDs in the United States, and that upper-class professionals and wealthy elderly live near CBDs in Europe.

(e) To earn the point, the response must use reasoning and/or examples to explain how much the characteristics of populations near the CBD described in Part D reflect the concentric zone model. The response should identify that in the model, the CBD is surrounded by the zone in transition, which typically includes residences of lower-income citizens intermixed with industrial zones. The response must relate this description to the characteristics identified. For example, the model reflects that lower-income residents often live near the CBD in

U.S. cities, but does not explain that wealthier residents are moving to gentrified areas of U.S. cities or that wealthier residents live near the CBDs of European cities.

(f) To earn the point, the response must use details to describe a current issue of urban development in U.S. or European cities. Examples include housing affordability, housing discrimination practices, lack of access to services, overcrowding, crime, environmental strains, zones of abandonment, adverse effects of gentrification, and obstacles to addressing issues due to shared responsibilities across different levels of government.

(g) To earn the point, the response must use reasoning and/or examples to explain how a solution could address a current issue of urban development. Examples include inclusionary zoning practices to address inequalities in housing, gentrification and revitalization movements to address zones of abandonment, local food movements to address environmental strains, and community programs and education reforms to address crime.

2. A successful response to the free-response question accomplishes all tasks set forth by the prompt. Each part of the prompt is worth 1 point, for a total of 7 possible points.

(a) To earn the point, the response must identify a trend demonstrated in the table for less developed countries, which include some of the countries listed from Africa, Asia, and Latin America. Examples of trends include the average median age of some less developed countries, such as Vietnam, and the relatively low median age of most less developed countries, such as Niger and Mali.

(b) To earn the point, the response must compare the trends for more developed and less developed countries. The response must address not just the trend for one group of countries, but must identify how the trends compare: the median age is higher for more developed countries and lower for less developed countries.

(c) To earn the point, the response must describe the shapes of *both* population pyramids. The pyramid for Germany, with a median age of 47.1, would be narrow at the bottom for the youngest age brackets and bulge toward the middle and top to represent the skewing toward older age brackets. The pyramid for Mali, with a median age of 15.8, would be wide at the bottom for the youngest age brackets and narrow at the middle and top for the older age brackets.

(d) To earn the point, the response must use evidence and/or reasoning to explain how a specific factor affects birth rates in more developed countries. Examples of factors that lead to lower birth rates include children being an economic liability in industrial and service-based economies, more women opting to delay or forgo childbirth since they have more economic opportunities outside the home, and increased access to birth control.

(e) To earn the point, the response must use evidence and/or reasoning to explain how a specific factor affects birth rates in less developed countries. Examples of factors that lead to higher birth rates include the increasing access to quality food and medicine in some farming-based societies; women having more total births despite high infant mortality rates; children being an economic asset in farming-based societies; children providing social security for elderly relatives; traditional cultures being more likely to favor large families and traditional roles for women; government policies and patriarchal values limiting women's opportunities outside the home; and demographic momentum.

(f) To earn the point, the response must use evidence and/or reasoning to explain how a demographic trend in more developed countries impacts such countries. Examples of impacts of a relatively high median age include a stagnant or even negative population growth, a dependency ratio skewed toward the elderly, a possible shortage of young adult workers, a possible shrinking workforce and resulting labor shortages, segments of the population migrating away due to decreasing economic opportunity, more retired workers straining social support systems, and a possible diversion of resources away from education.

(g) To earn the point, the response must use evidence and/or reasoning to explain how a demographic trend in less developed countries impacts such countries. Examples of impacts of a relatively low median age include a growing population, a dependency ratio skewed toward the young, a possible straining of countries' economic and environmental resources, a possible need to find ways to increase agricultural productivity or food imports to feed growing populations, a possible job shortage when young people enter the workforce, potential overcrowding in urban areas, and potential political conflict as groups compete over limited resources.

3. A successful response to the free-response question accomplishes all tasks set forth by the prompt. Each part of the prompt is worth 1 point, for a total of 7 possible points.

(a) To earn the point, the response must identify a state added to the United Nations in the 1960s. The states include Algeria, Barbados, Benin, Botswana, Burkina Faso, Burundi, Cameroon, Central African Republic, Chad, Côte d'Ivoire, Cyprus, Democratic Republic of the Congo, Gabon, Gambia, Guyana, Jamaica, Kenya, Kuwait, Lesotho, Madagascar, Malawi, Maldives, Mali, Malta, Mauritania, Mauritius, Mongolia, Niger, Nigeria, Republic of the Congo, Rwanda, Senegal, Sierra Leone, Singapore, Somalia, Swaziland, Togo, Trinidad & Tobago, Uganda, and Zambia.

(b) To earn the point, the response must identify a geopolitical circumstance of the 1960s and use reasoning and/or evidence to explain how it led to a new state being created or added to the United Nations. Examples include colonialism ending in Africa, the Caribbean (Barbados, Jamaica, and Trinidad & Tobago), and Mediterranean islands (Cyprus and Malta); Cold War tensions between the Soviet Union and China (impacting Mongolia, for example); and Singapore's establishment as an independent state from Malaysia.

(c) To earn the point, the response must identify a world region from which states were added to the United Nations in the 1990s. Examples include Africa, especially the sub-Saharan region; Central Asia, for example, Azerbaijan, Kazakhstan, Kyrgyzstan, Tajikistan, Turkmenistan, and Uzbekistan; Eastern Asia, for example, North Korea and South Korea; Eastern Europe, for example, Armenia, Bosnia and Herzegovina, and Croatia; European microstates, for example, Andorra, Liechtenstein, Monaco, and San Marino; and the Pacific islands, for example, Micronesia, Palau, and Tonga.

(d) To earn the point, the response must identify a geopolitical circumstance of the 1990s and use reasoning and/or evidence to explain how it led to a new state being created or added to the United Nations. Examples of geopolitical circumstances include social pressure from European states toward independence, the political breakup of the former Soviet Union, the balkanization of Yugoslavia, the Pacific islands breaking away from colonial powers, the United Nations' goal to include small states in the organization's membership, and the ultimately unsuccessful discussions in the early 1990s about the reunification of North and South Korea.

441 | **K**

(e) To earn the point, the response must identify a historic political boundary and use details to describe how it followed cultural or national divisions. Examples include Portuguese Brazil's historical separation from Spanish colonies in South America and the division between predominantly Islamic Pakistan and Hindu India.

(f) To earn the point, the response must identify a historic political boundary and use details to describe how it did not follow cultural or national divisions. Examples include the division of African colonies, without regard to local cultural or tribal divisions by European powers, in the Berlin Conference and the political boundary established between culturally similar populations of North and South Korea.

(g) To earn the point, the response must use reasoning and/or examples to explain how political boundaries can lead to an economic or a cultural impact. Examples include creating barriers between trade, which prompted the creation of the European Union and use of the euro; strengthening regional and local identities; creating cultural conflict such as seen during the displacement of families after the separation of India and Pakistan and in the violence between ethnic groups in Bosnia after the dissolution of Yugoslavia.

Practice Exam 2

Practice Exam 2 Answer Grid

1. (A)(B)(C)(D)(E)	16. (A)(B)(C)(D)(E)	31. (A)(B)(C)(D)(E)	46. (A)(B)(C)(D)(E)
2. (A)(B)(C)(D)(E)	17. (A)(B)(C)(D)(E)	32. (A)(B)(C)(D)(E)	47. (A)(B)(C)(D)(E)
3. (A)(B)(C)(D)(E)	18. (A)(B)(C)(D)(E)	33. (A)(B)(C)(D)(E)	48. (A)(B)(C)(D)(E)
4. (A)(B)(C)(D)(E)	19. (A)(B)(C)(D)(E)	34. (A)(B)(C)(D)(E)	49. (A)(B)(C)(D)(E)
5. (A)(B)(C)(D)(E)	20. (A)(B)(C)(D)(E)	35. (A)(B)(C)(D)(E)	50. (A)(B)(C)(D)(E)
6. (A)(B)(C)(D)(E)	21. (A)(B)(C)(D)(E)	36. (A)(B)(C)(D)(E)	51. (A)(B)(C)(D)(E)
7. (A)(B)(C)(D)(E)	22. (A)(B)(C)(D)(E)	37. (A)(B)(C)(D)(E)	52. (A)(B)(C)(D)(E)
8. (A)(B)(C)(D)(E)	23. (A)(B)(C)(D)(E)	38. (A)(B)(C)(D)(E)	53. (A)(B)(C)(D)(E)
9. (A)(B)(C)(D)(E)	24. (A)(B)(C)(D)(E)	39. (A)(B)(C)(D)(E)	54. (A)(B)(C)(D)(E)
10. (A)(B)(C)(D)(E)	25. (A)(B)(C)(D)(E)	40. (A)(B)(C)(D)(E)	55. (A)(B)(C)(D)(E)
11. (A)(B)(C)(D)(E)	26. (A)(B)(C)(D)(E)	41. (A)(B)(C)(D)(E)	56. (A)(B)(C)(D)(E)
12. (A)(B)(C)(D)(E)	27. (A)(B)(C)(D)(E)	42. (A)(B)(C)(D)(E)	57. (A)(B)(C)(D)(E)
13. (A)(B)(C)(D)(E)	28. (A)(B)(C)(D)(E)	43. (A)(B)(C)(D)(E)	58. (A)(B)(C)(D)(E)
14. (A)(B)(C)(D)(E)	29. (A)(B)(C)(D)(E)	44. (A)(B)(C)(D)(E)	59. (A)(B)(C)(D)(E)
15. (A)(B)(C)(D)(E)	30. (A)(B)(C)(D)(E)	45. (A)(B)(C)(D)(E)	60. (A)(B)(C)(D)(E)

SECTION I

Time—60 Minutes

60 Questions

You have 60 minutes to answer the following 60 multiple-choice questions. Each of the questions or incomplete statements is accompanied by five possible answers or completions. Select the one that best answers the question or completes the statement.

Questions 1–2 refer to the sources below.

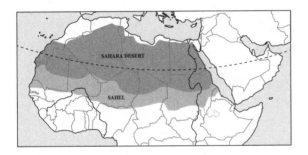

Country	Population (in millions)	Annual Rate of Natural Increase (%)	Total Fertility Rate
Burkina Faso	17.9	3.1	5.9
Chad	13.3	3.3	6.6
Eritrea	6.5	2.6	4.7
The Gambia	1.9	3.1	5.6
Guinea-Bissau	1.7	2.5	5.0
Mali	15.9	2.9	6.1
Mauritania	4.0	2.6	4.1
Niger	18.2	3.9	7.6
Senegal	13.9	3.2	5.3
Sudan	39.8	2.5	5.2

1. Suppose a person who was born in the desert region of Sudan self-identifies as "a proud immigrant from East Africa." Which of the following would most accurately describe the type of region the person has described?

   (A) Formal region

   (B) Functional region

   (C) Saharan region

   (D) Perceptual region

   (E) The Sahel region

2. Based on the table, which of the following statements is correct regarding the Sahel region?

   (A) The region's high total fertility rate is above replacement levels, leading to population increase.

   (B) The region's annual rate of natural increase exceeds its total fertility rate.

   (C) The region's birth and death rates are approximately equal.

   (D) The average population per country is less than five million.

   (E) The region's population is steadily declining due to a low total fertility rate.

GO ON TO THE NEXT PAGE

3. The sub-Saharan and Saharan regions of Africa are suffering from which of the following environmental problems due to the overgrazing of animals?

   (A) Climate change

   (B) Acid rain

   (C) Polluted rivers

   (D) Carbon dioxide pollution

   (E) Desertification

4. Which of the following is a common negative consequence of gentrification?

   (A) Older neighborhoods are revitalized.

   (B) New development creates urban sprawl.

   (C) Property taxes are increased.

   (D) New transportation systems replace older ones.

   (E) More restaurants and shops move into the gentrified area.

5. Languages that develop from a common ancestral tongue are classified as a language family. Chinese belongs to the

   (A) Indo-European family

   (B) Sino-Tibetan family

   (C) Afro-Asiatic family

   (D) Austro-Asiatic family

   (E) Niger-Congo family

6. Which of the following best describes the total fertility rate needed to maintain or grow a population?

   (A) Below 0.5

   (B) 0.5 to 1.0

   (C) 1.0 to 1.5

   (D) 1.5 to 2.0

   (E) Above 2.0

GO ON TO THE NEXT PAGE

Questions 7–9 refer to the sources below.

Winter Wheat 2009 (Planted Acres by County)

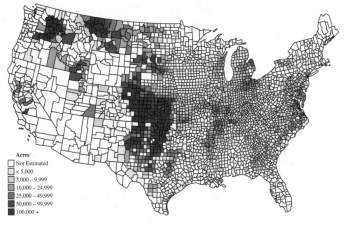

Acres
- Not Estimated
- < 5,000
- 5,000 – 9,999
- 10,000 – 24,999
- 25,000 – 49,999
- 50,000 – 99,999
- 100,000 +

**Wheat Yields in Less Developed
Countries (kg/harvested area)**

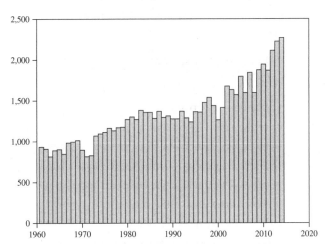

7. Based on the map, the Wheat Belt in the United States corresponds with which of the following regions?

   (A) Pacific Northwest

   (B) Southeast

   (C) Midwest

   (D) Desert Southwest

   (E) Great Plains

8. Which of the following would most directly account for the trend shown in the graph from 1960 to 2010?

   (A) First Agricultural Revolution

   (B) Industrial Revolution

   (C) Green Revolution

   (D) Second Agricultural Revolution

   (E) Advances in organic farming

9. Compared to wheat producers in less developed countries, wheat producers in the United States are more likely to rely on

   (A) plant domestication

   (B) intensive subsistence agricultural methods

   (C) collective farming

   (D) high-yield seed varieties

   (E) large-scale commercial agriculture

10. Which of the following is one of the main reasons the United Nations created the Human Development Index?

   (A) To promote Western-style education

   (B) To prevent inflation

   (C) To measure life expectancy

   (D) To promote international peace

   (E) To encourage economic reform

GO ON TO THE NEXT PAGE

11. Which of the following best represents a potential centrifugal force?

    (A) Religious diversity

    (B) Homogeneous population

    (C) A common language

    (D) Government-supported education

    (E) National anthem

12. The Hmong tradition of bringing family members to the United States after some family members have migrated is an example of

    (A) cyclic migration

    (B) interregional migration

    (C) intraregional migration

    (D) chain migration

    (E) intervening opportunity

13. Just-in-time delivery is a process that primarily aims at

    (A) getting food to the market before it spoils

    (B) getting products to the market to meet demand

    (C) getting food to the market for customized orders

    (D) eliminating long-distance transportation to reduce cost

    (E) eliminating competition in order to control prices

14. Which of the following best describes the outsourcing of labor from more developed countries to less developed countries in order to take advantage of cheaper labor costs?

    (A) The new international division of labor

    (B) The core/periphery relationship

    (C) Economic factors of development

    (D) Standards of industrial development

    (E) Inadequate debt financing of employment

15. Recent immigrants from China have established commercial activities in Chinatown in Washington, D.C. Their cultural imprint has given this neighborhood a distinctive flair, creating

    (A) an ethnic neighborhood

    (B) a gated community

    (C) a blockbusted neighborhood

    (D) a redlined area

    (E) an adaptive strategy

16. City A has improved its transportation system over the past 10 years, including constructing a light rail line that runs west/east through the core downtown. Construction firms have requested a large number of permits for new high-income residential buildings along the length of the tracks. Which of the following models most directly describes City A's growth?

    (A) Concentric zone model

    (B) Sector model

    (C) Galactic model

    (D) Keno-capitalism model

    (E) Gravity model

GO ON TO THE NEXT PAGE

Questions 17–19 refer to the map below.

17. Based on the map, which of the following best describes the city of Istanbul?

(A) Capital city

(B) Gateway city

(C) City-state

(D) Edge city

(E) Colonial city

18. Suppose a cartographer were to make a map of one of the individual locations shown on the map above. Which of the following locations would be mapped using the largest scale?

(A) The Mediterranean Sea

(B) Turkey

(C) Istanbul

(D) Syria

(E) Georgia

19. As shown on the map, the state of Bulgaria would most accurately be described as

(A) a Middle Eastern country

(B) a formal region

(C) a vernacular region

(D) a perceptual region

(E) an Asian country

20. Historically, steel production in Pittsburgh and automobile manufacturing in Detroit have been examples of which of the following?

(A) Multiplier effects

(B) Non-basic industries

(C) Site factors

(D) Situation factors

(E) Basic industries

21. Suppose a country has been experiencing a population explosion for the last five years. Which of the following most likely describes a true statement about this country's situation?

(A) Advances in technology will allow the country to adequately support the increased population.

(B) The death rate must have significantly decreased over the past five years.

(C) The birth rate must have been higher 10 years ago compared to now.

(D) The country must have increased its amount of habitable land.

(E) There is a diminishing ability of the land to sustain the population.

22. Which of the following most accurately explains why the North Atlantic Treaty Organization was created?

(A) To start the process of creating the European Union

(B) To replace the League of Nations

(C) To oppose the Warsaw Pact

(D) To counter the spread of communism

(E) To bring an end to World War II

GO ON TO THE NEXT PAGE

23. The movement of Mexicans from farmland to Mexico City is best described by which migration pattern?

    (A) Cyclical movement

    (B) Intercontinental

    (C) Interregional

    (D) Urban to rural

    (E) Transhumance

24. As a country's economy moves from relying on industry to being more service based, which of the following would most likely happen to the country's population?

    (A) An increase in migration to the country will increase its total population.

    (B) The population will stabilize because of zero population growth.

    (C) The proportion of the population that is elderly will start to rapidly decline.

    (D) Its birth and death rates will likely start moving closer together.

    (E) The birth rate will stay high, but the death rate will fall sharply.

25. The Hoover Dam best illustrates which of the following theories on human-environmental interaction?

    (A) Possibilism

    (B) Environmental determinism

    (C) Malthusian theory

    (D) Global environmentalism

    (E) Ecotourism

26. Which of the following business developments in a certain town would best indicate that the town's economy is moving into the quaternary economic sector?

    (A) A nearby ore-mining operation opens a new ore-processing facility.

    (B) A major cabinet and furniture manufacturer opens a large factory near a lumber yard.

    (C) The local airport becomes the hub for a large regional airline.

    (D) Business developers transform unused land into a multi-million dollar retail shopping center.

    (E) Local technology firms partner to open a space and satellite research and development laboratory.

27. A large agribusiness conglomerate recently contracted with local growers. Some of the growers will produce bananas, and others will produce sugarcane. These crops are traditionally associated with which of the following?

    (A) Plantation farming

    (B) Double-cropping

    (C) Triple-cropping

    (D) Mediterranean agriculture

    (E) Crop rotation farming

GO ON TO THE NEXT PAGE

28. In the United States, the South is experiencing rapid population growth due to the relocation of industrial activities from the Northeast and Midwest. Based on the core-periphery model, this is because the South is in

    (A) the industrial core

    (B) a downward transition area

    (C) an upward transition area

    (D) a resource frontier

    (E) a warmer climate zone

29. Which of the following best describes the relationship between core and periphery countries according to the world systems theory?

    (A) Core countries usually engage in free and fair trade practices when dealing with periphery countries.

    (B) Core countries invest very little foreign capital in periphery countries.

    (C) Core countries transfer natural resources to periphery countries.

    (D) Core countries help the workers in periphery countries by providing them with higher-paying jobs.

    (E) Core countries refuse to give humanitarian assistance to periphery countries.

30. For the last 10 years, a medium-sized city in the Midwest has suffered from an increase in crime, pollution, traffic congestion, and housing costs. Because of these issues, a significant number of people have left the city. This process is best described as

    (A) blockbusting

    (B) redlining

    (C) counterurbanization

    (D) decentralization

    (E) pull factor migration

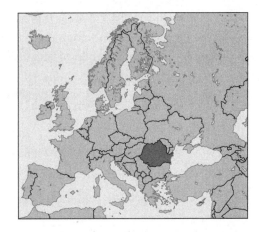

31. In terms of its relationship to the former Soviet Union, Romania could best be described as a

    (A) nation-state

    (B) shatterbelt

    (C) satellite state

    (D) microstate

    (E) unitary government

32. Romanian, Italian, and Portuguese are all part of the same

    (A) language family

    (B) dialect

    (C) toponym

    (D) trade language

    (E) isogloss

33. London, Paris, Buenos Aires, and Mexico City are all examples of

    (A) world cities

    (B) primate cities

    (C) edge cities

    (D) Spanish-speaking cities

    (E) megalopolises

GO ON TO THE NEXT PAGE

34. Which of the following lists of zones is presented in order of increasing distance from the market according to von Thünen's model of land use?

    (A) Dairy, commercial grain, livestock fattening

    (B) Market gardening, commercial grain, livestock fattening

    (C) Market gardening, livestock fattening, dairy

    (D) Dairy, livestock ranching, commercial grain

    (E) Dairy, commercial grain, livestock ranching

35. The Basque, Hmong, and Kurdish peoples are examples of which of the following?

    (A) Microstates

    (B) African ethnic groups

    (C) Southeast Asian nations

    (D) Nomadic tribes

    (E) Stateless nations

36. It can reasonably be inferred that the structure in the image above would be visited most frequently by adherents of which of the following faiths?

    (A) Judaism

    (B) Roman Catholicism

    (C) Eastern Orthodoxy

    (D) Hinduism

    (E) Islam

37. Which of the following best explains the inaccurate assumption underpinning Thomas Malthus's theory of overpopulation?

    (A) Birth rates would increase and contribute to an increasing population.

    (B) Death rates would decline and contribute to an increasing population.

    (C) Population control policies would not be able to keep up with an increasing population.

    (D) Agricultural productivity would increase with an increasing population.

    (E) Environmental disasters would result from an increasing population.

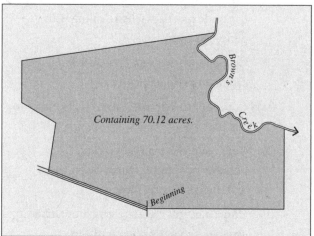

38. Which land-use system shown in the image above originated in Britain and is still used today in many parts of New England?

    (A) Metes and bounds

    (B) Long lots

    (C) Township and range

    (D) Environmental modification

    (E) Urbanization

GO ON TO THE NEXT PAGE

39. Which of the following incorrectly pairs a staple food with its geographic region?

    (A) Manioc and Northeastern South America

    (B) Coffee and Northeastern Africa

    (C) Millet and South Asia

    (D) Rice and Southeast Asia

    (E) Noodles and North China

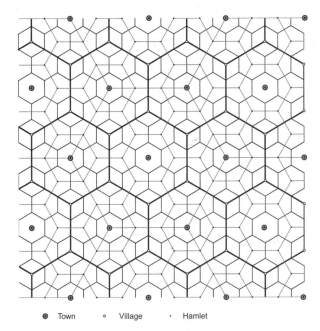

    ◉ Town   ○ Village   · Hamlet

40. The model of U.S. cities depicted above posits which of the following geographic principles as essential for the economic success of commercial establishments?

    (A) Threshold and range

    (B) Market area and economic structure

    (C) Threshold and globalization

    (D) Employment structure and range

    (E) Range and globalization

41. Which of the following is equal to the rate of natural increase?

    (A) Births minus deaths minus immigration

    (B) Births plus deaths plus immigration

    (C) Births minus deaths minus emigration

    (D) Births plus deaths plus emigration

    (E) Births minus deaths

42. Which of the following best explains why double-cropping is a common agricultural practice in Asia?

    (A) Double-cropping has allowed Asia to sell the second set of crops to more developed countries.

    (B) Double-cropping has ensured the food supply for much of Asia's population.

    (C) Double-cropping has helped Asia to triple its harvest.

    (D) Double-cropping is the best way to grow crops, though it creates desert areas due to overgrazing.

    (E) Double-cropping supports growing crops that require irrigation, such as rice.

GO ON TO THE NEXT PAGE

Questions 43–44 refer to the following images.

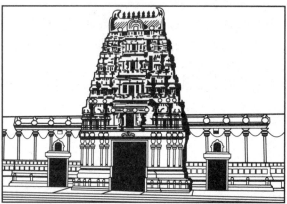

43. Which of the following was a pillar of the religion depicted by the first image?

(A) The triumvirate

(B) Feng shui

(C) Four Noble Truths

(D) The Torah

(E) A messiah

44. Which of the following beliefs is shared by the two religions represented by the images?

(A) Nirvana

(B) Polytheism

(C) Monotheism

(D) Reincarnation

(E) Ramadan

45. Olives, dates, and grapes are agricultural products that result from which type of farming?

(A) Plantation agriculture

(B) Mediterranean agriculture

(C) Subsistence agriculture

(D) Pastoral nomadism

(E) Slash-and-burn agriculture

46. Which of the following identifies the novel feature that allowed early automobile industrial workers high enough wages that they could afford the products that they were making?

(A) The outsourcing of low-paying jobs

(B) The long hours employees spent in poor working conditions

(C) The specialization of individual jobs

(D) The beginning of multinational companies

(E) The congregation of innovators in one area

47. According to the rank-size rule, if a region's biggest city has a population of 1,200,000, then the second-largest city will likely have a population of

(A) 200,000

(B) 240,000

(C) 300,000

(D) 600,000

(E) 850,000

GO ON TO THE NEXT PAGE

48. Many planned communities in third-ring suburbs are designed with pedestrians in mind due, in large part, to which of the following?

   (A) Brownfields

   (B) Urban sprawl

   (C) New Urbanism

   (D) Suburbanization

   (E) Tenements

49. Dividing a country's population by its total land area gives a geographer what statistic?

   (A) Physiological density

   (B) Arithmetic density

   (C) Agricultural density

   (D) Spatial distribution

   (E) Spatial density

Questions 50–51 refer to the following map.

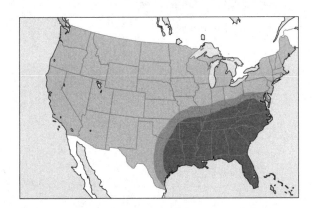

50. The concept of the American South means many things to different people, and many people draw the South using different boundaries. This is an example of

   (A) a formal region

   (B) a functional region

   (C) an industrial region

   (D) an agricultural region

   (E) a vernacular region

51. The region highlighted on the map has been most strongly influenced by which of the following institutions over the last century?

   (A) The Southern Baptist Convention

   (B) The Roman Catholic Church

   (C) The Mormon Church

   (D) The Southern Presbyterian Church

   (E) The Lutheran Church

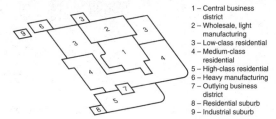

1 – Central business district
2 – Wholesale, light manufacturing
3 – Low-class residential
4 – Medium-class residential
5 – High-class residential
6 – Heavy manufacturing
7 – Outlying business district
8 – Residential suburb
9 – Industrial suburb

52. The above diagram best exhibits what model of urbanization?

   (A) Sector model

   (B) Concentric zone model

   (C) Central place theory

   (D) Multiple nuclei model

   (E) Gravity model

GO ON TO THE NEXT PAGE

Questions 53–55 refer to the following map.

--- Former Yugoslavia 2008

53. The boundary changes illustrated in the map were likely brought about by which of the following?

(A) Peaceful negotiation

(B) Infrastructure development

(C) Increased cultural cohesion

(D) Centrifugal forces

(E) The creation of relic boundaries

54. The breakup of the former Yugoslavia was most directly a result of which of the following?

(A) Ethnic conflict

(B) Soviet control

(C) U.S. involvement in the Balkans

(D) United Nations involvement

(E) NATO military occupation

55. Bosnia and Herzegovina has an internationally recognized border, but some of its territory is occupied by Serbian forces. This is an example of how a country's military forces can

(A) challenge state sovereignty

(B) put pressure on stateless nations

(C) gain international recognition

(D) foster alliances with other countries

(E) successfully conquer multiple states at once

56. Suppose a city mayor supports making major changes to improve the downtown area's transportation system by adding several new walkways, bike paths, and by improving all existing sidewalks. The mayor's approach is most similar to that called for by supporters of

(A) New Urbanism

(B) gated communities

(C) grid street systems

(D) symbolic landscapes

(E) disamenity zones

GO ON TO THE NEXT PAGE

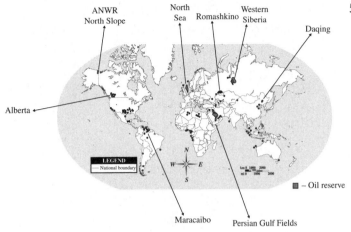

ANWR
North Slope
North Sea
Romashkino
Western Siberia
Daqing
Alberta
LEGEND
— National boundary
km 0 1000 2000
mi 0 1000 2000
■ – Oil reserve
Maracaibo
Persian Gulf Fields

57. The map indicates areas of interest that spurred the formation of which multinational organization?

(A) North Atlantic Treaty Organization (NATO)

(B) Arab League

(C) Organization of the Petroleum Exporting Countries (OPEC)

(D) United Nations (UN)

(E) Central Treaty Organization (CENTO)

58. Pork production is almost nonexistent in the Islamic world. Which of the following statements best explains this lack of pork production?

(A) The climate of most countries with large Islamic populations is not well-suited for pork production.

(B) Religious guidelines do not allow Muslims to eat pork.

(C) Pork is not a customary food preference in the Islamic diet.

(D) Muslims' dietary preferences tend more toward cattle production.

(E) The Islamic religion exalts vegans as having religious purity.

GO ON TO THE NEXT PAGE

Rostow's Model of Economic Development

Stage	Description
1	Traditional society
2	Preconditions of takeoff/Transitional
3	Takeoff
4	Drive to maturity
5	High mass consumption

59. A society engaged primarily in subsistence agriculture would be classified as being at which stage in Rostow's model of economic development?

   (A) Stage 1

   (B) Stage 2

   (C) Stage 3

   (D) Stage 4

   (E) Stage 5

60. Which crop is the most important grain for intensive subsistence farmers?

   (A) Maize

   (B) Barley

   (C) Sorghum

   (D) Rye

   (E) Rice

END OF SECTION I

IF YOU FINISH BEFORE TIME IS CALLED,
YOU MAY CHECK YOUR WORK ON SECTION I ONLY.
DO NOT GO ON TO SECTION II UNTIL INSTRUCTED TO DO SO.

SECTION II

Time—75 Minutes

3 Questions

You have 75 minutes to answer ALL THREE of the following questions. You should devote about 25 minutes to each question, including 5 minutes to plan each answer. While a formal essay is not required, it is not enough to answer a question by simply listing facts. Be sure that you number your answers, including each individual part.

1. Immanuel Wallerstein proposed the World Systems Theory in 1987 to describe the relative development of countries throughout the world.

    (A) Define the World Systems Theory.

    (B) Describe the typical employment sectors of countries categorized as core and countries categorized as periphery according to the World Systems Theory.

    (C) Identify a typical demographic trend in countries categorized as core according to the World Systems Theory.

    (D) Describe how core countries would be categorized in the demographic transition model.

    (E) Identify a typical demographic trend in countries categorized as periphery, according to the World Systems Theory.

    (F) Describe how periphery countries would be categorized in the demographic transition model.

    (G) Explain how the economic relationship between a specific periphery country and a specific core country demonstrates the dependency theory.

GO ON TO THE NEXT PAGE

WORLD CATTLE PRODUCTION

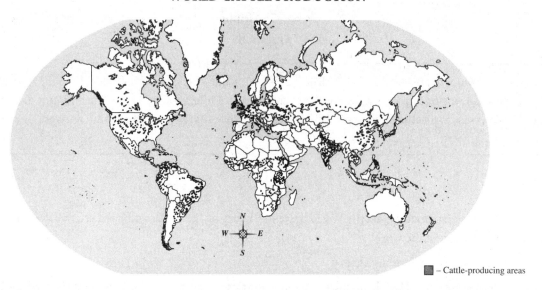

☐ – Cattle-producing areas

2. The map above shows locations of cattle production throughout the world.

  (A) Explain a way in which climate affects cattle production around the world, as shown on the map.

  (B) Explain whether livestock ranching is an intensive or extensive agricultural activity.

  (C) Describe von Thünen's model of agriculture.

  (D) Explain a way in which von Thünen's model relates to cattle production.

  (E) Explain a way in which culture impacts cattle production.

  (F) Explain how the impact identified in Part E affects the extent to which the organization of agriculture in a region reflects the von Thünen model.

  (G) Explain a reason why cattle production is absent from some world areas, as shown on the map.

GO ON TO THE NEXT PAGE ⟩

WHEAT CROP YIELDS IN BUSHELS PER ACRE, ENGLAND, SELECTED YEARS

Year	Bushels Per Acre
1400–1449	5.89
1550–1559	7.88
1600–1649	10.45
1700–1749	13.79
1750–1799	17.26
1800–1849	23.16
1850–1899	26.69

WHEAT PRODUCTION IN METRIC TONS, MEXICO

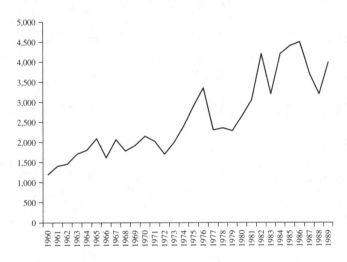

3. Developments in farming, over time, have revolutionized agricultural practices and impacted crop yields.

(A) Identify the type of farming most likely practiced during the years 1400–1449 as shown in the data table.

(B) Describe a development that impacted crop yields as shown in the data table.

(C) Describe an impact of the increase in crop yields as shown in the data table.

(D) Describe a development that impacted crop yields as shown in the graph.

(E) Describe a way in which the Green Revolution was successful.

(F) Describe a way in which the Green Revolution did not meet expectations or brought about criticism.

(G) Explain the significance of the Green Revolution in light of population trends in less developed countries.

END OF SECTION II

ANSWER KEY

Section I

1.	D	13.	B	25.	A	37.	D	49.	B
2.	A	14.	A	26.	E	38.	A	50.	E
3.	E	15.	A	27.	A	39.	C	51.	A
4.	C	16.	B	28.	C	40.	A	52.	D
5.	B	17.	B	29.	B	41.	E	53.	D
6.	E	18.	C	30.	C	42.	B	54.	A
7.	E	19.	B	31.	C	43.	C	55.	A
8.	C	20.	E	32.	A	44.	D	56.	A
9.	E	21.	E	33.	B	45.	B	57.	C
10.	C	22.	D	34.	E	46.	C	58.	B
11.	A	23.	C	35.	E	47.	D	59.	A
12.	D	24.	D	36.	E	48.	C	60.	E

Section II

See Answers and Explanations and self-score your responses.

Section I Number Correct: _____

Section II Points Earned: _____

Sign into your online account at kaptest.com and enter your results in the scoring section to see your 1–5 score.

Haven't registered your book yet? Go to kaptest.com/moreonline to begin.

ANSWERS AND EXPLANATIONS

Section I

1. D

A perceptual region is a region that exists primarily in the individual's perception or feelings (e.g., the concept of "the West" as a region of the United States differs depending on where someone lives). Thus, **(D)** is correct, as someone self-identifying as "a proud immigrant from East Africa" would be describing a perceptual region. Formal regions are areas in which everything has the same characteristic or experiences the same phenomenon, such as a political boundary or language. Broad areas such as the Sahara and the Sahel, each including multiple countries, are not considered formal regions, making (A) incorrect. A functional region is defined by its organization around a focal point, or node. An example would be New York City's financial district, which is centered around Wall Street. (B) is incorrect. While the person technically lives in the Sahara, the person's description is that of a perceptual region, making (C) incorrect. (E) is incorrect because the person lives in the desert in Sudan—thus the Sahara Desert—and therefore cannot live in the Sahel, which is a semi-arid savannah and grassland.

2. A

The total fertility rate is the number of children that an average woman has during her childbearing years. When a region's total fertility rate is above replacement levels, the total population is increasing. From the table, we can see that for each country in the Sahel, the rate is 4.1 or higher, which is well above replacement levels (which typically vary by region from about 2.1 to about 3.3). Therefore, the Sahel's population is growing. **(A)** is correct, and (E) is incorrect. (B) is incorrect because the rate of natural increase is a percentage, while the total fertility rate is a whole value corresponding to average children per woman, so the two values are not comparable. While the table gives the fertility rate, it does not give either the birth or death rates for the Sahel; (C) is incorrect. According to the table, most of the countries in the Sahel have populations of more than five million. Therefore, the average population will be more than five million—not less. (D) is incorrect.

3. E

Desertification occurs when livestock overgraze an area that is prone to drought, often near a desert region. In many areas of sub-Saharan Africa, herds of goats, sheep, and camels overgraze large swaths of land, damaging root systems and in turn leading to soil erosion. Once the topsoil disappears, desert-like conditions result. Thus, **(E)** is correct. Both climate change and polluted rivers have been problems in Africa, but these concerns are not directly related to overgrazing, so (A) and (C) are incorrect. While acid rain has been a problem in North America, Europe, and East Asia, it has not been a significant issue in Africa, making (B) incorrect. Carbon dioxide pollution is typically caused by human activity in urban or industrial areas, not sparsely settled areas such as the Saharan and sub-Saharan regions; (D) is also incorrect.

4. C

When people from the middle and upper classes move into low-income neighborhoods, the process is called gentrification. As the newcomers buy homes and fix them up, demand for housing and property values increase. The result is a gradual increase in property taxes. Eventually, the original inhabitants can no longer afford the high property taxes and are forced to move; **(C)** is correct. (A), (D), and (E) are incorrect because these are often considered positive results of gentrification. The gentrification of an area does not always lead to the building of newer neighborhoods farther out; (B) is incorrect.

5. B

There are a number of varieties of Chinese, all of which are classified as belonging to the Sino-Tibetan family of languages; **(B)** is correct. The most common variety, Mandarin Chinese, is spoken by more than one billion people, making it the most spoken language in the world. Other languages in the Sino-Tibetan group include Thai and Burmese. (A), (C), (D), and (E) are incorrect because these language families do not include Chinese. Indo-European languages include English, Spanish, German, and Hindi. Afro-Asiatic languages are common in North Africa and the Middle East; examples include Arabic and Hebrew.

The Austro-Asiatic language family is found in Southeast Asia and the South Pacific; Vietnamese is an example of a language within this family. The Niger-Congo language family is common to southern Africa and includes languages such as Swahili and Zulu.

6. E

The number of children needed to sustain a population is known as the replacement rate. For a population to increase without immigration, the total fertility rate must be higher than this replacement rate. In developed countries, the replacement rate is about 2.1; in countries where the mortality rate is higher, the replacement rate is higher. **(E)** is correct because it is the only choice that includes values in the required range. (A)–(D) are incorrect because they are below replacement levels for any population.

7. E

The map clearly indicates that the majority of wheat is grown in the middle of the United States, which is the Great Plains region. This area, known as the Wheat Belt, is usually relatively dry and therefore suitable for the production of wheat, which does not require a lot of moisture to grow; **(E)** is correct. The Pacific Northwest and the Desert Southwest are both capable of growing wheat; however, these regions are not known for growing mass quantities like the Great Plains region is, making (A) and (D) incorrect. The Southeast is too wet to grow wheat, making (B) incorrect. While wheat is grown in the Midwest, this region is known as the Corn Belt because corn is the predominant crop; (C) is incorrect.

8. C

The Green Revolution began in the mid-twentieth century and had a revolutionary impact on food production due to the development of biotechnology and genetic engineering. During this time, scientists created hybrids of plants and animals, farmers increased the use of chemical fertilizers, and agribusiness began mass agricultural production. The increase in wheat yields in least developed countries, as shown in the graph, is an example of a Green Revolution outcome, making **(C)** correct. (A) is incorrect because the First Agricultural Revolution was the transition from hunting and gathering to planting and sustaining, occurring many centuries earlier. (B) is incorrect because the Industrial Revolution began in the 1750s in Great Britain and diffused into the United States in the 1800s. During

the Industrial Revolution, a more mechanized system of farming was developed, coinciding with the Second Agricultural Revolution. Therefore, (D) is incorrect. Farmers during the Green Revolution relied heavily on chemical fertilizers; (E) is incorrect because organic farming involves producing food crops without such chemicals.

9. E

Large-scale commercial farming is a common style of farming in the United States as well as other developed countries. It involves the mass production of specialty crops, such as wheat, using machinery and modern technology. These farms often consist of tens of thousands of acres. Wheat fields in Kansas and the Dakotas, for example, are measured at that scale. Thus, **(E)** is correct. (A) is incorrect because wheat farmers in both the United States and the least developed countries depend on plant domestication in order to have seeds for planting wheat. Poorer countries tend to rely more heavily on intensive subsistence agricultural methods, such as manual planting and harvesting, than does the United States. (B) is incorrect. A collective farm is a type of farm where workers are not paid with money but instead receive a share of the crop. While once common in the United States, it is no longer common, making (C) incorrect. Due to the Green Revolution, many less developed countries grow high-yield varieties of wheat, so this is not more true of U.S. farmers; (D) is incorrect.

10. C

Ever since the Industrial Revolution, researchers have worked to establish a meaningful way to measure economic development. In the 1970s, the United Nations created one such measure: the Human Development Index (HDI). In addition to measuring a country's overall economic development, the HDI rating is based on factors such as literacy rates, life expectancy, and per capita income. **(C)** is therefore correct. While the HDI measures educational and economic factors, the United Nations did not develop this index in order to promote a particular type of education, to prevent inflation, or to encourage economic reform; (A), (B), and (E) are incorrect. While one of the United Nations' main functions is to promote international peace, the HDI itself wasn't developed as a tool to promote peace, so (D) is incorrect.

11. A

Centrifugal forces divide a state's citizens. Differences in political views, economic status, religion, and language are all types of centrifugal forces that sometimes make it difficult to politically unite a country. For example, the Irish War of Independence led to the creation of the Irish Free State out of the United Kingdom. British forces were largely Protestant, while many Irish fighters were Roman Catholic. Thus, religious diversity can be a centrifugal force; **(A)** is correct. In a homogeneous population, people share similar cultural or ethnic traits; this would not be a centrifugal force, so (B) is incorrect. Likewise, sharing a common language would not be a centrifugal force; (C) is incorrect. Public education and having a national anthem would most likely unite people, making (D) and (E) incorrect.

12. D

The Hmong is an ethnic group located mainly in China, Vietnam, Laos, and Thailand. In the 1970s, Christian organizations in the United States started sponsoring Hmong immigrants. First, a few family members were brought to the United States. Then, these family members sent money to their families back in their homeland, allowing their families to also come to the United States. When immigrants provide the financial resources for their family members to migrate and join them in the new country, the process is called chain migration; **(D)** is correct. (A) is incorrect because cyclic migration describes a seasonal migration pattern, such as when people move into an area to work in agriculture during the planting or harvest months and then return home. Interregional migration is usually done within a country's borders, from region to region, making (B) incorrect. (C) is incorrect because intraregional migration is the movement of people within the same region. An intervening opportunity occurs when a migrant stops and decides to stay at a location along the journey because of favorable economic opportunities or environmental amenities; (E) is also incorrect.

13. B

Just-in-time delivery refers to getting a product to the market just as the demand for the product occurs, thereby reducing stock and inventory. Thus, **(B)** is correct. (A) and (C) are incorrectly limited to food; while the just-in-time delivery system is often associated with agriculture, it can also be applied to most manufactured goods. (D) and (E) are incorrect because just-in-time delivery does not eliminate long-distance transportation, nor is its focus on eliminating competition.

14. A

The new international division of labor refers to the outsourcing of manufacturing jobs to less developed countries; **(A)** is correct. Wallerstein's world system analysis proposes that more developed countries (the core) keep their manufacturing jobs while less developed countries (the periphery) export raw materials, making (B) incorrect. Economic factors of development include a country's GDP and GNP; outsourcing is only a small element of these, so (C) is incorrect. Standards of industrial development refer to a wide range of factors that affect a country's growth, such as its economic system and access to natural resources; (D) is incorrect. Inadequate debt financing would stall business in less developed countries, causing the outsourcing of labor to be a non-issue. Thus, (E) is incorrect.

15. A

Chinatown in Washington, D.C., is an example of an ethnic neighborhood. It contains restaurants, shops, and other commercial establishments catering to its Chinese-speaking residents. Thus, **(A)** is correct. Gated communities are residential communities that are gated to ensure that only the residents and their guests are allowed to enter. This does not necessarily describe a neighborhood with a distinctive flair, so (B) is incorrect. Blockbusting is when real estate agents try to induce people to sell their homes because of a perception that a different race is moving into the neighborhood, which does not describe Chinatown, making (C) incorrect. Redlining is the refusal of lending institutions to give loans to those in high-risk areas and would be invoked in a neighborhood that had a high default rate on mortgages. This may or may not take place in an ethnic community, so (D) is incorrect. An adaptive strategy refers to how a person adjusts to a new culture or location (for example, an immigrant experiencing snow for the first time and adding a heavy jacket to her wardrobe). This is not clearly indicated from the example of Chinatown, so (E) is also incorrect.

16. B

The sector model of urbanization was described by Homer Hoyt in 1939. According to this model, social structure can be influenced by transportation systems. Hoyt based his model on Chicago, which had grown outward, especially on the north side of the city where high-income residences were being built. This model accurately describes City A's pattern of growth; **(B)** is correct. The other models fail to describe what has happened in City A. According to the concentric zone model, the lower classes live closest to the central business district, while the upper classes live farther out because they can afford the commute into the city to work, so (A) is incorrect. The galactic city model represents a city with growth independent of the central business district (CBD) that is traditionally connected to the central city by means of an arterial highway or interstate. Thus, (C) is incorrect. The Keno-capitalism model suggests that areas are zoned off or even gated off from other zones in the city, so (D) is incorrect. The gravity model suggests that the greater the sphere of influence a city has, the greater its impact on other cities around it. (E) is incorrect.

17. B

A gateway city serves as a connection point between two areas. Istanbul, the largest city in Turkey, is considered a gateway city because it connects Europe with Asia. Thus, **(B)** is correct. (A) is incorrect because the capital of Turkey is Ankara. A city-state is a small sovereign state that is made up of a town or city and the surrounding area. Since Istanbul is governed as part of Turkey, (C) is incorrect. (D) is incorrect because an edge city is a rapidly growing city found in the suburbs or just outside the main city area. Although Istanbul was once part of the Roman Empire and, later, the Ottoman Empire, today's modern Istanbul is not considered a colonial city, making (E) incorrect.

18. C

Scale is an essential concept that geographers use to create maps. Scale refers to the relationship between a location's size on a map and its actual size on Earth. A map depicting a small location is referred to as a large-scale map. This is because the location's area on the map has been scaled down less, making the scale larger. Therefore, a map depicting a relatively small area, such as a city, is considered a large-scale map. Istanbul, though a very large city, is the smallest location shown on the map,

making **(C)** correct. Maps of the Mediterranean Sea and the countries of Turkey, Syria, and Georgia would depict a greater amount of territory and would, therefore, be considered small-scale, making (A), (B), (D), and (E) incorrect.

19. B

In formal regions, nearly everything inside has the same characteristic, such as a common language or some other cultural trait. A formal region also shares a political and legal system. Bulgaria is an example of a formal region because it has a defined political boundary with sovereignty and because the people of Bulgaria share a culture and a political system; **(B)** is correct. Bulgaria is a European country—not a Middle Eastern or an Asian country. Thus, (A) and (E) are incorrect. A region that exists primarily in the individual's perception or feelings is called a vernacular, or a perceptual, region. An example of such a region in the United States is "the South," which differs depending on where someone lives. Since the two terms—vernacular and perceptual—are synonymous, both (C) and (D) are incorrect.

20. E

Steel production was once the main focus of Pittsburgh's economy, and automobile manufacturing remains the most prominent force in Detroit's economy. When an area's economy is dominated by a single industry, that industry is referred to as a basic industry, making **(E)** correct. Multiplier effects refer to an expansion of the area's economy that, in turn, results in even more growth, across multiple industries, so (A) is incorrect. (B) is incorrect because non-basic industries are industries that grow in conjunction with a basic industry, such as restaurants and retail shops. (C) and (D) are incorrect because they refer to factors that might cause an area to have a basic industry, but they are not used to describe the industry itself.

21. E

The term "carrying capacity" describes the ability of an amount of land to sustain a population. The more people who inhabit an area, the more likely the population will reach the carrying capacity of the environment. Once the carrying capacity is reached, the problems of overpopulation become apparent. Given that this country has been undergoing a population explosion, the ability of its land to sustain the population must be declining. Thus, **(E)** is correct. While some countries may be able to take advantage of technology to grow more food and harvest more resources, there is no guarantee that this is the situation here; (A) is incorrect. Likewise, there is no way to know whether the death rate has significantly changed over the past five years. In fact, it may be that during a population explosion, the death rate increases due to less food and other resources per person. (B) is incorrect. Given that the population has significantly increased over the last five years, there is no basis for (C), making it incorrect. Likewise, there is no basis for believing the country has gained more habitable land; (D) is incorrect.

22. D

The heartland theory suggests that whoever controls Eastern Europe and Western Asia has the political power and capital to rule the world. The heartland has abundant natural resources. The Soviet Union occupied most of the heartland after the end of World War II. The North Atlantic Treaty Organization (NATO) was established in 1949 to contain communism there; **(D)** is therefore correct. The goal of NATO was not to set the stage for the creation of the European Union, which was not officially established until 1993. (A) is incorrect. The League of Nations was an international organization created at the end of World War I and later replaced by the United Nations, so (B) is incorrect. While NATO's counterpart was the Warsaw Pact, an alliance of Soviet-backed Eastern European countries, this group was not created until 1955, making (C) incorrect. NATO was created to oppose the Soviet Union and communism—not to end World War II. (E) is incorrect.

23. C

Interregional migration involves citizens moving within a single country. Thus, **(C)** is correct. Cyclical movement is seasonal migration based on opportunities such as work or resources, but the movement of rural Mexicans to Mexico City has not been motivated primarily by seasonal opportunities, making (A) incorrect. Intercontinental migration occurs when people move from one continent to another, but Mexicans moving to their capital city are staying within North America; (B) is incorrect. Urban-to-rural migration would involve Mexicans moving from Mexico City to agricultural areas, not the other way around, making (D) incorrect. Transhumance is the movement of livestock to different elevations during various seasons; (E) is also incorrect.

24. D

According to the demographic transition model, as an economy advances from one that is industry based to one that is service based, the population tends to stabilize. This occurs because the birth rates and death rates start moving closer together. **(D)** is correct. (A) and (C) are incorrect because growth of the service sector does not correlate with an increase (or a decrease) in migration or a decline in the number of elderly people. A claim of zero population growth, meaning that the birth rate equals the death rate, is extreme, so (B) is incorrect. Generally, when a country transforms its economy from one that is industry based to one that is more service based, its birth rate is low, so (E) is incorrect.

25. A

The theory of possibilism suggests that humans are not products of their environment, but rather that they possess the skills necessary to modify their environment to fit their needs. In other words, people can determine their own outcomes without regard to location. Building a large, complex structure, such as the Hoover Dam, is an example of such an outcome, making **(A)** correct. The philosophy known as environmental determinism states that human behaviors are the direct result of their surrounding environment. This would not explain why a society would build a complex structure such as a dam, making (B) incorrect. Malthusian theory relates to modern-day trends in population and food production rather than building structures, so (C) is incorrect. (D) is incorrect because global environmentalism is a broad term that describes governmental and societal efforts to protect the Earth and its resources. While many people visit the Hoover Dam, promoting ecotourism is not the reason the dam was built, and indeed dams interrupt the natural flow of rivers, making (E) incorrect.

26. E

Quaternary sector activities include industries that are concerned with the creation and distribution of knowledge. Examples include research and development, finance, banking, marketing, and business consulting. Therefore, **(E)** is correct. Primary sector activities include agriculture, forestry, fishing, and the extraction and harvest of natural resources. Secondary sector activities include the processing of raw materials and natural resources and the creation of manufactured goods.

(A) and (B) are therefore incorrect. Tertiary sector activities are service-based economic activities that include the selling of goods and services as well as transportation. Thus, (C) and (D) are incorrect.

27. A

Plantation agriculture often occurs in less developed countries and usually involves the production of one crop, which is sold in more developed countries. Banana, sugarcane, coffee, and cotton plantations are common in many tropical areas. **(A)** is therefore correct, and (B) and (C) are incorrect. Mediterranean agriculture is a type of farming that must be practiced in a climate that has a dry summer and a cool, moist winter. The crops associated with the Mediterranean Sea region include grapes, dates, and olives. (D) is incorrect. Crop rotation farming involves the planting of different crops each year to replenish nutrients in the soil that were lost to the previous crops. Bananas and sugarcane have not traditionally been grown using such a method, so (E) is incorrect.

28. C

According to the core-periphery model, the industrial core is where the majority of industrial activities are located within a country. In the United States, the largest industrial core extends from the Northeast to the Midwest. The next major area in the core-periphery model is the upward transition area. Upward transition describes an area that is gaining jobs and attracting industry. The economy here grows rapidly, which in turn leads to further development. In the United States, the upward transition area is the South. Therefore, **(C)** is correct, and (A) is incorrect. The third area in the core-periphery model is the downward transition area, where companies are leaving and unemployment rates are high. In the United States, the Great Plains region is experiencing a downward cycle. (B) is incorrect. The last section of the core-periphery model is the resource frontier. Resource frontier areas provide resources that are used for energy production or manufacturing. The remote north section of Alaska, with crude oil resources, is the largest resource frontier in the United States. (D) is correct. While the South generally has a warm climate, this is not directly related to the core-periphery model, making (E) incorrect.

29. B

According to the world systems theory, the core areas are the more developed countries. These are located primarily in North America and Western Europe, as well as, Japan, Australia, and New Zealand. The periphery areas are the less developed countries. The theory holds that the core areas take advantage of the supply of natural resources and labor located in the periphery, furthering the success of the core. The periphery also lacks foreign investment from developed countries, thereby keeping peripheral countries in a permanent state of underdevelopment. **(B)** is correct, and (C) and (D) are incorrect. Based on this theory, there is no indication that core countries would typically engage in free and fair trade with periphery countries, so (A) is incorrect. While core areas invest little foreign capital in the periphery, there is no indication that they deny the periphery humanitarian assistance, so (E) is incorrect.

30. C

Counterurbanization is the process of moving away from urban areas, usually when people want to get away from traffic, crime, and pollution. Thus, **(C)** is correct. Blockbusting and redlining are methods of buying and selling homes in urban areas and are generally held to be unethical, or even illegal, because of their association with racial prejudice. They are not necessarily about moving away from cities, though, making (A) and (B) incorrect. Decentralization involves who has authority, not the movement of people; (D) is incorrect. A pull factor is a positive perception of a location that induces a person to move there. This does not directly describe the situation for this city, so (E) is incorrect.

31. C

Because Romania was under the former Soviet Union's control, it was considered a satellite state; **(C)** is correct. Although a satellite state possesses sovereignty, it is in essence under the control of a nation-state and is not a nation-state itself, making (A) incorrect. Because Romania was not located between two superpowers, it was not a shatterbelt; (B) is incorrect. A microstate is a country that is small in both population and area, making (D) incorrect. A unitary government means that the state holds authority over other subordinate governments; Romania actually lost some of its autonomy in decision making when it became a satellite state, making (E) incorrect.

32. A

All of these languages are part of the same language family, the Romance languages, so called because they developed from Latin, the language of the Roman Empire. Therefore, **(A)** is correct. (B)–(E) are incorrect terms for the languages listed in the question. Dialects are different forms of the same language. Toponyms are simply place names. Trade languages are established by traders to communicate more effectively with each other and avoid having to learn several languages. Lastly, isoglosses are the map boundaries for different languages.

33. B

London, Paris, Mexico City, and Buenos Aires are examples of primate cities. Each has more than double the population of the next-largest city within its country. Thus, **(B)** is correct. By Saskia Sassen's definition of the term, only New York City and London qualify as world cities, so (A) is incorrect. Edge cities are urban areas that grow around major metropolitan areas. Because the cities mentioned are at the center of their major metropolitan areas, (C) incorrect. (D) is incorrect because London and Paris are not Spanish-speaking cities. Lastly, (E) is incorrect because megalopolises are comprised of adjacent metropolitan areas that spread into one another (e.g., the Boston–Washington, D.C., corridor), and this does not accurately describe the listed cities.

34. E

The proper pattern for von Thünen's agricultural land use model is market gardening, dairy, livestock fattening, commercial grain, and finally livestock ranching. Thus, **(E)** is correct. (A)–(D) have at least one of the zones out of order. The position of each zone depends on the costs of transportation to market, the cost of land, and other market factors. For example, market gardening has to occur close to the market, because the cost to transport these products is greater based on their bulk and weight. As another example, livestock fattening has to come before livestock ranching, because more space is needed for livestock ranching, and land is more expensive closer to the market or the urban center.

35. E

The Basques, Hmong, and Kurds are examples of nations that are struggling for independence within the context of another state. The Basques are a small nation located in northern Spain and southern France and speak their own language. The Hmong are a nation located in Southeast Asia, primarily in Laos, and many seek to create their own homeland in that region. The Kurds are fighting for their independence within northern Iran and Iraq and in eastern Turkey. **(E)** is correct. A microstate is a country that is small in both population and area; (A) is incorrect. None of these groups are African ethnic groups or nomadic tribes, making (B) and (D) incorrect. While the Hmong are a Southeast Asian nation, the Basques and Kurds are not, making (C) incorrect.

36. E

The above image is of a mosque, which is a house of worship in the Islamic faith. Many mosques have minarets, which are the vertical extensions around the mosque, as shown in the image. In addition, the spires on top of the domes have crescent moons on them, which is a common symbol of Islam; thus, **(E)** is correct. The houses of worship for each of the other faiths mentioned have their own distinct architectural styles, making (A)–(D) incorrect.

37. D

In coining the term "overpopulation" in the late 1700s, Thomas Malthus suggested that the world's population was growing faster than the rate of food production and, as a result, mass starvation would occur. Malthus was correct in his assumption about world population increase, but he was incorrect in his prediction that agriculture would be unable to produce sufficient food; **(D)** is correct. Birth rates are one of the best indicators of population increase, which Malthus had right, eliminating (A). Malthus did not explicitly predict population control, death rates, or environmental disasters making (B), (C), and (E) incorrect.

38. A

The metes and bounds system uses the land's physical features to describe ownership claims. This type of land use came from Britain and is still used in parts of New England today, making **(A)** correct. The long lots system came from the French, whereas the township and range system began in response to the vast spaces of the Midwest and Great Plains regions of the United States; (B) and (C) are incorrect. (D) and (E) are incorrect because both of these terms are not land-use systems. Environmental modification is the introduction of human-made chemicals and practices to an area, and urbanization is the process of people living and working in a city.

39. C

Millet is a staple crop in many parts of Africa, not South Asia; **(C)** is correct. (A) is incorrect because manioc is grown in South America and is used in many dishes in Brazil. Northeastern Africa was a major agricultural hearth where coffee was the major crop, making (B) incorrect. China has a geographic "noodle line." North of the noodle line, where more wheat products are grown, noodles are produced and are a daily part of the diet. South of this "noodle line," rice is the most abundantly grown crop as the climate is warmer; eliminating (D) and (E).

40. A

Walter Christaller established the central place theory in the 1930s, which suggests that all cities and commercial establishments follow a similar pattern, based on the assumption that settlements are central places that provide services to the surrounding area. Within this theory, range refers to the maximum distance people are willing to travel to get a product or service, and threshold is the minimum number of people needed for a business to operate; accordingly, the same geometric pattern repeats itself across areas with multiple settlements. Thus, **(A)** is correct. While market area, economic structure, globalization, and employment structure are important to making a commercial business successful, these were not part of the central place theory; (B)–(E) are incorrect.

41. E

The rate of natural increase is equal to births minus deaths; **(E)** is correct. Immigration and emigration have nothing to do with natural increase because they simply involve people moving from one place to another, making (A)–(D) incorrect.

42. B

Asia is home to a vast population, and agricultural innovation has been required to ensure a consistent food supply. Double-cropping means growing more than one crop in a calendar year on the same plot of land, and Asians use this technique to increase output; **(B)** is correct. (A) refers to a major benefit of plantation agriculture, which typically occurs in less developed countries and usually

involves the production of one crop that is sold to more developed countries; this would not be a good strategy for feeding countries' own populations, so (A) is incorrect. (C) is incorrect because it describes triple-cropping, not double-cropping. (D) is incorrect because it describes desertification, which has a negative effect on agricultural production. (E) incorrectly describes terraced irrigation instead of double-cropping.

43. C

The first image is of a Buddhist temple, a pagoda; note the tall structure with ornate design. The Four Noble Truths form the cornerstone of Buddhism, making **(C)** correct. The triumvirate consists of Brahma, Shiva, and Vishnu, which are the three primary deities of the Hindu faith, making (A) incorrect. Feng shui concerns maintaining proper relationships in life through the positioning of items to keep the flow of energy in harmony; this is a principle of Confucianism, so (B) is incorrect. (D) is incorrect because the Torah consists of the five books that were written by Moses according to Jewish faith. Belief in or rejection of a messiah plays a role in many monotheistic religions predominant in the West, so (E) is incorrect.

44. D

The first image is of a Buddhist pagoda; the second image is a Hindu temple, as shown by the multi-tiered architecture with characteristic symmetry and repeating shapes. Reincarnation, or the belief that one has lived a previous life and will continue to live another life after death, is a shared belief between Buddhism and Hinduism, making **(D)** correct. Nirvana is the ultimate goal of the Buddhist faith, but is not shared with Hinduism; (A) is incorrect. Polytheism, the belief in many gods, and monotheism, the belief in one god, are not held by either Hinduism or Buddhism. While Hinduism includes several gods, particularly the triumvirate (Brahma, Shiva, and Vishnu), these deities are often seen as manifestations of a universal god, which is different from the idea of a single god as held by monotheistic religions, such as Christianity. Additionally, Buddhism doesn't truly include the worship of deities; there is no personal god in Buddhism, only the path of Siddhartha Gautama. Thus, (B) and (C) are incorrect. (E) is incorrect because Ramadan is part of the faith of Islam.

45. B

The climate for Mediterranean agriculture is characterized by warm, dry summers and cool, moist winters. This climate is conducive to growing such agricultural products as nuts, olives, dates, and grapes; **(B)** is correct. (A) is incorrect because plantation agriculture occurs in less developed countries and usually involves the production of one crop that is sold to more developed countries; however, grapes, olives, and dates are typically grown together in Mediterranean-type climates. Most farmers who produce olives, dates, and grapes take these to market, while subsistence farmers eat most of what they produce; (C) is incorrect. Pastoral nomadism is traditionally practiced in arid climates and focuses on animals rather than crops, eliminating (D). Slash-and-burn agriculture is the process of clearing land to plant new crops, which is not practiced when farming olives, dates, and grapes; (E) is incorrect.

46. C

In 1914, Henry Ford started paying his automobile manufacturing workers $5 per day (about $120 today). Such a generous daily wage, unheard of at this time, enabled auto industry workers to actually buy cars for themselves. This was made possible as the workers specialized in doing individual tasks, which increased their speed, efficiency, and quality, thereby reducing costs. As each person on Ford's assembly line specialized in a task, they were paid well for their task expertise; **(C)** is correct. (A) is incorrect because outsourcing of jobs was not a feature of the early automobile industry. Although workers in the automobile industry likely worked long hours, their working conditions were not considered particularly poor; such conditions were associated more with textile industry "sweatshops." (B) is incorrect. (D) and (E) are incorrect because neither influenced the early automobile industry and its workers' wages. (E) is also a feature of the technology industry of Silicon Valley rather than what would become the hub of the automobile industry in Detroit.

47. D

The rank-size rule is a concept in geography that describes the pattern of urban settlement in a country. The rule says that the population of a country's second-largest city will be approximately half the population of the largest city. The country's third-largest city will be approximately one-third the largest city's population. In general terms, the *n*th largest city is 1/*n* of the size of the largest city. If the largest city has a population of 1,200,000, then the second-largest city is roughly half that size, or 600,000. Thus, **(D)** is correct, and (A)–(C) and (E) are incorrect.

48. C

Suburban areas are often developed as planned communities, which include well-maintained landscapes, parks, recreational facilities, and other amenities to draw in more residents. Planned communities increasingly have been designed such that they are more walkable, rather than automobile dependent, with a diversity of jobs. This approach is called New Urbanism, making **(C)** correct. Brownfields are former industrial sites that cities are now attempting to redevelop. They are typical of first-ring suburbs, not third-ring, making (A) incorrect. Urban sprawl is the process of growing into and infringing on the surrounding rural areas. Urban sprawl is a second-ring suburb phenomenon, so (B) is incorrect. Suburbanization is a process by which a population expands from the city center to surrounding, less dense, areas. This is the general process by which suburbs are created but does not explain the design development of planned communities; thus (D) is incorrect. Tenements are rundown apartment buildings that are minimally kept up by landlords because their value is so low. They are typical of urban communities, making (E) incorrect.

49. B

Arithmetic density is calculated by dividing a country's total population by its total land area to determine the population density per square mile or kilometer. One of the downsides of using arithmetic density as a measure is that it does not account for areas in which people do not live, such as desert regions or other places where the climate forbids habitation. To correct for this problem, geographers can calculate the physiological density, found by dividing the total population by the amount of agricultural land. Therefore, **(B)** is correct and (A) is incorrect. Agricultural density, (C), is found by dividing the total number of farm workers by the amount of farmland. Spatial distribution, (D), is a term that describes where a population is located. Spatial density, (E), is a measure of how many people are in a particular space.

50. E

Because the South means many different things to many different people, it is an example of a vernacular, or perceptual, region. Definitions of "the South" vary; shared cultural values, climate, and language dialects are examples of criteria that people use to define the South. **(E)** is correct. (A), (B), and (C) are incorrect because these regions have more specific definitions than a perceptual region has. A formal region is an area that has a clearly marked boundary with no significant dispute over the region's location. A territory that is organized around something central, such as a city or an industry, is considered a functional region. An industrial region would be an area that is dominated by an economic activity such as manufacturing. While the South does have agricultural regions, (D) is incorrect because it does not describe the perceptual views of what it means to be in "the South."

51. A

One of the most prevalent Christian denominations in America is the Southern Baptist Convention, which is dominant in the South. In fact, the South is often described as the "Bible Belt," in part, due to its large number of Southern Baptist churches. **(A)** is correct. While popular in the United States as a whole, the Roman Catholic Church has fewer members in the South than does the Southern Baptist Convention. (B) is incorrect. Similarly, the Mormon, Southern Presbyterian, and Lutheran churches have more members in other regions of the country. (C)–(E) are incorrect.

52. D

The multiple nuclei model suggests that the growth of the urban area is independent of the central business district and occurs where development is needed. As such, growth may occur haphazardly and extend more in one direction than another. The diagram illustrates a typical multiple nuclei city design; **(D)** is correct. The sector model, (A), holds that different zones within the urban area are determined by transportation routes. With the concentric zone model, (B), development expands from the central business district in a series of rings, or concentric circles. The central place theory, (C), claims that within a region, there will be one large city that is encircled by smaller cities and towns. The large city provides goods and services, and the people living in the smaller areas provide part of the labor supply and market required by the city. The gravity model, (E), states that the interaction between two places can be determined by the product of the population of both places, divided by the square of their distance from one another.

53. D

In the former country of Yugoslavia, ethnic tensions grew to a volatile level in the 1980s, partly due to a myriad of centrifugal forces. There were many different ethnic groups within the same geographical area. Certain areas were dominated by Christian denominations, and other areas included large populations of Muslims. There were a variety of languages spoken in different parts of Yugoslavia. Some areas were more capitalistic and pro-Western, and other areas were more anti-West. These forces reached a critical level, and war broke out across the Balkan Peninsula. The end result was a balkanization of the former Yugoslavia, producing multiple independent states. **(D)** is correct. (A) is incorrect because a long, brutal war was fought. While later infrastructure development did occur, (B) is not the reason for the boundary changes. (C) is incorrect because there was a lack of cultural cohesion, which fueled the ethnic tensions. The political situation that drove the breakup of Yugoslavia had nothing to do with relic boundaries. A relic boundary is, just as the term implies, held over from the past but no longer functional. (E) is incorrect.

54. A

During the 1980s, ethnic tensions grew to a volatile level in the former country of Yugoslavia. As the Cold War came to a close, the state of Yugoslavia experienced a civil war that resulted in a breaking apart of the country into multiple states, including Bosnia and Herzegovina, Macedonia, Serbia, Montenegro, Croatia, and Slovenia. **(A)** is correct. The involvement of neither the Soviet Union nor the United States directly resulted in the breakup of Yugoslavia, making (B) and (C) incorrect. Similarly, the United Nations and NATO did not have a direct role in the breakup, so (D) and (E) are incorrect.

55. A

The question stem indicates that Bosnia and Herzegovina has an internationally recognized border while at the same time having some of its territory occupied by Serbian forces. This is an example of how a country's military forces can challenge another state's sovereignty; **(A)** is correct. (B) is incorrect because there is no information about stateless nations. While the question stem talks about internationally recognized boundaries, it does not provide any information about military forces gaining international recognition, so (C) is incorrect. Likewise, there is no indication given that military forces can foster, or promote, alliances with other countries or successfully conquer other states, making (D) and (E) incorrect.

56. A

The New Urbanism movement calls for urban and suburban planners to make streets more walkable and thus less automobile dependent. Proponents argue that bike paths and walkways will enhance the health of residents and improve transportation routes. Therefore, **(A)** is correct. Gated communities are closed off to ensure that only residents and their guests are allowed to enter. (B) is incorrect. In a grid street system, streets run east/west and north/south, creating a grid pattern on the landscape. This is not directly related to what the mayor is supporting, so (C) is incorrect. A symbolic landscape is an urban landscape that reflects the city's history and has become synonymous with the city, so (D) is incorrect. (E) is incorrect because disamenities are factors that cause people to not want to live in the city. However, bike paths and walkways would be considered amenities.

57. C

The Organization of the Petroleum Exporting Countries (OPEC) was founded in 1960 and currently consists of 14 states. The mission of OPEC is to coordinate and unify its members' petroleum policies and to provide a regular supply of oil to maintain a stable, healthy oil market. Because the map shows the locations of oil reserves, which are the prime focus of this group, **(C)** is correct. The North Atlantic Treaty Organization (NATO) was created after World War II as a military alliance of 16 states, consisting of the United States, Canada, and 14 European countries. The prime focus of NATO was to counter communism, specifically as exported by the Soviet Union, making (A) incorrect. (B) is incorrect because the Arab League aims to strengthen ties and coordinate foreign and domestic policies in the Middle East and North Africa on a state and local level, but it is not concerned specifically with the world's oil reserves. The United Nations (UN) was established in 1945; it currently consists of nearly 200 states. Although the UN plays an important role in trying to bring peace to conflict-prone areas such as the Middle East and sub-Saharan Africa, its

primary focus has never been oil reserves. Similar to NATO, the Central Treaty Organization (CENTO) was created in response to the spread of the communism around the world, making (E) incorrect.

58. B

The primary reason why pork is not eaten in the Islamic diet is that it is proscribed by the religion. Pigs are seen as unclean animals, and, therefore, Muslims around the world avoid any type of food with pork in it. **(B)** is correct. Pork is avoided for religious reasons, not for regional reasons or dietary preference, making (A), (C), and (D) incorrect. There is no special designation for vegans in Islam, making (E) incorrect.

59. A

W.W. Rostow's model of economic development explains the phases that a country goes through before it becomes modernized. In stage 1, a country is classified as a "traditional society." The majority of people are involved in primary economic activities, such as subsistence agriculture. There is a small amount of regional trading and minimal access to education during this stage. **(A)** is correct, and therefore (B)–(E) are incorrect. As a country starts to develop some manufacturing, it moves into the "preconditions to takeoff" stage. As manufacturing expands due to industrialization, the economy starts to grow more rapidly; this is called "the takeoff" stage. As living standards rise, technology advances, and economic growth stabilizes, a country enters "the drive to maturity." In the last stage, "the age of mass consumption," a country's economy shifts from one that is based on manufacturing to one that is based on services and advanced technology. In this phase, the economy is robust, and consumerism and mass consumption are widespread.

60. E

Rice is the world's most-consumed grain. To grow, rice needs flat, low-lying land with plenty of water and a long growing season. It is also very labor intensive, meaning that a lot of people are needed to plant and harvest the crop. Rice production is essential to the livelihoods of millions of people in South and Southeast Asia. **(E)** is correct. Maize (corn), barley, sorghum, and rye are all very important grains, but none of these involve the same high level of labor-intensive, subsistence-based agriculture as does rice. (A)–(D) are incorrect.

Section II

1. A successful response to the free-response question accomplishes all tasks set forth by the prompt. Each part of the prompt is worth 1 point, for a total of 7 possible points.

(a) To earn the point, the response must define the essential characteristic of the World Systems Theory; it classifies countries into more developed (core) and less developed (periphery) countries according to their location and economic development. The response may include details such as the recent addition of semi-periphery countries in an intermediate stage of development; that core countries include those north of 30 degrees north latitude (North America, Europe, Japan), as well as Australia and New Zealand; and that core countries benefit from the resources of periphery countries.

(b) To earn the point, the response must use details to describe typical employment sectors in core countries and in periphery countries. The response should describe core countries as engaging primarily in service-based or tertiary economic activities and periphery countries as engaging primarily in primary economic activities, such as agriculture and mining. The response may indicate that core countries may engage in some manufacturing as well as quaternary and quinary activities. The response may also address semi-periphery countries, which are most likely to be engaged in secondary, or industrial, economic activities.

(c) To earn the point, the response must identify a demographic trend common in core countries. Examples include low birth rates, low death rates, and low or zero population growth.

(d) To earn the point, the response must use details to describe that core countries would be identified as stage 4 countries in the demographic transition model, since core countries engage in tertiary economic activities and have low or zero population growth.

(e) To earn the point, the response must identify a demographic trend common in periphery countries. Examples include high birth rates, increasingly lower death rates, and population growth.

(f) To earn the point, the response must use details to show that periphery countries would be identified as stage 2 countries in the demographic transition model, since periphery countries engage in primary economic activities and have high population growth. The response may also address semi-periphery countries, which would be identified as stage 3 countries, with decreasing birth rates and an economy based on secondary economic activities.

(g) To earn the point, the response must identify an economic relationship between two specific countries and use reasoning and/or examples to explain how this relationship demonstrates the dependency theory. The response should define the dependency theory as a feature of the interconnected global economy, in which some countries' economies, particularly those of periphery countries, become dependent on the export of a particular primary sector commodity. The response should then identify two specific countries, describe their economic relationship, and explain how this reflects the dependency theory; for example, coffee exports make up a significant portion of Ethiopia's exports, which are inexpensively purchased and resold for higher prices in the United States, creating a dependency on coffee in Ethiopia and vulnerability to world coffee prices set by core countries such as the United States.

2. A successful response to the free-response question accomplishes all tasks set forth by the prompt. Each part of the prompt is worth 1 point, for a total of 7 possible points.

(a) To earn the point, the response must use reasoning and/or examples to explain a way in which climate affects cattle production. Examples include that more developed countries tend to do livestock ranching in drier areas that would not be effective for crop farming; that the typically dry climates in livestock-ranching areas necessitate irrigation technology and large ranches to support huge cattle operations; that cattle production in the Midwestern United States tends to depend on the Corn Belt, which supplies feed for the animals; and that less developed countries tend to engage in pastoral nomadism to raise cattle in drier areas.

(b) To earn the point, the response must identify livestock ranching as an extensive agricultural activity and explain that extensive agriculture is characterized by the use of relatively small amounts of labor and resources in relation to the land being used; since livestock ranching uses a small amount of labor relative to ranching land, it is an example of extensive agriculture.

(c) To earn the point, the response must use details to describe von Thünen's model of agriculture. Details of the model include that certain crops/livestock are produced in relation to their distance from the market; items that cost more to transport to market due to weight or spoilage must be grown closer to markets to offset the transportation costs. The response could list the products of the six concentric rings of the model that extend outward from the market at the center: market gardening, dairy, livestock fattening, commercial grain, livestock ranching, and nonagricultural regions.

(d) To earn the point, the response must use reasoning and/or examples to explain a way in which von Thünen's model relates to cattle production. Examples include that the model places dairy production in the second ring from the center market because dairy products spoil quickly and must be produced relatively close to the market; that in livestock fattening regions (zone 3), where the goal is to fatten livestock to increase their value at sale, cattle graze on relatively smaller pastures because land is closer to the urban market and thus more expensive; that feedlots are used in livestock-fattening regions (zone 3) as large-scale centers of cattle fattening; that the model includes a region for growing grain (zone 4) to feed cattle in the livestock-fattening region (zone 3); and that livestock ranching occurs farthest from urban markets (zone 5) and uses the most land to graze cattle.

(e) To earn the point, the response must use reasoning and/or examples to explain a way in which culture impacts cattle production. Examples include that beef is a large part of Western diets, so cattle production is prioritized in Europe, the United States, and South America; that beef is typically not consumed in subsistence farming locations because cattle are used as part of the workforce, not as a food source; and that eating beef in some regions, such as traditional Hindu communities in India, is uncommon due to religious beliefs.

(f) To earn the point, the response must use reasoning and/or examples to explain whether the impact used in the answer to Part E impacts the expression of the von Thünen model. Examples include that cattle production in locations that follow a Western diet generally follows the model, with large-scale livestock fattening and ranching occurring relatively far from urban markets, as in the Great Plains and Midwest in the United States and Argentina in southern South America; that the cattle zones of the model might be absent in regions that practice subsistence agriculture or in places that typically do not consume beef (although India is increasingly participating in the exportation and consumption of beef and is currently more likely to have the cattle zones represented by the von Thünen model than in the past).

(g) To earn the point, the response must use reasoning and/or examples to explain why cattle production is absent in some world areas. Examples include cultural reasons, such as the Hindu religious beliefs in India; climate or environmental reasons, such as deserts or cold regions not providing enough vegetation for cattle to eat; and economic reasons, such as tropical regions relying on cash-crop production, cattle production requiring a relatively high investment to make a profit, cattle being used as part of the workforce in subsistence farming, and other sources of protein, such as fish in coastal regions, being more easily obtainable and cheaper than beef.

3. A successful response to the free-response question accomplishes all tasks set forth by the prompt. Each part of the prompt is worth 1 point, for a total of 7 possible points.

(a) To earn the point, the response must identify that the type of farming most likely practiced in England from 1400 to 1449 was subsistence, family, or small-scale farming, as indicated by the relatively low crop yield, as it predated the Second Agricultural Revolution.

(b) To earn the point, the response must use details to describe a development that increased crop yields in England during the Second Agricultural Revolution, reflected in the years shown in the table. Examples include the development of more efficient crop rotation, the enclosure movement creating large-scale farming operations, the invention of more efficient farming equipment, the beginning of the mechanization of agriculture, and improved transportation infrastructure to transport farm products.

(c) To earn the point, the response must use details to describe an impact of increased crop yields in England during the Second Agricultural Revolution. Examples include improving the diets of the population, displacing farmers as large-scale farming replaced small family farms, and creating an excess food supply to support industrial and urban workers.

(d) To earn the point, the response must use details to describe a development that increased crop yields in Mexico during the Green Revolution. Examples include the hybridization of crops resulting in advances such as the development of high-yield varieties of crops, drought- and disease-resistant crops, and crops that can grow in less favorable environments; increased use of pesticides and herbicides to improve crop survival rates; increased use of farm techniques such as irrigation systems, effective fertilization, and erosion prevention; and increased use of agricultural machinery and/or computerization.

(e) To earn the point, the response must use details to describe a way in which the Green Revolution succeeded. Examples include increasing food production in some world areas that adopted Green Revolution practices, such as in East Asia (China), South Asia (India), Southeast Asia (Indonesia and the Philippines), and South and Central America (Mexico and Brazil) and successfully cultivating crops due to hybridization or implementation of new agricultural techniques, such as cassava (in sub-Saharan Africa), cotton (in Burkina Faso), maize (in Mexico and sub-Saharan Africa), rice (in India and the Philippines), soybeans (in Brazil), and wheat (in Mexico and India).

(f) To earn the point, the response must use details to describe a way in which the Green Revolution did not meet expectations or drew criticism. Examples of the Green Revolution not meeting expectations include instances in which food production did not substantially increase, such as in sub-Saharan Africa, due to issues

such as government corruption or lack of support, lack of systems to distribute seed and fertilizers to farmers, poor soil and lack of water access, political instability disrupting economic systems, and systemic poverty limiting the amount of capital available to invest in new agricultural techniques. Criticisms of the Green Revolution include that its practices decreased biodiversity; that the environmental and health impacts of hybridization, chemical fertilizers, and major alterations to landscapes are unknown; that the growth of large-scale agribusinesses led to the decline of small family farms; and that the establishment of primarily cereal-based diets in some world regions provided inadequate nutrition.

(g) To earn the point, the response must use reasoning and/or examples to explain how the Green Revolution is significant in relation to population trends in less developed countries. The response must identify a relevant population trend in developing countries, such as growing populations, high birth rates, or relatively young populations. The response must then link the trend to the Green Revolution; examples include explaining that traditional forms of agriculture, such as subsistence farming, were likely insufficient to feed rapidly growing populations and necessitated more agricultural production; speculating on what might have happened if Green Revolution practices had not been adopted; or providing examples of specific countries' experiences.

Practice Exam 3

Practice Exam 3 Answer Grid

1. Ⓐ Ⓑ Ⓒ Ⓓ Ⓔ
2. Ⓐ Ⓑ Ⓒ Ⓓ Ⓔ
3. Ⓐ Ⓑ Ⓒ Ⓓ Ⓔ
4. Ⓐ Ⓑ Ⓒ Ⓓ Ⓔ
5. Ⓐ Ⓑ Ⓒ Ⓓ Ⓔ
6. Ⓐ Ⓑ Ⓒ Ⓓ Ⓔ
7. Ⓐ Ⓑ Ⓒ Ⓓ Ⓔ
8. Ⓐ Ⓑ Ⓒ Ⓓ Ⓔ
9. Ⓐ Ⓑ Ⓒ Ⓓ Ⓔ
10. Ⓐ Ⓑ Ⓒ Ⓓ Ⓔ
11. Ⓐ Ⓑ Ⓒ Ⓓ Ⓔ
12. Ⓐ Ⓑ Ⓒ Ⓓ Ⓔ
13. Ⓐ Ⓑ Ⓒ Ⓓ Ⓔ
14. Ⓐ Ⓑ Ⓒ Ⓓ Ⓔ
15. Ⓐ Ⓑ Ⓒ Ⓓ Ⓔ

16. Ⓐ Ⓑ Ⓒ Ⓓ Ⓔ
17. Ⓐ Ⓑ Ⓒ Ⓓ Ⓔ
18. Ⓐ Ⓑ Ⓒ Ⓓ Ⓔ
19. Ⓐ Ⓑ Ⓒ Ⓓ Ⓔ
20. Ⓐ Ⓑ Ⓒ Ⓓ Ⓔ
21. Ⓐ Ⓑ Ⓒ Ⓓ Ⓔ
22. Ⓐ Ⓑ Ⓒ Ⓓ Ⓔ
23. Ⓐ Ⓑ Ⓒ Ⓓ Ⓔ
24. Ⓐ Ⓑ Ⓒ Ⓓ Ⓔ
25. Ⓐ Ⓑ Ⓒ Ⓓ Ⓔ
26. Ⓐ Ⓑ Ⓒ Ⓓ Ⓔ
27. Ⓐ Ⓑ Ⓒ Ⓓ Ⓔ
28. Ⓐ Ⓑ Ⓒ Ⓓ Ⓔ
29. Ⓐ Ⓑ Ⓒ Ⓓ Ⓔ
30. Ⓐ Ⓑ Ⓒ Ⓓ Ⓔ

31. Ⓐ Ⓑ Ⓒ Ⓓ Ⓔ
32. Ⓐ Ⓑ Ⓒ Ⓓ Ⓔ
33. Ⓐ Ⓑ Ⓒ Ⓓ Ⓔ
34. Ⓐ Ⓑ Ⓒ Ⓓ Ⓔ
35. Ⓐ Ⓑ Ⓒ Ⓓ Ⓔ
36. Ⓐ Ⓑ Ⓒ Ⓓ Ⓔ
37. Ⓐ Ⓑ Ⓒ Ⓓ Ⓔ
38. Ⓐ Ⓑ Ⓒ Ⓓ Ⓔ
39. Ⓐ Ⓑ Ⓒ Ⓓ Ⓔ
40. Ⓐ Ⓑ Ⓒ Ⓓ Ⓔ
41. Ⓐ Ⓑ Ⓒ Ⓓ Ⓔ
42. Ⓐ Ⓑ Ⓒ Ⓓ Ⓔ
43. Ⓐ Ⓑ Ⓒ Ⓓ Ⓔ
44. Ⓐ Ⓑ Ⓒ Ⓓ Ⓔ
45. Ⓐ Ⓑ Ⓒ Ⓓ Ⓔ

46. Ⓐ Ⓑ Ⓒ Ⓓ Ⓔ
47. Ⓐ Ⓑ Ⓒ Ⓓ Ⓔ
48. Ⓐ Ⓑ Ⓒ Ⓓ Ⓔ
49. Ⓐ Ⓑ Ⓒ Ⓓ Ⓔ
50. Ⓐ Ⓑ Ⓒ Ⓓ Ⓔ
51. Ⓐ Ⓑ Ⓒ Ⓓ Ⓔ
52. Ⓐ Ⓑ Ⓒ Ⓓ Ⓔ
53. Ⓐ Ⓑ Ⓒ Ⓓ Ⓔ
54. Ⓐ Ⓑ Ⓒ Ⓓ Ⓔ
55. Ⓐ Ⓑ Ⓒ Ⓓ Ⓔ
56. Ⓐ Ⓑ Ⓒ Ⓓ Ⓔ
57. Ⓐ Ⓑ Ⓒ Ⓓ Ⓔ
58. Ⓐ Ⓑ Ⓒ Ⓓ Ⓔ
59. Ⓐ Ⓑ Ⓒ Ⓓ Ⓔ
60. Ⓐ Ⓑ Ⓒ Ⓓ Ⓔ

SECTION I

Time—60 Minutes

60 Questions

You have 60 minutes to answer the following 60 multiple-choice questions. Each of the questions or incomplete statements is accompanied by five possible answers or completions. Select the one that best answers the question or completes the statement.

Questions 1–2 refer to the chart below.

Demographic Transition in Russia

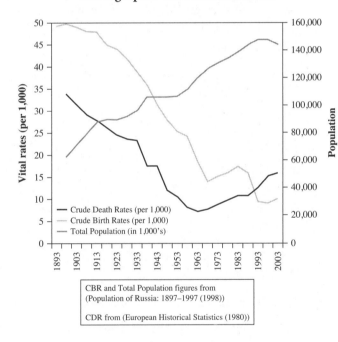

CBR and Total Population figures from
(Population of Russia: 1897–1997 (1998))

CDR from (European Historical Statistics (1980))

1. Based on the population data presented in the chart, Russia entered which stage of the demographic transition model in approximately 1993?

   (A) Stage 1

   (B) Stage 2

   (C) Stage 3

   (D) Stage 4

   (E) Stage 5

2. Which of the following results would be most likely to occur if the birth and death rates depicted in the chart stabilized at their 2003 levels?

   (A) Russia would reenter an agricultural phase of development.

   (B) The total population of Russia would experience a decline.

   (C) The Russian economy would suffer from a shortage of jobs.

   (D) The Russian government would likely encourage the use of birth control.

   (E) Russia would be unlikely to experience an increase in immigration rates.

GO ON TO THE NEXT PAGE

Country	City	Population
Brazil	São Paulo	12,176,866
	Rio de Janeiro	6,688,927
	Brasília	2,974,705
China	Shanghai	26,317,104
	Beijing	21,542,000
	Guangdong	14,904,400
Mexico	Mexico City	8,851,080
	Ecatepec	1,655,015
	Guadalajara	1,495,182

Cities listed are the three largest cities in their respective countries.

3. Which of the following is a primate city, based on the data shown in the table above?

(A) São Paulo

(B) Shanghai

(C) Beijing

(D) Mexico City

(E) Guadalajara

4. Which of the following forms of agriculture is traditionally practiced in more arid climates?

(A) Shifting cultivation

(B) Truck farming

(C) Commercial farming

(D) Subsistence farming

(E) Pastoral nomadism

Questions 5–6 refer to the table below.

Religion	Est. Number of Followers Worldwide
Islam	1,800,000,000
Catholicism	1,313,000,000
Evangelical Protestantism	619,000,000
Buddhism	520,000,000
Shinto	104,000,000

5. Based on the information in the table and your knowledge of geography, which of the following religions is most likely to be considered an ethnic religion?

(A) Islam

(B) Catholicism

(C) Evangelical Protestantism

(D) Buddhism

(E) Shinto

6. Which of the following correctly pairs a religion from the table with its hearth?

(A) Shinto and Western Europe

(B) Buddhism and South Asia

(C) Evangelical Protestantism and North Africa

(D) Catholicism and Latin America

(E) Islam and Central Asia

GO ON TO THE NEXT PAGE

Questions 7–8 refer to the map below.

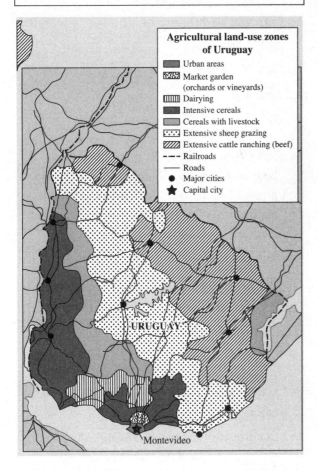

Agricultural land-use zones of Uruguay

- Urban areas
- Market garden (orchards or vineyards)
- Dairying
- Intensive cereals
- Cereals with livestock
- Extensive sheep grazing
- Extensive cattle ranching (beef)
- Railroads
- Roads
- ● Major cities
- ★ Capital city

URUGUAY

Montevideo

7. The designation of agricultural land-use zones in Uruguay, as depicted in the map, is most consistent with which of the following statements about von Thünen's model of agricultural land use?

(A) Agricultural products need to be close to market to minimize transportation costs.

(B) Raw materials need to be close to market to minimize transportation costs.

(C) Less-developed countries are considered periphery locations.

(D) Farmers practicing subsistence agriculture need to sell their products at a nearby market.

(E) Shepherds practicing pastoral nomadism move their herds to bring them to a commercial market.

8. Von Thünen's model of agricultural land use is usually represented by a series of concentric circles with the market at the center. Which of the following most likely explains why Uruguay's agricultural zones do not conform perfectly to von Thünen's concentric model?

(A) The presence of subsistence farming near markets has displaced some commercial farming activities.

(B) For cultural reasons, the people of Uruguay consume very little beef, leading to smaller zones for cattle ranching than is common in von Thünen's model.

(C) Geographical features can make some land unsuitable for certain types of commercial farming, regardless of the land's distance to markets.

(D) Uruguay has a primarily industrialized economy and relies almost exclusively on foreign imports of agricultural products.

(E) Grain is cheaper to transport to market in Uruguay than are most other agricultural products.

9. Which of the following theories, adopted by the Germans during World War II, proposed that whoever controls Eastern Europe and Western Asia could control the world?

(A) Rimland theory

(B) Heartland theory

(C) Domino theory

(D) World systems theory

(E) Core-periphery theory

GO ON TO THE NEXT PAGE

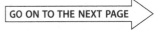

10. Which of the following most accurately describes how an economy develops, according to Rostow's development model?

    (A) Traditional society, transitional stage, drive to maturity, takeoff, age of mass consumption

    (B) Traditional society, takeoff, transitional stage, age of mass consumption, drive to maturity

    (C) Transitional stage, takeoff, traditional society, drive to maturity, age of mass consumption

    (D) Drive to maturity, traditional society, takeoff, transitional stage, age of mass consumption

    (E) Traditional society, transitional stage, takeoff, drive to maturity, age of mass consumption

11. The agricultural product that the majority of the world's population depends on for survival is

    (A) corn

    (B) wheat

    (C) barley

    (D) soybeans

    (E) rice

12. Which area of the world was the first to develop cotton, corn, and beans as primary agricultural products?

    (A) Southern India

    (B) Southeast Asia

    (C) Central America

    (D) Eastern Europe

    (E) Eastern Africa

13. Which of the following regions in the United States leads in coal production?

    (A) Appalachia

    (B) Gulf Coast

    (C) Western Pacific

    (D) Upper Midwest

    (E) Southwest Texas

14. Some countries, like Denmark, have state boundaries that closely coincide with the geographic boundaries of their dominant ethnic population. Which of the following terms best describes these countries?

    (A) Microstates

    (B) City-states

    (C) Stateless nations

    (D) Nation-states

    (E) Multistate nations

15. Which of the following illustrates the multiplier effect?

    (A) The steel industry has historically been the main focus of Pittsburgh's economy.

    (B) The steel industry in Pittsburgh has led to the expansion of the area's construction industries which has led to the expansion of raw material supply companies.

    (C) New restaurants have opened in Pittsburgh to help feed the community of steel workers.

    (D) The features of Pittsburgh's location make it an ideal spot to manufacture steel.

    (E) Pittsburgh's access to raw materials, clean water, and varied energy sources allows workers to propel the steel industry.

GO ON TO THE NEXT PAGE

Questions 16–18 refer to the maps below.

Map of Belgium

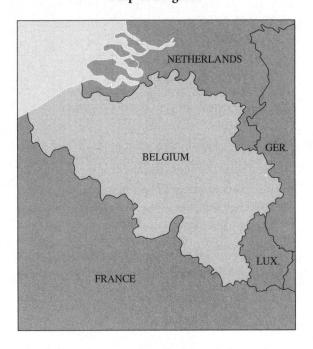

Map of Italy

16. Belgium's shape, as shown in the first map, is an advantage for which of the following reasons?

   (A) It allows for greater access to more natural resources.

   (B) It allows for more cultural cohesion.

   (C) It makes it easier to defend the country's borders.

   (D) It makes it difficult for another country to occupy Belgium.

   (E) It allows for lower tariffs for shipped goods.

17. Italy has two self-contained, autonomous states located within its borders: San Marino and Vatican City. Which of the following terms is most commonly used to describe countries, like Italy, with these types of political boundaries?

   (A) Enclave countries

   (B) Elongated countries

   (C) Fragmented countries

   (D) Perforated countries

   (E) Prorupted countries

18. Which of the following describes a consequence of Italy's shape, as shown in the second map?

   (A) Difficulty in transporting resources

   (B) A lack of natural resources

   (C) Central positioning of the government

   (D) Ease of monitoring political boundaries

   (E) Accessibility of government programs

GO ON TO THE NEXT PAGE

19. The Partition of India, in 1947, resulted in the creation of two newly independent countries: India, with a Hindu-majority population, and Pakistan, with a Muslim-majority population. The migration of Muslims from India and of Hindus from Pakistan following the Indian partition was most likely the result of which of the following types of factors that influence migration patterns?

    (A) An environmental push factor

    (B) An economic pull factor

    (C) An environmental pull factor

    (D) A political push factor

    (E) An economic push factor

20. Which statement best describes how European central business districts (CBDs) are different from those of most world cities?

    (A) European cities have their high-rises in their CBDs.

    (B) European cities' CBDs were designed to support modern transportation systems.

    (C) European cities have large areas devoted to foreign investment.

    (D) European cities' lower classes live in the CBDs.

    (E) European cities have narrow streets and low-rise buildings in their CBDs.

21. What do the languages of English, Spanish, and Hindi have in common?

    (A) They are all spoken primarily by people who share a common religion.

    (B) They are all spoken in the same countries.

    (C) All three derive from the Afro-Asiatic language family.

    (D) All three are spoken in their given locations primarily due to colonialism.

    (E) All three are in the Indo-European language family.

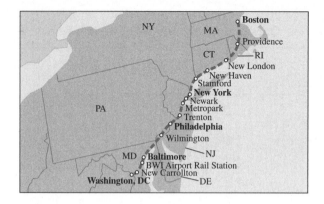

22. The map above shows Amtrak's main line in the Northeast corridor. The fact that there is more movement between Washington, D.C., and Baltimore than there is between Washington, D.C., and Philadelphia can best be characterized as a function of

    (A) distance decay

    (B) the gravity model

    (C) spatial interaction

    (D) cultural ecology

    (E) distribution

23. The term "formal region" refers to which of the following?

    (A) A region where everything has the same set of characteristics

    (B) A region where there are different characteristics

    (C) A region defined around a certain point or node

    (D) A region that exists primarily in an individual's perception or feelings

    (E) A region that speaks the same language

GO ON TO THE NEXT PAGE

24. The World Trade Center in New York City exemplified which of the following?

    (A) Symbolic landscape

    (B) Cityscape

    (C) Festival landscape

    (D) Cultural landscape

    (E) Folk landscape

25. Rapid population growth would likely lead to which of the following effects?

    (A) Increase in biodiversity

    (B) Environmental degradation

    (C) Improvement in air quality

    (D) Political stability

    (E) Environmental policy-making

Questions 26–27 refer to the map below.

Sector Model Applied to Chicago

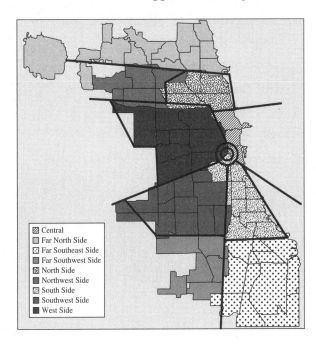

Legend:
- ▨ Central
- ☐ Far North Side
- ⊠ Far Southeast Side
- ▤ Far Southwest Side
- ▨ North Side
- ■ Northwest Side
- ▨ South Side
- ■ Southwest Side
- ■ West Side

---

26. Which of the following is true of the sector model for U.S. cities?

    (A) It demonstrates that areas are zoned off or gated off from other zones in the city.

    (B) It represents a city with growth that is connected to the central city by means of an arterial highway or interstate.

    (C) It suggests that lower classes live closest to the central business district, while the upper classes live farther out.

    (D) It describes a social structure based on transportation systems rather than on distance from the central business district.

    (E) It proposes that urban growth is independent of the central business district.

27. Most of the urban areas in the United States most accurately reflect which urban model?

    (A) Concentric zone model

    (B) Sector model

    (C) Multiple nuclei model

    (D) Central place theory

    (E) Von Thünen's model

28. Which vegetative hearth grew taro, bananas, and palm trees?

    (A) Southeast Asia

    (B) West Africa

    (C) Central America and northwestern South America

    (D) Northern China

    (E) Northeastern India

GO ON TO THE NEXT PAGE

29. Which of the following most directly produces a built environment?

    (A) Popular culture

    (B) Multicultural society

    (C) Folk culture

    (D) Non-material culture

    (E) Material culture

30. Democratization is more likely to occur in a country when that country has which of the following?

    (A) A relatively high level of wealth, a strong educational system, and strong social mobility

    (B) A relatively high level of wealth and a reliance on one or a few natural resources for its income

    (C) A relatively low level of wealth, a weak educational system, and little social mobility

    (D) A short cultural history and an unstable older population

    (E) A short cultural history and an unstable younger population

31. Which of the following boundary types best describes the western United States?

    (A) Cultural boundary

    (B) Subsequent boundary

    (C) Physical boundary

    (D) Geometric boundary

    (E) Antecedent boundary

32. Which of the following best explains a difference between eastern and western U.S. cities?

    (A) Eastern U.S. cities contain central business districts with skyscrapers.

    (B) Western U.S. cities rely on subway systems.

    (C) Western U.S. cities were built before the invention of the automobile.

    (D) Western U.S. cities have tightly packed residential areas.

    (E) Eastern U.S. cities tend to have narrow streets with parking in alleys.

33. Historically, the U.S. population has tended to move in which directions?

    (A) South, then east

    (B) North, then west

    (C) West, then south

    (D) North, then east

    (E) West, then north

GO ON TO THE NEXT PAGE

34. Which of the following types of farming involves abandoning fields and allowing the land to return to its natural state?

    (A) Intertillage

    (B) Mixed cropping

    (C) Pastoral nomadism

    (D) Plantation farming

    (E) Shifting cultivation

35. Which of the following correctly pairs the agricultural technique with its revolution?

    (A) Animal domestication and the First Agricultural Revolution

    (B) Planting of crops and the Second Agricultural Revolution

    (C) Hybridization and the Industrial Revolution

    (D) Planting of crops and the Third Agricultural Revolution

    (E) Animal domestication and the Green Revolution

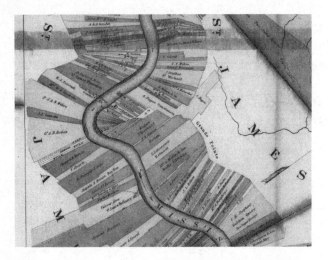

36. The land-survey pattern shown above is used in which part of the United States?

    (A) Midwest

    (B) New England

    (C) West Coast

    (D) Southwest

    (E) Southeast

37. According to Wallerstein's world systems analysis, which of the following areas represents less developed countries?

    (A) Core areas

    (B) Periphery areas

    (C) Semi-periphery areas

    (D) Industrial core areas

    (E) Upward transition areas

38. Which of the following is an example of a non-basic industry?

    (A) Manufacturing cars in Detroit

    (B) Producing steel in Pittsburgh

    (C) Milling in Minneapolis

    (D) Creating computer chips in Silicon Valley

    (E) Building homes in West Virginia

GO ON TO THE NEXT PAGE

City	Population	Land Area (square miles)
Boston	685 thousand	89.63
Madrid	3.17 million	233.3
Toronto	2.93 million	243.3
São Paulo	12.2 million	587
Washington, D.C.	633 thousand	68.34

39. Based on the chart above, which of the following metropolitan areas would most likely be considered a megacity?

    (A) São Paulo

    (B) Washington, D.C.

    (C) Toronto

    (D) Madrid

    (E) Boston

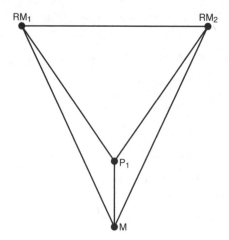

40. Which of the following best describes Weber's least cost theory?

    (A) The weight of the raw materials and the finished product will determine the location of the production facility.

    (B) A weight-gaining industry's production point will need to be located closer to the raw materials.

    (C) A weight-reducing industry's production point will need to be located closer to the market.

    (D) Variable costs fluctuate based on the volume of the order.

    (E) Fixed costs do not fluctuate based on the quantity ordered.

GO ON TO THE NEXT PAGE

41. Which of the following correctly pairs the area with its region type?

    (A) The South and formal region

    (B) Canada and formal region

    (C) Atlanta metropolitan area and vernacular region

    (D) The South and functional region

    (E) Canada and functional region

42. The United States and Canada are separated by the 49th parallel. Which of the following best describes this type of border?

    (A) Subsequent boundary

    (B) Geometric boundary

    (C) Superimposed boundary

    (D) Relic boundary

    (E) Antecedent boundary

Questions 43–44 refer to the map below.

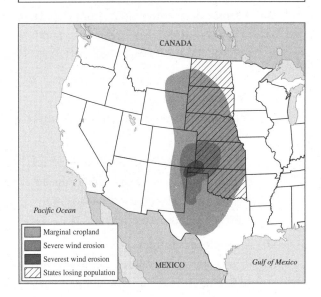

43. Which of the following factors most likely contributed to the Dust Bowl in the 1930s, pictured above?

    (A) Over-plowing the soil in the Great Plains

    (B) Under-plowing fields in the Great Plains

    (C) Massive migrations to the Great Plains

    (D) Heavy storms over the Great Plains

    (E) Weather conditions in California

44. Which of the following factors most likely led to migrations away from the Dust Bowl area of the Great Plains?

    (A) Economic pull factors

    (B) Economic push factors

    (C) Political pull factors

    (D) Political push factors

    (E) Environmental pull factors

GO ON TO THE NEXT PAGE

45. Which of the following is an example of an intervening opportunity?

    (A) A family decides to migrate from Florida to Chicago, only to later relocate to South Carolina for the warmer weather.

    (B) A family migrating from New York to California decides to stop in Chicago because of the high availability of premium jobs.

    (C) A family journeying from South America to New York is unable to continue due to a governmental restriction, so the family moves to Central America instead.

    (D) A couple moves from the city to the suburbs so that their children can receive an education in a specific school district.

    (E) A couple in Chicago relocates outside the city for employment opportunities in order to save enough money to move to San Francisco.

46. Which of the following best exemplifies the concept of commodity dependence?

    (A) The success of a core area depends on the use of a periphery area's labor supply.

    (B) The success of a core area depends on the use of a periphery area's natural resources.

    (C) A periphery area remains underdeveloped due to a lack of foreign investment.

    (D) A core area relies primarily on the export of oil for its economic growth.

    (E) A core area relies primarily on the import of oil for its economic growth.

47. Which of the following best describes one of Ravenstein's laws of migration?

    (A) Each migration produces a movement in the opposite direction.

    (B) Most migration is over a long distance.

    (C) Long-distance migrants usually move to rural areas.

    (D) People in cities migrate more than do people in rural areas.

    (E) Migration is mostly due to political causes.

48. Which of the following best describes a traditional society according to Rostow's model of development?

    (A) The majority of the workforce is involved in manufacturing.

    (B) Most people practice commercial farming.

    (C) Most people benefit from high mass consumption.

    (D) Most trade involves farmers and their agricultural products.

    (E) Growth takes place around large urban areas.

49. Renewable resources are an example of which of the following land-use models?

    (A) Sustainability

    (B) Economic

    (C) Environmental

    (D) Preservationist

    (E) Ecological

GO ON TO THE NEXT PAGE

50. Which of the following best explains how the Second Agricultural Revolution impacted populations?

    (A) People began to mechanize farming, increasing chemical use.

    (B) Fewer people were available for work in factories.

    (C) Populations decreased due to dangerous farming techniques.

    (D) Populations maintained healthier diets and longer life expectancies.

    (E) New crop hybridization methods increased food production for populations.

51. Which of the following best explains the bid-rent theory in the United States?

    (A) Wealthier families typically live within the central business district.

    (B) Only commercial landlords can afford the land within the central business district.

    (C) Shopping malls attract more customers than stand-alone stores.

    (D) Homes in the city are usually large and expensive.

    (E) It is more cost-effective to rent when living in the city.

52. Which of the following best identifies the region of Eastern Europe from the 1940s through the early 1990s?

    (A) Region unaffected by political conflict

    (B) Region dominated by theocracies

    (C) Core economic region

    (D) Homogeneous region

    (E) Shatterbelt region

53. In which of the following ways did the Industrial Revolution change many European cities?

    (A) More people migrated to suburbs.

    (B) Most rural villages experienced major population growth.

    (C) Cities became less crowded because of new transportation options.

    (D) Markets grew with increases in urban populations.

    (E) Agricultural products circulated primarily at the local level.

54. Which of the following best exemplifies the process of contagious diffusion?

   (A) The loss of parts of one's native culture after migration

   (B) A new video spreading rapidly online

   (C) The growing popularity of American-style pizza

   (D) The spread of rap music

   (E) The adoption of customs from a different culture

55. Which of the following urban design practices would a European urban planner most likely use to prevent urban sprawl?

   (A) Greenbelts

   (B) In-filling

   (C) Subway systems

   (D) City parks

   (E) Zoning laws

56. Which of the following best exemplifies traditional architecture?

   (A) Structures built in an area as it was first being established

   (B) Structures built after an area has been well established

   (C) Structures that are intrinsically linked to an area's culture

   (D) Structures not built by a professional craftsperson or artist

   (E) Structures that have two stories with chimneys on both sides

57. Which of the following is an example of national iconography?

   (A) Country flag

   (B) Official language

   (C) Dominant religion

   (D) Ports of trade

   (E) Governmental structure

58. Which of the following would most likely be considered a tertiary economic activity?

   (A) Gathering fruit from fields

   (B) Financial advising

   (C) Biomedical research

   (D) Repairing a cell phone

   (E) Manufacturing a car

GO ON TO THE NEXT PAGE

Questions 59–60 refer to the graphs below.

S-Curve

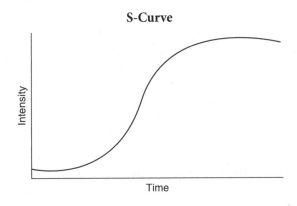

J-Curve

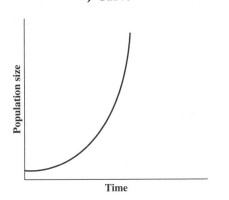

59. The S-curve is most often associated with what geographic factor?

(A) World population growth over time

(B) Immigration rates over time

(C) Economic development over time

(D) Cultural adaptation of ethnic groups over time

(E) The stability of countries' governments over time

60. A geographer who supports the conclusions of Thomas Malthus would most likely agree with which of the following statements?

(A) The J-curve illustrates the dangers presented by exponential population growth.

(B) The J-curve illustrates the ideal outcome offered through government-sponsored population control measures.

(C) The S-curve illustrates the dangers presented by exponential population growth.

(D) The S-curve illustrates the ideal outcome offered through government-sponsored population control measures.

(E) Neither the J-curve nor the S-curve has any connection with the work of Thomas Malthus.

END OF SECTION I

**IF YOU FINISH BEFORE TIME IS CALLED,
YOU MAY CHECK YOUR WORK ON SECTION I ONLY.
DO NOT GO ON TO SECTION II UNTIL INSTRUCTED TO DO SO.**

GO ON TO THE NEXT PAGE

SECTION II
Time—75 Minutes
3 Questions

You have 75 minutes to answer ALL THREE of the following questions. You should devote about 25 minutes to each question, including 5 minutes to plan each answer. While a formal essay is not required, it is not enough to answer a question by simply listing facts. Be sure that you number your answers, including each individual part.

1. Regionalization and globalization are two powerful, and sometimes opposing, trends occurring in today's world.

   (A) Define the concept of regionalization.

   (B) Define the concept of globalization.

   (C) Describe a specific example of regionalization.

   (D) Describe a specific example of globalization.

   (E) Describe a factor that has enabled globalization.

   (F) Explain the conflict that can exist between regionalization and globalization.

   (G) Explain a benefit that can result from globalization.

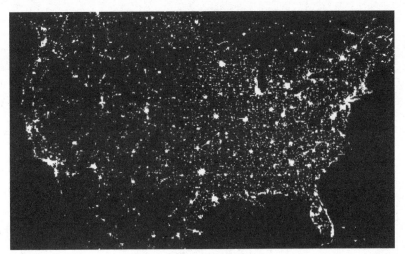

The United States at Night

2. This image is a composite of over 200 scans made by satellites of the U.S. Air Force Defense Meteorological Satellite Program (DMSP) Operational Linescan System. The DMSP satellites continue to help in the understanding and prediction of weather phenomena as well as provide key information about population patterns, city light levels, and even rural forest fires. The composite satellite image reveals electric usage, which is related to population distribution and density.

(A) Identify the difference between clustered and dispersed settlement patterns.

(B) Describe the overall population distribution in the contiguous United States as indicated by the satellite image using the terms *clustered settlement* and *dispersed settlement*.

(C) Describe a factor that has contributed to high population density in one specific region/metropolitan area of the contiguous United States.

(D) Describe a factor that has contributed to low population density in one specific region of the United States.

(E) Explain an impact of the settlement patterns shown on the satellite image on the economy of the United States.

(F) Explain an impact of the settlement patterns shown on the satellite image on the political situation in the United States.

(G) Assuming that the population distribution trends from the past 30 years continue, explain a way in which these trends will likely impact the satellite image in the future.

GO ON TO THE NEXT PAGE

POPULATION DATA

	World Averages	Argentina	United Kingdom	Zambia
Birth Rate per 1,000 People	20	19	12	45
Death Rate per 1,000 People	8	7	9	11

POPULATION PYRAMID, ANGOLA

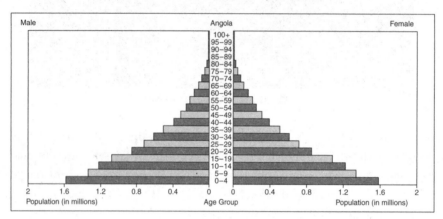

3. The demographic transition model uses statistics such as birth rates and death rates to describe both a country's demographics and economic development.

   (A) Identify how Zambia should be classified in the stages of the demographic transition model, based on the data in the table.

   (B) Explain Argentina's classification in the stages of the demographic transition model based on the data in the table.

   (C) Explain the United Kingdom's classification in the stages of the demographic transition model based on the data in the table.

   (D) Describe the likely features of Argentina's economy based on its placement in the demographic transition model based on the data in the table.

   (E) Describe the likely features of the United Kingdom's economy based on its placement in the demographic transition model based on the data in the table.

   (F) Explain which country—Argentina, the United Kingdom, or Zambia—would be most similar to Angola in terms of demographics and economics based on the data in the population pyramid.

   (G) Explain a likely economic or political impact of the demographic data shown in the population pyramid.

END OF SECTION II

ANSWER KEY

Section I

1. D	13. A	25. B	37. B	49. A
2. B	14. D	26. D	38. E	50. D
3. D	15. B	27. C	39. A	51. B
4. E	16. C	28. A	40. A	52. E
5. E	17. D	29. E	41. B	53. D
6. B	18. A	30. A	42. B	54. B
7. A	19. D	31. D	43. A	55. A
8. C	20. E	32. E	44. B	56. A
9. B	21. E	33. C	45. B	57. A
10. E	22. A	34. E	46. D	58. D
11. E	23. A	35. A	47. A	59. A
12. C	24. A	36. E	48. D	60. A

Section II

See Answers and Explanations and self-score your responses.

Section I Number Correct: _____

Section II Points Earned: _____

Sign into your online account at kaptest.com and enter your results in the scoring section to see your 1–5 score.

Haven't registered your book yet? Go to kaptest.com/moreonline to begin.

ANSWERS AND EXPLANATIONS

Section I

1. D

The demographic transition model is a tool used to categorize countries' population growth rates and economic structures. Traditionally, the model consists of four phases: Hunting and Gathering Societies (stage 1); Agricultural Societies (stage 2); Industrial Societies (stage 3); and Tertiary Societies (stage 4). Each phase is characterized by a certain set of trends in the birth, death, and overall population rates. According to the data in the chart, in 1993 Russia's birth and death rates were low and approximately equal, and its total population was entering a high-level plateau. These trends indicate a phase of zero population growth and are consistent with stage 4 of the demographic transition model, making **(D)** correct. The other choices are incorrect because they are not supported by the data in the chart. (A) is incorrect because stage 1 is characterized by low population growth rates and high-but-fluctuating birth and death rates. Similarly, (B) is incorrect because stage 2 is generally associated with a stable, high birth rate, which was not the case for Russia in 1993, according to the chart. (C) is incorrect because, during stage 3, the birth rate begins to fall but continues to exceed the death rate, leading to increases in the total population. Finally, (E) is incorrect because stage 5, currently a hypothetical stage of the demographic transition model, is characterized by long-term population decrease due to falling birth rates, but the Russian population reached a peak in 1993, and the decline thereafter is not sustained enough to fit stage 5.

2. B

According to the chart, in 2003 Russia's death rate exceeded its birth rate. Generally, this combination of trends, if it continues, means that the total population will decrease, making **(B)** correct. (A) is incorrect because agricultural development is associated with stage 2, and societies generally do not move backward in the demographic transition model unless they experience a nuclear attack or a similarly cataclysmic event. (C) is incorrect because low birth rates would be more likely to create a surplus of jobs than a job shortage. Similarly, (D) is incorrect because governments in countries with low birth rates tend to encourage people to have more children

rather than to use birth control. Finally, (E) is incorrect because information about birth and death rates cannot be used to make predictions about immigration rates, which depend on numerous other factors.

3. D

A primate city must have at least double the population of the second-largest city in that country, and it must be the cultural, political, and economic capital of the country. The table shows that Mexico City has a far greater population than the next two largest cities, Ecatepec and Guadalajara; therefore, **(D)** is correct and (E) is incorrect. São Paulo is not quite double the size of Rio de Janeiro; additionally, while it is a cultural center of Brazil, it is not a political center, so (A) is incorrect. The two largest cities in China, Shanghai and Beijing, are too close in size for either to be considered a primate city, making (B) and (C) incorrect.

4. E

Pastoral nomadism, which focuses on animal husbandry, is traditionally practiced in arid climates; **(E)** is correct. Shifting cultivation is a type of crop rotation that is practiced in multiple climates, but especially in tropical climates, making (A) incorrect. Truck farming, (B), is based on the exchange of commodities. Commercial farming, (C), is mainly concerned with profiting from crops or animals. Subsistence farmers, (D), primarily eat what they grow. All three of these types of agriculture are practiced in a variety of climates.

5. E

In ethnic religions, followers are typically born into the faith, and little to no effort is put forth to convert others. In universalizing religions, by contrast, members actively try to convert others. As a result, ethnic religions tend to have smaller numbers of followers than universalizing religions. Of the religions listed in the table, Shinto, **(E)**, has the smallest number of followers and it is, in fact, an ethnic religion. (A), (B), (C), and (D) are incorrect because Islam, Catholicism, Evangelical Protestantism, and Buddhism are all universalizing religions that actively promote conversion.

6. B

South Asia, specifically northern India, gave birth to two of the world's major religions, Buddhism and Hinduism. **(B)** is therefore correct. (A) is incorrect because Shinto originated in East Asia, specifically Japan. (C), (D), and (E) are incorrect because Judaism, Christianity (which includes both Evangelical Protestantism and Catholicism), and Islam all originated in Southwest Asia, specifically the areas that now include Israel and Saudi Arabia.

7. A

The von Thünen model represents the locations of agricultural production areas relative to the market in a commercial farming system. The type of product grown or raised by the farmer depends on the cost of transporting the product to the market; therefore, **(A)** is correct. Because von Thünen's model addresses an agricultural product's distance from the market, not a raw material's, (B) is incorrect. (C) is incorrect because it reflects the world systems theory, which speaks to the relationship between core and periphery countries. Subsistence farmers eat the majority of the products they produce, therefore not needing to transport their goods to the market, and pastoral nomadism is a form of subsistence agriculture; (D) and (E) are incorrect.

8. C

Von Thünen's model states that certain agricultural products are grown in direct relation to their distance from the market, with the items that are most expensive to transport being grown closest to the market. Usually, this means that dairy farming is conducted relatively close to market because of the costs associated with milk refrigeration, while grain production is carried out further from market since it can be transported more cheaply. However, in Uruguay, there is a zone of grain production that is closer to the market than the zone for dairy farming. One reason for this might be that the land closer to the market is unsuitable for dairy farming; another is that the land where dairy farming takes place is unsuitable for grain production. In other words, geographical features can impact the way that agricultural zones develop around a market, resulting in deviations from von Thünen's model. Thus, **(C)** is correct. Subsistence farmers produce food primarily for their families, so their location with respect to markets is far less important, making (A) incorrect. (B) is incorrect because, according to the map, Uruguay has a sizable zone for cattle ranching. (D) is also inconsistent with the map, as nearly all of the land area within Uruguay has been assigned a designated agricultural zone; if Uruguay were primarily industrialized and relied almost exclusively on imports for food, it is unlikely that so much of the country's land area would be devoted to commercial farming. Finally, (E) is incorrect because if grain was cheaper to transport, the zones for grain production would be located farther out from market; however, according to the map, one of the zones for grain production is actually closer to market than von Thünen's model predicts.

9. B

The heartland theory, proposed by Halford Mackinder, was the justification for the Germans to invade Poland and Eastern Europe during World War II; this theory states that whoever controls Eastern Europe and Western Asia will control the world. Thus, **(B)** is correct. An alternate theory, the rimland theory, was proposed by Nicholas Spykman; it states that whoever controls the seas and coasts will control Europe and Asia, making (A) incorrect. The domino theory holds that if a state adopts communism, surrounding states are more likely to adopt communism as well; thus, (C) is incorrect. The world systems theory and the core-periphery theory are both models of how global economies have developed and do not comment on geopolitical control, eliminating (D) and (E).

10. E

According to Rostow's model, societies start off as traditional societies, in which the economy is based on agriculture and mass production has not yet developed. The second phase is the transitional phase, in which a country starts to develop an infrastructure, an education system, and trade relations; business developers also emerge and begin to undertake money-making activities. Next is the takeoff stage, wherein more companies become involved in manufacturing; growth is generally limited to large urban areas and only a few industries. Then comes the drive to maturity stage, where technology advances and is integrated into all areas of industry. The final phase is the age of mass consumption; workers have become highly skilled, and the economy is stable. While manufacturing is still important, an economic sector emerges that is focused on service- and knowledge-based activities. Thus, **(E)** is correct. (A)–(D) are incorrect because they list the stages in the incorrect order.

11. E

The majority of the world's population, more than 58 percent, lives in Asia, where rice is typically eaten daily. Rice is an inexpensive crop that millions of people can afford, and subsistence farmers around the world, in warmer climates, grow rice to sustain themselves; **(E)** is correct. Although corn, wheat, soybeans, and barley are important, they are not eaten by as many people on a daily basis as rice; thus, (A)–(D) are incorrect.

12. C

Central America first developed cotton, beans, and corn, which are commonly cited as examples of crops introduced to Europe and other parts of the world via the Colombian Exchange; thus, **(C)** is correct. It is believed that agriculture developed in three areas of the world: Central America and northwestern South America, West Africa, and Southeast Asia. (A), (D), and (E) are incorrect because these are not agricultural hearths. Southeast Asia is where root crops such as taro, bananas, and palm trees were first domesticated; (B) is incorrect.

13. A

The leading coal-producing region in the United States is the Appalachia region; **(A)** is correct. The Gulf Coast is not a coal-producing region, eliminating (B). While some coal is mined in the West, Midwest, and Southwest, the volume and quality of coal is far less than that mined in the Appalachia region, making (C)–(E) incorrect.

14. D

A country whose state boundaries largely coincide with the boundaries of its dominant ethnic group is considered a nation-state, making **(D)** correct. (A) and (B) are incorrect because they refer to small states (microstates) and states that consist of a single urban center and its surrounding area (city-states); while some nation-states might be considered microstates or city-states, Denmark is not. (C) refers to an ethnic group that lacks a sovereign government, such as the Kurds in the Middle East or the Basque in Spain and France. (E) is incorrect because a multistate nation would consist of an ethnic group with multiple sovereign governments, such as the Korean people who live in North Korea and South Korea.

15. B

The multiplier effect describes the expansion of an area's economic base as a result of the basic and non-basic industries located there, which matches **(B)**. The fact that steel has historically been the main focus of Pittsburgh's economy is an example of a basic industry, not the multiplier effect, eliminating (A). (C) is incorrect because this describes a non-basic industry. The reference to Pittsburgh's surrounding area represents a situation factor; (D) is incorrect. Pittsburgh's access to raw materials, clean water, and varied energy sources refers to its site factors, making (E) incorrect.

16. C

Belgium has a compact shape. Because compact countries have relatively small and circular shapes, the distance from the center to any boundary doesn't vary much. As a result, the country is easier to defend than states of other shapes, making **(C)** is correct. Access to useful raw materials is an advantage for prorupted countries, not compact ones, so (A) is incorrect. While a compact state could have more cultural cohesion, this is not guaranteed. In Belgium's case, there have long been tensions between the Dutch-speaking (Flemish) and French-speaking (Walloon) populations based on differences in language, culture, and economic opportunities; thus, (B) is incorrect. An advantage of a fragmented, not compact, state is that it is so spread out that another country would have a hard time gaining control over it; thus, (D) is incorrect. Finally, Belgium's location near water, rather than its shape, would explain why tariffs would be lower, since imported goods wouldn't need to travel by land across other countries in order to get to Belgium; thus, (E) is incorrect.

17. D

A state that contains another state completely within its borders is called a perforated country; thus, **(D)** is correct. (A) is incorrect because it is used to describe countries like San Marino and Vatican City, which are contained completely within other countries. (B) and (C) are incorrect for similar reasons: while Italy is considered an elongated country because it is twice as long as it is wide, and could be considered a fragmented country because it has some islands, these features are unrelated to the presence of enclave countries within Italy's borders. Finally, prorupted countries are those land protrusions extending from the mainland; this is not the correct term for what is described in the question stem, making (E) incorrect.

18. A

A disadvantage of Italy's long and narrow shape is that it can make the transportation of resources challenging; **(A)** is correct. Compact countries, not elongated countries, typically suffer a lack of natural resources, making (B) incorrect. (C), (D), and (E) are incorrect because these represent advantages of compact countries like Belgium rather than features of elongated countries like Italy.

19. D

Following the Partition of India, Muslims living in India and Hindus living in Pakistan feared persecution within their respective countries. As a result, many Muslims living in India migrated to Pakistan, and many Hindus living in Pakistan migrated to India. Fear of persecution is an example of a political push factor, that is, a factor related to one's political status that prompts an individual to leave an area. **(D)** is correct. Environmental moves are often voluntary, such as when people relocate to a more desirable climate; (A) and (C) are incorrect. Economic factors cause people to move to where they can find employment, making (B) and (E) incorrect.

20. E

European cities have low-rise buildings, usually no higher than five or six stories, in their central business districts, along with narrow streets; **(E)** is correct. These cities were built hundreds of years ago, before the rise of modern transportation and high-rise buildings, making (A) and (B) incorrect. European cities are not unique in devoting areas to foreign investments; many other world cities, such as Shanghai, also do this, making (C) incorrect. In European cities, the wealthy live in the city center, and the lower classes live in the suburbs, eliminating (D).

21. E

English, Spanish, and Hindi are all languages within the Indo-European language family; thus, **(E)** is correct and (C) is incorrect. Religious systems do not play a major role in these three languages, eliminating (A). (B) is incorrect because English, Spanish, and Hindi are not all spoken in the same countries. None of the three languages are spoken where they are primarily due to colonialism; this is more primarily based on migration patterns, making (D) incorrect.

22. A

Distance decay means that there will be more interaction between two places that are closer to each other than between places that are farther apart. Because Washington, D.C., is closer to Baltimore than it is to Philadelphia, there is more interaction (movement of people, products, and ideas) between Washington, D.C., and Baltimore; **(A)** is correct. The gravity model suggests that the greater the sphere of influence a city has, the greater its impact on other cities around it. Because this does not address the distances between these cities, (B) is incorrect. Spatial interaction is concerned with how well an area is connected to the rest of the world, which would not specifically explain why there is more interaction and movement between D.C. and Baltimore, making (C) incorrect. (D) and (E) are incorrect because they are not relevant to the question at hand; cultural ecology is the study of how humans adapt to various environments, and distribution focuses on how people or objects are organized in an area.

23. A

A formal region (also called a "uniform region") is an area, such as a city or state, that is marked by a common set of characteristics; thus, **(A)** is correct and (B) is incorrect. A region defined around a certain point or node is a functional region, eliminating (C). (D) is incorrect because vernacular regions exist primarily in an individual's perception or feelings. While people in the same formal region may speak the same language, this is not necessarily true. The shared characteristic could instead include a political factor or other cultural trait; therefore, (E) is incorrect.

24. A

A symbolic landscape reflects a location's history and has become synonymous with the location. The World Trade Center represented a particular aspect of Western culture in their grandiose splendor; this was likely one reason they were targeted for the 9/11 terrorist attack. Thus, **(A)** is correct. A cityscape refers to a view or picture of an urban area. While the World Trade Center was once part of the New York cityscape, it was not itself the cityscape, so (B) is incorrect. (C), (D), and (E) are incorrect because they are not matches for the example of the World Trade Center. A festival landscape is a space that can accommodate a large number of people, such as Central Park in New York City. Cultural landscapes exhibit traits of the surrounding landscape and culture; examples are city parks. A folk landscape is defined by people's perception of an area; the Wild West is an example of a folk landscape in American culture.

25. B

Rapid population growth can lead to water pollution and a strain on an area's resources, causing environmental degradation; **(B)** is correct. A spike in population growth can lead to a decrease in biodiversity and an increase in air pollution, making (A) and (C) incorrect. Rapid growth in the population is more likely to cause political instability than political stability, making (D) incorrect. Lastly, there is no indication that population leads to an increase in any kind of policymaking; (E) is incorrect.

26. D

The sector model is based on class and describes the social structure in relation to transportation systems rather than to distance from the central business district; **(D)** is correct. (A) is incorrect because this statement describes the Keno-capitalism model, which suggests that zones in the city are randomly placed in the city but are separated from each other by walls. The galactic city model, not the sector model, shows that a city with growth independent of the central business district is traditionally connected to the central city by a highway or interstate; (B) is incorrect. In the concentric zone model, the upper classes tend to live farther away from the central business district than do the lower classes because the upper classes can better afford to commute to work, making (C) incorrect. The multiple nuclei model suggests that growth may begin in commercial, industrial, or residential areas outside of the central business district, making (E) incorrect.

27. C

The multiple nuclei model was created to better reflect the complexities of American cities, such as Chicago, the city it was based on. **(C)** is correct. The multiple nuclei model suggests that, even if there is a central business district, there are additional other CBDs within a city and on its outskirts. This is in opposition to the concentric zone model, which posits that there is one CBD surrounded by a series of concentric rings. Thus, (A) is incorrect. (B) is incorrect because the sector model suggests that growth extends along transportation routes, a pattern that does not describe most of the urban areas in the United States. Central place theory describes the mutually beneficial relationship between an urban area and its surrounding hinterlands; it is not an urban model that describes how a city is laid out, so (D) is incorrect. Von Thünen's model focuses on transportation in terms of agriculture, not urban areas; (E) is also incorrect.

28. A

There are three major vegetative hearths: Central America and northwestern South America, West Africa, and Southeast Asia. Southeast Asia was a hearth for taro, bananas, and palm trees; **(A)** is correct. (B) is incorrect because the major domesticated agricultural products in West Africa were yams and palm oil. Central America and northwestern South America grew manioc, squash, and sweet potatoes, eliminating (C). Northern China and northeastern India were seed hearths rather than vegetative hearths, making (D) and (E) incorrect.

29. E

A built environment results from the tangible impact of material culture on a landscape. Thus, **(E)** is correct and (D) is incorrect. (A), (B), and (C) are incorrect because popular culture, multicultural society, and folk culture do not directly impact the tangible, material landscape.

30. A

A country that has a relatively high level of wealth, a strong educational system, and strong social mobility tends to have a better chance at becoming a democracy. **(A)** is correct and (C) is incorrect. If a country relies on one or a few natural resources for most of its wealth, then democratization tends not to happen because the resources are typically controlled by the ruling authority or power elite; (B) is incorrect. Democratization also tends to happen in countries with longer cultural histories and stable populations, making (D) and (E) incorrect.

31. D

Many of the boundaries in the western United States, such as those of Colorado, Wyoming, and Utah, are geometric boundaries. Geometric boundaries are created using lines of longitude and latitude. Thus, **(D)** is correct and (A) is incorrect. Subsequent boundaries develop along with the development of the cultural landscape; (B) is incorrect. The western United States' boundaries were not decided based on natural features, making (C) incorrect. (E) is incorrect because antecedent boundaries exist before the settlement of an area and this is not true of the western United States.

32. E

Eastern U.S. cities tend to have narrow streets with parking in alleys because these cities were built prior to the invention of cars, making **(E)** correct and (C) incorrect. Both western and eastern U.S. cities have central business districts with skyscrapers, eliminating (A). Transportation in western U.S. cities relies on automobiles and mass public transportation, but not on subway systems, so (B) is incorrect. (D) is incorrect because eastern, not western, U.S. cities have tightly packed residential areas.

33. C

The U.S. population has consistently moved west and then south, which matches **(C)**. (A) is incorrect because the U.S. population only started to move south within the last 40 years and has not collectively moved east. The north is considered to have more environmental push factors than pull factors, making (B), (D), and (E) incorrect.

34. E

Shifting cultivation is a method in which a plot of land is cleared by burning, cultivated for a period of time, and then abandoned by the farmer so that the land can revert to its normal state. The farmer moves on to newer fields containing more productive soil. Thus, **(E)** is correct. (A) is incorrect because intertillage is the clearing of fields using hoes, rakes, and other manual equipment. Mixed cropping is a type of agriculture that involves planting two or more plants simultaneously in the same field, making (B) incorrect. Pastoral nomadism is a form of subsistence farming that involves moving herds from place to place, based on factors such as the weather and available grazing lands; (C) is incorrect. A plantation is a large farm in tropical and subtropical climates that specializes in the production of one or two crops for sale, making (D) incorrect.

35. A

In the First Agricultural Revolution, humans began to diversify their food supply by planting crops and domesticating wild animals, such as cows, chickens, and pigs; thus, **(A)** is correct. The Second Agricultural Revolution, which occurred during the Industrial Revolution, used new technology to increase the production and distribution of products, eliminating (B) and (C). The Third Agricultural Revolution, also called the Green Revolution, dealt with the hybridization of crops, not crop or animal domestication; (D) and (E) are incorrect.

36. E

The image depicts a long lots system, which is based around access to rivers; the narrow lots extend far back from the river, allowing distribution of various soil types to farms on the river plain and providing a means of transportation for agricultural goods. In what became the modern-day Southeast United States, the French initiated the long lots system, which is still in use in areas such as Louisiana. Thus, **(E)** is correct. (A) is incorrect because the Midwest, due to its relatively flat landscape and the earlier prominence of railroads, uses the township and range system, which divides up land in rectangular patterns. (B) is incorrect because New England has traditionally used the British metes and bounds system, in which the land's physical features are used to describe ownership claims. Newer geographical survey methods have been the primary ways in which land has been divided up in the West and Southwest, making (C) and (D) incorrect.

37. B

Wallerstein's world systems analysis is composed of three areas: the core, periphery, and semi-periphery. The less developed countries are found in the periphery; **(B)** is correct. Developed countries are in the core areas, and countries gaining in development are in the semi-periphery; (A) and (C) are incorrect. The industrial core and upward transition areas are part of the core-periphery model and were not included in Wallerstein's world systems analysis. Nearly all countries have certain areas that fall into the categories of industrial core and upward transition; therefore, (D) and (E) are incorrect.

38. E

Non-basic industries are secondary businesses that support employees who are working in an area's basic industry. **(E)** is correct because home construction is not West Virginia's basic industry; however, businesses that build homes in West Virginia support the state's main industry, which is coal mining. (A), (B), (C), and (D) are incorrect because all of these are the basic industries in the cities listed.

39. A

A metropolitan area inhabited by more than 10 million people is considered a megacity, and São Paulo has a population of more than 12 million. Therefore, **(A)** is correct. Land area is not a factor in determining whether a metropolitan area is a megacity. The cities in (B)–(E) have fewer than 10 million residents, so these choices are incorrect.

40. A

According to Weber's least cost theory, an industry selects its production location based on the weight of the raw materials and the finished product; **(A)** is correct. In a weight-gaining industry, the finished goods weigh more than the raw materials; (B) is incorrect because a weight-gaining industry would want its production facility closer to the finished goods market. In a weight-reducing industry, the final product weighs less than the raw materials. (C) is incorrect because a weight-reducing industry would want to be closer to the raw materials. While (D) and (E) are both true statements, these statements are not directly part of Weber's least cost theory.

41. B

A formal region is any area that is clearly marked with a border, such as a city, state, or a country, making **(B)** correct. A vernacular region (also known as perceptual region) is not defined by any borders or boundaries, but rather is defined by a person's own understanding of an area; an example in the United States is the South. Thus (A) and (D) are incorrect. A functional region contains a city and its surrounding suburbs, such as metropolitan areas, so (A) and (E) are incorrect.

42. B

The 49th parallel is based upon measurements of latitude and longitude. Thus, it is a geometric boundary and **(B)** is correct. Subsequent boundaries develop along with the development of the cultural landscape; (A) is incorrect. (C) is incorrect because a superimposed boundary is a political boundary that ignores the existing cultural organization on the landscape. A relic boundary is a boundary that no longer exists, making (D) incorrect. An antecedent boundary is one that existed before human settlement of the area, but the boundary between America and Canada was decided upon after settlement by various groups; (E) is incorrect.

43. A

During the 1930s, the Great Plains experienced severe drought-like conditions. The dry conditions were made worse by continued plowing of farm fields, leading to massive dust storms; therefore, **(A)** is correct and (B) is incorrect. During the 1930s, millions of people left the Great Plains. A majority went westward, seeking jobs and better lives for their families; (C) is incorrect. (D) is incorrect because the region's dust storms started with a drought. While many people migrated from the Great Plains to California, the weather in California did not cause the Dust Bowl, making (E) incorrect.

44. B

Between the drought and the Great Depression, many farmers went out of business during the 1930s, leading them to seek employment elsewhere in the United States. Thus, **(B)** is correct. (A) is incorrect because it would mean that people were moving from the Great Plains primarily because better economic opportunities were to be had elsewhere; while migrants hoped to be able to make a living in their new locations, the main impetus for moving was the desperately poor conditions in the Dust Bowl. Political push and pull factors are in play when migrants feel threatened by the government, which was not the case during the Dust Bowl, making (C) and (D) incorrect. (E) is incorrect because the Dust Bowl was an environmental disaster and thus an environmental push factor; as with economic opportunities, people certainly hoped for better conditions elsewhere, but they moved because conditions on the Great Plains were bad, not because the climate in California, for example, was good.

45. B

An intervening opportunity occurs when a migrant stops and remains at a particular point along the journey because of favorable economic opportunities or environmental amenities. **(B)** is correct because, in this example, the family stopped its migration to live in Chicago for employment. (C) is incorrect because this is an example of an intervening obstacle, not an intervening opportunity. (A), (D), and (E) are incorrect because the migrants did not stop and permanently settle while on their migratory paths.

46. D

Commodity dependence means that an area (whether core or periphery) relies primarily on the export of a product for its economic growth; thus, **(D)** is correct and (E) is incorrect. While (A)–(C) are true, these statements describe the broader world systems theory of Wallerstein rather than commodity dependence specifically.

47. A

E.G. Ravenstein, a nineteenth-century geographer, created 10 laws of migrations based on his research. One of these laws states that each migration produces a movement in the opposite direction; thus, **(A)** is correct. Ravenstein found that most migrations occur over a short distance, making (B) incorrect. He also found that since long-distance migrants usually move to cities, (C) is incorrect. Ravenstein's laws show that people in rural areas migrate more than people in cities, making (D) incorrect. Because migration is mostly due to economic causes, according to Ravenstein, (E) is incorrect.

48. D

In Rostow's five-stage model of development, stage 1 is called the traditional society. During this stage, society is based on subsistence farming, and most trade involves farmers and their agricultural products. **(D)** is correct. A large percentage of the workforce will not move into manufacturing until stage 3, the takeoff; (A) is incorrect. (B) is incorrect because commercial farming starts to develop in stage 2, the preconditions to takeoff. Stage 5 is characterized by high mass consumption; thus, (C) is incorrect. Growth begins to take place around large urban areas in stage 3; (E) is also incorrect.

49. A

Renewable resources are an example of the sustainability land-use model, which entails taking something from the land while ensuring there is enough of the resource for future generations. Thus, **(A)** is correct. (B), (C), and (D) are incorrect because the other three types of land-use models—economic, environmental, and preservationist—do not explain the concept of renewable resources. The economic land-use model is used to develop and build on a landscape. The environmental land-use model suggests that human development should impact the land as little as possible. Preservationists believe that land should go untouched by humans. Lastly, (E) is incorrect because "ecological" is not a type of land-use model.

50. D

The Second Agricultural Revolution brought new technology and an increase in food production, which eventually led to healthier diets, longer life expectancies, and more people being available for factory work. Thus, **(D)** is

correct and (B) is incorrect. (A) and (E) are incorrect because these describe the Green Revolution, not the Second Agricultural Revolution. The increased food production and technological advancements contributed to unprecedented population growth, making (C) incorrect.

51. B

The bid-rent theory states that only commercial landlords can afford the land within the central business district (CBD) and that as a person moves farther from the CBD, the value of the land decreases. Thus, **(B)** is correct. (A) is incorrect because the suburbs have more land per residence, on average, and families typically choose to move to the suburbs in the United States. The bid-rent theory does not address the idea of agglomeration or its advantages, eliminating (C). According to the bid-rent theory, homes in the inner city usually have smaller lots and are typically apartments; (D) is incorrect. Because of the limited land in the city, it is much more expensive to live near the CBD than in the suburbs, making (E) incorrect.

52. E

Eastern Europe from the 1940s to the early 1990s is considered a shatterbelt—a region caught between two stronger, conflicting powers—because it was an area sandwiched between the Soviet Union and Western Europe during the Cold War. Therefore, **(E)** is correct and (A) is incorrect. Though many countries in Eastern Europe have strong religious traditions, none were ruled by a theocracy, making (B) incorrect. (C) is incorrect because the region was economically depressed while under the influence of the Soviet Union. Eastern Europe is fairly mountainous and ethnically diverse, making it a region that is difficult to control and unite politically, so (D) is also incorrect.

53. D

The Industrial Revolution brought significant changes to Europe, including the growth of markets that went along with the increase in urban populations; **(D)** is correct. As fewer people were needed on farms, more migrated to cities searching for employment, making (A) and (C) incorrect. The Industrial Revolution did not dramatically increase the size of rural villages, making (B) incorrect. With new methods of transportation, agricultural products could be sent farther; (E) is also incorrect.

54. B

Contagious diffusion is the rapid transmission of an idea or cultural trend. This type of diffusion is called "contagious" because the information spreads quickly, like a virus. A new video going viral online is an example of contagious diffusion, making **(B)** correct. Losing parts of one's native culture after migration is assimilation; (A) is incorrect. The Americanization of pizza (an Italian food) is an example of stimulus diffusion, which occurs when a cultural trend is adopted and changed by another culture; (C) is incorrect. (D) is incorrect because rap music represents the diffusion of something from a powerful minority to the majority, which is hierarchical diffusion. Adopting the customs of a new culture is called acculturation, eliminating (E).

55. A

In order to prevent urban sprawl in Europe, city planners established greenbelts, which are tracts of farmland, forests, or other green spaces set aside to prevent development from extending too far outward. Thus, **(A)** is correct. In-filling is another phenomenon greenbelts help to prevent. In-filling occurs when neighboring cities merge together; thus (B) is incorrect. (C) and (D) are incorrect because subway systems and city parks do not slow the expansion of urban development. Zoning laws determine how land and buildings can be used; as they only help to determine how land is used, they do not directly address the issue of urban sprawl, eliminating (E).

56. A

Traditional architecture includes structures built prior to or very early in an area's establishment. The log cabin, for example, was a traditional form of architecture in early America. Therefore, **(A)** is correct and (B) is incorrect. (C) is incorrect because a structure could have been built in an area as it was first being established without continuing to be linked to its culture. Any structure not built by a professional or an artist is classified as indigenous rather than traditional, eliminating (D). Traditional architecture is not defined by size, so (E) is incorrect.

57. A

National iconography is any symbol of nationalism, such as a country's flag; **(A)** is correct. A country's official language and dominant religion are part of a nation's culture; however, these are not considered part of the national iconography, making (B) and (C) incorrect. Ports of trade and government structure are also not parts of the national iconography, making (D) and (E) incorrect.

58. D

Tertiary economic activities are service-oriented activities. Repairing a cell phone is an example of such an activity, making **(D)** correct. Gathering fruit from fields falls into the category of a primary economic activity, making (A) incorrect. Financial advising and biomedical research are quaternary economic activities, which are knowledge-based services; (B) and (C) are incorrect. (E) is incorrect because making a car is an activity of the secondary economic sector, which is centered on manufacturing.

59. A

The S-curve is most closely associated with world population growth over the past two centuries. After a period of exponential growth, the population increase eventually slows, owing to a lack of resources needed to sustain such a large population, and the population may even decline; the resulting graph resembles the letter S. Thus, **(A)** is correct. Immigration rates go up and down over time, eliminating (B). Economic development would not be modeled with an S-curve because economic growth goes up and down over time, making (C) incorrect. With cultural adaptation, an ethnic group's local traditions die out as new ones emerge, and this would not be modeled with an S-curve; (D) is incorrect. The stability of countries' governments over time is represented by a different J-curve, developed by Ian Bremmer; (E) is incorrect.

60. A

The J-curve graphically illustrates exponential growth. Thomas Malthus calculated that the human population would grow in a simple exponential way, outstripping the food supply and leading to famine. Thus, **(A)** is correct and (E) is incorrect. Malthus's theory does not assume the involvement of the government or any other human agency. Moreover, population control measures would have the opposite effect of that predicted by Malthus. (B) and (D) are incorrect. While the J-curve has no limit to its growth, the S-curve represents logistic growth, where natural limits restrict population growth, so (C) is incorrect.

Section II

1. A successful response to the free-response question accomplishes all tasks set forth by the prompt. Each part of the prompt is worth 1 point, for a total of 7 possible points.

(a) To earn the point, the response must define the concept of regionalization as classifying a geographic area according to its unique characteristics. The response may include the definition of a region (a geographic area with a common characteristic); that regions may be formal, functional, or perceptual; and that regionalization may also refer to a group's self-identification with a geographic region.

(b) To earn the point, the response must define the concept of globalization as the processes of growing interconnectedness throughout the world, resulting in an increasingly worldwide popular culture. The response may include the idea that globalization can refer to the characteristics of popular culture that make a place homogeneous with other places around it; the idea that globalization occurs in many spheres (economic, cultural, political, etc.); and terms related to the spread of cultural artifacts or ideas, such as contagious diffusion, stimulus diffusion, relocation diffusion, acculturation, cultural adaptation, or assimilation.

(c) To earn the point, the response must use details to describe a specific example of regionalization. Examples include regional foods (such as grits in the southern United States), regional dances (such as the Polish polka), regional languages (such as Welsh), regional religions (such as Shintoism), regional music (such as norteño), and regional architecture (such as log cabins).

(d) To earn the point, the response must use details to describe a specific example of globalization. Examples include any idea or trend that has spread throughout the world, such as food (for example, McDonald's), music (for example, American pop music), language (for example, the lingua franca of English in business), architecture (for example, skyscrapers), religion (for example, Christianity, Buddhism, and Islam), multinational organizations (for example, Apple and General Electric), and supranational organizations (for example, NATO, the U.N., and the E.U.).

(e) To earn the point, the response must use details to describe a factor that has enabled globalization. Examples include advances in transportation and communication technologies, the Digital Revolution, the development of international business and trade relationships, and the creation of supranational organizations.

(f) To earn the point, the response must use reasoning and/or examples to explain the potential conflict between regionalization and globalization. Examples include the ideas that conflict may naturally arise because regionalization refers to the unique features of and people's identification with a specific region, while at the same time all world regions are experiencing the worldwide homogenization of cultures, economies, and politics; that individuals and communities may struggle to maintain a regional identity while simultaneously partaking in a global culture; that a cultural shatterbelt refers to a region particularly experiencing the conflict between globalization/modernization and maintaining a traditional regional identity; and that the forces of globalization are powerful and sometimes irresistible.

(g) To earn the point, the response must use reasoning and/or examples to explain a benefit that can result from globalization. Examples include the spread of beneficial technologies and ideas, such as medicines, medical treatments, democracy, and education; more profitable businesses and increased job opportunities through multinational corporations; and the fostering of human creativity and innovation through increased cross-cultural contacts.

2. A successful response to the free-response question accomplishes all tasks set forth by the prompt. Each part of the prompt is worth 1 point, for a total of 7 possible points.

(a) To earn the point, the response must define both clustered and dispersed settlement and/or identify the essential difference between the terms. "Clustered" settlement refers to areas with closely concentrated populations, while "dispersed" settlement areas have spread out or scattered populations.

(b) To earn the point, the response must use details to describe the overall population distribution. The response must use the terms *clustered settlement* and *dispersed settlement*, and they must not only focus on one area of the United States, but describe the distribution in the country overall and/or describe distribution in all regions. An example description could identify the eastern coast as having clustered settlement, increasingly dispersed settlements moving westward across the country, and clustered settlements in the southwest portion of the country. The response could mention specific areas of clustered settlement, including the northeast (Boston to northern Virginia), the eastern United States, the Great Lakes region, the coasts of Florida, and coastal California and areas of dispersed settlement, including the western half of the country, the Rocky Mountain region, and the Great Plains region.

(c) To earn the point, the response must use details to describe how a factor has contributed to high population density. The response must identify a specific region or metropolitan area. Examples include the northeast and Mid-Atlantic coastal regions being historic locations of ports and factories and the first areas settled by immigrants, resulting in the development of urban business and financial centers. Another example is the southeast coast, Texas, the southwest, and southern west coast (Sun Belt region) having a growing population due to many pull migration factors, such as favorable weather and economic growth due to construction of factories, tax incentives for businesses, low unionization, and good weather for agriculture (e.g., western fruit farms). The Great Lakes region is a historic hub of industry and transportation due to the Great Lakes and Mississippi/Ohio River Systems (e.g., railroad and airline networks centered in Chicago, the auto industry in Detroit). The west coast has historic port cities and a temperate climate, and it is the location of modern economic opportunities such as the film industry and Silicon Valley.

(d) To earn the point, the response must use details to describe how a factor has contributed to low population density. The response must identify a specific region. Examples include push migration factors in the Great Lakes and Midwestern region Rust Belt, such as the closing of factories in some cities (e.g., Cleveland, Buffalo, Detroit); the growth of large-scale agriculture and feedlots in the Corn Belt pushing out small farmers; and geographic features such as mountains and arid climates limiting settlement in the Rocky Mountains and the southwest.

(e) To earn the point, the response must use reasoning and/or examples to explain how the settlement patterns in the United States have led to a particular economic impact. Examples include the continued economic growth in urban areas of dense settlement, such

as New York City and Los Angeles, that have become financial and technological hubs and the economic decline of rural areas of dispersed settlement that continue to see a decrease in small farming and other job opportunities.

(f) To earn the point, the response must use reasoning and/or examples to explain how the settlement patterns in the United States have led to a particular political impact. Examples include the higher relative political representation for dense areas of settlement in proportion to their geographic size and the emergence of different political concerns (such as the of overcrowding of cities versus the liabilities created by abandoned rural towns) across regions based on their relative population densities.

(g) To earn the point, the response must use reasoning and/or examples to explain how a continuation of current distribution trends will likely impact the satellite image in the future. Examples include the trend of continued migration to the Sun Belt (Florida, the Carolinas, Georgia, Houston, Austin, Dallas–Fort Worth, San Antonio, Arizona, and Southern California) due to continued factors such as favorable weather and economic growth. Other examples include the continued decline in population in Rust Belt cities that are unable to create new economic opportunities after the closing of factories, the continued stagnation or decline in population in the Corn Belt due to large-scale agriculture and feedlots, and the continued expansion or even merging of major urban areas, such as Seattle into Portland, due to suburbanization and urban sprawl.

3.   A successful response to the free-response question accomplishes all tasks set forth by the prompt. Each part of the prompt is worth 1 point, for a total of 7 possible points.

(a) To earn the point, the response must identify that Zambia would be classified as a stage 2 country in the demographic transition model. (This is due to its comparatively high birth rate and high, or near average, death rate, although the response is not required to explain the reason for the classification.)

(b) To earn the point, the response must use reasoning to explain why the data in the table indicates that Argentina is in stage 3 of the demographic transition model: its average birth and death rates, which are close to the world averages, reflect a country in stage 3.

(c) To earn the point, the response must use reasoning to explain why the data in the table indicates that the United Kingdom is in stage 4 of the demographic transition model: its low birth rate and average (or slightly high) death rate reflect a country in stage 4.

(d) To earn the point, the response must use details to describe a likely feature of Argentina's economy based on its status as a stage 3 country; stage 3 economies include involvement in industrial or manufacturing economic activities.

(e) To earn the point, the response must use details to describe a likely feature of the United Kingdom's economy based on its status as a stage 4 country; stage 4 economies include involvement in tertiary, or service-based, industries and may also include quaternary and/or quinary activities.

(f) To earn the point, the response must identify that Angola would be most similar to Zambia, a stage 2 country, in terms of demographics and economics and explain why the population pyramid indicates this similarity; the pyramid is widest at the bottom, indicating a high birth rate, and therefore, a large population of children and young people. The pyramid rapidly narrows as it moves upward, indicating smaller numbers of middle-aged and elderly people in the population. As indicated by the high birth rate of Zambia on the table, Angola's demographic trends are most similar to those of Zambia.

(g) To earn the point, the response must use reasoning and/or examples to explain a likely economic or political impact of a country that has a large young population and high birth rate, like Angola, as shown in the population pyramid. Examples of impacts include a dependency ratio skewed toward the young, a possible straining of countries' economic and environmental resources, a possible need to find ways to increase agricultural productivity or food imports to feed the growing population, a possible job shortage when young people enter the workforce, potential overcrowding in urban areas, and potential political conflict as groups compete over limited resources.